Harry R. G. Inglis

The Contour Road Book of England

Western Divison

Harry R. G. Inglis

The Contour Road Book of England
Western Divison

ISBN/EAN: 9783744735513

Printed in Europe, USA, Canada, Australia, Japan

Cover: Foto ©ninafisch / pixelio.de

More available books at **www.hansebooks.com**

INDEX MAPS

NUMBERS 1-28

Are in the Northern and South-East Divisions

INDEX

TO THE

KEY MAPS.

The Numbers on the Maps refer to the Routes.

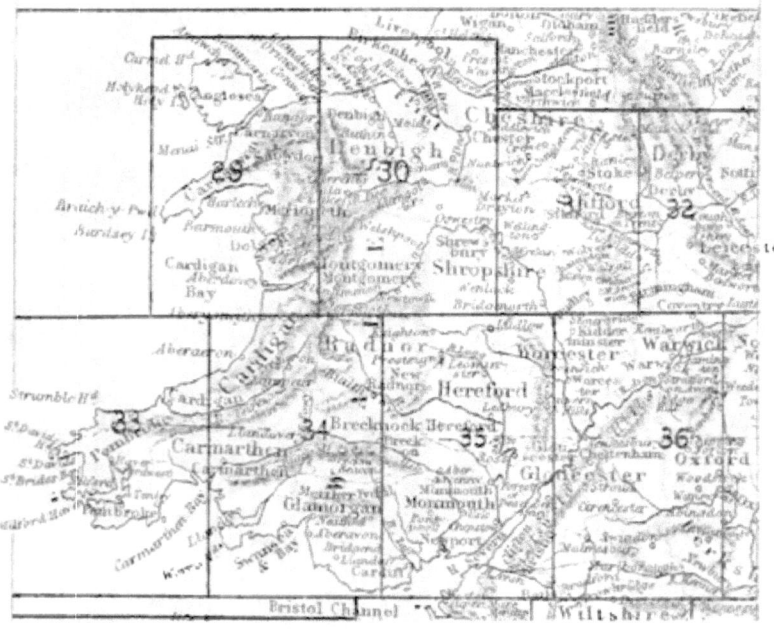

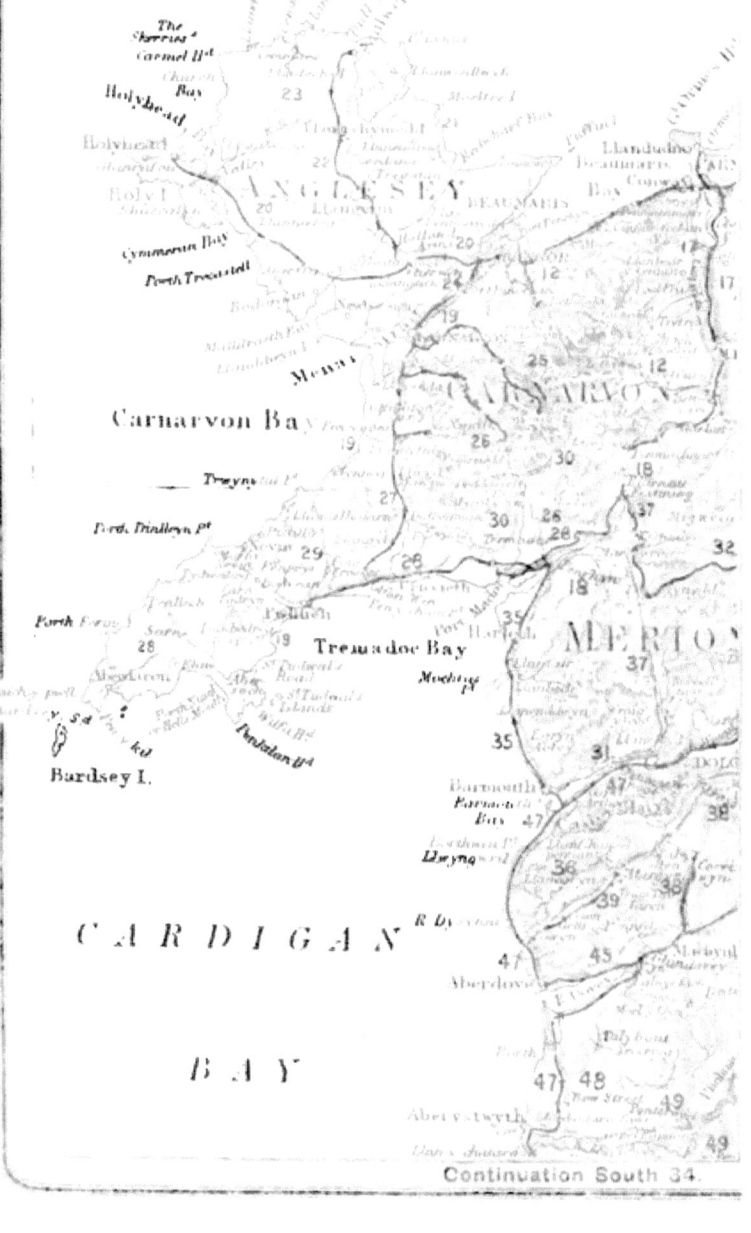

The Skerries
Carmel Hd
Church
Holyhead Bay

Holyhead
23

ANGLESEY
Holy I.
20
BEAUMARIS
Llandudno
Beaumaris
Bay
Conway

Cymmeran Bay
20

Porth Trecastell
24
12
17

19

Menai
25
12

Carnarvon Bay
CARNARVON
19
26
30
18

Trwyn Pt
27
30
28
37
32

Porth Dinlleyn Pt
Nevin
29
28

28

Porth Ferry
19
18

Pwllheli
Port Madoc
MERION

28
Tremadoc Bay
37

Mochras
Pt

35
31

Bardsey I.
Barmouth
Barmouth
Bay
47
47
38

Llwyn
36
38

39

CARDIGAN
R Dysynni
47
45

Aberdovey

BAY
47
48

47
48
49

Aberystwyth
49

Continuation South 35.

Continuation South 36

35

Continuation North 32.

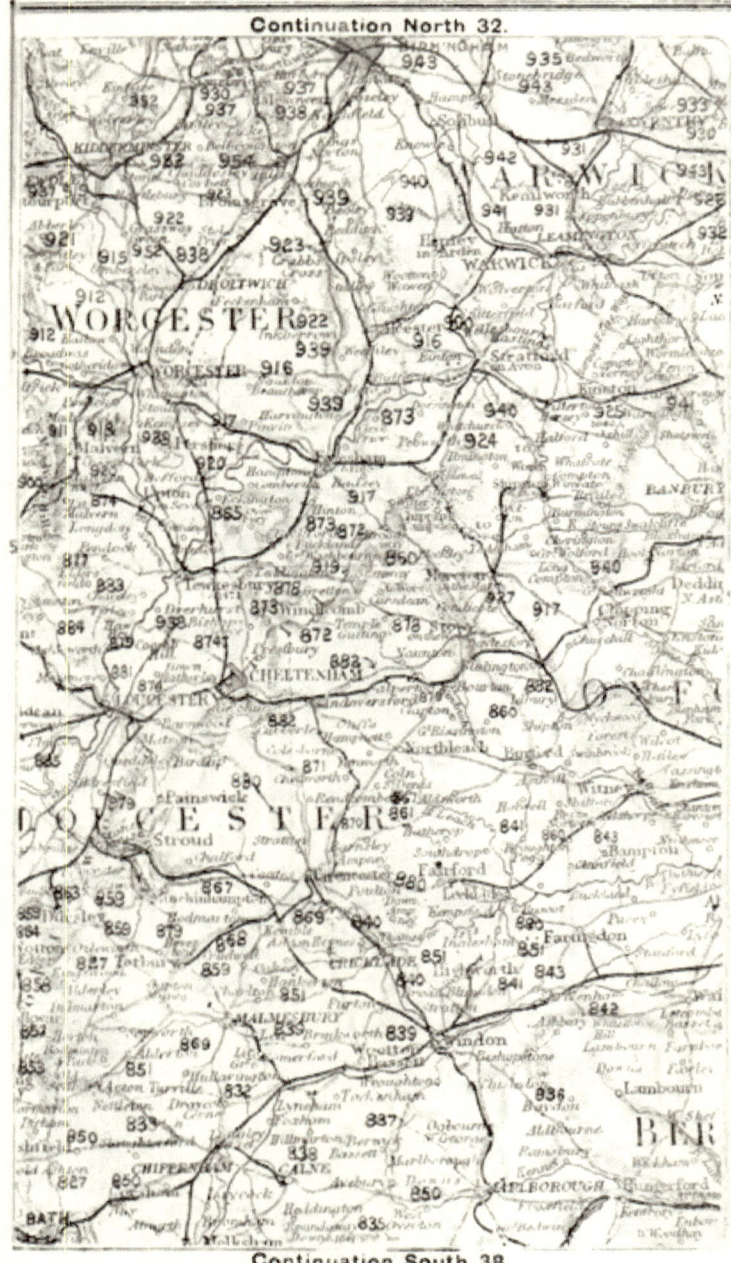

Continuation South 38.

Continuation West 40

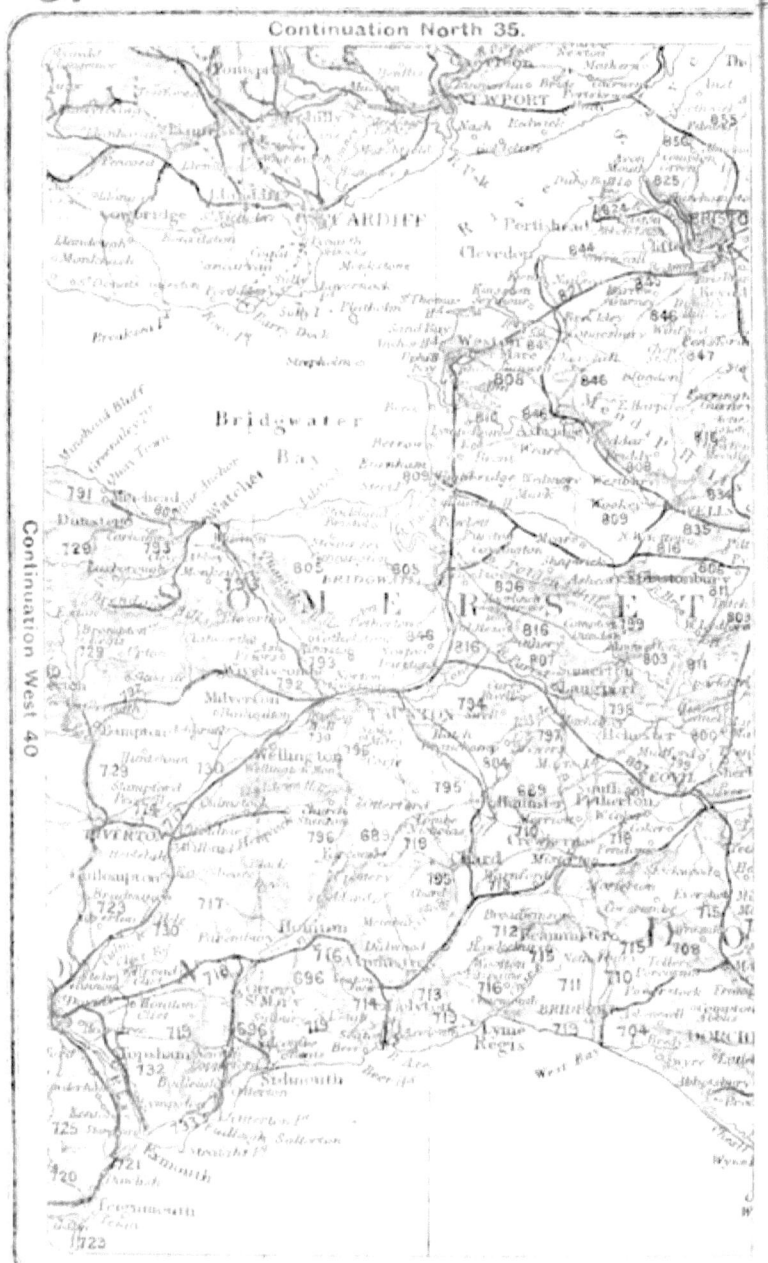

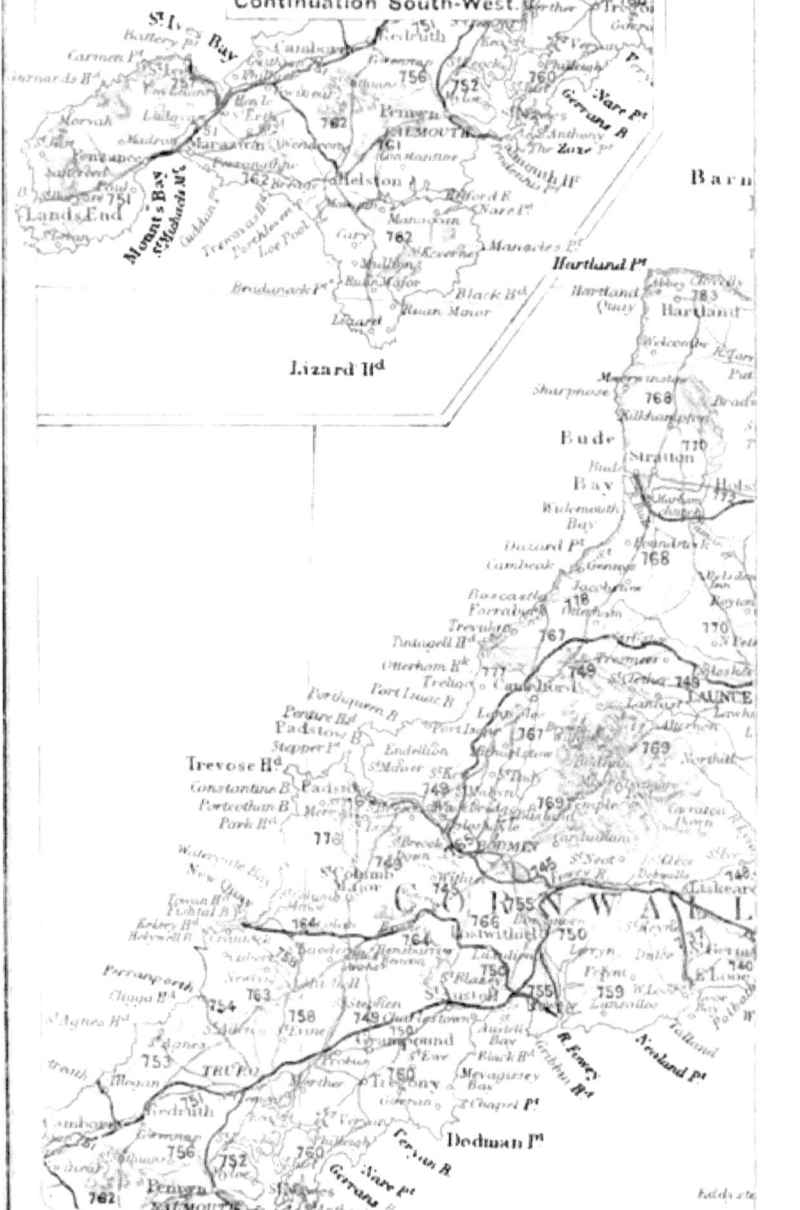

Continuation East 37

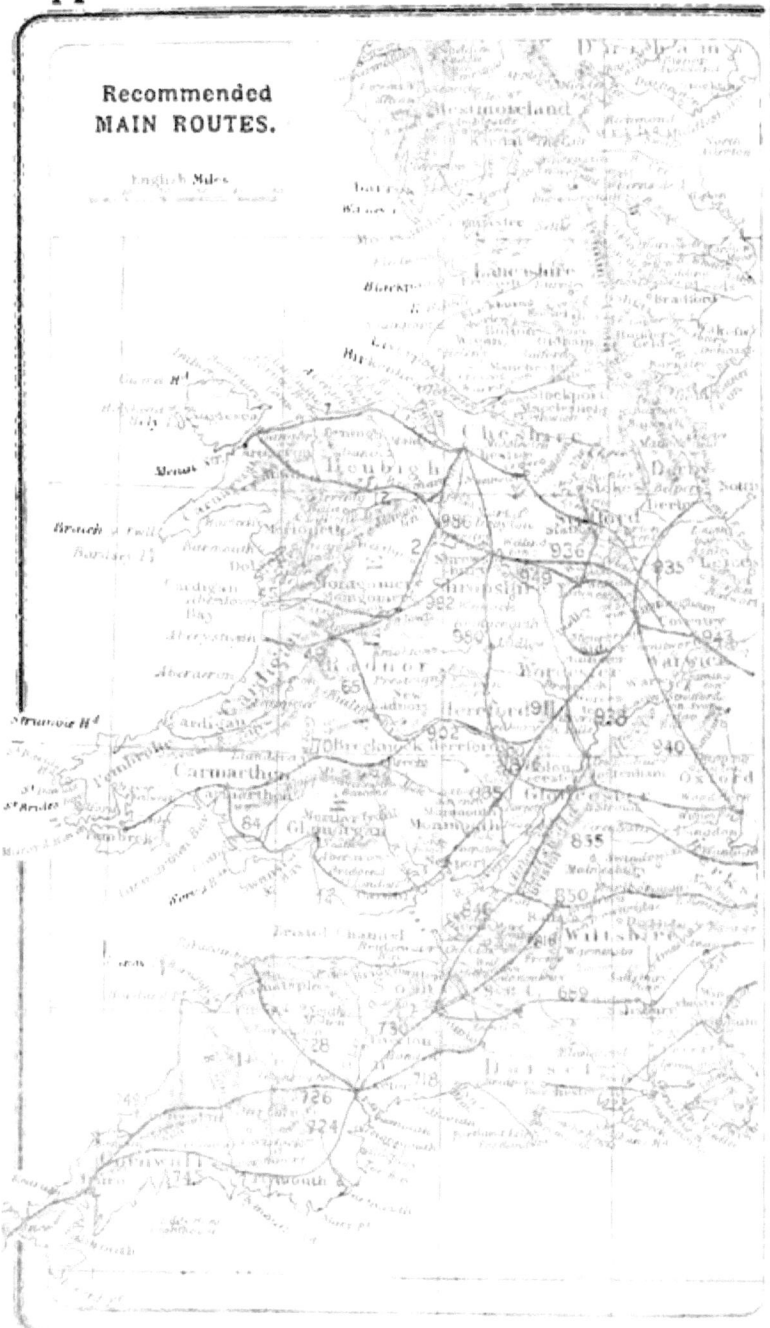

Recommended
MAIN ROUTES.

English Miles

Lichfield

Warwick

Walsall

Cambridge

Coventry

Leamington

Shrewsbury

Shrewsbury

THE
CONTOUR' ROAD BOOK
OF
ENGLAND

(WESTERN DIVISION.)
INCLUDING WALES.

*A Series of Elevation Plans of the Roads,
with Measurements and Descriptive
Letterpress.*

BY HARRY R. G. INGLIS.
author of the 'Contour Road Book of Scotland.'

With 500 Maps and Plans

London:
GALL AND INGLIS, 25 PATERNOSTER SQUARE;
AND EDINBURGH
1901-2

Uniform with this Volume.

ENGLAND. —
I. Northern Division.
II. South-East Division.

SCOTLAND.—Complete in One Vol.

Preface.

THIS volume, covering Wales, the Midlands, and South-West, completes the "Contour" Road Book of England in three volumes. The total mileage of the roads "contoured" in this volume is 9,500 miles, which shows that the work is complete in every respect.

The work has been compiled from entirely original sources, the information being obtained personally by the writer in a survey of each district. The utmost care has been taken to ensure perfect accuracy in regard to all the miscellaneous information compressed into these pages.

The Author's thanks are due to those gentlemen who have so kindly helped at various stages, and whose ready assistance has so largely contributed to the accuracy of the work.

Edinburgh, 1900.

CONTENTS.

The Routes are arranged Geographically from centres, so that the roads in each district are kept together.

As a general rule the Route, is from the larger place to the smaller.

GENERAL NOTES.

Routes 1-674 are in the North, and South-East Divisions.

The district covered by this volume is one of the most delightful parts of England for scenery. The rugged cliffs, and the bold headlands are the distinctive features of the whole coast from Dorset, round Cornwall, to North Wales. The tourist must therefore be content with following the hilliest of roads. Inland the country is either very hilly or undulating, with the exception of a portion of Somersetshire, where it is flat.

The roads are all more or less hilly, but some of the main routes through the best scenery are well engineered. During the Autumn Military Manœuvres the roads over Salisbury Plain are completely broken up with the traffic over them, and are often impassable.

The Cathedrals at Exeter, Truro, Wells, Bristol, Bath, Salisbury, Gloucester, Worcester, and Lichfield are worth visiting. Those in Wales are of no great interest. Visit also the fine ruins of Tintern Abbey and Glastonbury Abbey. Of Castles and ruins of castles there are few in the South, but in Wales, and near its borders; those at Chepstow, Raglan, Ludlow, Harlech, Carnarvon, and Conway, are in remarkably good preservation.

The best scenery is in Carnarvonshire and Merioneth; and at Llangollen, Barmouth, Aberystwyth, Wye Valley, Tenby, Ludlow, Warwick; the Devonshire, Cornwall, and Dorset Coast; and the Mendip and Malvern Hills. "Shakespeare's country" is at Stratford-on-Avon.

Ferries.—The length of the ferry is given in brackets after the name in the route, and is included in the road measurement.

Aberdovey Ferry, Ferry Boat.	Falmouth to St. Mawes, Steamer
Bangor (Garth Ferry) Ferry Boat.	,, Truro, Tidal Stmr.
,, to Beaumaris, Steamer.	Ferryside, Ferry Boat.
Dartmouth to Kingswear, Pontoon & Railway Stmr.	Laugharne, Ferry Boat.
	Lostwithiel, Ferry Boat.
,, Totnes, Tidal Stmr.	Newnham on Severn, Boat.
Devonport to Torpoint, Pontoon.	Pembroke Dock to New Milford,
,, Cremyll, Pontoon.	Pembroke Ferry, Boat. [Stmr.
,, Saltash, Steamer.	Saltash Ferry, Pontoon.
Exmouth to Starcross, Launch.	Truro to Falmouth, Tidal Stmr.

Tourist Approaches.—From London to Devonshire, &c., *via* Bath; to South Wales, *via* Cheltenham and Ross; to North Wales, *via* Coventry and Shrewsbury.

Steamers from London call at Torquay, Dartmouth, Plymouth, Falmouth, Penzance and Bristol.

Steamers from Cork to New Milford, Cardiff, Newport, Bristol, and Plymouth, and from Waterford to New Milford.

Steamers from Dublin to Holyhead; to Falmouth, and Plymouth.

Excursion steamers ply during the summer between Bournemouth and Swanage, and occasionally to Torquay, Dartmouth, &c. Also on the Bristol Channel, from Bristol and Cardiff to Weston and Ilfracombe, occasionally calling at Lynmouth, and from Swansea and Tenby to Ilfracombe. Also from Liverpool to Llandudno, and Bangor, &c.

DISTANCES BY RAIL.

London.

The mileage given below has been kindly supplied by the different Railway Companies, and is the distance upon which their charges for the conveyance of cycles is based.

```
113  Birmingham.
118   89  Bristol.
165  108   42  Cardiff.
170   74  149  144  Chester.
172  168   76  118  224  Exeter.
114   52   37   56  112  112  Gloucester.
224  219  128  170  277   53  165  Plymouth.
156   42  110  105   39  186   73  238  Shrewsbury.
208  133   88   45  145  163  102  216  106  Swansea.
114   26   66   82   91  142   28  104   52  107  Worcester.
237  124  161  132   86  132  147  289   82   88  132  Aberystwyth.
107   96   11   54  154   87   42  140  115   95   70  Bath.
248  142  218  213   69  295  180  345  107  213  159  Carnarvon.
109   45   44   64  112  119    6  170   73  110   22  Cheltenham.
 94   19  99½  122   91  169   62  222   65  150   40  Coventry.
158   53  143  138   21  218  105  271   33  139   79  Crewe.
224  112  174  144   62  249  138  302   69  185  117  Dolgelley.
144   55   67   55   80  143   30  195   51   78   30  Hereford.
264  158  233  228   84  308  196  360  123  228  175  Holyhead.
221  195  103  147  252   54  141   91  213  192  172  Ilfracombe.
 98   24   91  115   93  168   53  220   66  140   42  Leamington.
227  122  197  192   48  272  159  324   86  192  138  Llandudno.
185   72  140  134   23  215  103  267   30  135   82  Llangollen.
156   47   91   78   66  166   54  216   28   89   39  Ludlow.
123   34   65   72   99  140   26  193   60   98    8  Malvern.
153   96   34   12  132  109   45  162   93   58   70  Newport (Mon.).
260  174  156  114  183  231  170  284  144   71  136  Pembroke.
303  298  209  250  357  133  246   80  319  296  275  Penzance.
209  104  179  174   30  236  142  306   69  162  120  Rhyl.
134   28  111  119   46  186   75  238   30  131   48  Stafford.
163  134   45   87  194   31   82   84  155  132  111  Taunton.
187  180   91  133  240   15  128   38  201  178  157  Teignmouth.
193  191  102  144  251   26  139   39  212  189  168  Torquay.
277  270  181  225  330  107  220   54  293  270  249  Truro.
126  119   30   72  179   66   67  118  140  117   96  Wells.
137  108   19   61  168   58   57  110  129  107   85  Weston-s-Mare.
143  166   77  119  226   77  1..  130  186  164  141  Weymouth.
125   13   97  108   61  1..   6.  225   3.  129   32  Wolverhampton.
```

Railway Rates

FOR CONVEYANCE OF :—

Distances.	Bicycles.			Tricycles.		
	As Passenger's Luggage.	As Parcels. Owner's Risk.	Coy's Risk.	As Passenger's Luggage.	As Parcels. Owner's Risk.	Coy's Risk.
Up to 12 miles ..	6d.	9d.	1/-	1/-	2/-	3/-
12 to 25 ,, ..	9d.	1/2	1/6	1/6	3/-	4/6
25 to 50 ,, ..	1/-	1/6	2/-	2/-	4/-	6/-
50 to 75 ,, ..	1/6	2/3	3/-	3/-	6/-	9/-
75 to 100 ,, ..	2/-	3/-	4/-	4/-	8/-	12/-
100 to 150 ,, ..	2/6	3/9	5/-	5/-	10/-	15/-
150 to 200 ,, ..	3/-	4/6	6/-	6/-	12/-	18/-
200 to 250 ,, ..	3/6	5/3	7/-	7/-	14/-	21/-
250 to 300 ,, ..	4/-	6/-	8/-	8/-	16/-	24/-
300 to 350 ,, ..	4/6	6/9	9/-	9/-	18/-	27/-
350 to 400 ,, ..	5/-	7/6	10/-	10/-	20/-	30/-
Each additional 50 miles and portion thereof	6d.	9d.	1/-	1/-	2/-	3/-

Tandems, &c., 50 per cent. additional for seat.

Pronunciation of Names.

In Devonshire and Cornwall the names are pronounced a little sharper than in other parts; and a and u are short.

Abergavenny = Aberg(av)'enny.	Devizes = Devízes.
Almondsbury = Aamsbury.	Frome = Froom.
Alverdiscot = Alscot.	Gloucester = Gloster.
Beaminster = Bemminster.	Leominster = Lemster.
Berkeley = Barkly.	Rugeley = Rudgley.
Bideford = Biddyford.	Tintagel = Tintadjel.
Cirencester = Cicester.	Totnes = Tótnes.
Clun = Clŭn.	Weobley = Webley.

Wales.

At first glance, the spelling and pronunciation of the Welsh names is very puzzling, but this is owing to some of the letters of the Welsh alphabet being used to produce different sounds from the English. For all practical purposes it is enough to know that :—

$Ll=thl$; $dd=th$; $w=u$ or oo; $u=i$; $c=k$; $f=v$; and $ff=f$.

These will enable the beginner to master the initial stages, but, to be accurate, there is a subtle inflexion which has no English equivalent, and that can only be learned *vivâ voce*.

Amlwch = Amluch.	Llandudno = Thlandidno.
Beaumaris = Bomaris.	Llanfyllin = Thlanvothlen.
Bettws-y-coed = Bettus-y-coed.	Llangollen = Thlangothlen.
Builth = Bealth.	Machynlleth = Machynthleth.
Criccieth = Kriketh.	Maentwrog = Maen-turog.
Hawarden = Harden.	Pontypridd = Ponty-preeth.
Laugharne = Larne.	Pwllheli = Pultheli.

It is only right to say that the place names owe their length to being compound words, and when the letters are run together some extraordinary combinations are produced. The name that has suffered most is Llanfair-pwll-gwyngyll, in Anglesea, known as Llanfair (P.G.), which is made to appear as :—

Llanfairpwllgwyngyllgogerchwyrndrobwllttysiliogogoch, *or* Llanfairpwllgwyngyllfrisiliologogoch, *and other variations.*

The termination to the original name is apocryphal, and consists merely of a more minute description of the locality.

Llan means church, and the common compounds Llanfair (Church St. Mary); Llanfihangel (Church St. Michael); and Llansantffraid (Church St. Bride), are the initial stages of the longer words. The names are usually simple, thus, the church of St. Bride on the banks of the Conway : Llansantffraid-glan-Conway.

Concise Glossary.

The following gives the meaning of some of the commoner Welsh place names : as Pen-maen-mawr, The great rock headland.

Aber ..	river mouth.	Glyn ..	glen.	mawr }	
Afon ..	,,	Gwy ..	water.	fawr }	.. great.
Bedd ..	.. grave.	Llan ..	church.	bach }	
Bettws ..	.. chapel.	Llyn ..	lake.	fach }	.. little.
Blaenau ..	summit.	Maen ..	stone.	uchaf ..	.. highest.
Bwlch ..	.. pass.	Mynydd ..	moorland.	isaf ..	.. lowest.
Caer ..	.. fort.	Pen ..	.. headland.	eithaf ..	.. furthest.
Capel ..	chapel.	Pont, bont. bridge.		newydd ..	.. new.
Carn ..	.. cairn.	Pwll ..	.. pool.	hen ..	.. old.
Coed ..	.. wood.	Rhaiadr..	waterfall.	ddu ..	.. black.
Dwfr, dwr..	water.	Rhyd ..	.. ford.	wen (gwyn)	white.
Eglwys ..	.. church.	Tal ..	.. point.	coch ..	.. red.
Glan ..	.. bank.	Tomen ..	mound.	rhudd ..	,,

Lamp=Lighting Tables.
(See Index of Towns on next page.)

The time of sunset for each date varies from year to year, these Tables therefore are not absolutely exact, but give an average which is never more than a few minutes out, on any date.

To use the **Tables.**—Find the district required on the next page, and add the time allowance to the column named, and opposite the required date. For example, the average time for lighting lamps at Coventry on June 21 is obtained as follows:—Coventry, add 6 minutes to column **F** on June 21, which is 9.19. The average hour for lighting lamps is therefore 9.25 p.m.

For dates not in Table take the proportion between the two nearest.

	53°	52½°	52°	51½°	50½°
Date.	E P.M.	F P.M.	G P.M.	H P.M.	I P.M.
Jany. 1	4.47	4.49	4.52	4.55	5.0
,, 9	4.58	4.59	5.2	5.4	5.9
,, 15	5.8	5.7	5.11	5.13	5.18
,, 20	5.15	5.16	5.20	5.22	5.26
,, 24	5.23	5.25	5.27	5.29	5.33
,, 28	5.31	5.33	5.35	5.36	5.40
Feby. 1	5.38	5.39	5.41	5.42	5.46
,, 4	5.45	5.46	5.48	5.49	5.52
,, 8	5.51	5.52	5.54	5.55	5.58
,, 11	5.57	5.58	6.0	6.1	6.3
,, 14	6.3	6.4	6.5	6.6	6.9
,, 17	6.8	6.9	6.11	6.12	6.14
,, 19	6.13	6.15	6.16	6.17	6.19
, 22	6.19	6.21	6.22	6.23	6.24
,, 25	6.24	6.25	6.26	6.27	6.28
,, 28	6.30	6.31	6.32	6.32	6.33
Mar. 2	6.34	6.35	6.36	6.36	6.37
,, 5	6.40	6.39	6.40	6.40	6.41
,, 7	6.44	6.44	6.45	6.45	6.46
., 10	6.49	6.49	6.49	6.49	6.50
,, 13	6.53	6.53	6.54	6.54	6.54
,, 15	6.58	6.58	6.59	6.59	6.59
,, 18	7.3	7.3	7.3	7.3	7.3
,, 20	7.7	7.7	7.7	7.7	7.7
,, 23	7.12	7.11	7.11	7.11	7.11
,, 25	7.17	7.16	7.16	7.16	7.16
,, 28	7.21	7.20	7.20	7.20	7.19
,, 30	7.25	7.26	7.26	7.25	7.24
April 2	7.31	7.30	7.30	7.29	7.28
,, 5	7.36	7.34	7.34	7.33	7.32
,, 7	7.40	7.39	7.38	7.37	7.36
,, 10	7.44	7.43	7.42	7.41	7.40
,, 13	7.50	7.48	7.47	7.46	7.44
,, 15	7.54	7.53	7.52	7.51	7.49
,, 18	8.0	7.58	7.57	7.56	7.54
,, 21	8.5	8.3	8.2	8.1	7.59
,, 24	8.9	8.8	8.7	8.5	8.3
,, 27	8.15	8.13	8.12	8.11	8.8
May 1	8.20	8.18	8.17	8.15	8.12
,, 4	8.26	8.24	8.23	8.21	8.18
,, 8	8.33	8.31	8.29	8.27	8.24
,, 11	8.38	8.37	8.35	8.33	8.30
,, 16	8.45	8.43	8.41	8.39	8.35
,, 20	8.52	8.49	8.47	8.45	8.41
,, 25	8.58	8.56	8.54	8.51	8.47
,, 31	9.7	9.4	9.2	8.59	8.54
June 10	9.16	9.13	9.11	9.8	9.3
,, 21	9.22	9.19	9.16	9.13	9.8

	53°	52½°	52°	51½°	50½°
Date.	E P.M.	F P.M.	G P.M.	H P.M.	I P.M.
July 2	9.20	9.17	9.15	9.12	9.7
,, 11	9.15	9.12	9.10	9.9	9.2
,, 18	9.8	9.6	9.4	9.1	8.57
,, 23	9.2	8.59	8.57	8.55	8.51
,, 28	8.55	8.53	8.51	8.49	8.45
Aug. 1	8.48	8.46	8.44	8.42	8.39
,, 5	8.42	8.40	8.38	8.36	8.33
,, 8	8.34	8.32	8.31	8.29	8.26
,, 12	8.28	8.26	8.25	8.23	8.20
,, 15	8.21	8.19	8.18	8.17	8.14
,, 18	8.14	8.14	8.13	8.11	8.9
,, 21	8.9	8.7	8.6	8.5	8.3
,, 24	8.2	8.1	8.0	7.59	7.57
,, 27	7.55	7.54	7.53	7.52	7.50
,, 30	7.49	7.48	7.47	7.46	7.44
Sept. 2	7.43	7.42	7.41	7.40	7.39
,, 4	7.37	7.36	7.35	7.34	7.33
,, 7	7.30	7.29	7.29	7.28	7.27
,, 10	7.24	7.23	7.23	7.22	7.21
,, 12	7.17	7.17	7.17	7.16	7.15
,, 15	7.11	7.10	7.10	7.10	7.9
,, 17	7.5	7.4	7.4	7.4	7.4
,, 20	6.58	6.58	6.58	6.58	6.58
,, 22	6.53	6.53	6.53	6.53	6.53
,, 25	6.47	6.47	6.47	6.47	6.47
,, 28	6.40	6.40	6.41	6.41	6.41
,, 30	6.34	6.34	6.35	6.35	6.35
Oct. 3	6.28	6.28	6.28	6.28	6.29
,, 5	6.21	6.21	6.22	6.22	6.23
,, 8	6.15	6.15	6.16	6.16	6.17
,, 11	6.9	6.10	6.11	6.11	6.12
,, 13	6.3	6.4	6.5	6.5	6.6
,, 16	5.57	5.57	5.58	5.59	6.0
,, 19	5.51	5.52	5.53	5.54	5.55
,, 22	5.45	5.46	5.47	5.48	5.50
,, 25	5.38	5.39	5.41	5.42	5.43
,, 27	5.33	5.34	5.35	5.36	5.39
,, 30	5.27	5.28	5.30	5.31	5.33
Nov. 3	5.21	5.22	5.24	5.25	5.28
,, 6	5.15	5.16	5.18	5.19	5.22
,, 9	5.8	5.10	5.12	5.13	5.17
,, 13	5.3	5.5	5.7	5.8	5.12
,, 17	4.56	4.58	5.0	5.2	5.6
,, 21	4.50	4.52	4.53	4.57	5.1
,, 26	4.46	4.46	4.50	4.52	4.57
Dec. 2	4.40	4.42	4.45	4.47	4.52
,, 11	4.36	4.38	4.41	4.44	4.49
,, 21	4.38	4.40	4.43	4.45	4.50

Town.	Minutes.	Col.	Town.	Minutes.	Col.
Abergavenny,	add 12 to	F	Marlborough,	add 7 to	H
Aberystwyth,	,, 16 ,,	G	Merthyr,	,, 13 ,,	G
Bangor,	,, 16 ,,	E	Monmouth,	,, 11 ,,	G
Barmouth,	,, 16 ,,	F	Montgomery,	,, 12 ,,	F
Barnstaple,	,, 16 ,,	H	Newcastle-under-Lyme,	9 ,,	E
Bath,	,, 9 ,,	H	Newport (Mon.),	,, 12 ,,	H
Bideford,	,, 17 ,,	I	New Quay (Cornwall),	20 ,,	I
Birmingham,	,, 7 ,,	F	Newton Abbott,	,, 14 ,,	I
Blandford,	,, 8 ,,	I	Newtown,	,, 13 ,,	F
Bodmin,	,, 19 ,,	I	Nuneaton,	,, 6 ,,	F
Bournemouth,	,, 7 ,,	I	Okehampton,	,, 16 ,,	I
Bradford-on-Avon,	,, 8 ,,	H	Oswestry,	,, 12 ,,	E
Brecon,	,, 13 ,,	G	Pembroke,	,, 20 ,,	H
Bridgnorth,	,, 10 ,,	F	Penzance,	,, 22 ,,	I
Bridgwater,	,, 12 ,,	H	Plymouth,	,, 17 ,,	I
Bridport,	,, 11 ,,	I	Pontypool,	,, 12 ,,	H
Bristol,	,, 10 ,,	H	Poole,	,, 8 ,,	I
Burton-on-Trent,	,, 6 ,,	E	Portmadoc,	,, 16 ,,	E
Cardiff,	,, 13 ,,	H	Pwllheli,	,, 18 ,,	E
Cardigan,	,, 19 ,,	G	Radnor,	,, 12 ,,	G
Carmarthen,	,, 17 ,,	G	Redditch,	,, 8 ,,	F
Carnarvon,	,, 17 ,,	E	Redruth,	,, 21 ,,	I
Cheltenham,	,, 8 ,,	H	Rhyl,	,, 14 ,,	E
Chepstow,	,, 11 ,,	H	Ross,	,, 10 ,,	G
Chippenham,	,, 8 ,,	H	Rugby,	,, 5 ,,	F
Cirencester,	,, 8 ,,	H	Salisbury,	,, 7 ,,	H
Clevedon,	,, 11 ,,	H	St. Davids,	,, 21 ,,	G
Colwyn Bay,	,, 15 ,,	E	Shaftesbury,	,, 8 ,,	H
Coventry,	,, 6 ,,	F	Sherborne,	,, 10 ,,	I
Crediton,	,, 15 ,,	I	Sidmouth,	,, 13 ,,	I
Dartmouth,	,, 14 ,,	I	Stafford,	,, 8 ,,	E
Denbigh,	,, 13 ,,	E	Stratford-on-Avon,	,, 7 ,,	G
Devizes,	,, 8 ,,	H	Stroud,	,, 9 ,,	H
Dolgelley,	,, 15 ,,	F	Swansea,	,, 16 ,,	H
Dorchester,	,, 9 ,,	I	Swindon,	,, 7 ,,	H
Dudley,	,, 8 ,,	F	Taunton,	,, 12 ,,	H
Evesham,	,, 8 ,,	G	Tavistock,	,, 17 ,,	I
Exeter,	,, 14 ,,	I	Teignmouth,	,, 14 ,,	I
Exmouth,	,, 13 ,,	I	Tenby,	,, 19 ,,	H
Falmouth,	,, 20 ,,	I	Tiverton,	,, 14 ,,	I
Frome,	,, 9 ,,	H	Torquay,	,, 14 ,,	I
Glastonbury,	,, 11 ,,	H	Torrington,	,, 17 ,,	I
Gloucester,	,, 9 ,,	H	Totnes,	,, 15 ,,	I
Hereford,	,, 11 ,,	G	Trowbridge,	,, 8 ,,	H
Holyhead,	,, 19 ,,	E	Truro,	,, 20 ,,	I
Ilfracombe,	,, 16 ,,	H	Uttoxeter,	,, 7 ,,	E
Kidderminster,	,, 9 ,,	F	Walsall,	,, 8 ,,	F
Land's End,	,, 23 ,,	I	Warminster,	,, 8 ,,	H
Launceston,	,, 17 ,,	I	Warwick,	,, 6 ,,	F
Leamington,	,, 6 ,,	F	Wellington (Somerset),	,, 13 ,,	I
Leek,	,, 8 ,,	E	,, (Salop),	,, 10 ,,	F
Leominster,	,, 11 ,,	G	Wells,	,, 10 ,,	H
Lichfield,	,, 7 ,,	F	Welshpool,	,, 12 ,,	F
Liskeard,	,, 18 ,,	I	Weston-super-mare,	,, 12 ,,	H
Llandudno,	,, 15 ,,	E	Weymouth,	,, 9 ,,	I
Llanelly,	,, 17 ,,	H	Whitchurch,	,, 11 ,,	E
Llangollen,	,, 12 ,,	E	Wimborne,	,, 3 ,,	I
Longton,	,, 9 ,,	E	Wolverhampton,	,, 3 ,,	F
Ludlow,	,, 11 ,,	F	Worcester,	,, 9 ,,	G
Lyme Regis,	,, 11 ,,	I	Wrexham,	,, 12 ,,	E
Malvern,	,, 9 ,,	G	Yeovil,	,, 10 ,,	I

EXPLANATION OF DIAGRAMS.

The line bordering the shaded portion of the Plan is a facsimile of the profile of the Route, and is divided by vertical lines into miles, and by horizontal lines into contours of 100 feet, so that distances and heights are ascertained quickly.

The blocks show the positions of the villages and houses, while the signs are the road directions :— < Road Fork, forward journey, > ditto reverse, + Cross Roads, ⊥ Road Junction, ∩ Bridge, ⊤ indicates a sharp turn. The directions R (right) and L (left) for the forward journey are above the Road Line, those of the reverse below.

The vertical scale has necessarily been enlarged out of strict proportion, as otherwise the ordinary Gradients would almost have been imperceptible.

EXPLANATION OF LETTERPRESS.

The diagram should be consulted first, as the letterpress is appended to it. Places named in brackets are off the road.

The Description states the quality of the road, and it should be observed that the "Class" refers solely to the construction of the road, and not to its surface. Class I. is a superior, broad, and finely-made road. Class II. is the ordinary main road. Class III. is of inferior construction, usually narrow, or hilly. Roads of this class are usually very old, or have been constructed in an inferior manner.

Gradients.—1 in 25; *i.e.*, 1 foot of rise in 25, is a fairly easy hill, 1 in 20 is stiff. 1 in 15 is steep. Cyclists usually walk up a hill of 1 in 17. A descent does not generally become dangerous till it is 1 in 15 and then only with a sharp turn, but with anything steeper the danger increases. A little experience of one or two hills will be a permanent guide. On nearly every hill the gradient varies every few yards. Those given here represent approximately the general slope, and in most cases the maximum is given.

Milestones.—The exact points from which these are measured are named. Where the measurements in this work differ from those given on the milestones, the difference in distance between the starting points, and other variations, is the cause.

Measurements.—The tabular form gives the distance from any one point to another, the number below the one name and opposite the other being the distance required. For clearness the furlongs have been put in the tables as ⅛ths.

Principal Objects of Interest.—These are only notes—details can be found in almost any guide book.

Hotels or Inns.—It has been found difficult to decide whether certain small houses should be inserted or not. The tourist therefore should not expect much of some of them, as they are the only accommodation available.

At intervals throughout the book, numbers have been left blank, to enable new routes to be added when required.

NEWPORT TO BRADING, &C. 675

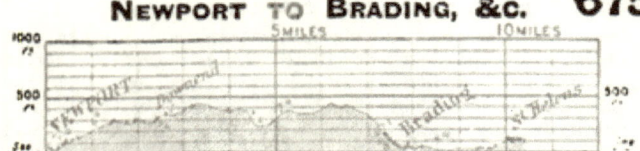

Description.—Class III. A very hilly road; fairly good surface.

Gradients.—At 1m. 1 in 17; 4½m. 1 in 11 (very dangerous); 5m. 1 in 13; 7½m. 1 in 8 (very dangerous); 10m. 1 in 16.

Milestones.—Measured from Coppins Bridge, Newport.

Measurements.—Newport,* St. James Sq.
    7¼ Brading,* P.O.
    10⅜ 2½ St. Helens.*

Principal Objects of Interest.—Brading: Church.

NEWPORT TO SANDOWN. 676

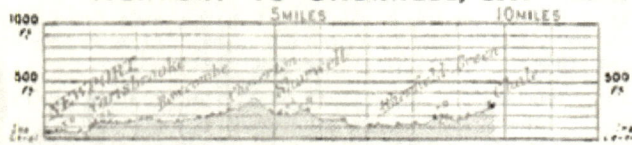

Description.—Class II. A slightly undulating road with good surface. This is about the best road in the island.

Gradients.—At ½m. 1 in 15; ¾m. 1 in 21; 2m. 1 in 15; 4m. 1 in 20; 6¾m. 1 in 18; 7½m. 1 in 22; 9m. 1 in 13; 9¼m. 1 in 19.

Milestones.—Measured from Newport, Town Hall.

Measurements.—Newport,* St. James Sq.
    4 Arreton.*
    8¾ 4½ Lake.*
    9¾ 5¾ 1¼ Sandown,* Hotel.

Principal Objects of Interest.—Sandown: Fort, Chines.

NEWPORT TO SHORWELL, &C. 677

Description.—Class III. A hilly road with fairly good surface, but poor after Shorwell, to Chale.

Gradients.—At 1m. 1 in 16; 4½m. 1 in 13; 4¾m. 1 in 10 (both dangerous); 8½m. 1 in 13.

Milestones.—Measured from Newport, Town Hall.

Measurements.—Newport,* St. James Sq.
    5¼ Shorwell.*
    9¾ 4½ Chale.*

Principal Objects of Interest.—Carisbrooke: Castle, Roman Villa.

678 CHRISTCHURCH TO BLANDFORD.

Description.—Class II. A very good, undulating road to
Longham, thereafter quite level and with magnificent sur-
face. The direct road from Wimborne to Blandford by
Badbury (6½m.) is very hilly.

Measurements.

Christchurch,* Town Hall.
7¼ Longham,* P.O.
11½ 3½ Wimborne,* Bridge.
18, 11½ 7½ Spettisbury,* Station.
21½ 14½ 10½ 3½ Blandford,* Market.

Principal Objects of Interest.—WIMBORNE: Minster,
Canford Manor. BLANDFORD: Bryanstone House, &c.

679 BOURNEMOUTH TO SOUTHAMPTON.

Description.—Class II. The best road is by Lyndhurst.
This road after Pokesdown has fine surface as far as Milton,
whence variable, but usually very good to Hythe, where ferry
to Southampton. Ford at 9½m. Toll at Lymington Bridge.

Gradients.—At 3m. 1 in 19; 9½m. 1 in 16; 12½m. 1 in 16; 18m.
1 in 11 (dangerous); 23m. 1 in 17; 24m. and 27½m. 1 in 18.

Measurements.

Bournemouth,* Square.
5¼ Christchurch,* Town Hall.
17¼ 11½ Lymington,*
23½ 17¼ 6¾ Beaulieu.*
28½ 23 11¼ 4¾ Hythe,* Pier.
30½ 25½ 13½ 7¼ 2, Southampton,* Bargate.

Principal Objects of Interest.—CHRISTCHURCH: Priory
Church. Beaulieu: Abbey ruin. SOUTHAMPTON: as R.512.

Hotels or Inns at places marked *, and at Newtown, &c.

680 BOURNEMOUTH TO WEYMOUTH.

Description.—Class II. Very lumpy to Parkstone, then
splendid to Wool, whence good but hilly to Weymouth.

Gradients. At ¼m. 1 in 18; 3m. 1 in 16; 25m. 1 in 18;
27½m. 1 in 15; 28½m. 1 in 16 (dangerous).

Measurements.

Bournemouth,* Square.
(… Poole,* Station.)
13½ 9½ Wareham,* Clock.
21½ 17½ 8 Winfrith,* Inn.
32½ 28½ 18½ 10½ Weymouth,* Bridge.
30½ 26½ 16½ 8½ Dorchester,* Clock.

Principal Objects of Interest.—Wool: Binden Abbey,
2½m. White Horse. WEYMOUTH: Sandsfoot Castle, Esplanade, George III. Statue, &c.

Hotels or Inns at places marked *, and at Wool, &c., &c.

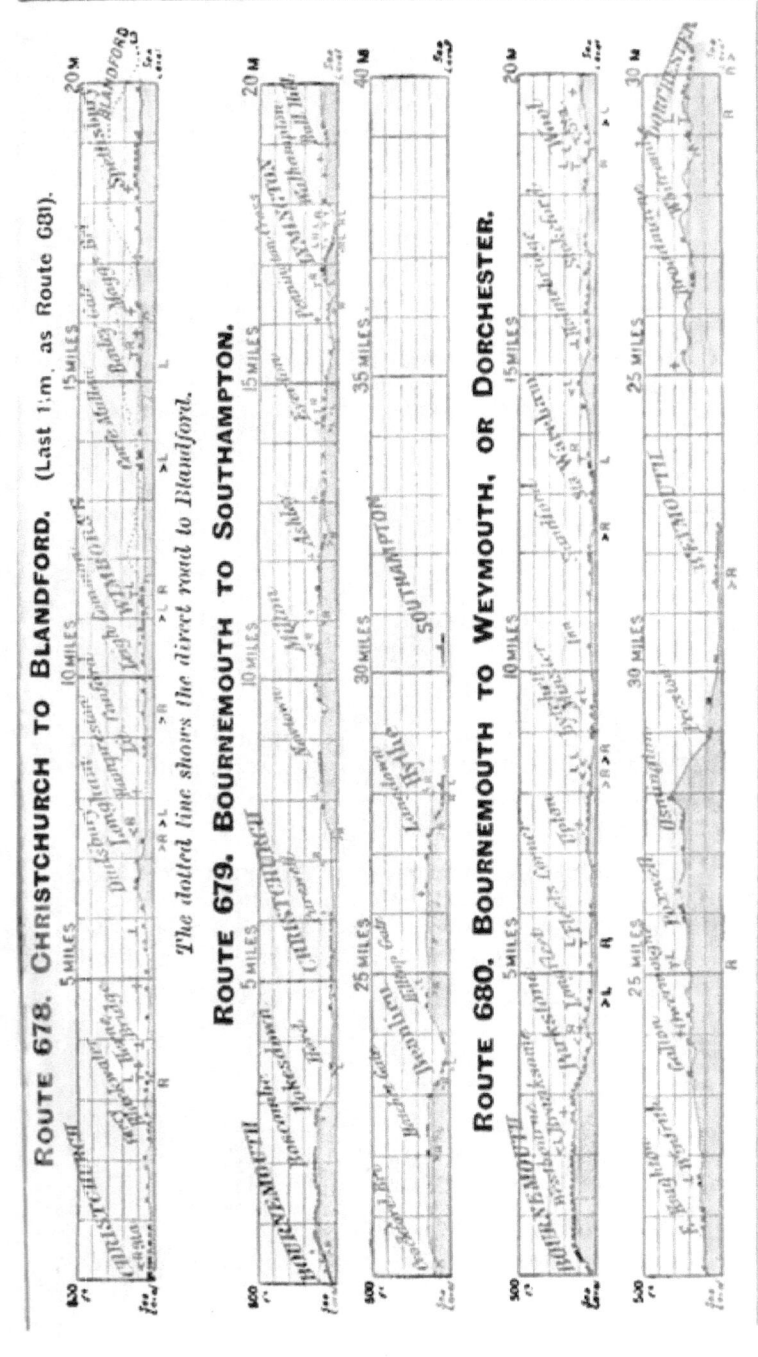

ROUTE 678. CHRISTCHURCH TO BLANDFORD. (Last 1½m, as Route 681).

The dotted line shows the direct road to Blandford.

ROUTE 679. BOURNEMOUTH TO SOUTHAMPTON.

ROUTE 680. BOURNEMOUTH TO WEYMOUTH, OR DORCHESTER.

681 BOURNEMOUTH TO SHERBORNE.

Description. Class II. Lumpy as far as Parkstone, whence very fine surface, but somewhat undulating to Sturminster; thereafter the road is more hilly, but the surface is fair.

Gradients. At ½m. 1 in 18; 3m. 1 in 16; 10½m. 1 in 22; 18½m. 1 in 15; 24m. and 25½m. 1 in 17; 28m. 1 in 16; 30½m. 1 in 14; 31m. 1 in 17; 32½m. 1 in 15; 33½m. 1 in 21; 36½m. 1 in 17.

Milestones. Measured from Blandford Market. After Bishop's Caundle measured from Sherborne.

Measurements.

Bournemouth,* Square.
(.. Poole,* Station.)
14½ 10½ Spettisbury,* Station.
17½ 13½ 3½ Blandford,* Market.
25½ 22½ 11½ 8½ Sturminster,* Bridge.
32½ 28½ 18 14½ 6½ Bishop's Caundle,* Church.
38 33½ 23½ 20½ 11½ 5½ Sherborne,* Cross.

Principal Objects of Interest. — 11½m. Charborough House. Blandford: Bryanstone House, Damory Court. Sturminster: Castle. SHERBORNE: Minster, Castle.

Hotels or Inns at places marked*, and at Durweston, &c.

682 ANDOVER TO STONEHENGE, &C.

Description. Class II. Splendid surface to Weyhill, thereafter a fair road over the downs as far as Stonehenge, when it becomes loose, and after Winterbourne is very rough and steep. Beyond Deptford it is also very rough; a much better and easier road is round by Salisbury. This is a rather monotonous road.

Gradients.—At 4½m. 1 in 18; 5½m. 1 in 22; 7½m. 1 in 23; 8m. 1 in 14; 10½m. 1 in 18; 12m. 1 in 14; 15m. 1 in 13; 15½m. 1 in 15; 16m. 1 in 22; 18½m. 1 in 14; 19½m. 1 in 18; 19½m. 1 in 15; 21m. 1 in 18; 22m., 25m., 29m., 31½m., and 35m. 1 in 13 (all dangerous); 36m. 1 in 24.

Milestones.—Continuation of those from London as far as Winterbourne, thereafter irregular and unreliable.

Measurements.

Andover.*
8 Park House Inn* (R. 684).
14 5½ Amesbury.*
19 10½ 5 Winterbourne Stoke.
23½ 14½ 9½ 4½ Deptford.
30½ 21½ 16½ 11½ 7½ Chicklade.
37½ 28½ 23½ 18½ 14 6½ Mere.*
39½ 30½ 27½ 20½ 16½ 8½ 2½ Zeals Green (R. 699).
(34½ 25 17 12 8 3 Hindon.*) [over.

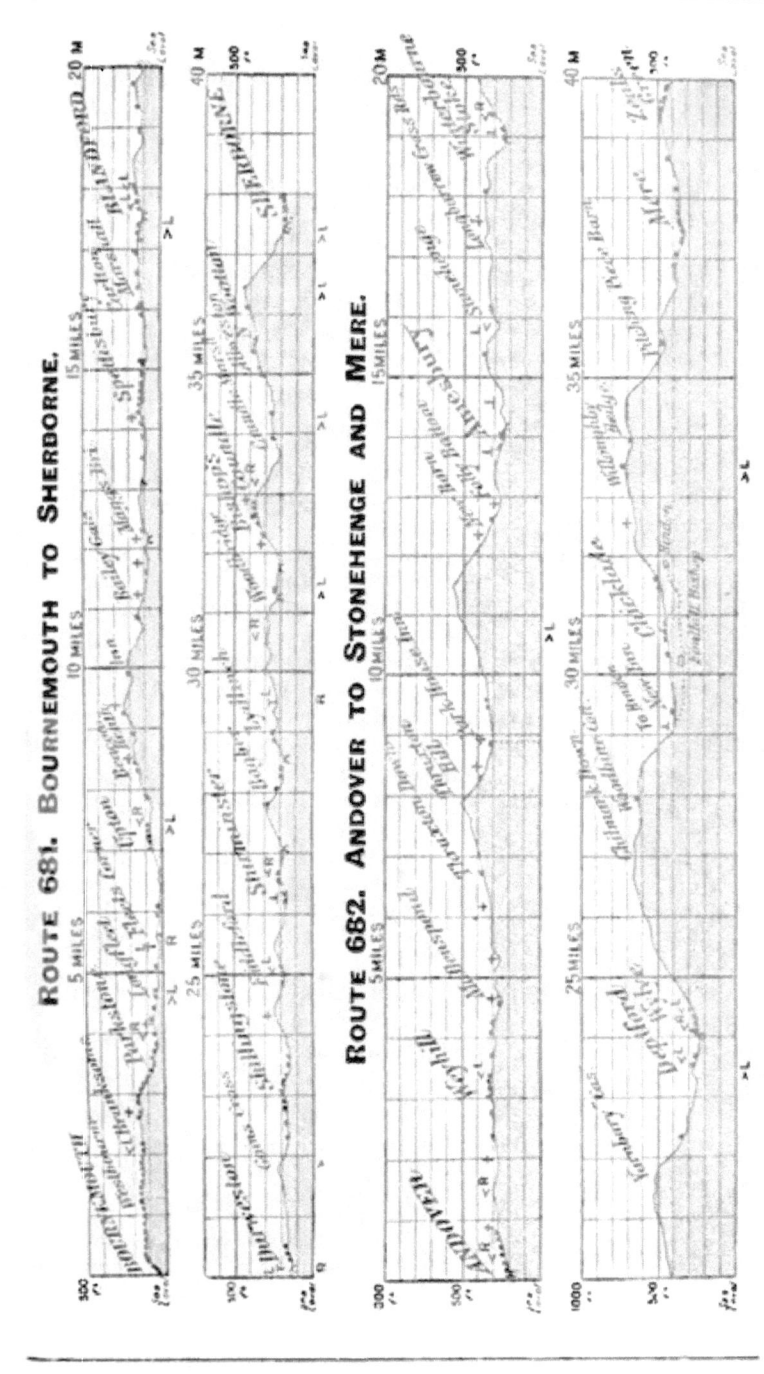

ROUTE 681. BOURNEMOUTH TO SHERBORNE.

ROUTE 682. ANDOVER TO STONEHENGE AND MERE.

Route 682—Continued.

Principal Objects of Interest. 16m. Stonehenge. 21½m. Yarnbury "Castle." Mere: Church, Castle Hill. Hindon: Fonthill Abbey.

Hotels or Inns at places marked *, and at Weyhill, Mullens Pond, and Wylye.

683 SALISBURY TO ROMSEY.

Description.—Class I. The surface is very good all the way to Romsey, although the road is slightly hilly.

Gradients. At 3½m. 1 in 25; 5m. 1 in 20; 5½m. 1 in 17; 6½m. 1 in 21; 8½m. and 9½m. 1 in 21; 13m. 1 in 22; 15m. 1 in 17.

Milestones.—Measured from Salisbury as far as Whiteparish; thereafter from Romsey, Market.

Measurements.

Salisbury,* Market.

8½	Whiteparish,* Inn.		
11½	3½	Sherfield English,* Inn.	
15½	7½	4½	Romsey,* Market.

Principal Objects of Interest.—Romsey: Abbey Church.

Hotels or Inns at places marked *.

684 SALISBURY TO HUNGERFORD.

Description.—Class II. An excellent, undulating but narrow road almost the whole way. The surface is usually in good order, but between Winterbourne and Collingbourne it is sometimes rough. The old road over the Downs is disused as far as Collingbourne, while the direct road from Collingbourne to Hungerford (shown in dotted lines) is exceedingly hilly and rough. The road given here is the best, and the one usually followed, though 3½m. further.

Gradients.—At 7½m. 1 in 17; 17½m. 1 in 16; 25½m. 1 in 15; 26m. 1 in 25; 29½m. 1 in 15; 31m. 1 in 14.

Measurements.

Salisbury,* Market.

5½	Porton.				
11½	5½	Park House Inn.* (R. 682).			
17½	12½	6½	Collingbourne Ducis.*		
(23	17½	11½	5½	Burbage.*) (R. 650).	
27½	22½	16½	9½	5½	Great Bedwyn.*
33½	27½	22	15½	11	5½	Hungerford,* Boar Hotel.

Principal Objects of Interest.—9m. Wilbury Park. East Grafton; Savernake Forest. HUNGERFORD: Town Hall.

Hotels or Inns at places marked *, and at Allington, Cholderton, Tidworth, and Little Bedwyn.

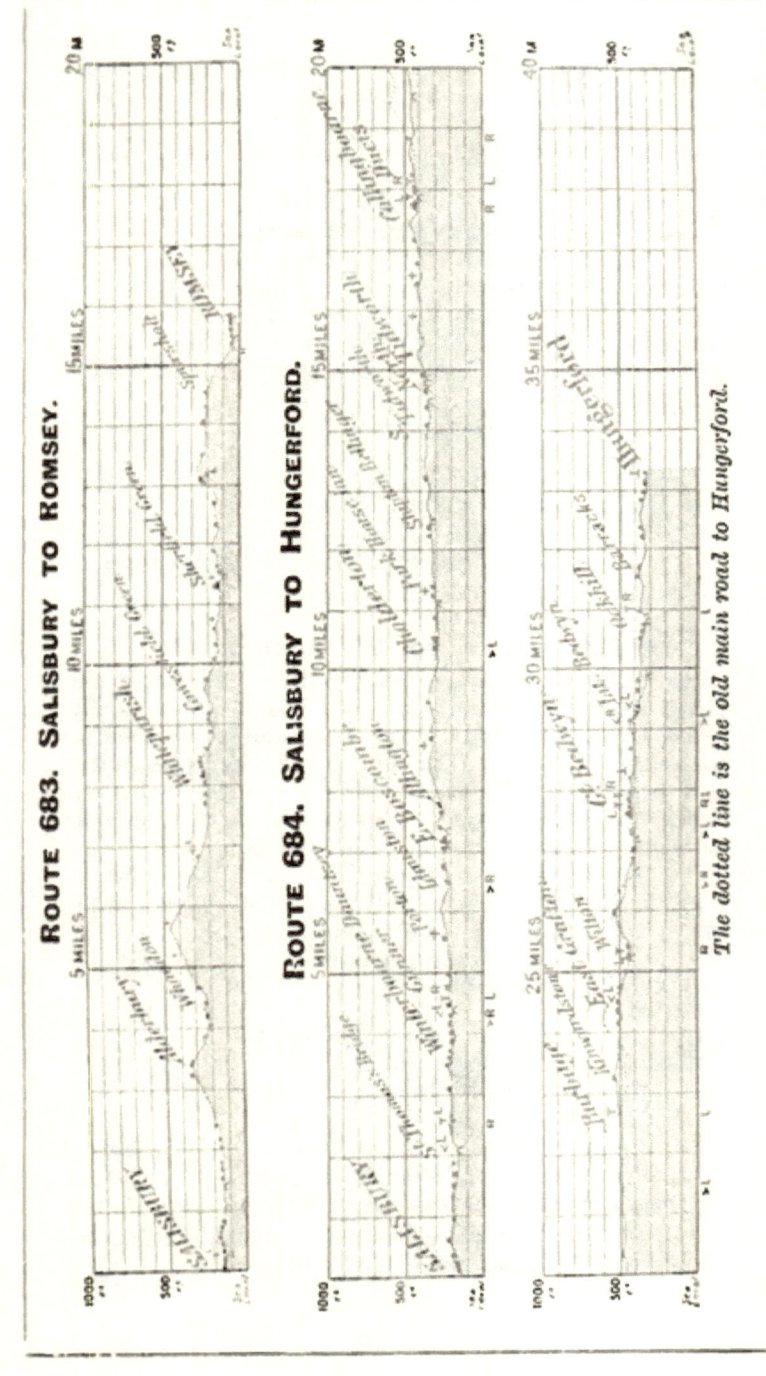

ROUTE 683. SALISBURY TO ROMSEY.

ROUTE 684. SALISBURY TO HUNGERFORD.

The dotted line is the old main road to Hungerford.

685   SALISBURY **TO SWINDON.**

Description. Class II. A hilly road as far as Amesbury, but with excellent surface; thereafter undulating with very fair surface to Marlborough, but with dangerous hills after Oare and into Marlborough. From Marlborough to Swindon the surface is usually good, but during and after the autumn military manoeuvres the surface of this road is wretched.

Gradients.—At 1½m. 1 in 21; 2m. 1 in 16; 4m. 1 in 19; 6m. 1 in 15; 6½m. 1 in 17; 7m. 1 in 19; 9½m. 1 in 18; 12½m. 1 in 15; 21½m. 1 in 16; 24m. 1 in 12†; 27½m. 1 in 13†; 28m. 1 in 11†; 28½m. 1 in 15†; 35½m. 1 in 17; 38m. 1 in 25; 39½m. 1 in 16. (†*Dangerous.*)

Milestones.—Measured from the Council House, Salisbury; after Marlborough from Swindon Market.

Measurements.

Salisbury,* Market Place.
7½	Amesbury.*					
16¼	9¼	Upavon.*				
21	13¾	4½	Pewsey,* P.O.			
27¾	20¼	11¼	6¾	Marlborough,* Town House.		
31¼	23¾	14¼	10½	3¾	Ogbourne,* Station.	
39½	31½	22¼	18¼	11¼	7½	Swindon,* Goddard Arms.
40¼	32½	23¾	19½	12½	8¼	1¼ Swindon,* Station.

Principal Objects of Interest.—1½m. Old Sarum. Amesbury: Stonehenge. MARLBOROUGH: College, Town Hall, Savernake, Devil's Den. SWINDON: Railway works. Rather monotonous road over the Downs.

Hotels or Inns at places marked *, and at Netheravon, &c.

686   SALISBURY **TO DEVIZES.**

Description.—Class I. & II. A splendid road to Stapleford; thereafter a fair road over the Downs—often very loose—to West Lavington, whence good surface to Devizes. The old road over the Downs is mostly grass-grown.

Gradients.—At 7m. 1 in 19; 10½m. 1 in 16; 18½m. 1 in 17; 23m. 1 in 23; 24½m. 1 in 18.

Milestones.—Measured from Salisbury, Council House as far as Shrewton; after Lavington, measured from Devizes.

Measurements.

Salisbury,* Market.
10⅛	Winterbourne Stoke.*	
19½	9¼	West Lavington,* Bridge Inn.
25¼	15¼	6¼ Devizes,* Cross.

Principal Objects of Interest.—1½m. Bemerton Church. 3m. Wilton: Church and House. 18½m. Robbers' Stone. DEVIZES: Castle, Cross, Town Hall, Museum.

Hotels or Inns at places marked *, and at S. Newton, &c.

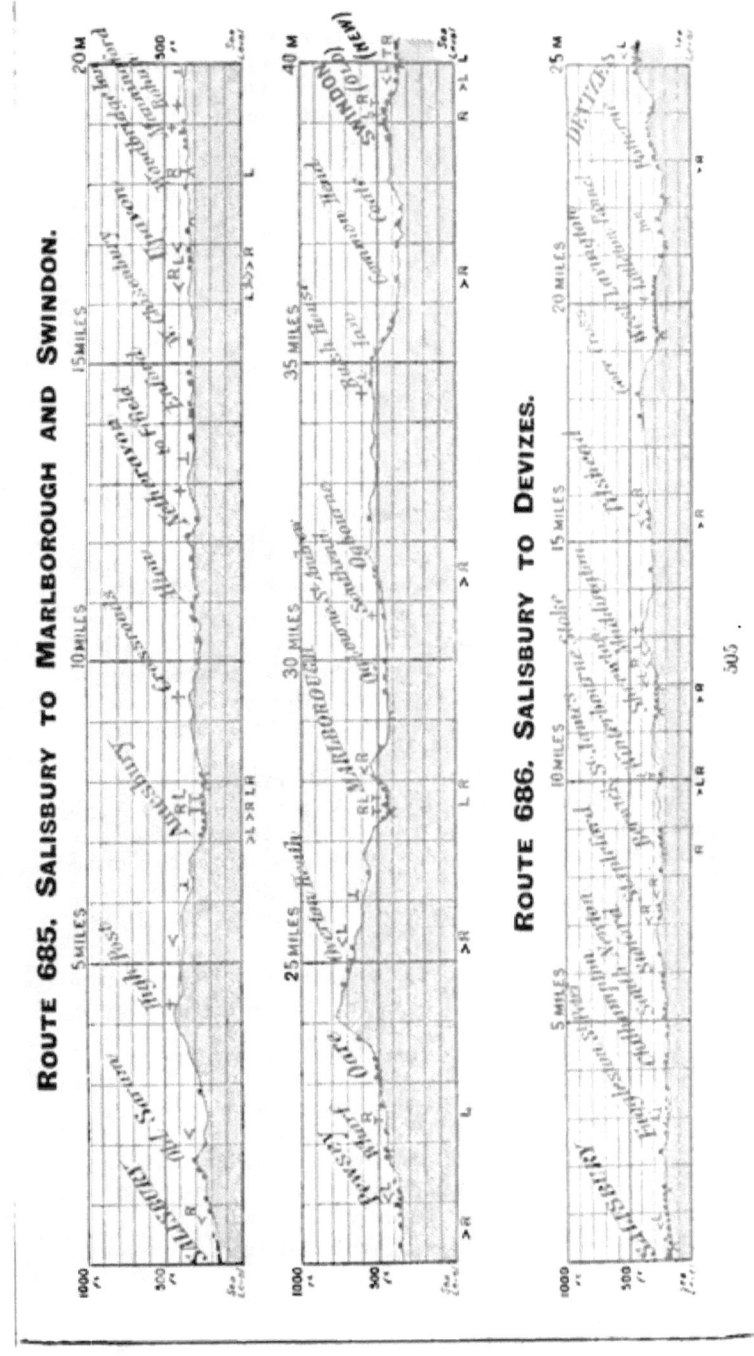

ROUTE 685. SALISBURY TO MARLBOROUGH AND SWINDON.

ROUTE 686. SALISBURY TO DEVIZES.

687   SALISBURY **TO** **FROME.**

Description.—Class I. The best road out of Salisbury. The road has splendid surface all the way to Warminster, and is in very fine condition except during the autumn military manœuvres. Splendid surface, but a slightly hilly road from Warminster to Frome; thereafter very hilly, but with good surface to Radstock; thereafter the road is narrow and winding, but with fair surface, joining the Bristol road at Farrington Gurney. The main part of Frome lies down a very steep hill from the "danger-board."

Gradients.—At 7m. 1 in 19; 17m. 1 in 22; 23m. 1 in 22; 23½m. 1 in 15; 25½m. 1 in 17; 26¾m. 1 in 23; 27m. 1 in 17; 29½m. 1 in 17; 31m. 1 in 11 (dangerous); 31¾m. 1 in 13; 34½m. 1 in 18; 35½m. 1 in 14; 36¼m. 1 in 12 (both dangerous); 38m. 1 in 20.

Milestones.—Measured from Salisbury, Council House, to Warminster, then from Frome.

Measurements.

Salisbury,* Market.						
5¼	South Newton.*					
11	5⅜	Deptford.*				
17½	12¼	6½	Heytesbury,* Church.			
21	15⅝	10	3½	Warminster,* Clock.		
28½	23¾	17½	11	7½	Frome,* Cross.	
36	30¼	25	18½	15	8	Radstock,* Bridge.
40¼	35¼	29¼	22¾	17½	12¼	4¼ Farrington Inn.*

Principal Objects of Interest.—1½m. Bemington Church. 3m. Wilton: House and Church. Heytesbury: Church. WARMINSTER: Minster. 23½m. Longleat Park. FROME: Cross, Church. Radstock: Collieries.

Hotels or Inns at places marked *, and at Wilton, South Newton, Serrington, Codford, Boreham, &c.

688   SALISBURY **TO** **WINCANTON.**

Description.—Class II. A very fine, level road to Dinton; thereafter very hilly and with poor surface as far as Mere, thence good to Wincanton. The best route is 689.

Gradients.—At 10m. 1/20; 11m. 1/14; 11¾m. 1/17; 13½m. 1/22; 14m. and 15½m. 1/20; 20m. 1/13; 20¾m. 1/19; 21¼m. 1/24.

Milestones.—Measured from Salisbury Council House as far as Willoughby Hedge; thereafter from Wincanton.

Measurements.

Salisbury,* Market.					
3¾	Wilton,* Market.				
12	8¾	Chilmark.*			
15¾	12½	3¾	Hindon.*		
22¾	19¼	10½	6⅝	Mere.*	
24¾	21¼	12¾	8¾	2¼	Zeals Green.
29¾	26¼	17¾	13¾	7¼	5 Wincanton.* [over.

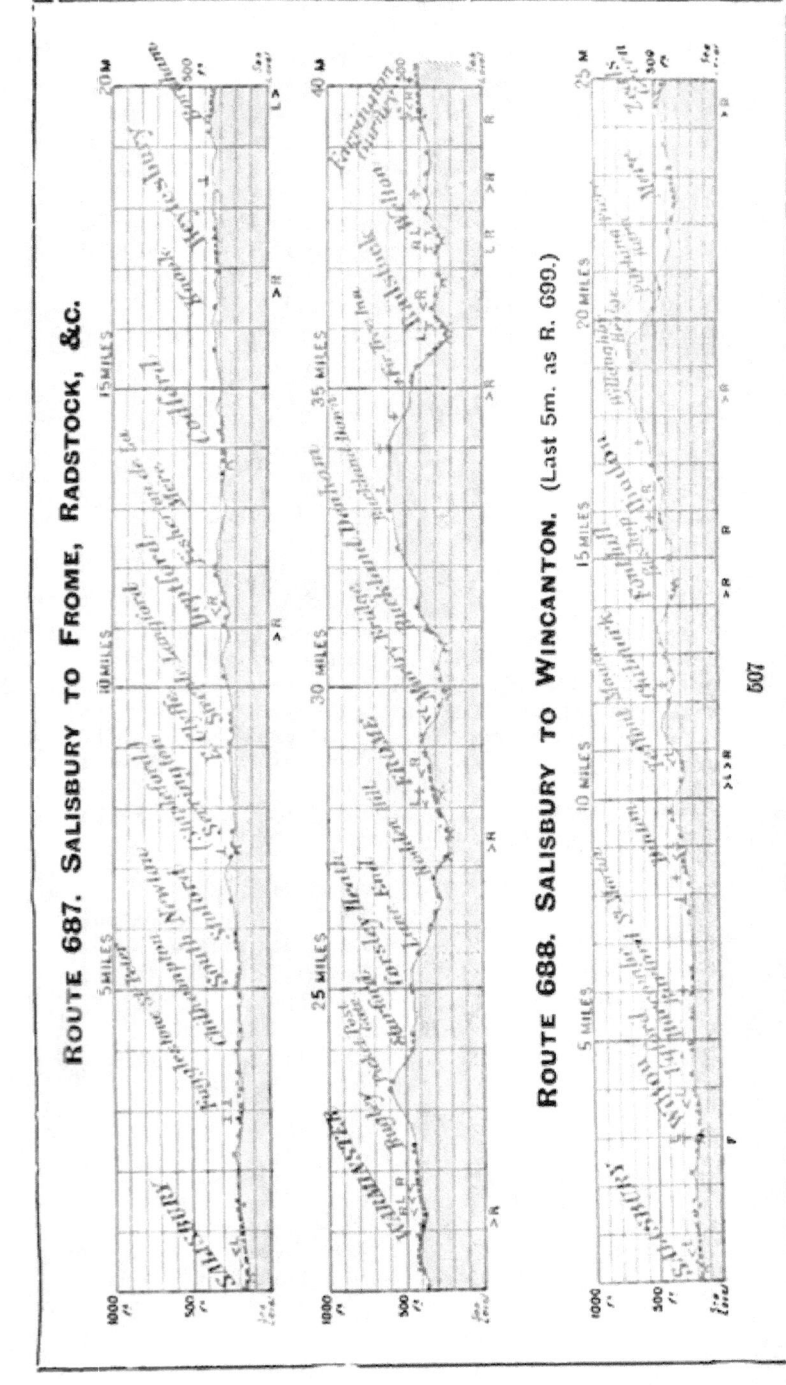

ROUTE 687. SALISBURY TO FROME, RADSTOCK, &C.

ROUTE 688. SALISBURY TO WINCANTON. (Last 5m. as R. 699.)

Route 688—Continued.

Principal Objects of Interest.—At 1½m. Bemerton Ch.
Wilton: Church, House. 8½m. Dinton House, Nickball
Castle. 14½m. Fonthill Abbey. Mere: Church, Castle Hill.

689   SALISBURY TO EXETER.

Description.—Class I. The road has splendid surface,
but is somewhat hilly as far as Shaftesbury. (By following
the road given here from Whitesand Cross to Knights Barn,
two steep hills are avoided, but the direct road should be
followed at night). From Shaftesbury to Wincanton—after
the dangerous descent from Shaftesbury—the surface is
splendid, and the gradients remarkably easy; thereafter
the road continues of very fine surface, and with easy undulations to Ilminster. From Ilminster to Honiton the road
is steep and rather rough. Honiton to Exeter, see R. 718.

Gradients.—At 7¼m. & 8¾m. 1 in 22; 10m. 1 in 17; 12¾m. 1 in
18; 14m. 1 in 13; (16½m. to 17m. on direct road, 1 in 12); 21¾m.
1 in 12 (dangerous turn); 32¼m. 1 in 17; 34m. 1 in 21; 34½m.
1 in 19; 35¼m. 1 in 21; 37m. 1 in 19; 43m. 1 in 20; 48m. 1 in 23;
50¾m. & 51¼m. 1 in 21; 58m. 1 in 18; 58¾m. 1 in 14; 62½m. 1 in
12 (dangerous); 65m. 1 in 14; 66½m. 1 in 15; 71½m. 1 in 16.

Milestones.—Measured from Salisbury Council House to
Barford, then from Cattle Market, Shaftesbury, then from
the Court House to Leigh Common, whence from Wincanton Town Hall on to Sparkford; thereafter from Ilminster
Town Hall to County boundary, after which from Honiton.

Measurements.

Salisbury,* Market.										
3½	Wilton,* Market.									
10	6½	Fovant.*								
21½	18	11¼	Shaftesbury,* Court House.							
25¼	22¼	15¼	4½	Gillingham,* P.O.						
32¾	29½	22¾	11½	7	Wincanton,* Town Hall.					
40½	37¼	30½	19¼	14½	7½	Sparkford,* Inn.				
46¼	42½	36½	24¼	20¼	13¼	5¾	Ilchester,* Town Hall.			
58¼	54¼	48¼	36¾	32¼	25¼	17¾	12	Ilminster,* Town Hall.		
75	71½	65	53½	49½	42½	34½	28¾	16¾	Honiton, Church.	
91½	88½	81½	70¼	65¾	58½	51½	45½	33½	16½	Exeter.

Principal Objects of Interest.—1½m. Bemerton Church.
Wilton: Ch., Wilton House. 15m. Wardour Cas. SHAFTES-
BURY: Court House, Church, fine view from Castle Hill.
Gillingham: Church, School. WINCANTON: site of Palace.
Sparkford: Cadbury "Castle," or Camelot. Ilchester: Ch.
Ilminster: Market House, Church. HONITON: Church.

Hotels or Inns at places marked *, and at Holton, Tintin-
hull, Seavington, Horton, and Marsh, &c.

ROUTE 689. SALISBURY TO EXETER. (Honiton to Exeter: see Route 718.)

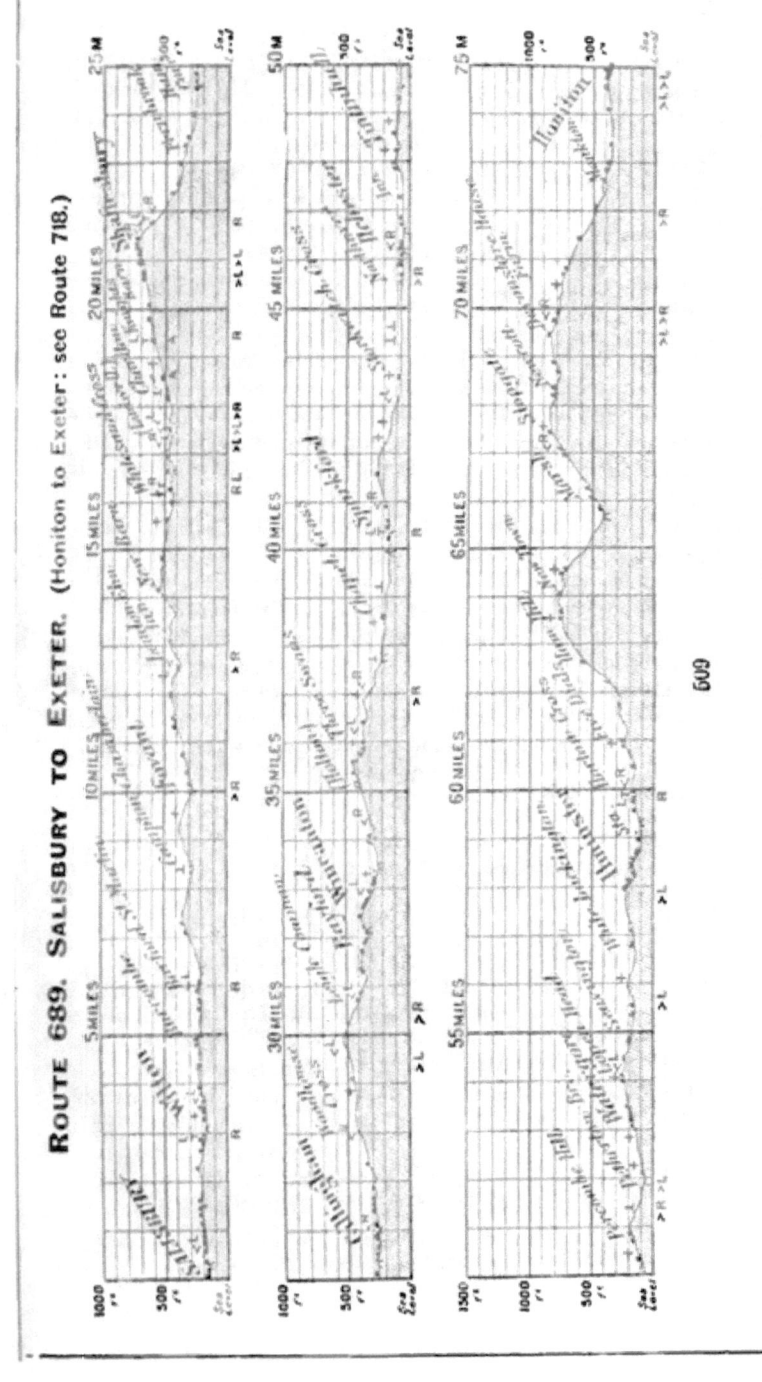

690 SALISBURY TO DORCHESTER.

Description.—Class II. A very hilly road, with only moderately good surface as far as Blandford. From Blandford to Dorchester the road is exceedingly hilly, with steep and dangerous hills as far as Puddletown, thereafter very good surface to Dorchester. The best road from Blandford to Dorchester is Route 681 to Spettisbury, thence by a cross lane to Almer, where join Route 705 (21⅜m.).

Gradients.—At 1m. 1/19; 2m. 1/23; 4¼m. 1/13; 5m. 1/17; 7m. 1/20; 7¾m. 1/18; 9¾m. 1/22; 12¾m. 1/16; 15m. 1/20; 15½m. 1/12; 16¾m. 1/22; 18m. 1/17; 18¼m. 1/23; 19½m. 1/22; 22¼m. 1/16; 23¼m. 1/15; 24m. & 24¼m. 1/18; 24¾m. 1/15; 25¼m. 1/16; 27¼m. 1/12; 28m. 1/14; 29m. 1/17; 30¼m. 1/14; 30¾m. 1/12; 32¼m. 1/11 (both dangerous); 33½m. 1/20; 35¼m. 1/16; 35¾m. 1/18.

Milestones.—Measured from Harnham Bridge, Salisbury, to Pimperne; thereafter from Shire Hall, Dorchester.

Measurements.

Salisbury,* Market.
10¾ Woodyates,* Inn.
15⅝ 4⅞ Cashmoor,* Inn.
22 10¼ 5⅜ Blandford,* Market.
27⅞ 17⅛ 12¼ 9⅝ 4⅜ Winterborne Whitchurch.*
30 20 15⅛ 12⅜ 7¾ 2⅝ Milborne,* St. Andrew.
38¼ 28¼ 23⅝ 20⅝ 16 11⅜ 8¼ Dorchester,* Clock.

Principal Objects of Interest.—A lonely road over the Downs. Cashmore: to Rushmere and Lamatree. Blandford: Bryanstone House, Damory Court. Milborne: Weatherbury "Castle." DORCHESTER: as Route 704.

Hotels or Inns at places marked *, and at Combe Bisset, Tarrant Hinton, Pimperne, and Puddletown.

---

691 SALISBURY TO CHRISTCHURCH.

Description.—Class II. A slightly undulating road for the first three miles, then a splendid road, quite level the rest of the way. It is sometimes a little loose.

Gradients.—At ¾m. 1 in 18; 2m. 1 in 23; 2¾m. 1 in 18.

Measurements.

Salisbury,* Market.
6¼ Downton Wick.*
10⅞ 4¼ Fordingbridge.*
16⅞ 10¾ 6 Ringwood,* Market Place.
26¼ 20¼ 15½ 9½ Christchurch,* Town Hall.

Principal Objects of Interest.—2m. Britford: Buckingham's Tomb. 2¾m. Longford Castle. Downton: Church. Moot, Maze. Breamore: House. Fordingbridge: Church. Ringwood: Monmouth's House. Sopley: Church. CHRISTCHURCH: Abbey Church, Town Hall, Staple Cross.

Hotels or Inns at places marked*, and at Breamore, &c

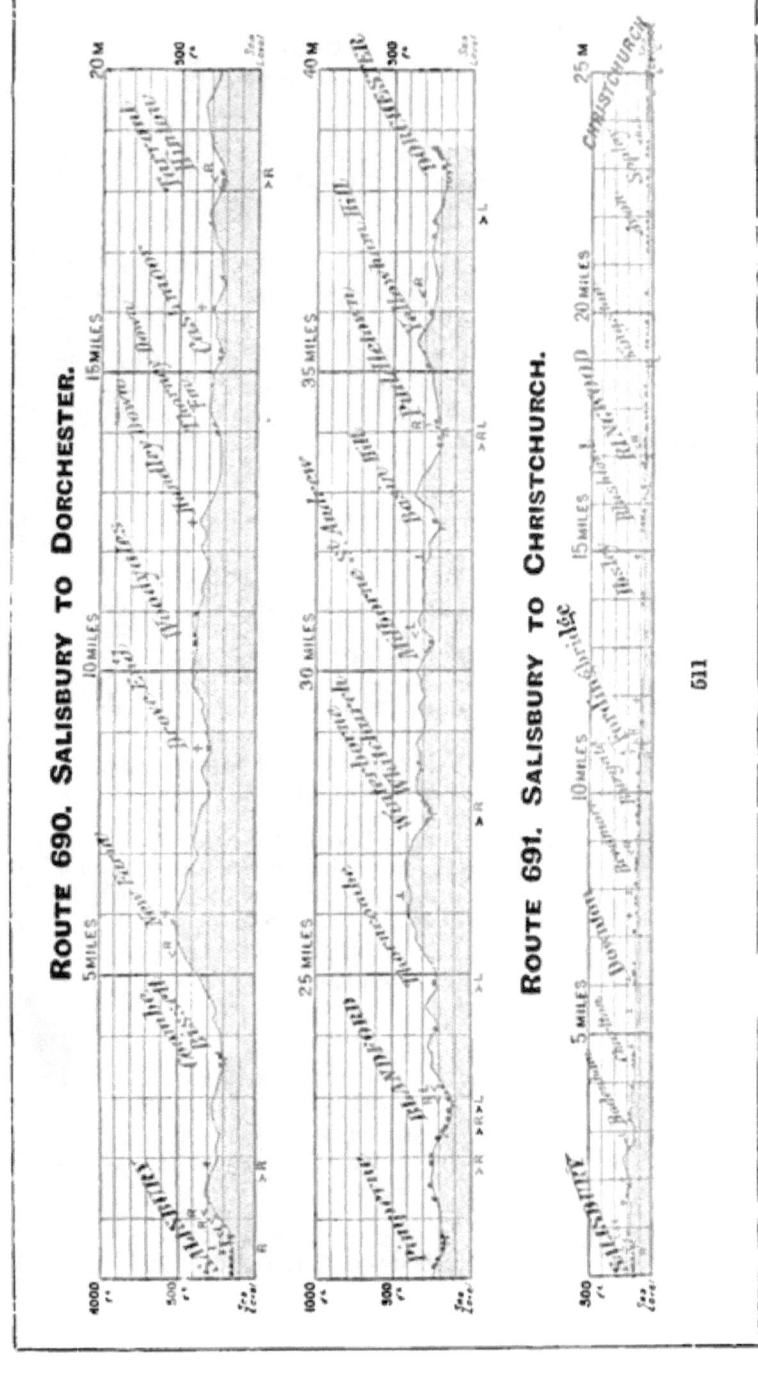

ROUTE 690. SALISBURY TO DORCHESTER.

ROUTE 691. SALISBURY TO CHRISTCHURCH.

692 SALISBURY TO STONEHENGE.

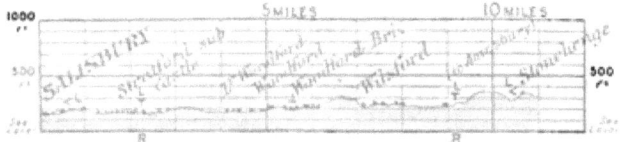

Description.—Class II.—A fine road, but with dangerous descent at Wilsford; surface rather loose approaching Stonehenge. This is an easier road than by Amesbury.

Measurements.—Salisbury,* Market Place.

5¾		Woodford Bridge.*
10¾	5	Stonehenge, or
(9½	4½	Amesbury.)

Principal Objects of Interest.—2m. Old Sarum. Stonehenge.

---

693 BOURNEMOUTH TO WIMBORNE.

Description.—Class II. Steep hill out of Bournemouth, then a good undulating country road.

Measurements.—Bournemouth,* Square.

4½		Kinson.*
9⅝	5	Wimborne Minster.*

Principal Objects of Interest.—Kinson: Church, Canford Manor. Wimborne: Minster.

---

694 WAREHAM TO LULWORTH.

Description.—Class II. Fine surface to Holme Bridge, then a fair country road.

Gradients.—At 6½m. 1 in 19; 8m. 1 in 10 (dangerous).

Measurements.—Wareham,* Town Clock.

6		East Lulworth.*
9	3	West Lulworth,* Cove Hotel.

Principal Objects of Interest.—East Lulworth: Castle. West Lulworth: Cove. Fine coast scenery.

Hotels or Inns at places marked *.

WEYMOUTH TO BRIDPORT. 695

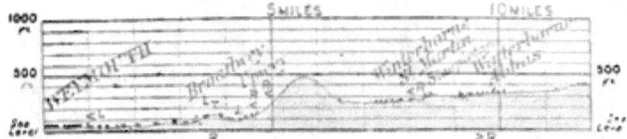

Description.—Class II. Excellent surface to Broadwey, then very steep for three miles, after which good surface. The Bridport road (R. 704) is joined at Winterborne Abbas.

Gradients.—At 5m. 1 in 10 (dangerous); 6¼m. 1 in 14, &c.

Milestones.—Measured from Bridport.

Measurements.—Weymouth,* Bridge.

9¾   Winterborne Abbas.*

19⅝   10   Bridport.*   (R. 704).

Principal Objects of Interest.—6½m. Maiden Castle, &c.

HONITON TO SIDMOUTH. 696

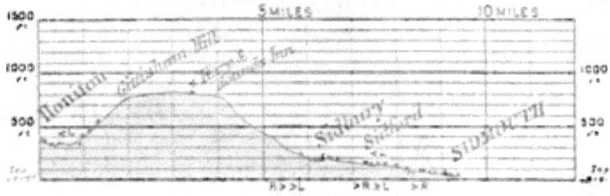

Description.—Class III. Very steep and rough to Sidbury, thence good surface. The road by Ottery is the best road to Sidmouth; excellent surface, but a continuously undulating road.

Gradients.—(†*Dangerous.*) 1½m. 1/10†; 4½m. 1 13†; 5½m. 1/17.

Milestones.—Measured from Honiton Church.

Measurements.—Honiton,* Church.

7¾   Sidford.*

9⅔   2   Sidmouth,* Esplanade.

By OTTERY.

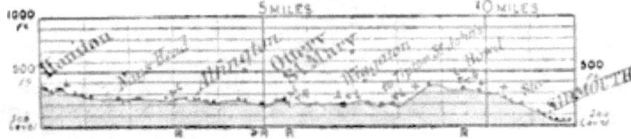

Gradients.—At 5 & 5½m. 1 in 19; 8½m. 1 in 22.

Milestones.—Measured from Honiton Ch., and Sidmouth.

Measurements.—Honiton,* Church.

5½   Ottery.*

9½   3¾   Bowd Inn.*   (R. 719).

11¾   6¼   2¾   Sidmouth,* Esplanade.

Principal Objects of Interest.—Sidbury: Castle, House. SIDMOUTH : fine coast, Peak Hill, &c   Ottery: Church.

2 O

698   DEVIZES TO ANDOVER.

Description.—Class II. Good surface at first, then rather looser to Upavon, whence rather rough to Everley; thereafter fine surface to Andover.

Gradients.—At 2m. 1 in 22; 2½m. 1 in 23; 11m. 1 in 19; 13½m. 1 in 17; 14m. 1 in 14; 17½m. 1 in 18.

Measurements.

Devizes,* Cross.
9¾ Upavon.*
14⅝ 5¼ Everley.*
19¼ 9¾ 4 Ludgershall,* Cross.
26½ 16⅝ 11 7½ Andover.*

Principal Objects of Interest.—11¼m. Chisenbury Camp. Ludgershall: Castle. ANDOVER: Bury Hill, &c.

699   WARMINSTER TO WINCANTON. &C.

Description.—Class II. An excellent, undulating road as far as Zeal's Green, thereafter hilly, but with good surface to Wincanton. From Wincanton to Sherborne the road has good surface, but Charlton Hill is very dangerous.

Gradients.—At ½m. 1 in 20; 8½m. 1 in 17; 12½m. 1 in 23; 14m. & 14½m. 1 in 20; 16½m. 1 in 17; 17m. 1 in 18; 18½m. 1 in 21; 19½m. 1 in 18; 21¼m. 1 in 12 (dangerous).

Milestones.—Measured from Warminster Clock.

Measurements.

Warminster,* Clock.
6¾ Maiden Bradley.*
17 10¼ Wincanton,* Town Hall.
25¼ 18½ 8¼ Milborne Port.*
28⅝ 21⅞ 11⅝ 2⅜ Sherborne.* (R. 718.)

Principal Objects of Interest. — 2¾m. Shear Water. Stourton: Stourhead House, Alfred's Tower. WINCANTON: Town Hall. SHERBORNE: Minster, Cross, Castle.

700   WARMINSTER TO SHAFTESBURY.

Description.—Class II. A good, undulating road for 3m. then very hilly to West Knoyle, with indifferent surface; thereafter good to Shaftesbury.

Gradients.—(† Dangerous.) At ½m. 1 in 20; 3m. 1 in 14; 4m. 1 in 15; 6m. 1 in 10†; 6½m. 1 in 23; 8m. 1 in 15; 8½m. 1 in 10†; 9½m. 1 in 11†; 13½m. 1 in 13.†

Measurements.

Warminster,* Clock.
10 East Knoyle.
(... 2¼ Hindon.)
15¼ 5¼ 7½ Shaftesbury,* Court House.

Principal Objects of Interest.—East Knoyle: Fonthill Abbey. SHAFTESBURY: Castle Hill, Court House.

Hotels or Inns at places marked *, and at Semley Station.

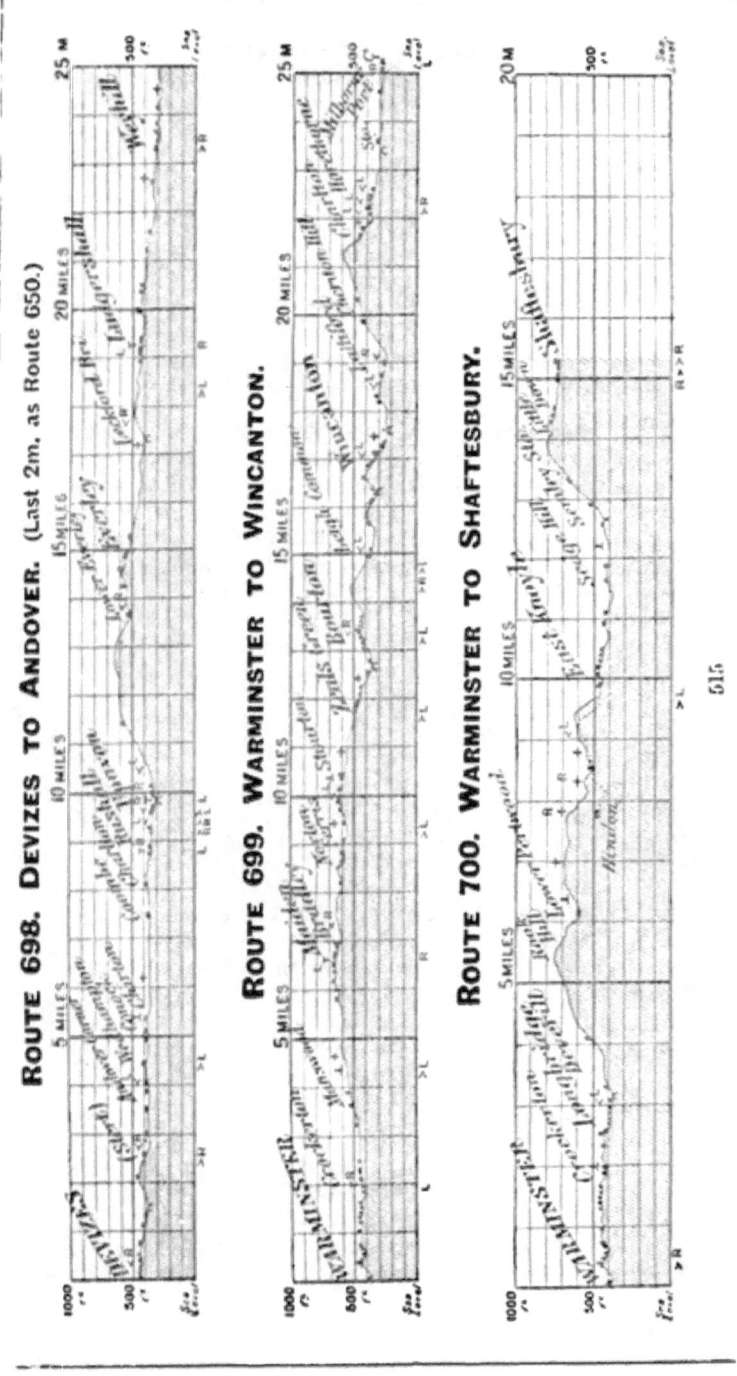

ROUTE 698. DEVIZES TO ANDOVER. (Last 2m. as Route 650.)

ROUTE 699. WARMINSTER TO WINCANTON.

ROUTE 700. WARMINSTER TO SHAFTESBURY.

515

701 BLANDFORD TO SHAFTESBURY.

Description.—Class II. A very good road, with slight hills to Fontmell, then steep, and with a highly dangerous hill near Shaftesbury.

Gradients.—At ¾m. 1 in 15; 2¼m. 1 in 13; 8¼m. 1 in 18; 10½m. 1 in 9; 11m. 1 in 13 (both dangerous).

Milestones.—Measured from Blandford Market.

Measurements.

Blandford,* Market.
8 Fontmell.*
12¾ 4¾ Shaftesbury,* Court House.

Principal Objects of Interest.—Rather a pretty road.

702 WIMBORNE TO SWANAGE.

Description.—Class II. Fine surface to Corfe Mullen, then narrow and hilly to Lytchett, whence fine to Wareham. Good undulating road from Wareham to Swanage.

Gradients.—At 3m. & 5¾m. 1/17; 13¼m. 1/13; 19½m. 1/15.

Milestones.—Measured from Wareham Clock.

Measurements.

Wimborne,* Bridge.
6¾ Lytchett Minster.*
11¼ 4½ Wareham,* Clock.
15½ 8¾ 4¼ Corfe Castle.*
21 14¼ 9¾ 5½ Swanage,* Town Hall.

Principal Objects of Interest.—Wareham: Ramparts, Potteries. Corfe Castle: Church. Swanage: Church, Mowlem Institute, Durlestone Head, Quarries, &c.

703 POOLE TO CRANBORNE, &C.

Description.—Class II. A slightly hilly road, but with good surface to Cranborne, thereafter exceedingly hilly and with poor surface to Coombe Bisset. The best road from Cranborne to Salisbury (16½m.), is to join R. 690 at Handley.

Gradients.—(†*Dangerous.*) At 3m. 1 in 23; 4¼m. 1 in 21; 7m. 1 in 16; 15m. 1 in 14; 15¾m. 1 in 17; 17¼m. 1 in 13†; 18½m. 1 in 11†; 19m. 1 in 13†; 19½m. & 20m. 1 in 12†; 23m. & 23½m. 1 in 16.

Measurements.

Poole,* Station.
6 Wimborne,* Bridge.
11¾ 5¾ Horton Inn.*
16 10 4¼ Cranborne.*
25 19 13¼ 9 Coombe Bisset.*
28¼ 22¼ 16½ 12¼ 3¼ Salisbury,* Market.

Principal Objects of Interest. — WIMBORNE: Minster. Cranborne: St. Giles Park, Priory Ch. 22¾m. Grimsditch.

Hotels or Inns at places marked *.

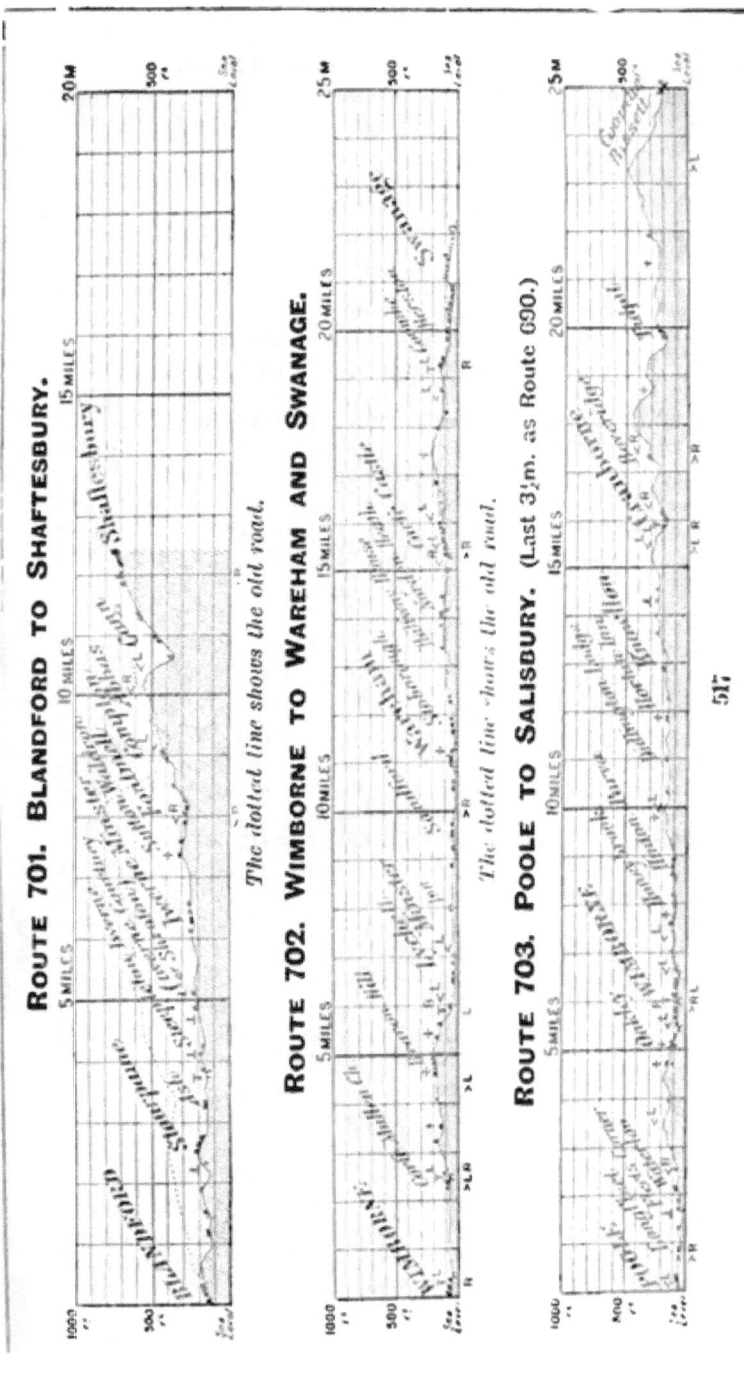

ROUTE 701. BLANDFORD TO SHAFTESBURY.

The dotted line shows the old road.

ROUTE 702. WIMBORNE TO WAREHAM AND SWANAGE.

The dotted line shows the old road.

ROUTE 703. POOLE TO SALISBURY. (Last 3½m. as Route 690.)

704 Poole to Bridport.

Description.—Class I. A magnificent and almost level road for the first ten miles, then slightly undulating, but with splendid surface to Dorchester. From Dorchester to Bridport the road is exceedingly hilly—several dangerous hills—but the surface is very fair.

Gradients.—(†*Dangerous.*) At 11¾m., 14m., 19½m., 20m. 1 in 18; 22¾m. 1 in 22; 23½m. 1 in 19; 26¾m. 1 in 13†; 27m. 1 in 21; 27½m. 1 in 12†; 30¼m. 1 in 13†; 31m. 1 in 11†; 32¼m. & 32½m. 1 in 15†; 33¼m. 1 in 17; 34½m. 1 in 12†; 35m. 1 in 14†; 35¾m. 1 in 9.†

Milestones.—Measured from Poole old toll-gate as far as Bere Regis, thereafter measured from Dorchester.

Measurements.

Poole,* Station.
.. Bournemouth,* Square. (R. 680 to Upton).
12½ 16¼ Bere Regis.*
18½ 22¼ 6 Puddletown.*
22¾ 27 10¾ 4¾ Dorchester,* Clock.
27½ 31¾ 15½ 9¼ 4¾ Winterborne Abbas.*
37½ 41¾ 25½ 19½ 14¾ 10 Bridport,* Market.

Principal Objects of Interest.—Bere: Woodbury Hill. DORCHESTER: Shirehall, Museum, Amphitheatre, Maiden Castle. 28m. Nine Stones. 29m. The Broad Stone. BRIDPORT: Church, Harbour, &c.

Hotels or Inns at places marked*, and at Lytchett, Tolpuddle, &c.

---

705 Dorchester to Ringwood.

Description.—Class I. The road has fine surface, but with one stiff hill to Puddletown; thereafter an easy road in splendid condition, and with hardly any perceptible gradient to Ringwood. This is the best road to London.

Gradients.—At 3m. 1 in 18; 3½m. 1 in 16; 8¾m. 1 in 19.

Milestones.—Measured from Dorchester Clock as far as Bailey Gate, thereafter from Ringwood.

Measurements.

Dorchester,* Clock.
10¾ Bere Regis.*
22 11¼ Wimborne,* Bridge.
31¾ 21 9¾ Ringwood.*
Dorchester to Blandford by Spettisbury, 21¼m.

Principal Objects of Interest.—Bere Regis: Woodbury Hill. 18m. Charborough House. WIMBORNE: Minster. Ringwood: Monmouth's House.

Hotels or Inns at places marked*, and at Tolpuddle and St. Leonards Bridge.

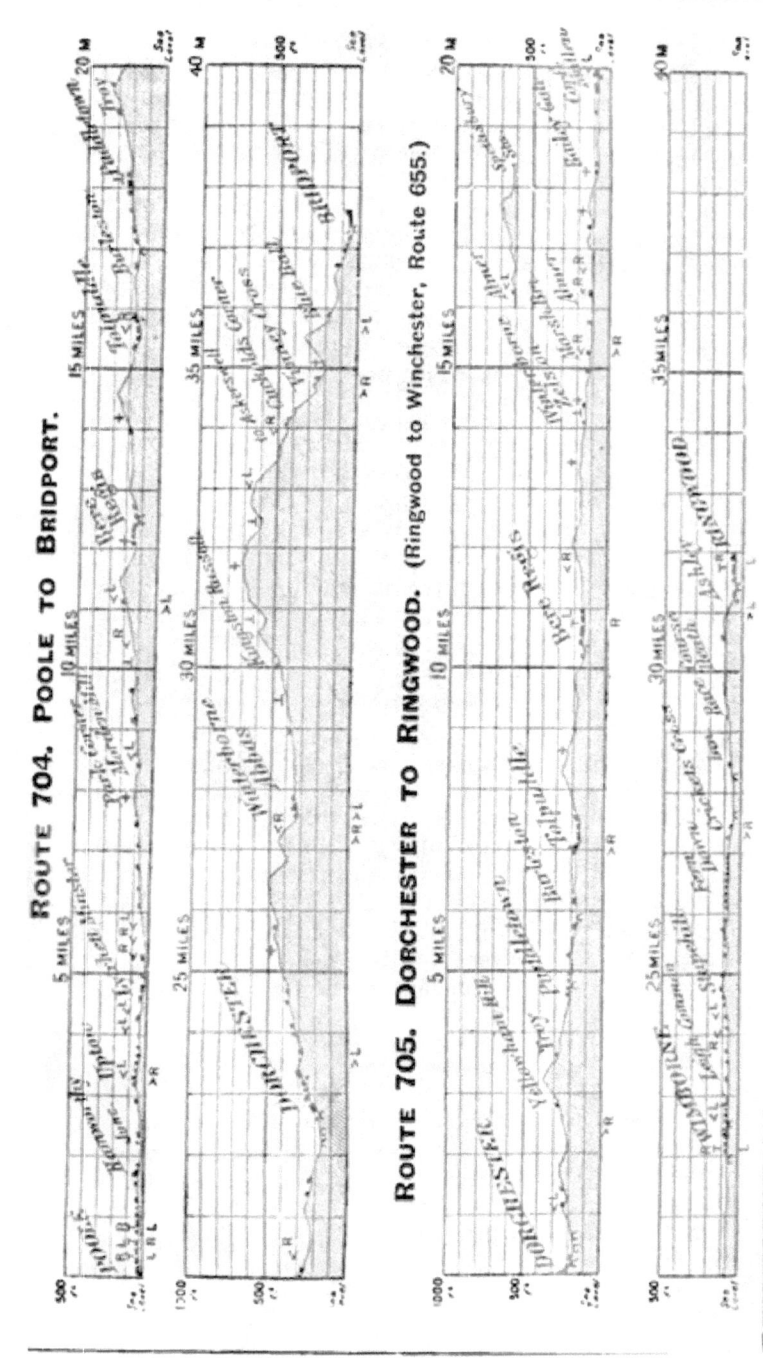

ROUTE 704. POOLE TO BRIDPORT.

ROUTE 705. DORCHESTER TO RINGWOOD. (Ringwood to Winchester, Route 655.)

706 DORCHESTER TO SHERBORNE, &C.

Description.—Class II. Splendid surface to Cerne, then a little rough to Lyons Gate, whence very good to Sherborne. From Sherborne to Marston, hilly but good.

Gradients.—(†*Dangerous.*) At 9½m. 1 in 18; 10½m. 1 in 11†; 17m. 1 in 21; 17½m. 1 in 17; 19½m. 1 in 15; 22½m. 1 in 10.

Milestones.—Measured from Sherborne Cross.

Measurements.

Dorchester,* Clock.
7½   Cerne Abbas.*
12¼   4½   Middlemarsh.*
18¾   11¼   6½   Sherborne,* Cross.
23¼   15¾   11¼   4¾   Marston,* Inn.   (R. 806).

Principal Objects of Interest.—Cerne: Abbey, Cerne Giant. SHERBORNE: Cross, Minster, Castle.

707   DORCHESTER TO YEOVIL.

Description.—Class II. Fine surface to Maiden Newton, then rather poor to Evershot, whence good to Yeovil; there are numerous steep and dangerous hills. Many therefore prefer going by Sherborne (R. 706 and 718).

Gradients.—(† *Dangerous.*) At 8½m. 1/9†; 12½m. 1/11†; 13¼m. 1/12†; 14½m. 1/12†; 15½m. 1/21; 19¼m. 1/16; 20¾m. 1/15.

Measurements.

Dorchester,* Clock.
8¼   Maiden Newton.*
13   5   Holywell.*
21¾   13¼   8¼   Yeovil,* Mermaid Hotel.

Principal Objects of Interest.—Maiden Newton: Cattistock Church. 15m. Melbury Park. YEOVIL: Church.

Hotels or Inns at places marked *, and at Grimstone, &c.

708 DORCHESTER TO CREWKERNE.

Description.—Class II. Fine surface to Maiden Newton, then a rather loose road over the Downs; the surface improves near Crewkerne.

Gradients.—At 9m. & 17m. 1/10 (dangerous); 20m. 1/15.

Milestones.—Measured from Shire Hall, Dorchester.

Measurements.

Dorchester,* Clock.
8¼   Maiden Newton.*
16¾   8¾   Toller Down.   (R. 715).
21¼   13¼   4¾   Crewkerne,* Market.

Principal Objects of Interest.—Maiden Newton: Cattistock Church. 17m. Winyards Gap. CREWKERNE: Church.

Hotels or Inns at places marked *, and at Stratton, Grimstone, Winyards Gap, and Misterton.

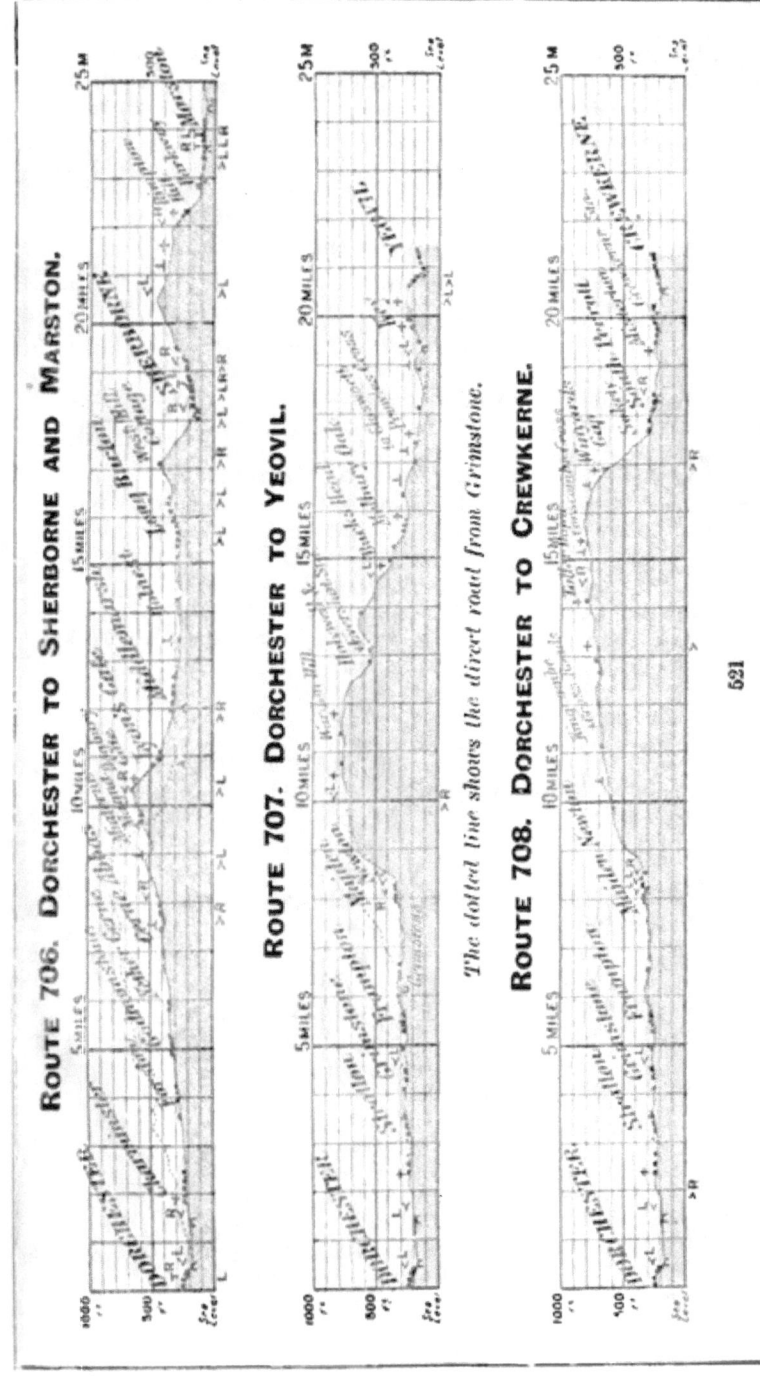

ROUTE 706. DORCHESTER TO SHERBORNE AND MARSTON.

ROUTE 707. DORCHESTER TO YEOVIL.

The dotted line shows the direct road from Grimstone.

ROUTE 708. DORCHESTER TO CREWKERNE.

709 DORCHESTER TO WEYMOUTH.

Description. Class I. A hilly road, with a steep and dangerous descent to Broadwey, thence splendid surface to Weymouth; thereafter to Portland the road is hilly to Portland Bridge, whence level but rough.

Gradients.—At 2m. 1 in 18; 3¾m. 1 in 15 (dangerous turn).

Milestones.—Irregular.

Measurements.

Dorchester,* Clock.
5   Broadwey.*
8¾ 3½ Weymouth,* Bridge.
12½ 7½ 4½ Portland,* Station.

Principal Objects of Interest. — 2m. Maiden Castle. WEYMOUTH: Esplanade, George III. Statue, Sandsfoot Castle. Portland: Castle, Breakwater, Prison.

710 BRIDPORT TO CREWKERNE, &c.

Description. —Class II. Fair surface, but very hilly road with steep and dangerous hills to Crewkerne. From Crewkerne to Ilminster good surface, but hilly. The next route is the best road between Bridport and Crewkerne.

Gradients.—(† *Dangerous.*) At 4½m. 5½m. & 7m. 1 in 13†; 8½m. 1 in 20; 9½m. 1 in 15; 10½m. 1 in 12†; 11¾m. 1 in 15; 12½m. & 13½m. 1 in 19; 15½m. 1 in 14; 15½m. 1 in 15; 19m. 1 in 13.†

Milestones.—Measured from Bridport to Beaminster, thereafter from Crewkerne.

Measurements.

Bridport,* Market.
6½ Beaminster.*
13½ 7 Crewkerne,* Market.
20½ 14 7 Ilminster,* Market House.

Principal Objects of Interest.—7½m. Tunnel.

Hotels or Inns at places marked *, and at Mosterton, &c.

711 CREWKERNE TO BRIDPORT.

Description.—Class III. Less hilly than the previous route, but the surface is hardly as good; it is, however, a much less trying route to travel.

Gradients.—At ½m. 1/16; 2m. 1/17; 9m. 1/16; 12m. 1/19.

Measurements.

Crewkerne,* Market.
6 Broadwindsor.*
13 7 Bridport,* Market.
14¾ 8½ 1½ Westbay,* Hotel.

Principal Objects of Interest. —Rather pretty road. BRIDPORT: Church, Harbour.

Hotels or Inns at places marked *, and at Drimpton, &c.

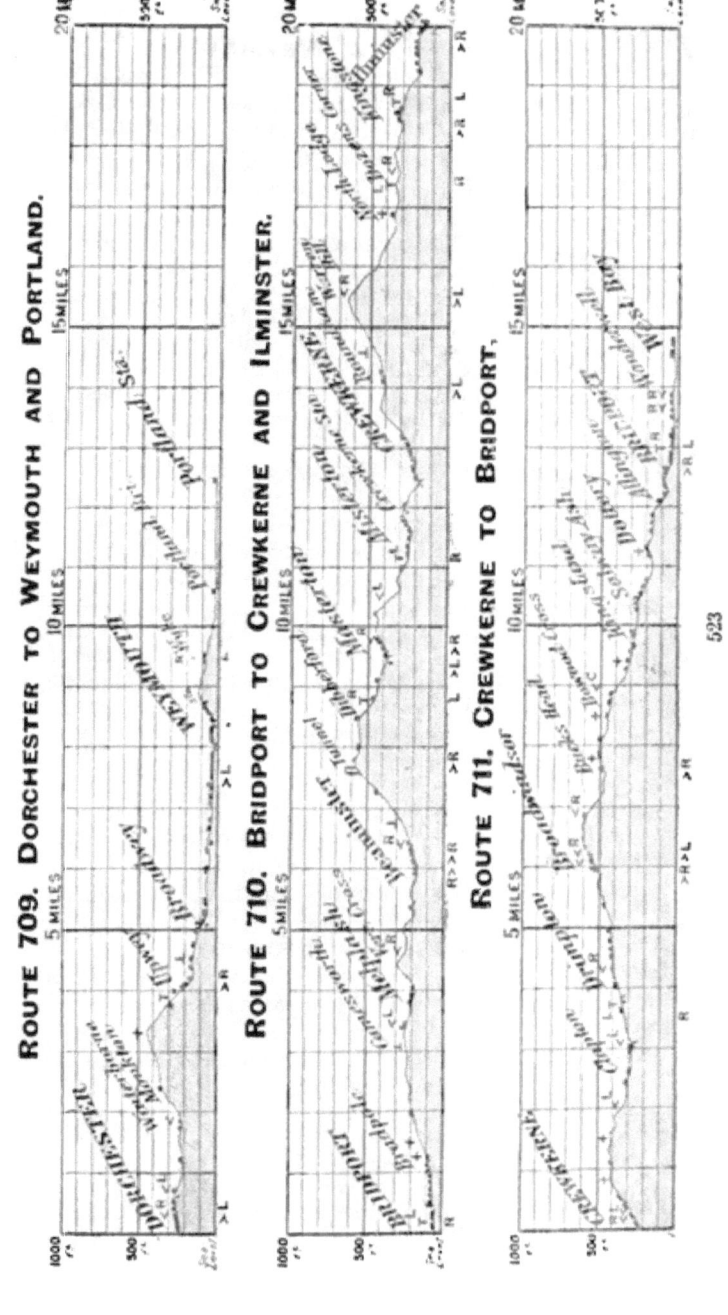

ROUTE 709. DORCHESTER TO WEYMOUTH AND PORTLAND.

ROUTE 710. BRIDPORT TO CREWKERNE AND ILMINSTER.

ROUTE 711. CREWKERNE TO BRIDPORT.

523

712 LYME REGIS TO CREWKERNE.

Description.—Class II. A steep and very hilly road, with poor surface. The road by Axminster is less trying.

Gradients.—(†*Dangerous.*) At ½m. 1/9†; 1½m. 1/16; 2¼m. 1/14†; 3½m. 1/14; 7¾m. 1/15; 8½m. 1/20; 9¼m. 1/14†; 9¾m. 1/12†; 10m. 1/11; 11½m. 1/18; 12½m. & 14¼m. 1/17; 16¾m. 1/16.

Measurements.

Lyme Regis.*
8 Marshwood Inn.*
16¾ 8¾ Crewkerne,* Market.

Principal Objects of Interest.—Fine views. 7¼m. Lambert's "Castle." CREWKERNE: Church.

Hotels or Inns at places marked *, and at Up Lyme, Hunter's Lodge, Birdsmoor Gate, Clapton, &c.

713 CREWKERNE TO AXMINSTER, &C.

Description.—Class II. & III. Splendid surface but hilly for five miles, then a narrow and poor road to Tytherleigh, whence fine surface but very hilly to Axminster; thereafter an undulating road, with very fair surface.

Gradients.—At ½m. 1 in 19; 2m. 1 in 14; 7½m. 1 in 21; 8¼m. 1 in 13; 10m. 1 in 10 (dangerous); 10½m. 1 in 16; 12¼m. 1 in 13; 15m. 1 in 14.

Milestones.—Rather irregular.

Measurements.

Crewkerne,* Market.
9¾ Tytherleigh,* Inn.
13¼ 3½ Axminster,* George Hotel.
18½ 8¾ 5¼ Colyford.*
20¾ 10½ 7¼ 1¾ Seaton.*

Principal Objects of Interest.—8m. Ford Abbey. AXMINSTER: Church. 15¼m. Ash House, Duke of Marlborough's birthplace. Seaton: Beer Head, Landslip, &c.

714 AXMINSTER TO SIDMOUTH.

Description.—Class II. The surface throughout is very fair, but most of the hills are dangerously steep.

Gradients.—(†*Very dangerous.*) At 1½m. 1 in 14; 2½m. 1 in 9†; 4½m. 1 in 10†; 5¼m. 1 in 13†; 13½m. 1 in 7†.

Milestones.—Measured from Colyton.

Measurements.

Axminster,* George Hotel.
5½ Colyton,* Market.
9¾ 4¼ Three Horse Shoes Inn.*
14¾ 9½ 5¾ Sidmouth,* Esplanade.

Principal Objects of Interest. — Colyton: Colcombe Castle. Sidmouth: fine coast, Peak Hill, &c.

Hotels or Inns at places marked *.

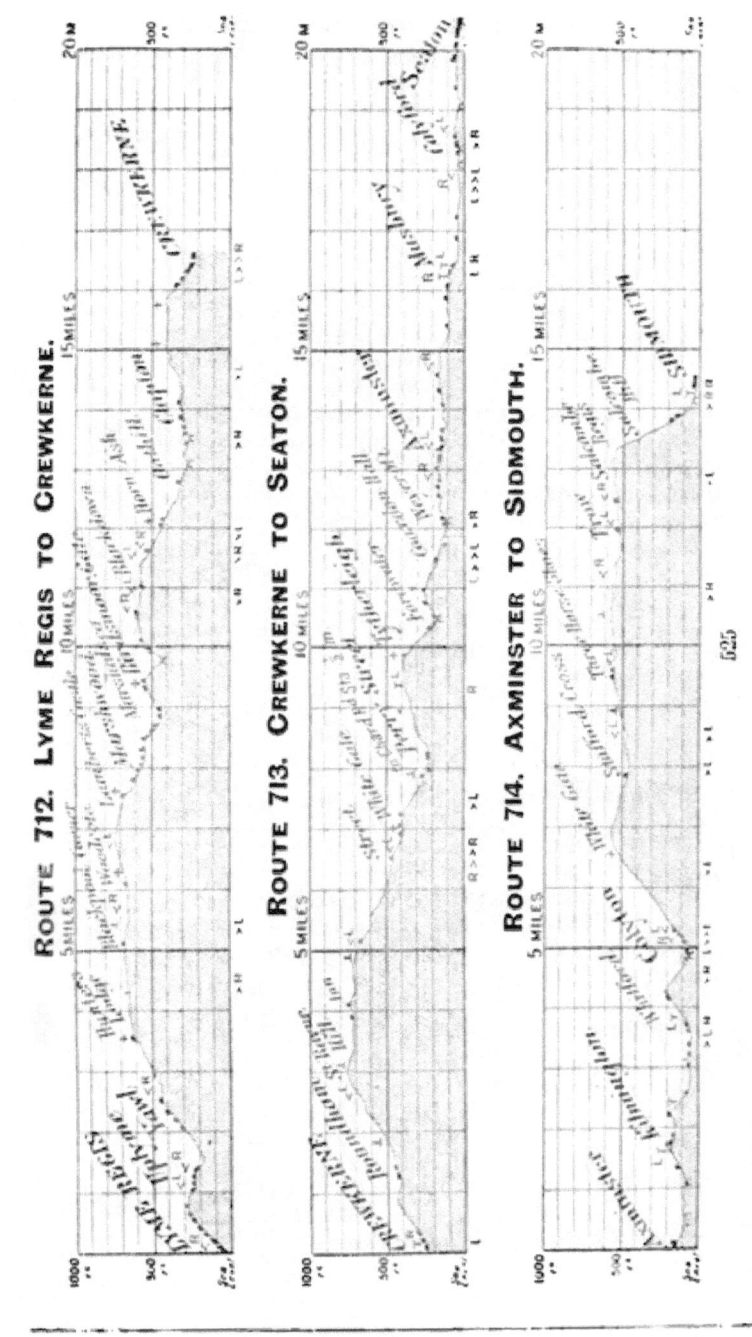

ROUTE 712. LYME REGIS TO CREWKERNE.

ROUTE 713. CREWKERNE TO SEATON.

ROUTE 714. AXMINSTER TO SIDMOUTH.

715 AXMINSTER TO BEAMINSTER, &C.

Description.—Class II. Exceedingly hilly, with poor surface and dangerous hills. R. 708 is joined at Toller Down.

Gradients.—(† *Dangerous.*) At ¼m. 1/19; ¾m. 1/10†; 1m. 1/9†; 1¾m. 1/7†; 7¼m. 1/16; 9m. 1/11†; 10m. 1/12†; 11m. 1/10†; 11¼m. 1/8†; 14¼m. 1/15; 15, 15¾, 16½, 17½, 19½, & 20m. 1/10.†

Measurements.

Axminster,* George Hotel.				
5½	Marshwood Inn.*			
10¼	4¾	Broadwindsor.*		
13⅛	7⅝	2⅞	Beaminster.*	
21⅝	16⅛	11⅜	8½	Evershot Station.*
25¾	20¼	15½	12⅝	Maiden Newton.* (R. 708).

Principal Objects of Interest.—5m. Lambert's Castle.

Hotels or Inns at places marked *, and at Birdsmoor Gate.

716 HONITON TO LYME REGIS.

Description.—Class II. Fine surface but rather hilly to Axminster; thereafter very steep but good to Lyme. For Charmouth turn to L. at 11⅝m. Good surface, but steep.

Gradients.—(† *Dangerous.*) At ½m. 1 in 13†; 3m. 1 in 14†; 8¼m. 1 in 13†; 10m. 1 in 15; 11¼m. 1 in 16; 13m. 1 in 14; 15m. 1 in 9.† To Charmouth: 12½m. 1 in 13†; 14½m. 1 in 14†; 15m. 1 in 9.†

Measurements.

Honiton,* Church.		
9¾	Axminster,* George Hotel.	
15½	5¾	Lyme Regis,* or
15¼	5½	Charmouth,* P.O.

Principal Objects of Interest.—AXMINSTER: Church. Uplyme: Church. Lyme Regis: Parade, Pier, Monmouth's landing, 1685. Fine views from this road.

Hotels or Inns at places marked *, and at Kilmington.

717 HONITON TO TIVERTON.

Description.—Class II. Good surface, but dangerously steep about Hembury Fort; thereafter a good, undulating road to Cullompton. The direct road to Tiverton is precipitous, that by Tiverton Junction is a good, undulating road.

Gradients.—At 3½m. & 4m. 1 in 10 (dangerous). Direct road to Tiverton: 1 in 10, 1 in 7, 1 in 10, & 1 in 8.

Measurements.

Honiton,* Church.				
7⅜	Dulford.			
11	3⅝	Cullompton.*		
14¼	6⅞	3¼	Tiverton Junction.*	
19¾	12⅜	8¾	5½	Tiverton.*
(16¾	9⅜	5¾	Tiverton,* direct).	

[over.

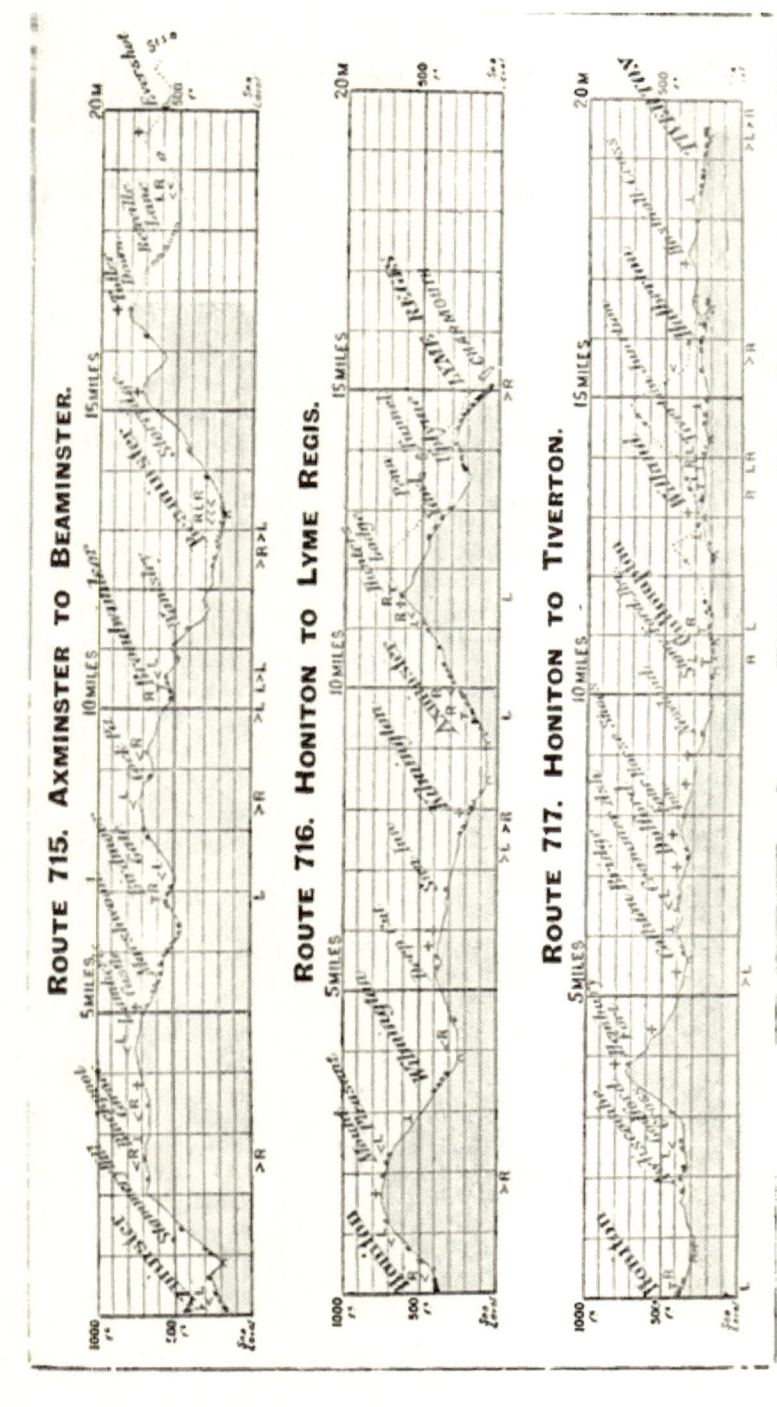

ROUTE 715. AXMINSTER TO BEAMINSTER.

ROUTE 716. HONITON TO LYME REGIS.

ROUTE 717. HONITON TO TIVERTON.

Route 717—Continued.

Principal Objects of Interest.—3¾m. Hembury Fort. Cullompton: Church. TIVERTON: Church, Castle ruins, Collipriest House.

Hotels or Inns at places marked *, and at Halberton.

718 EXETER TO SHAFTESBURY.

Description.—Class I. The London road, but Route 689 is rather easier after Honiton. The road has splendid surface, and is of uniform quality throughout, but it is unusually steep and hilly for such a superior road. Although many of the hills are very steep, the only ones with a dangerous turn are at Yarcombe and Shaftesbury, the others are all straight and wide. The old direct road from Honiton to Chard is shown in dotted lines.

Gradients.—At 9m. 1 in 16; 10½m. 1 in 21; 11¼m. & 11½m. 1 in 14; 23¼-24m. 1 in 13 (dangerous turn); 26m. 1 in 15; 29½m. 1 in 12 (dangerous); 32m. 1 in 18; 36m. 1 in 14; 37½m. 1 in 19; 38¼m. 1 in 20; 39m. 1 in 18; 40¼m. 1 in 16; 40½m. 1 in 20; 42¼m. 1 in 15; 46m. 1 in 15; 48½m. 1 in 17; 50m. 1 in 18; 54½m. 1 in 16; 55m. 1 in 19; 57m. 1 in 14; 58½m. 1 in 23; 62m. 1 in 12; 62½m. 1 in 23; 63½m., 65m., & 68m. 1 in 12 (dangerous).

Milestones.—Measured from road fork (½m. from Guild Hall, Exeter) as far as Fairmile, whence from Honiton Church; thereafter irregular to boundary, whence from Crewkerne Market as far as Chinnock, whence measured from Yeovil Market; after Sherborne measured from Shaftesbury, Court House.

Measurements.

Exeter,* Guild Hall.									
11⅜	Fairmile.*								
16⅝	5¼	Honiton,* Church.							
30	18⅝	13⅜	Chard,* Market.						
38	26⅝	21⅜	8	Crewkerne,* Market.					
46⅝	35¼	30	16⅝	8⅝	Yeovil,* Mermaid Hotel.				
52⅜	41	35¾	22⅜	14⅜	5¾	Sherborne,* Cross.			
58⅝	47¼	42	28⅝	20⅝	12	6¼	Henstridge.*		
68⅜	57	51¾	38⅜	30⅜	21¾	16	9¾	Shaftesbury, Court House.	
89¾	78⅜	73⅛	59¾	51¾	43⅛	37⅜	31⅛	21⅜	Salisbury.

Principal Objects of Interest.—Fairmile, Cadhay, Ottery Church. HONITON: Church. CHARD: Church, Town Hall, Battlefield. CREWKERNE: Church. YEOVIL: Church, Glove Factories. SHERBORNE: Minster, Cross, Castle. SHAFTESBURY: Court House, Castle Hill.

Hotels or Inns at places marked *, & at Clyst Honiton, &c.

ROUTE 718. EXETER TO SHAFTESBURY.

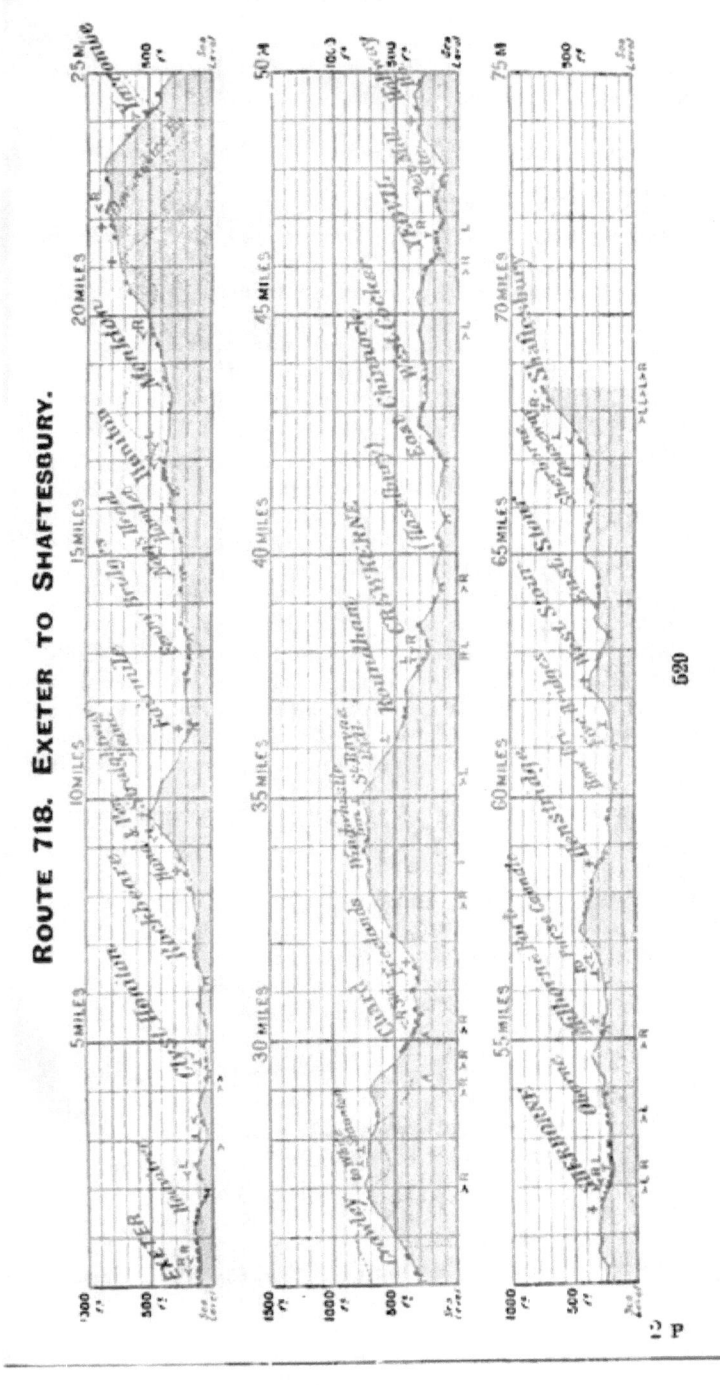

719 EXETER TO BRIDPORT.

Description.—Class II. Fine surface to Clyst St. Mary, thereafter good surface but exceedingly steep to Sidford, after which the road is a series of precipitous hills, with good surface between the summits; the worst hill is Trow-hill, just after Sidford, which has an acute turn, but most of the others are almost as bad.

Gradients.—(+ *Dangerous.*) At 7¼m. 1 in 20; 8½m. 1 in 14; 9¾m. 1 in 10†; 12m. 1 in 8†; 14½m. 1 in 9†; 15m. 1 in 8†; 21¾m. 1 in 10†; 24m. 1 in 10†; 28½m. 1 in 9†; 29½m. 1 in 9†; 31m. 1 in 10†; 34½m. 1 in 9†; 35½m. 1 in 12†; 36½m. 1 in 14.

Milestones.—Measured from road fork (½m. from Guild Hall), Exeter as far as Lyme Regis, thereafter from Dor-chester.

Measurements.

Exeter,* Guild Hall.
11   Newton Poppleford.
12¾   1¾   Bowd* (R. 697).
14¾   3¼   1½   Sidford* (R. 696).
18¾   7¼   5¼   4   Three Horse Shoes* (R. 714).
22¾   11½   10   8½   4½   Colyford* (R. 713).
28¾   17½   16   14½   10½   6¼   Lyme Regis.*
31   20   18¼   16¾   12¾   8¾   2¼   Charmouth,* P.O.   (R. 716).
37¼   26¾   25¼   23¾   19¾   15½   8½   6¼   Bridport,* Market.

Principal Objects of Interest.—Sidford: Sidmouth, Sid-bury Castle. Colyford: Seaton, Colcombe "Castle." Rous-don: Church, Landslip. Lyme: Parade, Pier, Monmouth landing, 1685. BRIDPORT: Church, Harbour, &c.

Hotels or Inns at places marked *, and at Clyst, White Cross. Morcombe Lake, &c.

720 EXETER TO TEIGNMOUTH.

Description.—Class II. Fine surface but undulating as far as Kennford, thereafter very hilly, and with a narrow and dangerous descent to Teignmouth. The best road is by Dawlish (R. 721).

Gradients.—At ½m. 1 in 16; 2¾m. 1 in 14; 4m. 1 in 16; 6m. 1 in 13; 9¾m. 1 in 12; 10¾m. 1 in 15; 13¾m. 1 in 10 (all dangerous).

Milestones.—Measured from Exeter Bridge.

Measurements.

Exeter,* Guild Hall.
4¼   Kennford,* Bridge.
14¼   10   Teignmouth,* P.O.

Principal Objects of Interest.—8½m. Mamhead landmark. Fine view at 12m. TEIGNMOUTH: the Den, Public Rooms, &c.

Hotels or Inns at places marked *.

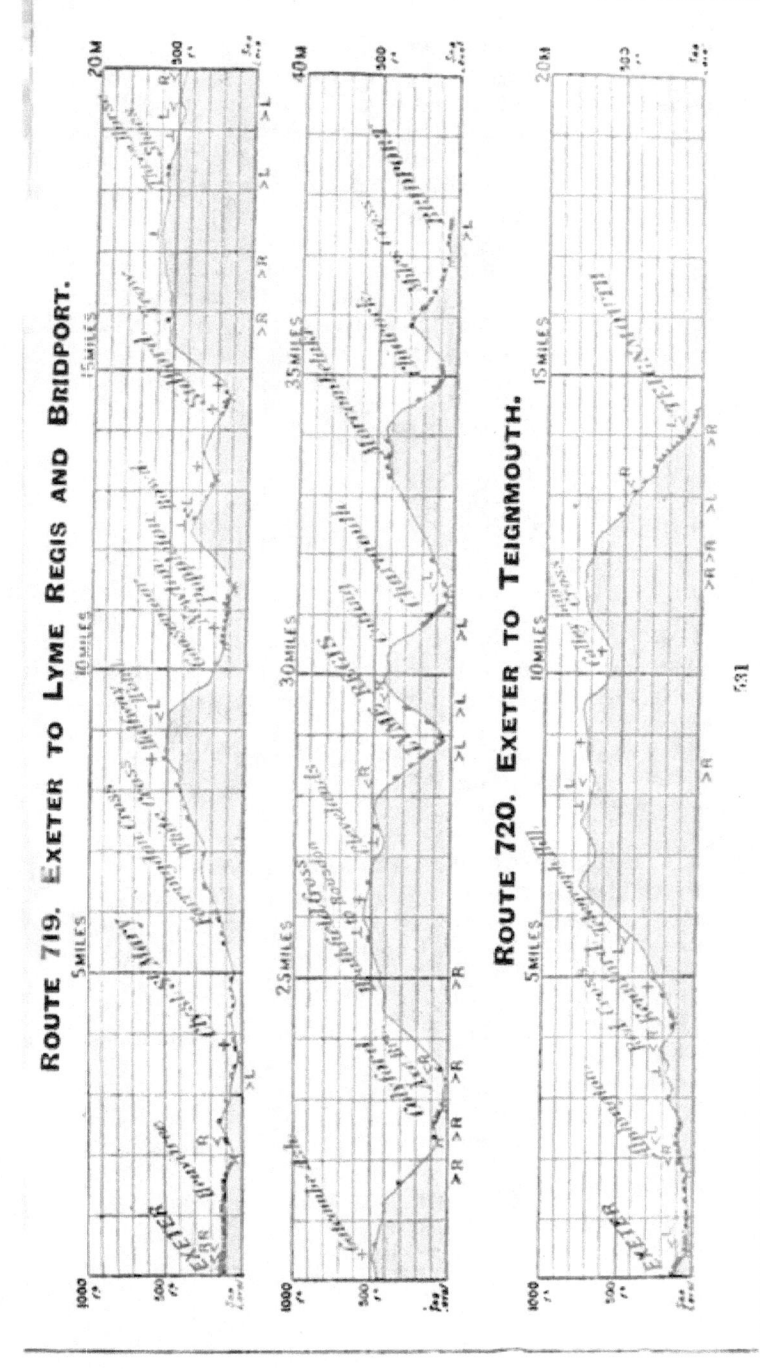

ROUTE 719. EXETER TO LYME REGIS AND BRIDPORT.

ROUTE 720. EXETER TO TEIGNMOUTH.

531

721 EXETER TO TORQUAY, &c.

Description.—Class II. An excellent but constantly undulating road to Dawlish (narrow and dangerous descent), whence very steep to Teignmouth; thereafter an easy, undulating road, with rather fine surface.

Gradients.—(†*Dangerous.*) At ¼m. 1 in 16; 6¼m. 1 in 15; 13¼m. 1 in 13†; 14¼m. 1 in 16; 14½m. 1 in 13†; 15¼m. 1 in 11†; 19½m. 1 in 25; 19¾m. 1 in 15; 27½m. 1 in 19; 32¼m. 1 in 18.

Milestones.—From Exeter Bridge to Exminster, then from Teignmouth; after Kingsteignton from Newton Abbot.

Measurements.

Exeter,* Guildhall.							
8¼	Starcross,* Station.						
13⅝	4⅜	Dawlish.*					
16	7¾	2⅜	Teignmouth.* (R. 723.)				
22	13⅝	8⅜	6	Newton Abbot.*			
(28⅝	20	15¾	12⅝	6⅝	Torquay,* Strand.)		
30⅝	21¾	17½	14⅝	8⅝	3	Paignton.* (R. 723.)	
36	27⅛	22⅝	20	14	8⅜	5¾	Brixham.*

Principal Objects of Interest.—4m. Asylum. Kenton: Powderham Castle. DAWLISH: Promenade, Parson and Clerk Rocks. TEIGNMOUTH: the Den, Public Rooms, Churches, &c. NEWTON ABBOT: Clock Tower, Proclamation Stone. TORQUAY: Tor Abbey, Baths, Museum, &c. BRIXHAM: William of Orange landing, Caverns, &c.

722 EXETER TO KINGSBRIDGE.

Description.—Class II. Splendid surface to Kennford, then hilly and loose to Chudleigh Arch, whence very good surface to Newton; thereafter hilly to Totnes, after which the road becomes even more hilly, but with smooth surface all the way to Kingsbridge. Dangerous hills at Totnes and Kingsbridge. An easier road to Newton Abbot is by R. 721.

Gradients.—(†*Dangerous.*) At ¼m. 1/16; 2¾m. 1/14; 4m. 1/16; 6m. 1/13†; 10¾m. 1/17; 11¾m. 1/23; 12m. 1/22; 12¾m. & 16½m. 1/16; 20m. 1/13†; 20½m. 1/12†; 22m. 1/15; 22¼m., 23¼m., & 25m. 1/11†; 26¼m. 1/12†; 28¾m. 1/16; 30¼m. 1/21, 33¼m. 1/19; 32m. & 33½m. 1/15; 36¼m. 1/9.†

Milestones.—Measured from Exeter Bridge as far as Newton, whence from Totnes Bridge; irregular thereafter.

Measurements.

Exeter,* Guildhall.					
4¼	Kennford,* Bridge.				
15¾	11½	Newton Abbot.*			
24⅛	19⅞	8⅜	Totnes,* Plains.		
30	25¾	14¼	5⅝	Halwell.*	
36¾	32½	21	12⅜	6¾	Kingsbridge.*

Principal Objects of Interest.—10½m. Ugbrook House. NEWTON ABBOT: as above. TOTNES: Church, Castle, Berry Castle. KINGSBRIDGE: Church, Town Hall.

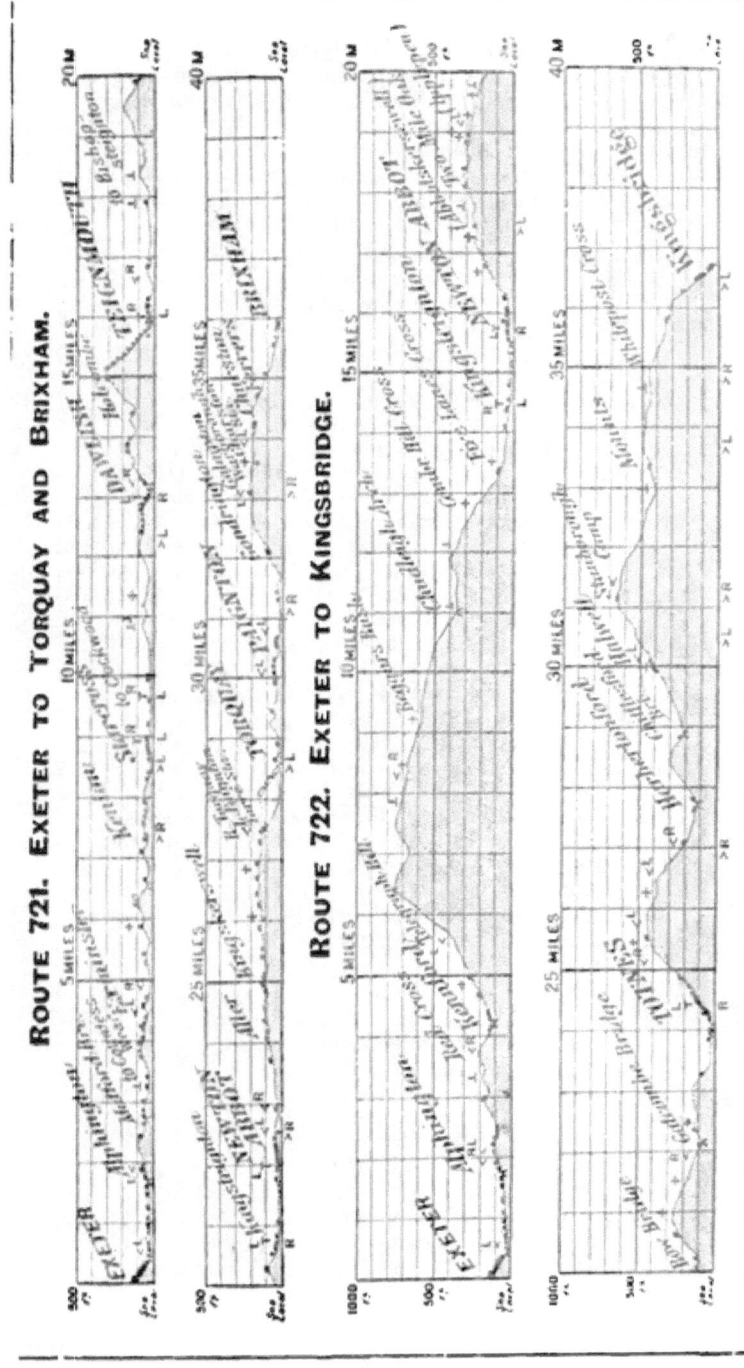

ROUTE 721. EXETER TO TORQUAY AND BRIXHAM.

ROUTE 722. EXETER TO KINGSBRIDGE.

723   EXETER TO DARTMOUTH.

Description.—Class II.　R. 721 to Teignmouth, thereafter a very hilly road to Torquay, whence undulating but good surface to Churston Station, then a rather dangerous descent to Kingswear, whence ferry to Dartmouth (½m.)

Gradients.—(† *Dangerous.*)　At 1½m.1 in 13†; 4m.1 in 18; 6m. 1 in 12†; 5½m. 1 in 13†; 8m. 1 in 16; 13m. 1 in 18; 15m. 1 in 16; 16m. 1 in 17; 17½m. 1 in 13.†

Milestones.—Measured from Teignmouth as far as Torquay, whence measured from Newton Abbot.

Measurements.

Exeter,* Guildhall.
16　Teignmouth.*
24½　8¾　Torquay,* The Strand.
27½　11½　3　Paignton.*
35½　19½　11　8　Dartmouth.*

Principal Objects of Interest. — TORQUAY : as above. Kingswear: Castle.　DARTMOUTH : Docks, Castle, Church.

724   EXETER TO PLYMOUTH.

Description.—Class I.　This road is very hilly throughout, but for Devonshire is a very fine road.　The surface is in splendid condition, and the only place on which it is a little loose is near the old Racecourse.　It is very bumpy near Plymouth. Route 725 has much finer scenery.

Gradients.—(† *Dangerous.*)　At ½m. 1/16; 2½m. 1/14; 4m. 1/16; 5½m. 1/13†; 7½m. 1/19; 8½m. 1/18; 10¾m. 1/13†; 15m. 1/13†; 16½m. 1/15; 17m. 1/13†; 18¾m. 1/14; 21¾m. 1/15; 22½m. 1/17; 24½m. 1/16; 25½m. 1/14; 26½m. & 27½m. 1/18; 28m. 1/19; 32½m. 1/18; 37¼m. 1/17; 38¼m. 1/19.

Milestones.—Measured from Exeter Bridge as far as Brentmill, thereafter from Plymouth.

Measurements.

Exeter,* Guildhall.
10　Chudleigh.*
17½　9½　Ashburton.*
22½　12½　3　Buckfastleigh.*
32½　22½　13½　10½　Ivybridge.*
38½　28½　19½　16½　6　Ridgeway* (Plympton.)
43½　33½　24　21　10½　4½　Plymouth,* Guildhall.
45½　35½　25½　22½　12½　6½　1¾　Devonport,* Fore Street.

Principal Objects of Interest.—Kennford: Haldon Ho. and Belvedere. 6½m. Old Racecourse. CHUDLEIGH: Church, Cavern, Rocks. Heathfield: Pottery. Ashburton: Church, Holne Chase. Buckfastleigh: Abbey. Dean Prior· Herrick's House. Ivybridge: Church. Plympton: Ch., Guildhall, &c. 40½m. Forts. PLYMOUTH : The Hoe, Smeaton Tower, Citadel, Town Hall, Public Library, Mount Edgecumbe. DEVONPORT: Dock Yard. Stonehouse: Victualling Yard.   [*over.*

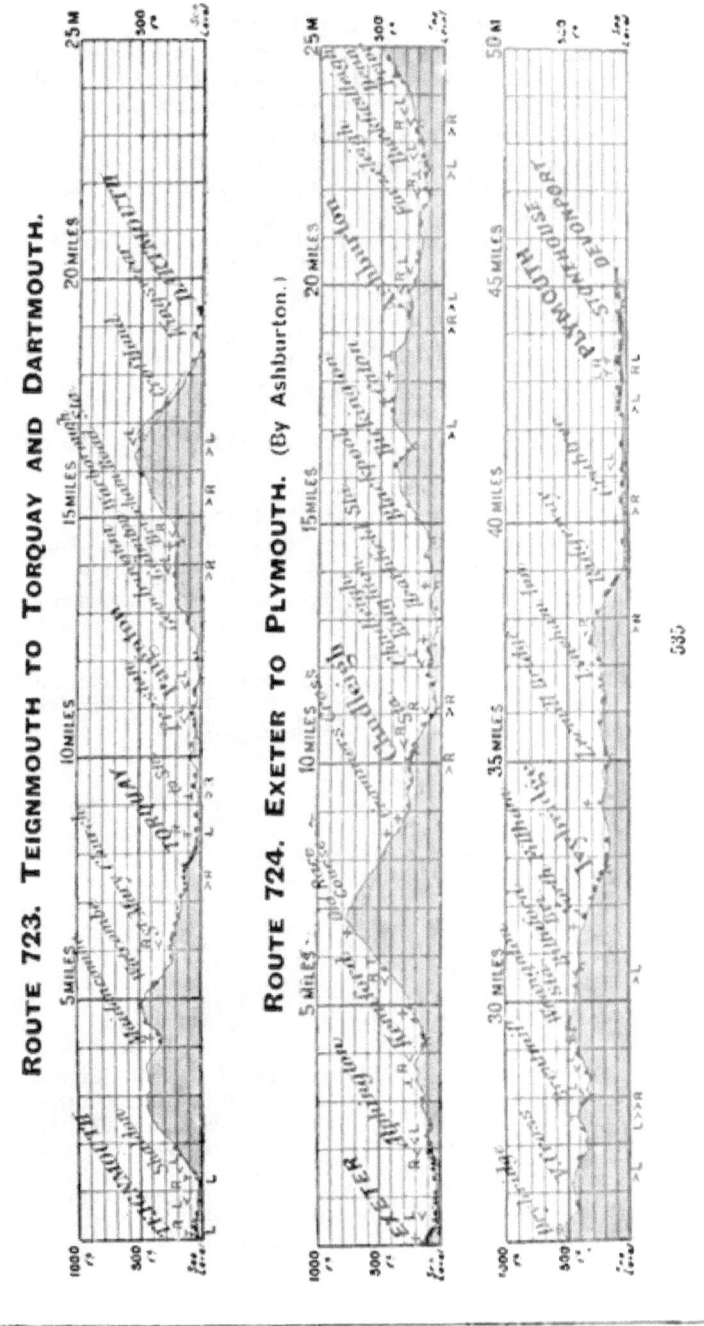

ROUTE 723. TEIGNMOUTH TO TORQUAY AND DARTMOUTH.

ROUTE 724. EXETER TO PLYMOUTH. (By Ashburton.)

Route 724—Continued.

Hotels or Inns at places marked*, and at Blackpool, Bickington, Brentmill, Wrangaton Station, Leemill Bridge, &c.

---

725 EXETER TO PLYMOUTH. (By Dartmoor.)

Description.—Class II. An exceedingly hilly road to within ten miles of Plymouth. The surface is very fair as far as Moreton Hampstead, but the hills are very steep and dangerous. From Moreton Hampstead to Princetown the road is loose on the moors, and is little else than a succession of dangerous hills, but they are nearly all straight. Awkward descent to Two Bridges. After Princetown the surface improves, and after Harrowbeer it is an excellent undulating road into Plymouth. For Devonport keep to R. at 40m. The best road is R. 724. Fine scenery.

Gradients.—Nearly all dangerous. At ¼m. 1/16; 1½ & 1¾m. 1/11; 2m. 1/9; 3¼m. 1/17; 5m. 1/14; 6½ & 7m. 1/8; 9m. 1/15; 11½m. 1/11; 12¾m. 1/10; 14½m. 1/9; 15¾m. 1/12; 16¼m. 1/9; 17 & 17¾m. 1/11; 18½ & 19m. 1/10; 19¼m. 1/15; 20¼ & 20¾m. 1/14; 21¼m. 1/9; 22½ & 23½m. 1/13; 23¾ & 25¼m. 1/20; 25½ & 26m. 1/12; 27m. 1/10; 27¾m. 1/11; 29m. 1/20; 30m. 1/14; 31m. 1/10; 40m. 1/14; 40¼m. 1/17; 41m. 1/13.

Milestones.—Irregular to Moreton Hampstead, from which place they are measured to Princetown, then from Plymouth.

Measurements.

Exeter,* Guildhall.							
13½	Moreton Hampstead.*						
22	8½	Postbridge.*					
25¾	12¼	3¾	Two Bridges.*				
27¼	13¾	5¼	1½	Princetown.*			
33	19½	11	7¼	5¾	Harrowbeer.*		
36¾	23¼	14¾	11	9½	3¾	Roborough.*	
42½	28⅝	20⅝	16⅝	15⅛	9⅝	5⅝	Plymouth,* Guildhall.
42	29¼	30¾	17	15½	9¾	6	Devonport,* Fore Street.

Principal Objects of Interest.—Moreton Hampstead: Church, Cross, Arcade. 16½m. Beeford Cross. 19½m. Bennet's Cross and Grimspound. 20¼m. Vitifer Mine. Postbridge: Clapper Bridge. 24m. Powder Mills. 25m. Crockern Tor, Wistman's Wood. Princetown: Convict Prison. 36m. Plymouth leat. 38¾m. Forts. Plymouth: as R. 724. There are many pretty places in the neighbourhood of Moreton Hampstead; and Chagford, a few miles to the north, is one of the best centres for exploring Dartmoor.

Hotels or Inns at places marked *, and at Dunsford.

ROUTE 725. EXETER TO PLYMOUTH. (By Dartmoor.)

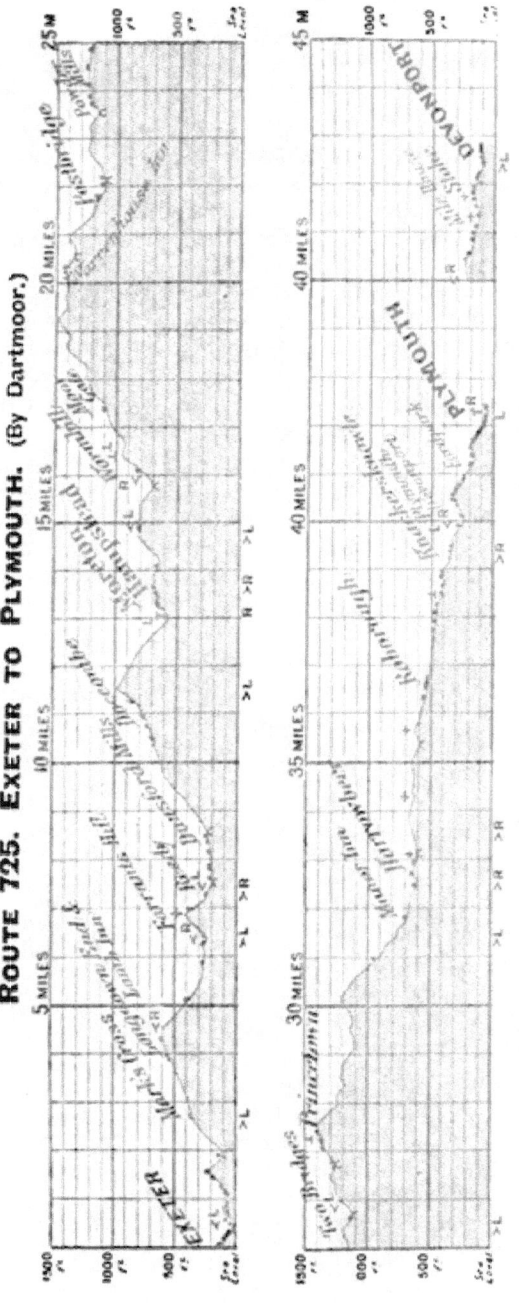

Signs. < Road Fork, forward journey. > ditto reverse. + Cross Road. ⊥ Road Junction. ○ Finger. T indicates a sharp turn. The directions R (right) and L (left) for the forward journey are above the Road Line, those of the reverse, below.

726 EXETER TO LAUNCESTON.

Description. Class I. The surface of this road is in splendid condition, and though it is a fine, broad highway many of the hills are very stiff—almost dangerous. For Devonshire it is a very good road. This, with R. 749, is the best road to Cornwall.

Gradients.—At ¼m. 1 in 16; 1½m. & 1¾m. 1 in 11 (dangerous); 5¼m. 1 in 13; 8m. 1 in 15; 8¼m. 1 in 14; 11m. 1 in 15; 11½m. 1 in 14; 15m., 16m., & 18½m. 1 in 17; 19½m. & 19¾m. 1 in 19; 22½m. 1 in 17; 53½m. 1 in 20; 24½m. 1 in 17; 25½m. 1 in 15; 29m. 1 in 19; 31m. 1 in 14; 32½m. 1 in 17; 35m. 1 in 23; 36½m. 1 in 17; 37m. 1 in 19; 39½m. & 41¼m. 1 in 13.

Milestones. — Measured from Exeter Bridge as far as Crockernwell, whence measured from Okehampton on as far as Lewdown; thereafter measured from Launceston Market.

Measurements

Exeter,* Guildhall.
11¼ Crockernwell.*
19¾ 7¼ Sticklepath.*
23 11¼ 3¾ Okehampton.*
33¼ 22 14¾ 10¾ Lewdown Inn.*
41½ 29⅝ 22¼ 18¾ 7¼ Launceston,* Market Clock.

Principal Objects of Interest.—Pretty country, with fine views of Dartmoor. Cheriton: Fulford House. Crockernwell: Preston Berry Castle, &c. Sticklepath: Lady Well. OKEHAMPTON: Castle, Yes Tor, &c. Bridestowe: Church. LAUNCESTOWN: Castle, Gateway.

Hotels or Inns at places marked*, and at Taphouse, Cheriton Cross, Whidden Down, Bridestowe, and Lifton.

727 EXETER TO TORRINGTON.

Description.—Class II. As R. 728 to Morchard Road Station. Thence an undulating country road of fair surface, but with some steep hills. For Torrington Station keep to L. at 34m.

Gradients.—At 22m. 1 in 15; 24½m. & 24½m. 1 in 17; 25m. 1 in 13; 30½m. & 31½m. 1 in 17; 33m. 1 in 23; 33½m. 1 in 18; 34½m. 1 in 12 (dangerous).

Milestones.—Measured from Torrington, Market House.

Measurements

Exeter,* Guildhall.
8¼ Crediton.*
14¼ 6¼ Morchard Road Station.
22¼ 14¼ 8 Winkleigh.*
29½ 21¼ 15¼ 7¼ Beaford.
34½ 26½ 20½ 12¾ 5¼ Torrington,* Market House.

Principal Objects of Interest. — CREDITON: Church. TORRINGTON: Castle remains, Frithelstock Priory.

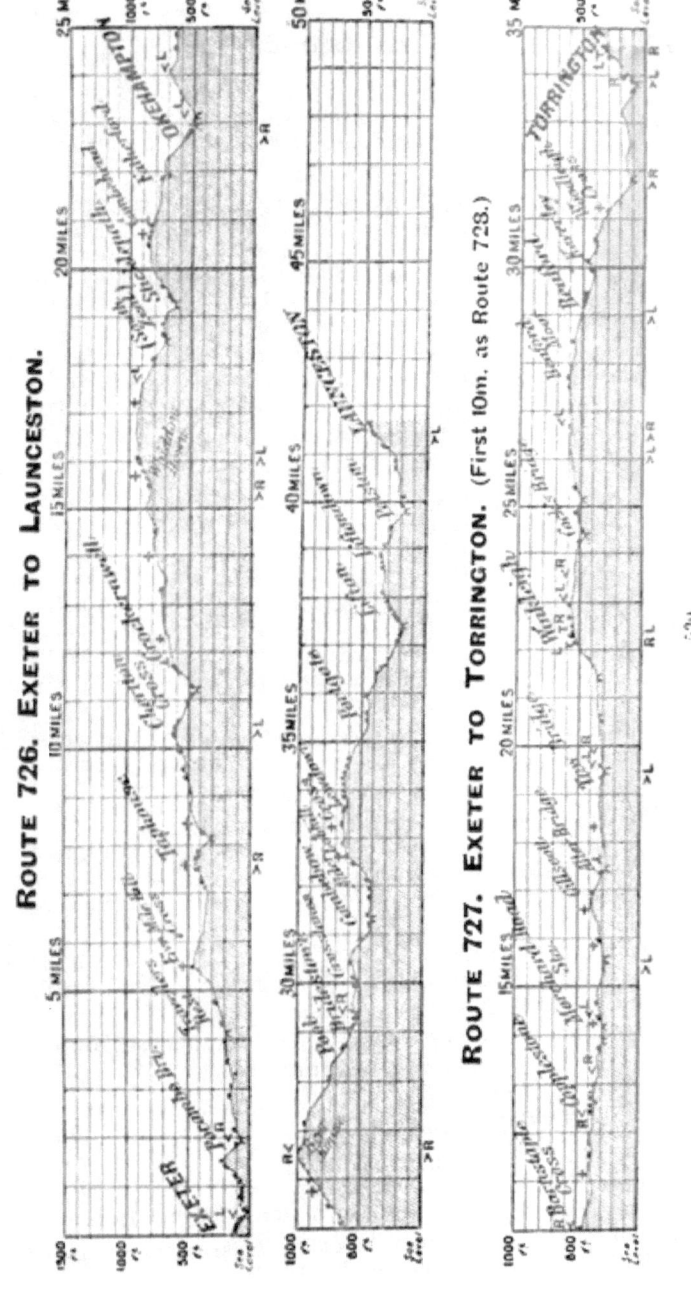

ROUTE 726. EXETER TO LAUNCESTON.

ROUTE 727. EXETER TO TORRINGTON. (First 10m. as Route 728.)

728 EXETER TO BARNSTAPLE.

Description.—Class I. The most level road in Devonshire. At first it is slightly hilly to Crediton; then after Lapford Station it becomes a smooth, finely-engineered road through very pretty scenery, close to the banks of River Taw to Bishops Tawton. Near Barnstaple it is hilly.

Gradients.—At 2¼m. 1/18; 2¾m. & 4¼m. 1/16; 4½m. 1/14: 4¾m. 1/15; 9½m. 1/21; 38¼m. 1/15; 38½m. 1/21; 39m. 1/15.

Milestones.—Measured from Guildhall, Exeter, as far as Lapford Station, thereafter from Barnstaple, Town Hall.

Measurements.

Exeter,* Guildhall.						
8⅛	Crediton.*					
14¼	6⅛	Morchard Road Station.*				
21	12⅞	6¾	Eggesford Station.*			
25¼	17⅛	11	4¼	So. Molton Road Station.*		
32½	24⅜	18¼	11½	7¼	Umberleigh Bridge.*	
40⅜	32¼	26⅛	19⅜	15⅛	7⅞	Barnstaple.*

Principal Objects of Interest.—CREDITON: Church. 21m. Eggesford. BARNSTAPLE: Bridge, Queen Anne's Statue, Church, School.

Hotels or Inns at places marked*, and at Lapford. &c.

729 EXETER TO MINEHEAD.

Description.—Class I. A finely engineered and smooth road, with very slight gradients, to Tiverton, thereafter a very good, undulating road to Exton; thereafter good surface to the summit, where it is a little rough, thence good into Minehead. Bampton lies 1¾m. to north of Exeter Inn.

Gradients.—At 5m. 1/20; 7¾m. 1/24; 10m. 1/20; 17½m. 1/14; 19m. 1/23; 35½m. 1/19; 36½m. 1/15; 39m. 1/16; 43m. 1/14.

Milestones.—Measured from Guildhall, Exeter, to Rewe; thereafter from Tiverton, Town Hall, to Exebridge, whence from Minehead.

Measurements.

Exeter,* Guildhall.								
11	Bickleigh Bridge.*							
14⅜	3⅜	Tiverton.*						
(22	11	7⅝	Bampton.*)					
25⅜	14⅜	10¾	6⅛	Exebridge,* Inn.				
32⅝	21⅝	17½	12⅞	6¾	Exton.*			
36⅛	25¼	21⅜	17	10⅞	4⅛	Wheddon Cross.*		
42¾	31¾	28⅛	23½	17	10⅞	6¾	Dunster.*	
45¼	34¼	30⅜	26	19⅞	13⅛	9	2½	Minehead.*

Principal Objects of Interest.—A very pretty road along the banks of the River Exe. TIVERTON: Church, Castle ruins, Collipriest House. 28¾m. Barlinch Abbey. Dunster: Eastle Priory Ch. MINEHEAD: Ch. Pretty near Pittbridge.

Hotels or Inns at places marked*, and at Stoke Canon, Exeter Inn, Okeford Bridge, and Timberscombe.

ROUTE 728. EXETER TO BARNSTAPLE.

ROUTE 729. EXETER TO MINEHEAD.

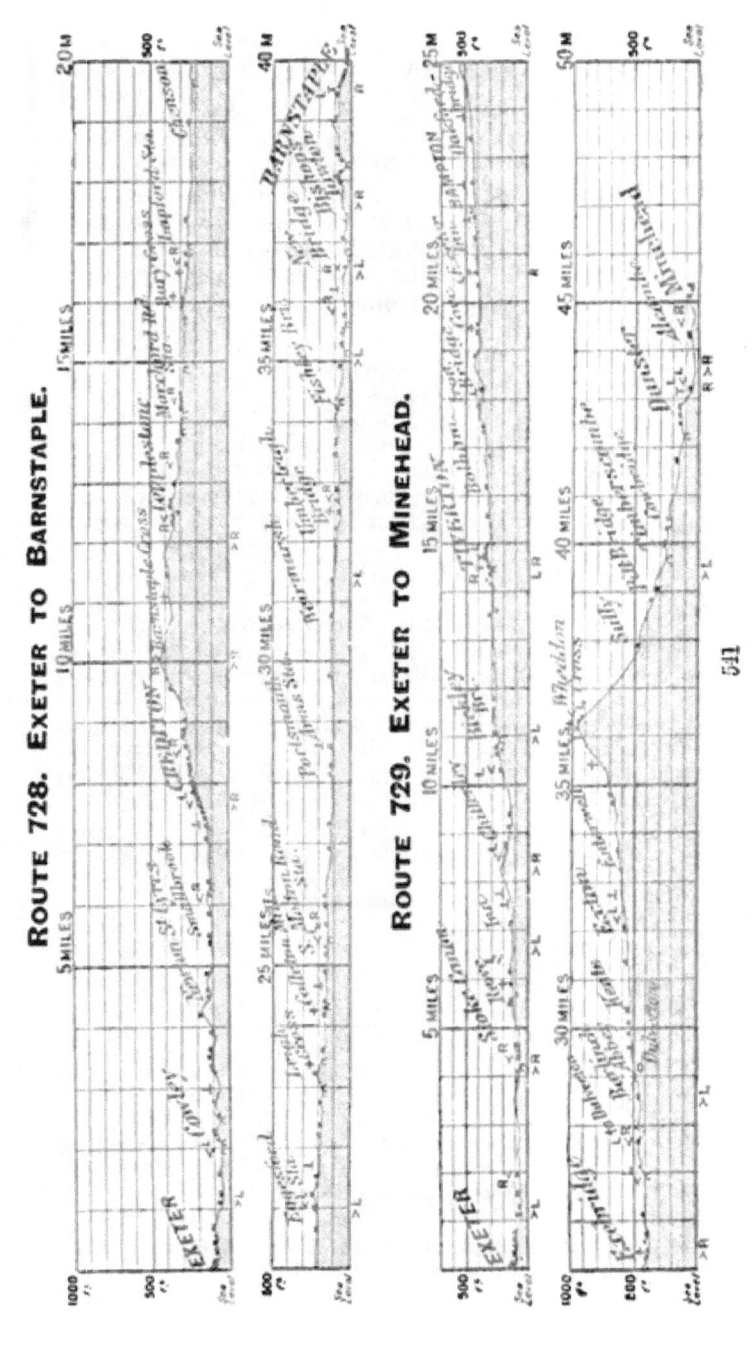

730 EXETER TO TAUNTON.

Description.—Class I. The Bristol road. Magnificent surface throughout and easy undulations, excepting the three dangerous hills. For Bristol, see R. 847; Bath, R. 823.

Gradients.—At 1¼m. 1 in 21; 3½m. 1 in 20; 14½m. 1 in 13 (dangerous); 18½m. 1 in 24; 19¼m. 1 in 10 (dangerous); 21½m. 1 in 23; 21¾m. 1 in 24; 22½m. 1 in 13 (dangerous); 23¼m. 1 in 17; 26½m. 1 in 20; 29¾m. 1 in 17; 30¼m. 1 in 23.

Milestones.—Measured from road fork, ½m. from Guildhall to Beare; whence from Taunton Market House.

Measurements.

Exeter,* Guildhall.
5¾	Broad Clyst.*			
13	7¾	Cullompton.*		
17¾	12½	4½	Waterloo Cross.*	
25¾	20	12¾	7½	Wellington.*
31½	26½	18¾	14	6½	Taunton,* Market House.

Principal Objects of Interest.—7m. Killerton Park. Cullompton: Church. Wellington: Church, Wellington Pillar. TAUNTON: Castle, Market House, Maids' Monument, Churches, Colleges, &c.

Hotels or Inns at places marked*, and at Hele Station, Appledore, Red Ball, Hawkaller, &c.

731 NEWTON ABBOT TO OKEHAMPTON.

Description.—Class III. Excellent surface, but hilly to Bovey Tracey, thereafter exceedingly hilly, and with poor surface to Moreton; thereafter the road is rather better, and the Exeter and Okehampton road (R. 726) is joined at Whiddon Down.

Gradients. —(† *Dangerous.*) At 1m. 1 in 17; 1¾m. 1 in 24; 2½m. 1 in 16; 6m. 1 in 14; 6¾ & 7¼m. 1 in 13†; 7¾ & 8½m. 1 in 14†; 9¼ & 11m. 1 in 13†; 12¼m. 1 in 18; 12½m. 1 in 14; 13m. 1 in 17; 9m. 1 in 21; 15½m. 1 in 19; 16m. 1 in 12†; 17m. 1 in 17.

Milestones.—Measured from Newton Bushel.

Measurements.

Newton Abbot.*
5¾	Bovey Tracey.*		
12¾	6½	Moreton Hampstead.*	
18¾	12¾	6¾	Whiddon Down.*
25¾	20	13½	7¼	Okehampton.*

Principal Objects of Interest.—Bovey Tracey: Potteries, Church. Moreton Hampstead: Church, Cross, Arcade. Easton: Chagford, Cranbrook "Castle," &c. A very pretty road in many places.

Hotels or Inns at places marked*, and at Sandypark.

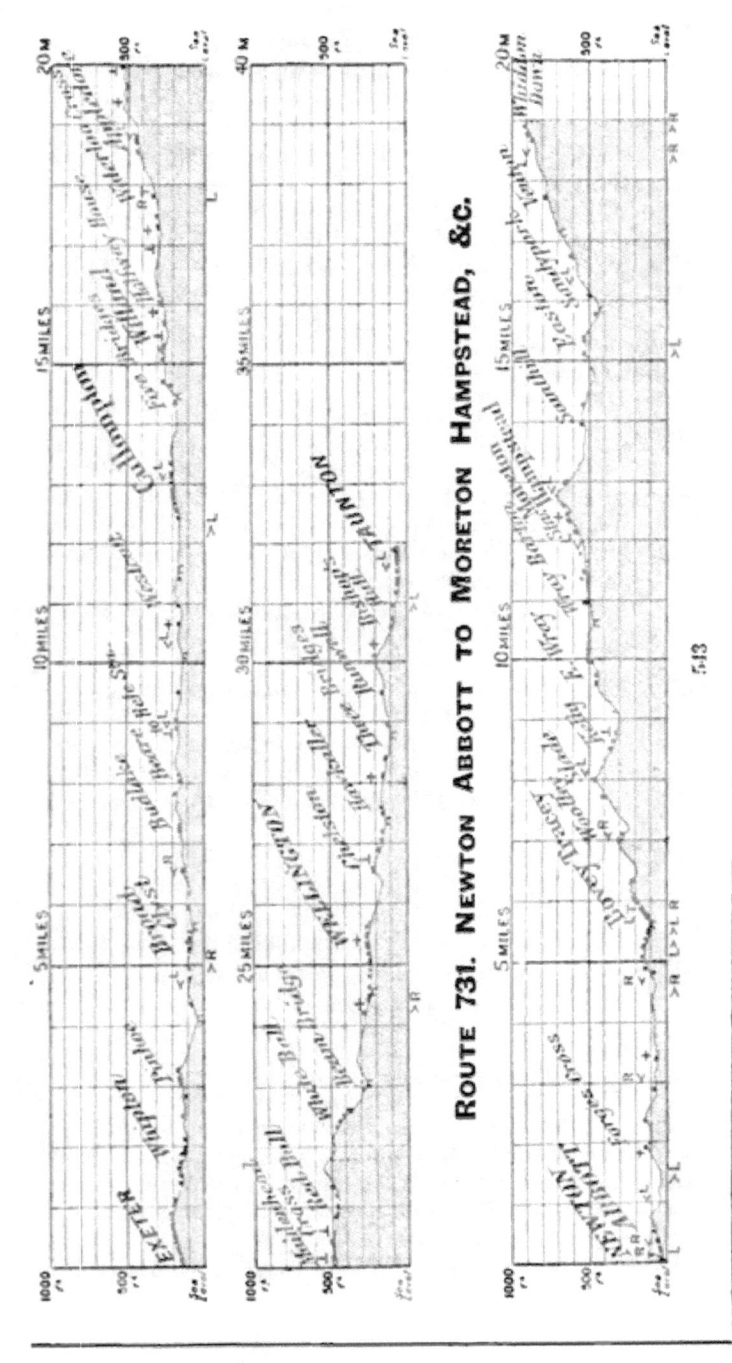

ROUTE 731. NEWTON ABBOTT TO MORETON HAMPSTEAD, &C.

543

732 EXETER TO EXMOUTH.

Description.—Class II. A very bumpy road to Topsham; thereafter better surface, but short and very steep hills.

Gradients.—Mostly 1 in 10, or 1 in 12.

Milestones.—Irregular.

Measurements.—Exeter,* Guildhall.

          4   Topsham.*

       10½ 6½ 3½ Exmouth,* Clock.

Principal Objects of Interest.—Exton: Nutwell Court. EXMOUTH: Esplanade, Black Hill, &c.

733 EXMOUTH TO SIDMOUTH.

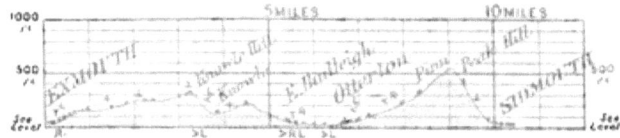

Description.—Class III. Fine surface to Otterton, then very steep, with a rough and precipitous descent.

Gradients. All dangerous. At ½m. 1 in 13; 3½m. 1 in 10; 9m. 1 in 12; 9½m. 1 in 7.

Measurements.—Exmouth,° Clock.

    (4½ Budleigh Salt'rt'n,* 1m.s.of Knowle.)

        6½ 2½ Otterton.*

      10½ 6½ 3½ Sidmouth,* Esplanade.

Principal Objects of Interest. — East Budleigh: Hays Barton, Sir W. Raleigh's birthplace. Otterton: Priory remains. Sidmouth: Peak Hill, Esplanade, fine coast.

734 NEWTON ABBOT TO ASHBURTON.

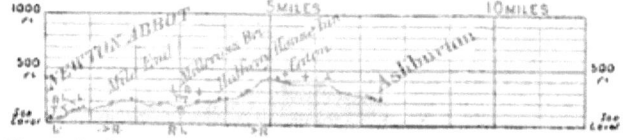

Description.—Class II. An excellent undulating road.

Gradients.—At ¾m. 1 in 18; 2¼ & 4½m. 1 in 14; 6½m. 1 in 14.

Measurements.—Newton Abbot.*

       3   Half-Way House Inn.°

       7½ 3½ Ashburton.*

Principal Objects of Interest.—Ashburton: Church. Hotels or Inns at places marked *.

NEWTON ABBOT TO CHUDLEIGH, 6½m. **735**

Description.—Class II. A poor road, cut up by heavy
Gradients.—At 5½m. 1 in 13.   [carting traffic.
Principal Objects of Interest.—Chudleigh: Ch., Cavern.

TAVISTOCK TO LYDFORD. **736**

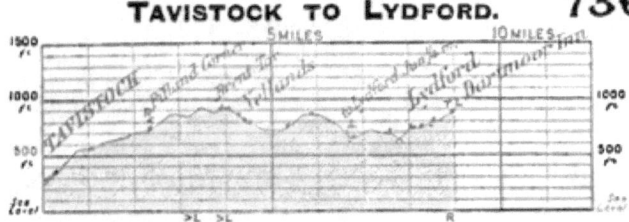

Description.—Class III. A good but steep road for 2m.,
then slightly loose and hilly to Brent Tor, after which
better surface, but still very steep.

    Gradients.—(*All Dangerous.*) At ½m. 1/9; 2½m. 1 16; 3
& 4½m. 1/15; 5½m. 1/11; 6½m. 1 13; 7m. 1/17; 7¾m. 1/12; 8m.
1/10; 9m. 1/16.

    Milestones.—Measured from Guildhall, Tavistock.
    Measurements.—Tavistock,* Guildhall.

(7		Lydford Junction.*)		
9	2¼	Dartmoor Inn.*		
17¼	10¼	8¼	Okehampton.*	R. 743.

    Principal Objects of Interest. — Brent Tor : Church.
Lydford : Castle, Cascades.

LISKEARD TO LOOE. **737**

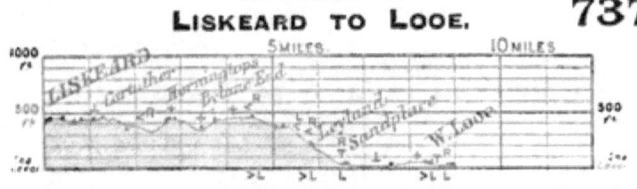

Description.—Class III. Fine surface for two miles, then
very hilly to Sandplace, after which very good to Looe.
    Gradients. –(†*Dangerous.*) 2½m. 1/11; 3½m. 1/13; 5½m. 1/9.
    Measurements.—Liskeard.*

6½		Sandplace.
8⅜	2¼	East Looe.*
or 9	2¾	West Looe.*

    Principal Objects of Interest.—Pretty country at Looe.
Hotels or Inns at places marked*.

738   ASHBURTON TO BRIXHAM.

Description.—Class II. Excellent surface, but rather hilly to Totnes; thereafter rather steep to Collaton.

Gradients.—(† *Dangerous.*) At 3¼m. 1/13†; 4½m. 1/17; 5¼m. & 6m. 1/15; 8½m. 1/12†; 9½m. 1/18; 10m. 1/19; 12m. 1/22.

Milestones.—Measured from Buckfastleigh, & Totnes Bri.

Measurements.

Ashburton.*
...   Buckfastleigh.*
8¼   6   Totnes,* Plain.
12½   10   4½   Collaton.
17¾   15   9½   5¼   Brixham,* or
20   18¼   12   7   Dartmouth.*   (R. 723).

Principal Objects of Interest.—TOTNES: Church, Castle, Brutus Stone, Berry Castle. Brixham: William of Orange landing, Caverns, &c. Very pretty near Buckfastleigh.

739   DARTMOUTH TO MODBURY.

Description.—Class II. Dangerously steep for 1½m., then a good undulating road to Halwell, where there is a rough and very dangerous hill; thereafter only fairly good surface, and with four dangerous hills. For Totnes turn to R. in Halwell, by Route 722. The direct road by Bowbridge is impassable.

Gradients.—(† *Dangerous.*) At ½m. 1 in 11†; 2¾m. 1 in 13; 3¾m. & 4½m. 1 in 18; 5½m. 1 in 21; 7½m. & 8m. 1 in 9†; 10½m. 1 in 13†; 11½m. 1 in 11†; 14¾m. 1 in 20; 16¼m. 1 in 18.

Measurements.

Dartmouth,* Quay.
7¾   Halwell.*   (R. 722).
11   3¾   Garabridge.*
16¾   8¾   5¾   Modbury.*   (R. 741).

Hotels or Inns at places marked *, and at Hemborough Post, &c.

740   PLYMOUTH TO LOOE.

Description. Class I. & III. Rough through Stonehouse and Devonport, where ferry to Torpoint; thereafter splendid surface to Polbathick, whence good, but dangerously steep.

Gradients.—(† *Dangerous.*) At 3¾m. 8½m. & 9½m. 1 in 18; 12m. 1 in 12†; 12¾m. 1 in 13†; 13½m. 1 in 11†; 16m. 1 in 9†; 16¼m. 1 in 12†; 17¾m. 1 in 13†.

Measurements.

Plymouth,* Town Hall.
1¾   Devonport,* Tore Street.
2¾   ⅞   Torpoint.*
10¼   8¾   7¾   Polbathick.*
18¼   16¾   15¾   8   East Looe,* Guildhall.
18¾   17   16½   8¼   West Looe,* Quay.

Principal Objects of Interest.—Antony: House, Forts.

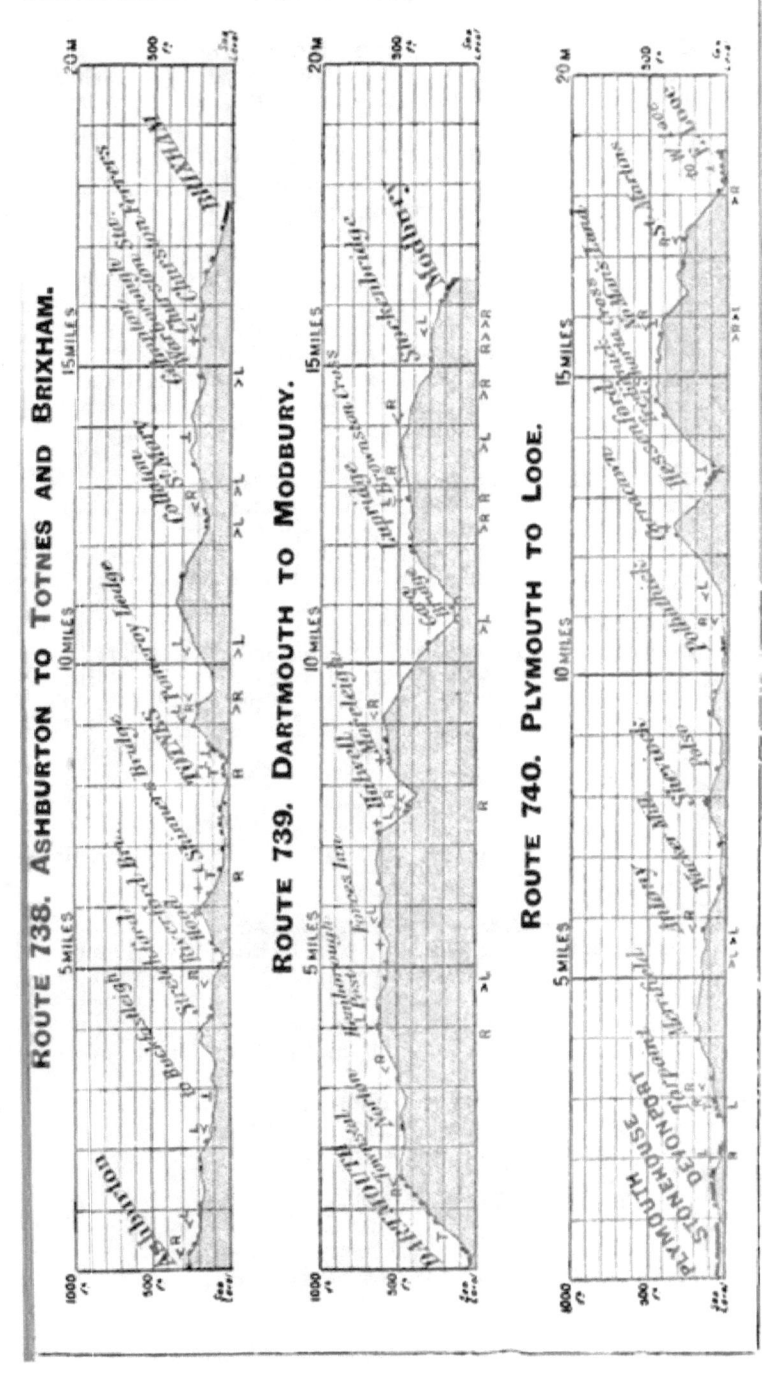

ROUTE 738. ASHBURTON TO TOTNES AND BRIXHAM.

ROUTE 739. DARTMOUTH TO MODBURY.

ROUTE 740. PLYMOUTH TO LOOE.

741 PLYMOUTH TO KINGSBRIDGE, &c.

Description.—Class II. Very bumpy to Brixton; thereafter excellent surface, but with steep and dangerous hills to Kingsbridge. From Kingsbridge to Dartmouth the surface is very good, but the hills are all very dangerous. From Dartmouth to Brixham the road is fair, but rather steep.

Gradients.—(†*Dangerous.*) At 3m.1/23; 4½m. & 5½m.1/15; 6m.1/14; 9m.1/20; 9¾m.1/18; 11¼m. & 12m.1/17; 12¼m.1/13; 13¼m.1/14; 13¾m.1/12†; 15m.1/13; 15½m.1/19; 15¾m.1/13; 16¾m.1/9†; 19½m.1/8†; 22¼m.1/15; 23¼m.1/12†; 25½m.1/14; 29¼m.1/13†; 31¼m. & 31¾m.1/10†; 33¾m.1/11†; 36m.1/18; 38m.1/10†; 38½m.1/12†.

Milestones.—Measured from Plymouth and Dartmouth.

Measurements.

Plymouth,* Town Hall.							
7	Yealmpton.*						
12¼	5¼	Modbury.*					
20¼	13¼	8	Kingsbridge.*				
26¾	19¾	14¾	6¾	Torcross.*			
28¼	21¼	16	8	1¾	Slapton Sands Hotel.*		
35	28	22¾	14¾	8½	6¾	Dartmouth,* Quay.	
40	33	27¾	19¾	13¼	11¾	5	Brixham.*

Principal Objects of Interest.—2m. Quarries. Brixton: Kitley House. 10¼m. Fleet House. Modbury: Church. Kingsbridge: Church, Town Hall, Museum. 28¼m. Slapton: Sands. Stoke Fleming: Church. DARTMOUTH: Castle, Docks, Training Ship, Church.

Hotels or Inns at places marked *, and at Brixton, &c.

742 PLYMOUTH TO TORQUAY.

Description.—Class I. Very bumpy to Ridgeway, then fine surface, but a slightly hilly road to Totnes; thereafter very steep to Collaton, whence good, but undulating.

Gradients.—At 5m.1/19; 6m.1/17; 11m.1/18; 15½m.1/19; 16½m. & 17m.1/18; 17¾m. & 19¼m.1/17; 24m.1/12 (dangerous); 24½m.1/18; 25m.1/19; 27¼m.1/22; 28½m.1/17; 30¾m.1/19.

Milestones.—Measured from Plymouth Fountain, as far as V. Cross, then from Totnes.

Measurements.

Plymouth,* Town Hall.					
4½	Ridgeway.*				
10¾	6	Ivybridge.*			
15¾	10¾	4¾	Brentbridge.*		
23¾	18½	12½	7¾	Totnes,* Plain.	
29¼	24¼	18¼	13¾	5¾	Paignton.*
32½	27¼	21¼	16¾	8¾	3 Torquay,* Strand.

Principal Objects of Interest.—3m. Forts. Plympton: Guild Hall, Church. TOTNES: Castle, Berry Castle. TORQUAY: as Route 721.

Hotels or Inns at places marked *, & Wrangaton Sta., &c.

ROUTE 741. PLYMOUTH TO KINGSBRIDGE AND DARTMOUTH, &C.

ROUTE 742. PLYMOUTH TO TORQUAY.

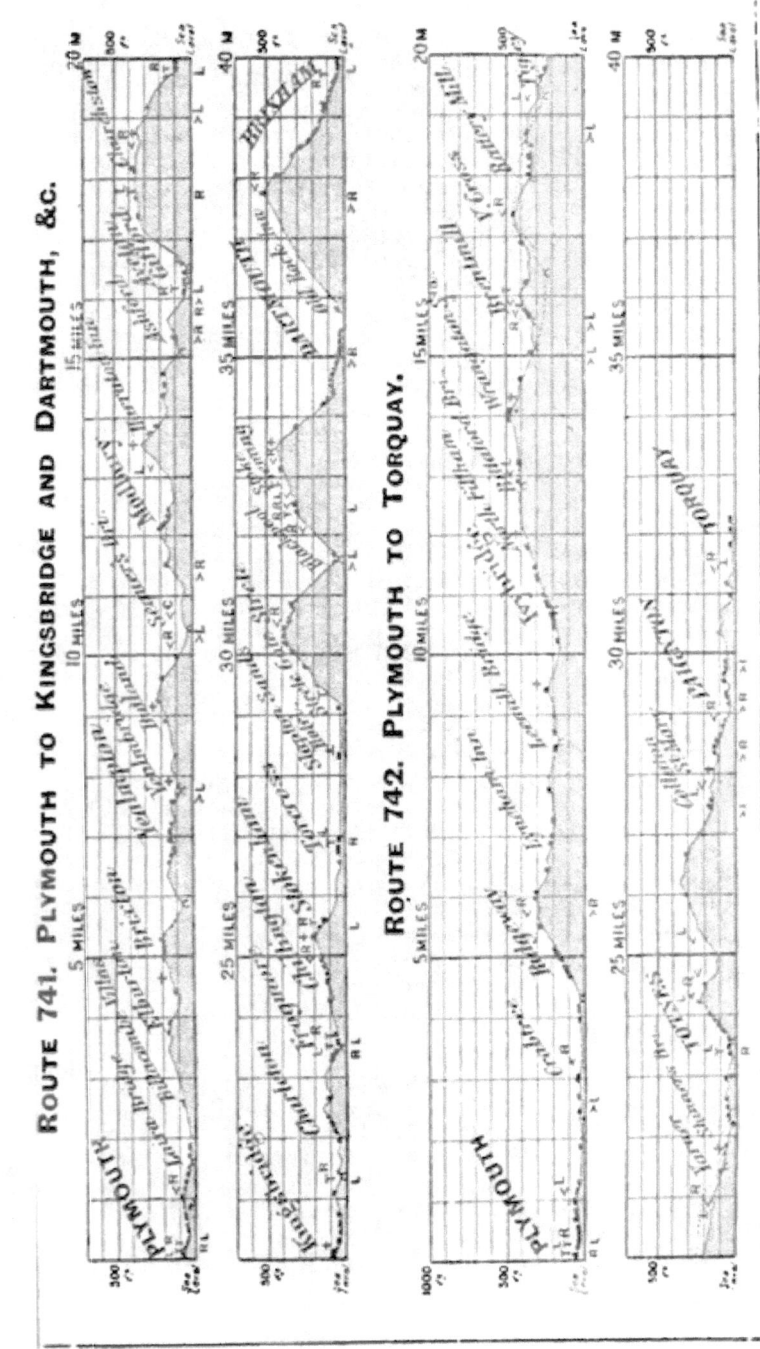

743 Plymouth to Okehampton.

Description. Class II. Somewhat hilly to Roborough—rather bumpy surface—then a fine road to Tavistock; thereafter the road is in good condition to Blackdown, after that it is rather poor for some miles, but after Sourton the surface is excellent.

Gradients.—At 1¼m. 1 in 13; 2¼m. 1 in 17; 2¾m. 1 in 14; 3½m. 1 in 15; 4m. 1 in 17; 9¾ & 10½m. 1 in 22; 11¾m. 1 in 17; 13½m. 1 in 24; 17¾ & 18m. 1 in 15; 19m. 1 in 13; 22¼m. 1 in 17; 23¼m. 1 in 23; 24¼ & 25m. 1 in 14; 28½m. 1 in 15; 29½m. 1 in 17; 30½m. 1 in 20.

Milestones.—Measured from beginning of Tavistock Street, Plymouth, to Tavistock, whence from Town Hall, Tavistock, to Dartmoor Inn; thereafter from Okehampton.

Measurements.

Plymouth,* Guildhall.					
5½	Roborough.*				
10¼	4¾	Horrabridge,* Station.			
14¾	9¼	4½	Tavistock,* Guildhall.		
22⅜	16⅞	12⅛	7⅝	Dartmoor Inn* (R. 736).	
30⅝	25⅛	20⅜	15⅞	8¼	Okehampton.*

Principal Objects of Interest.—Tavistock: Guildhall, Drake Statue, Church, Kelly College, Brent Tor. 22m. Lyd Cascade. Okehampton: Castle, Free Library.

Hotels or Inns at places marked *, and at Sourton, &c.

744 Plymouth to Launceston.

Description. Class II. Fair surface to Saltash Ferry (¼m.), thereafter excellent surface, but somewhat hilly to Callington, whence very good surface but continuous hills.

Gradients.—At 9½m. 1 in 17; 10¾m. 1 in 12; 11m. 1 in 13 (both dangerous); 13¾m. 1 in 16; 14m. 1 in 14; 15 & 15¼m. 1 in 20; 18m. 1 in 15; 19m. 1 in 17; 19½m. 1 in 19; 20¾m. 1 in 15; 21¼m. 1 in 18; 22¼m. 1 in 21.

Milestones.—Measured from North Road, Plymouth, then from Saltash; after Callington from Launceston Gateway.

Measurements.

Plymouth,* Guildhall.					
4¼	Saltash.*				
10⅜	6⅛	St. Mellion.*			
13¾	9½	3⅜	Callington.*		
18¾	14½	8⅜	5	Woodabridge.*	
24⅝	20⅜	14¼	10⅞	5⅞	Launceston,* Market Clock.

Principal Objects of Interest.—Saltash: Bridge, Market Hall, St. Nicholas Chapel. 10m. Pentillie Castle. Callington: Dupath Well. Launceston: Castle, Gateway. Very pretty views above Saltash.

ROUTE 743. PLYMOUTH TO OKEHAMPTON.

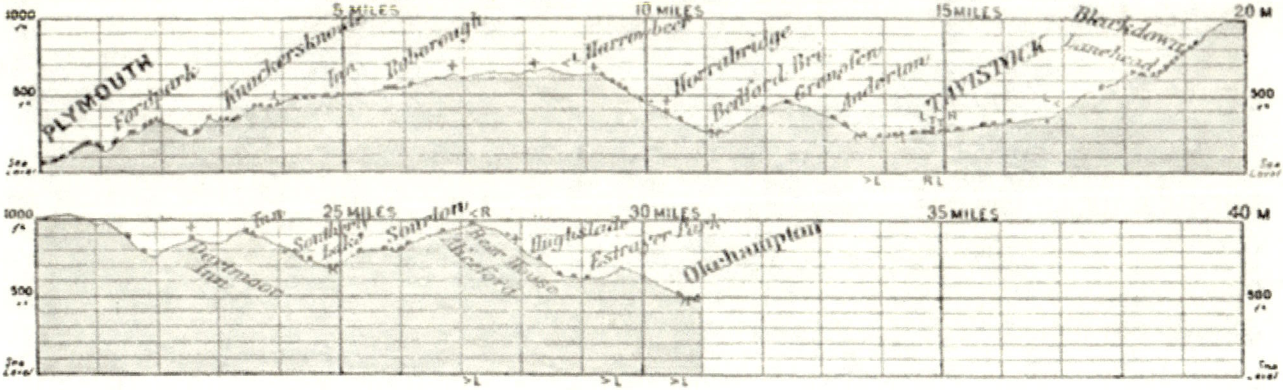

ROUTE 744. PLYMOUTH TO LAUNCESTON.

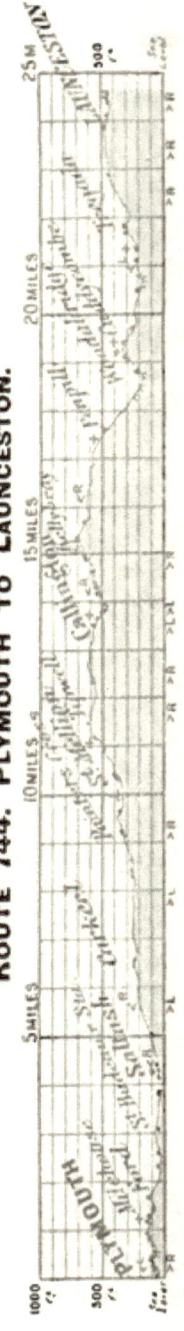

745 PLYMOUTH TO TRURO.

Description.—Class I. Rough through Devonport to Torpoint ferry (2m.). Thereafter the road has splendid surface, but approaching Liskeard it becomes very hilly, and there is a steep descent in that town. From Liskeard to Bodmin the surface is very fine, but the hills are a little stiff. From Bodmin to Truro is the best road in Cornwall, for after Lanivet, with the exception of the hills at Blue Anchor and near Truro, the gradients are of the slightest, and the surface magnificent. The hills near Bodmin can be avoided by following the road shown in dotted lines (1m. shorter), from Bodmin Road Station to the road fork beyond Lanivet. The road to Truro by St. Austell (R. 750) is a series of precipitous hills.

Gradients.—At 3¾m. 1/18; 8¼m. 1/18; 9¼m. 1/18; 12m. 1/20; 15¾m. 1/14; 16½m. 1/16; 17m. 1/14; 17½m. 1/15; 19½m. 1/20; 21½ & 23¼m. 1/17; 29m. 1/17; 31½m. 1/15; 33½ & 34m. 1/14; 34½ & 34¾m. 1/19; 35½m. 1/23; 39½m. 1/25; 39¾m. 1/22; 44½m. 1/13; 55 & 56m. 1/18.

Milestones.—Measured from Torpoint ferry to Liskeard; thereafter from Lostwithiel. After Dobwalls from Bodmin on to Blue Anchor, whence from Truro.

Measurements.

Plymouth,* Guildhall.
1¾ Devonport,* Fore Street.
2⅝ Torpoint.*
10½ 7⅞ Polbathick.
19¼ 16⅝ 8¾ Liskeard.*
(29 26⅜ 18½ 9¾ Bodmin Road Station.*)
32¼ 29⅝ 21¾ 13 3¼ Bodmin,* Court House.
39⅛ 36½ 28⅝ 19⅞ 10½ 6⅞ Victoria.*
44¾ 42⅛ 34¼ 25½ 16⅛ 12½ 5⅝ Blue Anchor,* Inn.
49⅜ 47 39⅛ 30⅜ 21 17⅜ 10½ 4⅜ Ladock.
56⅜ 54 46⅛ 37⅜ 28 24⅜ 17½ 11⅜ 7 Truro,* Market Place.

For St. Germans turn to R. at Polbathick.
For New Quay turn to R. at Indian Queen. (R. 764).
For St. Austell turn to L. beyond Lanivet. (R. 766).

Principal Objects of Interest.—5m. Antony House. 6¼m. Scrasdon Fort. LISKEARD: Church, St. Keyne's Well, Roundaberry, &c. 30½m. Castle Kynock. BODMIN: Church, County Hall, Court House, Gilbert Obelisk. Victoria: Roche Rock. TRURO: Cathedral, Infirmary, Library, Museum. Pretty scenery, but rather bleak between Lanivet and Blue Anchor.

Hotels or Inns at places marked*, and at Antony, Menheniot Station, Dobwalls, Lanivet, Tresillian, &c.

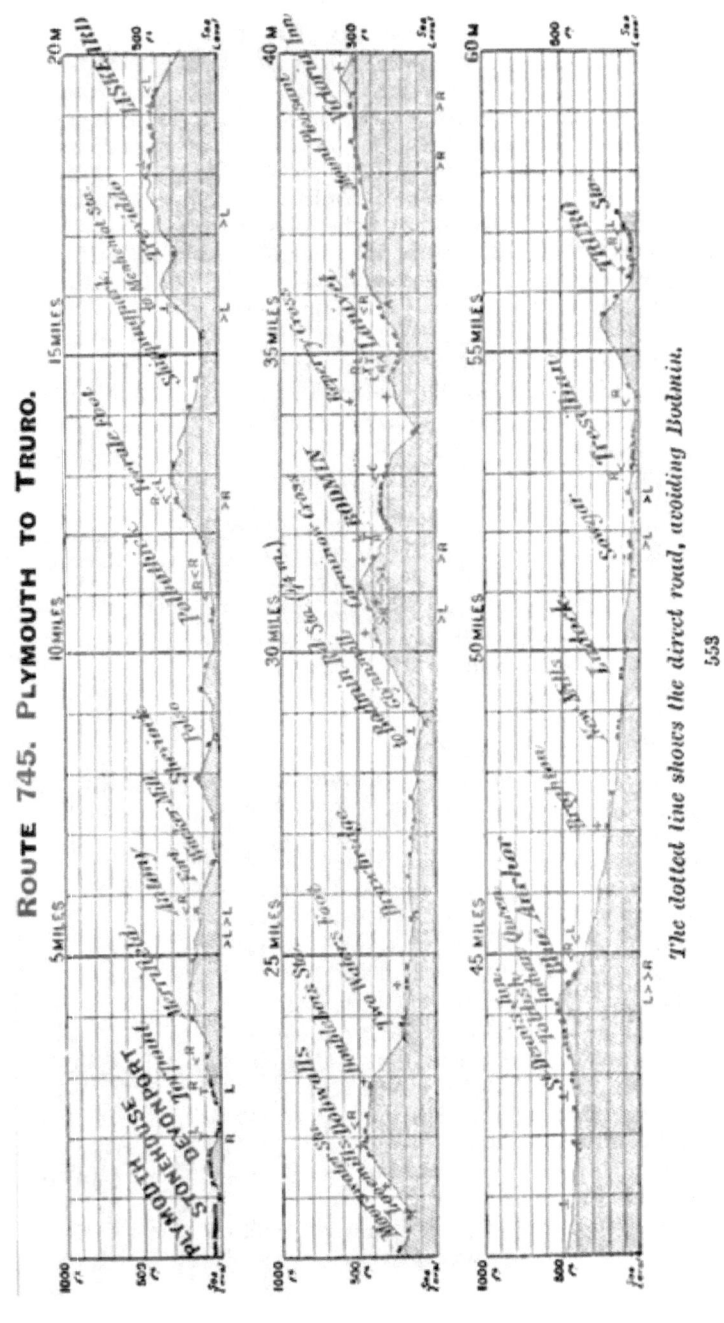

ROUTE 745. PLYMOUTH TO TRURO.

The dotted line shows the direct road, avoiding Bodmin.

558

746 TAVISTOCK TO ASHBURTON.

Description.—Class II. to Twobridges, then Class III. An exceedingly hilly road, with rather poor surface and innumerable precipitous hills. The scenery of Dartmoor is the only attraction.

Gradients.—At mostly 1 in 10 to Dunnabridge, then mostly 1 in 7 or 1 in 8. All highly dangerous.

Milestones.—Measured from Vigo Bridge, Tavistock.

Measurements.

Tavistock,* Guildhall.			
(7¾	Princetown.*)		
8¼	Twobridges.		
15⅜	7⅛	Poundsgate Inn.*	
19⅞	11⅝	4½	Ashburton.*

Principal Objects of Interest.—Splendid scenery.

Hotels or Inns at places marked*, and at Merrivale.

747 TAVISTOCK TO LAUNCESTON.

Description.—Class II. A very hilly road, but with good surface.

Gradients.—At ½m. 1 in 14; 1½m. 1 in 16; 3m. 1 in 17; 3½m. 1 in 19; 4½m. 1 in 17; 5¼ & 5¾m. 1 in 13; 6¼ & 6½m. 1 in 16; 9m. 1 in 14; 10m. 1 in 20; 13¾m. 1 in 11.

Milestones.—Measured from Tavistock in Devon; from Launceston Gateway in Cornwall.

Measurements.

Tavistock,* Guildhall.		
6⅛	Milton Abbott.*	
13½	7⅜	Launceston,* Market Clock.

Principal Objects of Interest.—LAUNCESTON: Castle, Gateway, St. Thomas Church.

Hotels or Inns at places marked*, and at Lamerton Green, &c.

748 TAVISTOCK TO LISKEARD.

Description.—Class II. Very fine surface, but long and very steep hills.

Gradients.—At ¾m. 1 in 15; 1½ & 2m. 1 in 15; 3¾m. 1 in 15; 4½m. 1 in 13; 5¼m. 1 in 8 (very dangerous); 8½m. 1 in 17; 10½m. 1 in 10 (dangerous); 12½m. 1 in 13; 15m. 1 in 13; 15½m. 1 in 10; 17m. 1 in 13; 17¼m. 1 in 10; 18¼m. 1 in 10.

Milestones.—In Devon measured from Tavistock, then from Callington, after which from Liskeard.

Measurements.

Tavistock,* Guildhall.				
4½	Gunnislake,* Cornish Inn			
9⅝	5⅛	Callington.*		
14⅛	9⅝	4½	St. Ive.	
18⅜	13⅞	8¾	4¼	Liskeard.*

[*over.*

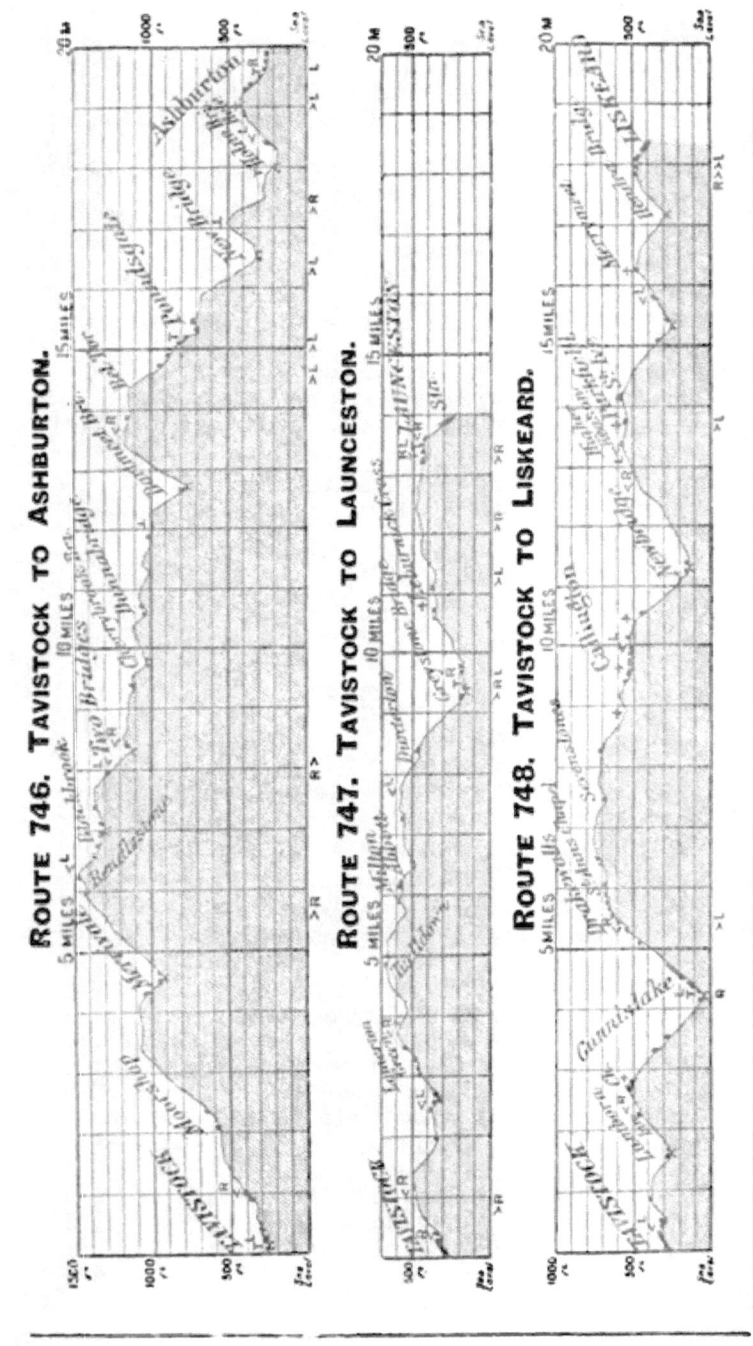

ROUTE 746. TAVISTOCK TO ASHBURTON.

ROUTE 747. TAVISTOCK TO LAUNCESTON.

ROUTE 748. TAVISTOCK TO LISKEARD.

Route 748—Continued.

Principal Objects of Interest. — Gunnislake: Bridge, Great Consols Mine. Callington: Dupath Well. LISKEARD: Church, St. Keynes Well.

749 TRURO TO LAUNCESTON.

Description.—Class I. Splendid surface to St. Columb, thence very good but hilly to Wadebridge; thereafter very good surface and pretty road to Knightsmill Bridge, whence steep to Camelford. From Camelford to Launceston the road is very fair, but with short, steep hills to Hallworthy, whence it is a very good, undulating road. This is the best through route to Exeter.

Gradients.—At ½ & 1½m. 1/18; 12½m. 1/19; 13¼m. 1/18; 14¼m. 1/12; 14½m. 1/16; 16m. 1/15; 17½m. 1/19; 18¼m. 1/23; 20½m. 1/19; 23½m. 1/12 (dangerous); 24¼m. 1/13; 27¾m. 1/14; 31¾m. 1/15; 34½m. 1/16; 35 & 38m. 1/17; 38½ & 39¼m. 1/13; 45¾ & 49½m. 1/18.

Milestones.—Measured from Truro to Blue Anchor, then after St. Columb from Wadebridge, whence from Camelford; thereafter measured from Launceston.

Measurements.

Truro,* Market Place.									
7	Ladock.								
11⅝	4⅝	Blue Anchor,* Inn.							
15½	8½	3⅞	St Columb,* Church.						
23⅞	16⅞	12	8⅜	Wadebridge,* Bridge.					
27¼	20¼	15⅝	11¾	3¼	St. Kew Highway,* Inn.				
34⅝	27⅝	22¾	19⅛	10¾	7⅜	Camelford,* Town Hall.			
40¼	33¼	28⅝	24¾	16½	13	5⅝	Hallworthy Inn.*		
46	39	34⅛	30⅛	22⅛	18¾	21⅜	5¾	Piperspool,* Inn.	
51	44	39⅝	35½	27⅛	23¾	16⅝	10¾	5	Launceston,* Mkt. Clock.

Principal Objects of Interest.—St. Columb: Church, Rectory. Wadebridge: Bridge, Egloshale Church. Camelford: Town Hall, Brown Willey, Delabole Quarries, Tintagel. LAUNCESTON: Castle, Gateway, St. Thomas Church.

Hotels or Inns at places marked *, and at Helstone.

750 TRURO TO LISKEARD.

Description.—Class II. The road has excellent surface, but the innumerable hills make this a very heavy road to travel. A better road is R. 745.

Gradients.—(† *Dangerous.*) At ½ & 1½m. 1/18; 5m. 1/16; 8½m. 1/13†; 9m. 1/16; 10m. 1/15; 11¼m. 1/14; 12½m. 1/13†; 13, 13½, & 14½m. 1/14; 17m. 1/13†; 17½m. 1/15; 19½m. 1/10†; 21m. 1/16; 21¼ & 21½m. 1/11†; 23m. 1/16; 24m. 1/12†; 24½ & 25m. 1/14; 26½m. 1/13†; 28¼ & 28½m. 1/17; 29m. 1/18; 30m. 1/14; 30¾ & 31½m. 1/17; 33¼m. 1/20.

Milestones.—Very irregular.

[*over.*

ROUTE 749. TRURO TO LAUNCESTON.

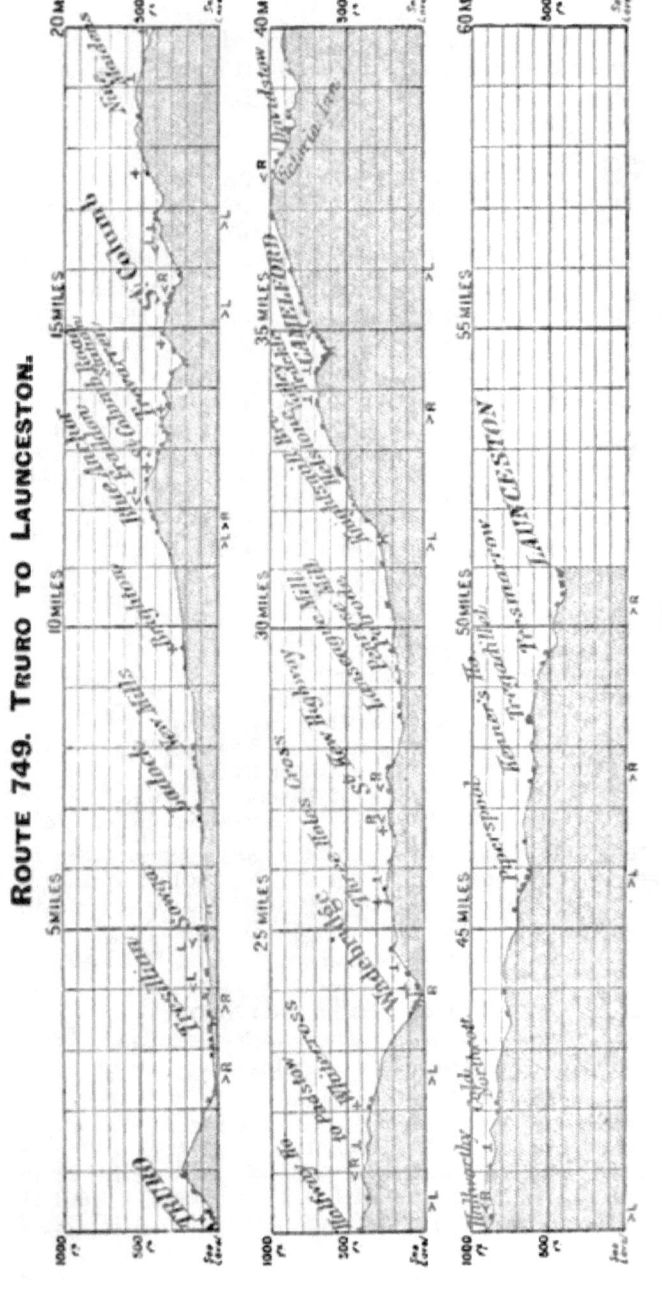

Route 750—Continued.

Measurements.

Truro.* Market Place.

8¼	Grampound.*				
14	5¾	St. Austell,* Church.			
18½	9¾	4¼	St. Blazey,* Market House.		
22¾	14¼	8¾	4¼	Lostwithiel,* Market House.	
33¾	25½	19¾	15½	11¾	Liskeard.*
53	44¾	39	34¾	30½	19¼ Plymouth.* (R. 745).

Principal Objects of Interest.—Probus : Church. St. Austell: Church, Carclaze Mines. Lostwithiel: Church, Palace ruins, Bridge, Restormel Castle. LISKEARD: Ch.

Hotels or Inns at places marked *, & Probus, Dobwalls, &c.

---

751   TRURO TO LAND'S END.

Description.—Class I. A somewhat hilly road, but with magnificent surface to Hayle, where it is bumpy for three miles; thereafter magnificent surface to Penzance. From Penzance to Lands End the road is a succession of short hills of varying length and steepness, but with good surface. The road by St. Just or St. Buryan is even more hilly.

Gradients. — († *Dangerous.*) At ¾m. 1/17 ; 4¾m. 1/13† ; 5¾m. 1/19 ; 8¾m. 1/17 ; 11¼m. 1/16 ; 14¼m. 1/18 ; 21m. 1/17 ; 27, 27¼, & 27½m. 1/15 ; 28 & 28½m. 1/10† ; 30¼ & 30½m. 1/14.

Milestones.—Measured from Truro as far as Redruth, whence from Davy Statue, Penzance; then from the County Hall.

Measurements.

Truro,* Market Place.

5	Chacewater,* Inn.				
8¾	3¾	Redruth.*			
12½	7½	3¾	Camborne,* Market House.		
18¾	13¾	9¾	6¼	Hayle,* Institute.	
(23¾	18¾	15	11¾	5¼	St. Ives.* R. 757.)
26	21	17½	13½	7½	10 Penzance,* Town Hall.
34¾	29¾	25¾	22¼	16	18¾ 8¾ Sennen,* Inn.
36	31	27½	23½	17½	20 10 1¼ Land's End,* Hotel.

For St. Ives keep to R. at 19¾m. ; coming from Penzance keep to L. after St. Erth Station.

From Redruth to Bodmin by Mitchell is 3½m. shorter than by Truro, but the latter road is far less hilly.

Principal Objects of Interest.—REDRUTH: Carn Brea, Dunstanville Monument, Copper Mines. CAMBORNE: Dolcoath Mine. 19½m. Hayle Causeway. PENZANCE: Market House, Humphrey Davy Statue, Battery, Public Buildings, St. Michael's Mount. 29m. Tresvennick Pillar. 20½m. "The Blind Fiddler." Land's End: splendid scenery, Longships Lighthouse, Armed Knights, &c.

Hotels or Inns at places marked *, and at Pool, &c.

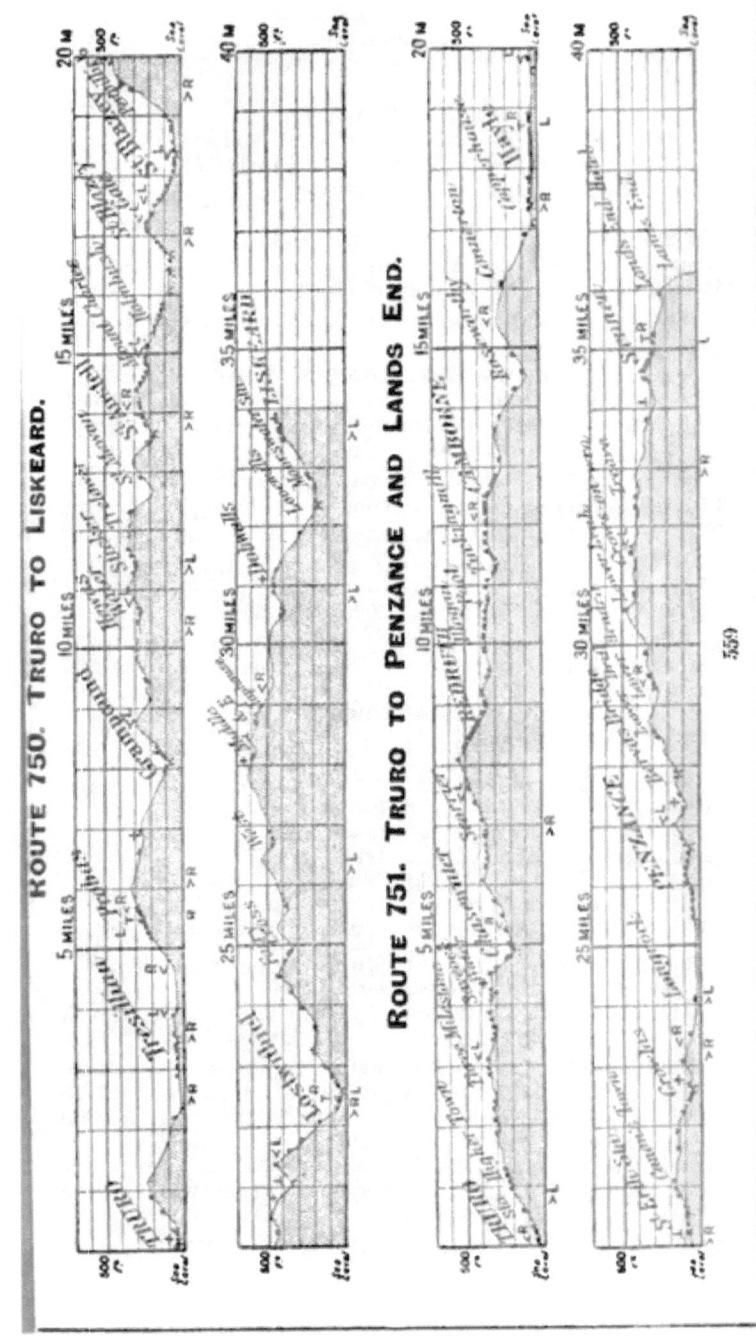

ROUTE 750. TRURO TO LISKEARD.

ROUTE 751. TRURO TO PENZANCE AND LANDS END.

752 TRURO TO FALMOUTH.

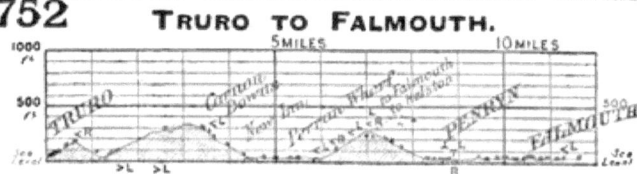

Description.—Class II. A very hilly road, but with fine surface to Penryn; thence very good to Falmouth. For Helston turn to R. at 7th milestone.

Gradients.—At ½ & 1m. 1/15; 1½m. 1/20; 3½, 6½, & 7m. 1/16.

Milestones.—Measured from Market Place, Truro; and Market Strand, Falmouth.

Measurements.

Truro,* Market Place.
5¼ Perran Wharf.*
8¾ 3½ Penryn,* Quay.
10¾ 5½ 1¾ Falmouth,* Market Strand.
16¾ 11½ Helston.* R. 761.

Principal Objects of Interest.— 6m. Carclew. Penryn: Stone Works. FALMOUTH: Church, Pendennis Castle, Kimberley Park, Trefusis.

753 TRURO TO ST. AGNES.

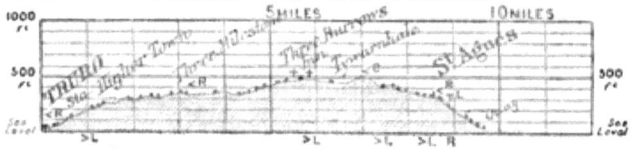

Description.—Class II. Splendid surface for three miles, then a very good country road.

Gradients.—At ½m. 1 in 17; 7½m. 1 in 14.

Measurements.—Truro,* Market Place.
5¾ Three Burrows' Inn.*
8⅝ 3 St. Agnes,* Church.

Principal Objects of Interest.—Fine coast scenery.

754 TRURO TO PERRANPORTH. 9½m.

Description.— Class II. Steep hill from Truro, and steep down to Perranporth, the rest a good country road.

Gradients.—At 1m. 1 in 10; 8½m. 1 in 14; both dangerous.

Principal Objects of Interest. — Perranporth: Chapel Rock, fine coast scenery.

Hotels or Inns at places marked *.

BODMIN TO FOWEY. 755

Description.—Class III. Fairly good surface, but precipitous hills. For Lostwithiel turn to L. at 3½m.

Gradients.—(*Dangerous.*) Mostly 1 in 10.

Measurements.—Bodmin,* Court House.
(5⅝ Lostwithiel.*)
11⅜ ... Fowey.*

Principal Objects of Interest.—2½m. Lanhydrock. Lostwithiel: Restormel Castle, Church. FOWEY: Ch., Castle, &c.

FALMOUTH TO REDRUTH. 756

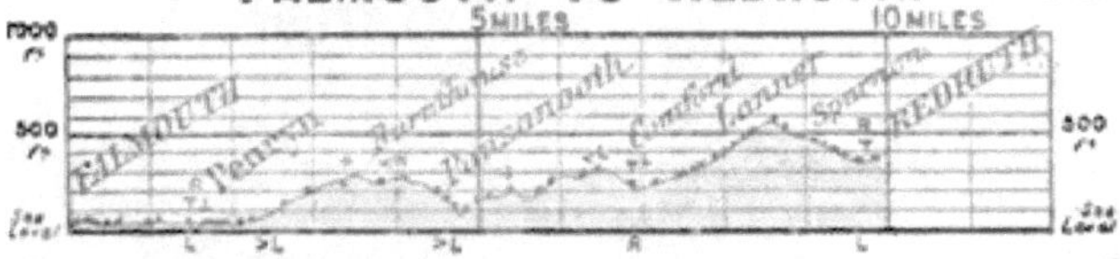

Description.—Class III. A fine road to Penryn, then very hilly with poor surface.

Gradients.—At 2½m. 1 in 16; 4¾ & 5m. 1 in 17; 6m. 1 in 12; 6¾m. 1 in 16; 8¼m. 1 in 13; 9m. 1 in 18.

Measurements.—Falmouth,* Market Strand.
1¾ Penryn,* Quay.
4¾ 3 Ponsanooth.*
9⅞ 8⅛ 5⅛ Redruth.*

Principal Objects of Interest.—Comford: Gwennap Pit 8½m. Carnbrea: Castle, Dunstanville Monument. REDRUTH: Copper Mines.

ST. IVES TO HAYLE OR PENZANCE. 757

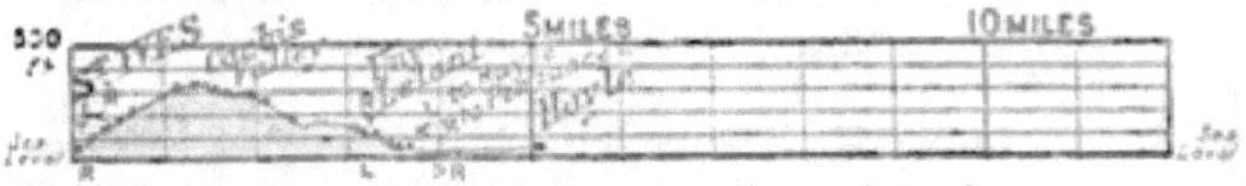

Description.—Class III. Good surface but very steep hills, till joining the Truro and Penzance Road.

Gradients.—At 1m. 1 in 19; 2¼m. 1 in 15; 3¼m. 1 in 14 (dangerous).

Measurements.—St. Ives,* Town Hall.
3¼ Lelant.*
5⅛ 1⅞ Hayle,*
or 10 6¾ Penzance.*

Principal Objects of Interest.—Carbis: Knill Obelisk, Cave. HAYLE: Copper Mines.

Hotels or Inns at places marked *

758   TRURO TO NEW QUAY.

Description.—Class III. Fine surface but very hilly road to Mitchell; thereafter fairly good surface, but less hilly.

Gradients. — († *Dangerous.*) At ¼m. 1/11†; 3¾m. 1/14†, 4¼m. 1/12 †; 5¼m. 1/11 †; 5¾m. 1/11†; 6¾m. 1/17; 8½m. 1/19; 8¾m. 1/17; 10¼m. 1/11†; 11m. 1/15; 12¾m. 1/22.

Milestones.—Measured from Truro as far as Mitchell, thereafter from New Quay.

Measurements.—Truro,* Market.
        7¼   Mitchell.*
        11½   4¾   Union Inn.*
        14¾   7¾   3¼   New Quay.*

Principal Objects of Interest. — New Quay : Beacon, Huers House, Towan Head, Pentire Point.

---

759   LISKEARD TO FOWEY, &C.

Description.—Class III. Good surface but very hilly for the first five miles; thereafter tolerably good surface and with numerous short hills, ending with a dangerous descent to Bodinick Ferry. From Fowey to Par the road is very steep, whence good to Liskeard.

Gradients. —(†*Dangerous.*) At ½m. 1/20; 2m. 1/17; 3½m. 1/14; 4¾m. 1/18; 5½m. 1/17; 6¾m. 1/14; 11½m. 1/13†; 14½ & 15½m. 1/11†; 17½m. 1/8†; 19½ & 20m. 1/13†; 22½m. 1/15.

Measurements.—Liskeard.*
        15¼   Fowey.*   R. 755.
        18¾   3¾   Par,* Inn.
        23¾   8¼   4¾   St. Austell,* Church.

Principal Objects of Interest. —6½m. Boconnoc Obelisk. FOWEY: Ch., Castle. ST. AUSTELL: Ch., Carclaze Mines.

Hotels or Inns at places marked *

---

760   ST. AUSTELL TO FALMOUTH.

Description.—Class III. An exceedingly hilly road, but with good surface to St. Mawes, where Ferry to Falmouth.

Gradients.—Mostly 1 in 14. At 8½m. 1 in 10 (dangerous).

Milestones.—Irregular.

Measurements.

St. Austell,* Church.
  8¼   Tregony,* P.O.
  14¾   6¼   Trewithian.*
  18¾   10½   4¼   St. Mawes.*
  21¾   13¼   7   2¾   Falmouth,* Market Strand.

Principal Objects of Interest. —St. Mawes : Castle. FALMOUTH: Pendennis Castle, Kimberley Park, &c

Hotels or Inns at places marked *.

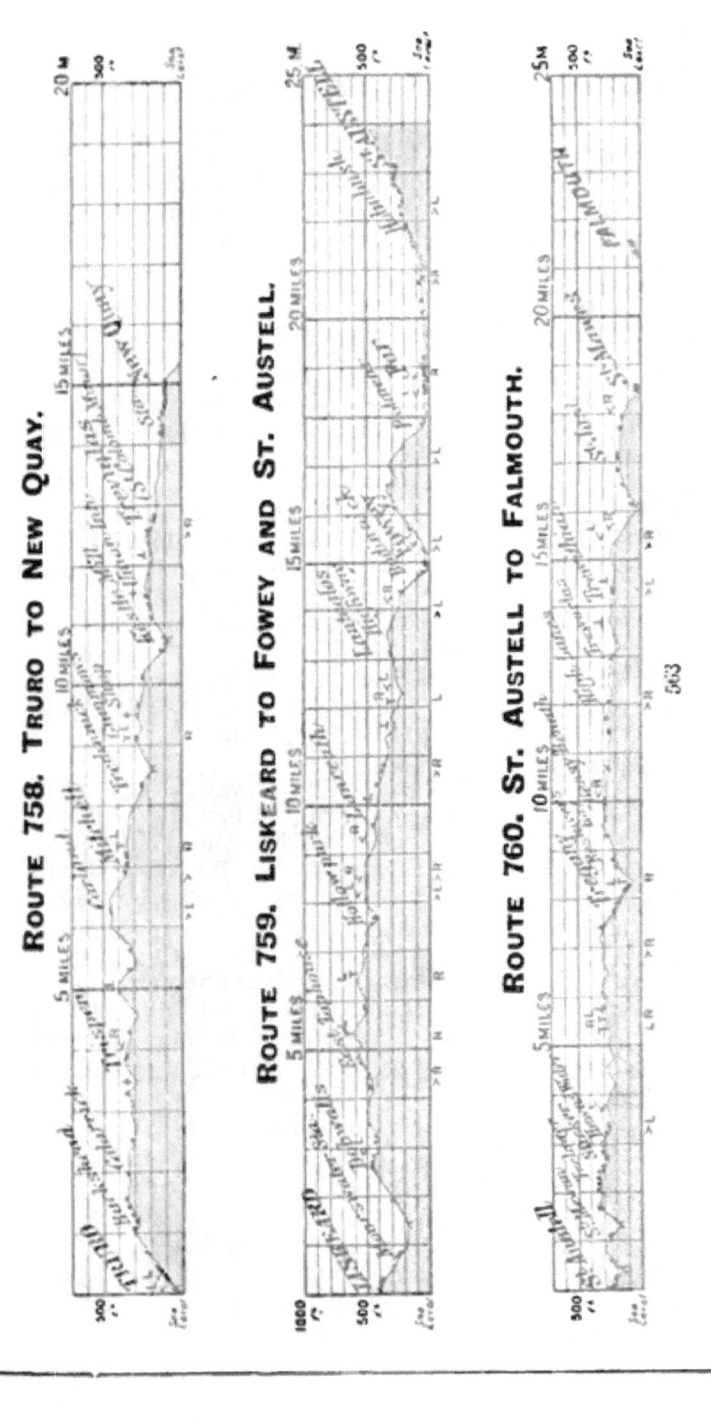

ROUTE 758. TRURO TO NEW QUAY.

ROUTE 759. LISKEARD TO FOWEY AND ST. AUSTELL.

ROUTE 760. ST. AUSTELL TO FALMOUTH.

761 FALMOUTH TO PENZANCE.

Description.—Class II. Fine surface but a hilly road to Helston, thence not quite so hilly, but with poorer surface to Marazion, whence fine to Penzance.

Gradients.—At 2½m. 1/19: 7 & 9m. 1/14: 10½m. 1/17; 12m. 1/12; 13m. 1/14; 14m. 1/22; 14¾m. 1/19; 17½ & 21½m. 1/20.

Milestones.—Measured from Market Strand, Falmouth.

Measurements.

Falmouth,* Market Strand.				
2	Penryn,* Market.			
12	10	Helston.*		
21⅝	19⅝	9⅝	Marazion,* Godolphin Hotel.	
25	23	13	3⅜	Penzance,* Town Hall.

Principal Objects of Interest.—Penryn: Stone Works. HELSTON: Church, Lizard Point. 16m. Pengersick Castle, Godolphin Park. Marazion: St. Michael's Mount. PENZANCE: Market House, Davy Statue, Public Buildings, Battery, Lescudjack Castle, Land's End.

762 REDRUTH TO LIZARD.

Description.—Class III. Very hilly, with poor surface to Helston; thereafter splendid surface to Lizard.

Gradients.—To Helston, mostly 1/14; 14, 14½, & 15½m. 1/13.

Milestones. — Irregular to Helston, thereafter from Helston.

Measurements.—Redruth.*

7⅝	Wendron.*			
10¼	2⅝	Helston.*		
14⅞	7¼	4⅝	Cross Lanes.*	
20¾	13⅛	10½	5⅞	Lizard.*

Principal Objects of Interest.—4m. "Nine Maidens. Lizard: Point, Lighthouses, Kynance Cove.

763 REDRUTH TO BLUE ANCHOR.

Description.—Class III. A very hilly road, but with fine surface to Zelah, then poor to Mitchell, after which good to Blue Anchor. Much easier grades and better surface by Truro, 3½m. longer. (R. 751 and 749.)

Gradients.—Mostly 1 in 13 or 1 in 15.

Milestones.—Very irregular after Mitchell.

Measurements.

Redruth.*			
9¾	Zelah.*		
13⅜	3⅝	Mitchell.	
17¼	7½	3⅞	Blue Anchor.* (R. 745 or 749).

Principal Objects of Interest.—Pleasant road.

Hotels or Inns at places marked *.

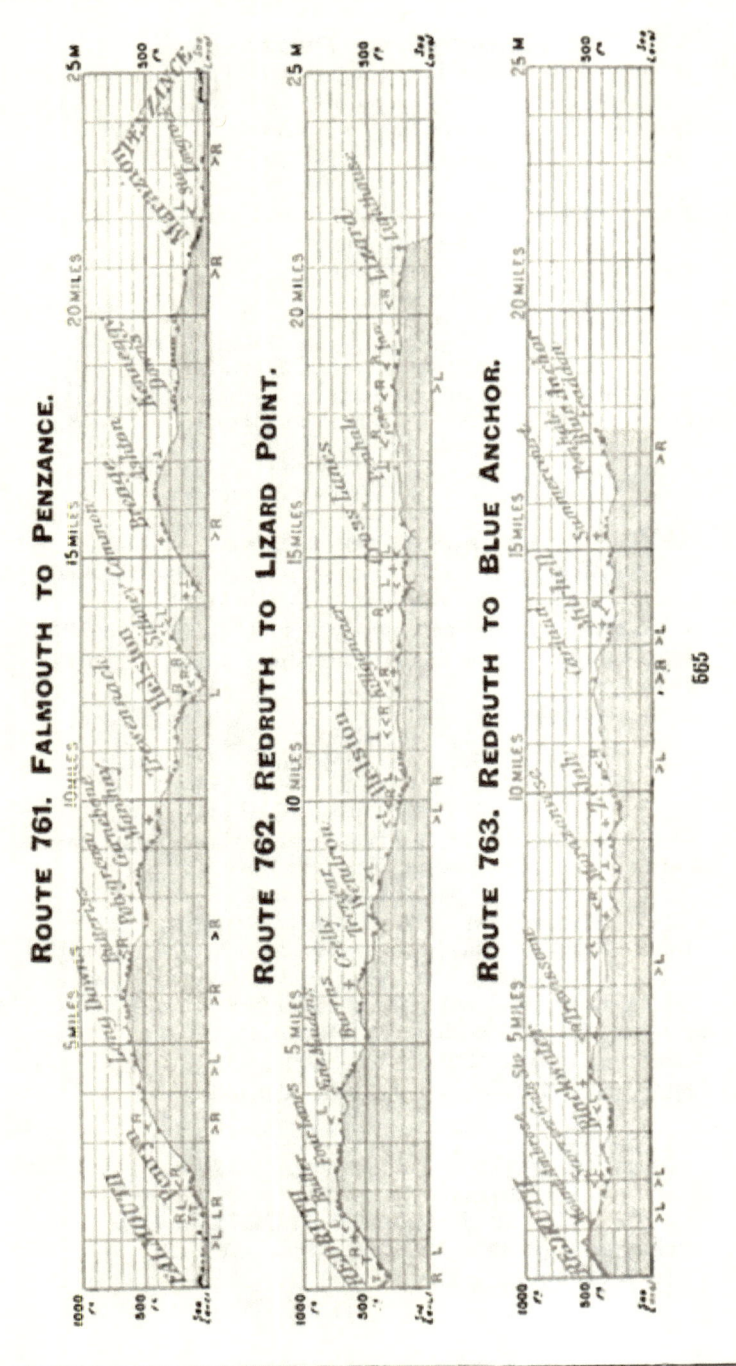

ROUTE 761. FALMOUTH TO PENZANCE.

ROUTE 762. REDRUTH TO LIZARD POINT.

ROUTE 763. REDRUTH TO BLUE ANCHOR.

764 New Quay to St. Austell.

Description.—Class III. Excellent surface to Roche, then poor, but improving after Carthew. Route 745 leading to Bodmin is joined at Indian Queen.

Gradients.—At 5½m. 1 in 19; 13m. 1 in 21; 14¼m. 1 in 16; 16m. 1 in 17; 17¾m. 1 in 15.

Milestones.—Measured from New Quay, Bodmin, and St. Austell.

Measurements.—New Quay.*
8 Indian Queen.*
13 5 Roche.*
19 11 6 St. Austell,* Church.
(19¾ 11¾ Bodmin.* R. 745.)

Principal Objects of Interest.—Roche: Rock, St. Michael's Chapel. St. Austell: Church, Carclaze Mine.

Hotels or Inns at places marked *, and at Union Inn and Carthew.

765 Bodmin to Padstow.

Description.—Class II. An exceedingly hilly road, with good surface, but there are six dangerous hills.

Gradients.—(*All dangerous.*) At 1¾m. 1/8; 2¼m. 1/11; 4m. 1/15; 7¼m. 1/12; 11¾m. 1/9; 12m. 1/10; 14¾m. 1/11.

Measurements.—Bodmin,* Court House.
7⅛ Wadebridge,* Market House.
14⅞ 7¾ Padstow.*

Principal Objects of Interest.—Wadebridge: Bridge, Egloshayle Ch. Padstow: Butter Hole, Permizen Bay.

Hotels or Inns at places marked *, and at Washaway.

766 Bodmin to St. Austell, &c.

Description.—Class II. Very hilly to Lanivet; then a splendid road to St. Austell; thereafter good surface to Pentewan, whence precipitous to Mevagissey.

Gradients.—At 1¼ & 1¾m 1/14, 2½ & 2¾m 1/19; 9¼m. 1/17; 10m. 1/15; 11¾m. 1/16, 15½ & 16¾m 1/8 (dangerous).

Milestones.—Measured from St. Austell

Measurements.—Bodmin,* Court House
7 Bugle*
11½ 4½ St. Austell,* Church.
17¼ 10¼ 5¾ Mevigissey.*

Principal Objects of Interest.—Lanivet: St. Bennetts Ruins. St Austell: Church, Carclaze Mine.

Hotels or Inns at places marked *.

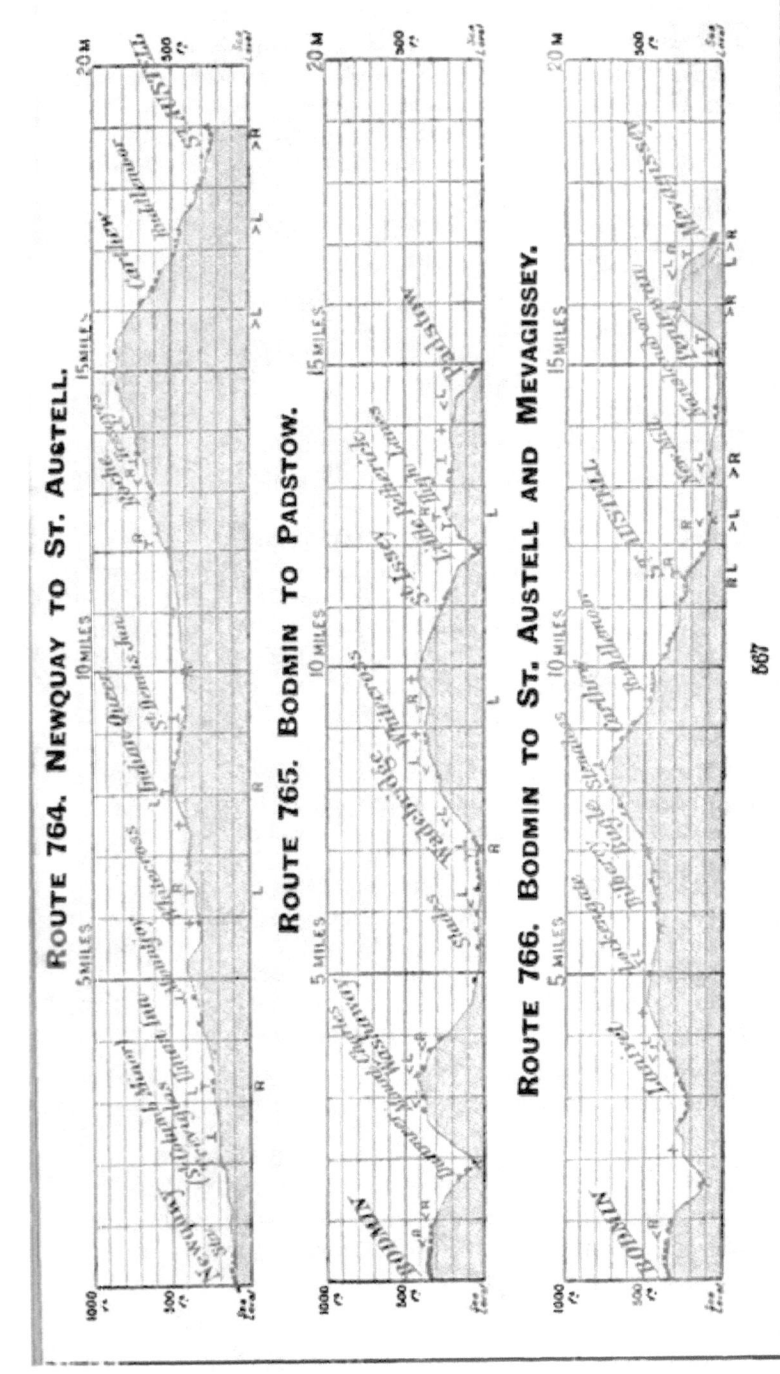

ROUTE 764. NEWQUAY TO ST. AUSTELL.

ROUTE 765. BODMIN TO PADSTOW.

ROUTE 766. BODMIN TO ST. AUSTELL AND MEVAGISSEY.

767 BODMIN TO CAMELFORD, &c.

Description.—Class II. Very steep for three miles, then a good undulating road all the way to Camelford. From Camelford to Boscastle the surface is good. The long winding descent to Boscastle is dangerously steep at the foot.

Gradients.—(†*Dangerous.*) At 1¾m. 1 in 8†; 2¼m. 1 in 11†; 6¾m. 1 in 13†; 7½m. 1 in 17; 9¾m. 1 in 18; 13¼m. 1 in 14; 13½m. 1 in 10†; 19m. 1 in 12†.

Milestones.—Measured from road fork in Bodmin.

Measurements.

Bodmin,* Court House.
5¾ Longstone.
13¼ 7½ Camelford,* Town Hall.
14⅞ 9⅛ 1⅝ Camelford Station.
18⅞ 13⅛ 5⅝ 4 Boscastle,* Wellington Hotel.

Principal Objects of Interest.—CAMELFORD: Brown Willey, Delabole Quarries. Boscastle: Fine Coast Scenery.

Hotels or Inns at places marked*, and at the Leathern Bottle.

768 CAMELFORD TO HARTLAND.

Description.—Class III. A continuously undulating road, usually with good surface, but often rather loose in parts according to season.

Gradients.—(*All Dangerous.*) At ½m. 1 in 17: 4¾m. 1 in 15; 5¼m. 1 in 22; 6¾m. 1 in 11; 10m. 1 in 10; 15¼m. 1 in 10: 17¼m. & 17½m. 1 in 10; 27¼m. 1 in 10; 32m. & 33¾m. 1 in 10. Other gradients mostly 1 in 15.

Measurements.

Camelford,* Town Hall.
9⅝ Wainhouse Corner. R. 778.
(17¼ 8⅝ Bude.* L. at 16m.)
17¼ 8⅝ Stratton.* R. 772.
21¼ 12⅝ 4 Kilkhampton.* R. 770.
27 17⅜ 9¾ 5¾ West Country Inn.*
31⅜ 22¼ 14⅛ 10⅛ 4⅜ Hartland.* R. 783.
34 24⅜ 16¾ 12¾ 7 2⅝ Hartland Quay.

Principal Objects of Interest.—Bude: Castle, Combe Valley. Stratton: Church, Battlefield (1643). Hartland: Church, Abbey.

Hotels or Inns at places marked*, and at Treskinnick Cross, and Stoke.

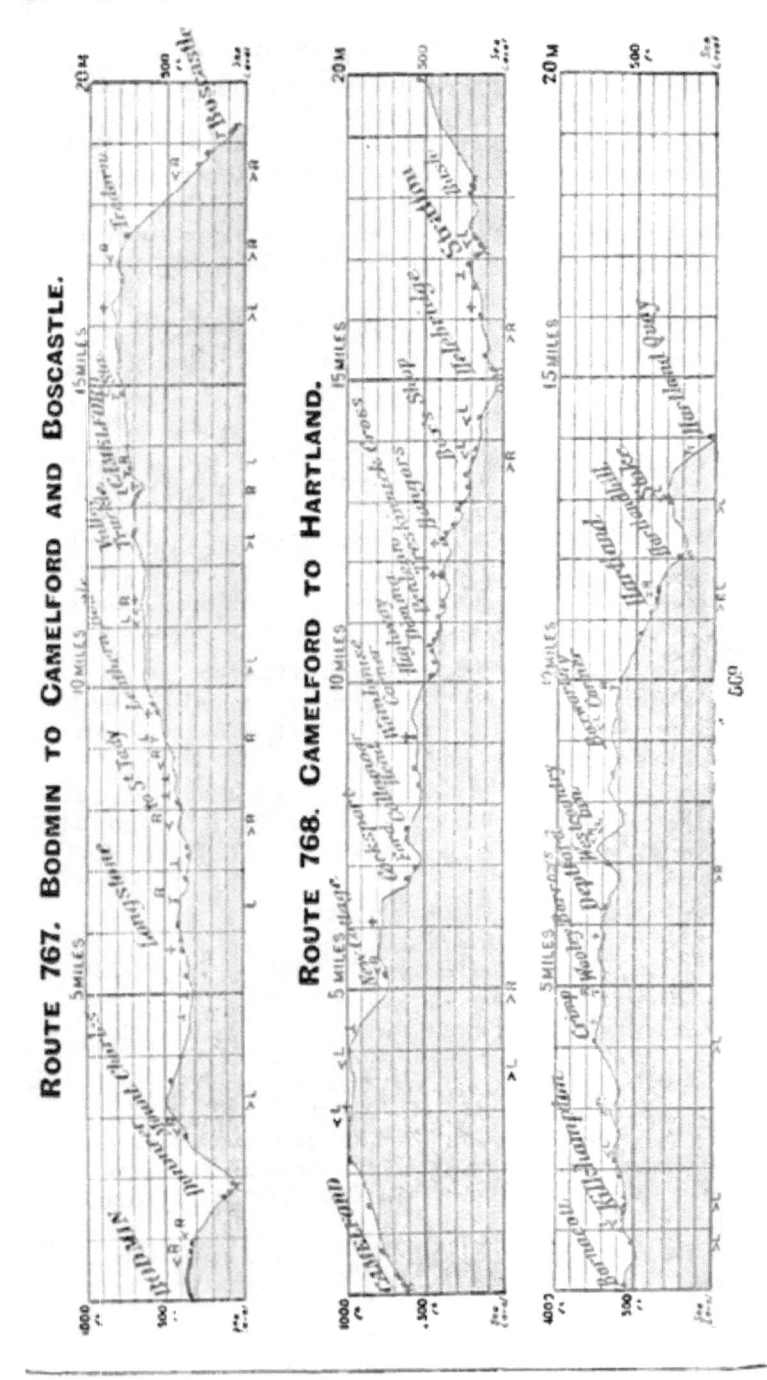

ROUTE 767. BODMIN TO CAMELFORD AND BOSCASTLE.

ROUTE 768. CAMELFORD TO HARTLAND.

609

769 LAUNCESTON TO BODMIN.

Description.—Class I. An exceedingly hilly road, good surface for four miles, then inferior till near Bodmin.

Gradients.—At 4m. 1 in 19; 5½m. 1 in 16; 8¼m. 1 in 17; 11m. 1 in 12 (dangerous); 11¾m. & 12¼m. 1 in 13; 14¼m. 1 in 17; 17¼m. & 21½m. 1 in 13.

Milestones.—Measured from Launceston as far as Five Lanes, thereafter from Bodmin Court House.

Measurements.

Launceston,* Market Clock.
11⅞ Bolventor.*
(15⅛ 3¼ Temple.)
17½ 5⅝ 2⅜ Pounds Cawsne Inn.*
22¼ 10⅜ 6⅞ 4⅜ Bodmin,* Court House.

Principal Objects of Interest.—Fine Scenery near Temple. 13¼m. Fourhole Cross. 17m. Peverell's Cross. BODMIN: Court House, Church, Gilbert Obelisk, "Castle Kynock."

770 LAUNCESTON TO HARTLAND, &c.

Description.—Class III. Steep for 3m., then a continuously undulating road with fair surface. For Stratton turn to L. at Red Post.

Gradients.—At ¼m. 1 in 11; ¾m. 1 in 9. Very dangerous. Other grades mostly 1 in 13, or 1 in 16.

Measurements.

Launceston,* Market Clock.
8 Dolsdon Inn.*
14½ 6½ Red Post.*
19 11 4½ Kilkhampton,* or
29¼ 21¼ 14¾ Hartland* (R. 768).
17½ 9½ 2¾ Stratton* (R. 772).

Hotels or Inns at places marked*, and at Whitstone.

771 LAUNCESTON TO HOLSWORTHY.

Description.—Class III. Dangerous hills for 2m., then numerous short hills of varying steepness, but the road has fairly good surface.

Gradients.—(+*Dangerous.*) At ½m. 1/11+; 1 & 1½m. 1/13+; 2½m. 1/16; 3¾m. 1/15; 4¾, 7, & 9m. 1/13+; 9½m. 1/15; 10½m. 1/12+; 11½ & 12¾m. 1/13+; 13¼m. 1/9+; 13½m. 1/10+.

Milestones.—Measured from Wooda Road, Launceston to Chudleigh Corner, thereafter from Holsworthy.

Measurements.

Launceston,* Market Clock.
6½ Chapman's Well.*
10⅝ 4⅛ Clawton.*
13⅝ 7⅛ 3 Holsworthy.*

[over.

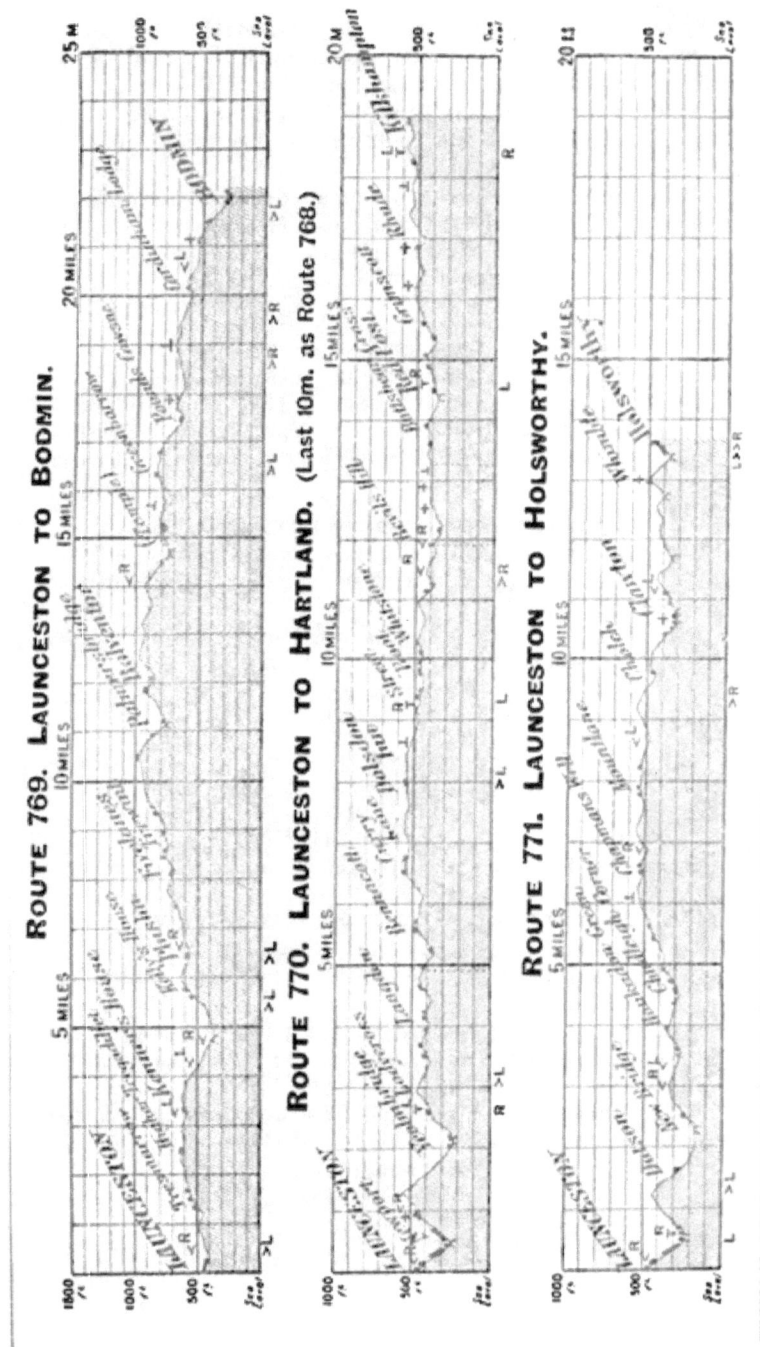

ROUTE 769. LAUNCESTON TO BODMIN.

ROUTE 770. LAUNCESTON TO HARTLAND. (Last 10m. as Route 768.)

ROUTE 771. LAUNCESTON TO HOLSWORTHY.

Route 771—Continued.

Principal Objects of Interest.—Pretty road near New Bridge, thereafter uninteresting. Holsworthy: Church.

772 OKEHAMPTON TO BUDE.

Description.—Class II. Rather a hilly road, but with tolerably good surface to Holsworthy, thereafter a better road, and with easier gradients.

Gradients.—(† *Dangerous.*) At ½m. 1 in 20; 3m. 1 in 12†; 3¼m. 1 in 8†; 10m. 1 in 11†; 11¾ & 12m. 1 in 19; 15m. 1 in 18; 19m. 1 in 13; 19¼m. 1 in 10†; 26¼m. 1 in 15†; 27½m. 1 in 11†; 28¼m. 1 in 14.

Milestones.—Measured from Okehampton, Holsworthy, and Stratton,

Measurements.—Okehampton.*

6¾	Broadbury Hotel.*				
11¼	4½	Halwill Sta.*			
19½	13¼	8¼	Holsworthy.*		
27½	21⅛	16¼	8	Stratton.*	
29⅛	22¾	17⅜	9⅝	1⅝	Bude,* Hotel.

Principal Objects of Interest.—½m. Okehampton Castle ruin. Broadbury: "Castle," fine views of Dartmoor. Holsworthy: Church. Stratton: Church, Battlefield 1643. Bude: Castle, Combe Valley.

Hotels or Inns at places marked *, and at Redpost.

773 OKEHAMPTON TO TORRINGTON.

Description.—Class III. A narrow and slightly hilly road, of good surface to Hatherleigh, then very steep to Meeth, after which the road is easy with good surface to Gribble Inn, whence there is a steep descent and ascent to Torrington. The old and direct road shown in dotted lines has good surface to Helebridge; after that it is precipitous, and with wretched surface in many places.

Gradients.—(†*Dangerous.*) At 2½m. 1 in 15; 4¾m. 1 in 15; 8½m. 1 in 14; 8¾m. 1 in 16; 9½m. 1 in 12†; 10m. 1 in 9†; 14½m. 1 in 17; 20m. 1 in 13†; 21m. 1 in 12.†

Measurements.—Okehampton.*

8½	Hatherleigh.*		
14¾	6¼	Merton.*	
21¼	12¾	6½	Torrington,* or
22¼	13¾	7½	Torrington Sta.

Okehampton to Hatherleigh, direct road, 7¼m.
Hatherleigh to Torrington, direct road by Petrockstow 11¾m.

Principal Objects of Interest.—7¼m. Basset's Cross. Hatherleigh: Church. TORRINGTON: Castle remains, Frithelstock Priory.

Hotels or Inns at places marked *, and at Gribble Inn.

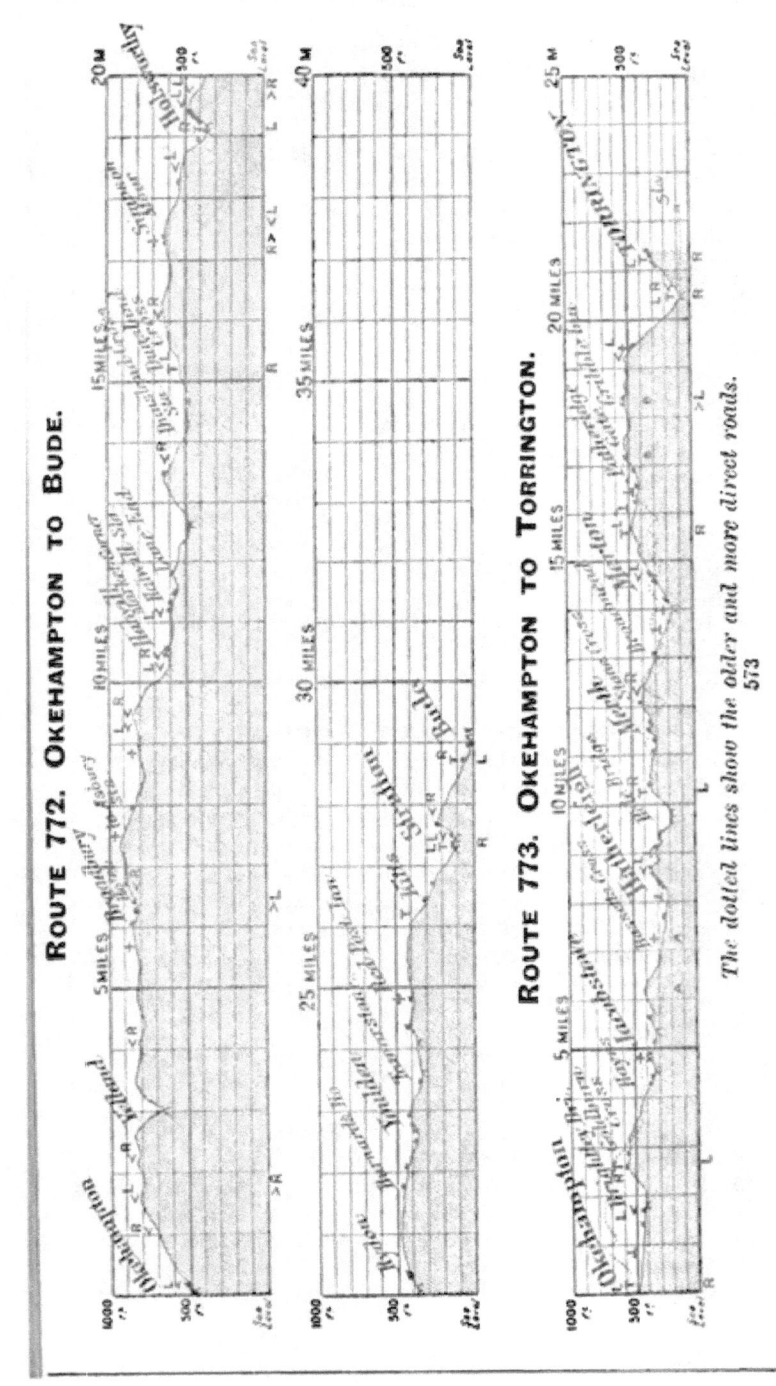

ROUTE 772. OKEHAMPTON TO BUDE.

ROUTE 773. OKEHAMPTON TO TORRINGTON.

The dotted lines show the older and more direct roads.

573

774 OKEHAMPTON TO TIVERTON, &c.

Description.—Class II. A very steep, hilly road for five miles, thence easier, and with better surface to Crediton; thereafter it is again hilly, with long steep hills and a precipitous descent to Bickleigh Bridge, after which the road has fine surface to Tiverton. After Tiverton the road is slightly undulating, and joins the Taunton Road (R. 730) at Waterloo Cross. The road from Bow to Crediton, by Coleford (shown dotted), is very steep.

Gradients.—Nearly all dangerous. The following are only the more severe gradients. At 1¼m. 1 in 10 ; 2½m. 1 in 11 ; 4¾m. 1 in 15 ; 10m. 1 in 19 ; 12⅞m. 1 in 16 ; 19m. 1 in 13 ; 19½m. 1 in 11 ; 20½m. 1 in 10 ; 22¼m. 1 in 11 ; 24¼m. 1 in 12 ; 26m. 1 in 9 ; 34m. 1 in 13 ; 35½m. 1 in 12.

Milestones.—Measured from Okehampton, Crediton, Tiverton, and Taunton.

Measurements.

Okehampton.*

9¾	Bow.*							
17⅜	7½	Crediton.*						
26¾	16½	9	Bickleigh Bridge.					
30	20½	12½	3½	Tiverton.*				
33¾	24	16½	7½	3¾	Halberton.*			
37½	27¼	19¾	10¾	7¼	3¼	Waterloo Cross.*		
44⅞	34¾	27¼	18¼	14⅜	10¾	7½	Wellington.*	
51⅝	41¼	33¾	24¾	21¼	17¼	14	Taunton.*	

Principal Objects of Interest. — Crediton : Church, Down Head. TIVERTON : Castle ruins, Church, Collipriest House. Halberton : Church.

Hotels or Inns at places marked*, and at Sampford Courtenay Station, Coleford, Sampford Peverell, &c.

775 HATHERLEIGH TO HOLSWORTHY.

Description.—Class III. A fairly good undulating country road, with two dangerous hills.

Gradients.—At ½m. 1/25 ; 4m. & 5½m. 1/12 (dangerous) ; 7½m. 1/22 ; 13m. 1/13 ; 13½m. 1/10 (both dangerous).

Milestones.—Measured from Holsworthy.

Measurements.—Hatherleigh.*

4	Highampton.*				
13½	9½	Holsworthy.*			
21¼	17¼	8	Stratton.	(R. 772).	
23¼	19¼	9¾	1⅝	Bude.	(R. 772).

Principal Objects of Interest.—Holsworthy : Church.

Hotels or Inns at places marked*, and at Brandis Corner.

ROUTE 774. OKEHAMPTON TO TIVERTON AND TAUNTON.

ROUTE 775. HATHERLEIGH TO HOLSWORTHY.

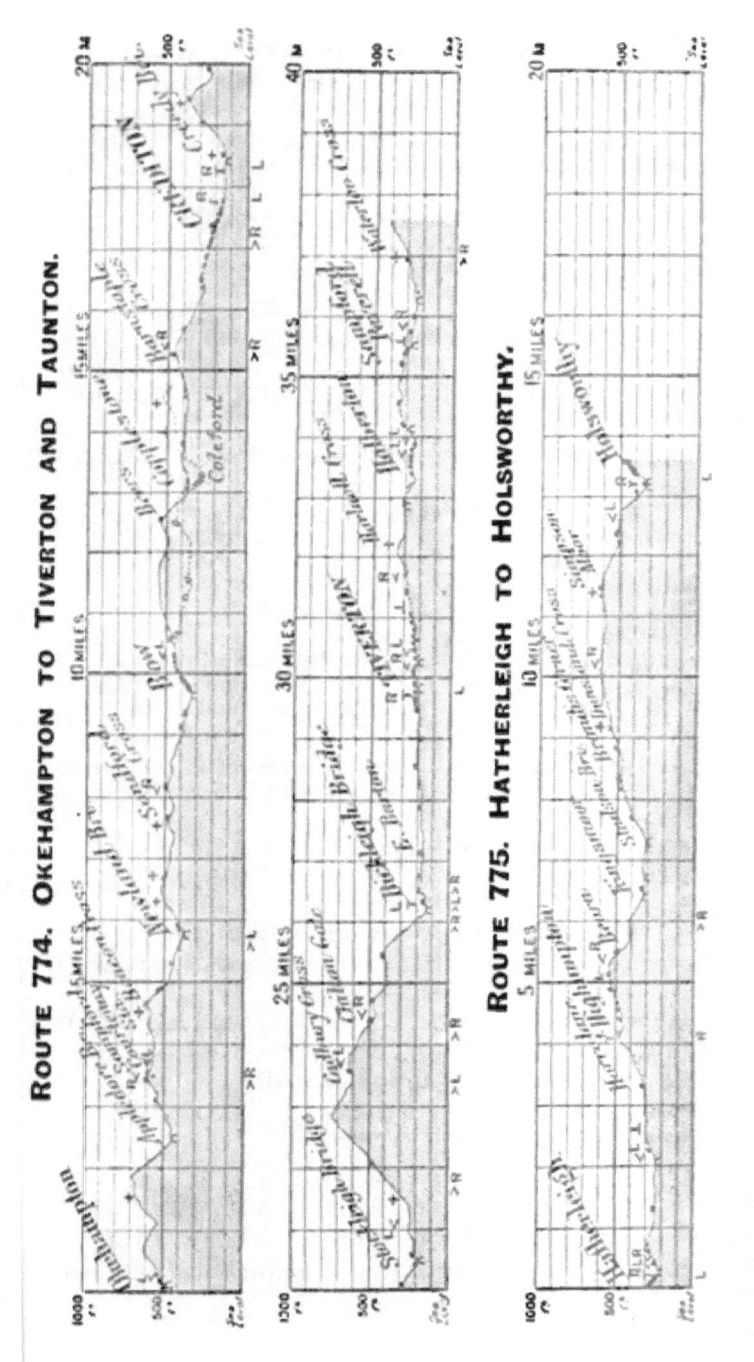

776 PADSTOW TO ST. COLUMB 8¾m.

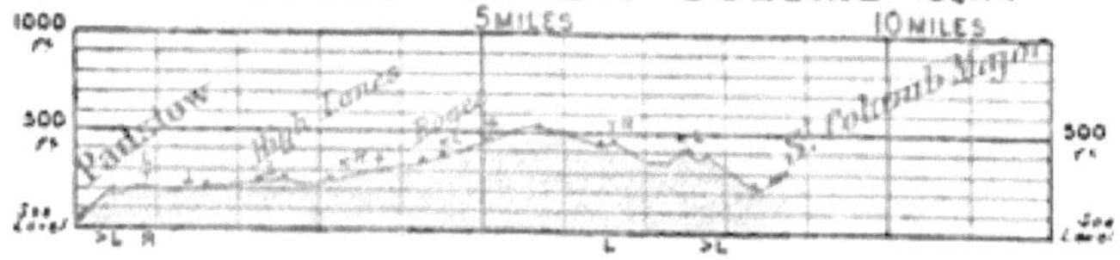

Description.—Class III. Very steep out of Padstow, then a fairly good road; improving surface, but very hilly near St. Colomb.

Gradients.—(*Dangerous.*) At ¼m. 1 in 11; 8m. 1 in 15.

Principal Objects of Interest.—St. Columb: Ch., Rectory.

777 CAMELFORD TO TINTAGEL.

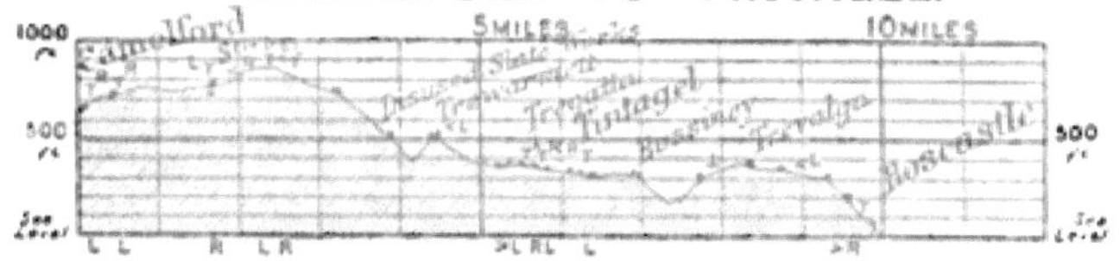

Description.—Class III. Good surface for two miles, then dangerously steep for three miles, after which good.

Gradients.—(† *Dangerous.*) At ¼m. 1 in 10†; 3½m. 1 in 13†; 4¼m. 1 in 10†; 4¾m. in 13†; 7m. 1 in 9†; 7½m. 1 in 11†; 9½m. 1 in 8†

Measurements.—Camelford,* Town Hall.
1¾ Camelford Sta.
6¼ 4½ Tintagel,* Wharncliff Arms.
9⅞ 8⅛ 3⅝ Boscastle.*

Principal Objects of Interest. — 4m. Disused Slate Works. TINTAGEL: King Arthur's Castle, Trebarwith Strand, &c.

778 BOSCASTLE TO STRATTON.

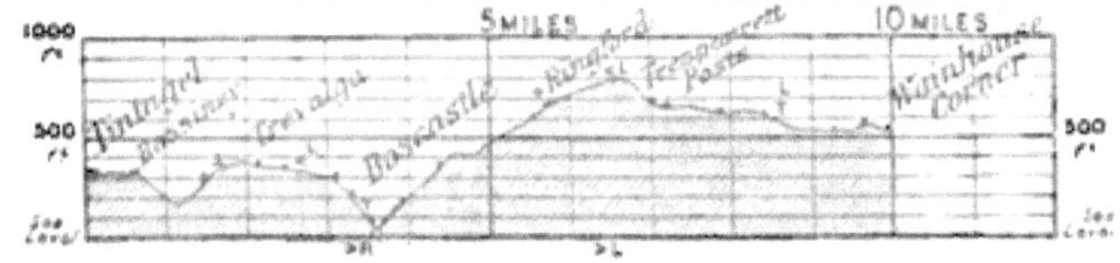

Description.—Class III. Tintagel to Boscastle, good surface but very steep. Boscastle to Wainhouse: rather poor surface, also very steep. Wainhouse to Stratton, R. 768.

Gradients. (*Dangerous.*) At 1m. 1 in 9†; 1½m. 1 in 11†; 3¼m. 1 in 8†; 4¼m. 1 in 9†; 7m. 1 in 11†.

Measurements.—Tintagel,* Wharncliffe Hotel.
3⅝ Boscastle,* Wellington Hotel.
10 6⅜ Wainhouse Corner. R. 768.
18⅛ 14½ 8⅛ Stratton.*

Principal Objects of Interest.—Boscastle: Fine coast.

Hotels or Inns at places marked *.

BARNSTAPLE TO LYNMOUTH. 779

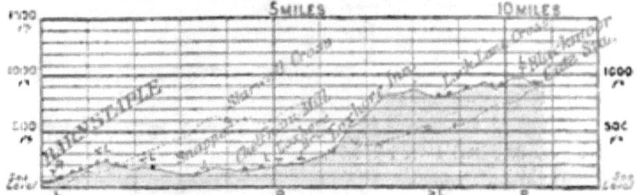

Description.—Class III. Excellent surface to Loxhore Inn, then a steep rough road. An easier road by Shirwell Cross is shown dotted. The grades on this latter road are not so steep, but the road is hardly as good.

Gradients.—At ½m. 1 in 21; 6½m. 1 in 7 (dangerous); 7½m. 1 in 13; 9½m. 1 in 13; 10m. 1 in 11.

Milestones.—Measured from Barnstaple, Town Hall.

Measurements.—Barnstaple.*

6¼	Loxhore Inn.*		
10¾	4¾	Blackmoor Sta.	
17¼	11½	7¼	Lynmouth.* R. 791.

Principal Objects of Interest.—Pretty scenery to Loxhore. Lynmouth as R. 791.

BAMPTON TO DULVERTON. 780

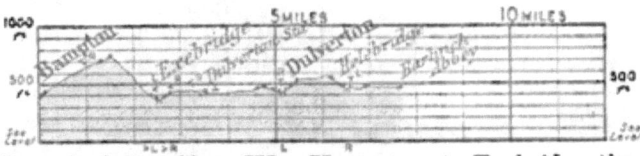

Description.—Class III.—Very steep to Exebridge, then good surface to Dulverton. The best road to Exebridge is by the river Exe, R. 729. From Dulverton towards Minehead the road is very steep to Helebridge, where join R. 729.

Gradients.—At ¼m. 1 in 9; 2m. 1 in 12; 6½m. 1 in 13. (All (dangerous).

Measurements.—Bampton.*

2½	Exebridge Inn.*	
5¼	2¾	Dulverton.*

Bampton to Dulverton, by river Exe 9m.

Dulverton to Exeton. (R. 729) 6m.

Principal Objects of Interest.—Dulverton: Pixton Park. Picturesque scenery.

Hotels or Inns at places marked*.

2 s

782 TORRINGTON TO SOUTH MOLTON.

Description.—Class III. While the surface is fairly good, the road is simply a series of precipitous hills as far as Umberleigh Bridge; thereafter it is not quite so steep. It is better to go round by Barnstaple.

Gradients.—(*All Dangerous.*) Mostly 1 in 12; but 5¼m. 1 in 8; 5¾m. & 6¼m. 1 in 7; 7m. 1 in 8.

Milestones.—Measured from South Molton.

Measurements.—Torrington,* Market.
8½ Umberleigh Bridge.*
15⅝ 7⅛ South Molton,* Guildhall.

Principal Objects of Interest.—Atherington: Church. South Molton: Church, Guildhall.

Hotels or Inns at places marked *, and at Atherington.

783 BIDEFORD TO HARTLAND.

Description.—Class III. A hilly road of very fair surface, but rather steep at several points. For Clovelly turn to R. at Clovelly Dykes; a very steep descent: better pay toll by Hobby Drive, a beautiful road turning off at 8½m.

Gradients.—(†*Dangerous.*) At ¼m. 1 in 10†; 3¼ & 4m. 1 in 13; 5 and 5¼m. 1 in 19; 5¾m. 1 in 14; 6¾m. 1 in 13; 12m. 1 in 15; 13½m. 1 in 17; 14¼m. 1 in 10†; 16m. 1 in 10†.

Measurements.—Bideford,* Bridge-end.
5⅝ Hoops Inn.*
(11¾ 5⅞ Clovelly.*)
13¾ 7⅞ 5¼ Hartland.*
16⅝ 10½ 7⅞ 2⅝ Hartland Quay.

Principal Objects of Interest.—10m. Clovelly Dykes, Clovelly Court, Gallantry Bower. Hartland: Ch., Abbey.

784 BIDEFORD TO HOLSWORTHY.

Description.—Class III. Good surface, but stiff gradients for the first ten miles, then rather steep with two dangerous hills and poorer surface to Holsworthy.

Gradients.—(†*Dangerous.*) At 2¼, 3½, 5½, & 6¼m. 1 in 17; 11m. 1 in 10†; 11½m. 1 in 11†; 12m. 1 in 15; 13½m. 1 in 10†; 14m. 1 in 12.†

Milestones.—Measured from Bideford and Holsworthy.

Measurements.—Bideford,* Bridge-end.
4⅜ Monkleigh.*
11⅜ 7 Woodford Bridge.*
18⅝ 14¼ 7¼ Holsworthy.*

Principal Objects of Interest.—Holsworthy: Church.

Hotels or Inns at places marked *.

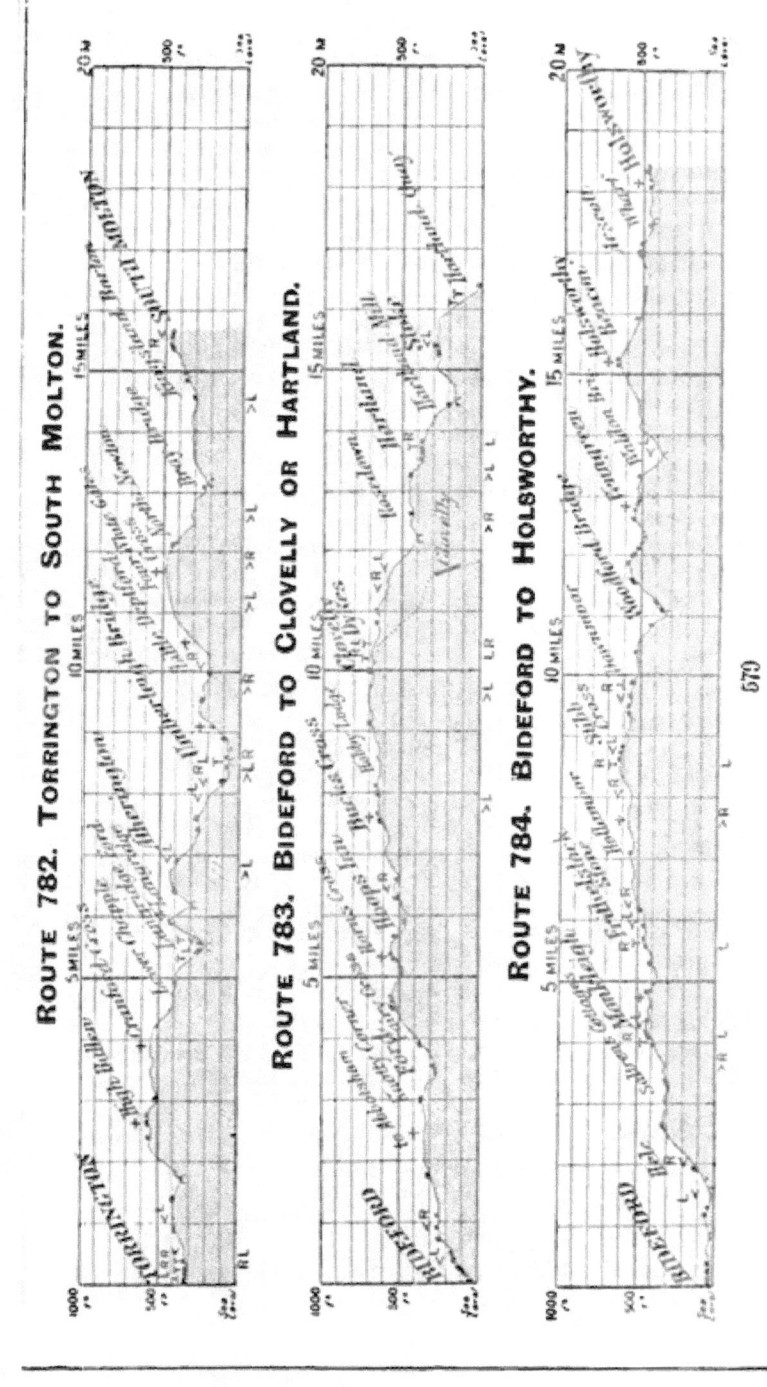

ROUTE 782. TORRINGTON TO SOUTH MOLTON.

ROUTE 783. BIDEFORD TO CLOVELLY OR HARTLAND.

ROUTE 784. BIDEFORD TO HOLSWORTHY.

785 SOUTH MOLTON TO CHULMLEIGH.

Description.—Class III. A narrow road, but with excellent surface and easy gradients, joining the Exeter and Barnstaple road at South Molton Road Sta.

Gradients.—At 11¼m. 1 in 12 (dangerous).

Milestones.—Measured from Guildhall, South Molton.

Measurements.—South Molton,* Guildhall.

5¼			Warkleigh Hotel.*
8¾	3½		South Molton Road Sta.'
12½	7¼	3½	Chulmleigh.*
(34½	28¾	25¼	Exeter,* Guildhall.)

Principal Objects of Interest.—7m. New Place. Chulmleigh: Church.

786 SOUTH MOLTON TO LYNTON.

Description.—Class III. Fairly good surface at first but steep, and with poor surface after Brayford Hill.

Gradients.—At ¾m. 1 in 19; 2½m. 1 in 23; 4m. 1 in 15; 7½m. 1 in 11 (dangerous); 9m. 1 in 14; 13½m. 1 in 17

Milestones.—Measured from Guildhall, South Molton.

Measurements.

South Molton,* Guildhall.

7				Brayfordhill.	
13¾	6¾			Blackmoor Sta.	
20¾	13¾	8½	7¼	Lynmouth.*	R 791.
or 18⅝	11⅝	6¼	4½	Combe Martin.*	R. 791.

Principal Objects of Interest.—Exmoor.

Hotels or Inns at places marked *.

787 BARNSTAPLE TO TORRINGTON.

Description.—Class II. Undulating road for 3m., thence an easy road with very good surface to Torrington Sta., whence steep up to Torrington. The direct road by Alverdiscot (10½m.) is a succession of precipitous hills.

Gradients.—At ¼m. 1 in 18; 1¾m. 1 in 15; 15¼m. 1 in 12 (dangerous).

Milestones.—Measured from Barnstaple, Town Hall.

Measurements.

Barnstaple.*

6¾				Instow,* Marine Hotel.
9¼	3			Bideford,* Bridge-end.
15¼	8⅞	5⅞		Torrington Sta.
16¼	10	7	1¼	Torrington,* Town Hall.

Principal Objects of Interest.—Instow: Church, Appledore. BIDEFORD: Bridge, Church, Chudleigh Fort, Westward Ho. Torrington: Frithelstock Priory, Castle remains.

Hotels or Inns at places marked *.

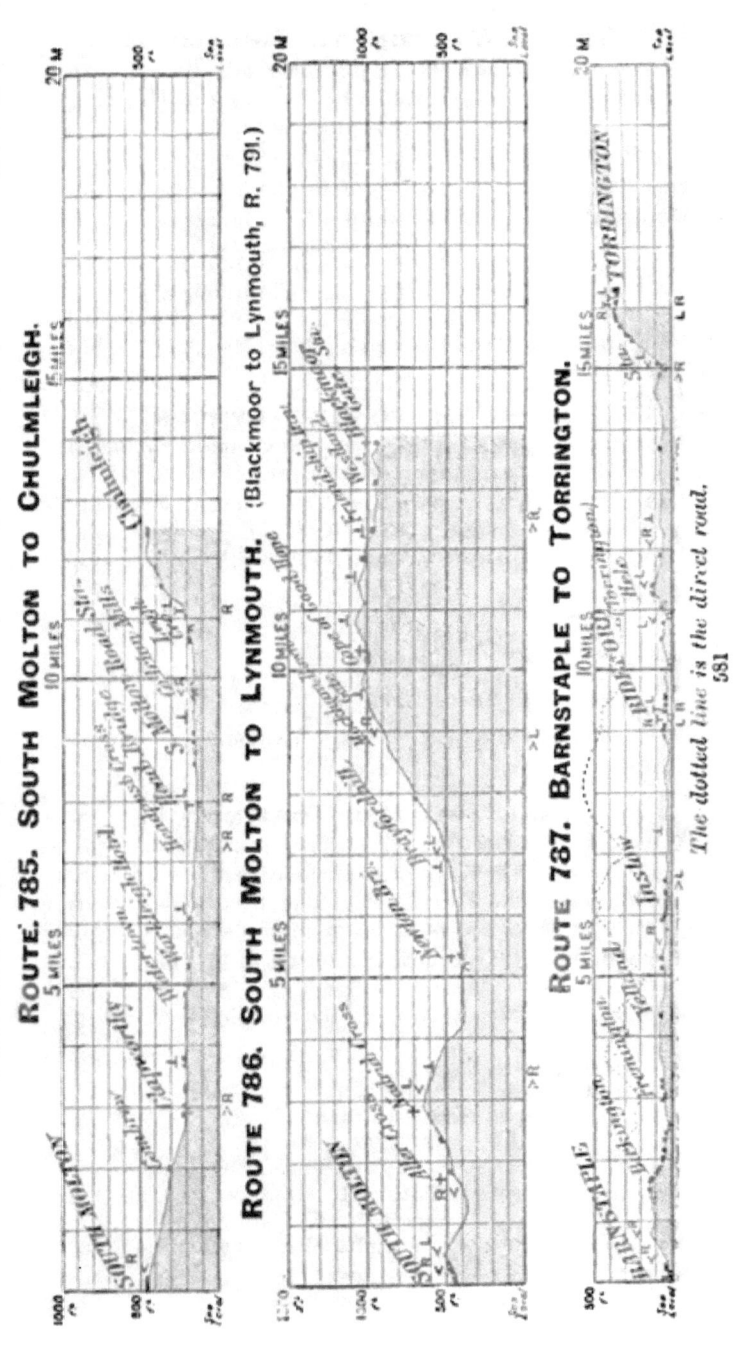

ROUTE 785. SOUTH MOLTON TO CHULMLEIGH.

ROUTE 786. SOUTH MOLTON TO LYNMOUTH. (Blackmoor to Lynmouth, R. 791.)

ROUTE 787. BARNSTAPLE TO TORRINGTON.

The dotted line is the direct road.

581

788 BARNSTAPLE TO ILFRACOMBE.

Description.—Class I. Fine surface, and a beautifully engineered road with long steady and easy gradients.

Gradients.—At 1m. 1 in 13; 5¾m. 1 in 25; 7¾m. 1 in 21; 10m. 1 in 24; 11m. 1 in 17.

Milestones.—Measured from Town Hall, Barnstaple.

Measurements.

Barnstaple.*
3¾ Muddiford.*
6¼ 2½ Bittadon.*
11⅝ 7⅞ 5⅜ Ilfracombe,* Town Clock.

Principal Objects of Interest. — ILFRACOMBE: Quay, Tors Walk, Capstone Hill, Lantern Hill, Morthoe, &c.

789 BARNSTAPLE TO BRAUNTON, &C.

Description.—Class III. Almost level road with good surface to Braunton, thence to Ilfracombe the road is narrow, with fair surface, but with rather a steep descent.

Gradients.—At 9½m. 1 in 18; 11½m. 1 in 15; 12½m. 1 in 17.

Milestones.—Measured from Barnstaple, Town Hall.

Measurements.

Barnstaple.*
5½ Braunton.*
9¼ 3¾ Foxhunters Inn.*
13½ 8 4¼ Ilfracombe,* Town Clock.

Principal Objects of Interest. — Braunton: Church.

Hotels or Inns at places marked *, and at Knowle.

790 TIVERTON TO SOUTH MOLTON.

Description.—Class II. Long and steep hills for the first six miles, thereafter rather easier gradients the rest of the way; good surface throughout. The old road to South Molton by Rackenford is far more hilly, and with bad surface.

Gradients.—(† *Dangerous.*) At 1½m. 1 in 15†; 2½ & 2¾m. 1 in 13†; 3½m. 1 in 15†; 5¼m. 1 in 16; 7½, 11, & 11¾m. 1 in 19; 12¼ & 13m. 1 in 15†; 14¾m. 1 in 21; 15¼m. 1 in 11†; 16¼m. 1 in 23.

Milestones.—Measured from Tiverton, after Witheridge from South Molton.

Measurements.

Tiverton.*
10¾ Witheridge.*
15½ 4¾ Meshaw.
21¼ 10½ 5¾ South Molton,* Guildhall.

Principal Objects of Interest.—So. Molton: Guildhall.

Hotels or Inns at places marked *, and at Mount Pleasant, Gidley Cross, and Alswear.

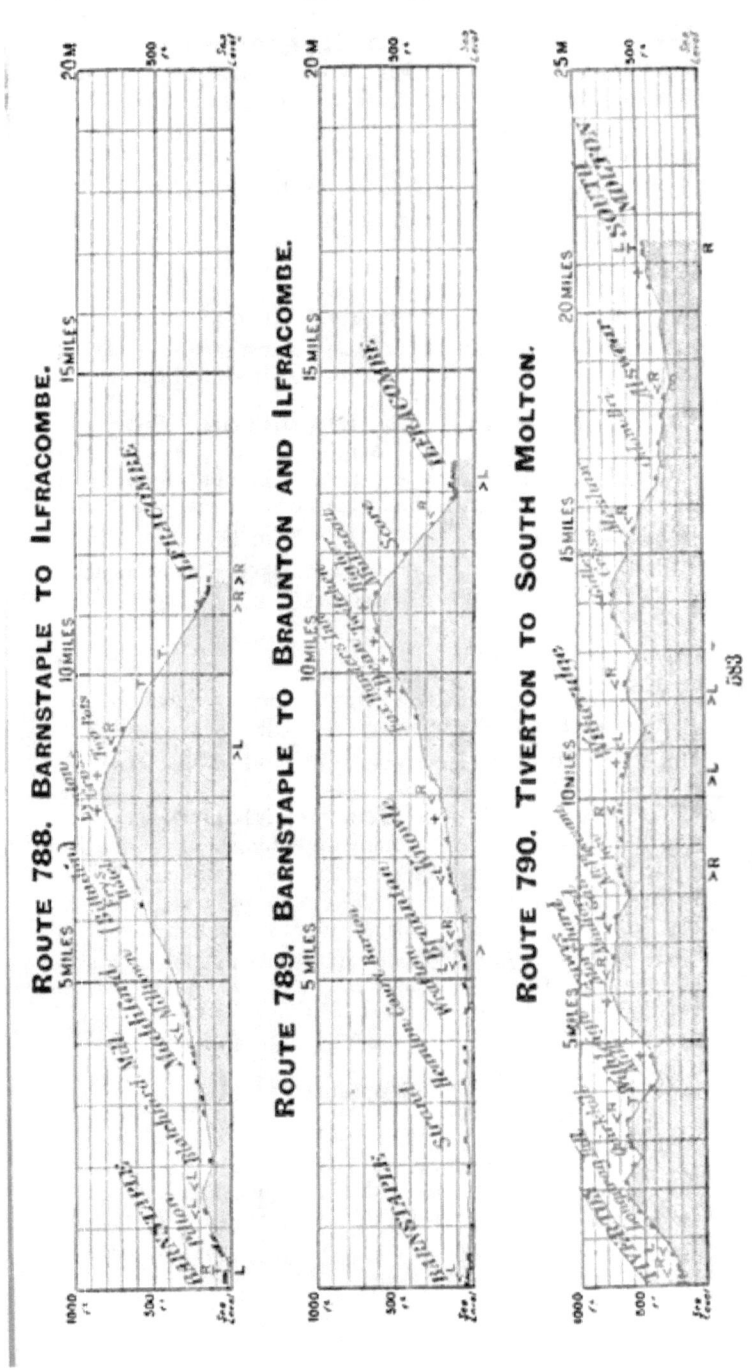

ROUTE 788. BARNSTAPLE TO ILFRACOMBE.

ROUTE 789. BARNSTAPLE TO BRAUNTON AND ILFRACOMBE.

ROUTE 790. TIVERTON TO SOUTH MOLTON.

791 Ilfracombe to Minehead.

Description.—Class II. The worst main road in the south of England. From Ilfracombe to Combe Martin the road has fine surface, but is very steep; thereafter it is a long ascent, very steep at first, then easier, then steep, but with good surface to Blackmoor Sta. From Blackmoor Sta. to Parracombe the surface is good to close to that place, when the road drops suddenly into the village and rises again on the other side with a perfectly precipitous gradient and with wretched surface; good surface again for the next four miles, then another dangerous descent before Barbrook Mill. The road then descends to Lynmouth by a sheer descent with an awkward twist at the bottom—about the most dangerous hill in the country. From Lynmouth the road rises by a two mile ascent of a somewhat similar description, but after Countisbury it is easier, and for the next 7m. is usually good, but inclined to be soft; the road then descends to Porlock by another sheer descent, with two twists near the bottom; there is scarcely any surface to this part of the road—it is more like a river bed—but a new descent (shown dotted) has been made to Porlock from Oar Post, a mile longer, with better surface. Fine surface, but a hilly road from Porlock to Minehead.

Gradients.—(*All dangerous.*) At 1m. 1 in 12; 1½m. 1 in 13; 3½m. 1 in 13; 4½m. 1 in 12; 6½m. 1 in 13; 8½m. 1 in 13; 12m. 1 in 7; 12½m. 1 in 9; 15¼m. 1 in 9; 16½m. 1 in 11; 17¼m. 1 in 5; 17¾m. 1 in 7; 19m. 1 in 9; 26½m. 1 in 10; 27½m. 1 in 8; 28½m. 1 in 6; 29¼m. 1 in 13; 32½m. 1 in 14.

Milestones.—Measured from Combe Martin.

Measurements.

Ilfracombe,* Town Clock.							
5½	Combe Martin,* Hotel.						
10⅜	4⅞	Blackmoor Sta.					
12⅛	6⅝	1¾	Parracombe,* Hotel.				
(17⅜	11⅞	7	5¼	Lynton.*)			
17½	12	7⅛	5⅜	Lynmouth.*			
19	13½	8⅝	6⅞	1½	Countisbury.*		
29	23½	18⅝	16⅞	11½	10	Porlock.*	
35⅛	29⅝	24¾	23	17⅝	16⅛	6⅛	Minehead.

Principal Objects of Interest.—Splendid scenery and views of Welsh Coast. 2¾m. Watermouth Castle. Barbrook Mill; Watersmeet. Lynton: Valley of Rocks, Mars Hill, Cliff, Doon Valley, East Lynn, Tramway. 26½m. White Stones. Porlock: Ch. Minehead: Ch., Quay, Dunster Castle.

Hotels or Inns at places marked *.

Route 791. Ilfracombe to Lynmouth and Minehead.

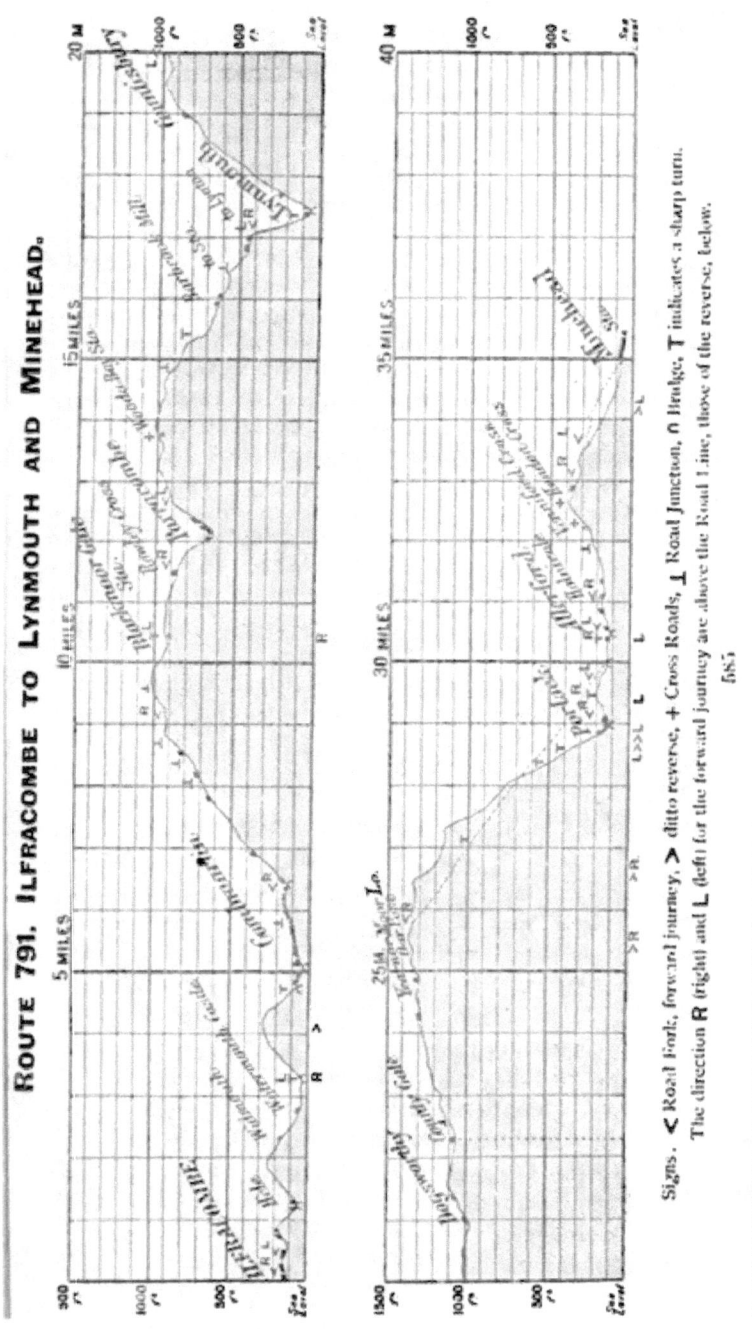

Signs. < Road Fork, forward journey, > ditto reverse, + Cross Roads, ⊥ Road Junction, ∩ Bridge, T indicates a sharp turn.
The direction R (right) and L (left) for the forward journey are above the Road Line, those of the reverse, below.

585

792 TAUNTON TO BARNSTAPLE.

Description.—Class II. As far as Milverton the road has fine surface, and slight gradients, but close to that place it becomes hilly, and after Wiveliscombe the hills are very long to Venn Cross Station, whence the gradients are easier to Bampton. From Bampton to South Molton the road is good at first, but after Stukeridge Bridge it rather degenerates in quality, and although the gradients are not very steep, it is sometimes a very heavy road. Near South Molton there are two very dangerous hills, and thereafter to Barnstaple the road is more or less hilly, with a dangerous descent to Swimbridge. There is a more direct road (shown by dotted lines) between Bampton and Stukeridge Bridge, a mile shorter, but rather steep.

Gradients.—(†*Dangerous.*) At 7m. in 15; 8m. 8⅝m. 9½m. & 10⅞m. 1 in 16; 11⅞m. 1 in 14†; 13½m. 1 in 25; 14m. 1 in 18; 24½m. 1 in 23; 31½m. 1 in 21; 35m. 1 in 22; 37¼m. 1 in 11†; 38m. 1 in 13†; 38¼m. 1 in 12†; 39½m. 1 in 19; 45½m. 1 in 11†; 46m. 1 in 19; 46½, 47, & 49m. 1 in 18.

Milestones.—Measured from Taunton Market House as far as Milverton, thereafter from Wiveliscombe through Bampton by the direct road to Newtown, whence measured from S. Molton as far as Swimbridge: thereafter from Barnstaple.

Measurements.

Taunton,* Market House.

7¾	Milverton.*							
10⅝	3⅛	Wiveliscombe.*						
20⅛	12⅜	9½	Bampton.*					
29½	21¾	18⅞	9⅜	Hare and Hounds Inn.				
38¾	31	27⅞	18⅝	9¼	South Molton,* Guildhall.			
45⅞	38⅛	35	25¾	16⅜	8⅛	Swimbridge.*		
50½	42¾	39⅞	30⅜	21	11¾	4⅝	Barnstaple.*	
62¼	54½	51¼	41¾	32⅜	23⅜	16¼	11⅝	Ilfracombe. R. 788.

Principal Objects of Interest.—Milverton: Ch. Wiveliscombe: Bishop's Palace. Bampton: Market House. Uninteresting road to South Molton. South Molton: Ch., Guildhall. Filleigh Bridge: Castle Hill, and imitation castle. Swimbridge: Ch. BARNSTAPLE: Bridge, Queen Anne Statue, Church, School, &c.

Hotels or Inns at places marked *, and at Norton Fitzwarren, Rockhouse, Shillingford, Exeter Inn, Bishmill, and Newland.

ROUTE 792. TAUNTON TO BARNSTAPLE.

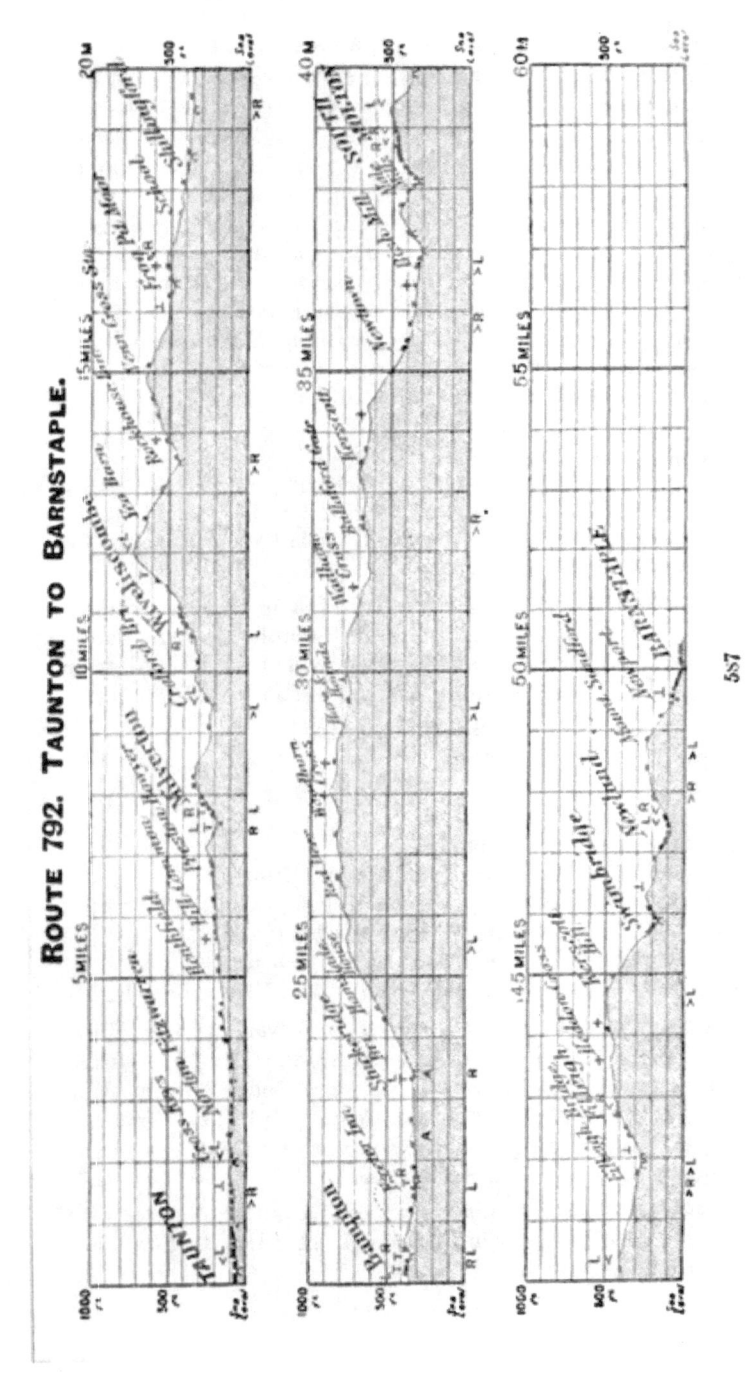

793 TAUNTON TO MINEHEAD.

Description.—Class II. Excellent surface for 7m., then very hilly to Williton, whence fine surface to Minehead.

Gradients.—At 7½m. 1 in 14; 9m. 1 in 16; 9½m. 1 in 11 (dangerous); 9¾m. 1 in 13; 12m. 1 in 15; 13m. & 15¼m. 1 in 13.

Milestones.—From Taunton for 5m., then from Minehead.

Measurements.—Taunton,* Market House.

10¾	Crowcombe.*			
15⅝	4⅞	Williton.*		
17½	6¾	1⅞	Washford.*	
23⅞	13⅛	8¼	6⅜	Minehead.*
(21⅞	11⅛	6¼	4⅜	Dunster).*
(29⅜	18⅝	13¾	11⅞	Porlock).* (R. 791).

Principal Objects of Interest.—Bishops Lydeard: Ch. Washford: Cleeve Abbey. Minehead: Church.

Hotels or Inns at places marked*, and at Carhampton.

---

794 TAUNTON TO WINCANTON.

Description.—Class II. A fine undulating road, specially good near Curry Rivel, and Sparkford.

Gradients.—At 4m. 1 in 14; 5m. 1 in 18; 7¾m. 1 in 25; 12¼m. 1 in 24; 13½m. 1 in 10; 16¾m. 1 in 16.

Measurements.

Taunton,* Market House.

5⅞	Wrantage Inn.*				
11⅜	5½	Curry Rivel.*			
13⅜	7½	2	Langport.*		
25⅝	19¾	14¼	12¼	Sparkford,* Inn.	
33¼	27⅜	21⅞	19⅞	7⅝	Wincanton.* R. 689.

Principal Objects of Interest.—Curry Rivel: Parkfield Monument, Ch. Langport: Ch., Museum. Somerton: Ch., Hurcot Quarries.

---

795 TAUNTON TO AXMINSTER.

Description.—Class II. A slightly hilly road to Chard, thereafter more hilly, and with a dangerous hill at Tytherleigh. Good surface throughout.

Gradients.—At 4m. 1 in 14; 4¼m. 1 in 17; 10¾m. 1 in 15; 17m. 1 in 16; 19½m. 1 in 10 (dangerous).

Milestones.—Measured from Taunton, as far as Ashill; near Chard, measured from Axminster.

Measurements.

Taunton,* Market House.

8¾	Ashill.*		
15½	6¾	Chard,* Town Hall.	
22½	13¾	7	Axminster,* George Hotel.

Principal Objects of Interest.—Chard: Ch., Town Hall.

Hotels or Inns at places marked*, and at Horton Cross, &c.

ROUTE 793. TAUNTON TO MINEHEAD.

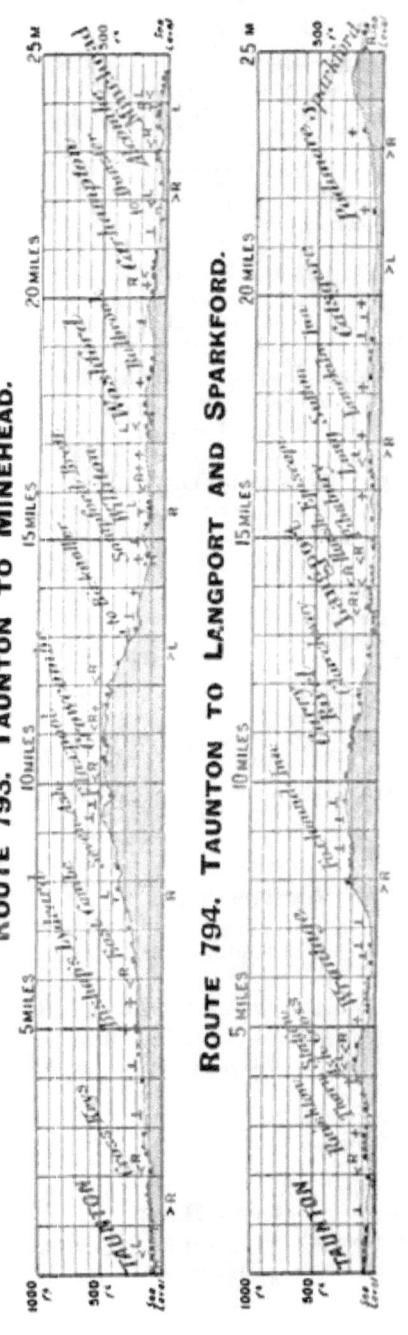

ROUTE 794. TAUNTON TO LANGPORT AND SPARKFORD.

ROUTE 795. TAUNTON TO CHARD AND AXMINSTER.

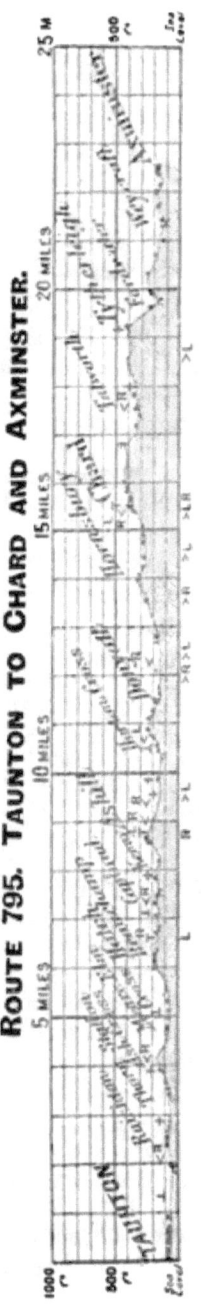

Signs — < Road Fork, forward journey. > ditto reverse; + Cross Roads, ⊥ Road Junction, ∩ Bridge, ⊤ indicates a sharp turn.

The direction: R (right) and L (left) for the forward journey are above the Road Line, those of the reverse, below

132

796 TAUNTON TO HONITON.

Description.—Class II. Good surface to Blagdon, then a very hilly and poor road to Upottery, whence good surface.

Gradients.—At ½m. 1 in 22; 5m. 1 in 12 (dangerous turn); 6¼m. 1 in 18; 11½m. 1 in 11 (dangerous).

Milestones.—Measured from Taunton Bridge in Somerset, irregular in Devon.

Measurements.—Taunton,* Market House.

4⅜	Blagdon.			
8½	4⅛	Churchingford.*		
12⅛	7¾	3⅝	Upottery.	
17¼	12⅞	8¾	5⅛	Honiton,* Church.

Principal Objects of Interest.—1m., College. Fine views from the Blackdown Hills. Honiton: Church.

797 CREWKERNE TO LANGPORT.

Description.—Class II. Slightly hilly at first, then easy after Lopenhead; very good surface.

Gradients.—At ½m. & ¾m. 1 in 17; 1¼m. 1 in 16; 1¾m. 1 in 21; 2½m. 1 in 17; 3½m. 1 in 20.

Milestones.—Measured from Crewkerne.

Measurements.—Crewkerne,* Fountain.

(5¾	South Petherton.*)		
8¾	4⅛	Kingsbury.*	
13	8⅜	4¼	Langport.*

Principal Objects of Interest.—Muchelney: Abbey ruin, Cross. Huish: Ch. Langport: Ch., Museum.

Hotels or Inns at places marked *, and at Lopenhead, &c.

798 CREWKERNE TO SOMERTON.

Description.—Class II. An excellent undulating road, usually with very good surface between Martock and Long Sutton.

Gradients.—At ½m. 1 in 17; ¾m. & 2½m. 1 in 18; 5m. 1 in 17; 6m. 1 in 17; 11¾m. 1 in 13; 12¾m. 1 in 14.

Milestones.—Measured from Crewkerne as far as Martock, thereafter from Somerton.

Measurements.—Crewkerne,* Fountain.

7	Martock,* Town Hall.		
11	4	Long Sutton,* Inn.	
14	7	3	Somerton,* Broadgate.

Principal Objects of Interest.—Martock: Cross. Somerton: Church.

Hotels or Inns at places marked *, and at Long Load.

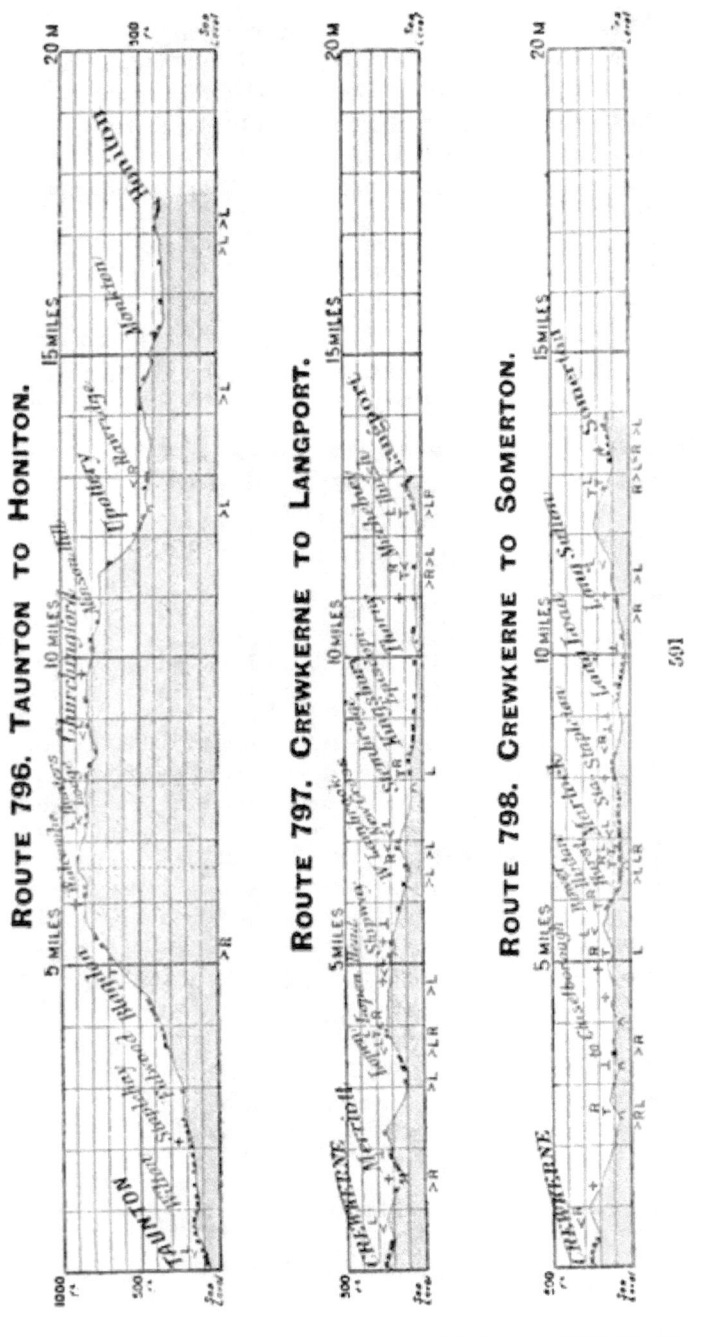

ROUTE 796. TAUNTON TO HONITON.

ROUTE 797. CREWKERNE TO LANGPORT.

ROUTE 798. CREWKERNE TO SOMERTON.

501

799 YEOVIL TO GLASTONBURY.

Description.—Class II. Fine surface to Ilchester, then a somewhat hilly road, but with very fair surface.

Gradients.—(† *Dangerous.*) At ½m. 1/20†; 1½m. 1/24; 7¾m. 1/13†; 8¾m. 1/11†; 10m. 1/14; 10½m. 1/17; 13m. 1/12†; 14m. 1/13†

Milestones.—From Market Yeovil, and from Somerton.

Measurements.—Yeovil,* Mermaid Hotel.

5			Ilchester,* Town Hall.
9⅞	4⅞		Somerton,* Cross.
16¾	11¾	7⅝	Glastonbury,* Cross.

Principal Objects of Interest.—Ilchester: Ch. Somerton: Ch. Compton: Hood's Monument. 13¼m. Wotton Obelisk. Glastonbury: Abbey, Cross, Church, Tor.

Hotels or Inns at places marked *, and at Street, &c.

800 YEOVIL TO BRUTON.

Description.—Class II. Slightly hilly at first, then a fine easy road to Castle Cary, whence steep and rough.

Gradients.—At ½m. 1 in 20; 2m. 1 in 17; 3m. 1 in 23; 7¼m. 1 in 19; 13, 13¼, & 14¾m. 1 in 16; 15¼m. 1 in 13; 16m. 1 in 16.

Milestones.—Measured from Yeovil Market to Sparkford, thereafter from Caatle Cary.

Measurements.—Yeovil,* Mermaid Hotel.

4⅞				Marston,* Inn. R. 706.
8	3⅛			Sparkford,* Inn.
12¾	7⅞	4¾		Castle Cary.*
16	11⅛	8⅜	3¼	Bruton,* P.O.

Principal Objects of Interest.—Sparkford: Cadbury Castle. Castle Cary: Camp. Bruton: Ch., Cross, Mkt. House.

Hotels or Inns at places marked *, and at Mudford, &c.

801 YEOVIL TO TAUNTON.

Description.—Class II. The best road out of Yeovil, fine surface to Ilminster, thereafter slightly hilly.

Gradients.—At 13½m. 1 in 18; 17¼m. 1 in 25; 20m. 1 in 15; 21½m. 1 in 17; 22m. 1 in 14.

Milestones.—Irregular to Montacute, thereafter measured from Ilminster as far as Ashill, then from Taunton.

Measurements.

Yeovil,* Mermaid Hotel.

4¼				Montacute,* Inn.
13¾	9½			Ilminster,* Market House.
17½	12⅞	3½		Ashill.*
25⅝	21⅜	12¼	8¼	Taunton,* Market House.

Principal Objects of Interest.—Montacute: Tower. Ilminster: Market House, Church. TAUNTON: Colleges, Castle, &c.

Hotels or Inns at places marked *, and at Lopenhead, &c.

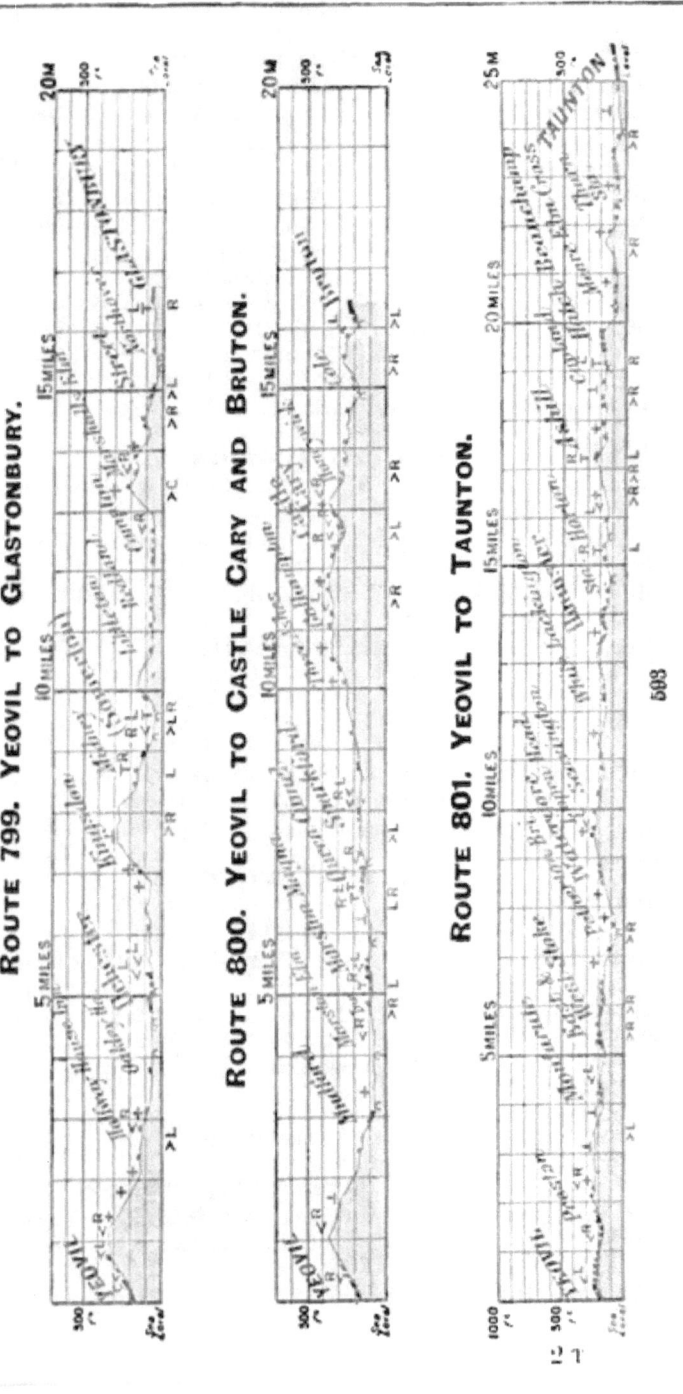

ROUTE 799. YEOVIL TO GLASTONBURY.

ROUTE 800. YEOVIL TO CASTLE CARY AND BRUTON.

ROUTE 801. YEOVIL TO TAUNTON.

802 WINCANTON TO STURMINSTER.

Description.—Class III. An excellent road, with short steep hills to Stalbridge, thereafter easier.

Gradients.—At 1m. 1 in 21; 2½m. 1 in 16; 4½m. 1 in 13; 5m. 1 in 23; 5½m. 1 in 18; 6¼m. 1 in 13; 13m. 1 in 16; 13½m. 1 in 21; 14½m. 1 in 25.

Measurements.

Wincanton,* Town Hall.				
4⅞	Templecombe.*			
6¾	1⅞	Henstridge Ash.*		
8⅜	3½	1⅝	Stalbridge.*	
14½	9⅝	7¾	6⅛	Sturminster,* Bridge. (R. 681.)

Principal Objects of Interest. — 10m. Obelisk. Sturminster: Castle.

803 LANGPORT TO BRUTON.

Description.—Class III. A hilly road to Somerton, where there is a steep descent, then with the exception of Snaphill it is a very easy road to Castle Cary; thereafter poor surface, and very steep to Bruton.

Gradients.—At 1 & 1¼m. 1 in 14; 1¾ & 3m. 1 in 16; 5m. 1 in 12 (dangerous); 7m. 1 in 14; 15½, 16, 17½, & 18½m. 1 in 16; 18m. 1 in 13.

Milestones.—Measured from Langport.

Measurements.—Langport.*

4¾	Somerton,* Cross.			
10¼	5½	Cross Keys Inn.* (R. 811.)		
15⅜	10⅝	5⅛	Castle Cary.*	
19	14¼	8¾	3⅝	Bruton,* P.O.

Principal Objects of Interest. — Somerton: Church. Castle Cary: Camp. Bruton: Market House, Church, Cross.

Hotels or Inns at places marked*, &c.

804 LANGPORT TO CHARD.

Description.—Class II. A slightly undulating road, but with splendid surface; there are several short hills.

Gradients.—At 1m. 1 in 24; 6¾ & 7¼m. 1 in 25; 9m 1 in 16.

Milestones.—Measured from Langport to Hambridge, thereafter from Ilminster Market House.

Measurements. Langport.*

4⅝	Hambridge Inn.*		
10⅜	5¾	Ilminster,* Town Hall.	
15⅜	10¾	5	Chard.*

Principal Objects of Interest. — Ilminster: Market House, Church. Chard: Church, Town Hall, School.

Hotels or Inns at places marked*, and at Westport.

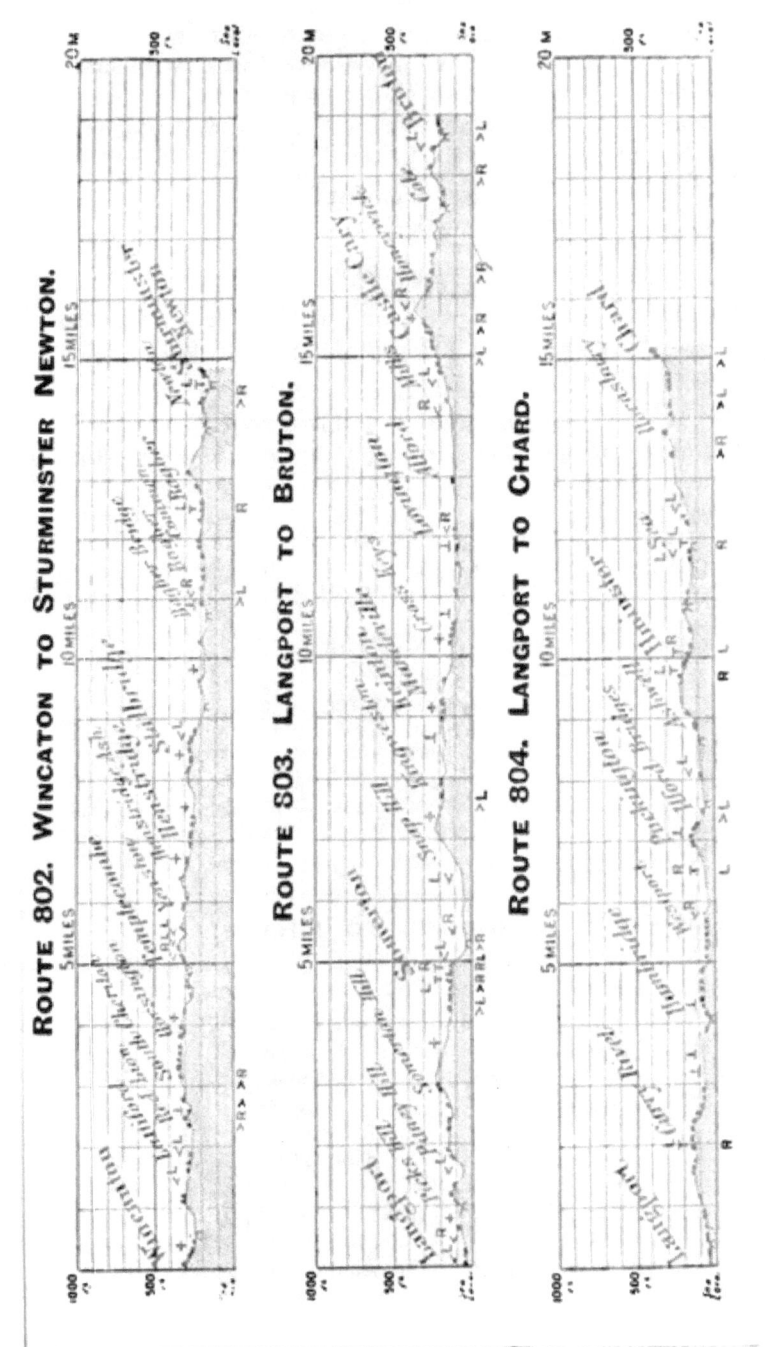

ROUTE 802. WINCATON TO STURMINSTER NEWTON.

ROUTE 803. LANGPORT TO BRUTON.

ROUTE 804. LANGPORT TO CHARD.

805   BRIDGWATER TO WATCHET.

Description. — Class II. Very good surface to Nether Stowey, when the road becomes very hilly, and continues so to Watchet; thereafter three dangerous hills. R. 793 is joined at Carhampton.

Gradients. — (†*Dangerous.*) At 1½m. 1/18; 2m. 1/21; 9½ & 12m. 1/14; 12½ & 15½m. 1/18; 17m. 1/9†; 18½m. 1/11†; 21m. 1/10†; 22m. 1/13†; 22½m. 1/9†.

Milestones. — Measured from Bridgwater and Minehead.

Measurements. — Bridgwater,* Cornhill.

8¼	Nether Stowey.*		
18¾	10¼	Watchet.*	
26½	18¼	8¼	Minehead.*
or 17¾	9¾		Williton,*
26½	17¾	8¼	Minehead.*

Principal Objects of Interest. — Nether Stowey: Coleridge's House. 15m. St. Audries House. Minehead: Ch.

806 BRIDGWATER TO GLASTONBURY.

Description. — Class II. A very good undulating road till within three miles of Shepton Mallet, when it becomes steep.

Gradients. — (†*Dangerous.*) At 3½m. 1/23; 10½m. 1/18; 16m. 1/16; 16½m. 1/22; 21½m. 1/11†; 22m. 1/13†; 23m. 1/14†; 23½m. 1/21

Milestones. — Measured from fork roads Bridgwater, and from Shepton Mallet, Cross.

Measurements.

Bridgwater,* Cornhill.

3½	Knowle Inn.*		
15¼	12	Glastonbury,* Cross.	
18½	15¾	3¾	West Pennard Inn.*
24¾	21¼	9¼	5¾ Shepton Mallet,* Cross.

Principal Objects of Interest. — Chilton: Museum. Sedgemoor Battlefield 1685. GLASTONBURY: Abbey, Cross, Church, Tor. SHEPTON MALLET: Church, Cross.

807   BRIDGWATER TO YEOVIL.

Description. — Class II. An almost level road with fairly good surface; one dangerous hill near Yeovil.

Gradients. — At 22m. 1 in 13 (dangerous).

Measurements.

Bridgwater,* Cornhill.

7¼	Othery Inn.*		
12¼	5	Langport.*	
17¾	10½	5½	Stapleton Inn.* R. 798.
24¾	17¾	12¾	6¾ Yeovil,* Mermaid Hotel.

Principal Objects of Interest. — Sedgemoor: Battlefield 1685. Middlezoy: Church. Langport: Church, Museum. Muchelney: Cross, Abbey ruins. YEOVIL: Church.

Hotels or Inns at places marked *.

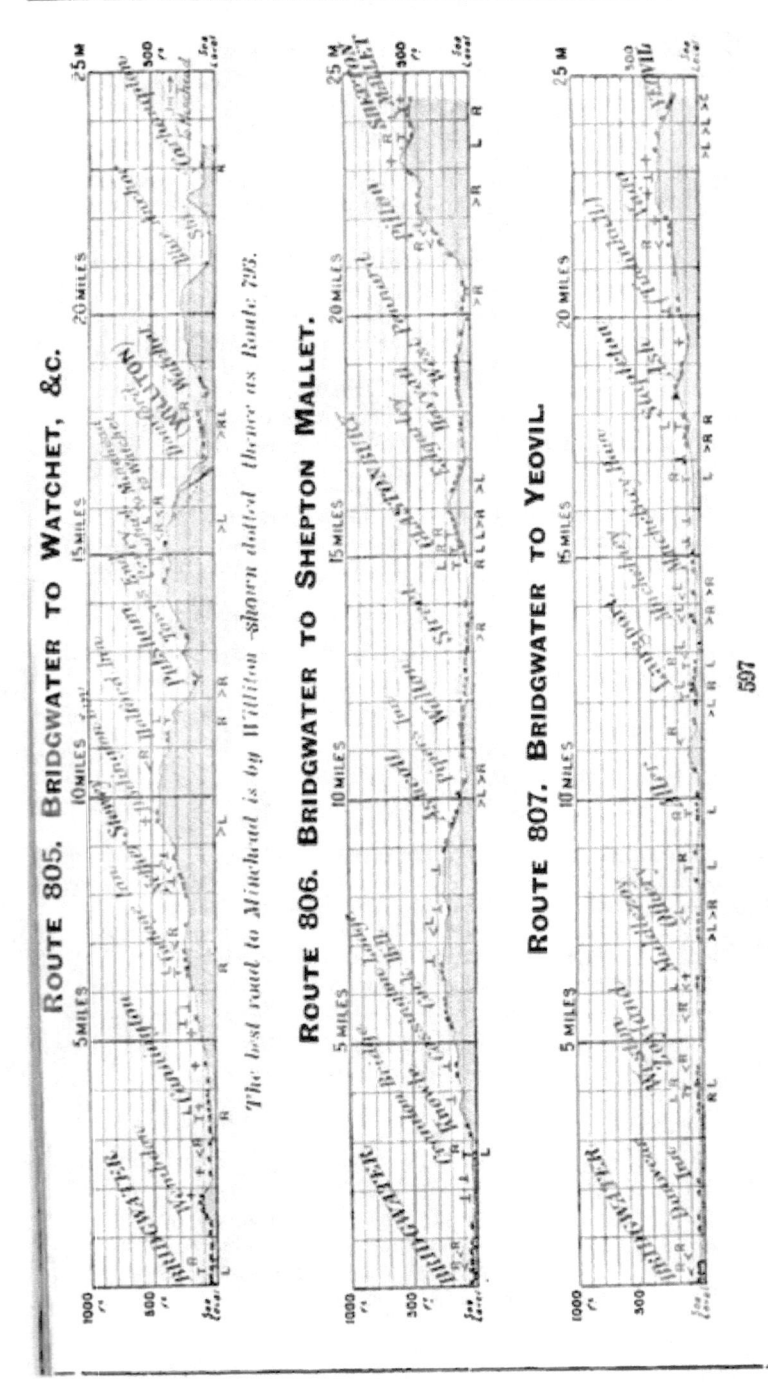

ROUTE 805. BRIDGWATER TO WATCHET, &C.

ROUTE 806. BRIDGWATER TO SHEPTON MALLET.

ROUTE 807. BRIDGWATER TO YEOVIL.

The best road to Minehead is by Williton shown dotted thence as Route 795.

808 WELLS TO WESTON-SUPER-MARE.

Description.—Class III. An undulating road with short steep hills to Cheddar; thereafter very good, except a stiff ascent at Axbridge, and a dangerous descent to Banwell.

Gradients.—Mostly 1 in 15 at first; 11½m. 1 in 19; 15m. 1 in 12 (dangerous).

Measurements.

Wells,* Market.
4⅝ Westbury.*
8⅜ 4 Cheddar,* Cross.
10½ 6¾ 2¾ Axbridge.*
15 10⅞ 6⅞ 4½ Banwell.*
21¼ 17½ 13¼ 10¾ 6¼ Weston-super-Mare,* High Street.

Principal Objects of Interest. — 1m. Wookey Hole. Cheddar: Cliffs, Caves. Axbridge: Church. Banwell: Castle. WESTON: Town Hall, Parade, Pier, &c.

Hotels or Inns at places marked*.

809   WELLS TO BURNHAM.

Description. Class III. An excellent undulating road, usually with very fair surface to Mark, after which it is often loose.

Measurements.— Wells.* Market.
8¼ Wedmore,* George Hotel.
11¾ 3½ Mark,* Church.
16 7¾ 4¼ Highbridge,* Market St.
17¾ 9½ 6 1¾ Burnham,* Sta.

Hotels or Inns at places marked *.

810   WESTON TO BRIDGWATER.

Description.—Class II. Fine surface on this road, but sometimes loose, as it lies very low. For the road from Highbridge to Bridgwater see R. 846. The road to Glastonbury (R. 806) is joined near Knowle Inn.

Gradients.— At 16m. 1 in 16; 16¼m. 1 in 13 (dangerous).

Measurements.

Weston-super-Mare,* High Street.
3¾ Bleadon,* Victoria Inn.*
7½ 3¾ Brent Knoll Inn.*
11¼ 7¾ 3½ Highbridge,* Market Street.
17¼ 13½ 9¾ 6¼ Knowle Inn.* (R. 806).
or 18⅜ 14⅝ 10⅞ 7¼ Bridgwater,* Cornhill. (R. 846).

Principal Objects of Interest. — Uphill: Cavern, Old Church, 8m. Brent Knoll. BRIDGWATER: Bridge, Church, Town Hall, &c.

Hotels or Inns at places marked *

ROUTE 808. WELLS TO WESTON-SUPER-MARE.

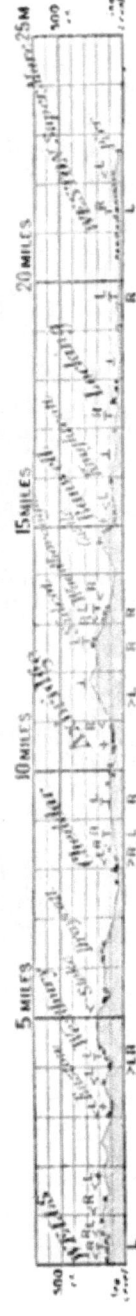

ROUTE 809. WELLS TO BURNHAM.

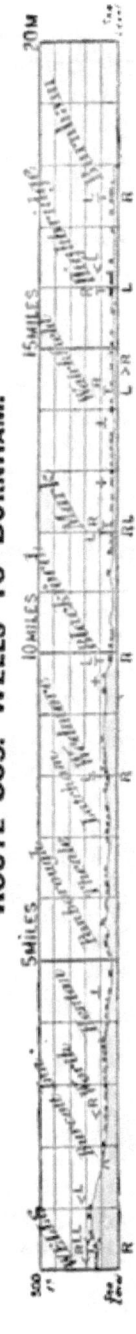

ROUTE 810. WESTON-SUPER-MARE TO BRIDGWATER OR GLASTONBURY.

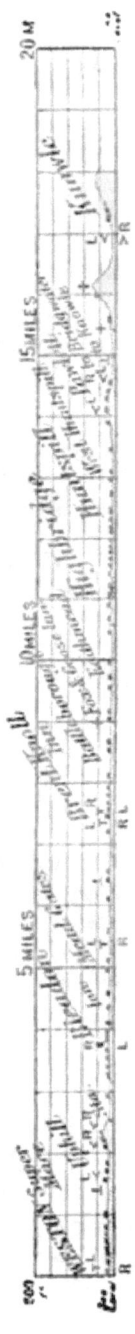

Signs: < Road Fork, forward journey, > ditto reverse, + Cross Roads, ⊥ Road Junction, o Bridge, T indicates a sharp turn.
The directions R (right) and L (left) for the forward journey are above the Road Line, those of the reverse, below.

811 Shepton Mallet to Ilchester.

Description.—Class II. Exceedingly steep and hilly for six miles, then a good and almost level road, but the surface is considerably cut up.

Gradients.—(*All Dangerous.*) At 2½m. 1 in 10; 4m. 1 in 13; 5½m. 1 in 8.

Milestones.—Measured from Shepton Mallet, Cross; and Ilchester, Town Hall.

Measurements.

Shepton Mallet,* Cross.
3¾   Pylle Street,* Inn.
9½   6¼   Cross Keys Inn.* R. 803.
15½   12¼   6   Ilchester,* Town Hall.

Principal Objects of Interest.—Ilchester; Town Hall, Church

Hotels or Inns at places marked *, and at Hornblotton.

812 Shepton Mallet to Wincanton.

Description.—Class II. The road by Castle Cary is easier than that by Bruton, and has excellent surface, but steep and stiff hills. The road by Bruton has fair surface, and very steep and dangerous hills.

Gradients—At 2½m. 1 in 12 (dangerous); 8½m. 1 in 14 (dangerous); 11½m. 1 in 17; 14m. 1 in 16.

By Bruton. At 2½m. 1 in 12; 5½m. 1 in 12; 6½m. 1 in 8; 7½m. 1 in 10; 8½m. 1 in 12; 12m. 1 in 11 (all dangerous).

Milestones.—Measured from Shepton Mallet Cross, and Wincanton Town Hall.

Measurements.

Shepton Mallet,* Cross.
4¾   Evercreech Junction.
8¼   3¼   Castle Cary *
14¾   9½   6¼   Wincanton.*

By Bruton.

Shepton Mallet,* Cross
7½   Bruton,* P.O.
12¼   5   Wincanton,* Town Hall

Principal Objects of Interest.—1½m. Canard's Grave. Castle Cary · Camp. Wincanton · Town Hall. Bruton : Market House, Church, Cross.

Hotels or Inns at places marked *, and at Prestleigh and Arthur's Bridge.

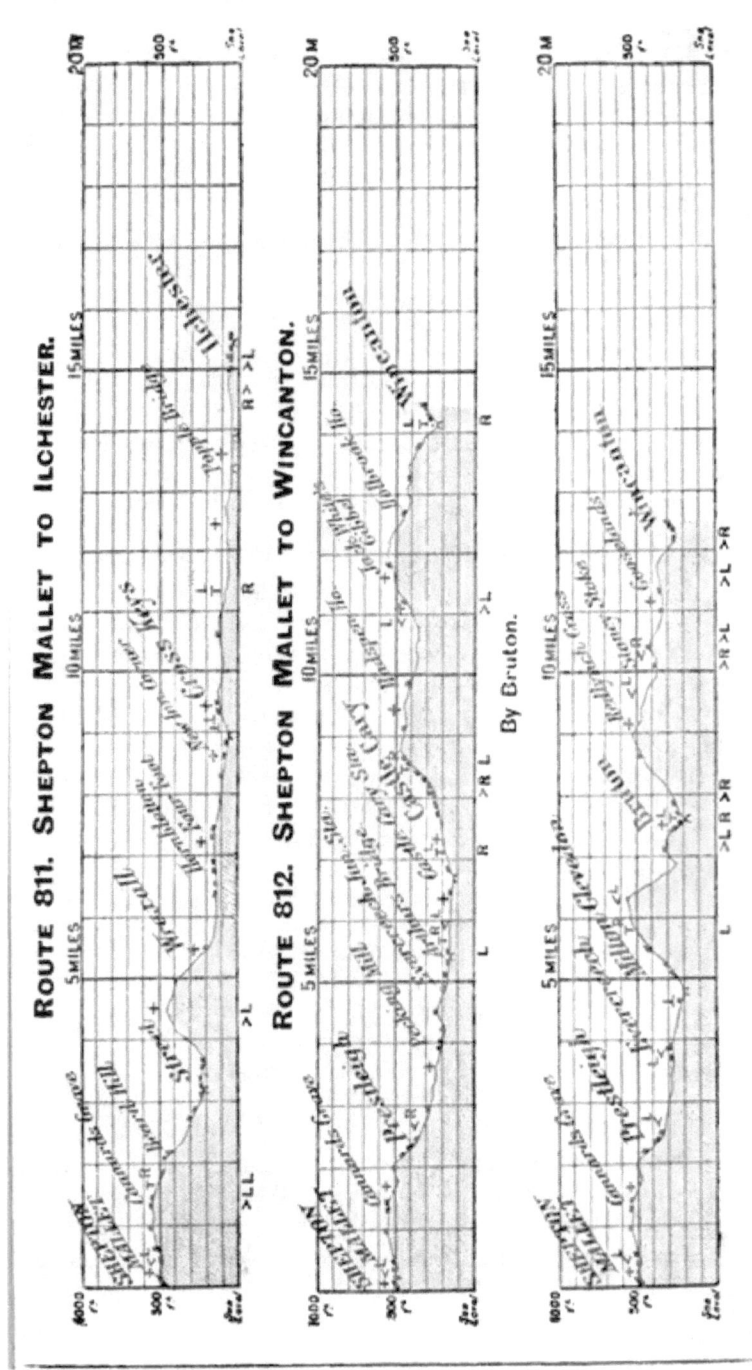

ROUTE 811. SHEPTON MALLET TO ILCHESTER.

ROUTE 812. SHEPTON MALLET TO WINCANTON.

By Bruton.

813 FROME TO YEOVIL.

Description.—Class II. After the dangerous hill in Frome, splendid surface to Bruton; thereafter hilly, and with poor surface to Galhampton, whence fine to Yeovil.

Gradients.—At ¼m. 1 in 9 (dangerous); 4½m. 1 in 14; 8½m. 1 in 23; 9¾m. 1 in 16; 11¼m. 1 in 18; 12¾m. 1 in 15.

Milestones.—Measured from Bruton.

Measurements.—Frome,* Cross.
5⅝ Wanstrow.*
10¾ 4⅞ Bruton,* P.O.
19 13⅜ 8¼ Sparkford,* Inn.
27 21⅜ 16¼ 8 Yeovil,* Mermaid Ho.

Principal Objects of Interest.—2½m., Marston House. Bruton: Market House, Church, Cross. Sparkford: Cadbury "Castle."

---

814 FROME TO SHAFTESBURY.

Description.—Class II. Excellent surface, but rather hilly to Maiden Bradley, thereafter good road; dangerous hill into Shaftesbury.

Gradients.—(† *Dangerous.*) At ¼m. 1 in 9†; 1¼m. 1 in 15; 5m. 1 in 14; 6m. 1 in 18; 7½ & 8m. 1 in 17; 19½m. 1 in 12†.

Milestones.—Measured from Frome, Danger Board, and from Gillingham.

Measurements.

Frome,* Cross.
6¼ Maiden Bradley.*
11½ 5¼ Zeal's Green.* R. 688.
15½ 9¼ 4 Gillingham,* P.O.
20 13¾ 8½ 4½ Shaftesbury,* Court House.

Principal Objects of Interest. Stourton: Stour Head House, Alfred's Tower. SHAFTESBURY: Court House.

---

815 FROME TO WESTBURY, &c.

Description.—Class III. A hilly road to Westbury, thereafter to Market Lavington it is a continuously undulating road with very fair surface.

Gradients.—At ¼m. 1 in 9 (dangerous); 1m. 1 in 14; 5¾m. 1 in 13; 10½m. 1 in 15; 13m. 1 in 18; 13¾m. 1 in 15.

Milestones.—Irregular.

Measurements.—Frome,* Cross.
7½ Westbury,* Market.
17 9½ Lavington,* Market.
26 18½ 9 Upavon.* (R. 698).

Principal Objects of Interest.—WESTBURY: Ch., White Horse. Earl Stoke: Park. Lavington: Church.

Hotels or Inns at places marked *.

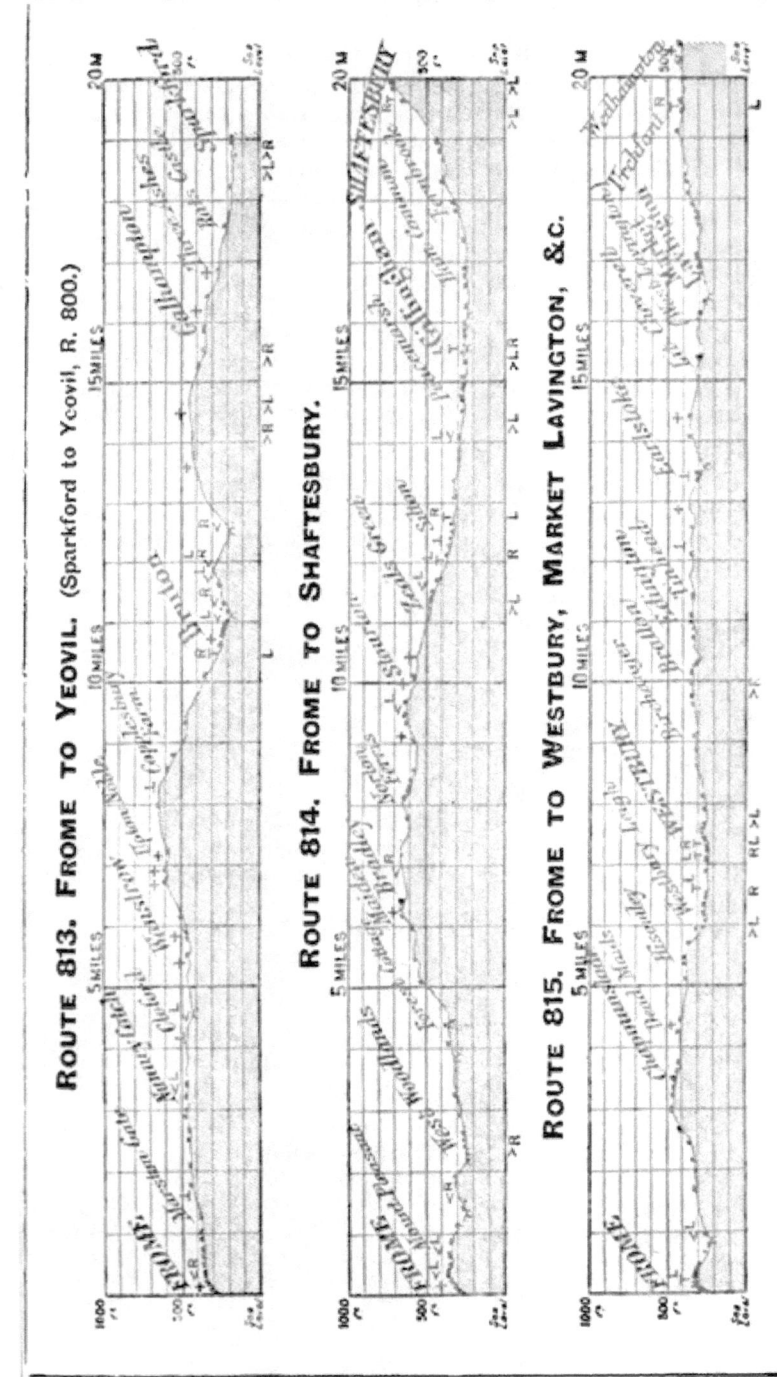

ROUTE 813. FROME TO YEOVIL. (Sparkford to Ycovil, R. 800.)

ROUTE 814. FROME TO SHAFTESBURY.

ROUTE 815. FROME TO WESTBURY, MARKET LAVINGTON, &C.

816 BATH TO TAUNTON.

Description.—Class I. Fine surface and easy gradients for ten miles, thence hilly, and with steep descent to Wells. Splendid surface between Wells and Glastonbury; thereafter good surface to Othery, whence it is slightly rough to Lyng, then undulating but fine to Taunton. The other road to Wells by Radstock is far more hilly.

Gradients.—(†*Dangerous.*) At 8m. 1 in 21; 8½m. 1 in 18; 10½m. 1 in 14; 12½m. 1 in 10†; 15 & 16½m. 1 in 14; 18½m. 1 in 16; 20½m. 1 in 13†; 37¾m. 1 in 16; 43½ & 44m. 1 in 17.

Milestones.—Measured from Town Hall, Bath, to Farrington, thereafter from Bristol. Near Wells, from Wells; after Piper's Inn, from Taunton, Market House.

Measurements.

Bath,* Town Hall.							
8	Farmborough.*						
12¼	4¼	Farrington Gurney,* Inn.					
15⅛	7⅛	2⅞	Chewton Mendip.*				
21	13	8¾	5⅛	Wells,* Market.			
26⅞	18⅞	14⅝	11¾	5⅝	Glastonbury,* Cross.		
37	29	24¾	21⅞	16	10⅛	Othery,* New Inn.	
48⅞	40⅞	36⅝	33¾	27⅞	22	11⅞	Taunton,* Market House.

Principal Objects of Interest. — 5½m., Stantonbury Camp. 9m., Barrow Hill. Chewton: Priory. WELLS: Cathedral, Bishop's Palace, Wookey Hole. GLASTONBURY: Abbey, Cross, Church, Pilgrim's Rest, Tor. 35m., Sedgemoor Battlefield 1685. Borough Bridge: Alfred Memorial, Chapel Ruins. TAUNTON: Market House, Church, Colleges, Castle, Monuments.

Hotels or Inns at places marked *, and at Pipers Inn, &c.

817 BATH TO SHEPTON MALLET.

Description.—Class II. An exceedingly steep road. The best road is by Farrington, Routes 816 and 848 (20¾m.)

Gradients.—(†*Dangerous.*) At ¾m. 1 in 14; 4½ & 5¼m. 1 in 13†; 8m. 1 in 17; 8½m. 1 in 12†; 12m. 1 in 17; 13m. 1 in 14†; 13¾m. 1 in 15; 16¾m. 1 in 14†.

Milestones.—Measured from Bath, Town Hall; and from Shepton Mallet, Cross.

Measurements.

Bath,* Town Hall.				
4⅝	Dunkerton.*			
8¾	3¾	Radstock.*		
11⅞	7¼	3½	Stratton-on-Fosse.*	
17⅜	12¾	9	5½	Shepton Mallet,* Cross.

Principal Objects of Interest. — Radstock: Collieries. Midsummer Norton: Ch. SHEPTON MALLET: Ch., Cross.

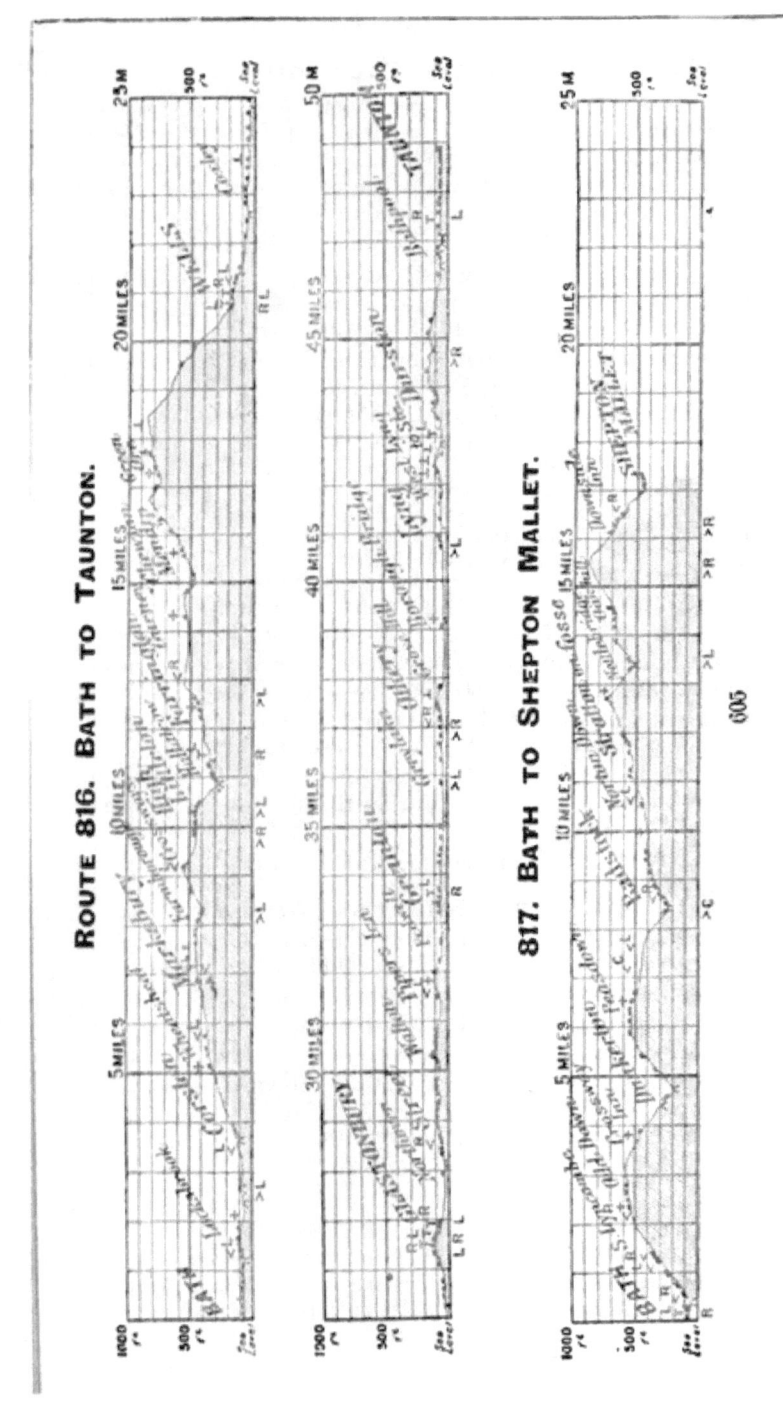

ROUTE 816. BATH TO TAUNTON.

817. BATH TO SHEPTON MALLET.

605

818 BATH TO WARMINSTER.

Description.—Class II. Although slightly hilly the road has very fine surface.

Gradients.—At 1, 5½, & 14½m. 1 in 18.

Milestones.—Measured from Bath *via* Midford—the old road.

Measurements.—Bath,* Town Hall.

	5½	Limpley Stoke.*		
	11⅝	6⅛	Beckington.*	
	18⅝	13⅛	7	Warminster.*
or	14⅝	9⅛	3	Frome Cross.* R. 835.

Principal Objects of Interest.—Pretty road near Limpley Stoke. WARMINSTER: Minster.

Hotels or Inns at places marked *, and at Wolverton.

819 BATH TO TROWBRIDGE, &C.

Description.—Class II. A rather lumpy road to Bath Easton, then rather steep for 3m., after which it is an easy road. For the road by Bradford-on-Avon see R. 829.

Gradients.—At 3½m. 1 in 15; 4¼m. 1 in 16; 15½ & 7¾m, 1 in 20.

Milestones.—Measured from Town Hall, Bath: and from Town Hall, Westbury.

Measurements.—Bath,* Town Hall.

9½	Staverton.*		
11¾	2¼	Trowbridge,* Church.	
16¾	7¼	5¼	Westbury,* Town Hall.

Principal Objects of Interest.—4½m., Warley House. TROWBRIDGE: Church. WESTBURY: Church, White Horse.

Hotels or Inns at places marked *, and Bath Easton, &c.

820 BATH TO DEVIZES.

Description.—Class I. Rather lumpy for three miles, then a splendid road, with finely engineered gradients.

Gradients.—At 8½m. 1 in 17; 18m. 1 in 18.

Milestones.—Measured from Bath, Town Hall, and Devizes Cross.

Measurements.

Bath,* Town Hall.

5¾	Box.*			
12⅜	6⅝	Melksham,* Market Place.		
19⅜	13⅝	7	Devizes,* Cross.	
33½	27¾	21⅛	14⅛	Marlborough,* Town Hall.

Principal Objects of Interest.—Box: Quarries. Melksham: Church. DEVIZES: Cross, Museum, St. Johns.

Hotels or Inns at places marked *, and at Bath Easton, Atworth, &c.

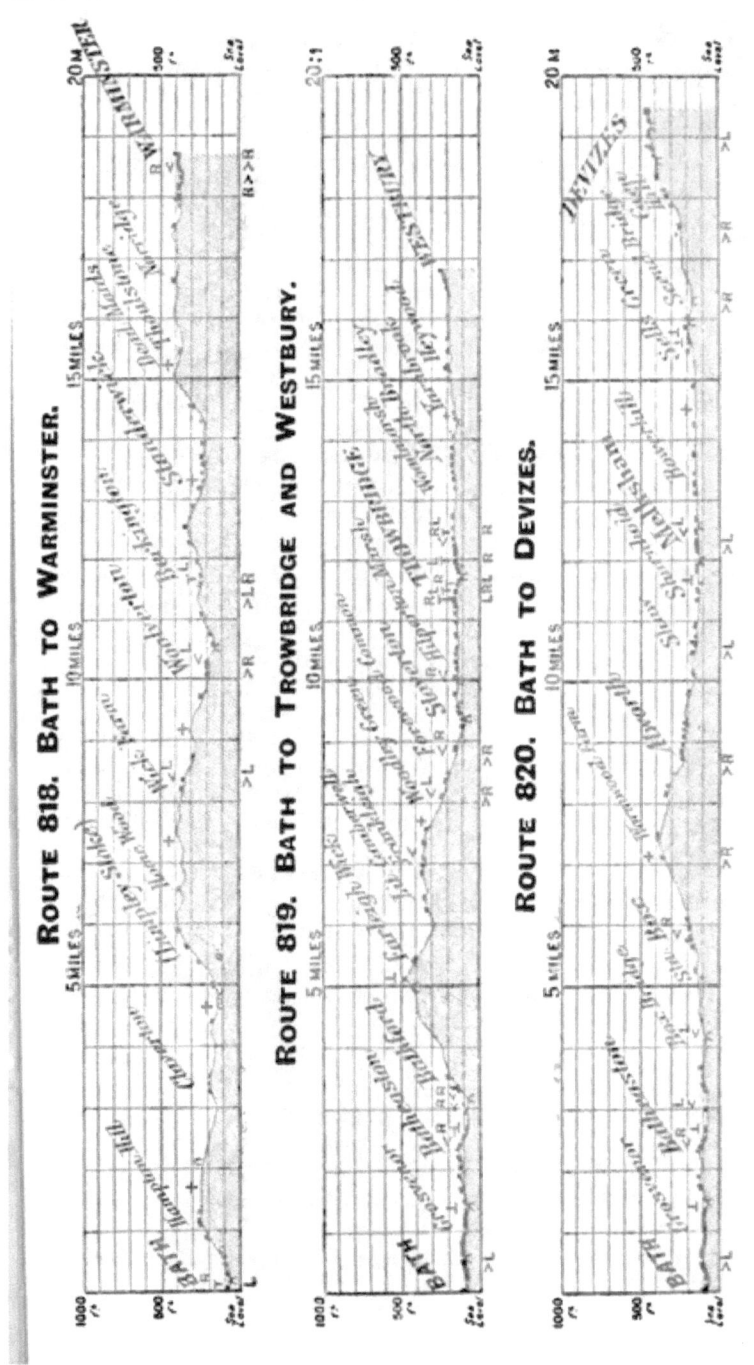

ROUTE 818. BATH TO WARMINSTER.

ROUTE 819. BATH TO TROWBRIDGE AND WESTBURY.

ROUTE 820. BATH TO DEVIZES.

821 Clevedon to Congresbury.

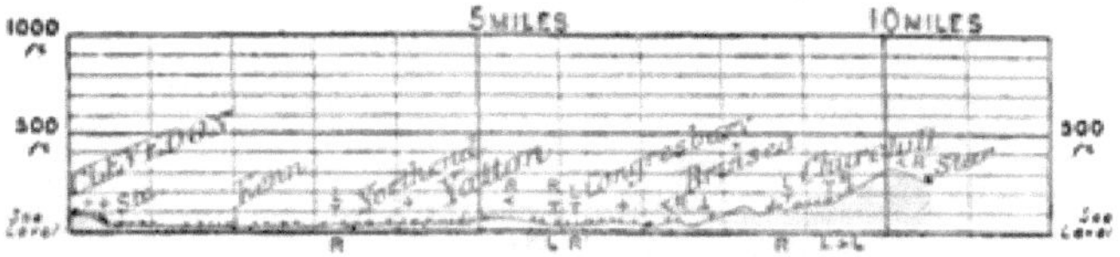

Description.—Class III. Level road with tolerably good surface to Congresbury, then undulating with fair surface to Churchill, where join Route 846.

Gradients.—At ¼m. 1 in 10; 8½m. 1 in 11 (dangerous).

Measurements.

Clevedon.*				
⅜	Clevedon Sta.			
4¼	3⅞	Yatton,* Sta.		
6⅛	5¾	1⅞	Congresbury,* Bridge.	
10½	10⅛	6¼	4⅜	Star Inn.* R. 846.

Principal Objects of Interest.—Uninteresting country.

822 Chippenham to Devizes.

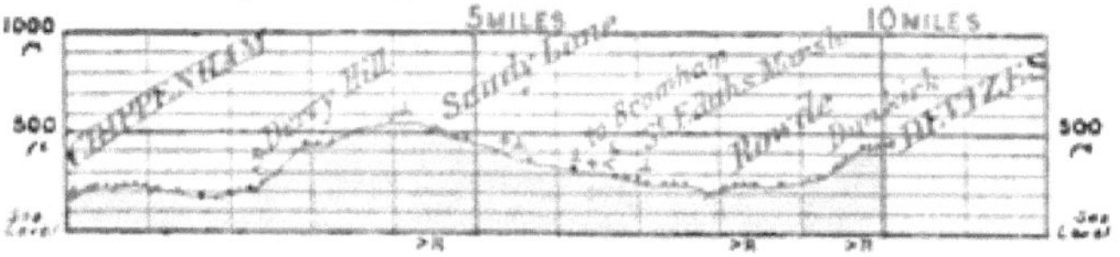

Description.—Class II. Fine surface to Derry Hill, then very steep for 2m., after which a good road to Devizes.

Gradients.—At 2½m. 1 in 10 (dangerous); 3½m. 1 in 20; 9½m. 1 in 9 (dangerous).

Milestones.—Measured from Devizes, Cross.

Measurements.

Chippenham,* Market.		
4¾	Sandy Lane, P.O.	
10⅛	5⅜	Devizes,* Cross.

Principal Objects of Interest. — 3m., Bowood House. DEVIZES: Cross, Museum, St.

823 Calne to Melksham.

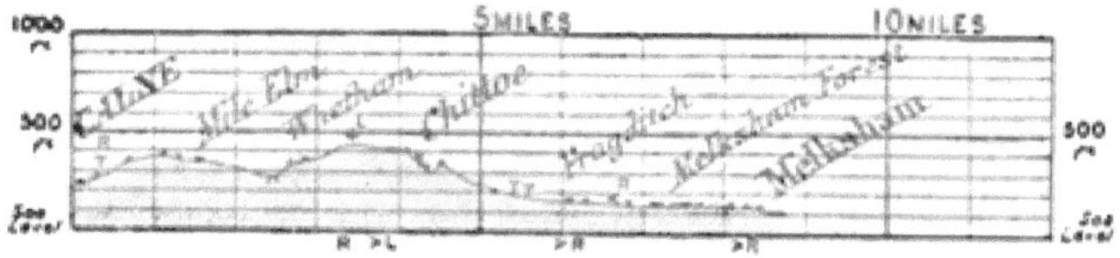

Description.—Class III. Fairly good surface, but very steep at Chittoe. For Devizes keep straight on at 3½m.

Measurements.—Calne,* Town Hall.
8½ Melksham,* Market.
or 8¾ Devizes,* Cross.

Principal Objects of Interest.—Melksham: Church.

Hotels or Inns at places marked *.

BRISTOL TO PORTISHEAD. 824

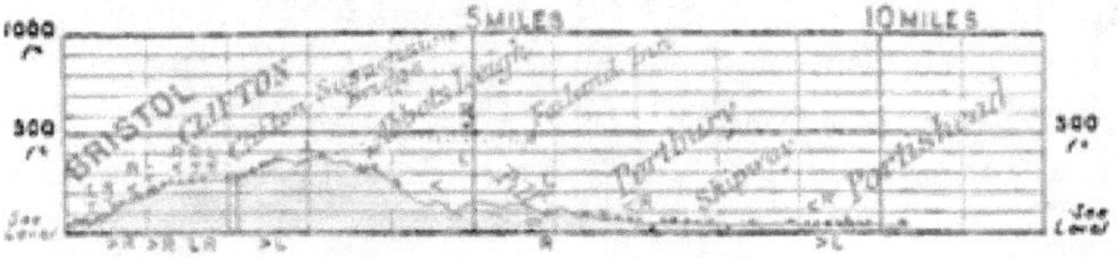

Description.—Class II. Bumpy surface to the Suspension Bridge, thence good surface, but somewhat hilly. Good surface between Portbury and Portishead.

Gradients.—At ½m. 1 in 13; 4m. 1 in 13.

Measurements.—Bristol,* Bridge.
2 Clifton,* Suspension Bridge.
(5¾ 3¾ Pill.)*
6⅞ 4⅞ Portbury.*
9¾ 7¾ 2⅞ Portishead.*

Bristol to Failand Inn, (R. 845) by Clifton, 5¾m.

Principal Objects of Interest. -- Suspension Bridge. Portishead: Dock.

Hotels or Inns at places marked*

BRISTOL TO AVONMOUTH. 825

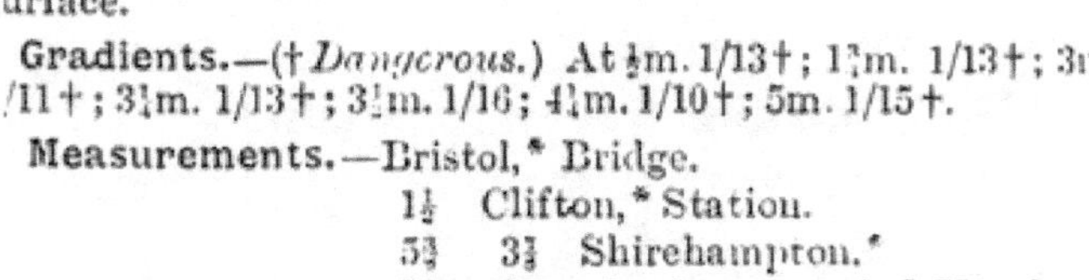

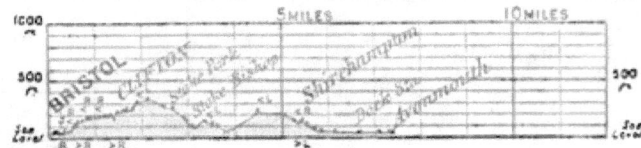

Description.—Class III. Rather steep hills, but very fair surface.

Gradients.—(† *Dangerous.*) At ½m. 1/13†; 1¾m. 1/13†; 3m. 1/11†; 3¼m. 1/13†; 3½m. 1/16; 4¼m. 1/10†; 5m. 1/15†.

Measurements.—Bristol,* Bridge.
1½ Clifton,* Station.
5⅝ 3⅝ Shirehampton.*
7⅝ 5⅝ 2 Avonmouth,* Hotel.

Principal Objects of Interest.—CLIFTON: Hot Wells, Suspension Bridge, &c. Avonmouth: Dock.

Hotels or Inns at places marked*.

827 BATH TO CHELTENHAM.

Description.—Class II. A bumpy road for 1½m., then a stiff two-mile hill, after which the road is undulating on the Downs for twenty miles, then descends to Nailsworth. Rather bumpy surface between Nailsworth and Stroud. From Stroud to Cheltenham excellent surface, with a long hill up and steep descent; the last six miles are level, with fine surface.

Gradients.—At 2½m. 1 in 15; 3¼m. 1 in 17; 8½m. 1 in 17; 10m. 1 in 16; 10¼m. 1 in 22; 13m. 1 in 17; 23¼m. 1 in 15; 28m. 1 in 14; 32m. 1 in 18; 36¾m. 1 in 13 (dangerous).

Milestones.—Measured from Bath, Town Hall, to Dunkirk; thereafter measured from Gloucester to Stroud, after which measured from Painswick and Cheltenham.

Measurements.

Bath,* Town Hall.								
8½	Tolldown Inn.							
11⅜	2⅞	Crosshands.*						
15⅛	6	3¾	Dunkirk.					
24¾	16¼	13⅜	9⅝	Nailsworth,* George Hotel.				
28⅞	20⅜	17½	13¾	4⅛	Stroud.*			
32⅜	23⅞	21	17¼	7⅝	3½	Painswick.*		
37¼	28¾	25⅞	22⅛	12½	8⅜	4⅞	Crosshands.*	
42¾	34¼	31⅜	27⅝	18	13⅞	10⅜	5½	Chelt'nh'm* Town Clock

Principal Objects of Interest.—3m., Reservoir. 10m., Dodington Park. Dunkirk: Badminton Park. STROUD: Mills, Subscription Rooms. Painswick: Church. CHELTENHAM: Spa, Promenade, Assembly Rooms, &c., &c.

Hotels or Inns at places marked *, &c.

828 BATH TO THORNBURY.

Description.—Class II. The surface on this road is not very good, and it is somewhat hilly; after Hambrook it is less so, and the surface is slightly better.

Gradients.—At 1¼m. 1 in 18; 3 & 4½m. 1 in 17; 6¾m. 1 in 13; 21½m. 1 in 14.

Milestones.—Measured from Bath, Town Hall, as far as Hambrook, thereafter from Bristol.

Measurements.—Bath,* Town Hall.

5⅞	Bitton.*				
11⅛	5¼	Mangotsfield.*			
13¾	7⅞	2⅝	Hambrook.*		
21¼	15⅜	10⅛	7½	Ship Inn.* R. 835.	
22½	16⅝	11⅜	8¾	1¼	Thornbury.*

Principal Objects of Interest.—Thornbury: Ch., Castle.

Hotels or Inns at places marked *, and at Kelston, &c.

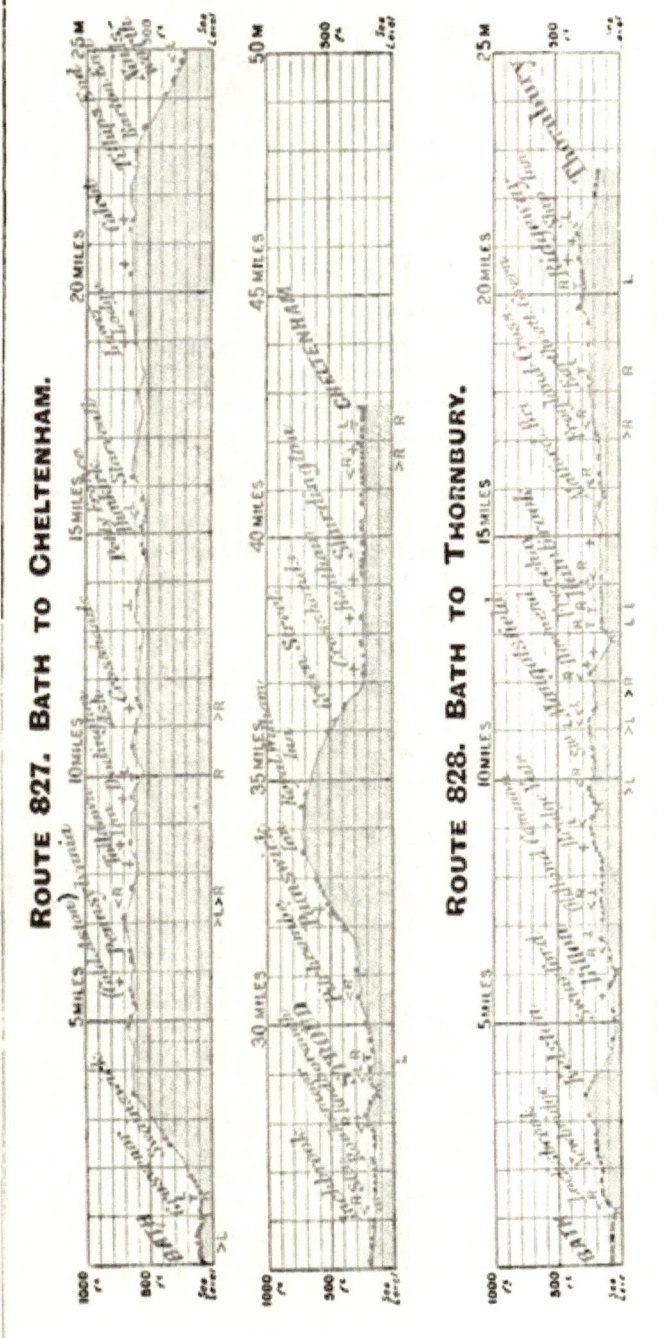

ROUTE 827. BATH TO CHELTENHAM.

ROUTE 828. BATH TO THORNBURY.

Signs: < Road Fork, forward journey, > ditto reverse, † Cross Roads, ⊥ Road Junction, ∩ Bridge, T indicate a sharp turn. The directions R (right) and L (left) for the forward journey are above the Road Line, those of the reverse, below

829 WARMINSTER TO BRADFORD-ON-AVON.

Description.—Class II. Steep hills to Westbury, then a fine level road to Bradford; dangerously steep hill in that town, after which it is a good hilly road to Bath.

Gradients.—(†*Dangerous*). At 2½m. 1/16†; 2½m. 1/13†; 2⅓ & 3½m. 1/16†; 12m. 1/10†; 14½m. 1/22; 15¾m. 1/16; 16¾m. 1/15.

Milestones.—From Warminster, Westbury, and Bath.

Measurements.

Warminster,* Clock.
4.　Westbury,* Market.
9½　5½　Trowbridge,* Church.
11½　7½　3½　Bradford-on-Avon,* Town Hall.
20　15¾　10½　8½　Bath,* Town Hall.

Principal Objects of Interest.—WESTBURY: Ch., White Horse. TROWBRIDGE: Ch., Bridge. BRADFORD: Church.

Hotels or Inns at places marked*, and at Yarnbrook, &c.

830 CHIPPENHAM TO WARMINSTER.

Description.—Class II. An undulating road for four miles, then level, with very good surface to Semington, whence poorer, and with slight hills to Yarnbrook; thereafter fine surface, but steep near Warminster.

Gradients.—(†*Dangerous*.) At 10½m. 1 in 23; 16½m. 1 in 20; 16⅔ & 17½m. 1 in 16†; 17½m. 1 in 13†; 18m. 1 in 16†.

Milestones.—Irregular.

Measurements.—Chippenham,* Market.
7½　Melksham,* Market Place.
9½　2½　Semington,* Crossroads.
15¾　8½　6½　Westbury,* Town Hall.
20⅛　12½　10⅔　4½　Warminster,* Clock.

Principal Objects of Interest.—Lacock: Abbey. Melksham: Church. WESTBURY: Ch., White horse. WARMINSTER: Minster.

Hotels or Inns at places marked*, and at Lacock, &c.

831 CHIPPENHAM TO BRADFORD-ON-AVON.

Description.—Class II. Undulating for 4m., then a fine level road till near Bradford-on-Avon. Onwards to Frome, slight hills, but good surface. R. 835 is joined at Beckington.

Gradients.—At 13½m. 1 in 14.

Measurements.—Chippenham,* Market.
7½　Melksham,* Market Place.
12½　5½　Bradford-on-Avon,* Tn. Hall.
18¾　12　6½　Beckington.*
21¾　15　9½　3　Frome,* Cross.

Principal Objects of Interest.—Lacock: Abbey.

Hotels or Inns at places marked*.

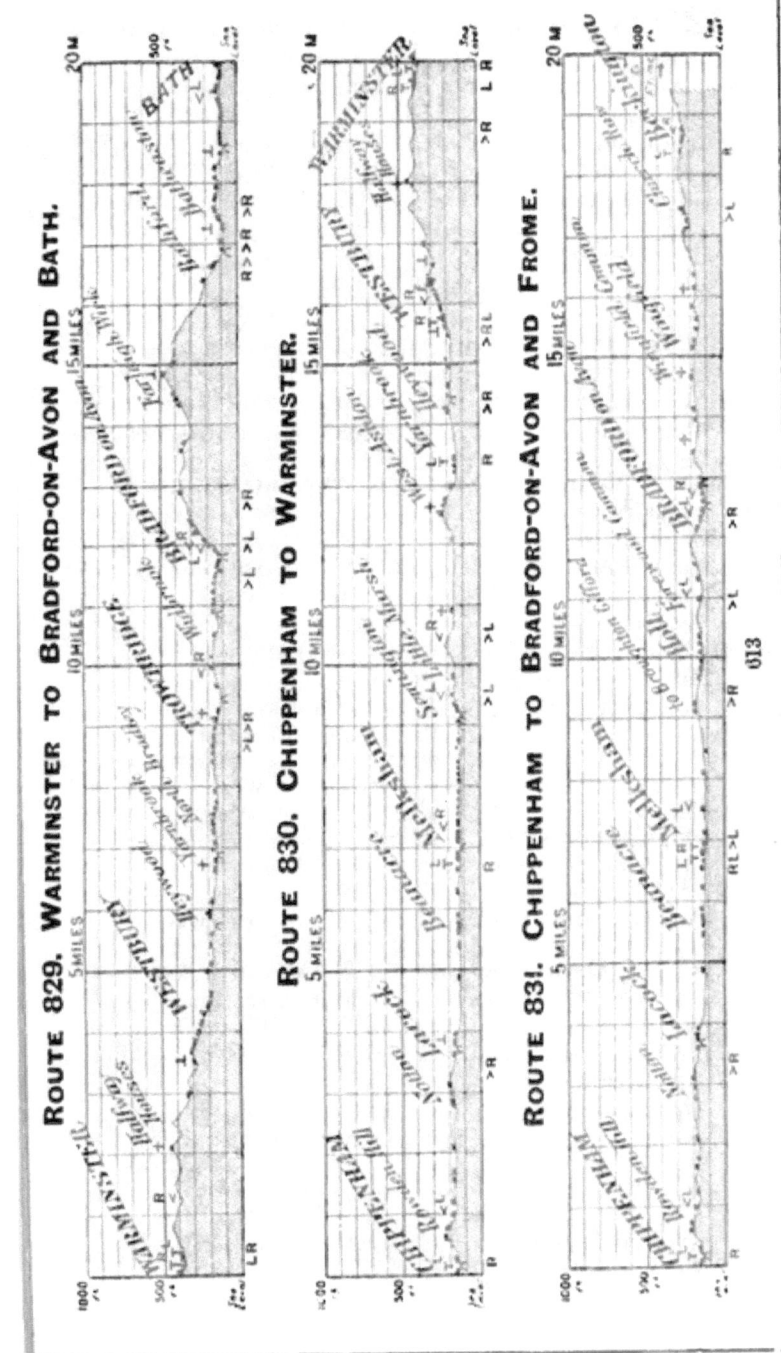

Route 829. Warminster to Bradford-on-Avon and Bath.

Route 830. Chippenham to Warminster.

Route 831. Chippenham to Bradford-on-Avon and Frome.

613

832 CHIPPENHAM TO SWINDON.

Description.—Class II An excellent undulating road, but often very loose.

Gradients.—At ¼m. 1 in 18; 8½m. 1 in 17; 19¼m. 1 in 18.

Measurements.

Chippenham,* Market.				
5½	Christian Malford,* Inn.			
9⅞	4⅜	Lyneham,* White Hart.		
14½	9	4⅝	Wooton Basset,* Town Hall.	
19⅞	14⅜	10	5⅜	Swindon,* Goddard Arms.

Principal Objects of Interest. — 3½m., Draycot Park. Wooton Basset: Town Hall. SWINDON: Railway Works.

Hotels or Inns at places marked *, and at Dauntsey Sta.

833 CHIPPENHAM TO THORNBURY.

Description.—Class II. Excellent surface throughout, and easy gradients, but not much traffic.

Gradients. At 8½m. 1 in 19; 12½m. 1 in 18; 13½ & 15¼m. 1 in 16; 22¼m. 1 in 17; 24½m. 1 in 14.

Milestones.—Continuation of the London milestones to Acton Turville, thereafter from Chipping Sodbury.

Measurements.

Chippenham,* Market.					
9¼	Acton Turville.*				
15⅛	5⅞	Chipping Sodbury.*			
18½	9¼	3⅜	Iron Acton,* Crown Inn.		
24	14¾	8⅞	5½	Ship Inn.*	
25¼	16	10⅛	6¾	1¼	Thornbury,* The Plain.

Principal Objects of Interest.—5½m., Castle Combe. Acton Turville: Badminton Park. Sodbury: Doddington Pk.

Hotels or Inns at places marked *, and at Yate, &c.

834 TROWBRIDGE TO WELLS.

Description.—Class II. A very hilly road, with fairly good surface, and shorter than R. 836, which is, however, the best road. The more direct road through Kilmersdon (shown by dotted lines) is ⅝m. shorter, but more hilly.

Gradients.—(† *Dangerous.*) At 1¼ & 3¾m. 1 in 21; 6m. 1 in 13†; 6½m. 1 in 20; 10¼m. 1 in 18; 11¾m. 1 in 14†; 12¼m. 1 in 12†; 20¾m. 1 in 22; 21½m. 1 in 16.

Milestones.—Measured from Trowbridge, and from Wells.

Measurements.—Trowbridge,* Church.

5⅞	Norton St. Philip.*		
12	6⅛	Radstock.*	
23⅜	17½	11⅜	Wells,* Market.

Principal Objects of Interest. — Radstock: Collieries. Midsummer Norton: Ch. 22m., Asylum. WELLS: Cathedral.

Hotels or Inns at places marked *, and at Chilcompton, &c.

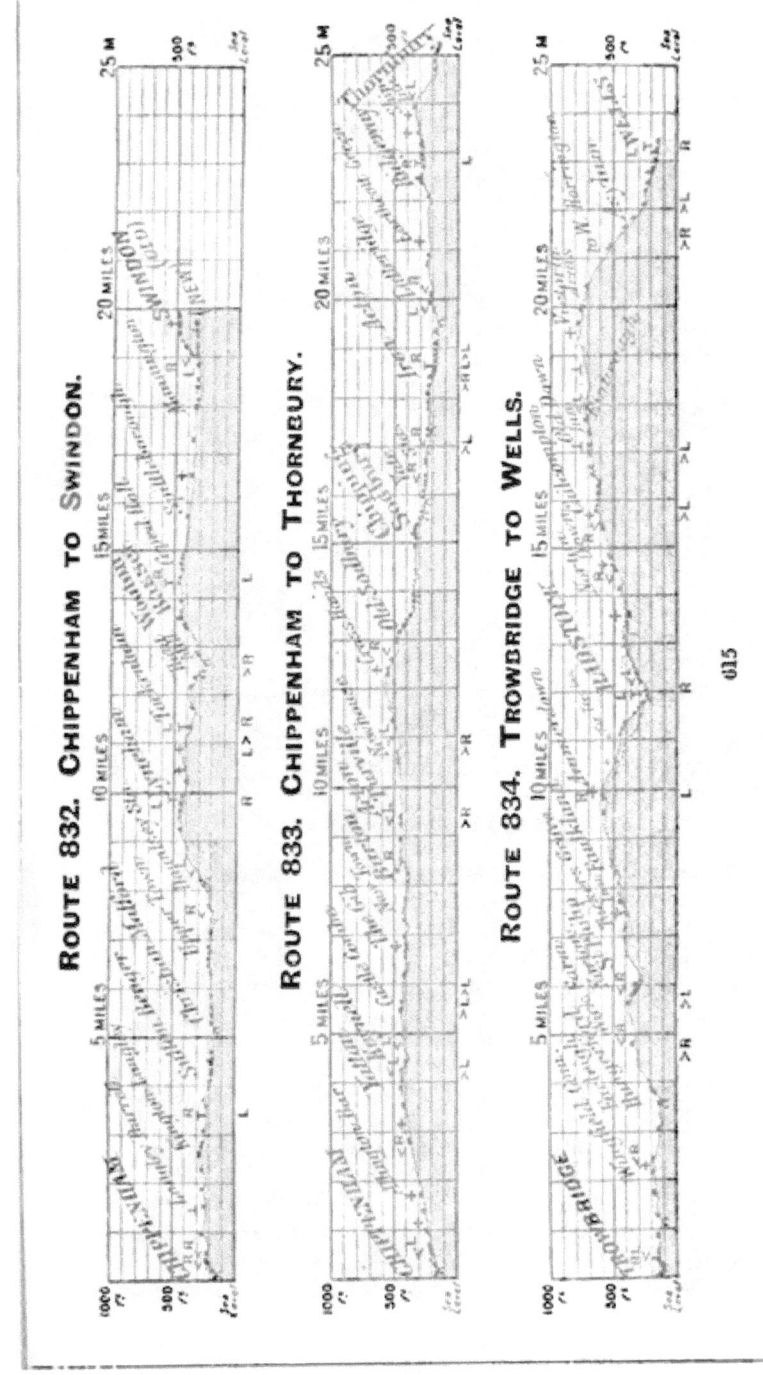

ROUTE 832. CHIPPENHAM TO SWINDON.

ROUTE 833. CHIPPENHAM TO THORNBURY.

ROUTE 834. TROWBRIDGE TO WELLS.

835   MARLBOROUGH TO WELLS.

Description.—Class I. & II. This road has splendid surface, but is slightly undulating to Beckhampton; thereafter almost level—surface apt to be loose—then slightly undulating approaching Devizes. From Devizes to Trowbridge the road is slightly hilly for five miles, but thereafter the gradients are very easy. After Trowbridge, on as far as Beckington it is a fine road, but it then becomes very hilly with steep gradients to Frome, where there is a dangerous hill; but thereafter to Shepton Mallet it is a splendid undulating road with only one steep hill. From Shepton Mallet to Wells the road has splendid surface, but there is a dangerous hill a mile before the latter place. There is a shorter road between Trowbridge and Wells, R. 834 (23¾m.), but this route is the better.

Gradients.—At 3m. 1 in 20; 4½ & 4¾m. 1 in 17; 12m. 1 in 18; 15½m. 1 in 18; 17½m. 1 in 20; 18½m. 1 in 17; 31½m. 1 in 17; 32m. 1 in 14; 33¾m. 1 in 9 (dangerous); 40m. 1 in 23; 43½m. 1 in 17; 44½m. 1 in 20; 45½m. 1 in 17; 49½m. 1 in 10 (dangerous.

Milestones.—Continuation of those from London to Shepherds Shore, then from Devizes Cross on to Seend, after which from Trowbridge, as far as Beckington; thereafter irregular to Leighton, whence from Shepton Mallet Cross, and Wells Market Place.

Measurements.

Marlborough,* Town Hall.

6½	Beckhampton Inn.*								
14⅜	7½	Devizes,* Cross.							
21½	15	7½	Semington,* Crossroads. R. 830.						
24½	18	10½	3	Trowbridge,* Church.					
30⅝	23⅞	16¼	8⅞	5¾	Beckington.* R. 831.				
33⅝	26⅞	19¼	11⅞	8⅞	3	Frome,* Cross.			
39¼	32½	25¼	17⅞	14⅜	8⅜	5⅜	Leighton.		
45¼	38½	31	23½	20⅜	14⅜	11⅜	6	Shepton Mallet,* Cross	
50½	43¾	36⅜	28¾	25⅜	20½	17¼	11¼	5¼	Wells,* Market.

Principal Objects of Interest.—Fyfield: Grey Wethers, Devil's Den. 6m., Silbury Hill. Beckhampton: Avebury Ring. 9m., Three Barrows. 10m., Wansdyke. DEVIZES: Cross, Museum, St. Johns. TROWBRIDGE: Church, Bridge. FROME: Church, Cross. 34¾m., Marston House. SHEPTON MALLET: Church, Cross. WELLS: Cathedral: Bishop's Palace, Wookey Hole.

Hotels or Inns at places marked*, and at Fyfield, West Overton, Seend, Horse Shoes, Hilperton, Southwick, Road, Holwell, Croscombe, &c.

ROUTE 835, MARLBOROUGH TO WELLS.

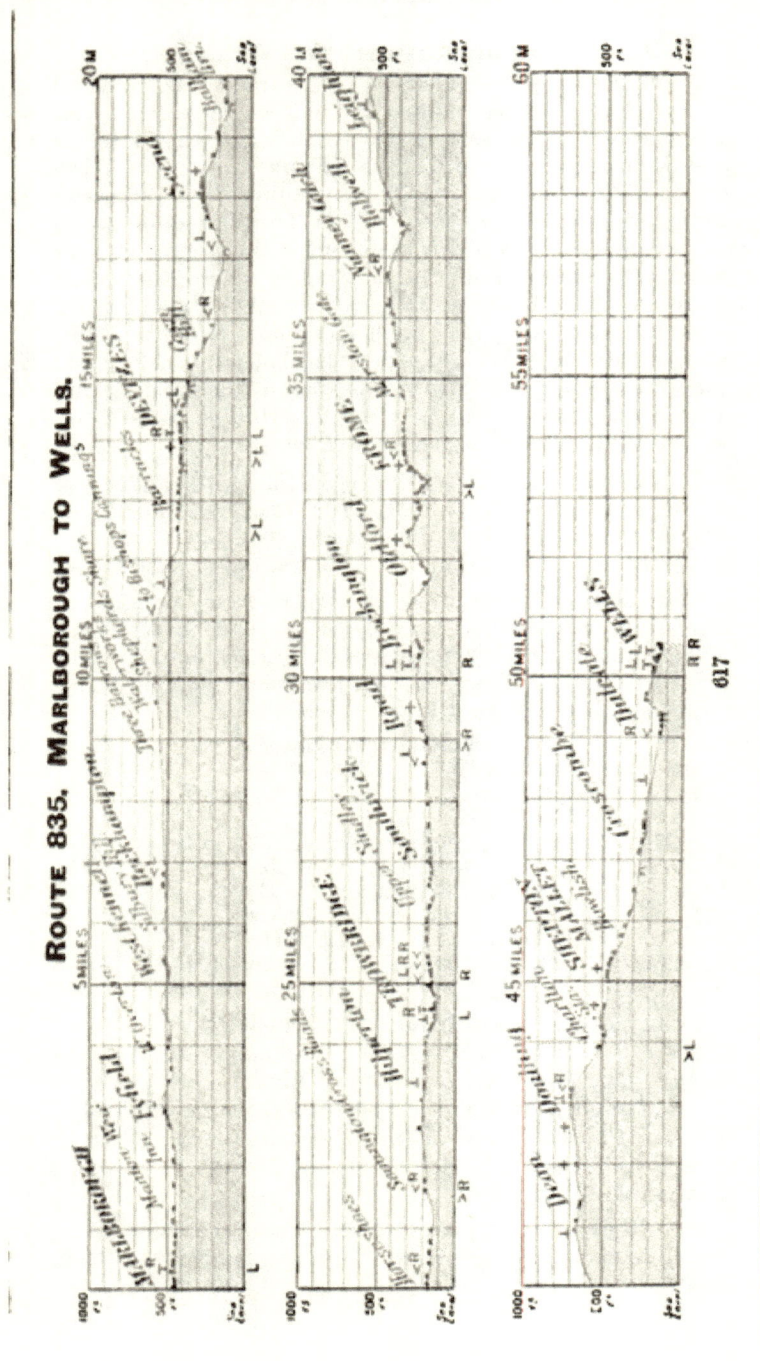

836 SWINDON TO HUNGERFORD.

Description.—Class II. The London road. Rather hilly for eight miles, with variable but usually good surface; thereafter a splendid undulating road.

Gradients.—At 3½m. 1 in 16; 4½ & 5¼m. 1 in 14.

Milestones.—Measured from Swindon Town Hall.

Measurements.

Swindon,* Goddard Arms Hotel.				
3¾	Liddington.*			
9	5¼	Aldbourne.*		
16	12¼	7	Hungerford,* Bear Hotel.	
83¾	79¾	74¾	67¾	London,* G.P.O.

Principal Objects of Interest.—5m., Liddington "Castle." Knighton: Littlecote Park. Hungerford: Town Hall.

Hotels or Inns at places marked*, and at Chilton

837 SWINDON TO DEVIZES.

Description.—Class II. Good surface, but somewhat undulating to Beckhampton, with one steep hill; thereafter a splendid road to Devizes.

Gradients.—At 3m. 1 in 20; 3½m. 1 in 13 (dangerous); 7m. 1 in 18.

Measurements.—Swindon,* Goddard Arms Hotel.

5¾	Broad Hinton.*			
10½	4¾	Avebury.*		
11¾	5¾	1¼	Beckhampton.*	
19	13¼	8½	7¼	Devizes,* Cross.

Principal Objects of Interest.—Avebury: Ring. Beckhampton: Silbury Hill. 15m. Wansdyke. DEVIZES: Cross, St. John's, Museum.

Hotels or Inns at places marked*, and at Wroughton, &c.

838 SWINDON TO CALNE.

Description.—Class II. An excellent road to Wooton Basset; thereafter slightly hilly to Calne.

Gradients.—At ¾m. 1 in 18; 6½m. 1 in 19; 7¼m. 1 in 21; 12½m. 1 in 15; 12¾m. 1 in 22.

Milestones.—Measured from Swindon P.O. to Lyneham.

Measurements.—Swindon,* Goddard Arms Hotel.

6¾	Wooton Basset,* Town Hall.		
10	3¾	Lyneham,* White Hart Inn.	
16	9¾	6	Calne,* Town Hall.

Principal Objects of Interest.—Wooton Basset: Town Hall. Calne: Town Hall.

Hotels or Inns at places marked*, and at Hilmarton.

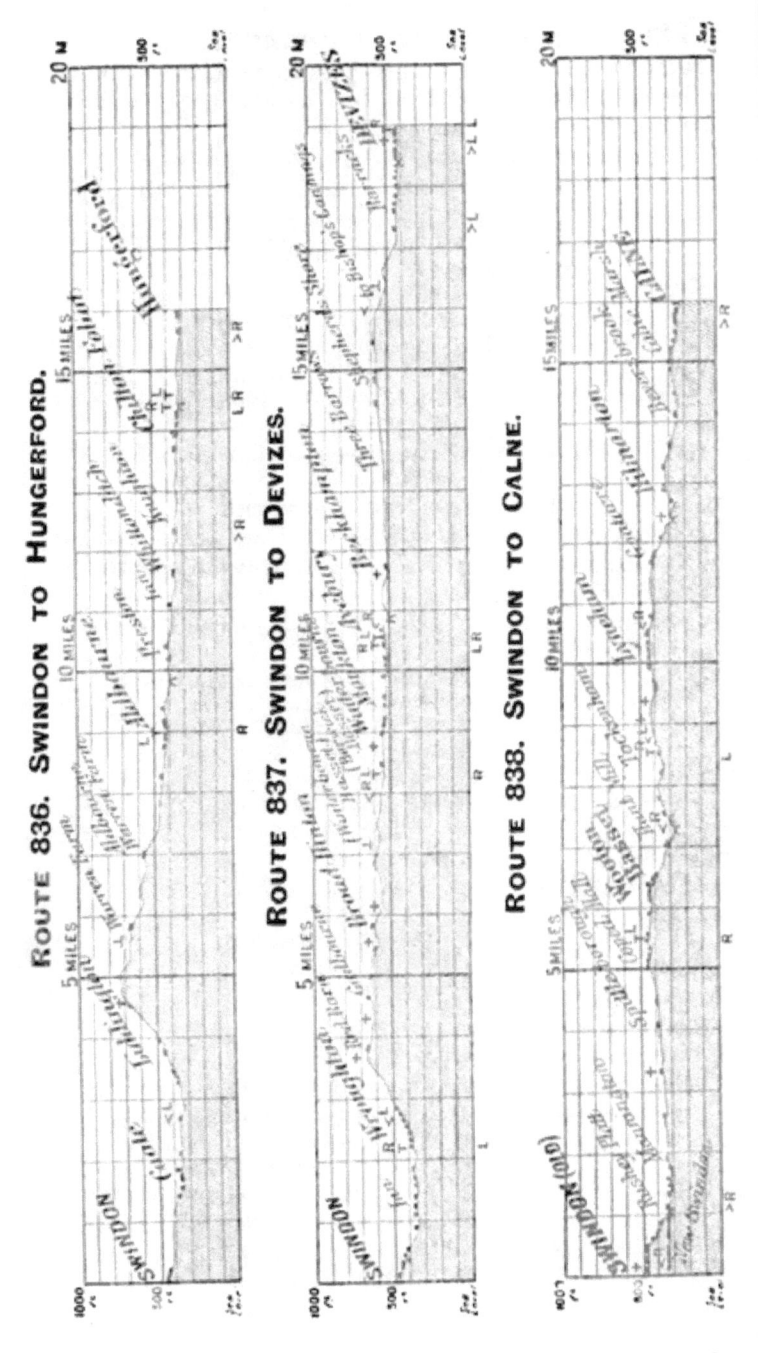

ROUTE 836. SWINDON TO HUNGERFORD.

ROUTE 837. SWINDON TO DEVIZES.

ROUTE 838. SWINDON TO CALNE.

839 SWINDON TO MALMESBURY.

Description.—Class II. A remarkably easy road, of excellent surface, but rather steep approaching Malmesbury.

Gradients.—At ¾m. 1 in 18; 9½m. 1 in 21; 14½m. 1 in 20; 14¾m. 1 in 13 (dangerous); 15m. 1 in 20.

Milestones.—Measured from Swindon and Malmesbury.

Measurements.—Swindon,* Goddard Arms Hotel.
(6¾ Wooton Basset, Town Hall.)
9⅞ 5½ Brinkworth,* Church.
15⅝ 11 5¾ Malmesbury,* Town Hall.

Principal Objects of Interest.—Malmesbury: Abbey Church.

840 SWINDON TO CIRENCESTER.

Description.—Class II. Dangerous hill in Swindon, then good surface to Blunsdon Hill—also dangerous—after which it is a splendid and almost level road.

Gradients.—At ¼ & 4¾m. 1 in 12 (both dangerous).

Milestones.—Measured from Swindon, and from Crickdale

Measurements.—Swindon,* Goddard Arms Hotel.
(... New Swindon,* Station).
8 7½ Cricklade,* White Horse.
15⅜ 14⅞ 7⅜ Cirencester,* Church.

Principal Objects of Interest.—Cricklade: Ch., Town House. CIRENCESTER: Town Hall, Church, Museum, Oakley Park, Agricultural College.

Hotels or Inns at places marked*, and at Coldharbour Inn, Blunsdon Hill, and The Foss.

841 SWINDON TO BURFORD.

Description.—Class II. Dangerous descent in Swindon, then a good undulating road to Highworth, after which another dangerous descent, when it becomes an excellent road, almost level, but with slightly inferior surface approaching Burford.

Gradients.—At ¼m. 1 in 12 (dangerous); 5½m. 1 in 18; 6¾m. 1 in 12 (dangerous); 19½m. 1 in 16.

Milestones.—Measured from Swindon, and from Lechlade.

Measurements.—Swindon,* Goddard Arms Hotel.
6⅜ Highworth,* High Street.
11 4⅝ Lechlade,* Market.
14½ 8⅛ 3½ Broughton Poggs,* P.O.
19⅝ 13¼ 8⅝ 5⅛ Burford.*

Principal Objects of Interest.—Highworth: Church, Coleshill Park. Lechlade: Church. Burford: Church.

Hotels or Inns at places marked*, and at Stratton, &c.

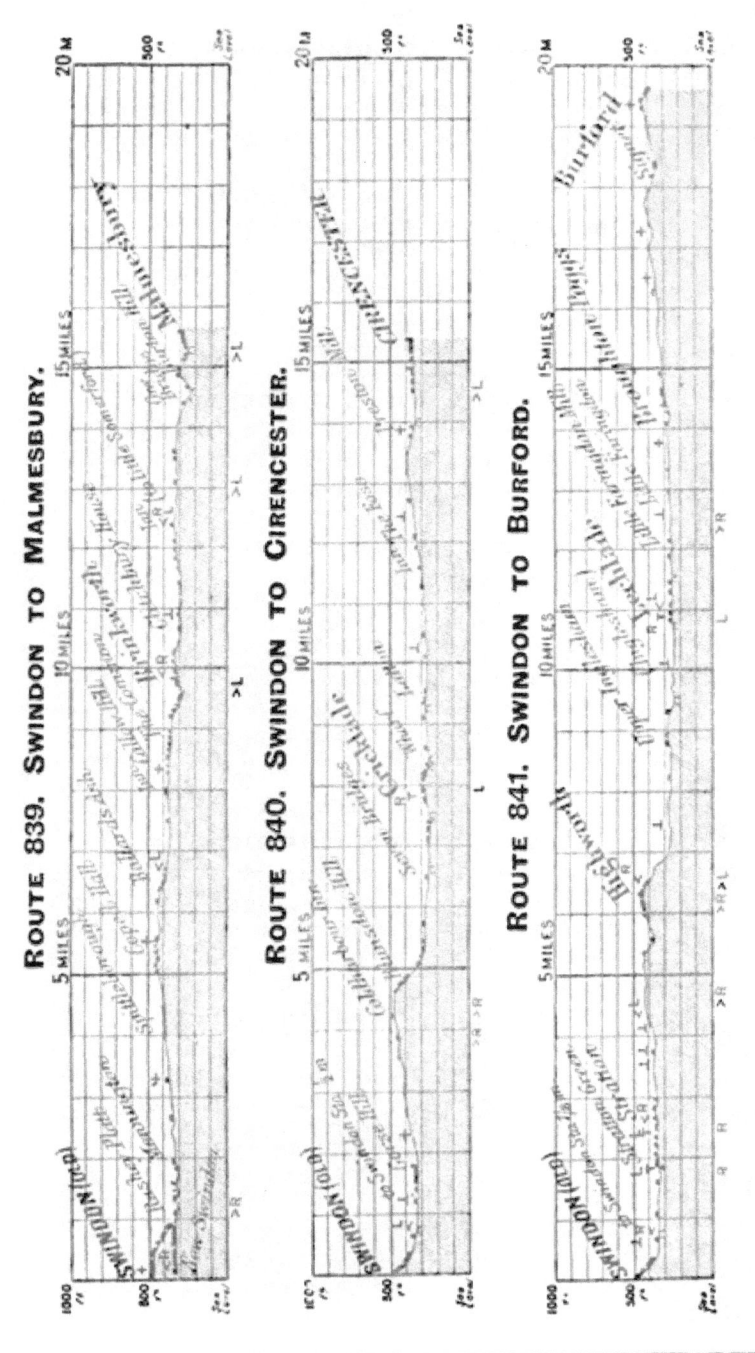

ROUTE 839. SWINDON TO MALMESBURY.

ROUTE 840. SWINDON TO CIRENCESTER.

ROUTE 841. SWINDON TO BURFORD.

842 SWINDON TO WANTAGE.

Description. — Class II. Dangerous descent from Swindon, then an almost level road for 9m., usually with excellent surface; it then becomes very hilly—short steep hills—but with good surface.

Gradients.—At ¼m. 1 in 12 (dangerous); 10m. 1 in 13; 11½m. 1 in 20; 12½m. 1 in 18; 13m. 1 in 17; 14m. 1 in 19; 14½m. 1 in 15; 16m. 1 in 23; 16¾m. 1 in 21.

Milestones.—Measured from Wantage.

Measurements.—Swindon,* Goddard Arms Hotel.

6¾	Shrivenham,* P.O.		
13¼	6¾	Blowing Stone Inn.*	
18	11¼	4½	Wantage,* Market.

Principal Objects of Interest. — 10¾m., White Horse. 13½m., Blowing Stone. Wantage : Alfred-the-Great statue.

843 SWINDON TO WITNEY.

Description.—Class II. Dangerous descent from Swindon, then an almost level road for 11m. to Faringdon, where there is a steep descent, after which level for 7m. to Bampton, but this section is often very loose; thereafter it is a good undulating road to Witney.

Gradients.—At ¼m. 1 in 12 (dangerous); 12½m. 1 in 15.

Milestones.—Measured from Faringdon.

Measurements.—Swindon,* Goddard Arms Hotel.

6¾	Shrivenham.*		
12¼	5½	Faringdon,* Market.	
18¼	11½	6¼	Bampton,* Town Hall.
24⅛	17¾	12	5¾ Witney,* Town Hall.

Principal Objects of Interest. — Shrivenham: Becket House. Faringdon: Church, Faringdon House. Radcot: Bridge. Bampton: Church, Castle. Witney: Church.

Hotels or Inns at places marked*, and at Radcot, &c.

844 BRISTOL TO CLEVEDON.

Description.—Class II. A slightly hilly road, with fairly good surface. The direct road by Failand Inn (13½m.) shown in dotted lines, has very steep hills.

Gradients.—At 8m. 1 in 20.

Measurements.—Bristol,* Bridge.

7½	Wraxall,* Inn.	
13¾	6¼	Clevedon,* The Triangle.
14	6½	Clevedon, Town Hall.

Principal Objects of Interest. — Stonedge : Cadbury Camp. Clevedon: Pier, Old Ch., Walton Castle, Dial Hill.

Hotels or Inns at places marked*, and at Long Ashton.

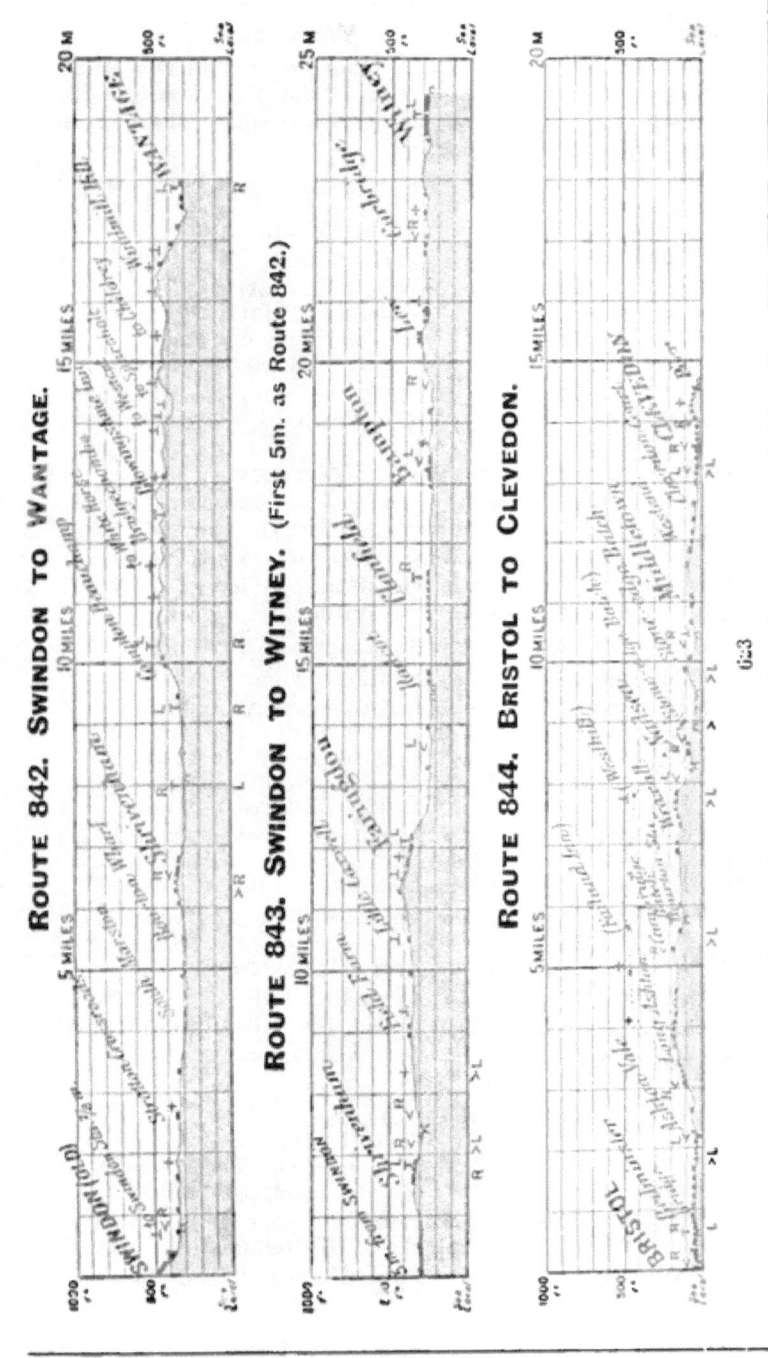

ROUTE 842. SWINDON TO WANTAGE.

ROUTE 843. SWINDON TO WITNEY. (First 5m. as Route 842.)

ROUTE 844. BRISTOL TO CLEVEDON.

623

845 BRISTOL TO WESTON-SUPER-MARE.

Description.— Class II. The road has good surface, but is somewhat undulating as far as Congresbury, with several rather steep pitches; thereafter level to Weston, usually with very good surface, but sometimes it is loose.

Gradients.—At 11m. 1 in 14; 11½m. 1 in 12.

Milestones.—Measured from Bedminster Bridge, Bristol, as far as Cleave.

Measurements.— Bristol,* Bridge.

7		Farleigh.*		
12¾	5¾	Congresbury,* Bridge.		
16¾	9¾	4¾	Puxton Station,*	
20⅞	13¾	8½	4¼	Weston,* High St.

Principal Objects of Interest. — 3m., Ashton Court. 11½m., Cadbury Camp. WESTON: Pier, Town Hall, &c.

Hotels or Inns at places marked *, and at Long Ashton, &c.

846 BRISTOL TO TAUNTON.

Description.—Class I. Although this road has splendid surface, it is exceedingly hilly as far as Cross; thereafter it is almost level for 18m., with splendid surface, but then becomes slightly undulating to Taunton. An easier road is R. 845 to Congresbury, thence R. 821 to Churchill; this avoids the very steep hills.

Gradients.—At 2m. 1 in 14; 4m. 1 in 16; 6 & 7m. 1 in 17; 9m. 1 in 11 (dangerous); 13½, 14½, & 15m. 1 in 17; 15½ & 16m. 1 in 15; 16¾m. 1 in 13; 38½m. 1 in 17.

Milestones.—Measured from Bedminster Bridge, Bristol, as far as Bridgwater; then from Bridgewater, and Taunton, Market House.

Measurements.

Bristol,* Bridge.							
13¼	Churchill Gate.*						
14¾	1½	Star Inn.* (R. 821).					
(17½	4¾	4¼	Axbridge.*)				
17¼	4¼	2¾	1	Cross,* White Hart.			
25¾	12½	11¼	9¾	8¾	Highbridge,* Market Street		
32¾	19¾	18½	16¾	15¾	7½	Bridgwater,* Cornhill.	
38½	25¾	24½	22½	21¼	12¾	5¾	Thurloxton.*
43¾	30¾	29¾	27¼	26½	18¼	10¾	5¼ Taunton,* Market Ho.

Principal Objects of Interest.—5m., Dundry Reservoirs, Tower. Churchill: Dolebury Camp. AXBRIDGE: Church, 22m., Brent Knoll. BRIDGWATER: Bridge, Church, Town Hall, Castle Field. North Petherton: Church. TAUNTON: Market House, Castle, Colleges, Church, Monuments.

Hotels or Inns at places marked *, and at Fox and Goose, Redhill, Langford, Brent Knoll, Dunball, &c.

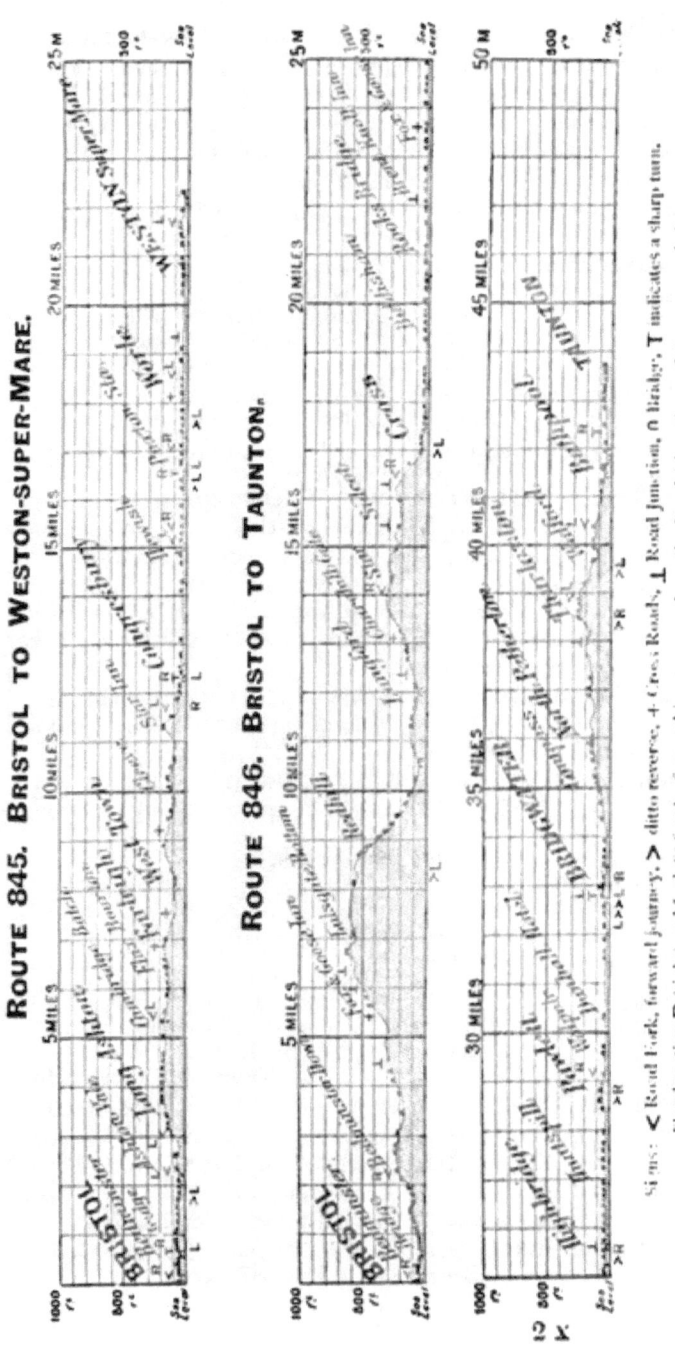

ROUTE 845. BRISTOL TO WESTON-SUPER-MARE.

ROUTE 846. BRISTOL TO TAUNTON.

Signs: < Road fork, forward journey, > ditto reverse, + Cross Road, ○ Bridge, ⊥ Road junction, T indicates a sharp turn. The direction R (right) and L (left) for the forward journey are above the Road Line, those of the reverse, below.

625

847 BRISTOL TO WELLS.

Description.—Class III. Fairly good surface, but precipitous hills. The proper road is by Farrington and Chewton Mendip, routes 848 and 816, 20⅝m.

Gradients.—All dangerous. Mostly 1 in 8, or 1 in 9.

Milestones.—Measured from Bedminster Bridge.

Measurements.—Bristol,* Bridge.

8	Stoke Inn.*	
19	11	Wells,* Market.

Principal Objects of Interest.—Dundry: Tower, Roman Camp. WELLS: Cathedral, Bishop's Palace, Wookey Hole.

Hotels or Inns at places marked*, and at Dundry, &c.

848 BRISTOL TO SHEPTON MALLET.

Description.—Class I. A very hilly road, but with splendid surface; many of the hills are dangerous.

Gradients.—(†*Dangerous.*) At 1¼m. 1 in 20; 2¼m. 1 in 10†: 2½m. 1 in 14; 5m. 1 in 12†; 6m. 1 in 14; 7½m. 1 in 25; 8½m. 1 in 11†; 10m. 1 in 18; 10¾m. 1 in 16; 12½ & 16m. 1 in 15; 17m. 1 in 12†; 18½m. 1 in 24: 20m. 1 in 14.†

Milestones.—Measured from Bristol Bridge; and Shepton Mallet, Cross.

Measurements.—Bristol,* Bridge.

6½	Pensford,* Bridge.		
12⅛	5⅝	Farrington,* Inn.	
20⅝	14⅛	8½	Shepton Mallet,* Cross.

Principal Objects of Interest. — Pensford: Druidical Stones. SHEPTON MALLET: Church, Cross.

Hotels or Inns at places marked* and at Temple Cloud, &c.

849 BRISTOL TO WESTBURY.

Description.—Class III. As R. 850 to Keynsham; thereafter very steep to Charterhouse Hinton, after which easier to Westbury. The best road is by Bath.

Gradients. — All 1 in 12, or 1 in 10 to Charterhouse (dangerous).

Milestones.—Measured from Town Hall, Bath.

Measurements.

Bristol,* Bridge.

5¼	Keynsham.*				
(...	...	Bath,* Town Hall.)			
14½	8⅞	4	Midford.*		
20¼	15½	10⅜	6⅝	Beckington,* (R. 818).	
26¾	21½	16⅝	12⅝	6	Westbury,* Market.

Principal Objects of Interest.—Odd Down: Wansdyke, Workhouse. Norton St. Philip: George Inn. WESTBURY: Church, White Horse.

Hotels or Inns at places marked*, and at Odd Down, &c.

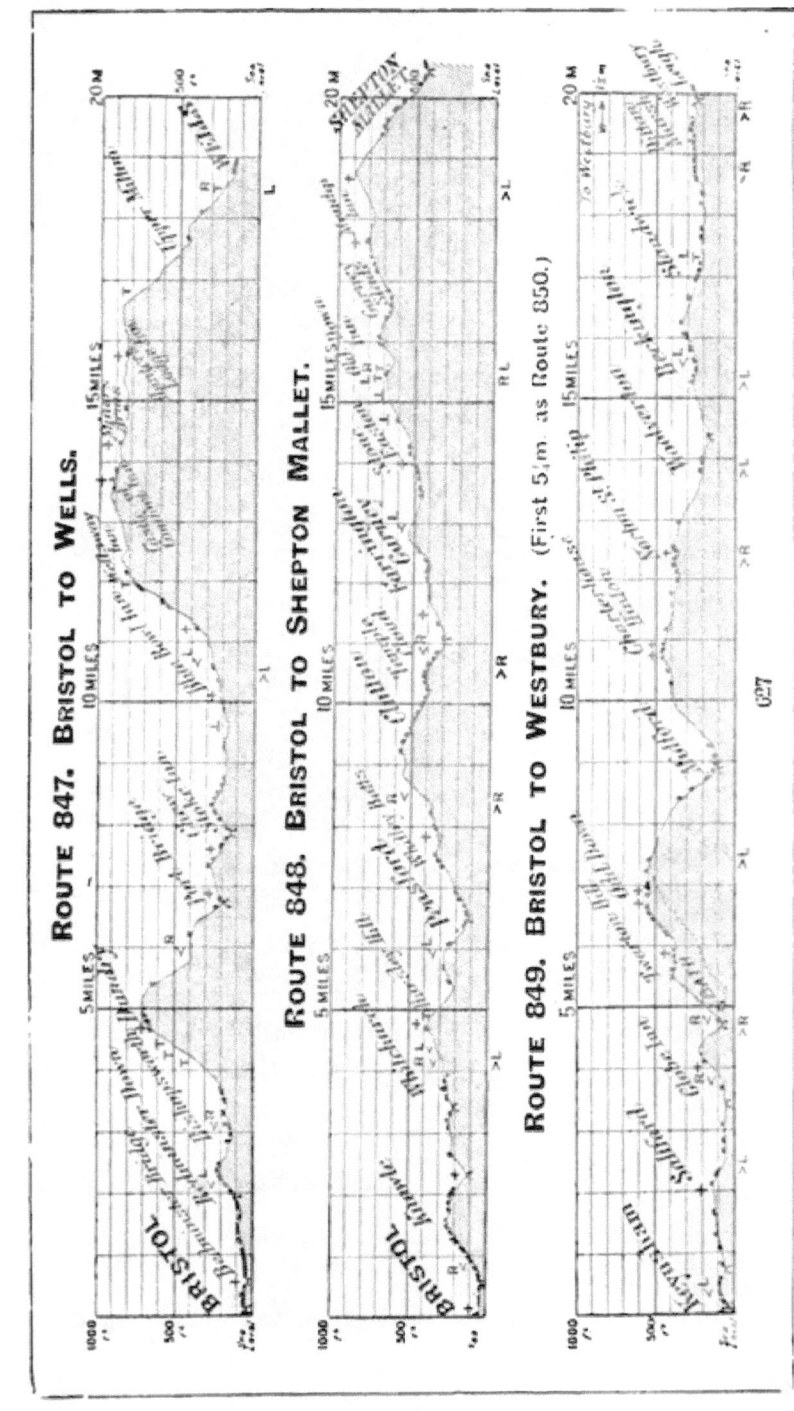

ROUTE 847. BRISTOL TO WELLS.

ROUTE 848. BRISTOL TO SHEPTON MALLET.

ROUTE 849. BRISTOL TO WESTBURY. (First 5½ m. as Route 850.)

850 BRISTOL TO LONDON.

Description.—Class I. A bumpy road to Keynsham, beyond which the road has fine surface the whole way to Marlborough, excepting a short piece on the Downs between Cherhill and Beckhampton. The hills between Chippenham and Calne are somewhat steep, but hardly dangerous. The more direct road to Chippenham by Marshfield is much inferior to that by Bath. It is very bumpy for five miles, then very steep and hilly for the next five, after which fine surface and easy gradients. From Marlborough to London see Route 517.

Gradients.—At 2¾m. 1 in 15; 7¾m. 1 in 17; 19m. 1 in 20; 23m. 1 in 18; 24½ & 25m. 1 in 20; 28¼m. 1 in 17; 29½ & 30m. 1 in 13: 33¼m. 1 in 20; 34½m. 1 in 17; 39½m. 1 in 17; 41¼m. 1 in 20.

Milestones.—Measured from Bristol, to Globe Inn; thereafter from Bath, Town Hall, on as far as Box, whence they are measured from Hyde Park Corner, London.

Measurements.

Bristol,* Bridge.								
5¼	Keynsham,* Lamb and Lark Hotel.							
12½	7¼	Bath,* Town Hall.						
18¼	13	5¾	Box.*					
25½	20¼	13	7¼	Chippenham,* Market Place.				
31	25¾	18½	12¾	5½	Calne,* Town Hall.			
37¾	32½	24¾	19½	11⅞	6½	Beckhampton.*		
44½	38¾	31½	25⅞	18⅝	13½	6¾	Marlboro',* Town Hall.	
121½	116¼	109	103¼	96	90½	84¼	77¾	London. R. 517.

Principal Objects of Interest. — Keynsham: Bridge. BATH: Guild Hall, Pump Room, Roman Bath, Colleges, Sham Castle, Beckford Tower. Box: Quarries. CHIPPENHAM: Church, Cross. Studley: Bowood House. Cherhill: White Horse, Oldbury Castle. Beckhampton: Silbury Hill, Avebury Ring. Fyfield: Grey Wethers, Devil's Den. MARLBOROUGH: Town Hall, Bradley Memorial College, Savernake Forest.

BY MARSHFIELD.
Measurements.

Bristol,* Bridge.					
7⅞	Wick Inn.*				
12⅝	5¼	Marshfield,* Market Place.			
16⅝	9¼	4	Ford,* P.O.		
22	14⅜	9⅜	5⅜	Chippenham,* Market Place.	
118	110⅝	105⅜	101⅜	96	London,* G.P.O.

Hotels or Inns at places marked *. and at Brislington, Saltford, Bath Easton, &c.

[*over.*

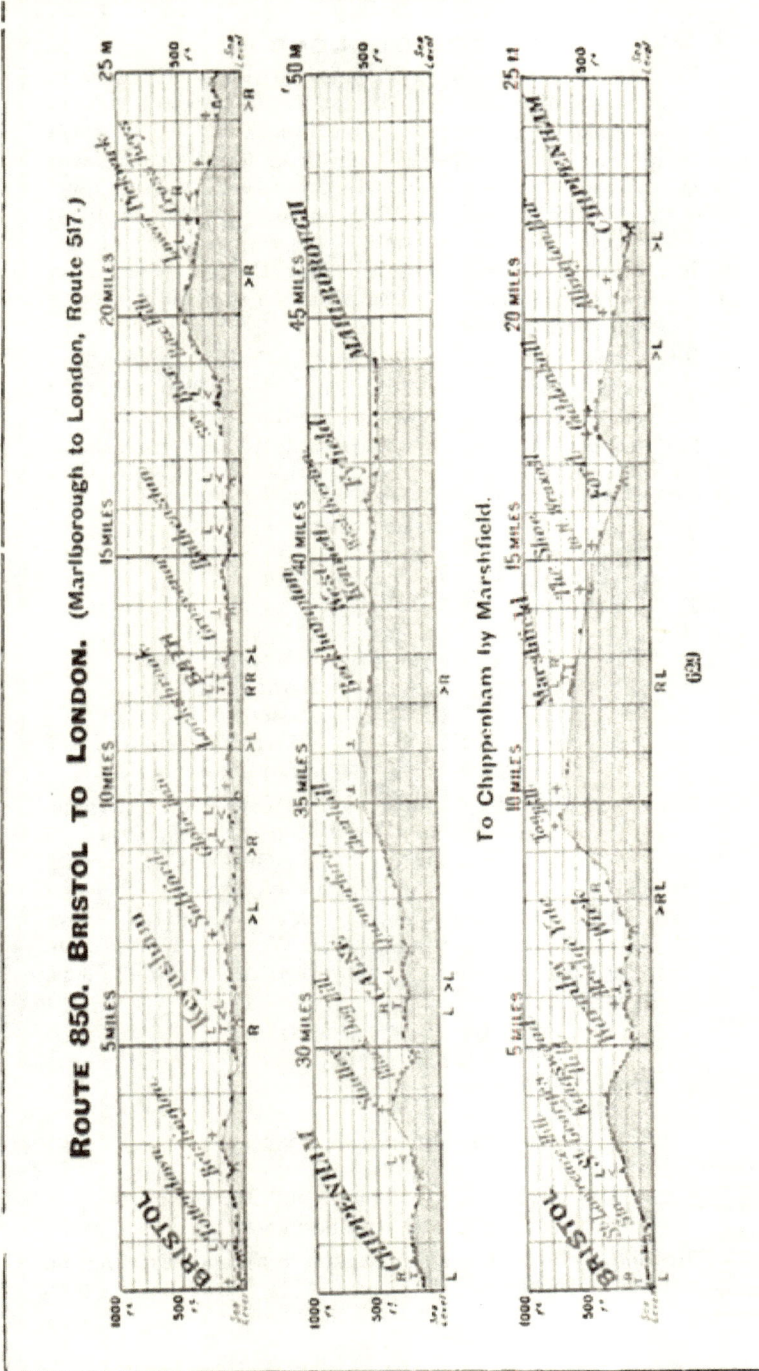

ROUTE 850. BRISTOL TO LONDON. (Marlborough to London, Route 517.)

To Chippenham by Marshfield.

629

Route 850—Continued.

Gradients.—At 2, 3, & 4¾m. 1 in 17; 6¼m. 1 in 13; 6¾m. 1 in 16; 7½m. 1 in 17; 9m. 1 in 12 (dangerous); 16¼m. 1 in 24; 17¼m. 1 in 17.

851   BRISTOL TO OXFORD.

Description.—Class II. Bumpy surface for 5m., thereafter the road has some rather steep grades, but has good surface to Acton Turville; these can be avoided by the less hilly road through Chipping Sodbury. Route 853. After Acton Turville it is a fine undulating road as far as Cricklade, with a very steep hill at Sherston. Thence to Highworth splendid surface, but Blunsdon Hill is dangerous. From Highworth to Faringdon the road is very steep and hilly; a better road—a mile and a quarter longer, avoiding the hills, and with better surface—is by Watchfield. The best route to Faringdon, however, is by Bath, Chippenham, and Swindon: Routes 850, 832, and 843. From Faringdon to Oxford, see Route 493.

Gradients.—(†*Dangerous.*) At 8½m. 1 in 14; 10m. 1 in 18; 12m. 1 in 15; 18½m. 1 in 19; 20½m. 1 in 11†; 26½m. 1 in 17; 29½m. 1 in 20; 30½m. 1 in 17; 37m. 1 in 19; 41m. 1 in 12†; 43m. 1 in 19; 44¾ & 46m. 1 in 15; 48m. 1 in 12†; 49½m. 1 in 10†.

Milestones.—Measured from Bristol; after Acton Turville measured from Malmesbury, thereafter from London.

Measurements.

Bristol,* Bridge.

3½	Fishponds.*							
10¼	6¾	Codrington.*						
15½	12¼	5¾	Acton Turville.*					
26	22¾	15½	10¼	Malmesbury.*				
33¼	29½	22¼	17¾	7¼	Minety Station.*			
37¾	34¼	27¾	22	11¾	4½	Cricklade,* White Horse Inn.		
45¾	41¾	34¼	29½	19¾	12¼	7½	Highworth.*	
51¾	48¼	41¼	35¾	25¾	18¼	13¾	6¾	Faringdon.*
69	65½	58½	53¼	43	35¾	31¼	23¾	17¼ Oxford,* Rt. 493.

Principal Objects of Interest. — 12½m., Dodington Park. Acton Turville: Badminton Park. 17m., Shire Stone. Malmesbury: Abbey Church, Market Cross. Cricklade: Town House, Church. Highworth: Church. Coleshill: Park. Faringdon: Church, &c.

Hotels or Inns at places marked*, and at Down End, Sherston, Charlton, Coleshill, &c.

ROUTE 851. BRISTOL TO OXFORD. (Faringdon to Oxford, Route 493.)

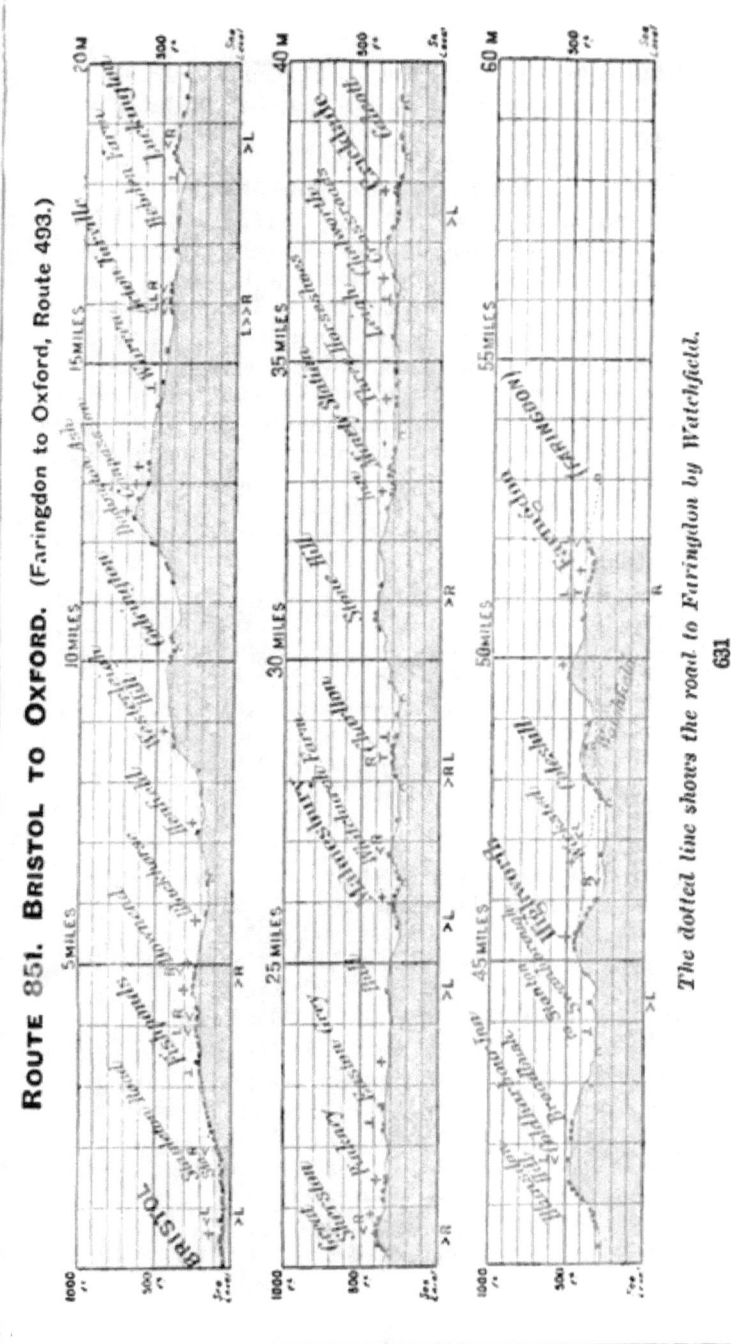

The dotted line shows the road to Faringdon by Watchfield.

631

852 BRISTOL TO BATH.

Description.—Class II. A very bumpy and hilly road to Bitton, whence better surface, but also hilly. The best road is by Keynsham (Rt. 850).

Gradients.—At 2¼m. 1 in 18; 3 & 3¼m. 1 in 15; 5½m. 1 in 13 (dangerous); 8½m. 1 in 17; 9½m. 1 in 17; 11¼m. 1 in 18.

Milestones.—Measured from Town Hall, Bath.

Measurements.—Bristol,* Bridge.

6¾	Bitton,* P.O.	
12⅝	5⅞	Bath,* Town Hall.

Principal Objects of Interest.—BATH: Guildhall, Pump Room, Colleges, Sham Castle, Beckford Tower, &c.

Hotels or Inns at places marked *, and at Kelston, &c.

853 BRISTOL TO CHIPPING SODBURY.

Description.—Class II. The road is rather bumpy for five miles, but after that it has excellent surface and easy gradients. This is the best road for Acton Turville.

Gradients.—At 7¼m. 1 in 23; 13¼m. 1 in 16.

Milestones.—Measured from Bristol.

Measurements.

Bristol,* Bridge.

4⅞	Downend,* Inn.				
10⅞	6	Yate.*			
11⅞	7	1	Sodbury,* Clock Tower.		
14⅝	9¾	3¾	2¾	Crosshands.*	
17¾	12⅞	6⅞	5⅞	3⅛	Acton Turville.*

Principal Objects of Interest.—Uninteresting country.

Hotels or Inns at places marked *, and at Coalpit Heath.

854 BRISTOL TO WOOTON-UNDER-EDGE.

Description.—Class II. This is a poor and rather hilly road, though fairly level near Iron Acton.

Gradients.—At 2¾m. 1 in 17; 6½m. 1 in 15; 16¼ & 18¾m. 1 in 11 (dangerous).

Milestones.—Irregular.

Measurements.

Bristol,* Bridge.

5¼	Hambrook.			
9⅝	4⅜	Iron Acton.*		
15	9¾	5⅜	Bibstone.*	
19⅛	13⅞	9½	4⅛	Wooton-under-Edge.*

Principal Objects of Interest.—Pretty country near Wooton. Wooton: Tyndale Monument.

Hotels or Inns at places marked *, and at Stapleton, Rangeworthy, Charfield Green, &c.

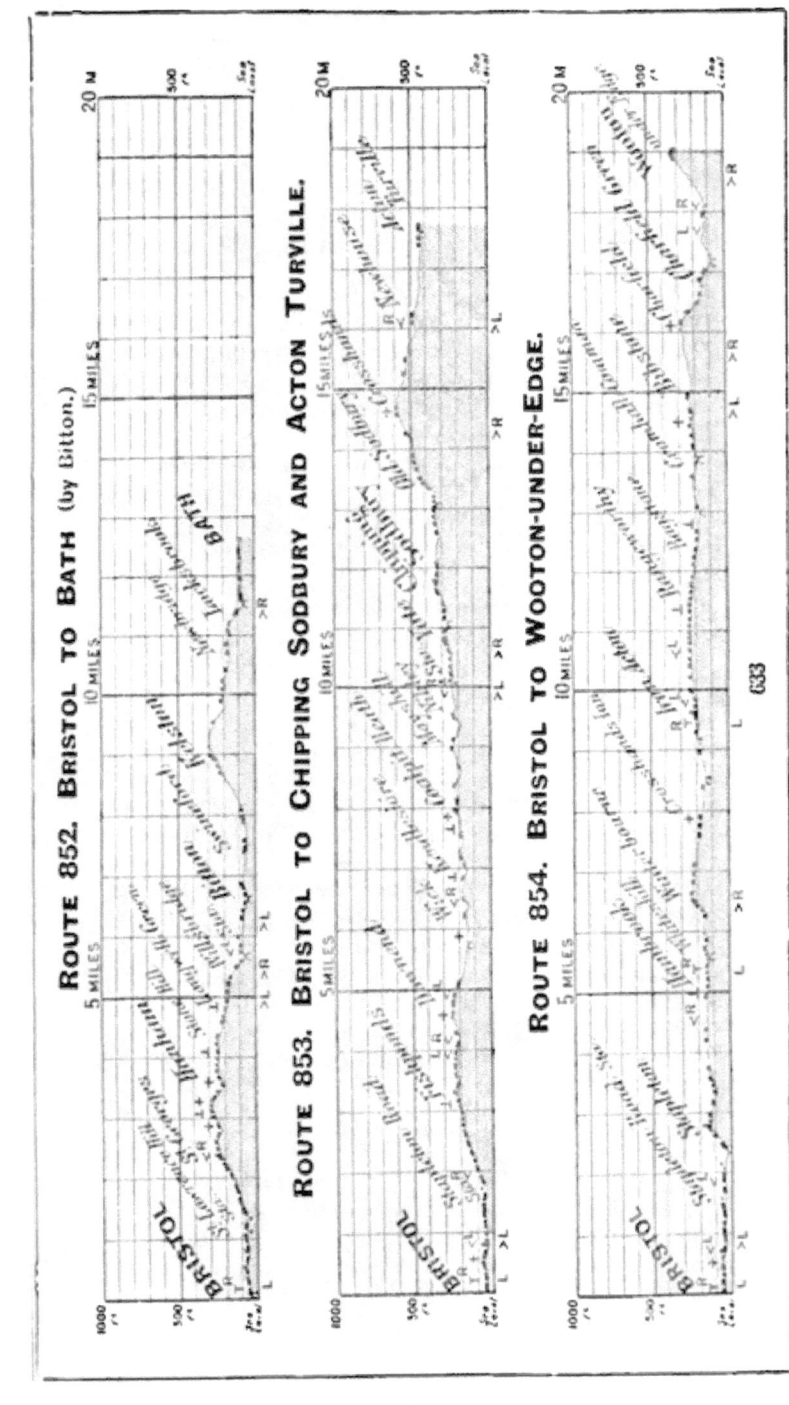

ROUTE 852. BRISTOL TO BATH (by Bitton.)

ROUTE 853. BRISTOL TO CHIPPING SODBURY AND ACTON TURVILLE.

ROUTE 854. BRISTOL TO WOOTON-UNDER-EDGE.

633

855 BRISTOL TO GLOUCESTER.

Description.—Class I. The road is rather bumpy for the first four miles, but after that it is a magnificent undulating road, usually with splendid surface the whole way to Gloucester—indeed all the way to Birmingham. The gradients are all very easy. It is one of the best main roads in the country. For the road through Thornbury or Berkeley which lie to the west of the main route, see route 862.

Gradients.—At 4½m. 1 in 16; 14m. 1 in 19; 17m. 1 in 17.

Milestones.—Measured from beginning of Cheltenham Road Bristol, to Whitminster; then from Gloucester Cross.

Measurements.

Bristol,* Bridge.									
5⅜	Patchway,* Station								
10¾	4⅜	Ship Inn.*							
16⅜	11	6⅝	Stone.*						
20¾	14⅜	10	3⅜	Berkeley Road Station.*					
23¾	17⅜	13	6⅜	3	Cambridge.*				
26⅞	21	16⅝	10	6⅝	3⅝	Whitminster.*			
30½	24⅝	19¾	13⅝	9¾	6¾	3⅝	Hardwick.*		
34½	28⅝	23¾	17⅝	13¾	10¾	7⅝	4	Gloucester,* Cross.	
43¼	37⅜	32½	26¾	22½	19½	16¾	12¾	8¾	Cheltenham.
60¾	54⅞	50	43⅝	40	37	33⅜	30¼	26¼	Worcester
86¾	80⅞	76	69⅝	66	63	59⅜	56¼	52¼	Birmingham.
60¼	54⅜	49⅝	43¼	39⅝	36⅝	33¼	29¾	25¾	Malvern
72⅞	67	62¼	56	52¼	49¼	46	42⅝	38⅝	Stratford-on-Av

Principal Objects of Interest.—3m., Barracks. Pretty country near Patchway. (Thornbury: Castle, Church. Berkeley: Castle.) GLOUCESTER: Cathedral, Guildhall, Museum, New Inn, Lanthony Priory.

Hotels or Inns at places marked*, and at Filton, Almondsbury, Patchway, Buckover, &c., &c.

856 BRISTOL TO NEWPORT.

Description.—Class II. A hilly road for seven miles, then level to Pilning Station, where train to Severn Tunnel Junction. Thence fairly good surface to Caerwent, where the Gloucester and Newport road is joined (Route 886), which has fine surface to Newport.

Gradients.—At ½m. 1 in 13 (dangerous); 3½m. 1 in 15; 6m. 1 in 15; 6¾m. 1 in 12 (dangerous); 17m. 1 in 21; 17¾m. 1 in 11.

Milestones.—Measured from top of Park Street, Bristol.

Measurements.

Bristol,* Bridge.						
1½	Clifton,* Station.					
3¾	2¼	Westbury.*				
8¾	7¼	5	Pilning Station.*			
15¾	14¼	12	7	Severn Tunnel Junction.		
18⅜	16⅞	14⅝	9⅝	2⅝	Caerwent.*	
29¼	27¾	25½	20½	13½	10⅞	Newport.*

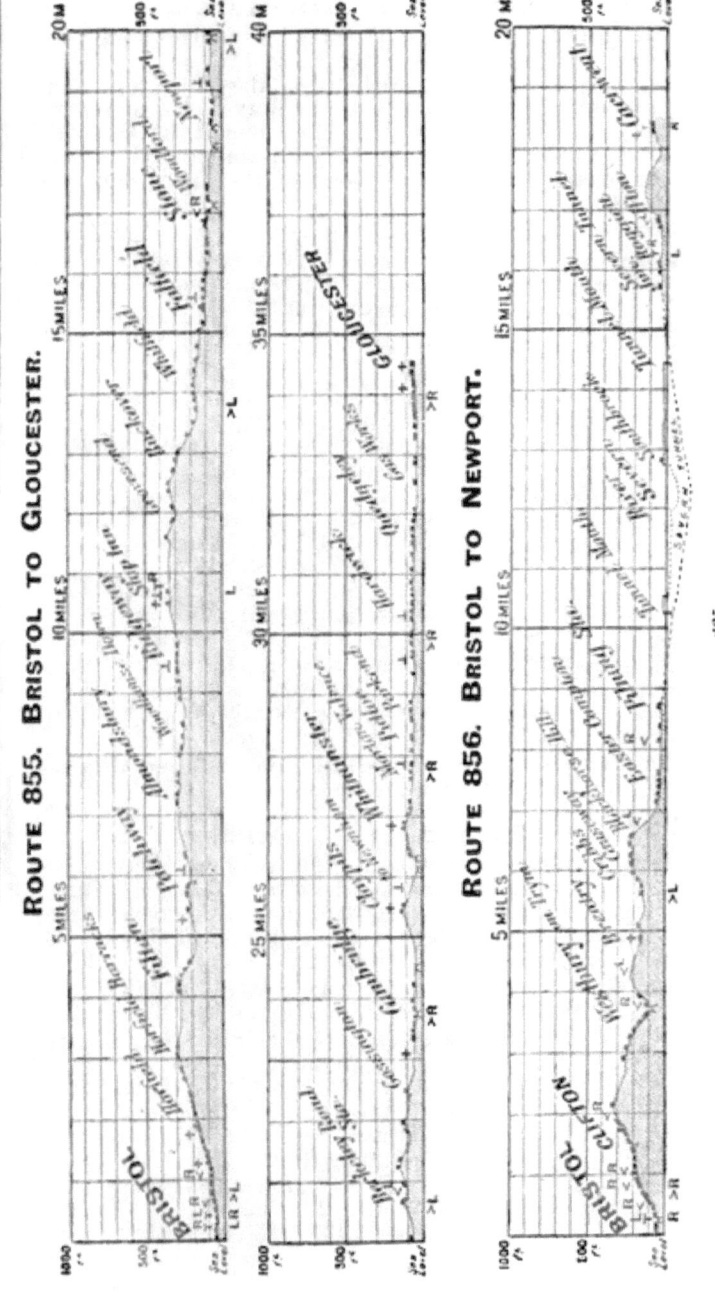

ROUTE 855. BRISTOL TO GLOUCESTER.

ROUTE 856. BRISTOL TO NEWPORT.

Route 856—Continued.

Principal Objects of Interest.—Severn Tunnel. Caerwent: Walls, &c.

Hotels or Inns at places marked *, &c.

857   SODBURY TO BERKELEY.

Description.—Class II. An excellent road throughout, with one dangerous hill.

Gradients.—At 4m. 1 in 14; 8m. 1 in 13 (dangerous)

Milestones.—Measured from Chipping Sodbury.

Measurements.—Chipping Sodbury,* Clock Tower
	4		Wickwar,* Town Hall.
10¼	6¼		Stone.*
13¼	9¼	2¾	Berkeley.*

Principal Objects of Interest.—Berkeley: Castle.

---

858 THORNBURY TO MINCHINHAMPTON.

Description.—Class II. This is a fair cross-country road, slightly hilly at first to Wooton-under-Edge, then very steep to Minchinhampton, but very fair surface.

Gradients.—(†*Dangerous.*) At 5m. 1 in 13; 6½m. 1 in 11†; 9¼m. 1 in 11†; 10½m. 1 in 12†; 14½m. 1 in 18; 16½m. 1 in 11†; 18½m. 1 in 10†.

Milestones.—Measured from Thornbury, and Wooton.

Measurements.—Thornbury.*
9¾			Wooton-under-Edge.*
17¼	8¼		Nailsworth.*
19¼	10½	2¼	Minchinhampton.*

Principal Objects of Interest.—Wooton · Tyndale Monument. Minchinhampton: Church. Pretty district.

Hotels or Inns at places marked *, and at Horsley, &c.

---

859   BERKELEY TO MALMESBURY.

Description.—Class II. A very steep road for the first eight miles, then a fine road to Malmesbury.

Gradients.—(†*Dangerous.*) At 3½m. 1 in 13; 6½m. 1 in 8†; 8m. 1 in 10†.

Milestones.—After Dursley, measured from Malmesbury.

Measurements.—Berkeley.*
2¼					Berkeley Road Station.*
5½	3¼				Dursley.*
9¼	7½	4¾			Huntershall Inn.*
15¼	12½	9¾	5¼		Tetbury,* Market.
20	17⅜	14½	10½	4¾	Malmesbury*.

Principal Objects of Interest.—Dursley: Market House. Beverstone: Castle. Tetbury: Church, Market. Malmesbury: Abbey Church, Cross, Charlton Park.

Hotels or Inns at places marked *.

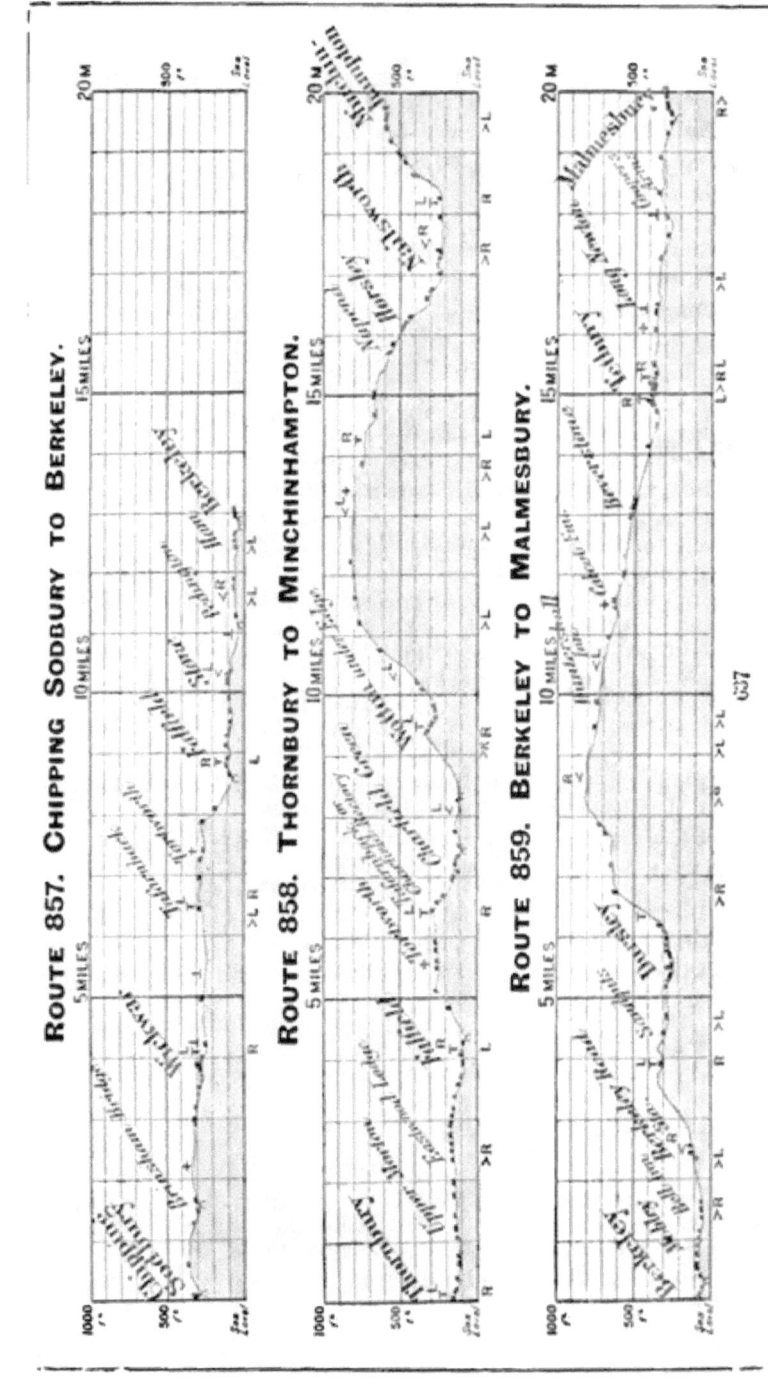

ROUTE 857. CHIPPING SODBURY TO BERKELEY.

ROUTE 858. THORNBURY TO MINCHINHAMPTON.

ROUTE 859. BERKELEY TO MALMESBURY.

860 FARINGDON TO EVESHAM.

Description.—Class II. After the steep hill out of Faringdon, the road has fairly good surface though inclined to be loose to Burford, whence poorer to Stow-on-the-Wold. The road then continues in a poor state for five miles, when the Oxford road is joined ; thereafter the surface improves, but is rough on the dangerous descent to Broadway Thence fine surface to Evesham.

Gradients.—(†*Dangerous.*) At ¼m. 1 in 15; 11¼m. 1 in 12†; 11¾m. 1 in 13; 19¼m. 1 in 14; 20½m. 1 in 11†; 22m. 1 in 17; 30m. 1 in 11†; 35¼m. 1 in 17.

Milestones.—Measured from Faringdon and from Evesham.

Measurements.

Faringdon,* Market.						
5⅝	Black Bourton.*					
11¼	5⅝	Burford.*				
15½	9⅞	4¼	Merrymouth Inn.*			
21	15⅜	9¾	5½	Stow-on-the-Wold.*		
31½	25⅞	20¼	16	10½	Broadway,* Lygon Arms.	
37⅛	31½	25⅞	21⅝	16⅛	5⅝	Evesham,* Town Clock.

Principal Objects of Interest.—Burford: Church. Stow: Church. EVESHAM: Bell Tower, Battlefield 1265.

Hotels or Inns at places marked *, and at Radcot, Clanfield, Ganborough, Fish, Wickhamford.

861 CIRENCESTER TO BURFORD.

Description.—Class II. An undulating road of rather poor surface, and some short steep hills.

Gradients.—At 5½m. 1 in 15; 6¾m. 1 in 20; 7½m. 1 in 15; 9¼m. 1 in 19; 10m. 1 in 16.

Milestones.—Measured from Cirencester.

Measurements.

Cirencester,* Town Hall.				
4⅛	Barnsley.*			
6⅞	2¾	Bibury.*		
10½	6⅜	3⅝	Aldsworth,* Inn.	
16¾	12⅝	9⅞	6¼	Burford.*

Principal Objects of Interest.—Dreary road. Burford: Church.

Hotels or Inns at places marked*.

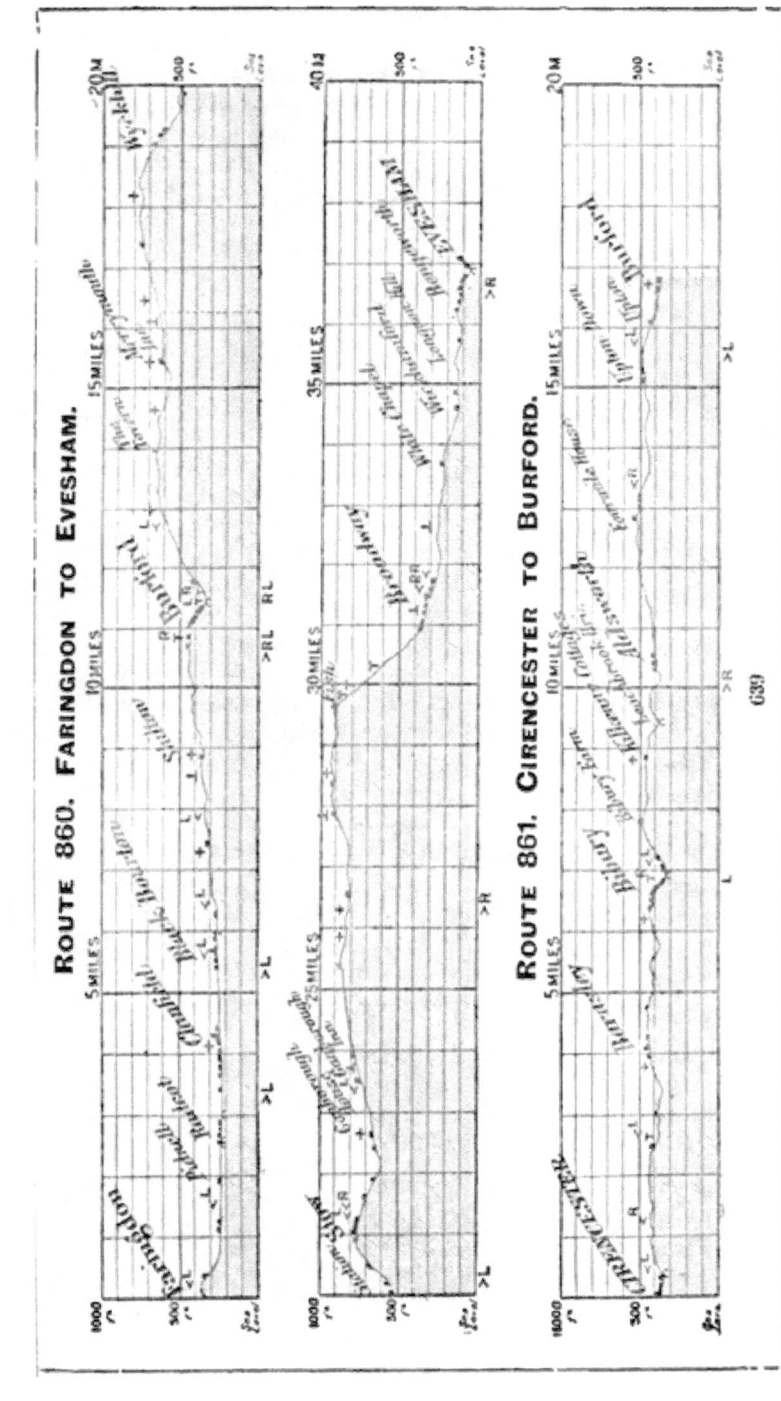

ROUTE 860. FARINGDON TO EVESHAM.

ROUTE 861. CIRENCESTER TO BURFORD.

862 Bristol to Thornbury or Berkeley.

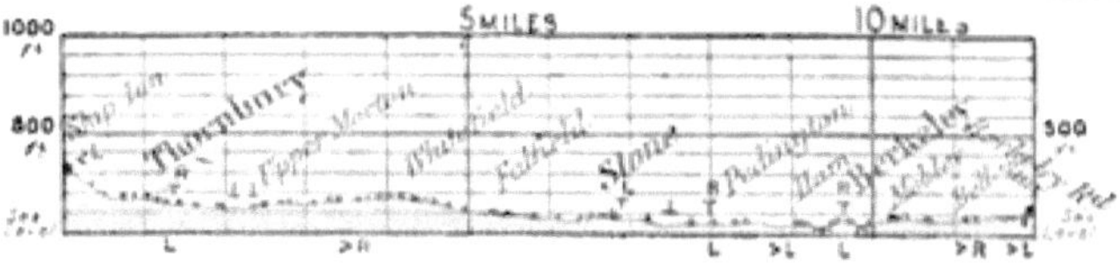

Description.—Class I. For Thornbury, as R. 855 to Ship Inn. For Berkeley, as R. 855 to Stone. From Gloucester to Berkeley, as R. 855 to Berkeley Road Station. For Thornbury, to Stone as R. 855. Fine surface. The direct road between Thornbury and Berkeley, shown below, has only fair surface.

Gradients.—At ½m. 1 in 14.

Measurements.

Bristol,* Bridge.
10¾ Ship Inn.*
12 1¼ Thornbury,* The Plain.
17½ 6¾ 5½ Stone.*
20⅜ 9⅝ 8⅜ 2⅞ Berkeley.*
22¾ 12 10¾ 5¼ 2⅜ Berkeley Road Station.*
36½ 24⅞ 23½ 17⅝ 16⅛ 13¾ Gloucester,* Cross.

Direct Road.

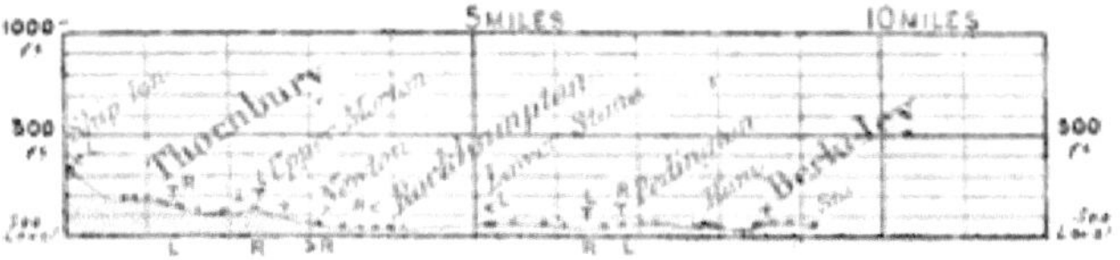

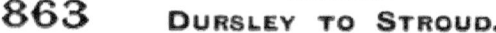

Measurements.—Bristol,* Bridge.
10¾ Ship Inn.*
12 1¼ Thornbury,* The Plain.
19¼ 8½ 7¼ Berkeley.*

Principal Objects of Interest.—Thornbury: Church, Castle. Berkeley: Castle.

863 Dursley to Stroud.

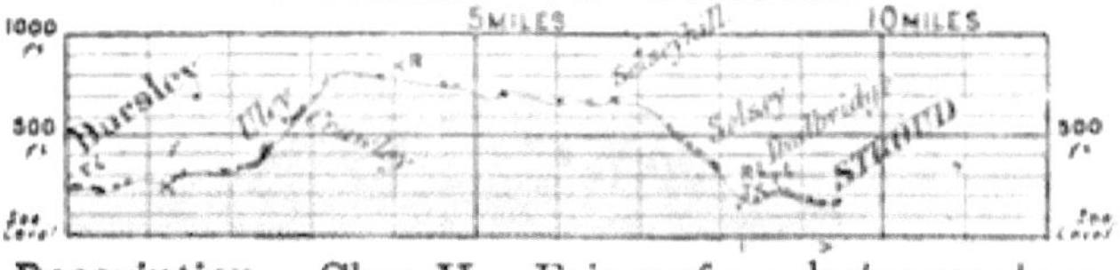

Description.—Class II. Fair surface, but very steep.

Gradients.—At 1¼m. 1 in 13; 3m. 1 in 8; 7¼m. 1 in 12; 8m. 1 in 10. All dangerous.

Milestones.—Measured from Dursley and Stroud.

Measurements.—Dursley,* Market House.
2⅜ Uley,* Crown Inn.
9½ 7⅛ Stroud.*

Principal Objects of Interest.—Pretty country.

GLOUCESTER TO WOOTON. 864

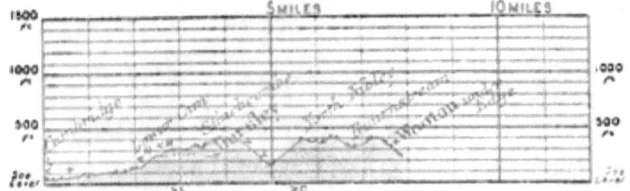

Description.—Class III. Good surface, but a very hilly road, with dangerous hills. Follow Route 855 to Cambridge Inn. For Dursley turn to L., 2½m. beyond Cambridge.

Gradients.—(†*Dangerous.*) *From Cambridge.*—At 2¼m. 1 in 15; 4¾m.1 in 10†; 5½m.1 in 13†; 6½m.1 in 16; 6¼m.1 in 14; 7m.1 in 12†; 7¼m.1 in 13†.

Milestones.—Continuation of those on R. 855.

Measurements.

Gloucester,* Cross.
10¾ Cambridge Inn.*
(14¼ 3½ Dursley,* Market House;) or
18¾ 7¼ Wooton-under-Edge.*

Principal Objects of Interest.—Dursley: Market House, 5½m., Tyndale's Monument.

Hotels or Inns at places marked*.

TEWKESBURY TO PERSHORE. 865

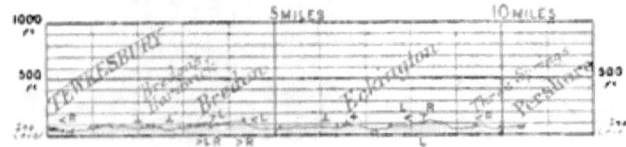

Description.—Class II. An undulating country road, with good surface.

Gradients.—At 4½m. 1 in 19; 7 & 7½m. 1 in 18.

Milestones. — Measured from Tewkesbury, and from Pershore.

Measurements.

Tewkesbury.*
6½ Eckington.*
10½ 4 Pershore.*

Principal Objects of Interest.—Pershore: Church.

Hotels or Inns at places marked *.

867 CIRENCESTER TO STROUD, &C.

Description.—Class II. Excellent surface the whole way; ferry at Newnham (¼m.).

Gradients.—At 1½m. 1/16; 4½m. 1/22; 8¼m. 1/11 (dangerous).

Milestones.—Measured from Cirencester Market, to White Horse, thence from Stroud Town Hall.

Measurements.

Cirencester,* Church.
16⅝ White Horse Inn.*
12⅜ 5¾ Stroud,* Town Hall.
18½ 11⅞ 6⅛ Claypits. R. 855.
25 18⅜ 12⅝ 6½ Newnham.*

Principal Objects of Interest.—1¼m., Agricultural College, Oakley Park. STROUD: Town Hall, Library. Fretherne: Church, Court. Newnham: Forest of Dean.

868 CIRENCESTER TO SODBURY.

Description.—Class II. The Bristol road. The road has fine surface throughout.

Gradients.—At ½m. 1 in 20; 4m. 1 in 23; 5m. 1 in 19; 10¼m. 1 in 14; 20m. 1 in 17; 21m. 1 in 18; 22½m. 1 in 16.

Milestones.—Measured from Cirencester Mkt. to Dunkirk.

Measurements.

Cirencester,* Church.
10¼ Tetbury.*
14⅝ 4⅜ Knockdown Inn.*
21¼ 11⅜ 7 Crosshands. R. 827.
24½ 14⅜ 9¾ 2¾ Sodbury,* Clock.
36⅝ 26¼ 21⅝ 14⅝ 11⅞ Bristol.* R. 853.

Principal Objects of Interest.—3m., Thames Canal. Tetbury: Church, Market, Beverstone Castle.

869 CIRENCESTER TO CHIPPENHAM.

Description.—Class II. This is a fine road throughout, with only one steep hill. This is the best road to Bath.

Gradients.—At ½m. 1 in 20; 4½m. 1 in 18; 4¾m. 1 in 14; 11m. 1 in 17; 20m. 1 in 24.

Milestones.—From Cirencester Market for 4m., then from Malmesbury Cross to Stanton, whence from Chippenham Br.

Measurements.

Cirencester,* Church.
8 Crudwell.
11½ 3½ Malmesbury,* Market.
21¼ 13¼ 9¾ Chippenham,* Market Place.
34 26 22½ 13 Bath.* R. 850.

Principal Objects of Interest.—3m., Thames Canal. Malmesbury: Cross, Abbey House, Wall.

Hotels or Inns at places marked*.

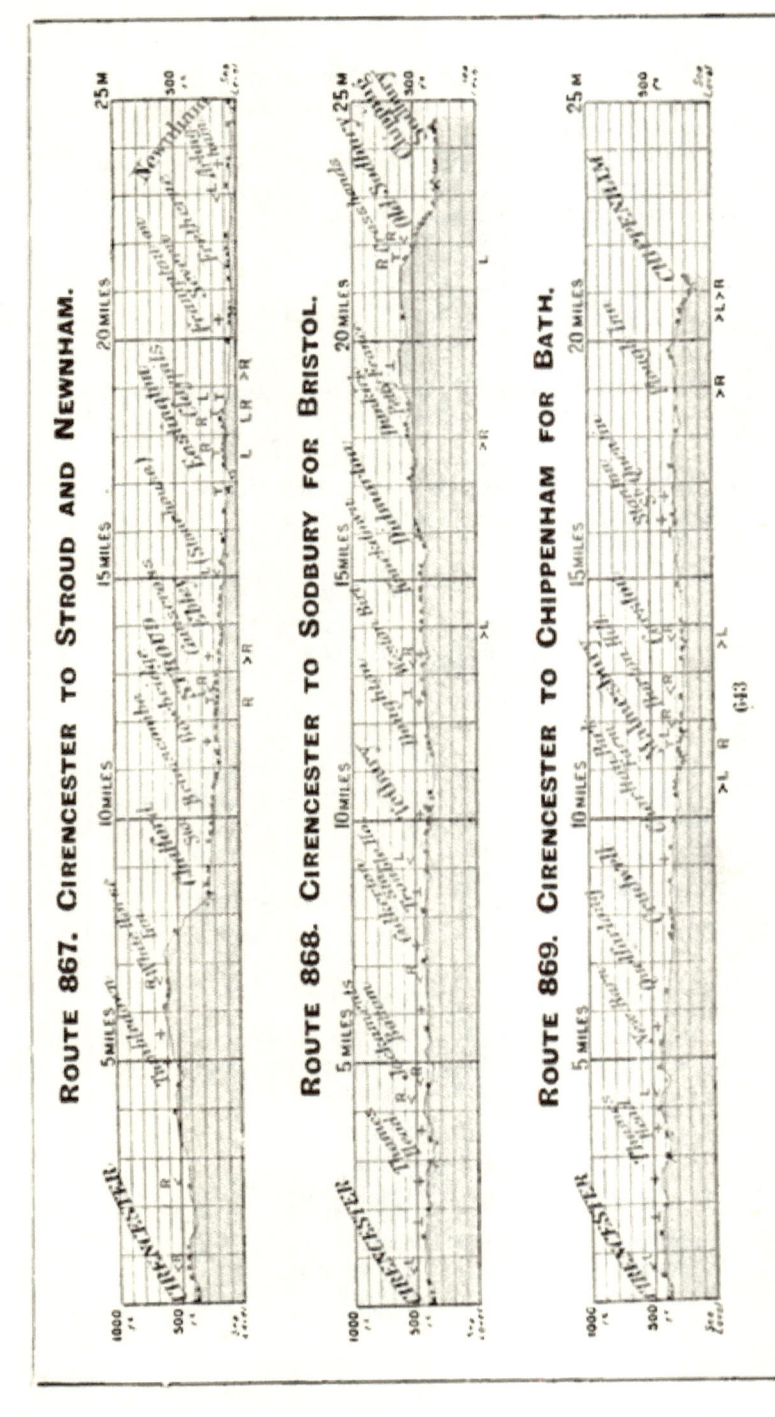

ROUTE 867. CIRENCESTER TO STROUD AND NEWNHAM.

ROUTE 868. CIRENCESTER TO SODBURY FOR BRISTOL.

ROUTE 869. CIRENCESTER TO CHIPPENHAM FOR BATH.

643

870 CIRENCESTER TO STOW-ON-THE-WOLD.

Description.—Class III.   An exceedingly hilly, and slightly rough road the whole way.   As the road is mostly quite straight, many of the hills are not very dangerous.

Gradients.—(*All dangerous*).   At 5m. 1 in 12; 7m. 1 in 8; 7½m. 1 in 7; 10 and 10½m. 1 in 11; 11m. 1 in 10; 12½m. 1 in 11; 13½m. 1 in 12; 14¾m. 1 in 13; 18¾m. 1 in 11.

Milestones.—Measured from Cirencester Church.

Measurements.

Cirencester,* Church.
7¼ Fossbridge.*
(10½ 3¼ Northleach.*)
18⅝ 11⅝ 9¼ Stow,* Unicorn Inn.

Principal Objects of Interest.—6m., Foss Cross.   8½m., Stowell Park.   Northleach: Prison.   Stow: Church.

Hotels or Inns at places marked*, and at Foss Cross.

871 CHELTENHAM TO CIRENCESTER.

Description. Class II.   After the dangerous hill out of Charlton Kings, the road has fine surface to Cirencester.

Gradients.—At 3m. 1 in 12-14 (dangerous).

Milestones.—Measured from Plough Hotel, Cheltenham.

Measurements.

Cheltenham,* Town Clock.
7½ Colesborne.*
11¾ 3¾ North Cerney.*
15½ 8 4⅛ Cirencester,* Church.

Principal Objects of Interest. - Seven Springs, one source of Thames.   CIRENCESTER: Abbey Church, Town Hall, Museum, Agricultural College, Oakley Park.

Hotels or Inns where marked*, and at Perrot's Brook, &c.

872 CHELTENHAM TO BROADWAY.

Description.—Class II.   Steep and dangerous to Winchcomb, thence excellent surface to Broadway.

Gradients.—(†*Dangerous*.) At 3¾m. 1 in 10†; 5m. 1 in 13†; 6m. 1 in 16.

Milestones.—Measured from Plough Hotel, Cheltenham.

Measurements.

Cheltenham,* Town Clock.
7½ Winchcomb.*
15½ 8 Broadway,* Lygon Arms.

Principal Objects of Interest.—2½m., Southam House. Winchcomb: Sudeley Castle.   Broadway: pretty district.

Hotels or Inns at places marked*, and at Prestbury, &c.

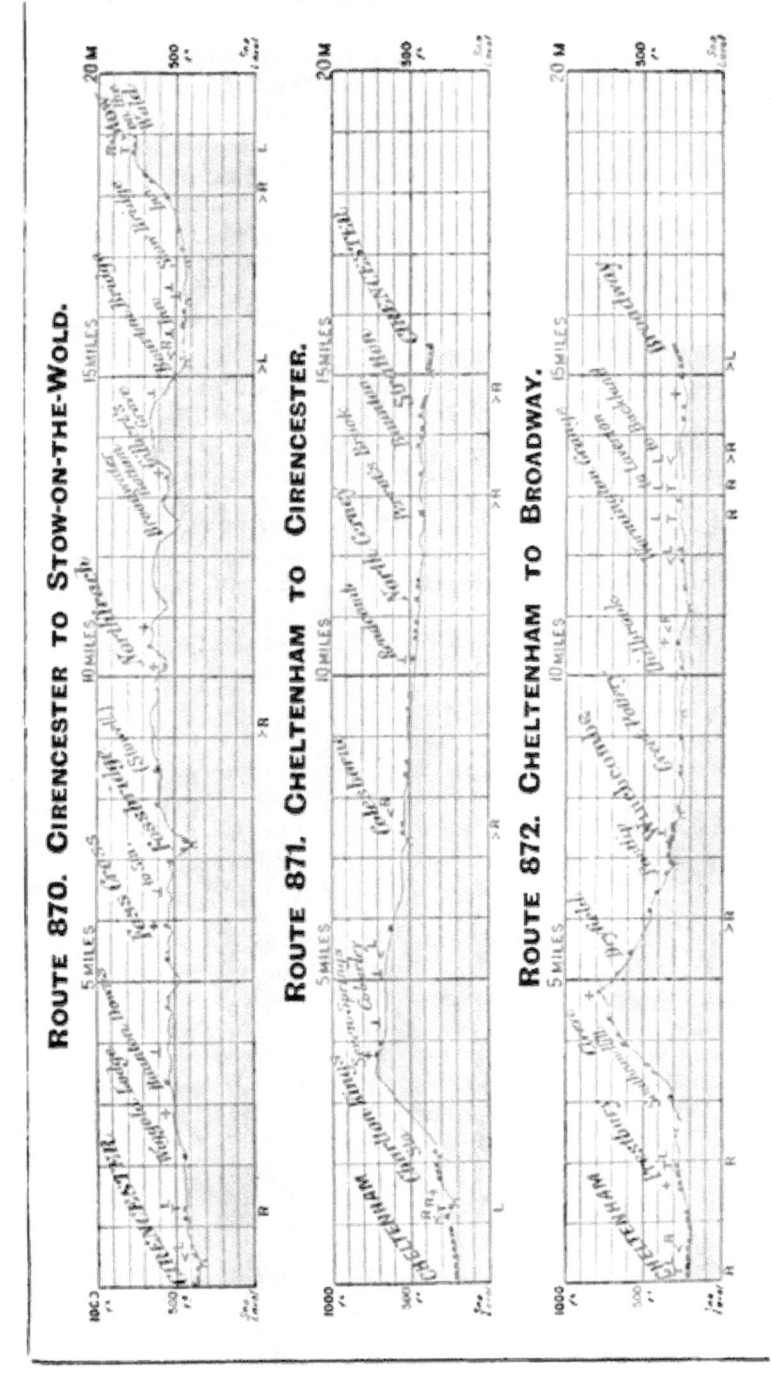

ROUTE 870. CIRENCESTER TO STOW-ON-THE-WOLD.

ROUTE 871. CHELTENHAM TO CIRENCESTER.

ROUTE 872. CHELTENHAM TO BROADWAY.

873 CHELTENHAM TO STRATFORD-ON-AVON.

Description.—Class II. With the exception of several slight hills the road is almost level, with splendid surface to Evesham; thereafter it becomes rather more hilly, and near Stratford there is a dangerous hill. Excellent surface.

Gradients.—At 12¼m. 1 in 18; 12½m. 1 in 14; 17m. 1 in 23; 20½ and 23m. 1 in 13; 24m. 1 in 17; 29¼m. 1 in 10 (dangerous).

Milestones.—Irregular to Beckford, then from Evesham Bridge.

Measurements.

Cheltenham,* Town Clock.					
9⅛	Beckford,* Hotel.				
12⅝	3½	Sedgebarrow.*			
16¼	7⅛	3⅝	Evesham,* Clock.		
23¾	14⅝	11⅛	7½	Bidford,* Church.	
30¾	21⅝	18⅛	14½	7	Stratford-on-Avon.*

Principal Objects of Interest.—EVESHAM: Battlefield, 1265, Bell Tower. Bidford: Bridge. STRATFORD: Shakespeare Memorial, Church, Anne Hathaway's Cottage, &c.

Hotels or Inns at places marked *, and numerous others.

874 CHELTENHAM TO MALVERN.

Description.—Class II. Splendid surface to Upton, then a good road, but rather steep through Malvern Wells. Route 920 is shorter from Upton, but not so good.

Gradients.—At 9½ and 21½m. 1 in 15.

Milestones.—Measured from Town Hall, Cheltenham.

Measurements.

Cheltenham,* Town Clock.				
8⅝	Tewkesbury.*			
15¾	7⅛	Upton.*		
21⅝	13	5⅞	Malvern Wells,* Hornyold Arms Hotel.	
23⅝	15	7⅞	2	Malvern,* Bellevue Terrace.

Principal Objects of Interest.—6m., Deerhurst Church to W. TEWKESBURY: Battlefield, 1471, Abbey. MALVERN: Spa, Priory Church, St. Anne's Well, Malvern Hills, &c.

875 CHELTENHAM TO LEDBURY.

Description.—Class II. A good undulating country road.

Gradients.—At 10¼m. 1 in 21; 15m. 1 in 16; 19 & 20½m. 1 in 13.

Measurements.

Cheltenham,* Town Clock.				
4¾	Coombe Hill.*			
9½	4¾	Haw Bridge.*		
13¼	8½	3¾	Staunton.*	
22	17¼	12½	8¾	Ledbury,* Market House.

Principal Objects of Interest.—Ledbury: Market House. Church, Eastnor Castle.

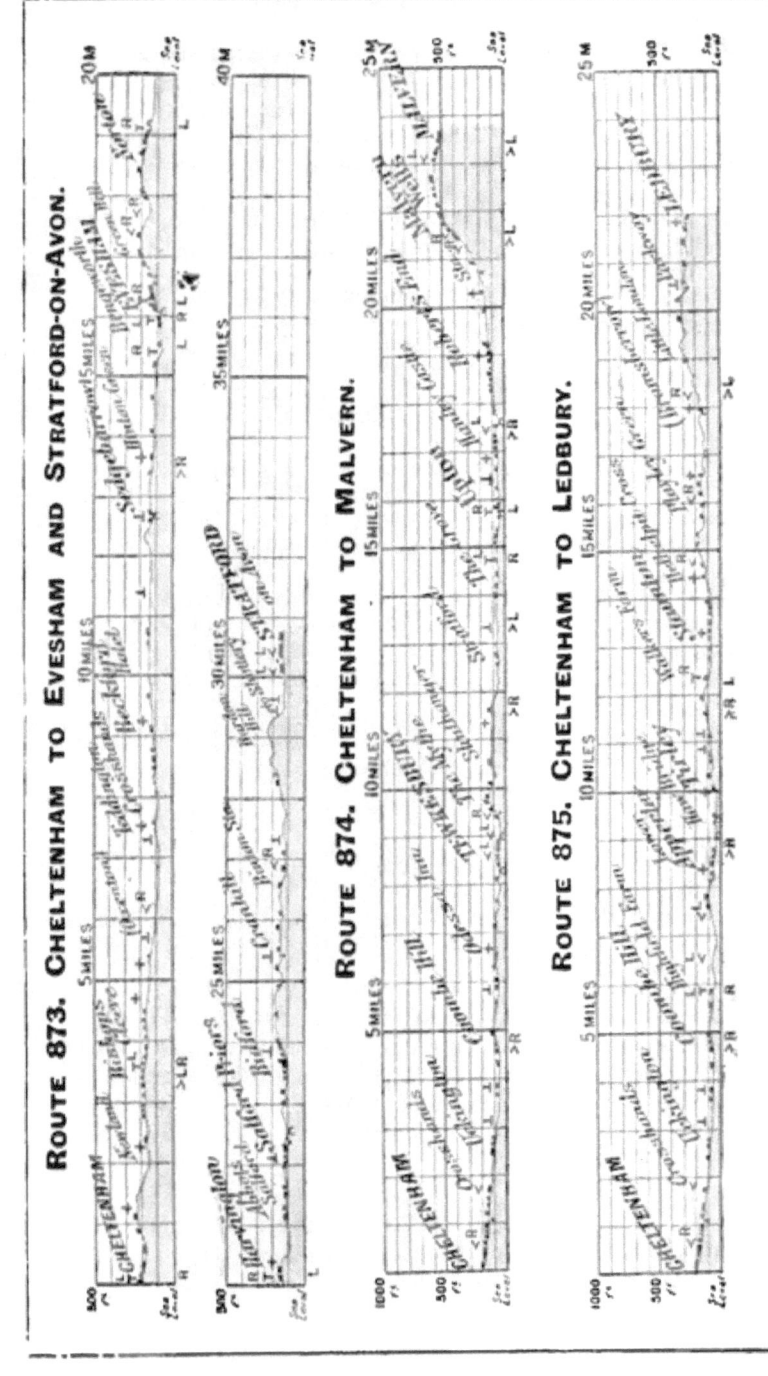

ROUTE 873. CHELTENHAM TO EVESHAM AND STRATFORD-ON-AVON.

ROUTE 874. CHELTENHAM TO MALVERN.

ROUTE 875. CHELTENHAM TO LEDBURY.

876 CHELTENHAM TO HEREFORD.

Description.—Class I. The road has excellent surface from Cheltenham to Gloucester, but near these towns it is generally very bumpy. After Gloucester, the road, though slightly hilly, has fine surface throughout, and is much to be preferred to the more direct roads which are much steeper.

Gradients.—At 17 & 18m. 1 in 20; 19½m. 1 in 18; 20½m. 1 in 22; 22¼m. 1 in 17; 26¼m. 1 in 22; 31¼ & 35½m. 1 in 18.

Milestones.—Measured from Town Clock, Cheltenham. Beyond Gloucester, from Gloucester Bridge as far as Harewood End, whence from Hereford Cross.

Measurements.

Cheltenham,* Town Clock.						
8¾	Gloucester,* Cross.					
17⅝	8⅞	Dursley Cross.*				
20¾	12	3⅛	Lea.*			
25¼	16½	7⅝	4½	Ross,* Market House.		
30⅜	21⅝	12¾	9⅝	5⅛	Harewood End.*	
39¾	31	22⅛	19	14½	9⅜	Hereford,* Town Hall.

Principal Objects of Interest.—GLOUCESTER: Cathedral, Guildhall, Museum, Public Park, Llanthony Priory. Dursley Cross: Longhope. ROSS: Church, Market Hall. 26m., Wilton Castle (ruin). 28¼m., Winters Cross. HEREFORD: Cathedral, Bridge, Shire Hall, Castle Green, Nelson Monument, White Cross.

Hotels or Inns at places marked*, and at Staverton Bridge, Over, Birdwood, Weston, Wilton, Peterstow, &c.

877 TEWKESBURY TO LEDBURY.

Description.—Class II. A good road for eight miles, then very hilly.

Gradients.—At 2½m. 1 in 22; 5½m. 1 in 15; 7 & 9m. 1 in 17; 9¾m. 1 in 13 (dangerous); 10¼m. 1 in 17; 13¾m. 1 in 21.

Milestones.—Measured from Tewkesbury to Hollybush, then from Ledbury Cross-roads.

Measurements.

Tewkesbury.*			
8½	Duke of York Inn.*		
11¾	3⅝	Eastnor.*	
14	5⅞	2¼	Ledbury,* Market House.

Principal Objects of Interest.—1m., Mythe Bridge. Eastnor: Castle, Bransill Castle, Hollybush Hill. LEDBURY: Church, Market House.

Hotels or Inns at places marked*.

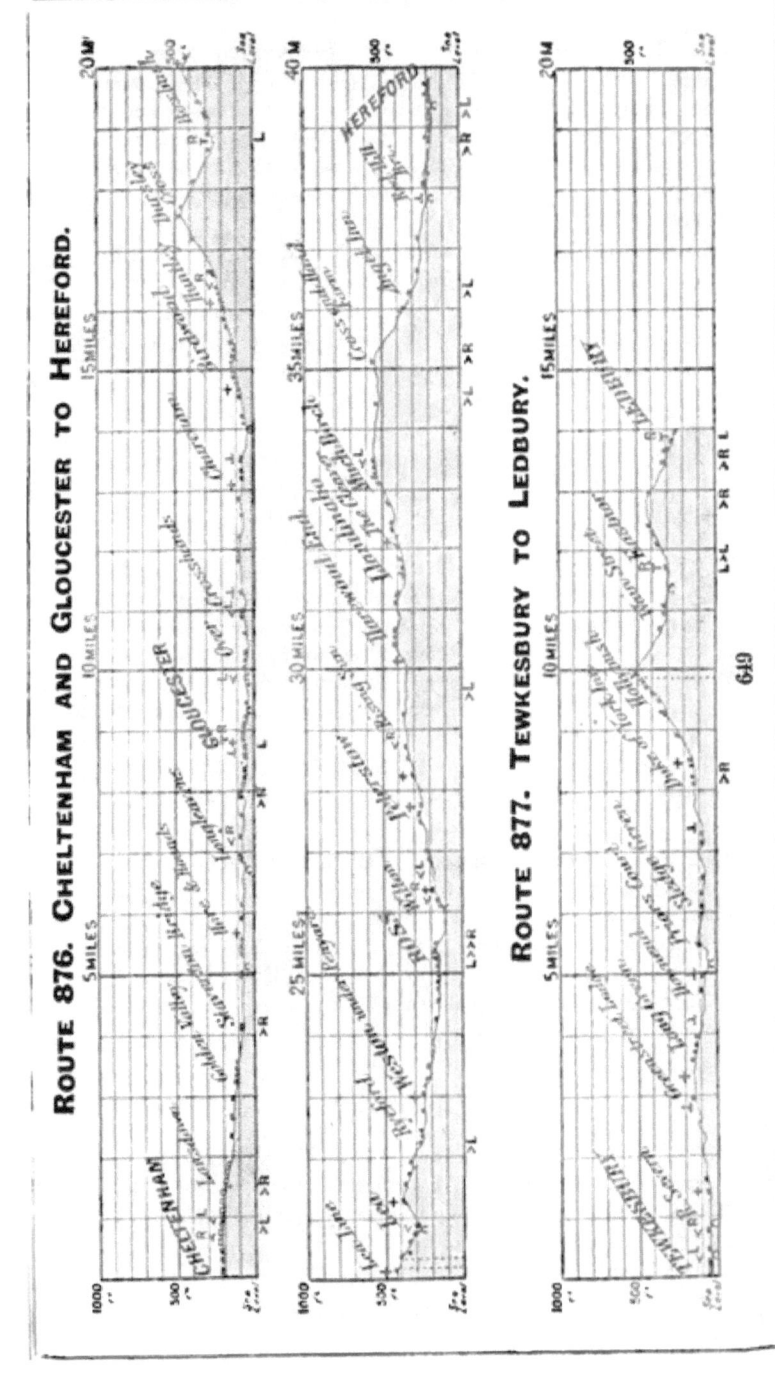

ROUTE 876. CHELTENHAM AND GLOUCESTER TO HEREFORD.

ROUTE 877. TEWKESBURY TO LEDBURY.

649

878 TEWKESBURY TO STOW.

Description.—Class II. Fine surface to Stanway, then a very steep road, with dangerous hills.

Gradients.—(† *Dangerous.*) At 12m. 1 in 13†; 13½m. 1 in 9†; 15m. 1 in 12†; 15½m. 1 in 16; 19m. 1 in 14; 20½m. 1 in 14.

Milestones.—Measured from Gloucester as far as Stanway, thereafter from Stow.

Measurements.

Tewkesbury.*			
4⅝	Teddington,* Cross Hands.		
13⅞	9¼	Ford.*	
21	16⅜	7⅛	Stow,* Unicorn Inn.

Principal Objects of Interest.—4⅝m., Teddington Stone. 9½m., Toddington House. Stow: Church.

Hotels or Inns at places marked *, and at Aston Cross, Hobnails Inn, &c.

---

879 GLOUCESTER TO MALMESBURY.

Description.—Class II. The first diagram shows the main route to both Stroud and Malmesbury, the second indicates the old direct road by Stroud and Minchinhampton. The first road has excellent surface throughout, and has only one steep hill at Avening. The second has also good surface, but the hills are dangerous.

Gradients.—(† *Dangerous.*) At 18m. 1 in 14. Second route. 5½m. 1 in 13†; 7¼m. 1 in 14†; 11¾m. 1 in 9†; 12½m. 1 in 8†; 15½m. 1 in 12†; 16m. 1 in 13.

Milestones.—Measured from Gloucester Cross Roads to Cainscross, whence from Stroud on to Nailsworth.

Measurements.

Gloucester,* Cross.				
9¼	Stonehouse,* Woolpack Inn.			
(12¼	3	Stroud,* Town Hall.)		
15	5¾	4⅛	Nailsworth,* George Hotel.	
21¼	12	10⅝	6¼	Tetbury.*
26⅛	16⅞	15¼	11⅛	4⅞ Malmesbury.*

By Minchinhampton.

Gloucester,* Cross.			
9⅜	Stroud,* Town Hall.		
13⅝	4¼	Minchinhampton.*	
19⅜	10	5¾	Tetbury.*
24¼	14⅞	10⅝	4⅞ Malmesbury.*

Principal Objects of Interest.—STROUD: Town Hall, Library. Woodchester: Park, R.C. Priory. Minchinhampton: Ch. Avening: Ch. Tetbury: Ch., Market, Beverstone Castle. Malmesbury: Abbey House, Market Cross, Wall.

Hotels or Inns at places marked*, &c., &c.

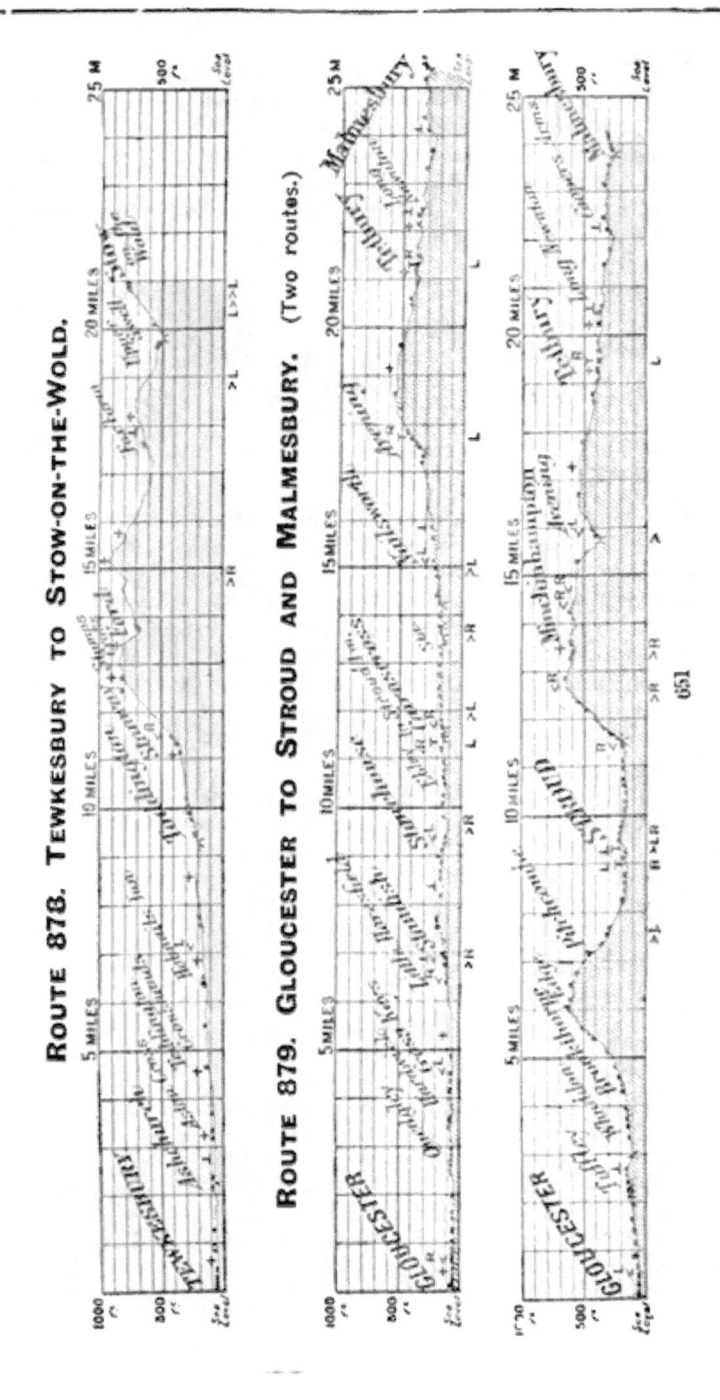

ROUTE 878. TEWKESBURY TO STOW-ON-THE-WOLD.

ROUTE 879. GLOUCESTER TO STROUD AND MALMESBURY. (Two routes.)

880   Gloucester to Faringdon.

Description.—Class I. The London Road. Although this has the highly dangerous Birdlip Hill, it is the best road to London, as the surface is rather better than the road by Northleach. Splendid surface throughout, especially between Cirencester and Faringdon.

Gradients.—At 6½m. 1 in 7 (highly dangerous); 8m. 1 in 17; 9½m. 1 in 14; 12½m. 1 in 18; 15½m. 1 in 16; 35½m. 1 in 20.

Milestones.—London milestones to Witcombe, then from Cirencester; after Cirencester from London.

Measurements.

Gloucester,* Cross.
6¾ Birdlip.*
16½ 10 Cirencester,* Church.
25½ 18¾ 8¾ Fairford,* Market.
29½ 23 13 4½ Lechlade,* Market.
35½ 29 19 10½ 6 Faringdon,* Market.
53 46½ 36½ 27½ 23½ 17½ Oxford.* R. 493.

To Oxford by Cheltenham and Northleach, 49¾m.

Principal Objects of Interest. — Birdlip: Magnificent view. Cirencester: Abbey Church, Town Hall, Museum, Agricultural College, Oakley Park. Fairford: Church Window. Lechlade: Church. Faringdon: Church, House.

Hotels or Inns at places marked *, and at Crosshands, Smith's Cross, Stratton, Poulton, Buscot, &c.

881   Gloucester to Evesham.

Description.—Class II. A splendid road throughout. It is somewhat undulating as far as Tewkesbury, but after that, with the exception of one hill at Sedgebarrow, it is practically level.

Gradients.—At 20m. 1 in 19; 20½m. 1 in 14.

Milestones.—Measured from Tewkesbury, beyond which from Evesham Bridge.

Measurements.

Gloucester,* Cross.
6½ Coombe Hill.*
10½ 3¾ Tewkesbury.*
16½ 9¾ 6½ Beckford Hotel.*
23⅞ 17 13½ 7½ Evesham,* Clock.

Principal Objects of Interest.—8m., Deerhurst Church to west. 10m., Tewkesbury Battlefield, 1471. Tewkesbury: Abbey. Teddington: Cross. Evesham: Bell Tower, Battlefield, 1265.

Hotels or Inns at places marked *, and at Norton, Odessa Inn, Sedgebarrow, &c.

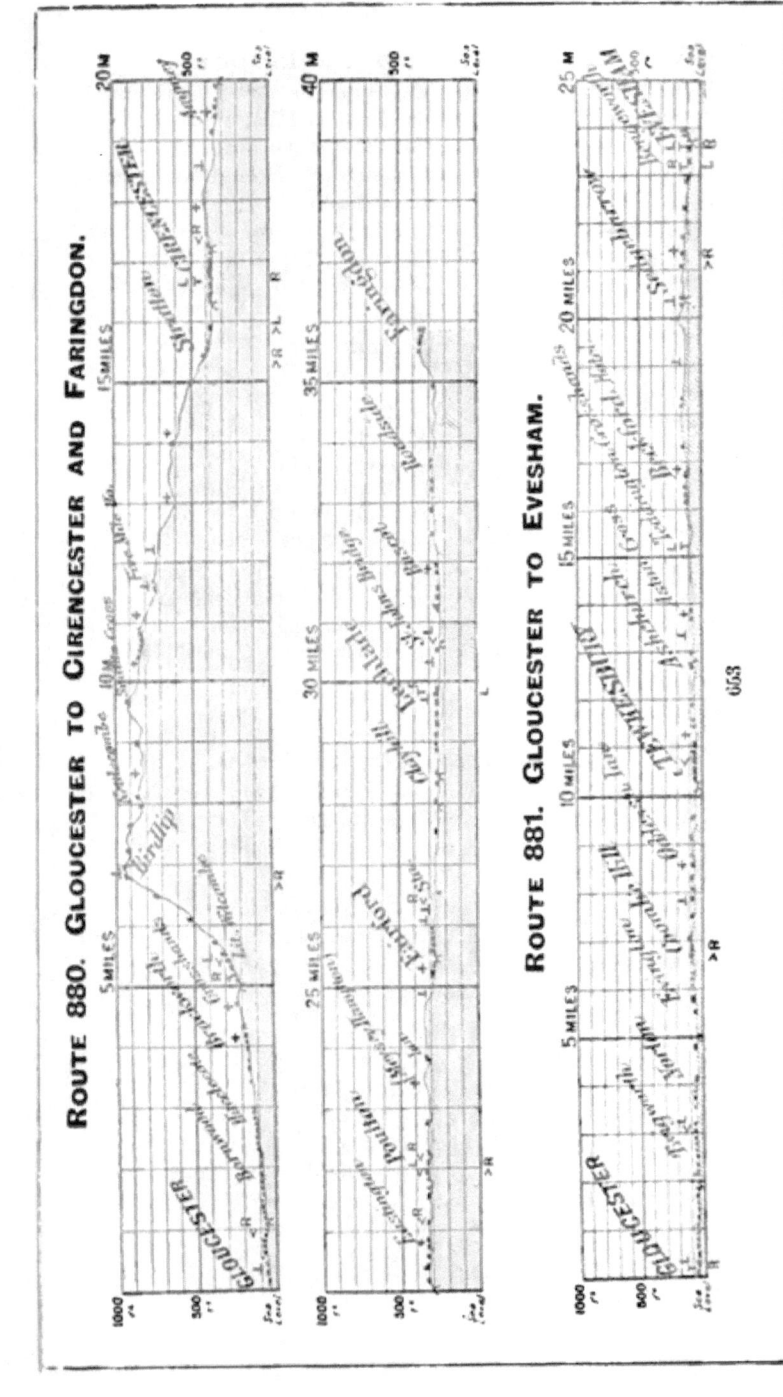

ROUTE 880. GLOUCESTER TO CIRENCESTER AND FARINGDON.

ROUTE 881. GLOUCESTER TO EVESHAM.

882 GLOUCESTER TO CHIPPING NORTON.

Description.—Class I. & III. The best road from Gloucester to Andoversford is through Cheltenham, the more direct road being dangerously steep, as shown at foot. Fine surface all the way to Andoversford, although the road near Cheltenham is at times very bumpy. This part is the London road. After Andoversford the road has fair surface all the way to Chipping Norton, but there are quite a number of steep and dangerous hills as far as Stow, but these can mostly be avoided by following a side road past Notgrove Station. From Stow to Chipping Norton, the direct road, shown dotted, is very steep; the longer route by Churchhill, that is usually followed, avoids the steep hills, and has excellent surface. There is another and almost better road by Adlestrop Station and Kingham to Churchhill. As a through route this road cannot be recommended; the road by Burford and Witney is much easier when going eastwards.

Gradients.—(† *Dangerous.*) At 13½m. 1/23; 16½m. 1/11†; 20m. 1/17; 21¾m. 1/16; 22¼m. 1/12†; 23¼m. 1/11†; 24m. 1/10†; 24½m. 1/14; 25½m. 1/11†; 26¾m. 1/16; 32¾m. 1/18.

Direct road.—At 6½m. 1 in 11†; 9¼m. 1 in 17; 10¼m. 1 in 11†; 20½m. 1 in 21.

Milestones.—From Cheltenham, Town Clock, as far as Andoversford; thereafter from Stow, but not very accurate.

Measurements.

Gloucester,* Cross.

8¾	Cheltenham,* Town Clock.					
14⅜	5⅝	Andoversford,* Inn.				
20¼	11½	5⅞	Naunton Inn.*			
26¼	17½	11⅞	6	Stow,* Unicorn Inn.		
30¼	21½	15⅞	10	4	Bledington.*	
36¼	27½	21⅞	16	10	6	Chipping Norton,* Town Hall.

Stow to Chipping Norton direct, 8⅝m.

Direct Road.

Gloucester,* Cross.

7¼	Air Balloon.*	
13½	6¼	Andoversford,* Inn.

Principal Objects of Interest.—CHELTENHAM: Spa. Promenade, Assembly Rooms, &c., &c. 12m., Cheltenham Reservoirs. Stow: Church. CHIPPING NORTON: Town Hall, Rollerich Stones.

Hotels or Inns at places marked*, and at Eyford, Church hill, &c.

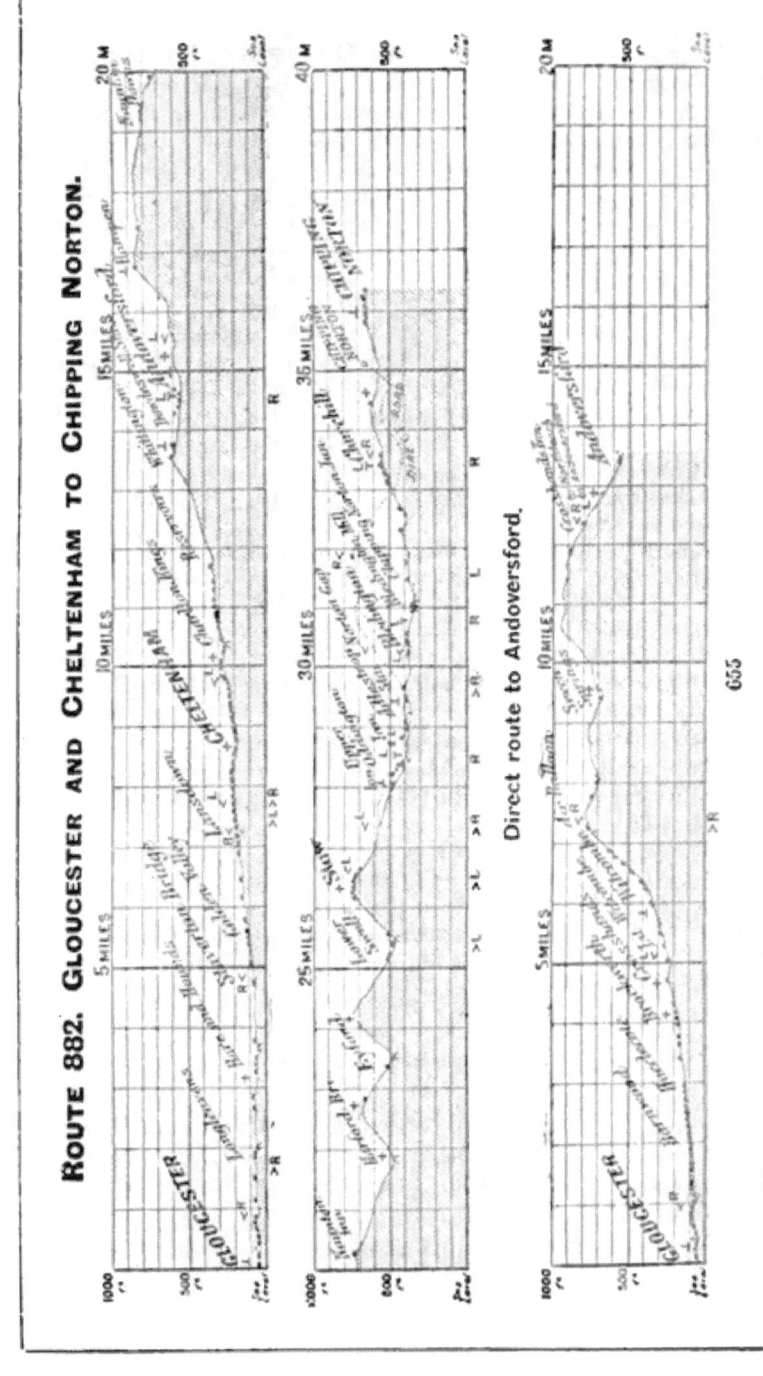

ROUTE 882. GLOUCESTER AND CHELTENHAM TO CHIPPING NORTON.

Direct route to Andoversford.

655

883 Gloucester to Upton.

Description.—Class III. This is not the main route, but a good country road on the west Bank of the Severn. The best road is Route 938.

Gradients.—At 4m. 1 in 21; 14m. 1 in 21; 16¾m. 1 in 19.

Milestones.—Measured from Gloucester Bridge to Hartpury; then from Upton,—irregular.

Measurements.

Gloucester,* Cross.
9⅝ Green Dragon Inn.*
13¾ 4⅛ Longdon,* Inn.
17 7⅜ 3¼ Upton.*

Principal Objects of Interest.—Green Dragon Inn. 15m., Ham Court.

Hotels or Inns at places marked *, and at Hartpury, Long Green, &c.

884 Gloucester to Ledbury.

Description.—Class II. Of the two roads given, the shorter one by Staunton is usually chosen, but in the reverse direction from Ledbury to Gloucester; the road by Newent is perhaps easier. The surface on the two roads is very much the same, but the first is slightly less hilly than the second.

Gradients.—By Staunton.—At 4m. 1 in 21; 9m. 1 in 14; 10½m. 1 in 16; 14m. 1 in 13; 15m. 1 in 13.

By Newent.—9¾m. 1 in 14; 11½m. 1 in 17.

Milestones.—By Staunton.—Measured from Gloucester Bridge. By Newent.—Measured from Gloucester Bridge, as far as High Leadon; after Newent, from Ledbury Cross-roads.

Measurements.

Gloucester,* Cross.
5⅜ Hartpury,* Inn.
8 2⅝ Staunton.*
16¾ 11⅜ 8¾ Ledbury,* Market House.

By Newent.

Gloucester,* Cross.
9¼ Newent,* Market.
12⅝ 3⅜ Dymock.*
17⅜ 8¼ 4½ Ledbury,* Market House.

Principal Objects of Interest.—Barbersbridge, Monument. Newent: Market House, Church. Dymock: Market House. LEDBURY: Market Hall, Church, Eastnor Castle.

Hotels or Inns at places marked *, and at Over, Playley Green, &c., &c.

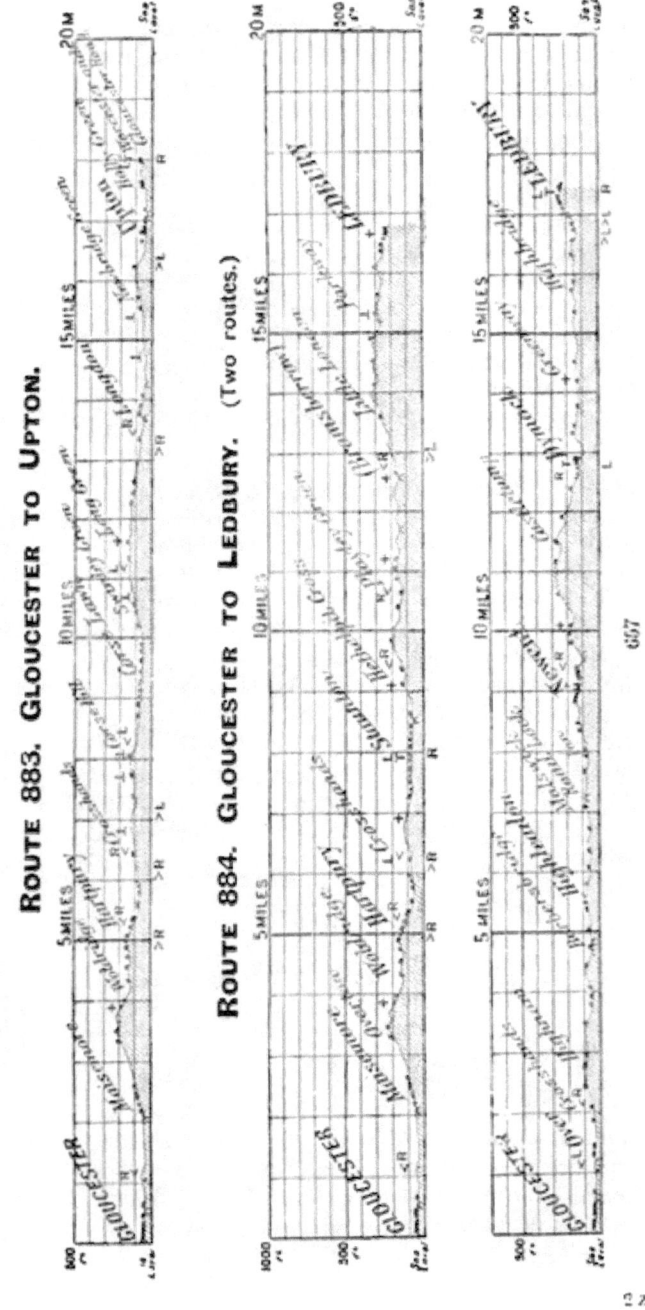

ROUTE 883. GLOUCESTER TO UPTON.

ROUTE 884. GLOUCESTER TO LEDBURY. (Two routes.)

657

2 Z

885 GLOUCESTER TO NEWPORT (Monmouth).

Description.—Class I. Although this seems a roundabout road, it is by far the best and quickest, owing to the hilly country intervening. The direct route to Monmouth *via* Coleford is shown below; the direct route to Newport is Route 886, but both are much steeper than this route.

From Gloucester to Ross, see Route 876; thereafter magnificent surface the whole way to Newport, but with a rough and dangerous hill at Whitchurch. The road by Coleford has fair surface, but dangerous hills; but from Coleford to Monmouth by Staunton is even better than by Redbrook.

Gradients.—(From Ross.) At ¾m. 1 in 13; 4m. 1 in 16; 4½m. 1 in 17; 6¾m. 1 in 10 (dangerous); 7¾m. 1 in 25; 20½m. 1 in 13; 22½ & 27m. 1 in 18.

By Coleford.—(From Westbury.) 2½m. 1 in 16; 4m. 1 in 11; 5m. 1 in 9; 5¼m. 1 in 12; 7½m. 1 in 9; 8¾ & 9¾m. 1 in 12; 12m. 1 in 20; 12½m. 1 in 14; 14¾m. 1 in 13; (all dangerous).

Milestones.—Measured from Market House, Ross, to Kerne Bridge; thereafter from Monmouth, Shire Hall.

Measurements.

Gloucester,* Cross.							
16½	Ross,* Market House.						
22½	6	Whitchurch,* Clock.					
26⅝	10⅛	4⅛	Monmouth,* Shire Hall.				
34¾	18¼	12¼	7⅝	Raglan.*			
39⅞	23⅜	17⅜	13	5¼	Usk.*		
47⅝	31⅛	25⅛	20¾	13	7¾	Caerleon.*	
50⅝	34⅛	28⅛	24	16¼	11	3¼	Newport,* Town Hall.

By Coleford.

Gloucester,* Cross.					
9⅜	Westbury-on-Severn,*				
14¾	5⅜	Cinderford,* Bridge Inn.			
16⅝	7¼	2	Speech House Hotel.*		
19¾	10⅜	5⅛	3⅛	Coleford,* Town Hall.	
26⅝	17½	12¼	10¼	7⅛	Monmouth,* Shire Hall.

Principal Objects of Interest.—Ross: Market Hall, Ch., Wilton Castle. Goodrich: Castle. Whitchurch: Symonds Yat. MONMOUTH: County Buildings, Troy House. Raglan: Castle. Usk: Castle. Llangibby: Castle. Caerleon: Llantarnam Abbey. NEWPORT: Castle, Docks, &c.

By Coleford.—Speech House: Verderers Court. Coleford: Buckstone. This is a beautiful road between Ross and Monmouth, but the beauty of the River Wye is best seen by sailing between these points in a boat.

Hotels or Inns at places marked*, and at Walford, Llangibby, &c.

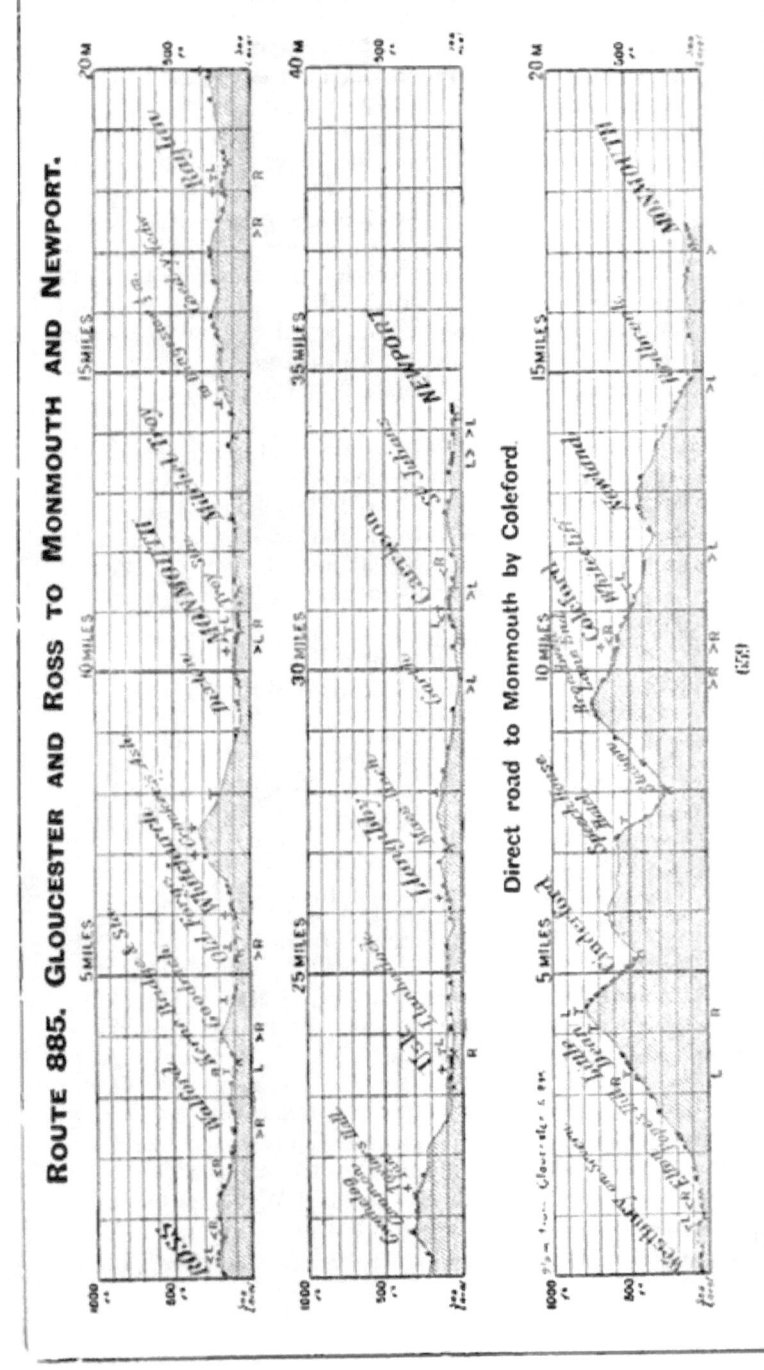

ROUTE 885. GLOUCESTER AND ROSS TO MONMOUTH AND NEWPORT.

Direct road to Monmouth by Coleford.

886 GLOUCESTER TO CARDIFF.

Description.—Class II. Although this is the direct road, it is exceedingly hilly between Newnham and Chepstow, and as these hills are very steep, the road round by Ross and Monmouth, Route 885, is much to be preferred. At first the surface is very good to Newnham, but after that there is a succession of steep and dangerous hills, but with very fair surface, to Chepstow; thereafter the road, though somewhat hilly as far as Caerwent, has very good surface, but is rather bumpy round about Newport and Cardiff, owing to heavy traffic.

Gradients.—Mostly dangerous. At 14m. 1 in 10; 14½m. 1 in 16; 15½m. 1 in 15; 16¼m. 1 in 12; 16¾m. 1 in 15; 17¼m. 1 in 21; 18m. 1 in 18; 19m. 1 in 10; 20½m. 1 in 12: 22 & 22¼m. 1 in 13; 26¼m. 1 in 21; 28m. 1 in 13; 29m. 1 in 12; 30m. 1 in 13; 31¼m. 1 in 14; 32¼m. 1 in 24; 33½m. 1 in 22; 35½m. 1 in 19; 38¼m. 1 in 18; 52m. 1 in 14; 53¾m. 1 in 17.

Milestones.—Measured from Gloucester Bridge as far as Newnham, thence from Chepstow, on as far as Newport, whence from Cardiff Town Hall.

Measurements.

Gloucester,* Cross.									
9⅜	Westbury-on-Severn.*								
12	2⅝	Newnham,* Town Hall.							
15¾	6⅜	3¾	Blakeney.*						
19¼	9⅞	7¼	3½	Lydney.*					
28½	19⅛	16½	12¾	9¼	Chepstow,* Beaufort Arms.				
33⅝	24¼	21⅝	17⅞	14⅜	5⅛	Caerwent.*			
44½	35⅛	32½	28¾	25¼	16	10⅞	Newport,* Town Hall.		
49⅞	40½	37⅞	34⅛	30⅝	21⅜	16¼	5⅜	Castletown.*	
56⅝	47	44⅜	40⅝	37⅛	27⅞	22¾	11⅞	6½	Cardiff,* Castle

Gloucester to Cardiff by Monmouth, R. 885, 62¾m.

Principal Objects of Interest.—Over: Bridge. Minsterworth: Ch. Tower. Newnham: pretty scenery on Severn. Blakeney: Severn Bridge. Lydney: Cross, Park. Chepstow: Castle, Wye Valley, Tintern Abbey. Caerwent: Roman remains, Caldicot Castle. Penhow: Castle. NEWPORT; Castle, Docks. St. Mellons: Church. CARDIFF: Castle, St. John's Church, Bute Docks, Tredegar Park, Penarth Docks, Barry Docks, &c., &c.

Hotels or Inns at places marked *, and at Hartlands Hill, Broadoak, Bullo, Aylburton, Stroat, Pwll Meyric, Penow, St. Mellons, Rumney, &c.

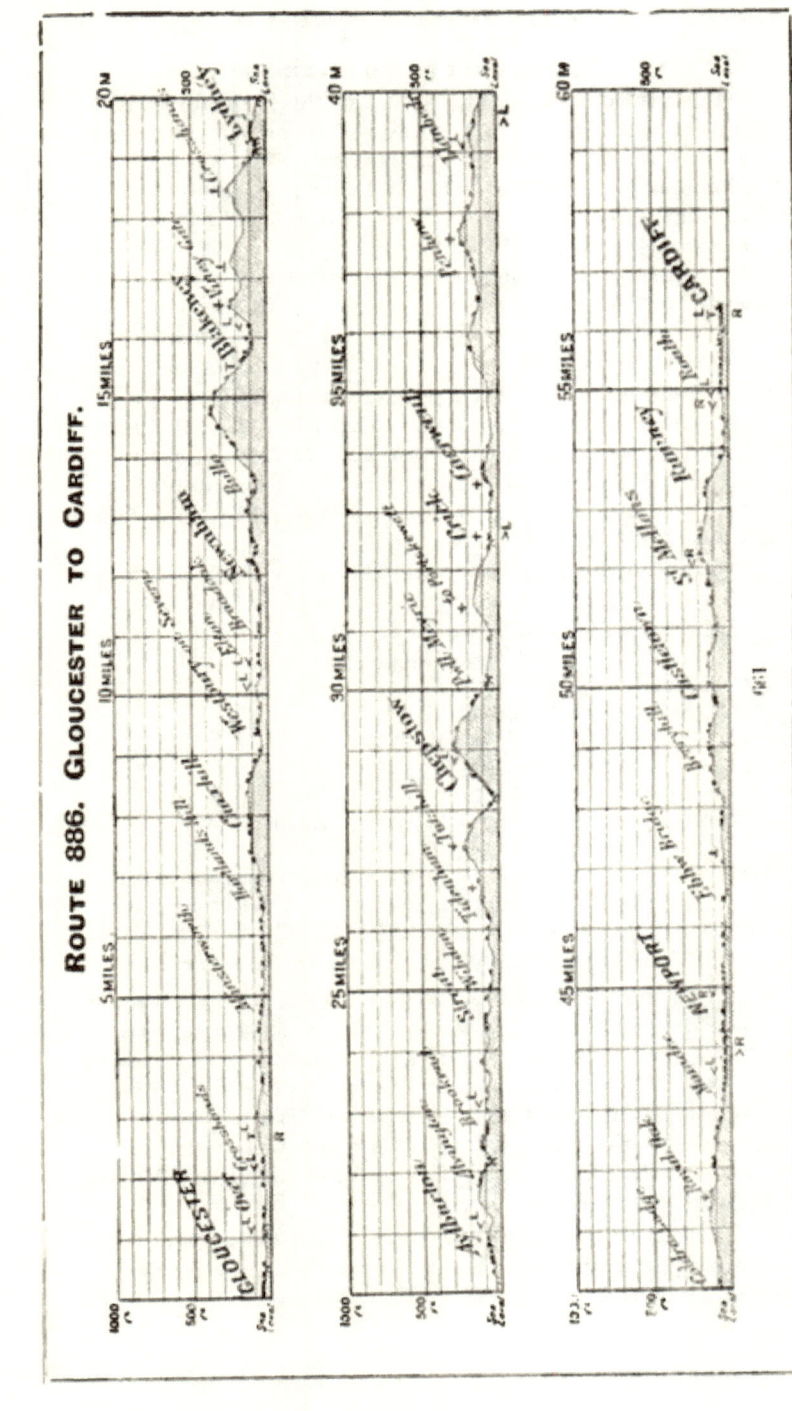

ROUTE 886. GLOUCESTER TO CARDIFF.

887 CHEPSTOW TO COLEFORD.

Description.—Class II. A fairly good country road, but very steep in parts. Another way is by Route 898 to Tintern; thence to St. Briavels, as shown by dotted line.

Gradients.—(*Dangerous.*) At ¾m. 1 in 13; 1¾m. 1 in 12; 3m. 1 in 16; 5½ & 6¼m. 1 in 12; 7¾m. 1 in 15; 11m. 1 in 16; 12m. 1 in 23.

Measurements.

Chepstow,* Beaufort Arms.
   8   St. Briavels.
  13½ 5¼ Coleford,* Town Hall.

Principal Objects of Interest.—Fine view of the Wye Valley at 2¾m. St. Briavels: Castle.

888 CHEPSTOW TO USK.

Description.—Class II. This road is finely engineered, and is kept in good order. After the first three miles the rise is very gradual.

Gradients.—At ¼m. 1 in 16; ¾m. 1 in 19; 2¼m. 1 in 20; 8m. 1 in 20; 9¾m. 1 in 17.

Measurements.

Chepstow,* Beaufort Arms.
  3¾ Mynyddbach Inn.*
  10 6¼ Llangwm,* Bridge Inn.
  13¾ 10¼ 3¾ Usk.*

Principal Objects of Interest.—Usk: Castle.

Hotels or Inns at places marked*, and at Cross Hands, and Maerdy.

889 NEWPORT TO PONTYPRIDD.

Description.—Class III. The surface of the road is in excellent condition to Caerphilly; thereafter it is narrow, and rather steep to Nantgarw, whence very good to Pontypridd. The road to Caerphilly, by Rudry (12m.), is steep.

Gradients.—At 6½m. 1 in 16; 7¾m. 1 in 16; 9m. 1 in 21; 13¾m. 1 in 14; 15m. 1 in 9-12-10 (dangerous).

Milestones.—Measured from Newport, and Caerphilly.

Measurements.

Newport,* Town Hall.
  3¾ Bassaleg.*
  8¼ 4¾ Machen Upper.*
  12¾ 8¾ 4¾ Caerphilly.*
  15¾ 11¾ 7½ 2¾ Nantgarw.*
  20¼ 16¾ 11¾ 7½ 4¾ Pontypridd,* Market.

Principal Objects of Interest. — Caerphilly: Castle. PONTYPRIDD: Bridge.

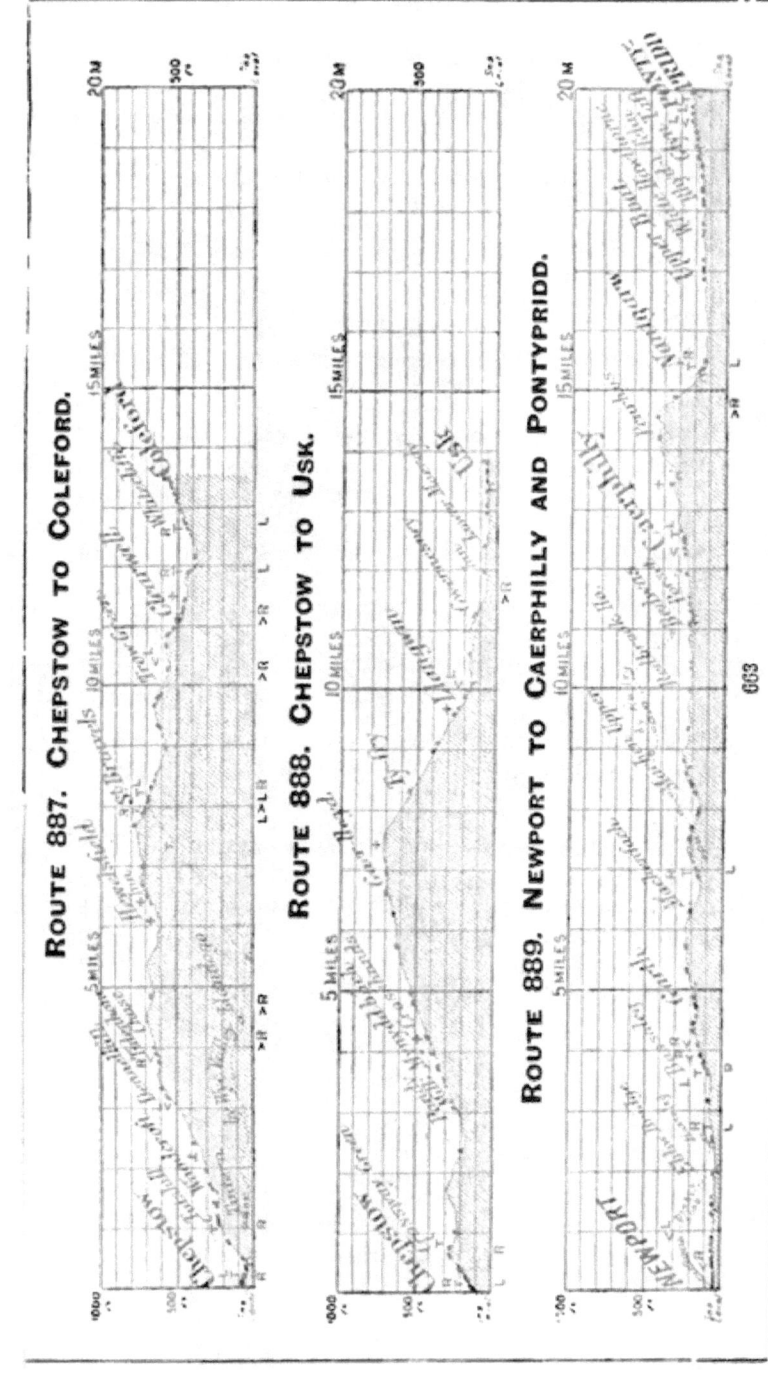

ROUTE 887. CHEPSTOW TO COLEFORD.

ROUTE 888. CHEPSTOW TO USK.

ROUTE 889. NEWPORT TO CAERPHILLY AND PONTYPRIDD.

890 NEWPORT TO BLAINA, &c.

Description.—Class III. An undulating road through colliery district, with fair surface as far as Crumlin; thereafter poor surface and very hilly.

Gradients.—(† *Dangerous.*) At ½m. 1 in 14; 7¼m. 1 in 12†; 9m. 1 in 19; 14½m. 1 in 15; 14½m. 1 in 13†; 15¾m. 1 in 14; 16½m. 1 in 11†; 19½m. 1 in 20: 21m. 1 in 22.

Milestones.—Measured from Newport, Town Hall.

Measurements.

Newport,* Town Hall.
5¾ Risca,* Exchange Inn.
11¼ 5½ Crumlin,* Viaduct Hotel.
16¼ 10¾ 4¾ Abertillery.*
19 13¼ 7½ 2¾ Blaina.*
21¾ 15¾ 10¼ 5¾ 2¾ Bryn Mawr.* R. 893.

Principal Objects of Interest.—Colliery District. Crumlin: Viaduct. BLAINA: Iron Works.

Hotels or Inns at places marked *, and at Abercarn, &c.

891 NEWPORT TO ABERGAVENNY.

Description.—Class II. The best road between these two towns is the longer route by Usk, which has splendid surface and easy gradients. The more direct road passing close to Pontypool has very fair surface, but there are a number of steep and dangerous hills. The first route is much the quicker, though of greater length.

Gradients.—(† *Dangerous.*) By Usk.—At 7¼m. 1 in 18; 15¾m. 1 in 12†.

By Pontypool.—At 1½m. 1 in 19; 3m. 1 in 18; 5½m. 1 in 16; 8½m. 1 in 19; 9m. 1 in 12†; 10¾m. 1 in 12†; 11½m. 1 in 11†; 13¾m. 1 in 14.

Milestones.—Measured from Newport, Town Hall, for 16m.; then from Monmouth.

By Pontypool.—Measured from Pontypool.

Measurements.

Newport,* Town Hall.
3¼ Caerleon.*
11 7¾ Usk.*
22 18¾ 11 Abergavenny,* Market.

By Pontypool.

Newport,* Town Hall.
(9¾ Pontypool.*)
10¾ 3½ Mamhilad.*
18½ 10¾ 7¼ Abergavenny,* Market.

Principal Objects of Interest.—By Usk.—Caerleon: Museum. Llangibby: Cas. Usk: Cas. 16m., Clytha Cas.

By Pontypool.—3¾m., Llantarnam Abbey. 14m., Llanover Court. Abergavenny: Market House, Castle, Church.

Hotels or Inns at places marked *, and at Llangibby, Llantarnam, Llanelen, &c.

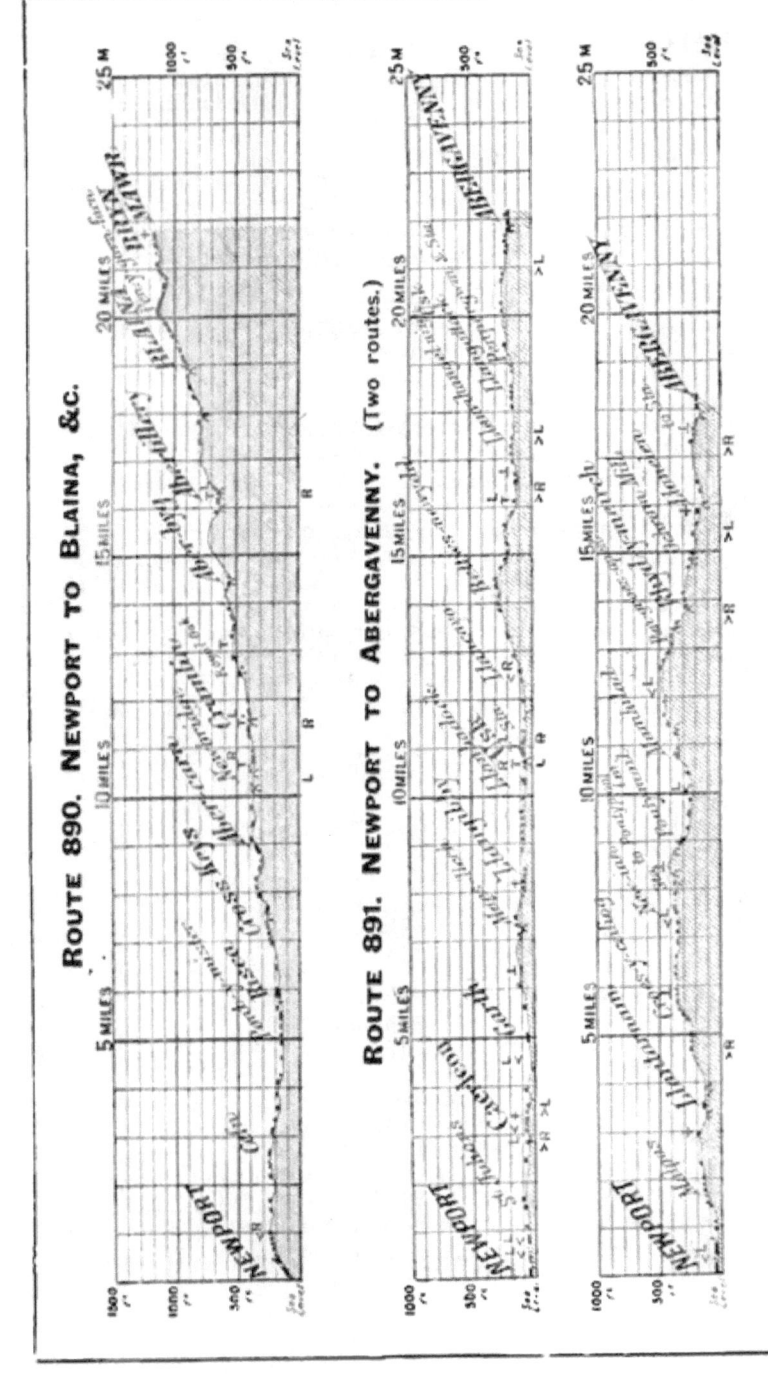

892 Usk to Pontypool, &c.

Description.—Class II. A very good road to Pontypool; thereafter, while mostly in excellent condition, it is very steep near Crumlin, & a little rough near Tredegar Junction.

Gradients.—At 6¾m. 1 in 19; 8¼m. 1 in 17; 12 & 13¾m. 1 in 12 (dangerous); 14½m. 1 in 22; 22m. 1 in 15; 22¼m. 1 in 21.

Milestones.—Measured from Pontypool.

Measurements.

Usk.*				
7¼	Pontypool,* Station.			
12	4¾	Crumlin,* Viaduct Hotel.		
17⅞	10⅝	5⅛	Ystrad Bridge.	
22	14¾	10	4⅛	Quaker's Yard,* or
22½	15¼	10½	4⅝	Caerphilly.*

Principal Objects of Interest.—Collieries and Iron Works. Crumlin: Viaduct. Caerphilly: Castle.

893 Abergavenny to Merthyr.

Description.—Class II. Excellent surface for five miles, then poor surface and long, steep hills.

Gradients.—(†*Dangerous.*) At 4¼m. 1/18; 5½m. 1/12†; 7m. 1/11†; 10m. 1/14†; 10¼m. 1/20; 11¾m. 1/15; 13¼m. 1/22; 14½m. 1/14†; 14¾m. 1/18; 17m. 1/12†; 17¾m. 1/16; 18½m. 1/18.

Milestones.—Measured from Abergavenny Market; irregular after Brynmawr.

Measurements.

Abergavenny,* Market.				
8¼	Brynmawr.*			
12	3¾	Tredegar,* Sirhowey Station.		
17¼	9	5¼	Dowlais,* Market.	
19	10¾	7	1¾	Merthyr,* Town Hall.

Principal Objects of Interest.—Clydach: Waterfall.

894 Abergavenny to Ross.

Description. Class III. This cross-country road is seldom used as a through route, as the road by Monmouth is much superior. It has fairly good surface, but the hills are long and stiff.

Gradients.—At 1¼m. 1 in 23; 2½, 3½, 3¾, & 7m. 1 in 17; 8¾m. 1 in 16; 10m. 1 in 12 (dangerous); 13¼ & 14m. 1 in 16; 15m. 1 in 17; 17m. 1 in 18; 18m. 1 in 17; 21¼m. 1 in 22.

Measurements.

Abergavenny,* Market.		
12½	Skenfrith.*	
22⅝	10⅛	Ross,* Market House.

Principal Objects of Interest.—Skenfrith: Castle. Wilton: Castle. Ross: Church, Market House.

Hotels or Inns at places marked*, and numerous others.

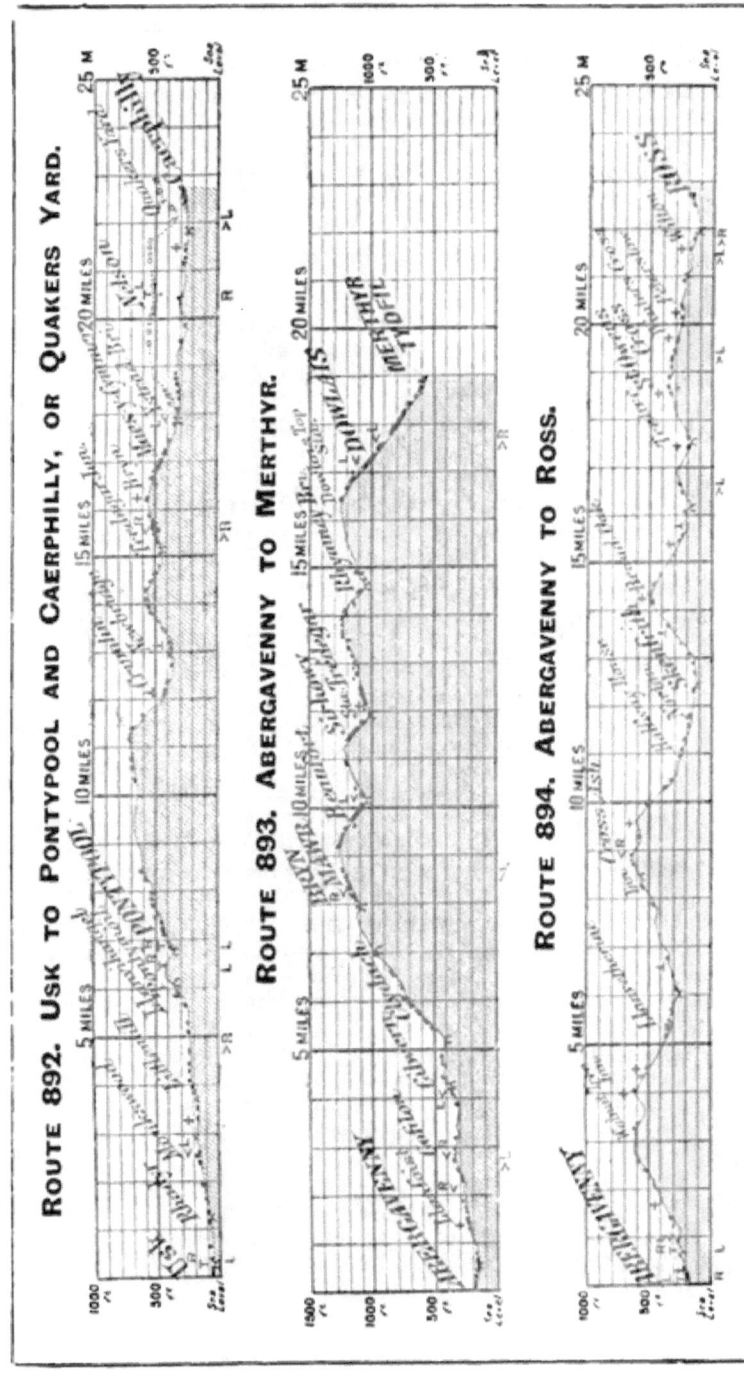

ROUTE 892. USK TO PONTYPOOL AND CAERPHILLY, OR QUAKERS YARD.

ROUTE 893. ABERGAVENNY TO MERTHYR.

ROUTE 894. ABERGAVENNY TO ROSS.

895 Abergavenny to Hay, &c.

Description.—Class II. The road has splendid surface to Crickhowell; thereafter it is beautifully engineered, and is in excellent condition to Talgarth, whence splendid to Hay. The road past Llangorse is much more hilly.

Gradients.—At 1¼m. 1 in 22; 6m. 1 in 21; 12m. 1 in 26; 16½m. 1 in 23.

By Llangorse.—Grades of 1 in 13 and 1 in 16.

Milestones.—Measured from Abergavenny Market, and from Crickhowell.

Measurements.

Abergavenny,* Market.					
6⅛	Crickhowell.*				
14½	8⅜	Castle Inn.*			
17⅞	11¾	3⅜	Talgarth.*		
18⅞	12¾	4⅜	1	Bronllys.*	
26¼	20⅛	11¾	8¾	7⅜	Hay,* or
32⅞	26¾	18⅜	15	14	Builth.*

Crickhowell to Llangorse, 9⅝m. Llangorse to Talgarth, 4⅝m.

Principal Objects of Interest. Llangorse: Pool. Hay: Castle.

896 Monmouth to Brecon.

Description.—Class I. This is a splendid road, with easy gradients as far as Crickhowell, when it becomes somewhat hilly, and for two miles on each side of Bwlch is rather steep; thereafter splendid surface to Brecon.

Gradients.—At 11m. 1 in 17; 18m. 1 in 22; 22½m. 1 in 21; 26¼m. 1 in 15; 27¼ & 28¼m. 1 in 16; 28¾m. 1 in 14; 30m. 1 in 15; 35m. 1 in 16.

Milestones.—Measured from Monmouth as far as Raglan, whence from Abergavenny to County Boundary. In Brecknockshire, measured from Brecon, Guildhall.

Measurements.

Monmouth,* Shire Hall.					
7¾	Raglan.*				
16¾	9	Abergavenny,* Market.			
22⅞	15⅛	6⅛	Crickhowell.*		
28½	20¾	11¾	5⅝	Bwlch.*	
36¾	29	20	13⅝	8¼	Brecon,* Guildhall.

Principal Objects of Interest. — ¾m., Troy House. Raglan: Castle, Church. 11m., Clytha Castle. ABERGAVENNY: Market House, Castle, Church. Fine views near Bwlch. BRECON: Barracks, Shire Hall, Castle, Priory Church, Brecon Beacons, Wellington Monument, Guildhall.

Hotels or Inns at places marked* and at Llangrwyne, Talybont, &c.

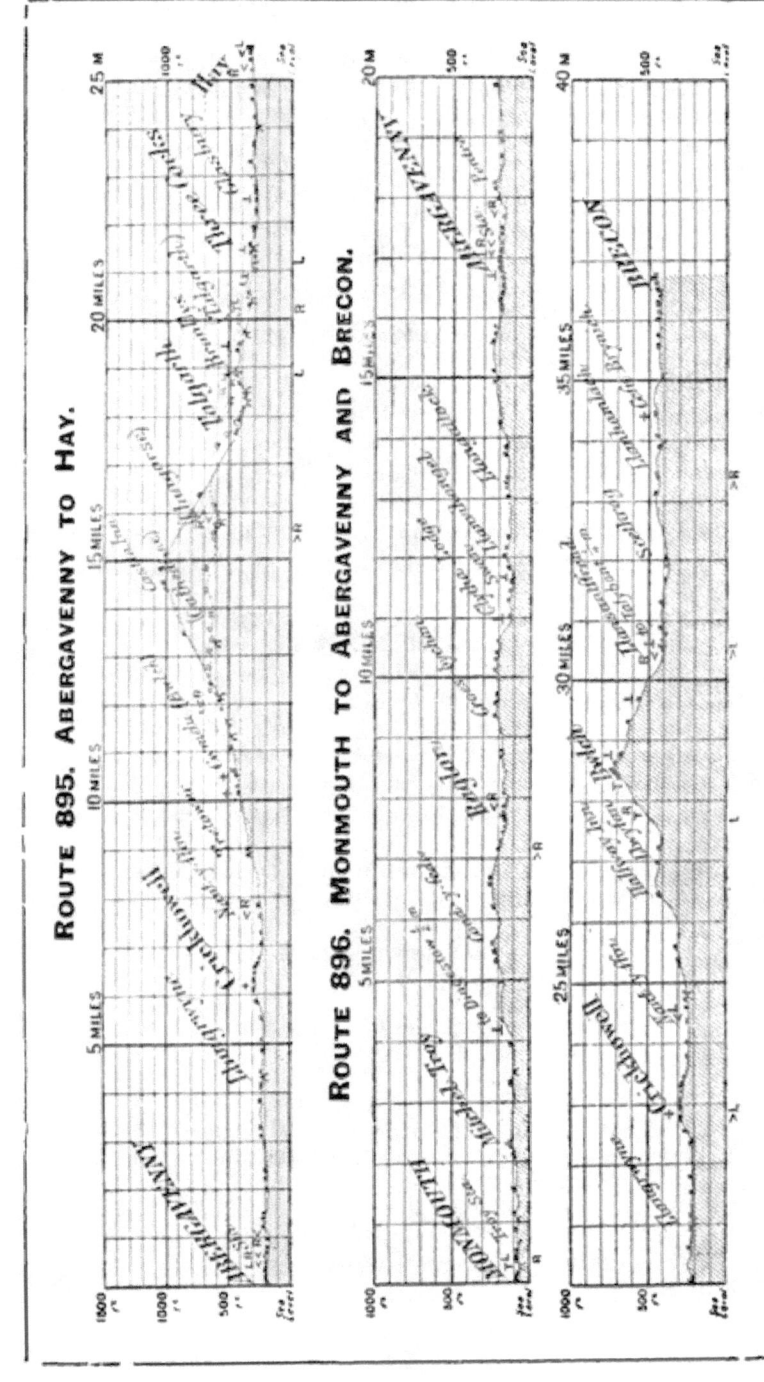

ROUTE 895. ABERGAVENNY TO HAY.

ROUTE 896. MONMOUTH TO ABERGAVENNY AND BRECON.

897 HEREFORD TO ABERGAVENNY.

Description.—Class II. The road has excellent surface throughout, and is practically level for the greater part of the distance. It is very finely engineered.

Gradients.—At 6m. 1 in 18; 18½m. 1 in 18; 22¾m. 1 in 16.

Milestones.—Measured from Hereford, to Pontrilas; thereafter from Abergavenny.

Measurements.

Hereford,* Market.
5¾ Horse-shoes * (Tram Inn Sta.).
11½ 5¾ Pontrilas.*
17½ 11¾ 6 Pandy Inn.*
23½ 17¾ 12 6 Abergavenny,* Market.

Principal Objects of Interest.—Pontrilas: Monastery remains. Llanvihangel: Llanthony Abbey and Capel-y-ffyn Monastery. ABERGAVENNY: Market House, Church, Castle.

Hotels or Inns at places marked*, and at Goose Pool, Wormbridge, and Llanvihangel.

---

898 HEREFORD TO CHEPSTOW.

Description.—Class II. An excellent, but somewhat hilly road to Monmouth, thence a splendid road to Tintern, whence hilly to Chepstow. There is a more direct road to Monmouth (18m.), by St. Weonards, shown dotted, but it is exceedingly hilly, and the surface is much inferior to the road by Whitchurch.

Gradients.—At 3¾m. 1 in 22; 8½m. 1 in 18; 14¾m. 1 in 12; 15m. 1 in 14; 16¾m. 1 in 10 (dangerous); 28m. 1 in 25; 29m. 1 in 20; 31¼m. 1 in 16; 32½m. 1 in 25; 33½m. 1 in 20; 34m. 1 in 19; 35m. 1 in 15; 36m. 1 in 9 (dangerous).

Milestones.—Measured from Hereford, Town Hall, and from Chepstow.

Measurements.

Hereford,* Market.
9¾ Harewood End.*
15¾ 6¾ Whitchurch,* Clock.
20½ 10¾ 4¾ Monmouth,* Shire Hall.
31½ 21¾ 15¾ 11 Tintern,* Abbey.
36½ 27 20¾ 16¼ 5¼ Chepstow,* Beaufort Arms.

Principal Objects of Interest.—Whitchurch: Symonds Yat. MONMOUTH: County Buildings, Troy House. Bigsweir: River Wye, tidal to this point. Tintern: Abbey. Chepstow: Castle. Fine scenery for the last fifteen miles.

Hotels or Inns at places marked*, and at Redbrook, Llandogo, &c.

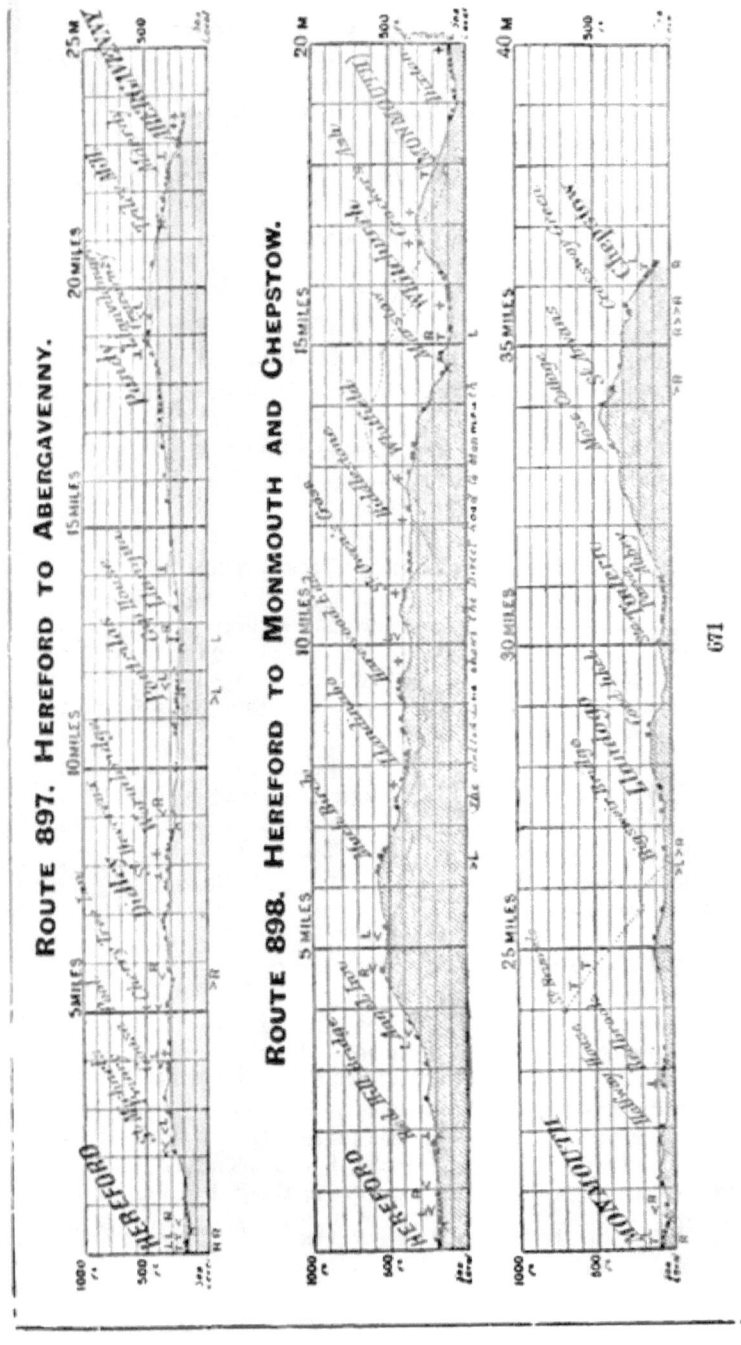

ROUTE 897. HEREFORD TO ABERGAVENNY.

ROUTE 898. HEREFORD TO MONMOUTH AND CHEPSTOW.

671

899   HEREFORD TO NEWENT.

Description.—Class III. Excellent surface, but a very hilly road. Many of the hills after Fownhope are dangerous.

Gradients.—(† *Dangerous*). At 6¾ & 7¼m. 1/9†; 8½m. 1/14; 9½m. 1/15; 10¼m. 1/17; 12½ & 12¾m. 1/10†; 13¼m. 1/14; 14m. 1/12†; 14¼m. 1/15; 15¼m. 1/23; 16¼m. 1/13†.

Milestones.—Measured from Hereford Town Hall.

Measuremeuts.

Hereford,* Market.
 6¼ Fownhope Inn.*
 12¾ 6½ Crow Hill.
 18½ 12¼ 5½ Newent,* Market House.

Principal Objects of Interest.—Newent: Market Ho., Ch.

Hotels or Inns at places marked *, and at Mordiford, &c.

900   HEREFORD TO MALVERN.

Description.—Class I. A splendid and easy undulating road to Ledbury, thence excellent surface, but dangerous hills to Malvern. The best road to Malvern is through Eastnor Park and Wyche Cut (shown dotted). See also R. 911.

Gradients.—(† *Dangerous.*) At 3m. 1/19; 4½m. 1/20; 13m. 1/17; 13¾m. 1/19; 15¼m. 1/20; 18m. 1/11†; 19m. 1/9†.

Milestones.—Measured from Hereford Town Hall, to Tarrington, thence from Ledbury, Cross-roads.

Measurements.

Hereford,* Market.
 7¾ Tarrington,* Foley Arms Inn.
 14½ 7 Ledbury,* Market House.
 20¾ 13¼ 6¼ Malvern Wells,* Hornyold Arms Hotel.
 22¾ 15¼ 8¼ 2 Malvern,* Bellevue Terrace.

Principal Objects of Interest. — Stoke Edith: Park. LEDBURY: Market Hall, Ch., Eastnor Castle. 19m., British Camp. MALVERN: Wells, Priory Ch., St. Anne's Well, &c.

Hotels or Inns at places marked *, &c.

901   HEREFORD TO BROMYARD.

Description.—Class II. A very good road to Burley Gate; thence somewhat hilly, but with fair surface.

Gradients.—At ¾m. 1 in 16; 1¼m. 1 in 14; 9½m. 1 in 13; 10¼m. 1 in 14; 12½m. 1 in 22; 14m. 1 in 13 (dangerous).

Milestones.—Measured from Hereford Town Hall

Measurements.

Hereford,* Market.
 7¾ Burley Gate,* Inn.
 14½ 6¾ Bromyard.*

Principal Objects of Interest.—Bromyard: Church.

Hotels or Inns where marked *, and at Withington Marsh.

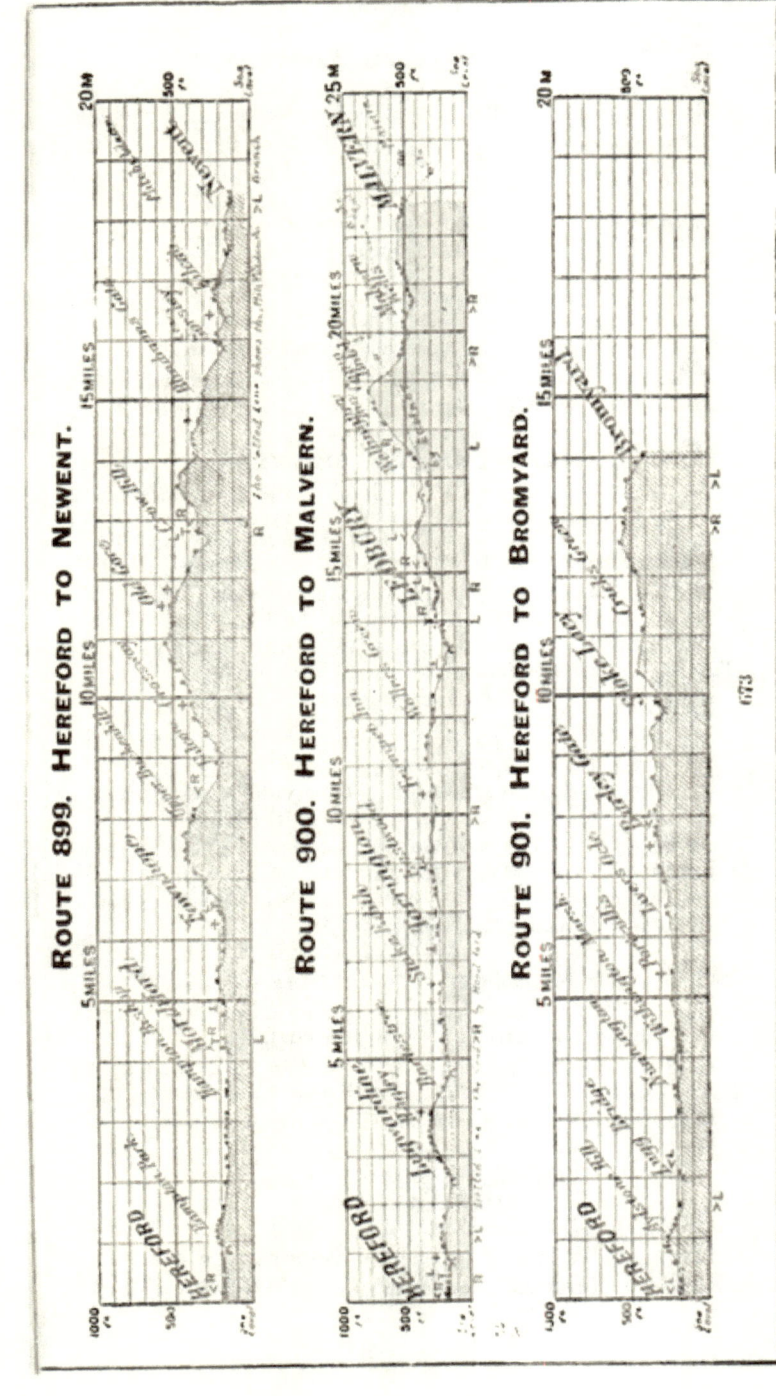

ROUTE 899. HEREFORD TO NEWENT.

ROUTE 900. HEREFORD TO MALVERN.

ROUTE 901. HEREFORD TO BROMYARD.

902 HEREFORD TO BRECON.

Description.—Class I. This is a magnificent road the whole way to Brecon. The best part is between Hereford and Hay, as there is only one hill of any consequence. Note to cross Whitney Bridge, as the road straight forward, though also leading to Hay, is very poor. After Hay the surface is hardly so perfect, but it is a fine road right into Brecon. There is one steep hill in this section. There is a more direct road to Hay, by Bredwardine (shown dotted), but it is very steep.

The road to Hay, by Peterchurch, is a good cross-country road, with one or two slight hills.

Gradients.—At 10½m. 1 in 21; 11¼m. 1 in 17; 20¾m. 1 in 17; 32m. 1 in 17; 35¾m. 1 in 16.

By Peterchurch.—At 4m. 1 in 15; 8m. 1 in 14; 8½m. 1 in 17; 17m. 1 in 16; 18¾m. 1 in 23.

Milestones.—Measured from Hereford, Town Hall, as far as Whitney, whence from Hay Station; thereafter from Guildhall, Brecon.

Measurements.

Hereford,* Market.								
5⅞	Bridge Sollers.*							
11½	5⅝	Letton,* Inn.						
13¼	7⅜	1¾	Willersley.* R. 903.					
18¼	12⅜	6¾	5	Clifford.*				
20¾	14⅞	9¼	7½	2½	Hay,* Market House.			
25½	19⅝	14	12¼	7¼	4¾	Three Cocks Inn.*		
28⅛	22¼	16⅝	14⅞	9⅞	7⅜	2⅝	Bronllys.	
36⅜	30½	24⅞	23⅛	18⅛	15⅝	10⅞	8¼	Brecon,* Guildhall.

By Peterchurch.

Hereford,* Market.			
12	Peterchurch.*		
15	3	Dorstone,* Station.	
21½	9½	6½	Hay,* Market Ho.

By Bredwardine.

Hereford,* Market.			
5⅞	Bridge Sollers.*		
11⅞	6	Bredwardine.*	
19½	13⅝	7⅝	Hay.*

Principal Objects of Interest.—¾m., White Cross. Clifford: Castle. Hay: Castle. Three Cocks: Inn. BRECON: Castle, Priory Church, Barracks, County Buildings. Pretty scenery near Whitney. The fine peaks known as the Brecnock Beacons come into view approaching Brecon.

Hotels or Inns at places marked*, and at Kings Acre, Sugwas Pool, Portway, Winforton, Glasbury, and Felinfach; and at Coldwell, and Hardwick, by Peterchurch.

ROUTE 902. HEREFORD TO HAY AND BRECON.

By Peterchurch.

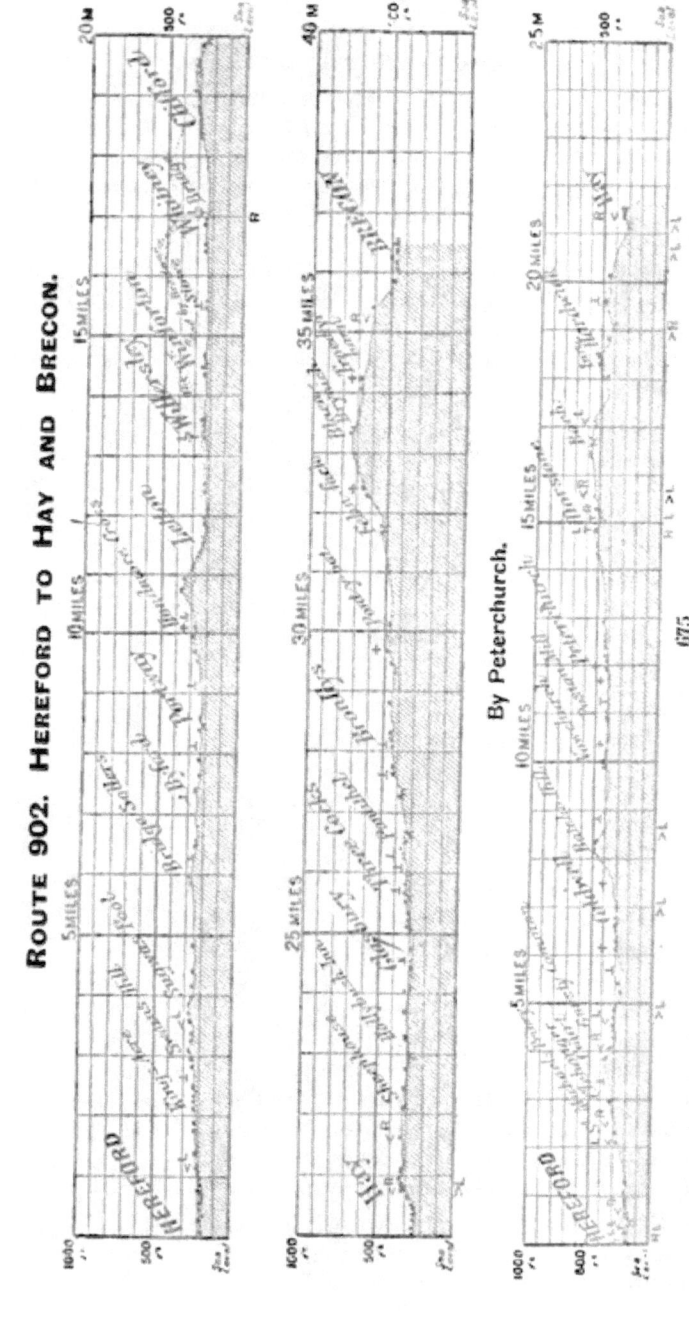

903 HEREFORD TO KINGTON.

Description.—Class I. & II. Of the two roads shown, that by Eardisley is much the best; the surface is in perfect condition, but the hill after Eardisley is somewhat stiff. The road by Lyonshall has excellent surface to Woonton, but approaching Kington there are then some rather steep hills. For Weobley (shown dotted), turn to right at 9¾m. on second route.

From HAY to KINGTON, follow R. 902 to Willersley, thence this route, 14¼m. The direct road is rough.

Gradients.—At 10½m. 1 in 21; 11m. 1 in 17; 15m. 1 in 17; 17m. 1 in 14; 17¾m. 1 in 23; 18¾m. 1 in 23.

Second route.—At 15m. 1 in 22; 15¼m. 1 in 20; 15¾m. 1 in 14; 16¾m. 1 in 15; 18¼m. 1 in 14.

Milestones.—Measured from Hereford, Town Hall, to Willersley; thereafter from Kington.

Measurements.

Hereford,* Market.
5⅜ Bridge Sollers,* Inn.
13¼ 7¾ Willersley.* R. 902.
14⅜ 8¾ 1⅛ Eardisley,* Inn.
19⅝ 14 6⅜ 5¼ Kington,* Town Clock.

By Lyonshall.

Hereford,* Market.
(9½ Moorhampton Station.*)
(12 3¾ Weobley.*)
13¾ 4¾ Woonton.*
19½ 10½ 5¾ Kington,* Town Clock.

Principal Objects of Interest.—1m., Whitecross. Letton: Court, Credenhill Camp. Kington: Good scenery.

Hotels or Inns at places marked*, and at Portway, Letton, Lyonshall, &c.

904 LEOMINSTER TO HAY.

Description.—Class II. An excellent, undulating country road to Willersley, whence splendid surface to Hay.

Gradients.—At 5m. 1 in 23; 10m. 1 in 23; 11m. 1 in 21.

Milestones.—Measured from Leominster, Town Hall, to Willersley; thereafter from Hay Station.

Measurements.

Leominster.*
9¼ Weobley.*
15⅝ 8½ 1¼ Winforton.*
22⅛ 14¾ 7½ 6¼ Hay,* Market House.

Principal Objects of Interest.—4½m., Golden Cross. Weobley: Castle. Clifford: Castle. Hay: Castle.

Hotels or Inns at places marked*, and at Dilwyn, &c.

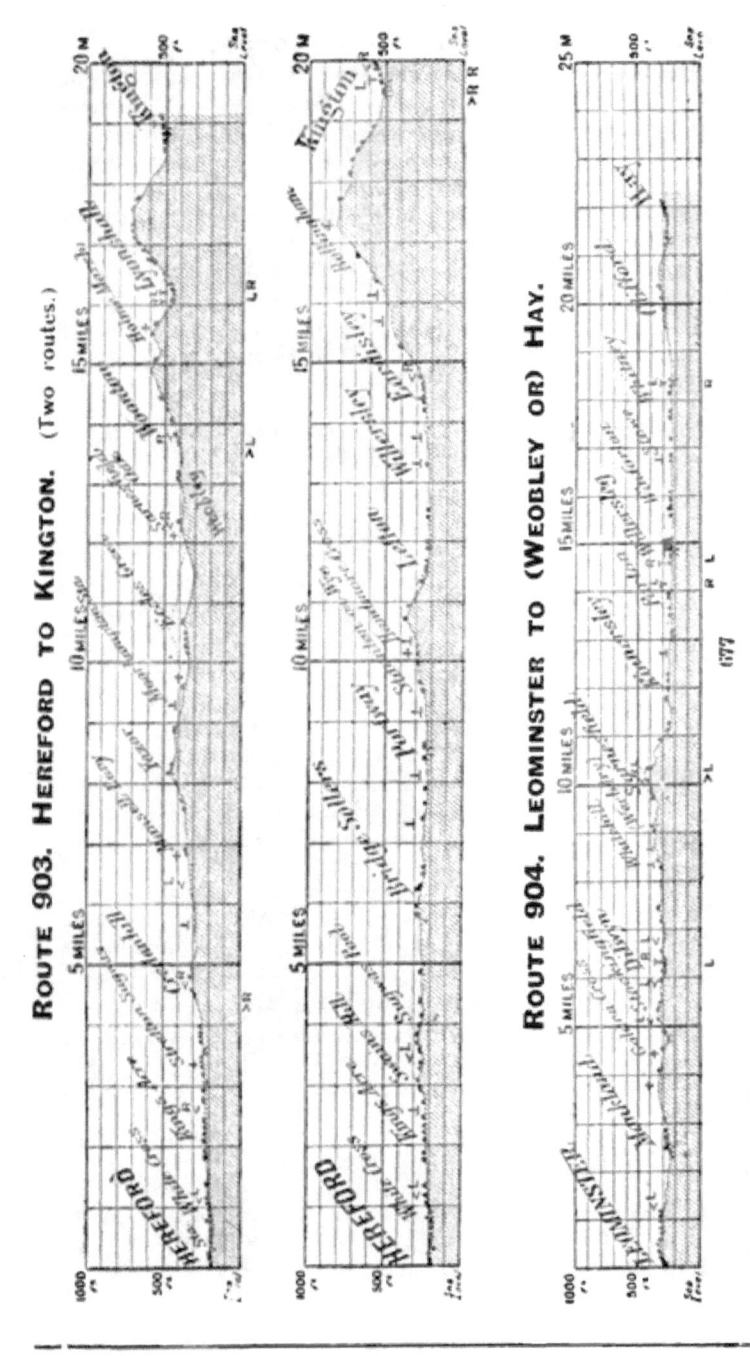

ROUTE 903. HEREFORD TO KINGTON. (Two routes.)

ROUTE 904. LEOMINSTER TO (WEOBLEY OR) HAY.

905   LEOMINSTER TO RADNOR.

Description.—Class II. There are two routes to Radnor; the direct road by Kington has good surface, but several dangerous hills. The best, and a practically level route, is by Presteign, turning off, however, half a mile before that town. This road has splendid surface, and no hills of any consequence.

Gradients.—By Presteign. At 9¾m. 1 in 25; 14m. 1 in 19.

By Kington.—(† *Dangerous.*) At 1½m. 1 in 20; 3½m. 1 in 18; 11¾m. 1 in 15; 13m. 1 in 14†; 14½m. 1 in 13†; 14½m. 1 in 18; 16¼m. 1 in 12†; 17¼m. 1 in 10†.

Milestones.—Measured from Leominster Town Hall; after Presteign, measured from that place to Walton.

Measurements.

Leominster.*
5   Eardisland.
7½   2½   Pembridge.
14   9   6½   Kington,* Town Clock.
20½   15½   13   6½   Radnor,* P.O.

By Presteign.

Leominster.*
7   Shobdon.
13   6   Presteign,* Clock.
20¼   13¾   8¾   Radnor,* P.O.

Principal Objects of Interest.—Pretty scenery beyond Kington and near Presteign,

Hotels or Inns at places marked *, and at Lyonshall, &c.

---

906   LEOMINSTER TO KNIGHTON.

Description.—Class II. An exceedingly good country road, slightly undulating, but in excellent condition.

Gradients.—At 10m. 1 in 22; 1½m. 1 in 20; 11½m. 1 in 16; 19m. 1 in 17; 19½m. 1 in 22 and 1 in 13.

Milestones.—Measured from Leominster to Kingsland; thereafter from Town Clock, Knighton.

Measurements.

Leominster.*
6½   Mortimers Cross.*
9¾   3½   Wigmore Castle Inn.*
12½   6½   2½   Walford.
19½   13¾   9¾   7   Knighton,* Norton Arms Hotel.

Principal Objects of Interest.—Mortimers Cross: Battlefield, 1461, Croft Castle. Wigmore: Castle. 17m., Stannage Park. Knighton: Offa's Dyke, Caer Ditches, &c.

Hotels or Inns at places marked *, and at Aymestrey, &c.

ROUTE 905. LEOMINSTER TO NEW RADNOR. (Two routes.)

ROUTE 906. LEOMINSTER TO KNIGHTON.

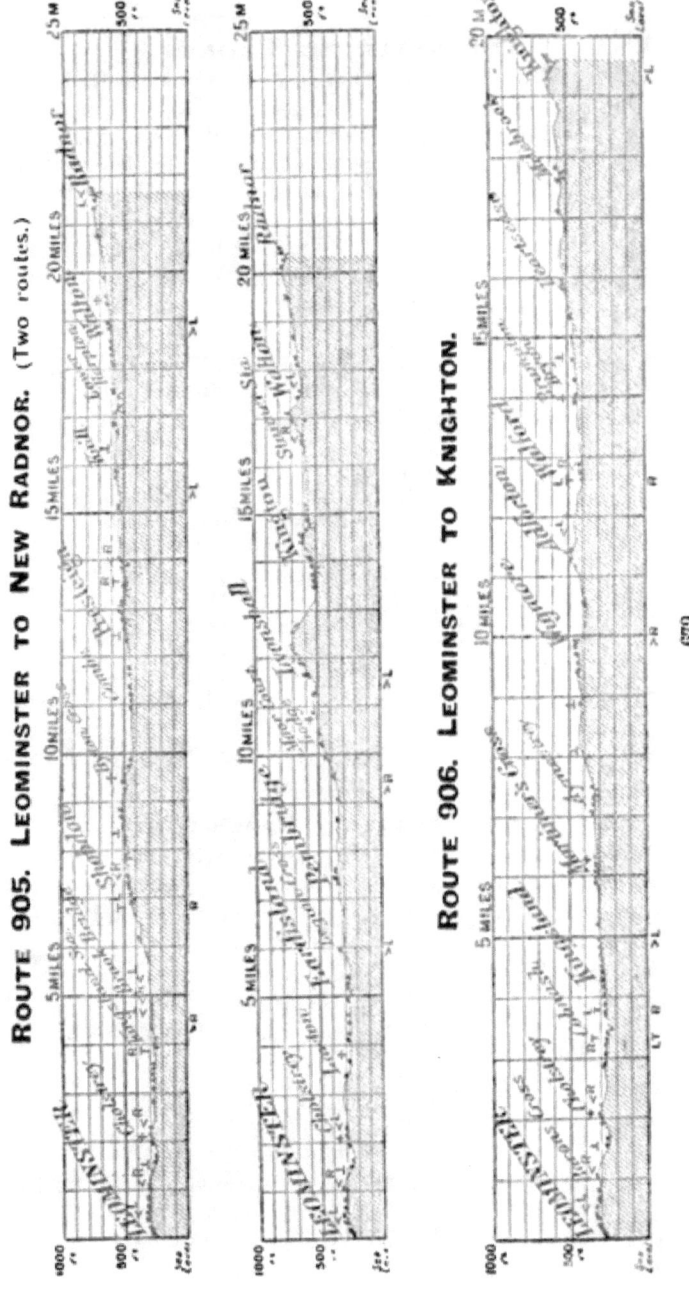

907 LEOMINSTER TO LEDBURY.

Description.—Class II. Splendid surface for eight miles, then a good undulating country road.

Gradients.—At 19½m. 1 in 17 ; 20½m. 1 in 19.

Milestones.— Measured from Leominster Town Hall, and from Cross-roads, Ledbury.

Measurements.—Leominster.*
13   Newton.
21¾   8¾ Ledbury,* Market House.

Principal Objects of Interest.—5m., Hampton Co. 15m., disused Canal. Ledbury: Market Ho., Ch., Eastnor Castle.

Hotels or Inns at places marked *, and at Saffrons Cross, England's Gate, and Ashperton.

908 LUDLOW TO PRESTEIGN.

Description.—Class II. The direct road by Wigmore has precipitous hills. The best road, by Mortimers Cross, has splendid surface to Comberton, is then somewhat hilly and poor to Shobden, whence good surface.

Gradients.—(† *Dangerous.*) At ½m. 1 in 12† ; ½m. 1 in 15 ; 7m. 1 in 20 ; 7¾m. 1 in 16 ; 8½ & 8¾m. 1 in 15 ; 10½m. 1 in 20 ; 11¼m. 1 in 15 ; 12m. 1 in 10† ; 16m. 1 in 25.

Milestones.—Measured from Ludlow Market House to Wooferton ; thereafter from Mortimers Cross.

Measurements.—Ludlow,* Bull Ring.
4   Wooferton,* Hotel.
11½   7½ Mortimers Cross.*
19¾ 15¾   7⅞ Presteign,* Clock.

Principal Objects of Interest. — 9m., Croft Castle. Mortimers Cross: Battlefield, 1461. 12m., Mortimers Rock.

Hotels or Inns at places marked *, and at Comberton, Shobden, Byton Cross, Combe, &c.

909 LUDLOW TO KNIGHTON.

Description.—Class II. The road has good surface, but is exceedingly hilly to Leintwardine,

Gradients.—At ½m. 1 in 16 ; 3½m. 1 in 20 ; 4m. 1 in 16 ; 5½m. 1 in 14 ; 6¼m. 1 in 14 ; 8m. 1 in 16 ; 16½m. 1 in 17 ; 16¾m. 1 in 22 ; 17m. 1 in 13.

Milestones.—Measured from Market House, Ludlow.

Measurements.—Ludlow,* Bull Ring.
8½ Leintwardine.*
17   8½ Knighton,* Norton Arms Hotel.

Principal Objects of Interest.—Bromfield Church. 5m., Downton Castle. Knighton: Offa's Dyke, Caer Ditches, &c.

Hotels or Inns at places marked *, and at Todding, &c.

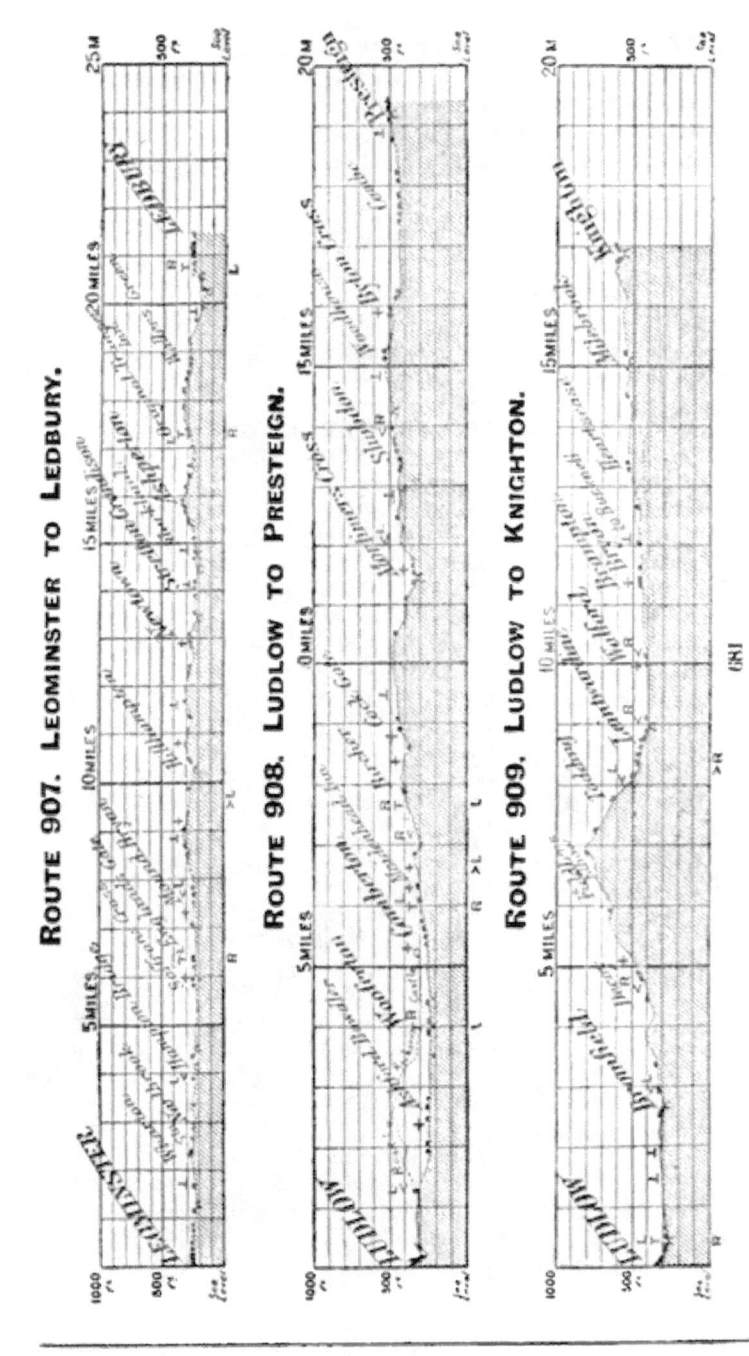

ROUTE 907. LEOMINSTER TO LEDBURY.

ROUTE 908. LUDLOW TO PRESTEIGN.

ROUTE 909. LUDLOW TO KNIGHTON.

910 LUDLOW TO BISHOPS CASTLE.

Description.—Class II. This road has magnificent surface throughout, and is one of the best roads in the district; the more direct roads between Craven Arms and Bishops Castle are very hilly. For Clun, turn to L. at 12m.

Gradients.—At ½m. 1 in 16; 11¾m. 1 in 17; 19½m. 1 in 8.

Milestones.—Measured from Market House, Ludlow, to Craven Arms; thereafter from Bishops Castle, Clock.

Measurements.

Ludlow,* Bull Ring.				
7¼	Craven Arms,* Hotel.			
10¼	2¾	Aston-on-Clun.*	R. 1062.	
(16¼	8¼	6	Clun.*)	
19⅗	11⅞	9¼	12¼	Bishops Castle,* Town Clock.

Principal Objects of Interest. — Bromfield: Church. Stokesay: Castle. Bishops Castle: Town Ho. Clun: Cas.

Hotels or Inns at places marked *, and at Stokesay, &c.

911 WORCESTER TO MONMOUTH.

Description.—Class I. Splendid surface between Worcester and Malvern, then steep, with dangerous descent to Colwell, whence good surface to Ledbury; thereafter a splendid undulating road all the way to Monmouth, except one dangerous hill, with very rough surface, at Whitchurch. There are several roads between Malvern and Ledbury; the best is by Wyche Cut, Camp Hotel, and through Eastnor Park. The steepest is through Malvern Wells, by Camp Hotel, Route 900.

Gradients.—(† *Dangerous*) At 4m. 1 in 23; 4½m. 1 in 21; 7½m. 1 in 15-20; 9m. 1 in 17; 10m. 1 in 11†; 10½m. 1 in 14†; 12m. 1 in 12†; 14¾m. 1 in 22; 15¼m. 1 in 20; 17¼m. 1 in 17; 23m. 1 in 17; 26m. 1 in 15; 27¾m. 1 in 21; 28¼m. 1 in 12; 32m. 1 in 16; 32½m. 1 in 17; 35m. 1 in 10†.

Milestones.—Measured from Worcester Cross to Ledbury, then from Ross Market House to Whitchurch, whence from Monmouth, Shire Hall.

Measurements.

Worcester,* Cross.						
8¼	Malvern,* Bellevue Terrace.					
11¼	2¾	Colwall Stone.*				
16¼	7¾	5	Ledbury,* Market House.			
20⅗	12⅗	9½	4¾	Much Marcle.*		
28¼	20	17¼	12¾	7⅗	Ross,* Market House.	
34¼	26	23½	18¾	13⅗	6	Whitchurch.* Clock.
38⅞	30¾	27½	22¾	18	10¼	4¾	Monmouth,* Shire Hall.

Principal Objects of Interest.—6m., Newlands Almshouses. MALVERN: Priory Church and Gateway, St. Anne's

[over.

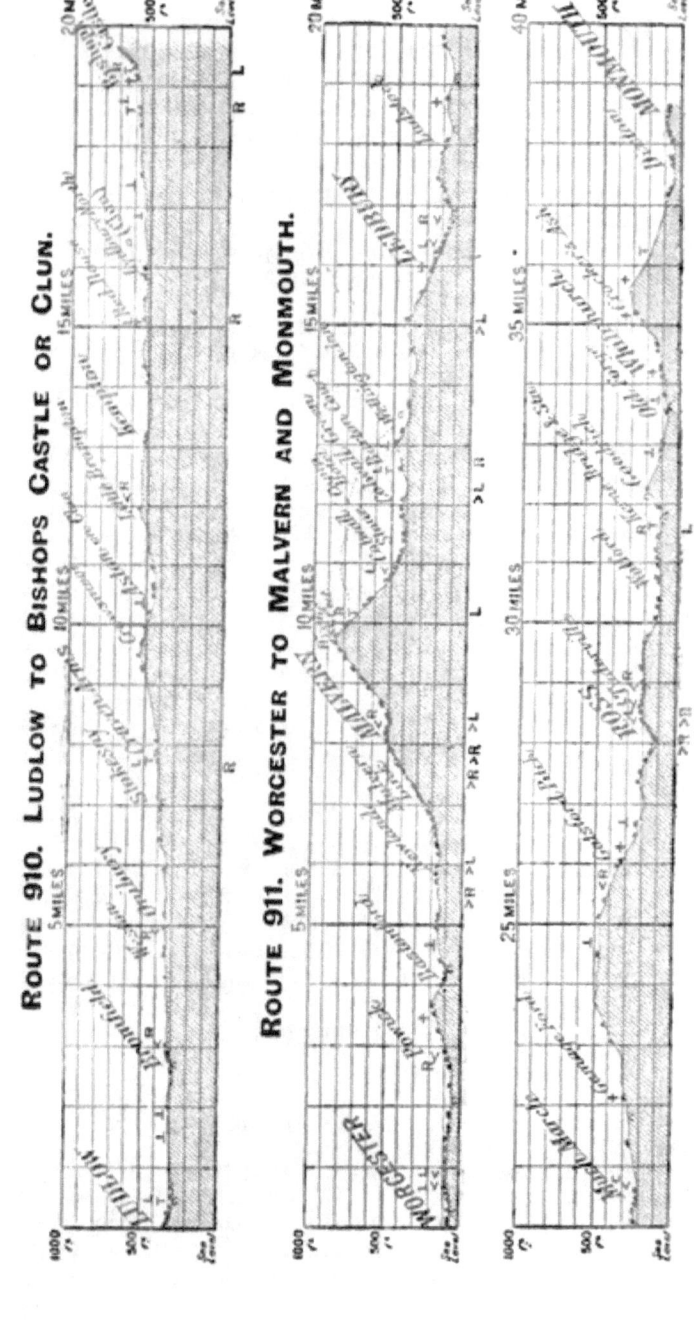

ROUTE 910. LUDLOW TO BISHOPS CASTLE OR CLUN.

ROUTE 911. WORCESTER TO MALVERN AND MONMOUTH.

Route 911—Continued.

Well, Worcestershire Beacon, &c. 9¾m., Wyche Cutting. LEDBURY: Eastnor Cas., Market House, Ch. ROSS: Market Hall, Church, Wilton Castle (ruin). 32m., Goodrich Castle. Whitchurch: Symonds Yat. MONMOUTH: County Bdgs.. Troy House. Splendid view from Wyche Cut on Malvern Hills. Very pretty road from Ross to Monmouth.

Hotels or Inns at places marked*, and at Powick, Bastonford, Newland, Malvern Link, Wellington Inn, &c.

912   WORCESTER TO LUDLOW.

Description.—Class II. There are several roads between Worcester and Tenbury. The usual road is by Witley, which has very good surface to that place, but then becomes exceedingly steep for four miles,—several of the hills dangerous,—but after that it is splendid all the way to Ludlow. The direct road by Clifton has several precipitous hills. There is also a road from Hambridge along the banks of the Teme, but the surface is not good. The road from Droitwich, joining this road at Holt Heath, is given at end of second diagram. The measurement is ¼m. less than from Worcester.

Gradients.—(† *Dangerous.*) At 8¼m. 1 in 14; 9¼m. 1 in 19; 11¼m. 1 in 13†; 12m. 1 in 14†; 13¼m. 1 in 11†; 13¾m. 1 in 12†; 14¾m. 1 in 13†; 15m. 1 in 11†; 31m. 1 in 15; 31¼m. 1 in 12†.

By Marley.—3¼m. 1 in 21; 6¼m. 1 in 20; 7¾m. 1 in 12†; 8m. 1 in 11†; 9¼m. 1 in 10†; 16¼m. 1 in 7†.

Droitwich Road.—2¼m. 1 in 23; 2½m. 1 in 14; 5m. 1 in 15; 5¼m. 1 in 11†.

Milestones.—Measured from Worcester Cross to Tenbury, thereafter from Ludlow.

Measurements.

Worcester,* Cross.

6¼	Holt Heath.*	(6½m. from Droitwich.)			
11	4¾	Witley,* Hundred House.			
18¼	12¾	7¼	Newnham.*		
22¼	15¾	11¼	3¾	Tenbury,* Swan Hotel.	
27¾	21	16¾	8½	5¼	Wooferton,* Hotel.
31¾	25	20¾	12¾	9¼	4 Ludlow,* Bull Ring.

By Martley.

Worcester,* Cross.

7½	Martley,* Crown Inn.	
10¾	3¼	Clifton.*
20¾	13¼	9¾ Tenbury,* Swan Hotel.

Principal Objects of Interest.—4m., Thorn Grove. 10m., Witley Park. 13¾m., Stockton House. Tenbury: Market House, Spa, Church. LUDLOW: Castle, Bridge, Church.

Hotels or Inns at places marked*, and at Hallow, &c.

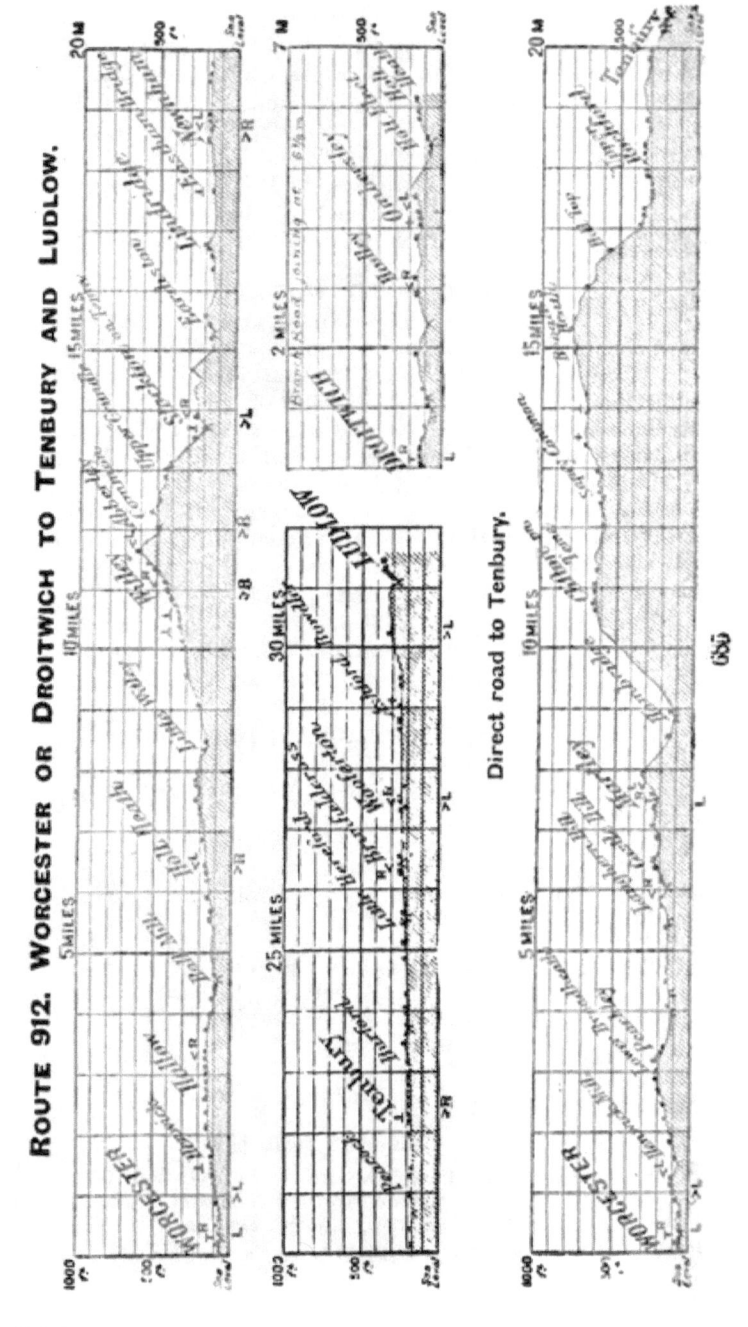

ROUTE 912. WORCESTER OR DROITWICH TO TENBURY AND LUDLOW.

Direct road to Tenbury.

913 WORCESTER TO HEREFORD.

Description.—Class III. Good surface for seven miles, then steep and dangerous hills for seven miles, whence undulating to Hereford. Better surface by Malvern.

Gradients.—(† *Dangerous.*) At 7¼m. 1 in 23; 8¼m. 1 in 18; 10m. 1 in 13†; 10¾m. 1 in 14†; 11½, 12, & 12¼m. 1 in 12†; 13¾m. 1 in 8†; 16¾m. 1 in 17; 24½m. 1 in 14; 25¼m. 1 in 16.

Milestones.—Measured from Worcester Cross, and from Hereford, Town Hall.

Measurements.—Worcester,* Cross.

9⅛	Stiffords Bridge,* Inn.		
17¼	8⅛	Newton,* Inn.	
25⅜	16¼	8⅛	Hereford,* Market.

Principal Objects of Interest.—Good views of the Malvern Hills. HEREFORD: Cathedral, Shire Hall, &c.

Hotels or Inns where marked*, and at Five Bridges, &c.

914 WORCESTER TO LEOMINISTER.

Description.—Class II. An excellent road for ten miles, then somewhat hilly, but with very fair surface.

Gradients.—(† *Dangerous.*) At 3m. 1/17; 10m. 1/16; 11m. 1/15; 12m. 1/11†; 12¾m. 1/17; 14¼m. 1/13†; 15½m. 1/17; 16m. 1/18; 17m. 1/15†; 17¼ & 22m. 1/18; 22¼m. 1/22.

Milestones.—Measured from Worcester Cross, in Worcestershire. From Bromyard and Leominster, in Hereford.

Measurements.—Worcester,* Cross.

8⅝	Knightsford Bridge,* Talbot Inn.			
14⅛	5½	Bromyard.*		
20¾	12⅛	6⅝	Docklow.*	
25¾	17⅛	11⅝	5	Leominster.*

Principal Objects of Interest.—Pretty scenery about Knightsford Bridge. Bromyard: Church. LEOMINSTER: Church, Town Hall.

Hotels or Inns at places marked*, and at Broadwas, &c.

915 WORCESTER TO STOURPORT, &C.

Description.—Class II. Exceedingly good surface to Dunhampton, thence slightly hilly to Stourport; thence a good road, but with a dangerous hill before Bewdley.

Gradients.—At 8¾m. 1 in 22; 10m. 1 in 19; 13½m. 1 in 13.

Milestones.—Measured from Worcester Cross.

Measurements.—Worcester,* Cross.

5⅝	Ombersley.*		
11⅝	6	Stourport.*	
14⅞	9¼	3¼	Bewdley.*

Principal Objects of Interest.—Uninteresting road. Bewdley: Bridge, Town Hall, Wyre Forest.

Hotels or Inns at places marked*, &c., &c.

ROUTE 913. WORCESTER TO HEREFORD.

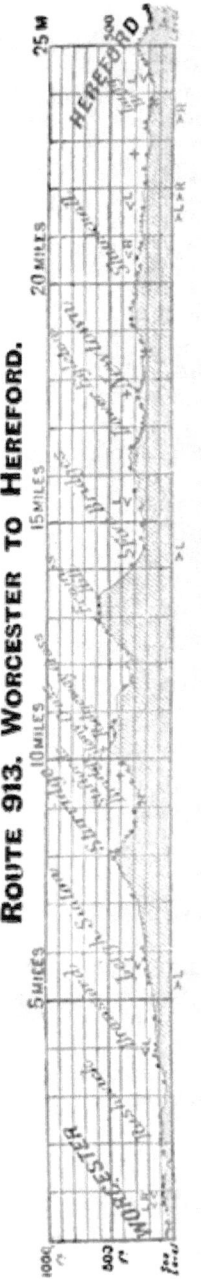

ROUTE 914. WORCESTER TO LEOMINSTER.

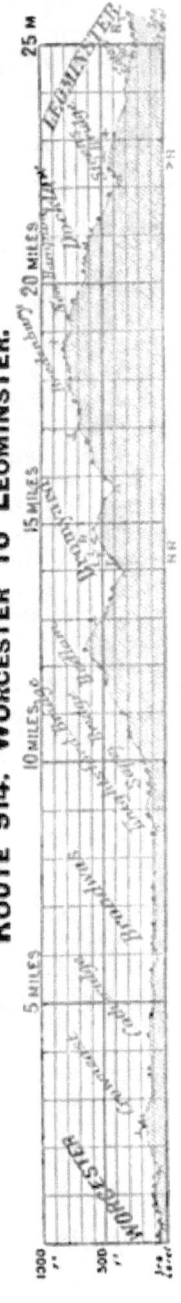

ROUTE 915. WORCESTER TO STOURPORT AND BEWDLEY.

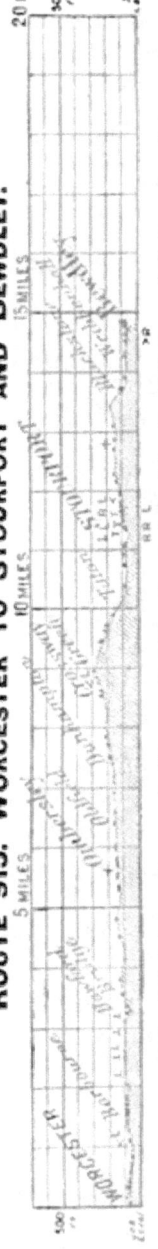

Signs. < Road Fork, forward journey. > ditto reverse. + Cross Roads. ⌐ Road Junction. ∩ Bridge. T indicates a sharp turn. The directions R (right) and L (left) for the forward journey are along the top of line, those of the reverse, below.

(187)

916 WORCESTER TO STRATFORD.

Description.—Class II. A very good, but somewhat undulating road, with a dangerous hill at Redhill.

Gradients.—At 1½m. 1 in 20; 6½m. 1 in 19; 11½m. 1 in 21; 13m. 1 in 20; 15¾m. 1 in 15; 21¼m. 1 in 13 (dangerous).

Milestones.—Measured from Worcester Cross, & Alcester.

Measurements.

Worcester,* Cross.			
9	Flyford Flavell.*		
17¾	8¾	Alcester.*	
25⅝	16⅝	7⅞	Stratford-on-Avon.*

Principal Objects of Interest.—16m., Ragley Park. Alcester: Town Hall. STRATFORD: see Route 873.

917 WORCESTER TO OXFORD.

Description.—Class I. Both roads to Evesham have good surface, but the best is by Wyre Piddle, that by Pershore being more hilly. From Evesham to Broadway, the road has also splendid surface, but after that there is a precipitous hill to the Fish; after which there are dangerous hills at Bourton, Little Compton, and two before Chipping Norton. The surface on these steep hills is rather rough, otherwise the road is good.

Gradients.—(†*Dangerous.*) At 1¼m. 1 in 20; 5m. 1 in 24; 12m. 1 in 15; 17¼m. 1 in 17; 22½m. 1 in 11†; 27m. 1 in 18; 28m. 1 in 10†; 34m. 1 in 12†; 35½m. 1 in 11†; 36½m. 1 in 17; 37½m. 1 in 13†.

By Pershore.—At 1¼ and 5¼m. 1 in 20; 7¼m. 1 in 23; 8m. 1 in 25; 8½m. 1 in 18; 10m. 1 in 17; 12½m. 1 in 21; 13½m. 1 in 18; 13¾m. 1 in 23; 14½m. 1 in 20.

Milestones.—Measured from Worcester Cross, and from Pershore; thereafter from Evesham.

Measurements.				By Pershore.		
Worcester,* Cross.				Worcester,* Cross.		
9¾	Wyre Piddle.*			9¼	Pershore.*	
15½	5¾	Evesham,* Clock.		15¾	6½	Bengeworth.*
15¾	6¼	¼ Bengeworth.*		16	6¾	¼ Evesham,* Clock.

21⅛	11½	5¾	5⅜	Broadway,* Lygon Arms Hotel.			
29¾	20½	14¼	14	8⅝	Moreton-in the-Marsh.*		
37¼	28½	22¼	22	16⅝	8	Chipping Norton,* Town Hall.	
57¼	47⅝	41¾	41½	36⅝	27½	19½	Oxford.* R. 495.

Principal Objects of Interest.—Pershore: Church. EVESHAM: Abbey remains, Bell Tower, Battle Monument, 1265. Broadway: pretty village. Magnificent view from the 'Fish.' 31¼m. Four-shire stone. CHIPPING NORTON: Rollerich Stone.

Hotels or Inns at places marked *, and at Cropthorn, Fish, Bourton, Little Compton, &c.

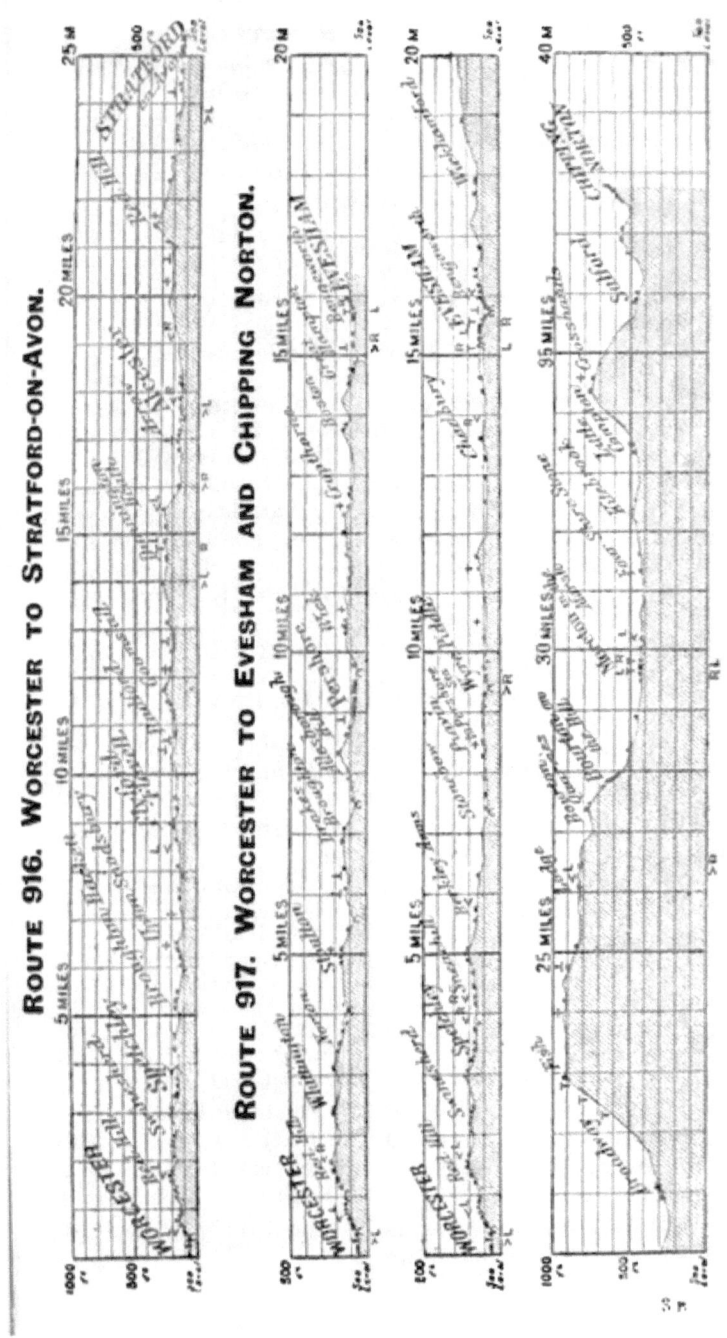

ROUTE 916. WORCESTER TO STRATFORD-ON-AVON.

ROUTE 917. WORCESTER TO EVESHAM AND CHIPPING NORTON.

918 Worcester to Upton.

Description.—Class III. Good surface.

Gradients.—Mostly 1 in 17.

Measurements.—Worcester,* Cross.
2¾ Powick.*
10½ 7¾ Upton.*

919 Evesham to Winchcomb.

Description.—Class II. A very good road.

Gradients.—At 8½m. 1 in 16.

Measurements.—Evesham,* Clock.
3⅝ Sedgebarrow.*
10½ 6⅞ Winchcomb.*

Principal Objects of Interest.—Winchcomb: Sudeley Castle (ruins).

920 Evesham to Malvern.

Description.—Class II. Splendid surface to Pershore, thence good, but with short steep hills to Upton; thereafter fairly good, but Route 874 is usually preferred.

Gradients.—(† *Dangerous.*) At 1¾m. 1 in 20; 2½m. 1 in 18; 3½m. 1 in 21; 6m. 1 in 17; 8½m. 1 in 22; 9m. 1 in 12†; 11¾ and 12m. 1 in 17; 21m. 1 in 13†; 21½m. 1 in 12†.

Measurements.—Evesham,* Clock.
7¾ Pershore.*
14⅝ 7⅞ Upton.*
21¾ 15 7⅛ Malvern,* Bellevue Ter.

Principal Objects of Interest.—Pershore: Church. Malvern: Wells, Priory Church, Malvern Hills, &c.

921 Kidderminster to Bromyard.

Description.—Class III. Very good surface through Stourport to Witley; thereafter, while the surface is fair, the hills are dangerous.

Gradients.—At 7 & 9m. 1 in 17; 9¾m. 1 in 10; 10¾m. 1 in 9; 11½m. 1 in 10; 13m. 1 in 8; 15m. 1 in 10; 18¾ & 19m. 1 in 13; 20m. 1 in 11 (all dangerous).

Milestones.—Measured from Kidderminster.

Measurements.—Kidderminster,* Town Hall.
3¾ Stourport.*
9⅛ 5⅜ Witley,* Hundred House.
11¾ 8 2⅝ Stanford Bridge.*
20¾ 17 11⅝ 9 Bromyard.*

Principal Objects of Interest.—Witley: Court, Woodbury Hill. Bromyard: Church.

Hotels or Inns at places marked*, and at Dunley, &c.

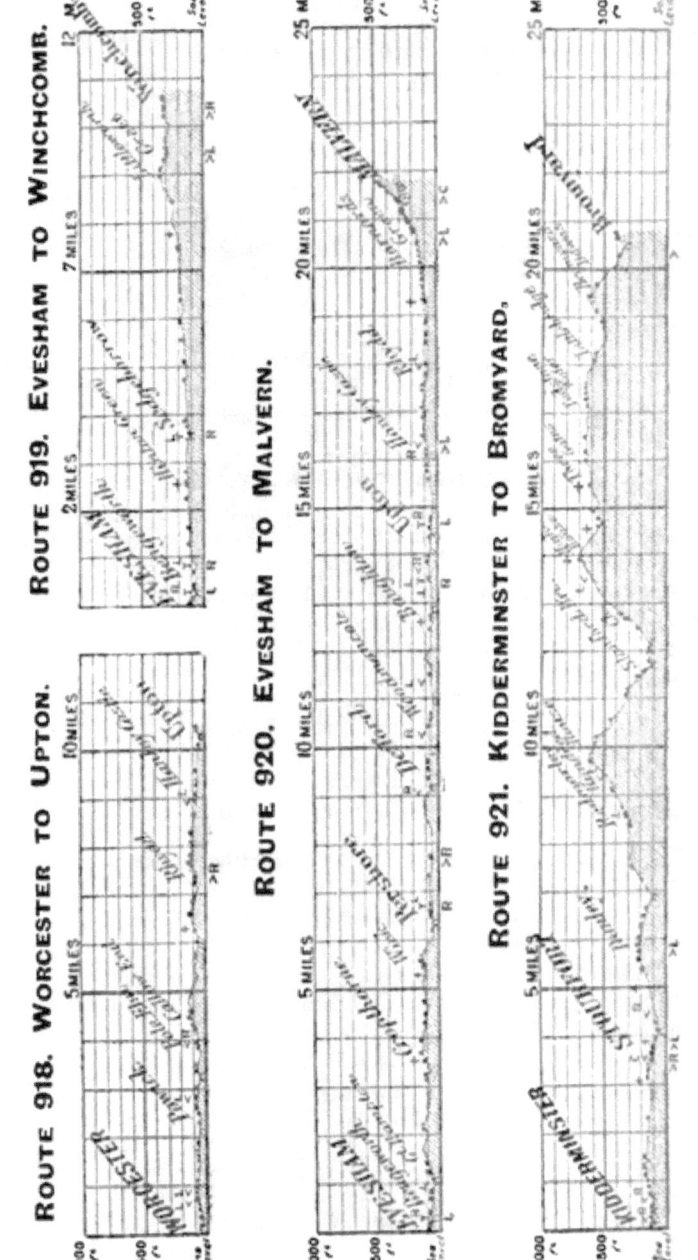

ROUTE 918. WORCESTER TO UPTON.

ROUTE 919. EVESHAM TO WINCHCOMB.

ROUTE 920. EVESHAM TO MALVERN.

ROUTE 921. KIDDERMINSTER TO BROMYARD.

(29)

922 KIDDERMINSTER TO ALCESTER, &c.

Description.—Class II. An excellent, but slightly undulating road to Droitwich, then good, but with a dangerous hill at New End.

Gradients.—At 1½m. 1 in 17; 2¼m. 1 in 20; 3m. 1 in 16; 15m. 1 in 14; 19¼m. 1 in 14; 21m. 1 in 13 (dangerous).

Milestones.—Measured from Kidderminster, & Droitwich.

Measurements.

Kidderminster,* Town Hall.
10¼ Droitwich,* Town Hall.
17⅝ 7⅜ Feckenham.
23⅞ 13⅝ 6¼ Alcester.*
31½ 21¼ 13⅞ 7⅝ Stratford.* R. 916.

Principal Objects of Interest.—DROITWICH: Baths, Salt Works, Westwood Park. Alcester: Town Hall.

Hotels or Inns where marked *, and at Cutnall Green, &c.

923 KIDDERMINSTER TO REDDITCH, &c.

Description.—Class II. A somewhat hilly road, many of the hills being very stiff. For Alcester, keep straight forward at 14½m.

Gradients.—At ½m. 1 in 17; 1m. 1 in 21; 2¼m. 1 in 15; 8½m. 1 in 24; 5¼m. 1 in 14; 7½m. 1 in 21; 10m. 1 in 13; 10¾m. 1 in 14; 11m. 1 in 13; 12¼m. 1 in 21; 13¼m. 1 in 20; 17m. 1 in 18.

Milestones.—From Kidderminster, and Bromsgrove.

Measurements.

Kidderminster,* Town Hall.
4¾ Chaddesley Corbett,* Fox Inn.
9½ 4¾ Bromsgrove.*
(15⅝ 11½ 6⅛ Redditch.*)
16⅝ 11⅞ 7⅛ Crabbs Cross.* R. 939.
22⅝ 17⅞ 13⅛ 6 Alcester.* R. 939.

Principal Objects of Interest.—Chaddesley Corbett: Church. BROMSGROVE: Church. 12½m., Hewell Park. Fine views near Headless Cross.

Hotels or Inns at places marked *, and at Park Gate, Finstall, &c.

924 STRATFORD TO BROADWAY.

Description.—Class II. A country road in splendid condition. For Chipping Campden turn to L. at Mickleton, steep ascent (1 in 13).

Gradients.—At 9½m. 1 in 23.

Measurements.

Stratford-on-Avon.*
8½ Mickleton.*
(11¾ 3¼ Chipping Campden.*)
15⅛ 6⅝ Broadway,* Lygon Arms Hotel. R. 872.

[*over*.

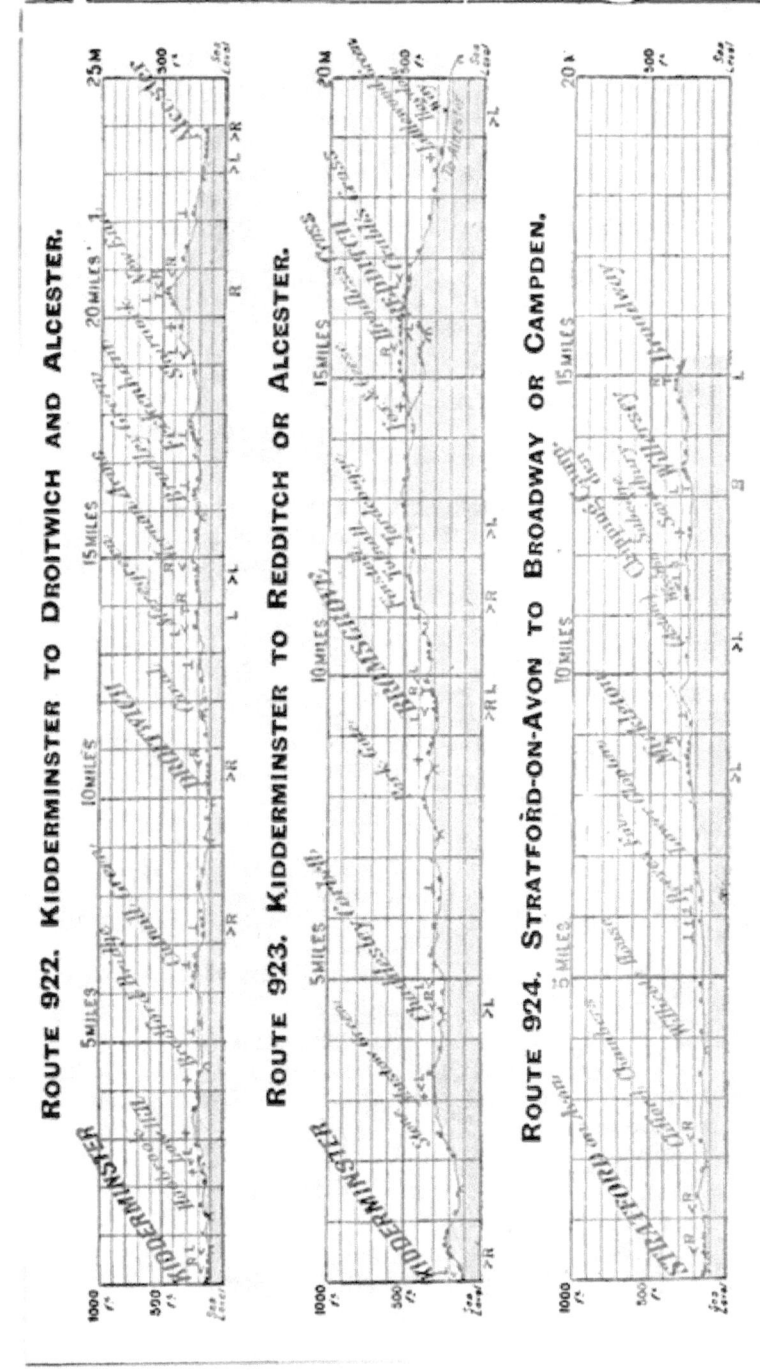

ROUTE 922. KIDDERMINSTER TO DROITWICH AND ALCESTER.

ROUTE 923. KIDDERMINSTER TO REDDITCH OR ALCESTER.

ROUTE 924. STRATFORD-ON-AVON TO BROADWAY OR CAMPDEN.

Route 924—Continued.

Principal Objects of Interest.—Chipping Campden: Market House, Court House. Broadway: pretty village, splendid view from the hill above.

925   STRATFORD TO BANBURY.

Description.—Class II. This road by Kineton is not so good as the direct route, and is more hilly: splendid surface to Wellesbourne Hastings, then rather poor.

Gradients.—All dangerous. At 7m. 1 in 13; 8m. 1 in 11; 9½m. 1 in 13; 13½m. 1 in 8.

Milestones.—Measured from Stratford Bridge, and from Banbury Cross.

Measurements.

Stratford-on-Avon.*
5½	Wellesbourne Hastings,* Talbot Hotel. R. 927.			
10	4½	Kineton,* Church.		
14¾	8¾	4¾	Edgehill Tower Inn.*	
22½	17	12½	8¼	Banbury,* Cross.

Principal Objects of Interest.—Edgehill; Battlefield, 1642. BANBURY: Cross, &c.

926   WARWICK TO RUGBY.

Description.—Class II. The direct route has excellent surface, but several stiff hills; the easiest road is through Bubbenhall and Ryton. From Blueboar to Rugby the direct road is somewhat stiff, and many prefer to follow the longer road, with better surface, through Dunchurch.

Gradients.—At 7½m. 1 in 15; 8m. 1 in 13; 9½m. 1 in 16; 13¾m. 1 in 21; 15½m. 1 in 17; 16m. 1 in 16.

By Bubbenhall.—At 10m. 1 in 17.

Measurements.

Warwick.* Court House.
(2¼	Leamington,* Town Hall.)			
9½	7¼	Princethorpe,* Three Horse Shoes.		
12¾	10¾	3½	Blueboar Farm.	
16¾	14¾	7½	4	Rugby,* Market.

By Bubbenhall.

Warwick,* Court House.
(2¼	Leamington,* Town Hall.)			
7¼	5¼	Bubbenhall.		
13¾	11¾	6½	Blueboar Farm.	
15½	13½	8¼	2¼	Dunchurch.*
18¾	16¾	11½	5	2¾	Rugby,* Market.

Principal Objects of Interest.—LEAMINGTON: Town Hall, Spa, Free Library, &c. RUGBY: School.

Hotels or Inns at places marked*, and at Cubbington, Wetherley, and Bilton.

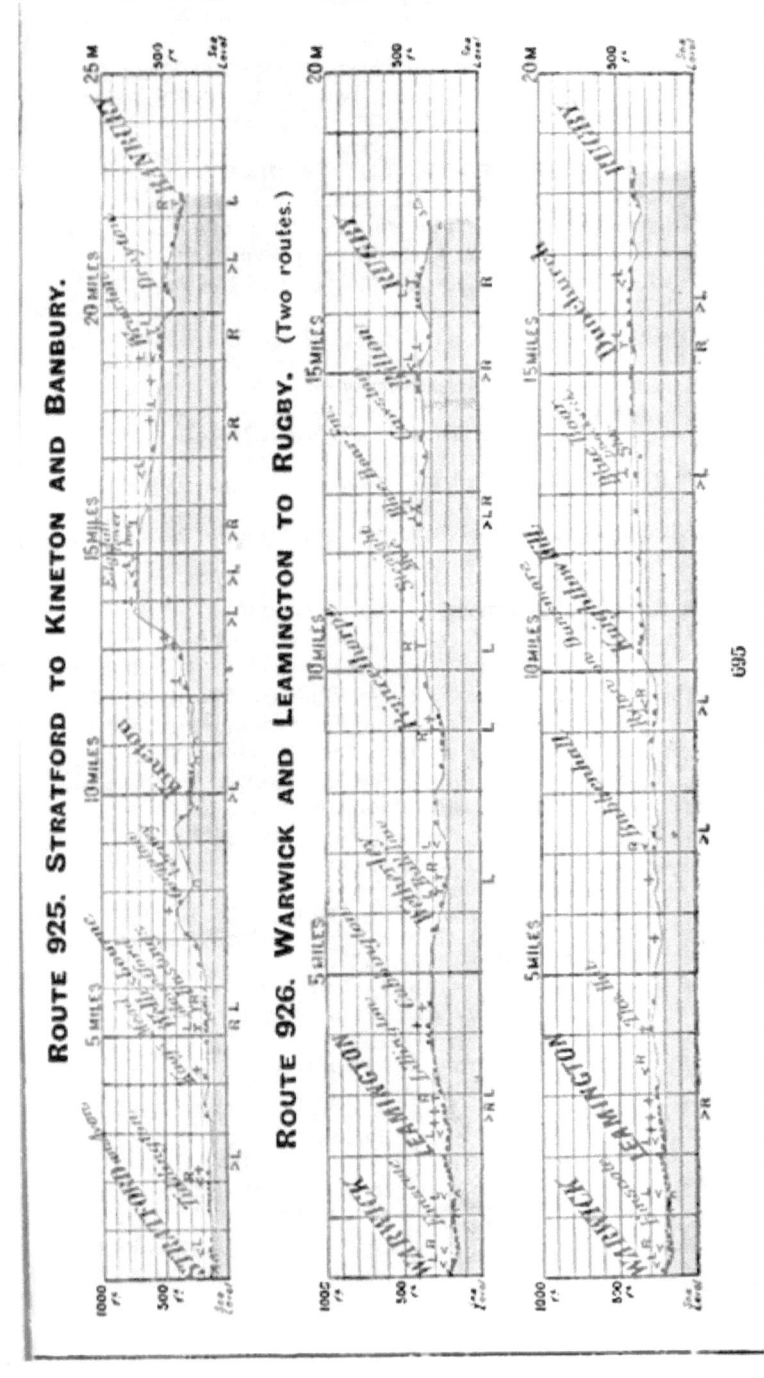

ROUTE 925. STRATFORD TO KINETON AND BANBURY.

ROUTE 926. WARWICK AND LEAMINGTON TO RUGBY. (Two routes.)

927 WARWICK TO STOW-ON-THE-WOLD.

Description.—Class III. Splendid surface to Wellesbourne; thereafter it is a somewhat hilly road, but with very fair surface to Halford, whence rather poorer to Stow.

Gradients.—At 7¾m. 1 in 16; 10¼m. 1 in 23; 11m. 1 in 18; 13m. 1 in 20; 14¼m. 1 in 18; 17m. 1 in 25; 18m. 1 in 14; 18¾m. 1 in 15; 19½m. 1 in 16; 20m. 1 in 20; 25¼m. 1 in 17.

Milestones.—Measured from Warwick Court House.

Measurements.

Warwick,* Court House.
6¾ Wellesbourne Hastings,* Talbot Hotel. R. 925.
13 6¼ Halford,* White Lion Inn.
(16¾ 10 3¾ Shipston-on-Stour,* Church.)
21¾ 15¼ 8¾ Moreton-in-the-Marsh.*
26¼ 19¾ 13¼ 4½ Stow-on-the-Wold,* Unicorn Inn.

Principal Objects of Interest.—Old Roman Fosse Way from Halford to Stow.

928 RUGBY TO HINCKLEY.

Description. — Class III. A slightly hilly country road, with excellent surface.

Gradients.—At ¾m. 1 in 18; 2 & 5m. 1 in 17: 6¼m. 1 in 22; 8m. 1 in 16; 8½m. 1 in 17; 11¼m. 1 in 13; 14¾m. 1 in 17.

Measurements.

Rugby,* Market.
5¼ Pailton.*
10¾ 5¼ Wolvey.*
15¼ 10 4½ Hinckley.*

Principal Objects of Interest.—Street Ashton: Newbold Revel. 13¼m., Watling Street. HINCKLEY: Castle Hill.

929 RUGBY TO SOUTHAM.

Description.—Class II. A good road.

Gradients.—At 3½m. 1 in 13; 8½m. 1 in 22.

Milestones.—Irregular.

Measurements.—Rugby,* Market.
2¾ Dunchurch.*
10¾ 8 Southam,* Market Hall.

Principal Objects of Interest.—Southam: Church.

930 RUGBY TO COVENTRY.

Description.—Class II. A good country road; but the main road by Dunchurch or Bilton has finer surface.

Gradients.—At 7¾m. 1 in 18.

Measurements.—Rugby,* Market.
6¾ Brandon.*
11¾ 5¼ Coventry,* Broadgate.

Hotels or Inns at places marked*.

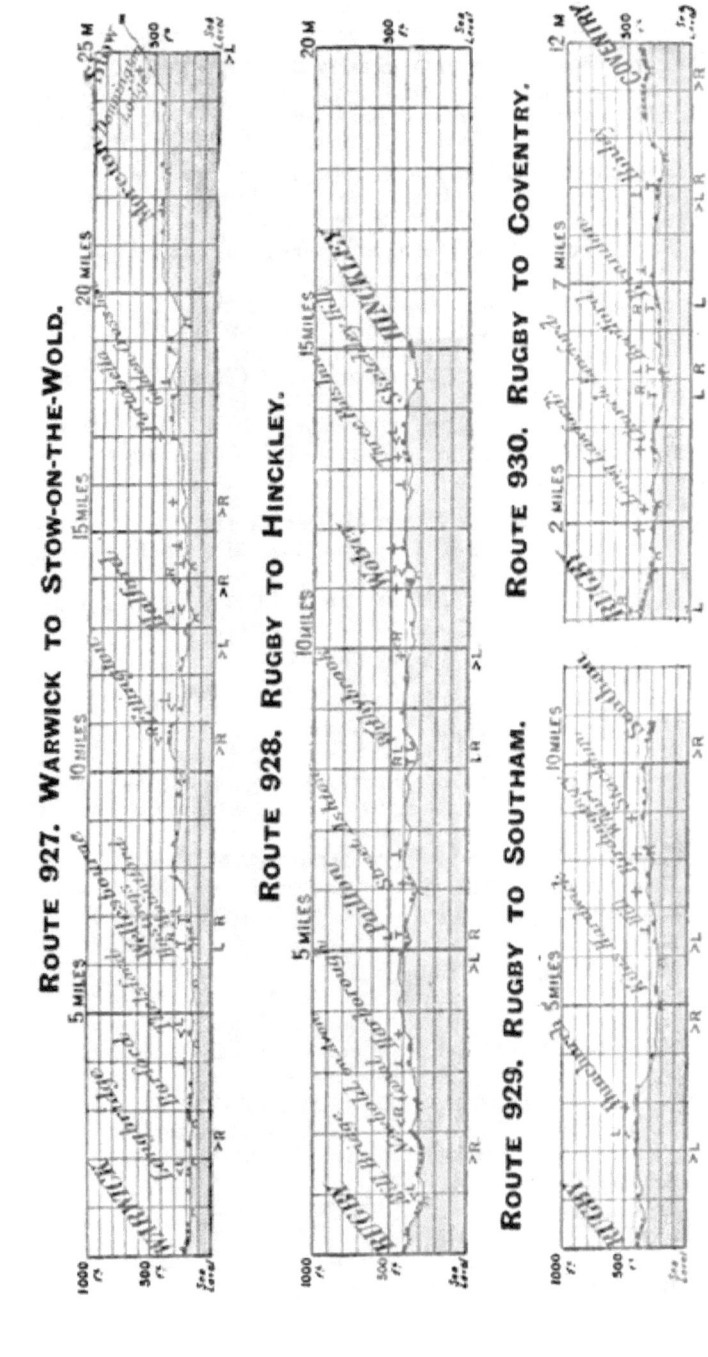

ROUTE 927. WARWICK TO STOW-ON-THE-WOLD.

ROUTE 928. RUGBY TO HINCKLEY.

ROUTE 929. RUGBY TO SOUTHAM.

ROUTE 930. RUGBY TO COVENTRY.

931 COVENTRY TO STRATFORD-ON-AVON.

Description.—Class II. This favourite road has splendid surface all the way, but is bumpy near Stratford.

Gradients.—At 3m. 1 in 21; 3¼m. 1 in 22; 4½m. 1 in 21; 5m. 1 in 22; 5¼m. 1 in 15; 10½m. 1 in 19; 13½m. 1 in 21; 15½m. 1 in 19.

Milestones.—Measured from Warwick Road, Coventry, and from Court House, Warwick.

Measurements.

```
Coventry,* Broadgate.
  5¾   Kenilworth.*
 10¾   4¾   Warwick,* Court House.
(10¼   4½   2¼   Leamington,* Town Hall.   R. 924.)
 18⅝  12¾   8¼  10¼  Stratford-on-Avon.*
```

Principal Objects of Interest. — KENILWORTH: Castle. 9m., Guy's Cliffe. WARWICK: Gateway, Court House, Cas., Church. STRATFORD: Shakespeare Memorial, Birthplace, Church, School, Anne Hathaway's Cottage.

. Hotels or Inns where marked *, and at Windmill Inn, &c.

932 COVENTRY TO BANBURY.

Description.—Class II. The road has very good surface, but there are several rather stiff hills.

Gradients.—At 11½m. 1 in 21; 16½m. 1 in 18; 18½m. 1 in 11; 19¼m. 1 in 14; 20¾m. 1 in 16; 21m. 1 in 16; 25m. 1 in 15.

Milestones.—Measured from Birmingham.

Measurements.

```
Coventry,* Broadgate.
  6¾   Princethorpe,* Three Horse Shoes.
 12¾   6    Southam,* Market Hill.
 18¼  11¾   5¾   Fenny Compton Wharf.*
 26⅞  20   14    8¾   Banbury,* Cross.
```

Principal Objects of Interest.—Southam: Church. BANBURY: Cross, Wroxton Abbey, &c.

Hotels or Inns at places marked *, and at Marton, &c.

933 COVENTRY TO LUTTERWORTH.

Description.—Class II. An excellent undulating road.

Gradients.—At 2½m. 1 in 18; 5½m. 1 in 16; 6m. 1 in 14; 7½m. 1 in 22; 9½m. 1 in 20; 14m. 1 in 21; 14½m. 1 in 18.

Milestones.—Measured from Broadgate, Coventry.

Measurements.

```
Coventry,* Broadgate.
  6¾   Brinklow.*
 10¾   3½   Pailton.*
 15½   8¾   5¾   Lutterworth,* Hotel.
 28½  21¾  18¾  13   Market Harborough.*
```

Principal Objects of Interest.—Lutterworth: Church, and Wickliffe Relics.

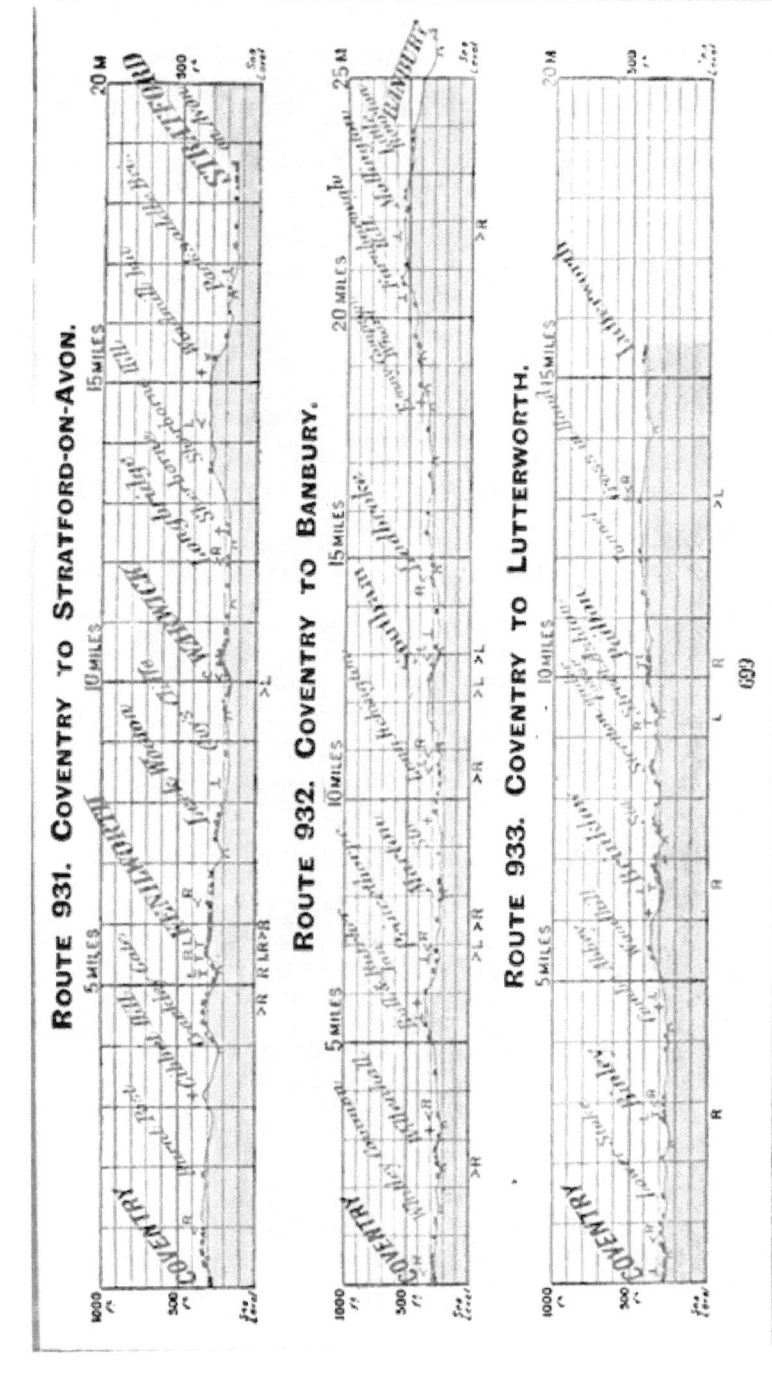

ROUTE 931. COVENTRY TO STRATFORD-ON-AVON.

ROUTE 932. COVENTRY TO BANBURY.

ROUTE 933. COVENTRY TO LUTTERWORTH.

934 COVENTRY TO HINCKLEY, &c.

Description.—Class II. The main route to Hinckley is through Nuneaton, but that road is very bumpy, and there are car lines. The best road is by Wolvey.

Hinckley to Market Bosworth, good surface. Nuneaton to Atherstone, good surface; but there is a dangerous hill between those two towns, in either direction.

Gradients.—By Wolvey.—At 5m. 1/16; 9m. 1/13; 12m. 1/17. By Nuneaton.—At 7½m. 1/21.

Nuneaton to Atherstone, 1/15, both hills.

Milestones.—Measured from Coventry.

Measurements.

Coventry,* Broadgate.
8¾	Wolvey.*		
12¾	4¼	Hinckley.*	
20¾	11¾	7½	Market Bosworth.*

By Nuneaton.

Coventry,* Broadgate.
5¾	Bedworth,* Market.		
8½	3½	Nuneaton,* Market.	
13½	7¾	4½	Hinckley,* or,
14	8½	5½	Atherstone.*

Principal Objects of Interest. — NUNEATON : Church. Hinckley: fine view. Market Bosworth: Battlefield, 1485.

Hotels or Inns at places marked*, and at Ansty, &c.

935 COVENTRY TO NEWCASTLE.

Description.—Class I. The main route to Manchester, Liverpool, Chester, and the north-west of England, avoiding Birmingham, and other manufacturing towns.

The best road is shown on next page; but some prefer Route 936 to Stonebridge, thence to Lichfield as on opposite diagram. A hilly and slightly loose road.

The **Gradients** on the road from Stonebridge to Lichfield are as follows: at ¼m. 1 in 15; 4m. 1 in 10 (dangerous); 4½m. 1 in 16; 5m. 1 in 14; 6¾ & 7m. 1 in 18; 9m. 1 in 19; 10 & 10¼m. 1 in 20; 14¾m. 1 in 23; 15m. 1 in 19.

Measurements.

Coventry,* Broadgate.
8½	Stonebridge,* Hotel.		
12	3½	Coleshill.*	
20	11¾	8	Bassetts Pole Inn.*
27½	19	15½	7½	Lichfield,* Clock Tower.

Principal Objects of Interest. — A rather uninteresting road ; views not very extensive.

Hotels or Inns at places marked*.   [*over.*

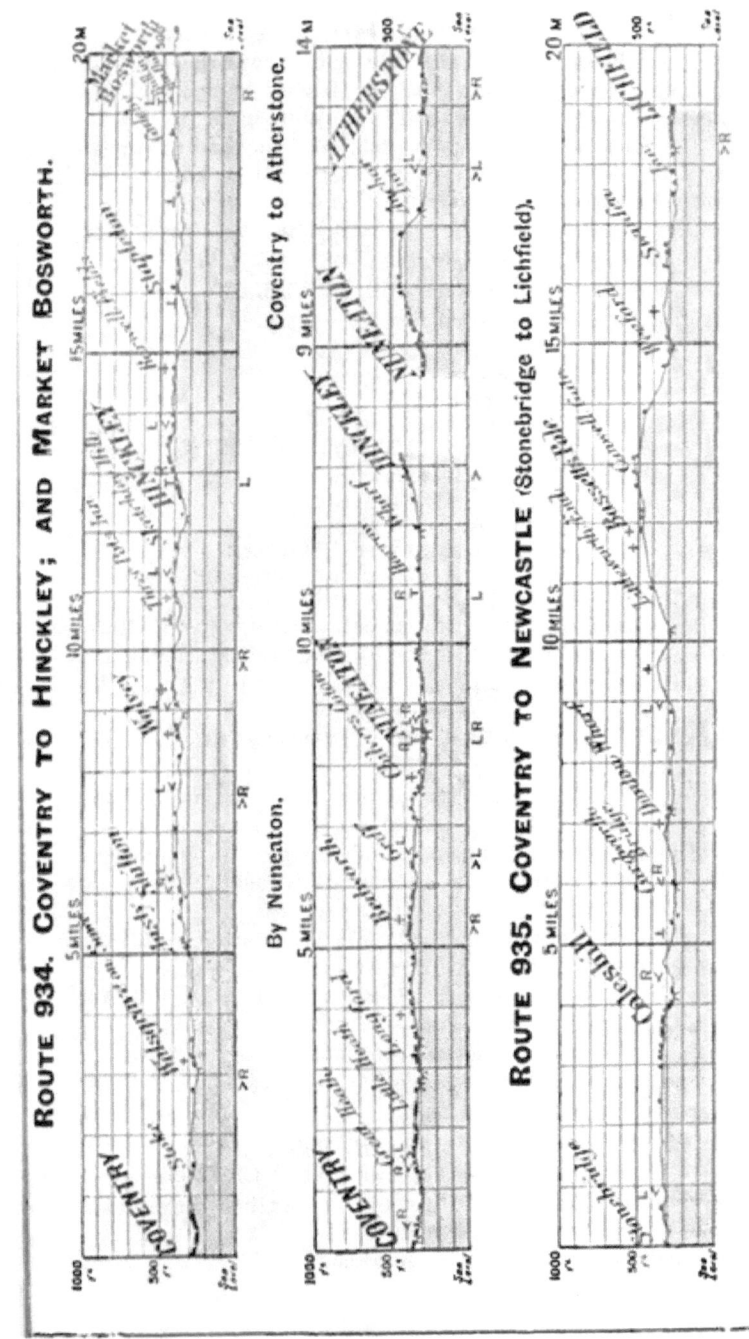

ROUTE 934. COVENTRY TO HINCKLEY; AND MARKET BOSWORTH.

Coventry to Atherstone.

By Nuneaton.

ROUTE 935. COVENTRY TO NEWCASTLE (Stonebridge to Lichfield).

935 COVENTRY TO NEWCASTLE (Continued).

Between Coventry and Lichfield there are a number of hills as far as Whitacre, and beyond that, only slight inclines to Fazeley; thereafter only one hill to Lichfield. (Note to turn to left at Two Gates, thus avoiding Tamworth, and a bumpy piece of road.) From Lichfield to Rugeley the road given here, though not the most direct, has fine surface and easy grades. The direct road (shown dotted) has some rather stiff inclines. From Rugeley to Newcastle the road is flat for ten miles, to Sandon, whence there are some slight hills between that place and Newcastle. The road throughout has magnificent surface, and is a splendid, broad highway.

For Chester (R. 265), turn off at Meaford, 50½m. For Stafford (R. 967), at Wolseley Bridge, 36⅞m. For Longton, at Trentham, 54m. For Stoke and Hanley (R. 958), at Trent Vale, 55⅛m. Newcastle to Manchester (R. 244), 36¾m.; to Liverpool (R. 231), 52¼m.

Gradients.—At 4¼m. 1 in 15; 7½m. 1 in 14; 8¼m. 1 in 18; 21¼m. 1 in 16; 27m. 1 in 21.

Milestones.—Measured from Coventry to Whitacre, whence from Tamworth on to Lichfield; thereafter, from Lichfield Clock Tower on to Newcastle.

Measurements.

Coventry,* Broadgate.
14⅛ Kingsbury,* Swan Inn.
18⅜ 4¼ Fazeley.*
(19⅜ 5¼ 1 Tamworth.*)
26⅛ 12 7¾ 7⅜ Lichfield,* Clock Tower.
34⅝ 20½ 16¼ 15⅞ 8½ Rugeley,* Market.
42½ 28¾ 24⅜ 23¾ 16⅜ 7⅞ Weston.*
44¾ 30⅝ 26⅜ 26 18⅜ 11 2¼ Sandon.*
49 34⅞ 30⅝ 30¼ 22⅜ 15 6½ 4¼ Stone,* Square.
54 39⅞ 35⅝ 35¼ 27⅞ 20 11½ 9¼ 5 Trentham.*
57⅜ 43½ 39¼ 38⅞ 31½ 23 15⅛ 12⅜ 8⅝ 3⅜ Newcastle.*
57½ 42¾ 39⅛ 38¾ 31⅜ 22⅜ 15 12¾ 8½ 3½ Longton,* Market
57⅛ 43 38¾ 38⅜ 31 22½ 14⅝ 12⅜ 8⅛ 3⅛ Stoke.*
58⅝ 44¾ 40½ 40⅛ 32¾ 24¼ 16⅜ 14⅛ 9⅜ 4⅞ Hanley.*

Principal Objects of Interest.—Two Gates: Watling Street. TAMWORTH: Castle. LICHFIELD: Cathedral, Johnson's Birthplace, Statue, St. John's Hospital. Armitage: Church. RUGELEY: Cannock Chase. 40m., Ingestre Park. Sandon: Park. Trentham: Hall. NEWCASTLE: Keele Hall, Iron Works, Pottery District. Pretty scenery near Whitacre; flat and uninteresting near Tamworth; pretty between Rugeley and Newcastle, specially so near Trentham.

Hotels or Inns at places marked*, and at Dosthill, Wolseley Bridge, Haywood, Meaford, Trentham, & Trent Vale.

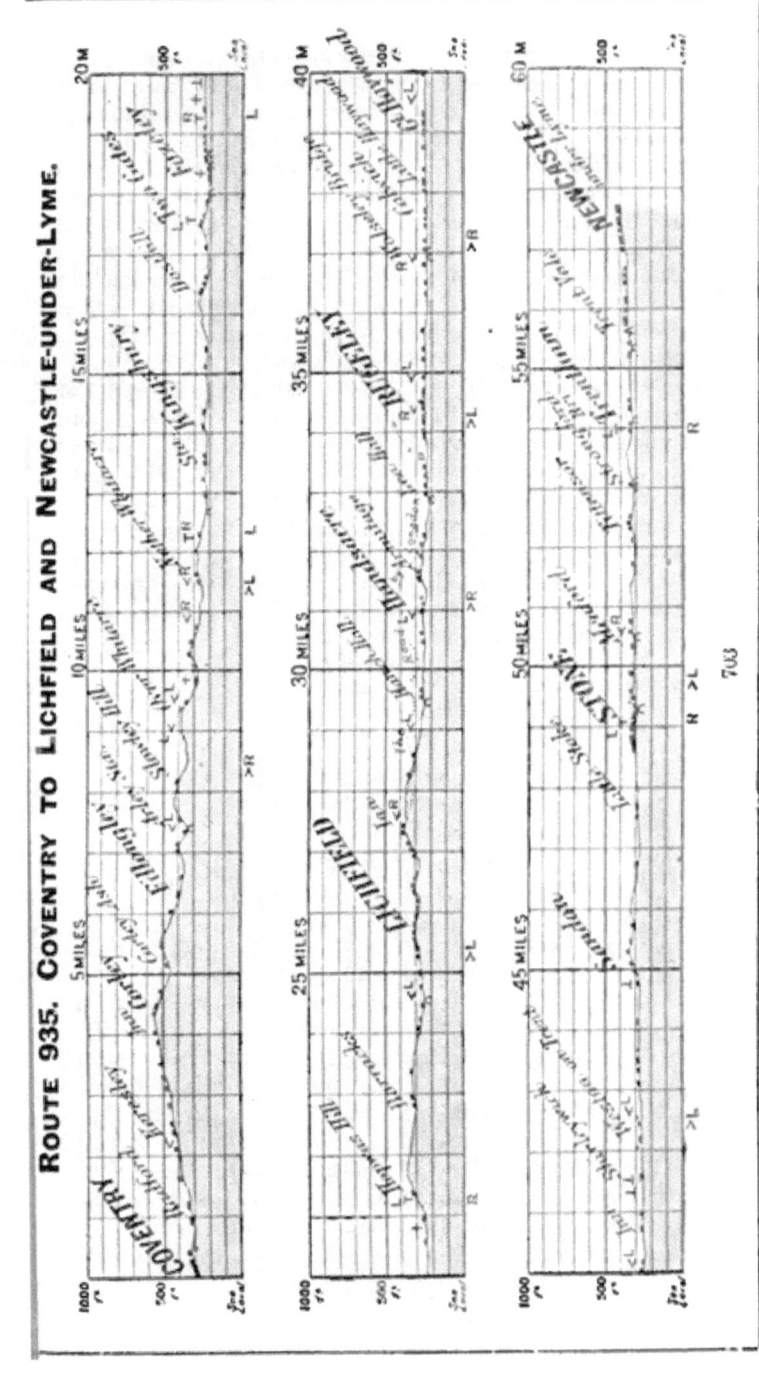

ROUTE 935. COVENTRY TO LICHFIELD AND NEWCASTLE-UNDER-LYME.

936 COVENTRY TO SHREWSBURY.

Description.—Class II. Although the main route to Shrewsbury is through Birmingham, this road avoids the 18 miles of Black Country that is most objectionable, both owing to heavy traffic, slag heaps, and spouting furnaces. At several points the surface on this road is a little loose, but the surface is generally in good condition to Cannock, whence the road has splendid surface to Crackley Bank. From there to Wellington the road is rough and steep, and it is almost better to go round by Shifnal. Note not to go straight forward past Oakengates, as the road is narrow and very steep; follow the route by Snedshill and Ketley Bank, or by Shifnal. From Wellington to Shrewsbury, see Route 949.

The road from Lichfield (shown dotted) joins in at Brownhills (Rising Sun Inn); it has good surface. The old Chester Road to Newport branches off to R. at 43⅛m.

Gradients.—At 5¼m. 1 in 20; 8¼m. 1 in 14; 8½m. 1 in 22; 11¼m. 1 in 15; 14¾m. 1 in 20; 15½m. 1 in 15; 25m. 1 in 20; 42½m. 1 in 18; 43m. 1 in 20; 47m. 1 in 17; 47¼m. 1 in 13; 48m. 1 in 22; 49¾m. 1 in 20.

Milestones.—Irregular to Brownhills, whence from Chester. Irregular after Weston.

Measurements.

Coventry,* Broadgate.
8⅛ Stonebridge,* Hotel.
14½ 6⅜ Castle Bromwich.*
27 18 12½ Brownhills,* Station Hotel.
(... ... ... Lichfield,* Clock Tower.)
31⅛ 23 16⅝ 4⅛ 9⅛ Church Bridge,* (Cannock).
(32⅞ 24¾ 18⅜ 5⅞ 10⅞ 1¾ Cannock,* Market Hall.)
35⅝ 27¾ 21⅛ 8⅝ 13⅝ 4⅜ 4⅝ Gailey,* Spread Eagle. R. 958.
40⅝ 32½ 26⅛ 13⅝ 18⅝ 9½ 9⅜ 4¾ Ivetsey Bank.*
(49⅛ 41 34⅝ 22⅛ 27⅛ 18 17⅞ 13¼ 8½ Newport.* R. 951.)
45⅜ 37¼ 30⅞ 18⅜ 23⅜ 14¼ 14⅛ 9½ 4¾ Crackley Bank.*
52⅜ 44½ 38⅛ 25⅜ 30⅝ 21½ 21⅜ 16¾ 12 7¼ Wellington,* Mkt.
63⅜ 54⅜ 48 35½ 40½ 31⅜ 31¼ 26⅝ 21⅜ 17⅛ 11¼ Shrewsbury.*

Principal Objects of Interest.—Meriden: Cross. Stonebridge: Favourite Cyclists' resort. 22m., Sutton Park. BROWNHILLS: Collieries. Cannock: Chase. 34m., Canal Reservoirs. Weston: Park. Ketley Bank: Iron Works. WELLINGTON: The Wrekin.

Hotels or Inns at places marked*, and at Meriden, Five Ways, Four Crosses, Horse Brook, Snedshill, &c., &c.

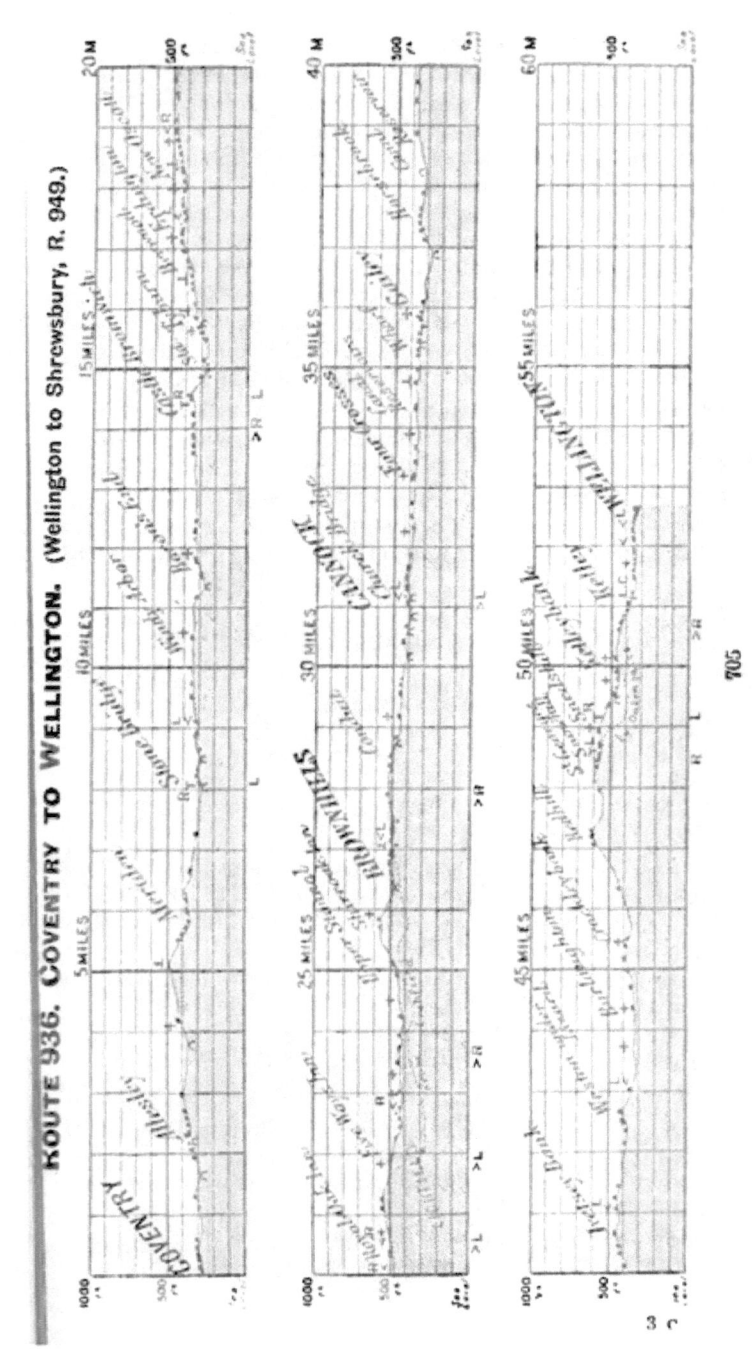

ROUTE 936. COVENTRY TO WELLINGTON. (Wellington to Shrewsbury, R. 949.)

705

937 BIRMINGHAM TO LEOMINSTER.

Description.—Class II. The paving is good for three miles from Birmingham, but the road then becomes bumpy, with two very dangerous hills to Hagley; after that good surface, but hilly to Kidderminster. (Better to train to Stourbridge, and join at Kidderminster, see last diagram). Excellent surface, but a stiff hill thence to Bewdley. From Bewdley to Tenbury there are very steep hills, with a dangerous turn in Mamble, but after reaching Newnham the road at once improves, and is in perfect condition to Leominster. The road from Bewdley, through Cleobury Mortimer to Tenbury, is a succession of dangerous hills.

Gradients.—(† *Dangerous.*) At 5m. 1 in 16; 6½m. 1 in 12†; 7¾m. 1 in 13; 10½m. 1 in 12†; 11½ & 13¼m. 1 in 18; 14¼m. 1 in 16; 17m. 1 in 19; 18m. 1 in 16; 18½m. 1 in 15; 20¾m. 1 in 14†; 22m. 1 in 17-15; 24½m. 1 in 18; 26m. 1 in 9†; 26½m. 1 in 12†; 27½m. 1 in 15†; 28¾ & 29m. 1 in 11†; 31m. 1 in 17; 40 & 43½m. 1 in 22.

Second route.—At 2¾m. 1 in 14†; 5¼m. 1 in 21; after 14m., frequent grades of 1 in 8† and 1 in 11†.

Milestones.—Measured from Market, Birmingham, as far as Hagley; thereafter from Kidderminster Town Hall. After that, measured from Bewdley, then from Ludlow and Leominster.

Measurements.

Birmingham,* Exchange.								
7⅜	Halesowen.*							
11⅛	3¾	Hagley.*						
17⅛	9¾	6	Kidderminster,* Town Hall.					
20¼	12⅞	9⅛	3⅛	Bewdley.*				
26	18⅝	14⅞	8⅞	5¾	Clows Top.			
34¾	27⅜	23⅝	17⅝	14½	8¾	Tenbury,* Swan Hotel.		
39⅜	32	28¼	22¼	19⅛	13⅜	4⅝	Brimfield.*	
46	38⅝	34⅞	28⅞	25¾	20	11¼	6⅝	Leominster,* To. Hall.

Second route.

Stourbridge.*				
6¾	Kidderminster,* Town Hall.			
9⅞	3⅛	Bewdley.*		
17⅞	11⅛	8	Cleobury Mortimer.*	
25⅞	19⅛	16	8	Tenbury,* Swan Hotel.

Principal Objects of Interest.—Very uninteresting to Halesowen. Hagley: Church, Park, Clent Hills. KIDDERMINSTER: Church, Town Hall, Baxter's Statue. Bewdley: Town Hall, Bridge, Wyre Forest. Tenbury: Spa, Market House, St. Michaels College. LEOMINSTER: Town Hall, Butter Cross, Church. Pretty scenery on River Severn at Bewdley; also at Newnham Bridge, near Tenbury.

Hotels or Inns at places marked*, and at Blakedown, Mamble, Newnham, &c.

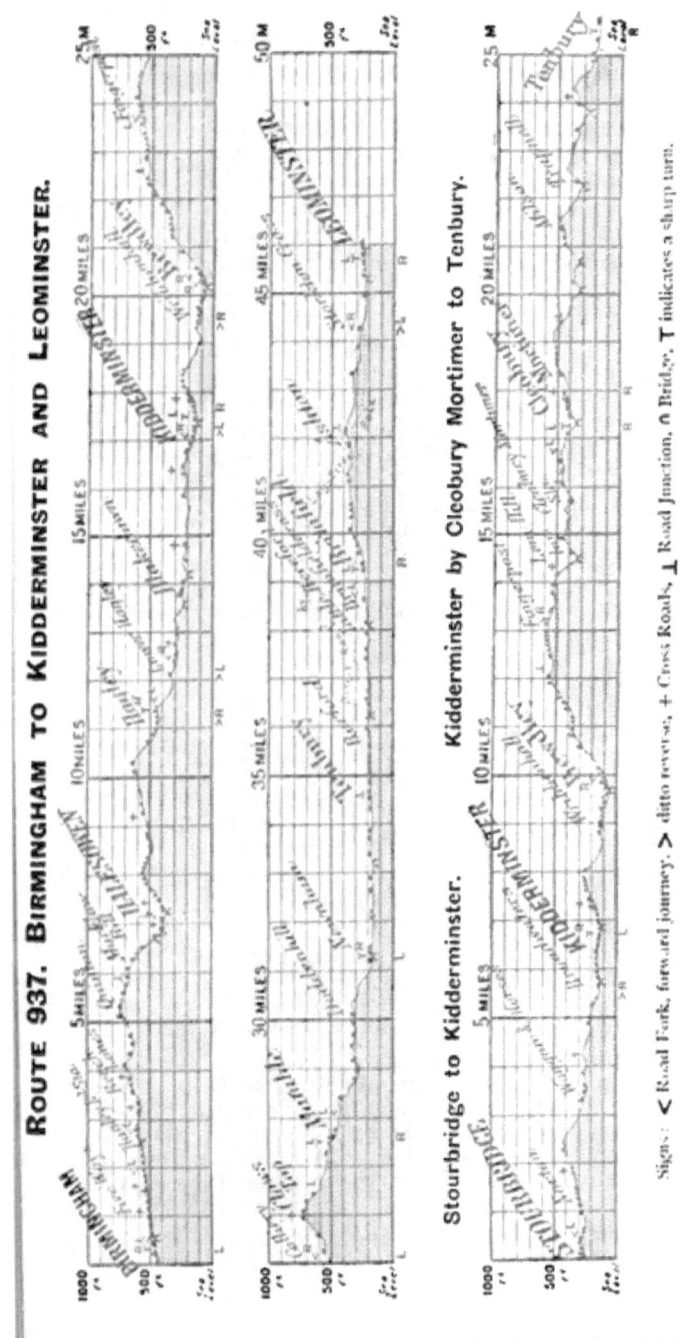

ROUTE 937. BIRMINGHAM TO KIDDERMINSTER AND LEOMINSTER.

Stourbridge to Kidderminster.

Kidderminster by Cleobury Mortimer to Tenbury.

Signs: < Road Fork, forward journey. > ditto reverse. + Cross Roads. ⊥ Road Junction. ∩ Bridge. T indicates a sharp turn.

The direction R (right) and L (left) for the forward journey are above the Road Line, those of the reverse, below.

707

938 BIRMINGHAM TO GLOUCESTER.

Description.—Class I. Car lines for four miles, then a bumpy road to Longbridge, whence splendid surface to Worcester. Fine surface thereafter to Gloucester. This is the main road to Bristol. Upton is off the main road. For Cheltenham, turn to L. at Coombe Hill.

Gradients.—At 4¼m. 1/17; 6m. 1/23; 15m. 1/21; 18½m. 1/19; 21½m. 1/20; 33¾m. 1/16; 34m. 1/19; 40¼m. 1/15.

Milestones.—Measured from Bull Ring, Birmingham, to Bromsgrove, thence from Worcester Cross to Severn Stoke; after that, from Tewkesbury.

Measurements.

Birmingham,* Exchange.								
13⅜	Bromsgrove.*							
19⅛	5¾	Droitwich.*						
26	12⅝	6⅞	Worcester,* Cross.					
33¼	19⅞	14	7¼	Severn Stoke.*				
(36½	22⅞	16⅜	10½	2⅜	Upton.*)			
41⅜	28	22¼	15⅜	8⅛	7½	Tewkesbury.*		
(50	36⅝	30⅞	24	16¾	15¾	8⅝	Cheltenham.*)	
52	38⅝	32⅞	26	18¾	17¼	10⅝	Gloucester,* Cross.	
86½	73⅛	67⅜	60½	53¼	52¼	45⅛	34½	Bristol.*

Principal Objects of Interest.—BROMSGROVE: Church. DROITWICH: Baths, Salt Works, Westwood Park. WORCESTER: Cathedral, Edgar Tower, Guildhall, Porcelain Works, Battlefields, 1651. Severn Stoke: Coombe Park. Tewkesbury: Abbey, Battlefield, 1471. 44m. to Deerhurst Church. GLOUCESTER: Cathedral, Guildhall, Museum, &c.

Hotels or Inns at places marked*, and numerous others.

939 BIRMINGHAM TO EVESHAM.

Description.—Class II. This road by Redditch has very fair surface, but it is not nearly so good as the road by Alcester, shown on the next page.

Gradients.—At 4½ & 8m. 1 in 17; 13¼m. 1 in 15; 22m. 1 in 16.

Milestones.—Measured from Bull Ring, Birmingham, and from Evesham.

Measurements.

Birmingham,* Exchange.					
5½	Kings Norton.*				
13⅝	8⅛	Redditch,* Church.			
15⅝	10⅛	2	Crabb's Cross,* P.O. R. 923.		
23	17½	9⅜	7⅜	Dunnington. R. 939.	
29¾	24¼	16⅛	14⅛	6¾	Evesham,* Clock.

Principal Objects of Interest.—Fine views of Worcestershire from about Crabb's Cross. [over.

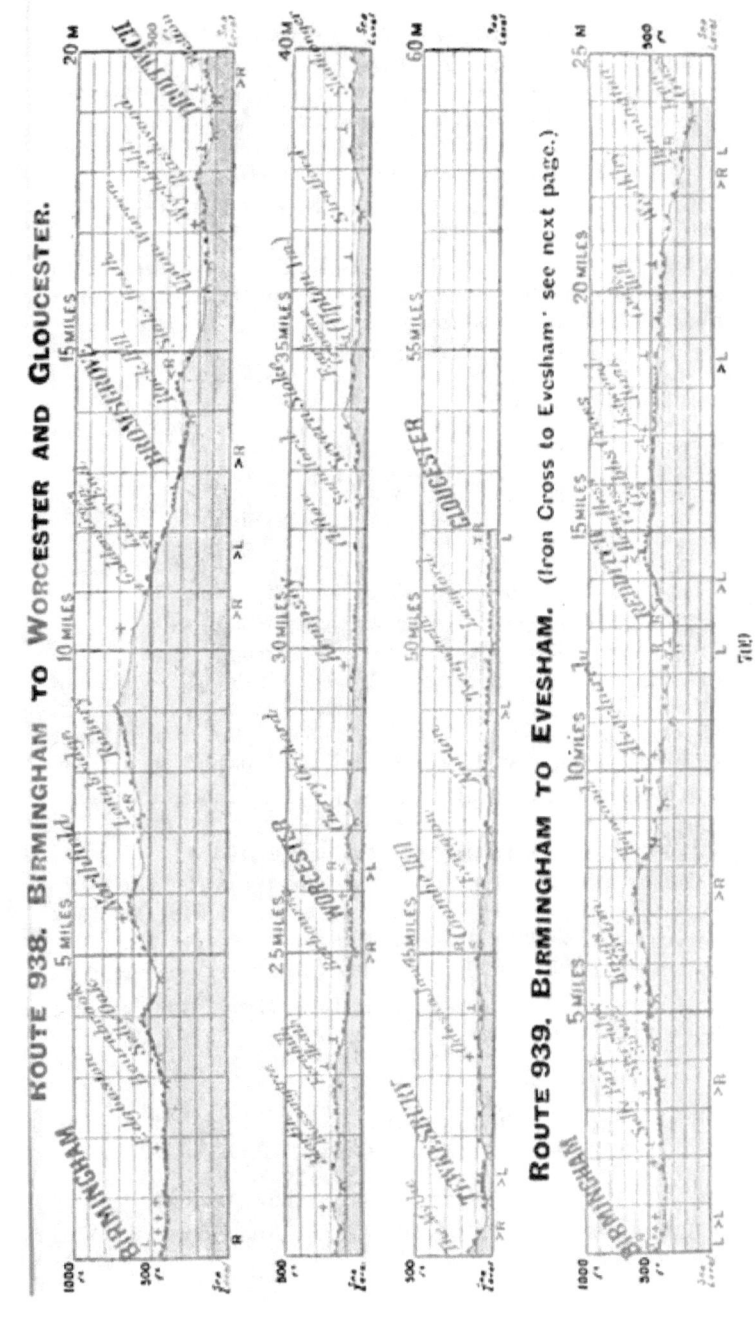

ROUTE 938. BIRMINGHAM TO WORCESTER AND GLOUCESTER.

ROUTE 939. BIRMINGHAM TO EVESHAM. (Iron Cross to Evesham: see next page.)

939 BIRMINGHAM TO EVESHAM (Contd).

Description.—Class I. The Cheltenham Road. Splendid surface throughout; but Gorcott Hill is dangerous.

Gradients.—At 1¾m. 1 in 20; 4½m. 1 in 21; 5m. 1 in 23; 7¼m. 1 in 12 (dangerous); 21½m. 1 in 15; 28½m. 1 in 23.

Milestones.—Measured from Bordesley as far as Studley; thereafter from Evesham.

Measurements.

Birmingham,* Exchange.
8¾ Inkford.*
15½ 6¾ Studley,* Bell Inn.
19¾ 11 4¼ Alcester.*
22¾ 14 7¼ 3 Dunnington.
29½ 20¾ 14 9¾ 6¾ Evesham,* Clock.
45¾ 37 30½ 26 23 16½ Cheltenham.* R. 873.

Principal Objects of Interest. — Alcester : Town Hall. EVESHAM: Abbey ruins, Bell tower, Battle monument, 1265.

Hotels or Inns at places marked *, and numerous others.

ALCESTER to HENLEY (8½m.). A road joining this and the next route; excellent surface, but short, steep hills.

940 BIRMINGHAM TO OXFORD.

Description.—Class I. For the first few miles the road is rather bumpy, but after Shirley it has splendid surface to Stratford-on-Avon. Thereafter very fine surface to Long Compton, where the stiff ascent commences. Fine surface on to Enstone, where join Route 495.

Gradients.—At 3½m. 1 in 22; 12m. 1 in 24; 12½, 13½, & 16½m. 1 in 17; 17½m. 1 in 19; 21m. 1 in 20; 34½m. 1 in 14; 38m. 1 in 22; 40m.1 in 21; 41½m.1 in 24; 42m.1 in 20; 46¾m.1 in 25; 48m.1 in 20.

Milestones.—Measured from Bordesley to Hockley Heath, whence from Stratford-on-Avon; thereafter from Oxford.

Measurements.

Birmingham,* Exchange.
6¼ Shirley.*
15 8¾ Henley-in-Arden.*
23 16¾ 8 Stratford-on-Avon.*
33½ 27¾ 18½ 10½ Shipston-on-Stour.*
39½ 33 24½ 16½ 5¾ Long Compton.*
47½ 41 32½ 24½ 13½ 8 Enstone.*
53¾ 47¾ 38½ 30¾ 20¾ 14½ 6¾ Woodstock.* R. 495.
61¾ 55¾ 46¾ 38¾ 28¾ 22¾ 14½ 8 Oxford,* Carfax.

Principal Objects of Interest.—Rather a pretty road. STRATFORD-ON-AVON: Shakespeare Memorial, Birthplace, Church, Anne Hathaway's Cottage. Long Compton: Rollerich Stone.

Hotels or Inns at places marked *, and numerous others.

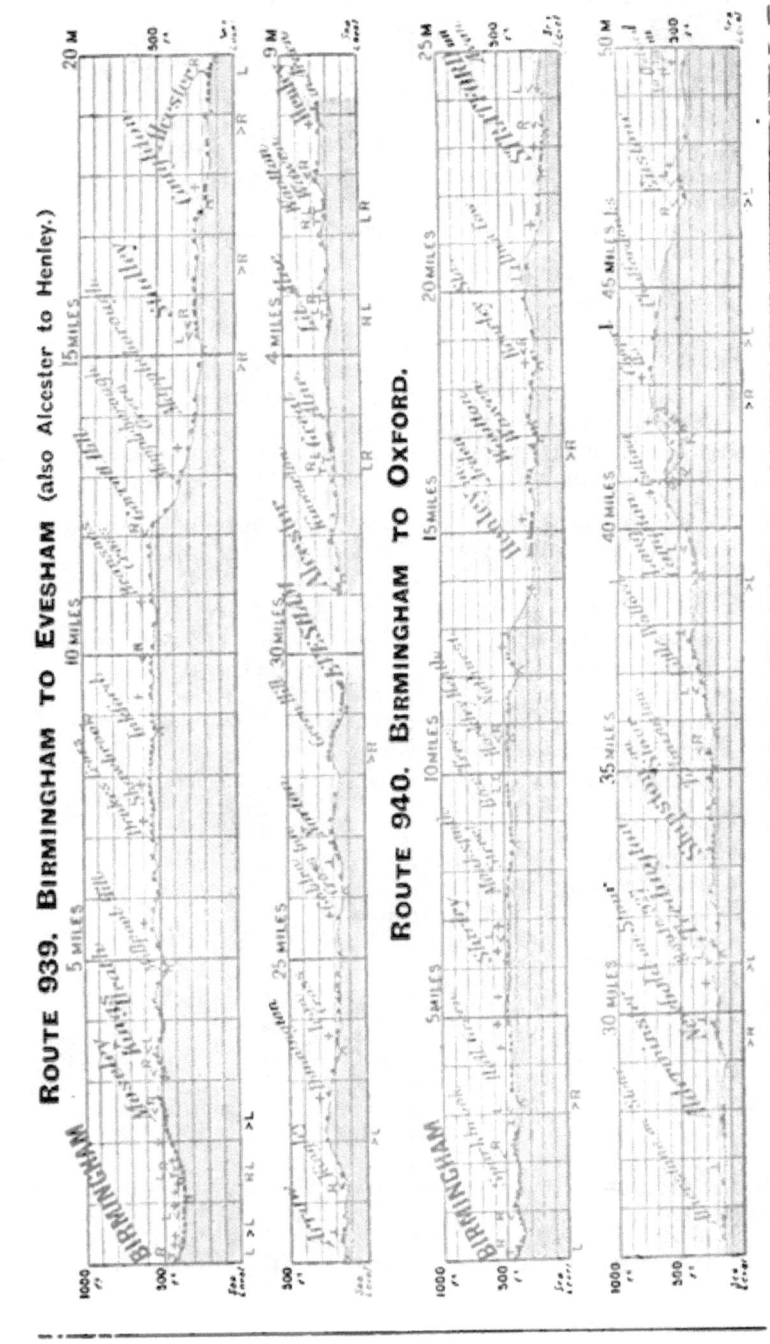

ROUTE 939. BIRMINGHAM TO EVESHAM (also Alcester to Henley.)

ROUTE 940. BIRMINGHAM TO OXFORD.

941 Birmingham to Banbury.

Description.—Class II. This is a splendid road to Warwick; thereafter, although the surface is very good, there are a number of steep hills which make this road very trying. This route to London is often preferred to the direct road by Coventry.

Gradients.—At 8 & 8¼m. 1 in 23; 10½ & 18m. 1 in 17; 20¾m. 1 in 18; 21¼m. 1 in 25; 22m. 1 in 21; 22¼m. 1 in 20; 23½m. 1 in 15; 24 & 26¼m. 1 in 21; 27½m. 1 in 16; 32½m. 1 in 12; 35¼m. 1 in 10 (dangerous); 29½m. 1 in 20.

Milestones.—Measured from Bordesley.

Measurements.

Birmingham,* Exchange.							
7¼	Solihull.*						
10	2¾	Knowle.*					
21	13¾	11	Warwick,* Court House.				
(23¼	16	13¼	2¼	Leamington.*)			
30⅛	22⅞	20⅛	9⅛	9½	Gaydon,* Inn.		
35¾	28½	25¾	14¾	15½	5⅝	Warmington,* Inn.	
40¾	33½	30¾	19¾	20⅝	10⅝	5	Banbury,* Cross.

Principal Objects of Interest.—Wroxall: Abbey. 18½m., Asylum. Warwick: Court House, Castle, Church, Gateway. Banbury: Cross, Bear Garden, Wroxton Abbey.

Hotels or Inns at places marked*, and at Acock's Green, Chadwick End. Hatton, &c.

942 Birmingham to Leamington.

Description.—Class I. & II. The best road to Leamington is R. 941. Bumpy for four miles, then splendid surface to Stonebridge; thereafter the road is good to Kenilworth, but with a ford (footbridge) just beyond the Castle. Splendid surface to Leamington.

Gradients.—At 9½m. 1/25; 16¼ & 17¼m. 1/18; 20½m. 1/17.

Milestones.—Measured from Bull Ring, Birmingham, and from Coventry.

Measurements.

Birmingham,* Exchange.			
9⅝	Stonebridge,* Hotel.		
19	9⅜	Kenilworth.*	
22½	13⅞	4½	Leamington,* Town Hall, or
(23¾	14	4⅝	Warwick,* Court House.)

Principal Objects of Interest.—Stonebridge: Favourite Cyclists' resort. Kenilworth: Castle. Leamington: Town Hall, Spa, Free Library, &c.

Hotels or Inns at places marked*, and at Yardley, George in the Tree, and Kenilworth Castle.

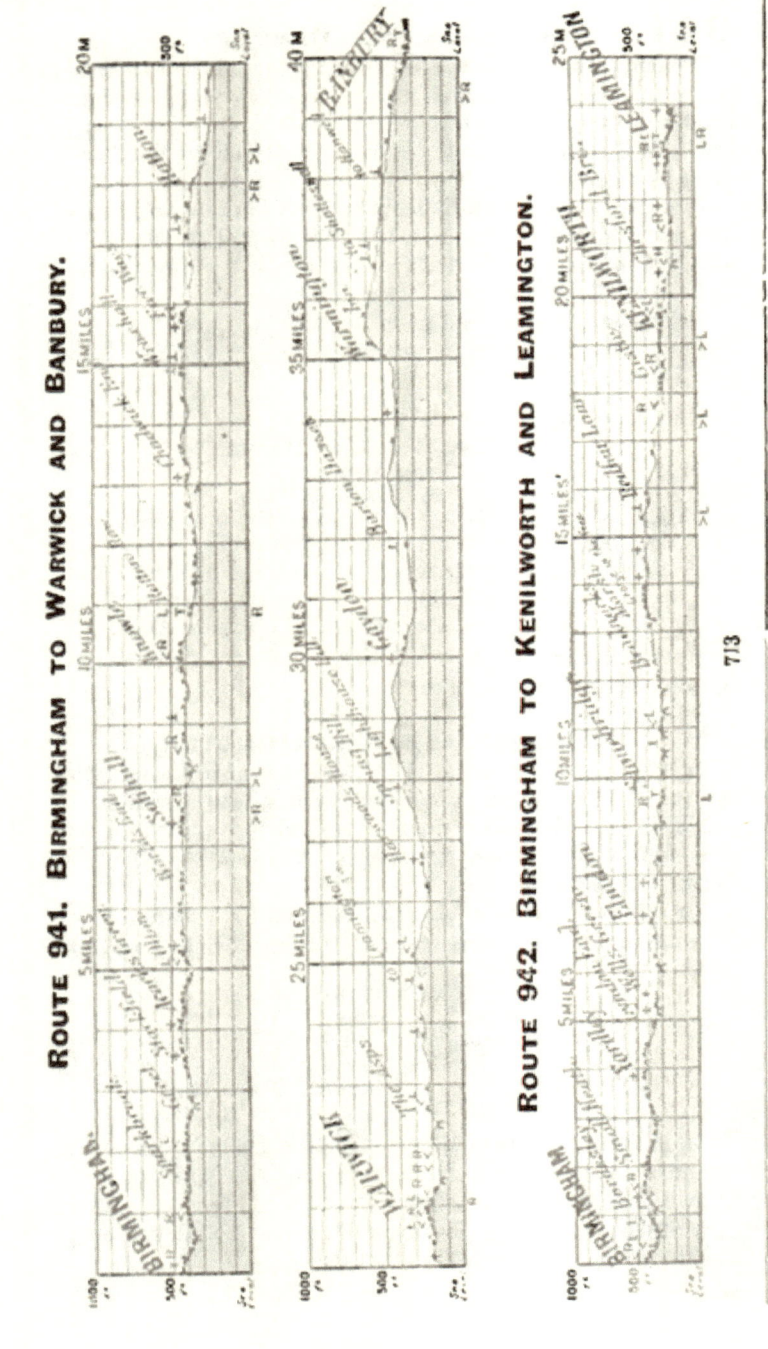

ROUTE 941. BIRMINGHAM TO WARWICK AND BANBURY.

ROUTE 942. BIRMINGHAM TO KENILWORTH AND LEAMINGTON.

943 BIRMINGHAM TO LONDON.

Description.—Class I. A rather bumpy road for four miles, then splendid surface, but a slightly undulating road to Coventry. From Coventry to Dunchurch, the road is equally good, the last five miles being like an avenue. Fine surface to Daventry, where join Route 524.

For Rugby, turn to left at Blue Boar Farm, or Dunchurch, preferably the latter. For Northampton, join Route 357 at Daventry.

Gradients.—At 9½m. 1 in 25; 12m. 1 in 20; 23½ & 29m. 1 in 17; 34m. 1 in 24; 36¾m. 1 in 18.

Milestones.—Measured from Bull Ring, Birmingham.

Measurements.

Birmingham,* Exchange.								
9⅝	Stonebridge,* Hotel.							
11¾	1¾	Meriden,* Cross.						
17¾	8⅛	6⅜	Coventry,* Broadgate.					
22¼	12⅝	10⅞	4½	Ryton.*				
26¾	17⅛	15⅜	9	4½	Blue Boar Farm. R. 925.			
28⅞	19¼	17½	11⅛	6⅝	2⅛	Dunchurch * (to Rugby, 2⅜m.)		
36⅞	27¼	25½	19⅛	14⅝	10⅛	8	Daventry.*	
49½	39⅞	37⅞	31½	27	22½	20¾	Northampton. R. 357.	
108⅝	99	97¼	90⅞	86⅜	81⅞	79¾	London,* G.P.O. R. 524.	

Principal Objects of Interest.—Stonebridge: Favourite Cyclists' resort, Packington Park. Meriden: Cross. COVENTRY: Churches, Cycle Works, Old Gateway. RUGBY: School.

Hotels or Inns at places marked*, and at Yardley, Ryton, Willoughby, Braunston, &c.

944 BIRMINGHAM TO NUNEATON.

Description.—Class II. A good road to Coleshill, after which it is hilly, and approaching Nuneaton it is bumpy.

Gradients.—At 9½m. 1 in 16; 10¼m. 1 in 23; 12¾m. 1 in 22; 13½m. 1 in 18; 14¾m. 1 in 16; 18½m. 1 in 20; 19½m. 1 in 17; 21m. 1 in 15.

Milestones.—Measured from Bull Ring, Birmingham, and from Nuneaton.

Measurements.

Birmingham,* Exchange.				
5½	Castle Bromwich.*			
9¾	4¼	Coleshill,* Market.		
22	16½	12¼	Nuneaton,* Market.	
39⅞	34⅜	30⅛	17⅞	Leicester,* direct.
40⅞	35⅜	31⅛	18⅞	Leicester, by Sapcote (best road).

Principal Objects of Interest.—Coleshill: Park. 18m., Reservoirs, Ansley Hall. NUNEATON: Church.

Hotels or Inns at places marked*, and at Shustoke, &c.

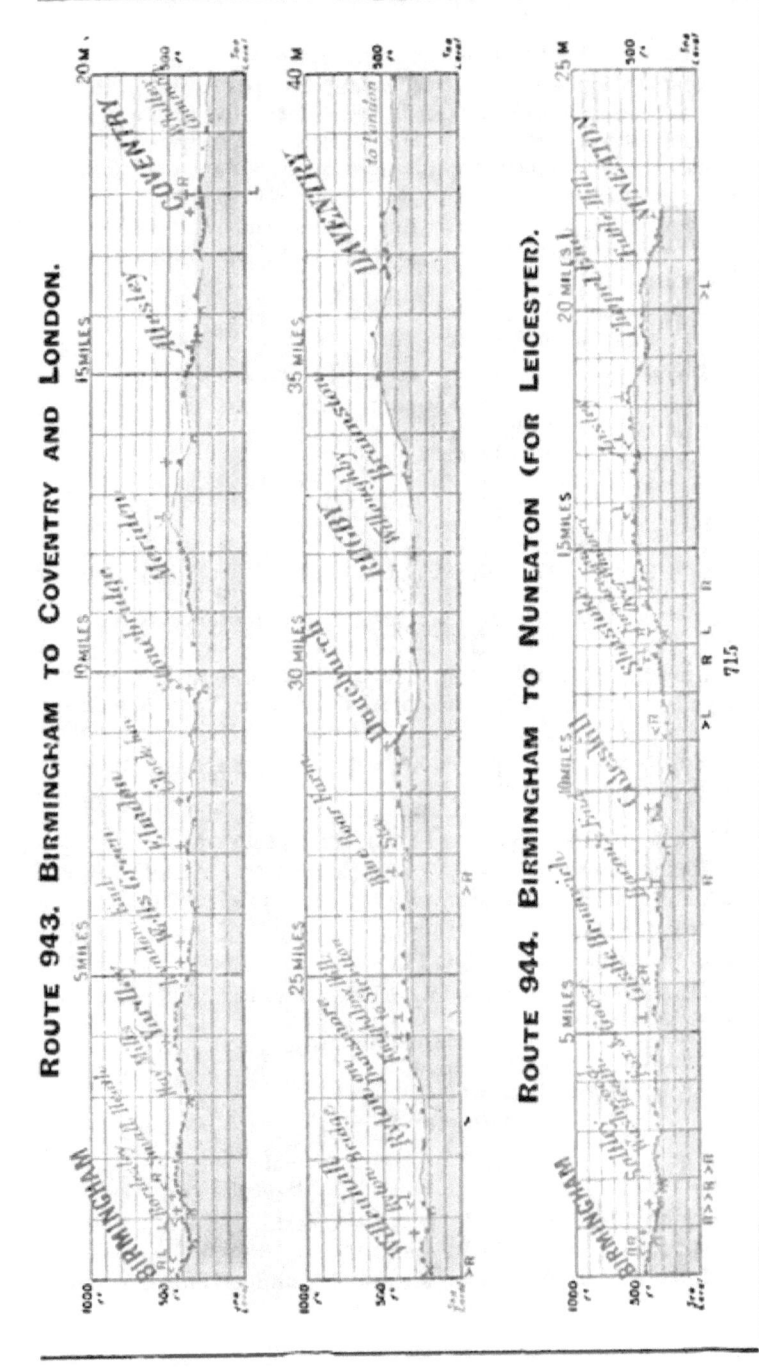

ROUTE 943. BIRMINGHAM TO COVENTRY AND LONDON.

ROUTE 944. BIRMINGHAM TO NUNEATON (FOR LEICESTER).

715

945 BIRMINGHAM TO ATHERSTONE.

Description.—Class II. An excellent undulating road as far as Coleshill, after which, though of very fair surface, the road has several dangerous hills.

Gradients.—(† *Dangerous.*) At 9½m. 1 in 16; 10¼m. 1 in 23; 12¾m. 1 in 22; 13¾m. 1 in 13†; 15m. 1 in 15; 17¾m. 1 in 11†; 18¼m. 1 in 14; 19m. 1 in 17.

Milestones.—Measured from Bull Ring, Birmingham, and from Atherstone.

Measurements.

Birmingham,* Exchange.			
5¼	Castle Bromwich.*		
9¾	4½	Coleshill,* Market.	
19⅜	13⅞	9⅝	Atherstone.

Principal Objects of Interest.— Coleshill: Park, Maxstock Cas. 11m., Reservoir. ATHERSTONE: Mancetter Camp.

Hotels or Inns at places marked *, and at Bentley, &c.

946 BIRMINGHAM TO ASHBY.

Description.—Class I. The Nottingham Road. The main route is by Sutton Coldfield, but the route given here is almost level, and has splendid surface to Tamworth. From Tamworth to Ashby is slightly hilly, but the surface is splendid. (From Sutton to Tamworth, see end of this diagram.)

Gradients.—At 3¼m. 1 in 25; 45m. 1 in 18; 45¾m. 1 in 19; 46¾m. 1 in 23.

By Sutton.—At ½m. 1 in 12 (dangerous); 1½m. 1 in 14; 3¼m. 1 in 17; 4½m. 1 in 18.

Milestones.—Rather irregular. Measured from Aston Road; after Curdworth, from Coleshill; after Tamworth, from Ashby.

Measurements.

Birmingham,* Exchange.						
8⅜	Curdworth,* White Horse.					
14⅞	6⅜	Fazeley.*				
16⅝	7¾	1¾	Tamworth.*			
25⅜	17½	11⅜	9¾	Measham.*		
29¼	20⅝	14½	13⅜	3⅝	Ashby de la Zouch.*	
51⅜	43	36⅜	35¼	25½	22⅜	Nottingham.*

By Sutton.

Birmingham.*			
4¾	Erdington.*		
7¼	2½	Sutton Coldfield.*	
14⅝	10½	7⅜	Tamworth.*

Birmingham to Kingsbury, 12m.

Principal Objects of Interest.—Flat, uninteresting road. Drayton Basset: Manor House. TAMWORTH: Castle. ASHBY: Castle, Baths, Church, Spa, Mount House.

Hotels or Inns at places marked *, and at Minworth and No Man's Heath.

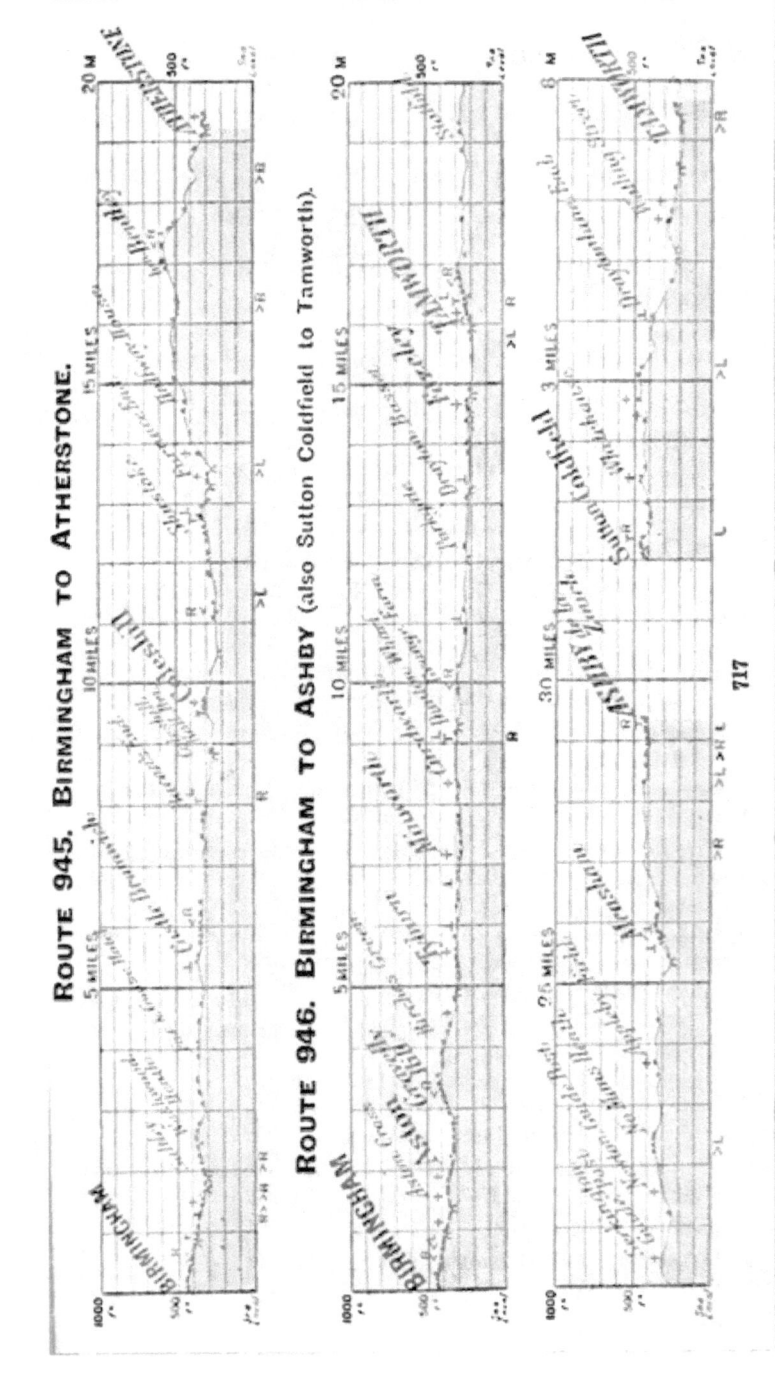

ROUTE 945. BIRMINGHAM TO ATHERSTONE.

ROUTE 946. BIRMINGHAM TO ASHBY (also Sutton Coldfield to Tamworth).

717

947 BIRMINGHAM TO DERBY.

Description.—Class I. The road is more or less bumpy for the first eight miles, but thereafter it is in fine condition to Lichfield, whence after a slight hill there is sixteen miles of flat road, only varied by the bridges over the canals and railways. In Burton there are a number of level crossings. Thence to Derby the surface is splendid, but there are several slight hills approaching that town.

Gradients.—At 3m. 1 in 25; 7¼m. 1 in 23; 16¼m. 1 in 20; 35m. 1 in 25; 37m. 1 in 21; 38½, 39, and 39½m. 1 in 20.

Milestones.—Measured from the Exchange to Watford Gap, then from Lichfield to Burton; thereafter from Derby.

Measurements.

Birmingham,* Exchange.					
7¼	Sutton Coldfield.*				
15¾	8½	Lichfield,* Clock Tower.			
21	13¾	5¼	Alrewas,* Paul Pry Inn.		
28½	21¼	12½	7¼	Burton-on-Trent,* Bridge St.	
39⅝	32⅜	23⅝	18⅝	11⅛	Derby,* Market.

Principal Objects of Interest.—Sutton Coldfield: Sutton Park. LICHFIELD: Cathedral, Johnson's Birthplace, Statue, St. John's Hospital, School. BURTON: Breweries, Bridge. DERBY: Free Library, All Saints Church, Railway Works.

948 BIRMINGHAM TO STAFFORD.

Description.—Class I. The surface is indifferent through the "Black Country" for seventeen miles, but after Cannock is splendid through Penkridge (where join Route 958) to Stafford. Better to train to Wolverhampton, thence as R. 958. The direct road from Cannock to Stafford (9⅝m.), shown dotted, is hilly, and with indifferent surface.

Gradients.—At 5½m. 1 in 21; 6½m. 1 in 22.

Milestones.—Measured from Colmore Row, Birmingham, and from Stafford Town Hall.

Measurements.

Birmingham,* Exchange.						
9	Walsall,* The Bridge.					
11½	2½	Bloxwich.*				
15¾	6¾	4¼	Church Bridge.* R. 936.			
17	8	5½	1¼	Cannock,* Market.		
21⅝	12⅝	10⅛	5⅜	4⅝	Penkridge,* Town Bridge.	
27⅝	18⅝	16⅛	11⅞	10⅝	6	Stafford.* R. 958.

Principal Objects of Interest.—Uninteresting manufacturing district. WALSALL: Statue. CANNOCK: Collieries. Penkridge: Teddesley Park. STAFFORD: Brine Baths, Shire Hall, Churches, Castle.

Hotels or Inns at places marked*, and numerous others.

ROUTE 947. BIRMINGHAM TO LICHFIELD AND DERBY.

ROUTE 948. BIRMINGHAM TO STAFFORD (Penkridge to Stafford: see R. 948).

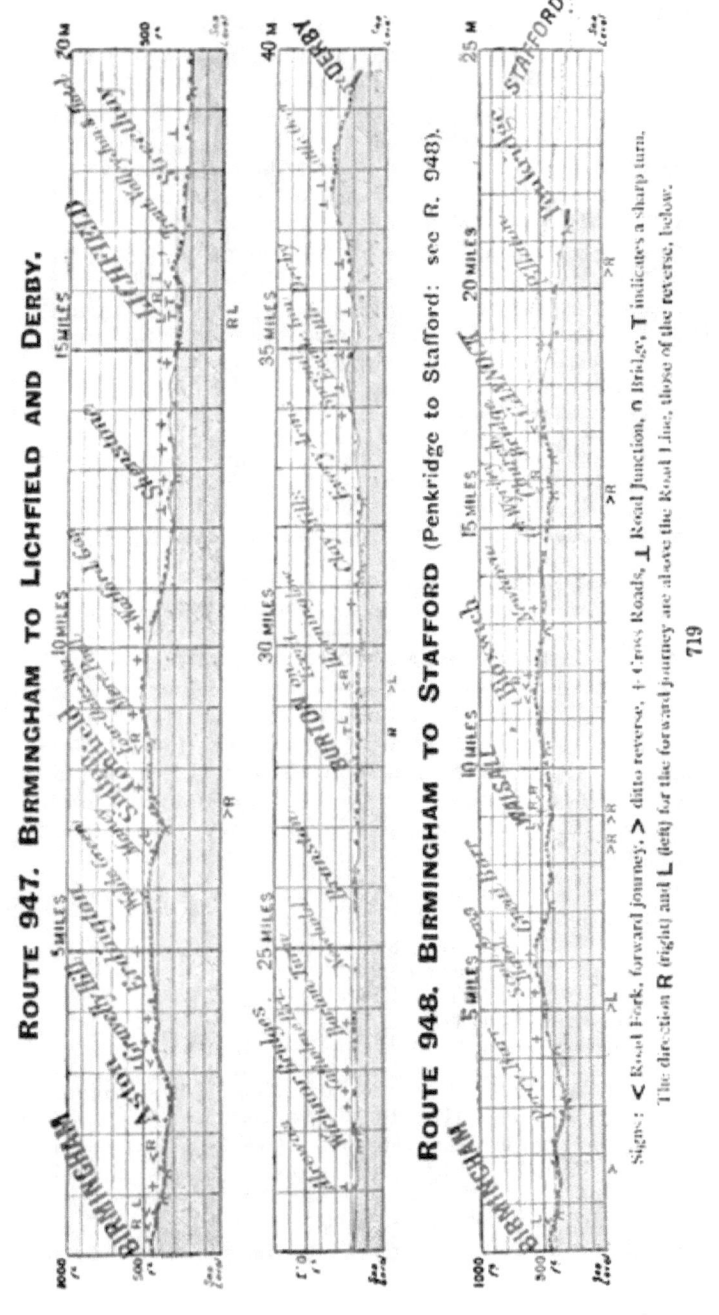

Signs : **<** Road Fork, forward journey, **>** ditto reverse, **+** Cross Roads, **⊥** Road Junction, **∩** Bridge, **T** indicates a sharp turn. The direction **R** (right) and **L** (left) for the forward journey are above the Road Line, those of the reverse, below.

949 BIRMINGHAM TO SHREWSBURY.

Description.—Class I. The main road to North Wales, and Holyhead. The first fourteen miles of this road lies through the "Black Country" and has car lines and paving; but after Wolverhampton there is a splendid stretch of road, until the collieries are met at Priors Lea, whence bumpy surface and level crossings to Wellington. Thence magnificent surface, but the hill in Shrewsbury is dangerous. The principal part of Wellington lies to the north of the main road.

Gradients.—At 7¼m. 1 in 21; 13½m. 1 in 18; 15½m. 1 in 21; 19m. 1 in 23; 26½m. 1 in 22; 28½m. 1 in 25; 29½m. 1 in 20; 43¼m. 1 in 13 (dangerous).

Milestones.—Measured from Birmingham Exchange to Wolverhampton, thence from Queen's Square in that town to Wellington, after that from Shrewsbury Market House.

Measurements.

Birmingham,* Exchange.

5¾	West Bromwich,* Town Hall.				
8	2¼	Wednesbury,* Market Place.			
10½	5¼	2¾	Bilston,* Town Hall.		
13¼	7¾	5½	2¾	Wolverhampton,* Queen's Square.	
25¾	20½	18	15¼	12¼	Shifnal,* Bridge.
32¼	27¼	24¾	22	19¼	6¾ Wellington,* Market.
43½	38⅜	35¾	33	30¼	17¾ 11¼ Shrewsbury,* Market Clock.

Principal Objects of Interest.—WEST BROMWICH: Town Hall. WOLVERHAMPTON: Prince Albert Statue, Agricultural Hall, St. Peter's Church. Shifnal: Church. 29m., Iron Works, Tunnel, and railway cuttings. 38m., Uriconium (Roman City). Atcham: Church. 42½m., Lord Hill Column. SHREWSBURY: Castle, Free Library, Market House, Churches, Town Walls, Public Gardens, Battlefield 1403, &c. View of the Wrekin, near Wellington.

Hotels or Inns at places marked*, and numerous others.

950 BIRMINGHAM TO BRIDGNORTH.

Description.—See next page.

Gradients.—(†*Dangerous.*) At 4½m. 1 in 18; 5m. 1 in 16; 6½m. 1 in 12†; 8½m. 1 in 13†; 8½m. 1 in 12†; 13m. 1 in 18; thence nearly all 1 in 13†.

Measurements.

Birmingham,* Exchange.

7¾	Halesowen.*			
11¾	4⅓	Stourbridge.*		
17¼	10	5⅝	Enville.*	
25½	18½	13¾	8½	Bridgnorth,* Lower.
26⅜	19¼	14¾	9¼	Bridgnorth,* Market. [*over.*

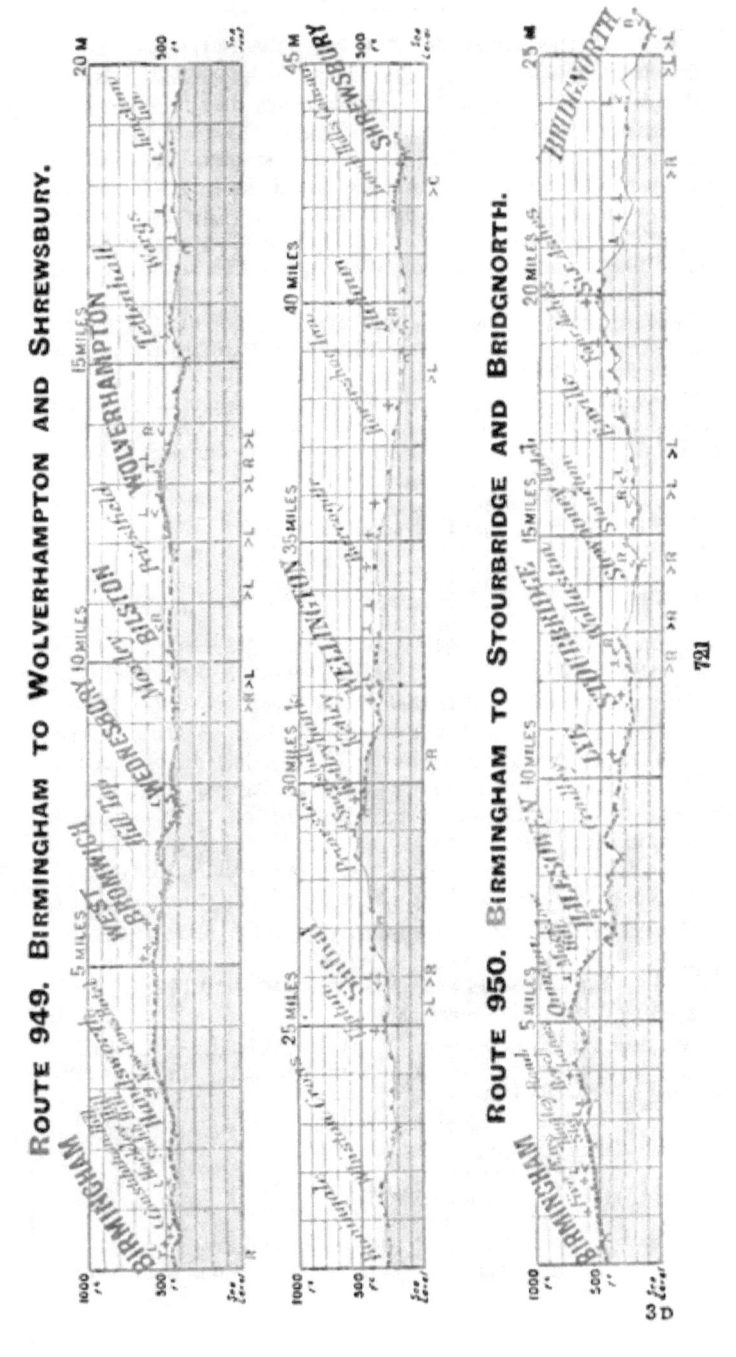

ROUTE 949. BIRMINGHAM TO WOLVERHAMPTON AND SHREWSBURY.

ROUTE 950. BIRMINGHAM TO STOURBRIDGE AND BRIDGNORTH.

721

3 D

950 BIRMINGHAM TO BRIDGNORTH (Contd).

Description.—Class II. Of the two routes, the best is by Dudley, as there are fewer bad hills, but the surface is wretched for the first ten miles, with car lines and paving. After Dudley excellent surface, but it is a hilly road, with a dangerous descent to Bridgnorth.

The road to Stourbridge has wretched surface, thence good surface, but short, steep hills. Bridgnorth is in two parts, the lower town beside the Severn, the upper town perched on a cliff above it.

Gradients.—At 2½m. 1 in 21; 8m. 1 in 17; 8¾m. 1 in 16; 10m. 1 in 15; 11m. 1 in 13; 11¾m. 1 in 18; 14¼m. 1 in 23; 19¼m. 1 in 17; 21m. 1 in 15; 24m. 1 in 19; 25m. 1 in 11-14 (dangerous).

Milestones.—Measured from Birmingham, and from Dudley Fountain; and from Birmingham, and Stourbridge.

Measurements.

Birmingham,* Exchange.						
3⅝	Smethwick.*					
5¾	2⅛	Oldbury,* Town Hall.				
8⅞	5¼	3⅛	Dudley,* Fountain.			
13¼	9⅝	7½	4⅜	Himley,* Dudley Arms Inn.		
25½	21⅞	19¾	16⅝	12¼	Bridgnorth,* Lower.	
26¼	22⅝	20½	17⅜	13	¾	Bridgnorth,* Market.

Principal Objects of Interest.—DUDLEY: Cas., Fountain, Museum. Stourton: Castle, Enville Hall. BRIDGNORTH: Bridge, Castle, Market House.

Hotels or Inns at places marked*, and numerous others.

951 WOLVERHAMPTON TO CHESTER.

Description.—Class II. Splendid surface to Tong, after which poor for four miles, then splendid surface to Whitchurch. There is a sharp turn on the hill at Hinstock.

Gradients.—At ¼m. 1 in 18; 2m. 1 in 21; 6m. 1 in 21; 13¼m. 1 in 21; 24½m. 1 in 14.

Milestones.—Measured from Queen's Square, Wolverhampton, to Junction Inn. London milestones by Watling Street, after Weston Heath.

Measurements.

Wolverhampton,* Queen's Square.						
7⅝	Albrighton.*					
18¼	10⅝	Newport,* Town Hall.				
24⅝	17	6⅜	Hinstock.			
29½	21⅞	11¼	4⅞	Ternhill. R. 977.		
39	31⅜	20¾	14⅜	9½	Whitchurch.*	
58⅝	51¼	40⅜	34¼	29⅛	19⅞	Chester.* R. 263. [over.

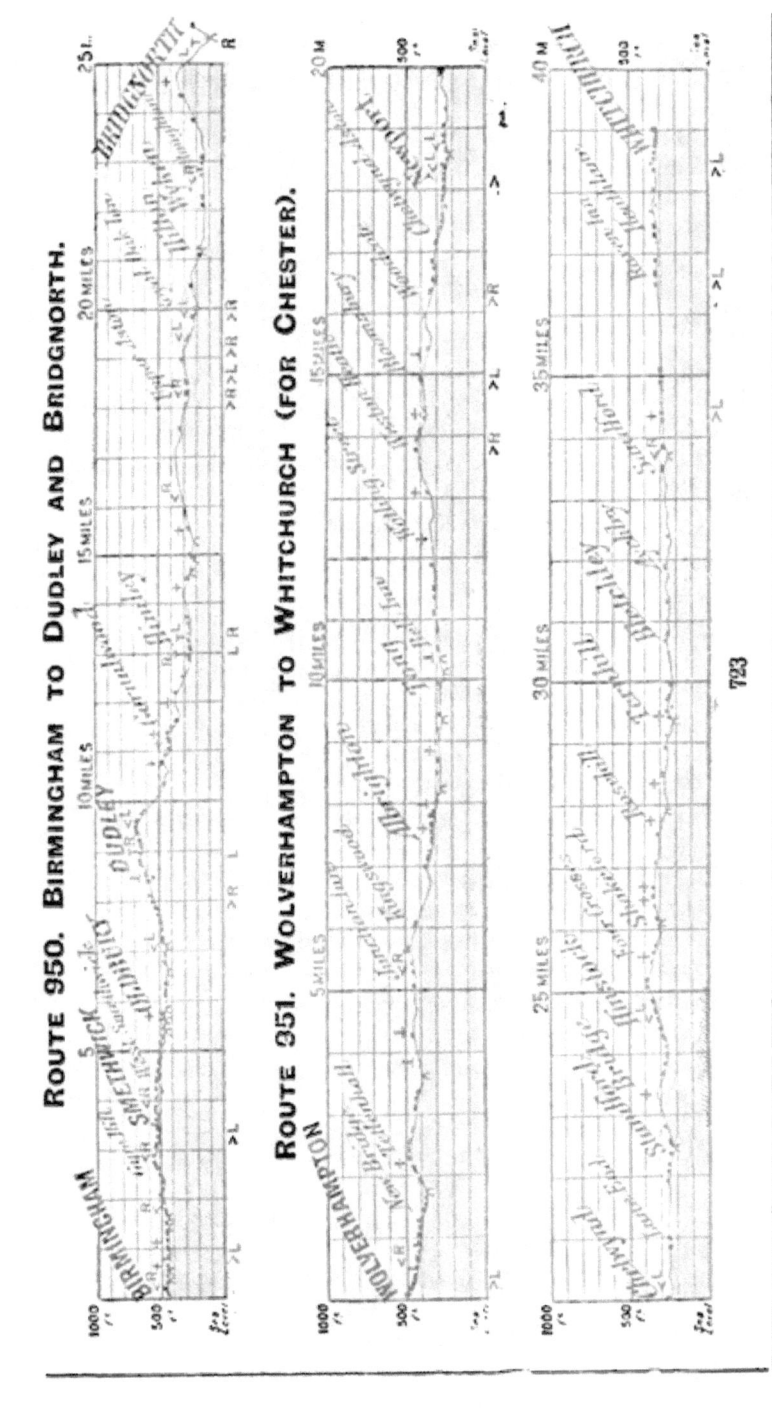

ROUTE 950. BIRMINGHAM TO DUDLEY AND BRIDGNORTH.

ROUTE 351. WOLVERHAMPTON TO WHITCHURCH (FOR CHESTER).

723

Route 951—Continued.

Principal Objects of Interest.—Tong: Castle, Church Bell. Newport: Church. WHITCHURCH: Church. The road is somewhat uninteresting, but is rather pretty near Tong and Chetwynd.

Hotels or Inns at places marked*, and numerous others.

952 WOLVERHAMPTON TO WORCESTER.

Description.—Class II. The best road is by Kidderminster; the road by Stourbridge being rather more hilly. From Wolverhampton to Kidderminster is a splendid undulating road all the way; after Hartlebury it becomes practically level, with fine surface to Worcester. The road by Stourbridge, passing through manufacturing district, is rather more bumpy, and between Stourbridge and Hartlebury there are several very steep hills.

Gradients.—At 3m. 1 in 21; 4½m. 1 in 23; 7m. 1 in 14; 9m. 1 in 15; 17½ and 19½m. 1 in 17; 20m. 1 in 16; 21¾m. 1 in 22.

By Stourbridge.—At 3m. 1 in 21; 4½m. 1 in 23; 8½m. 1 in 19; 14¾m. 1 in 25; 15m. 1 in 16; 15¼m. 1 in 14; 19m. 1 in 17.

Milestones.—Measured from Queen's Square, Wolverhampton.

Measurements.

Wolverhampton,* Queen's Square.

5⅝	Himley,* Dudley Arms.					
10	4⅜	Stewponey Hotel.*				
15⅝	10¼	5⅜	Kidderminster,* Town Hall.			
20	14⅜	10	4⅜	Hartlebury.*		
24¾	19⅜	14¾	8⅝	4¾	Ombersley.*	
30⅝	24¾	20⅝	14½	10⅝	5⅝	Worcester,* Cross.

By Stourbridge.

Wolverhampton,* Queen's Square.

10⅛	Stourbridge.*			
17	6⅞	Harvington.*		
20¼	10⅛	3¼	Hartlebury.*	
30⅝	20½	13⅜	10⅜	Worcester,* Cross.

Principal Objects of Interest.—6½m., Holbeach Mansion. Stewponey: Stourton Castle. KIDDERMINSTER: Town Hall, Baxter's Statue, Church. WORCESTER: Cathedral, Edgar Tower, Guild Hall, Porcelain Works.

Hotels or Inns at places marked*, and at Penn, Whittington, Crossway Green; also at Kingswinford, &c.

ROUTE 952. WOLVERHAMPTON TO WORCESTER.

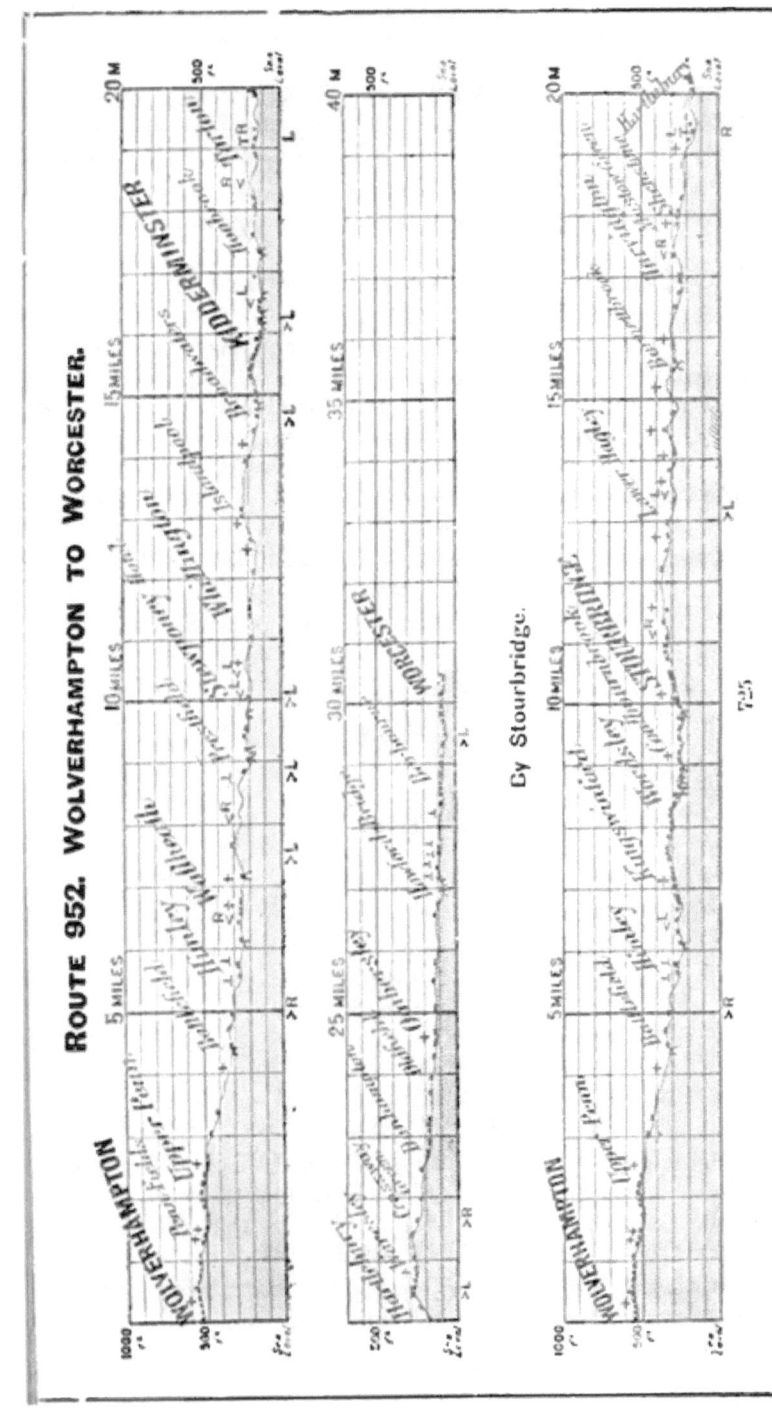

By Stourbridge.

953 WOLVERHAMPTON TO BRIDGNORTH.

Description.—Class II. The road has splendid surface, but there is a dangerous descent to Bridgnorth.

Gradients.—At 9½m. 1 in 15; 12m. 1 in 18; 13¼m. 1 in 11.

Milestones.—Measured from Wolverhampton.

Measurements.

Wolverhampton,* Queen's Square.

8¼ Royal Oak Inn.*

13⅞ 5⅝ Bridgnorth,* Lower.

14⅝ 6⅜ ¾ Bridgnorth,* Market.

Principal Objects of Interest.—BRIDGNORTH: Bridge, Castle.

Hotels or Inns at places marked*, and at Wightwick, &c.

---

954 WOLVERHAMPTON TO BROMSGROVE.

Description.—Class II. The road by Stourbridge, although slightly longer, has rather better surface, and although for several miles near that town it is a trifle bumpy, the rest is usually in excellent condition. The road by Dudley, on the other hand, while fairly good, has car lines for a good part of the way, and between Halesowen and Bromsgrove it is steep and rough at one or two points.

Gradients.—(†*Dangerous.*) By Stourbridge.—At 3m. 1 in 25; 4½m. 1 in 23; 8½m. 1 in 19; 16½m. 1 in 22; 17¾m. 1 in 16.

By Dudley.—At 2½m. 1 in 19; 6¾m. 1 in 13†; 8½m. 1 in 20; 9¾m. 1 in 18; 10m. 1 in 14; 12m. 1 in 13; 13m. 1 in 13; 14m. 1 in 10†; 14¼m. 1 in 12†; 15m. 1 in 15; 15½m. 1 in 12†; 16¾m. 1 in 11†.

Milestones.—Measured from Queen's Square, Wolverhampton, to Dudley and Stourbridge; thereafter from Stourbridge.

Measurements.

Wolverhampton,* Queen's Sqnare.

5⅝ Himley.*

10⅛ 4½ Stourbridge.*

12½ 6⅞ 2⅜ Hagley.*

20⅛ 14½ 10 7⅝ Bromsgrove.*

By Dudley.

Wolverhampton,* Queen's Square.

6¼ Dudley,* Fountain.

11½ 5¼ Halesowen,* Bull Ring.

19¾ 13½ 8¼ Bromsgrove.*

Principal Objects of Interest.—Himley: Hall, Holbeach Mansion. Hagley: Park, Clent Hills. BROMSGROVE: Church. Dudley: Fountain, Museum.

Hotels or Inns at places marked*.

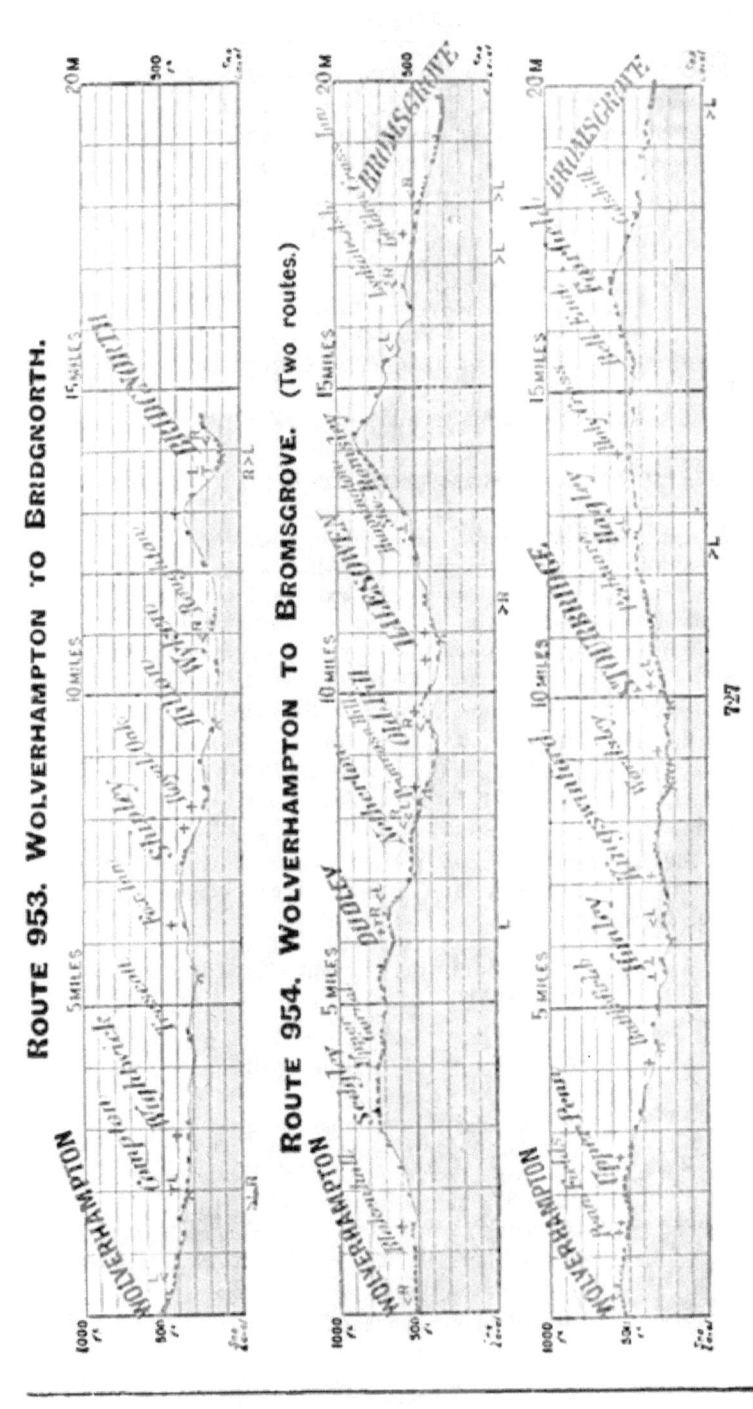

Route 953. Wolverhampton to Bridgnorth.

Route 954. Wolverhampton to Bromsgrove. (Two routes.)

270

955 Wolverhampton to Tamworth.

Description.—Class II. A rather bumpy road, with car lines, to Walsall, thereafter very fair surface, but a winding country road, somewhat difficult to follow owing to the numerous turns and forks. It is not a main road, but is extensively used.

Gradients.—At 16½m. 1 in 17; 17¾m. 1 in 18.

Measurements.

Wolverhampton,* Queen's Square.				
3⅛	Willenhall,* Market.			
6⅜	3¼	Walsall,* The Bridge.		
13⅜	10¼	7	Watford Gap.	
20⅞	17¾	14½	7½	Tamworth.*

Principal Objects of Interest.—Manufacturing district between Wolverhampton and Walsall; some fairly good views are obtained from the higher parts.

956 Wolverhampton to Lichfield.

Description.—Class II. & III. Of the two roads shown, the direct route by Bloxwich is by no means the better; it lies through the manufacturing districts of Wednesfield and Bloxwich, and through the collieries at Brownhills; the surface is therefore much cut up, and there is often loose material on the road. By Walsall the road is considerably superior, and is kept in better order.

Gradients.—At 10½m. and 11½m. 1 in 20; 14½m. 1 in 22.

Milestones.—Measured from Five Ways, Wolverhampton, and from Lichfield, Clock Tower.

Measurements.

Wolverhampton,* Queen's Square.				
3⅛	Willenhall,* Market.			
6⅜	3¼	Walsall,* The Bridge.		
10	6⅞	3⅝	Walsall Wood,* Bridge.	
16	12⅞	9⅝	6	Lichfield,* Clock Tower.

Direct Road.

Wolverhampton,* Queen's Square.				
2¼	Wednesfield.*			
6	3¾	Bloxwich.*		
9⅝	7⅜	3⅝	Brownhills,* Station.	
14⅞	12⅝	8⅞	5¼	Lichfield,* Clock Tower.

Principal Objects of Interest. — Uninteresting road, through manufacturing district. LICHFIELD: Cathedral, Johnson's Birthplace & Statue, St. John's Hospital, School.

Hotels or Inns at places marked*, &c.

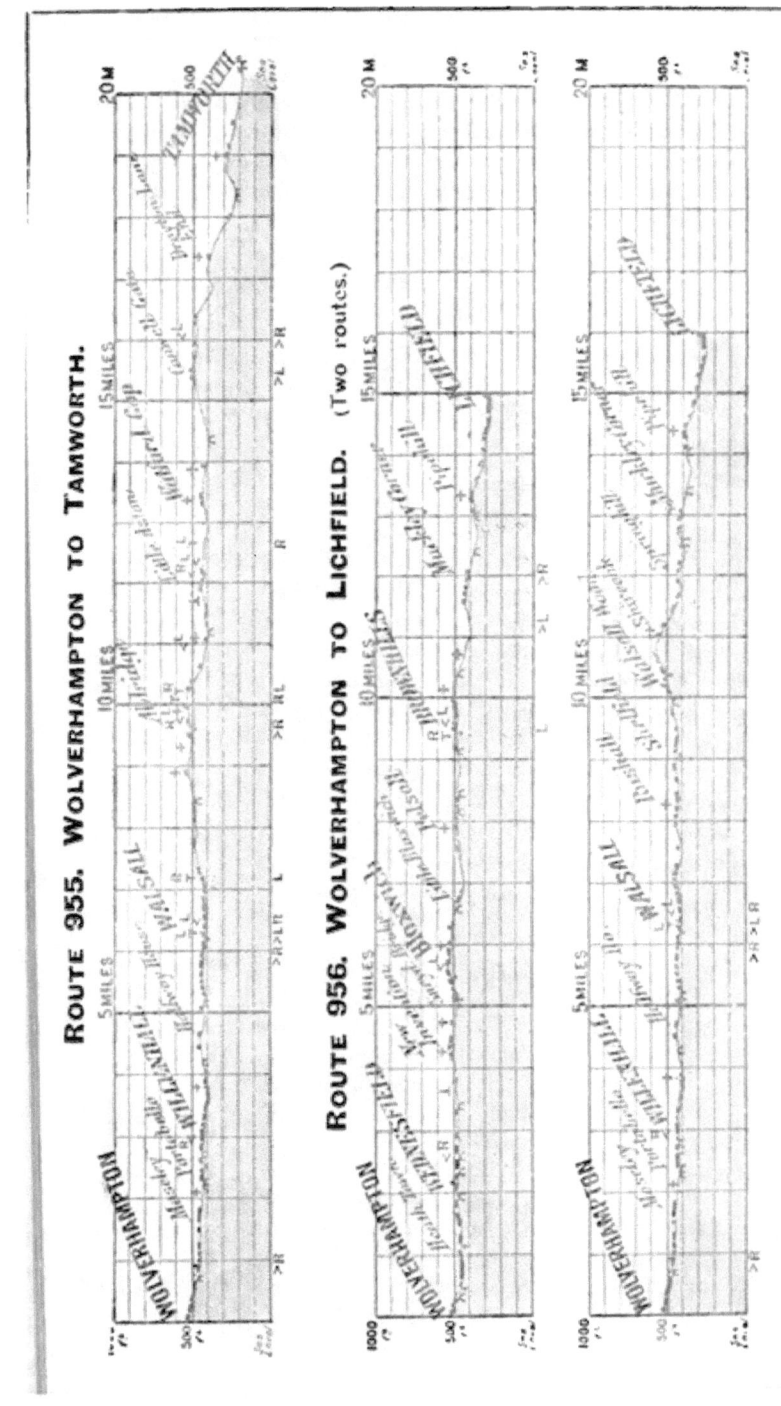

ROUTE 355. WOLVERHAMPTON TO TAMWORTH.

ROUTE 956. WOLVERHAMPTON TO LICHFIELD. (Two routes.)

957 WOLVERHAMPTON TO CANNOCK, &c.

Description.—Class II. A good undulating country road to Cannock; thence to Rugeley it is slightly loose.

Gradients.—At 7¾ & 10½m. 1/21; 15m. 1/14 (dangerous).

Milestones.—Measured from Queen's Sq., Wolverhampton.

Measurements.

Wolverhampton,* Queen's Square.			
5½	Shareshill.*		
9	3½	Cannock,* Market.	
15¾	10¼	6¾	Rugeley,* Market.

Principal Objects of Interest.—CANNOCK: Collieries. A pleasant road over Cannock Chase.

958 WOLVERHAMPTON TO NEWCASTLE.

Description.—Class II. The main route to Liverpool, Manchester, &c. For the first mile the road is bumpy, but immediately after, the surface improves, and is in perfect condition to Newcastle. The road is almost level, excepting a few slight undulations before Stafford, the hill over to Stone, and some hills near Trentham.

For Longton (30½m.), turn to right at Stone, or Trentham, preferably the latter. For Stoke and Hanley, turn to right at Trent Vale. Newcastle to Manchester (R. 244), 36¾m.; to Liverpool (R.231), 52¼m. The road avoiding Stone (which the telegraph wires follow), saves a very small distance.

Gradients.—At 15½, 18, and 20¼m. 1 in 25.

Milestones.—Measured from Queen's Square, Wolverhampton, as far as Gailey; thereafter from Stafford Town Hall to Stone, then from London.

Measurements.

Wolverhampton,* Queen's Square.						
7⅜	Gailey,* Spread Eagle. R. 936.					
10¼	2⅞	Penkridge,* Crown Bridge.				
16¼	8⅞	6	Stafford,* Town Hall.			
23½	15⅝	13¼	7¼	Stone.*		
28½	20⅝	18¼	12¼	5	Trentham.*	
32⅛	24¼	21⅞	15⅞	8⅝	3⅝	Newcastle-under-Lyme.*
32	24⅝	21¾	15¾	8½	3½	Longton,* Market Hall.
31⅝	23¾	21⅜	15⅜	8⅛	3⅛	Stoke.*
33⅜	25½	23⅛	17⅛	9⅞	4⅞	Hanley.*

Principal Objects of Interest.—8m., Watling Street. Penkridge: Teddesley Park. STAFFORD: Castle, Brine Baths, Shire Hall, Churches. Trentham: Park. NEWCASTLE: Iron Works and Potteries, Hall. Uninteresting as far as Stafford; fine scenery in the Trent Valley.

Hotels or Inns at places marked*, and numerous others.

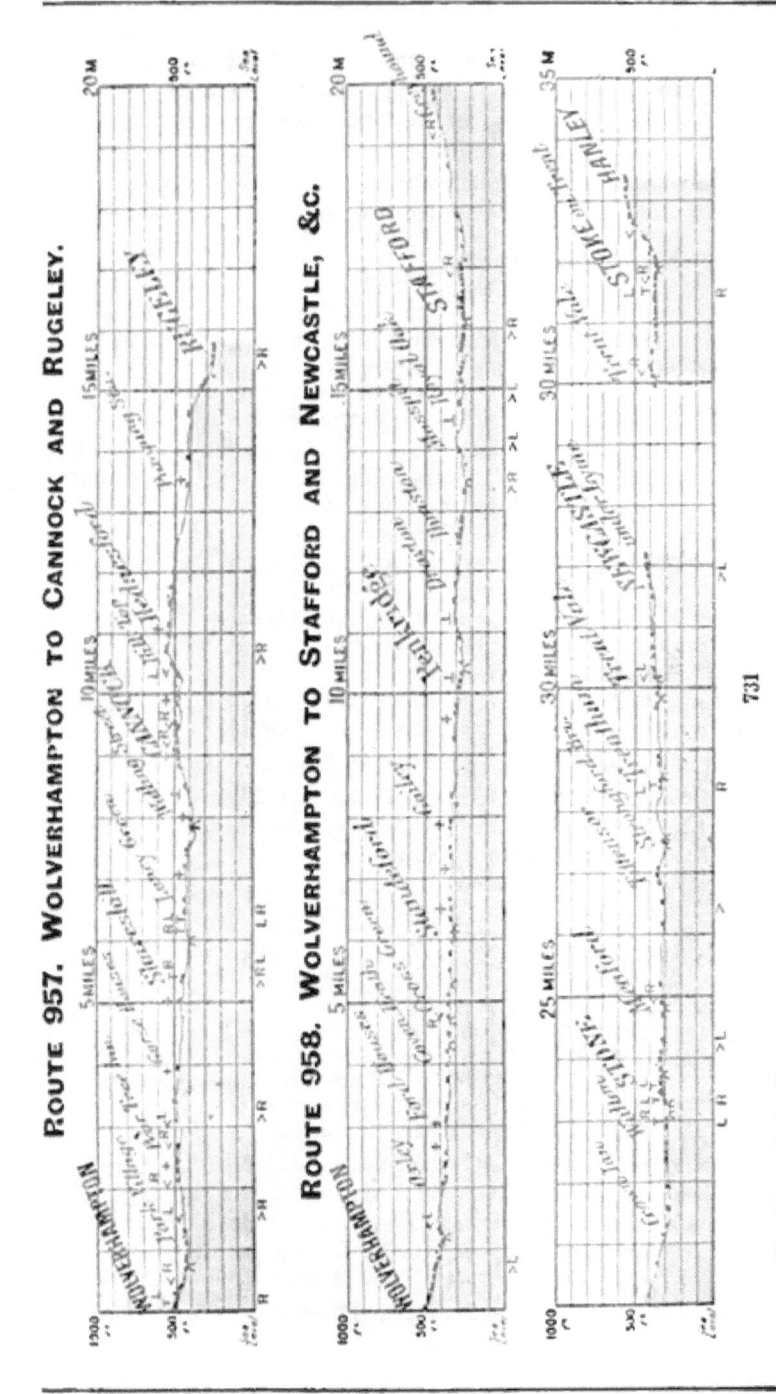

ROUTE 957. WOLVERHAMPTON TO CANNOCK AND RUGELEY.

ROUTE 958. WOLVERHAMPTON TO STAFFORD AND NEWCASTLE, &C.

959 WALSALL TO KIDDERMINSTER.

Description.—Class II. A bumpy road through manufacturing district, with car lines almost the whole way to Stourbridge, thereafter good surface.

Gradients.—At 7½m. 1 in 16; 8¾m. 1 in 24; 11m. 1 in 25; 12m. 1 in 18; 15½m. 1 in 20; 16m. 1 in 14.

Milestones.—Irregular.

Measurements.

Walsall,* The Bridge.						
3	Wednesbury,* Market.					
6⅜	3⅜	Tipton.*				
8	5	1⅝	Dudley,* Fountain.			
10¾	7¾	4⅜	2¾	Brierley Hill.		
13¾	10¾	7	5¾	2⅝	Stourbridge.*	
20⅛	17⅛	13¾	12⅛	9⅜	6⅜	Kidderminster,* Town Hall.

Principal Objects of Interest.—WEDNESBURY: Church. DUDLEY: Cas., Fountain, Museum. Kidderminster: Baxter's Statue, Church.

Hotels or Inns at places marked*, and numerous others.

960 LICHFIELD TO ASHBOURNE.

Description.—Class II. An excellent undulating country road through Abbots Bromley to Uttoxeter, thence splendid surface to Rocester, when the road becomes exceedingly hilly, with a dangerous hill at Ellastone. The road from Uttoxeter to Alton, 7¾m., is shown at end of diagram.

Gradients.—At 8¾m. 1 in 17; 9¾m. 1 in 23; 10¾m. 1 in 20; 13½m. 1 in 18; 16¾m. 1 in 15; 17½m. 1 in 20; 23m. 1 in 17; 24m. 1 in 18; 25¾m. 1 in 12 (dangerous); 26¼m. 1 in 13; 27½m. 1 in 20; 28 and 28¼m. 1 in 22.

Milestones.—Measured from Lichfield Clock to Handsacre, thereafter from Uttoxeter Bridge, after which from Uttoxeter Market to Rocester, then from Ashbourne.

Birmingham. **Measurements.**

15¾	Lichfield,* Clock Tower.					
20⅞	5⅛	Handsacre,* Crown Inn.				
27	11¼	6⅛	Abbots Bromley.*			
33⅝	17⅞	12¾	6⅝	Uttoxeter,* Market.		
38⅛	22⅜	17¼	11⅛	4½	Rocester.*	
45¾	30	24⅞	18¾	12⅛	7⅝	Ashbourne.*

Principal Objects of Interest.—Abbots Bromley: Bagots Park. UTTOXETER: Church, Dove Bridge. Ellastone: Calwich Abbey. ASHBOURNE: Church, School, Dovedale. The prettiest part of this road is between Uttoxeter and Ashbourne. Alton Towers is a favourite resort.

Hotels or Inns at places marked*, and at Blithbury, Red Cow Inn, Ellastone, Mayfield, &c.

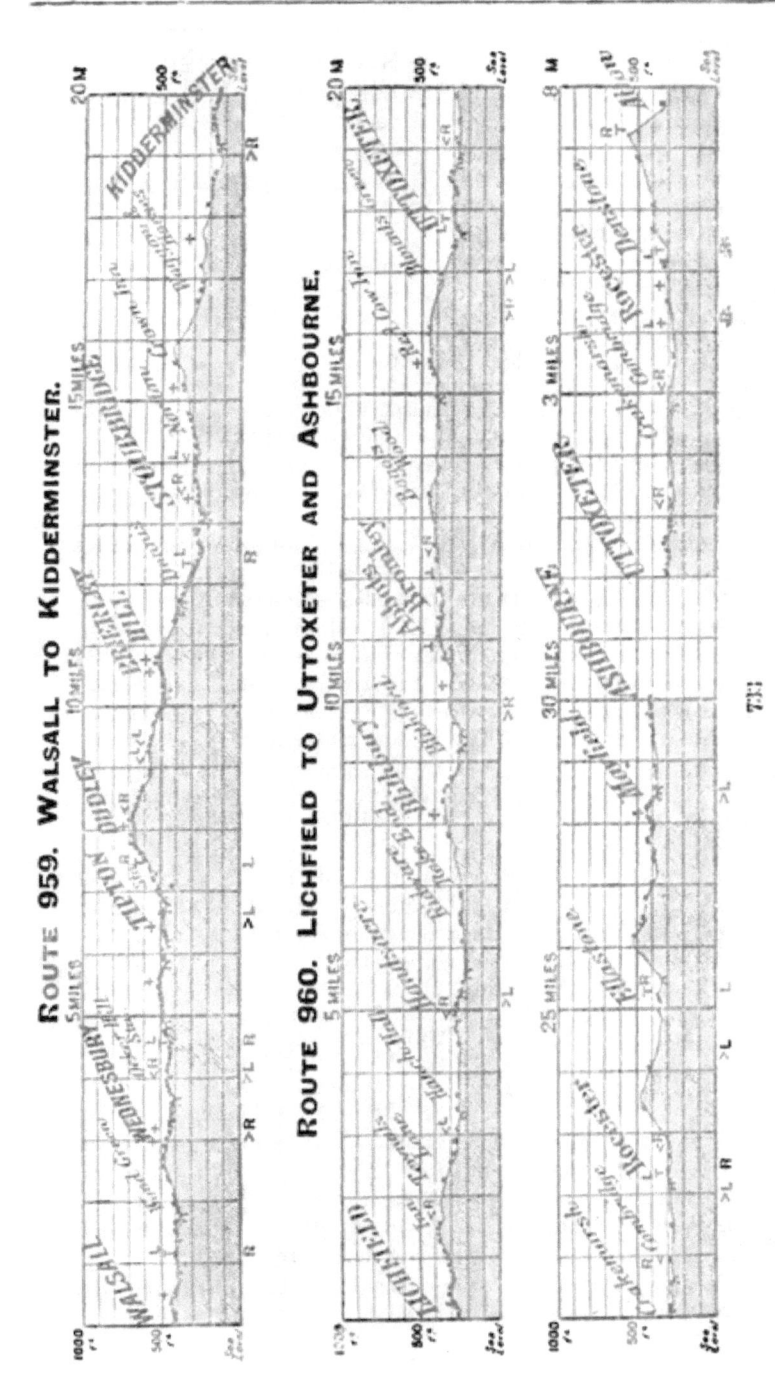

ROUTE 959. WALSALL TO KIDDERMINSTER.

ROUTE 960. LICHFIELD TO UTTOXETER AND ASHBOURNE.

961 LICHFIELD TO NUNEATON.

Description.—Class II. Very good surface to Tamworth, undulating on to Atherstone, then fine surface, but there is a dangerous hill near Nuneaton.

Gradients.—(†*Dangerous.*) At 5m. 1 in 16; 9½m. 1 in 23; 10m. 1 in 21; 18¼m. 1 in 15†; 20m. 1 in 15†.

Milestones.—Measured from Tamworth, and Nuneaton.

Measurements.

Lichfield,* Clock Tower.
7¼ Tamworth.*
15¼ 8 Atherstone.*
20¼ 13½ 5¼ Nuneaton,* Market.

Principal Objects of Interest.—3¼m., Barracks. TAMWORTH: Castle. Mancetter: Roman Camp. NUNEATON: Church.

Hotels or Inns at places marked *, and at Hopwas, &c.

962 BURTON-ON-TRENT TO ATHERSTONE.

Description.—Class II. The surface is not very good for five miles, but it then becomes very good on to Atherstone. The road by Appleby (shown dotted) is a mile shorter than the road by Measham; surface equally good.

Gradients.—At 1½m. 1 in 15; 4½m. 1 in 17.

Milestones.—Measured from Atherstone, by Measham.

Measurements.

Burton-on-Trent,* Bridge Street.
4½ Gresley,* Inn.
10¼ 5½ Measham.*
14½ 10 4½ Twycross.*
20 15½ 10½ 5½ Atherstone.*

Principal Objects of Interest.—Collieries near Gresley.

Hotels or Inns at places marked*, and at Overseal, Acresford, &c.

963 BURTON-ON-TRENT TO TAMWORTH.

Description.—Class II. An almost flat road, with the exception of a slight rise at Branston over the railway, and a short hill at Elford. Fine surface throughout.

Gradients.—At 11¼ and 12m. 1 in 17.

Milestones.—Measured from Tamworth.

Measurements.

Burton-on-Trent,* Bridge Street.
7½ Alrewas,* Paul Pry Inn. R. 967.
11½ 4 Elford,* Inn.
15¾ 8¼ 4½ Tamworth.*

Principal Objects of Interest.—An uninteresting road. TAMWORTH: Castle.

Hotels or Inns at places marked *.

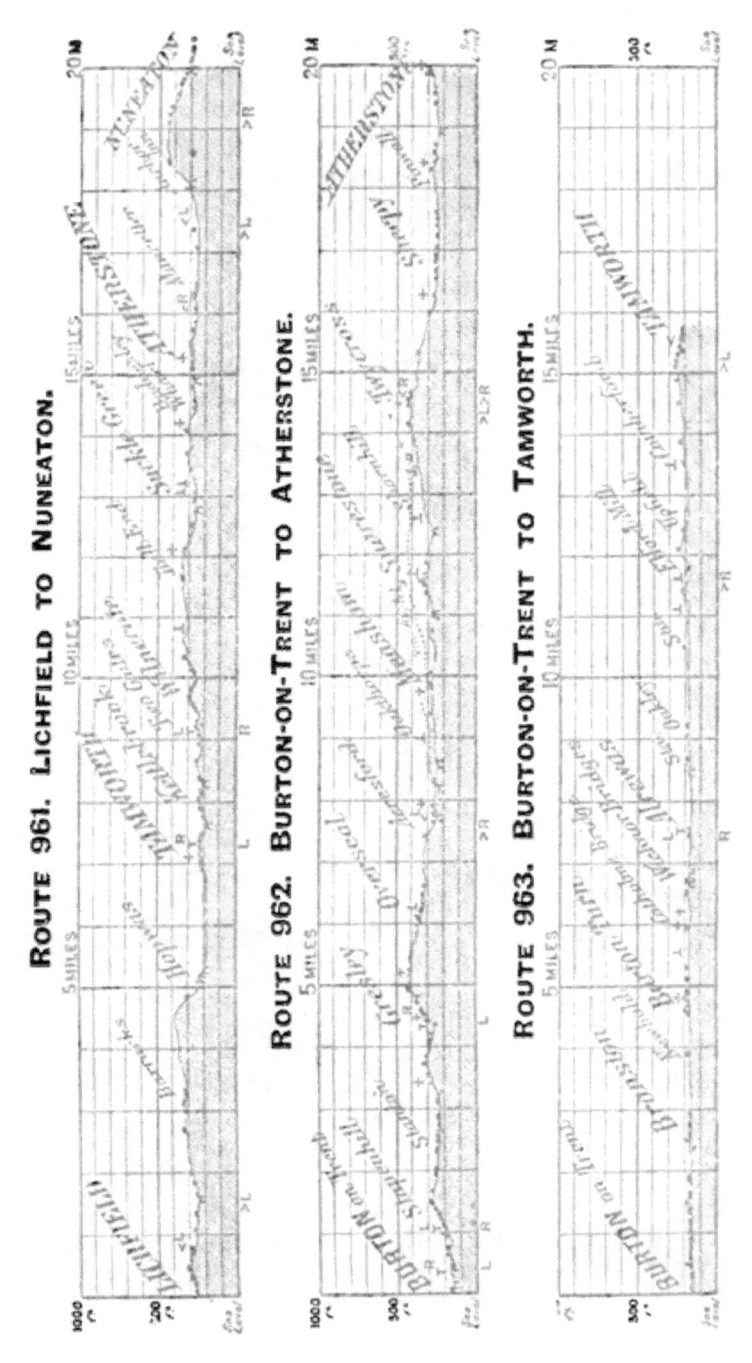

ROUTE 961. LICHFIELD TO NUNEATON.

ROUTE 962. BURTON-ON-TRENT TO ATHERSTONE.

ROUTE 963. BURTON-ON-TRENT TO TAMWORTH.

964 BURTON-ON-TRENT TO UTTOXETER.

Description.—Class II. An easy undulating road, with a steep descent in Tutbury, thence splendid surface.

Gradients.—At 3¼m. 1 in 21; 4½m. 1 in 15; 13¼m. 1 in 23.

Milestones.—Measured from London, and Derby.

Measurements.

Burton-on-Trent,* Bridge Street.
4⅝ Tutbury.*
9½ 4⅞ Sudbury.
14⅞ 10¼ 5⅜ Uttoxeter,* Market.

Principal Objects of Interest.—Tutbury: Castle. Sudbury: Park. UTTOXETER: Dove Bridge, Church.

965 UTTOXETER TO STONE, &c.

Description.—Class II. A steep and very hilly road, but with excellent surface to Stone. Good surface to Eccleshall.

Gradients.—(†*Dangerous.*) At 1½m. 1 in 17; 2¼m. 1 in 11†; 4½m. 1 in 13†; 6m. 1 in 20; 7½m. 1 in 12†; 8¼m. 1 in 14; 9m. 1 in 13; 11m. 1 in 11†; 11½m. 1 in 17; 16½m. 1 in 21; 18¼m. 1 in 14.

Milestones.—Measured from Stone.

Measurements.

Uttoxeter,* Market.
8¼ Milwich.*
13¼ 5 Stone,* Square.
18⅜ 10⅛ 5⅛ Eccleshall.*

Principal Objects of Interest.—Eccleshall: Bishop's Castle, Church.

Hotels or Inns at places marked *, and at Bramshall.

966 UTTOXETER TO LEEK.

Description.—Class I. & II. Splendid surface to Cheadle, then fair, but slightly hilly to Wetley Rocks, then steep.

Gradients.—(†*Dangerous.*) At 4m. 1 in 20; 7½m. 1 in 24; 9¼ & 11½m. 1 in 22; 12¾m. 1 in 19; 14½m. 1 in 20; 16m. 1 in 12†; 16½m. 1 in 13†; 17½m. 1 in 14†; 18m. 1 in 19; 19m. 1 in 17.

Milestones.—Measured from London; after Upper Tean, measured from Cheadle.

Measurements.

Uttoxeter,* Market.
6¾ Upper Tean.*
(13¼ 6½ Longton. R. 971).
9¼ 2½ Cheadle.*
14¼ 7½ 5¼ Wetley Rocks.*
19½ 12¾ 10⅜ 5¼ Leek.*

Principal Objects of Interest.—CHEADLE: R. C. Ch. LEEK: Church.

Hotels or Inns at places marked *, and at Cheddleton, &c.

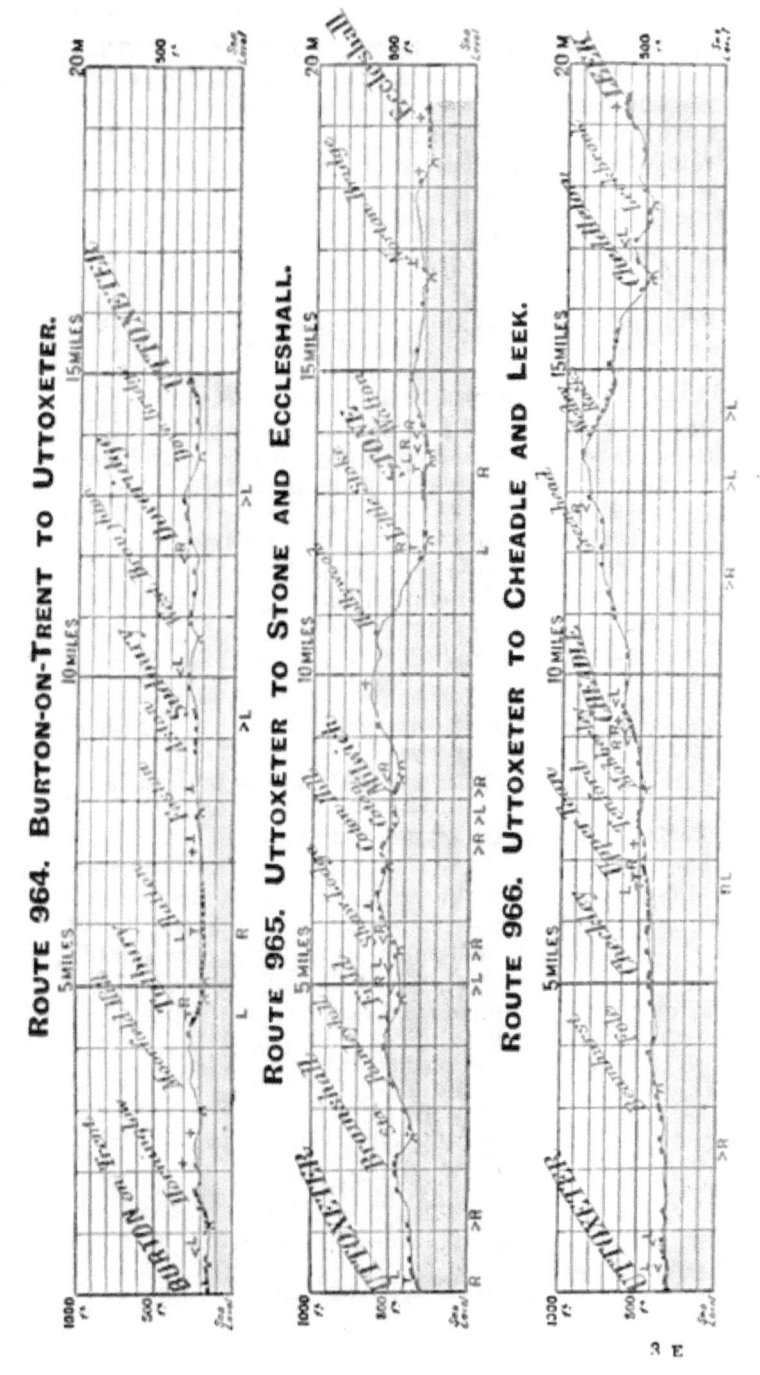

ROUTE 964. BURTON-ON-TRENT TO UTTOXETER.

ROUTE 965. UTTOXETER TO STONE AND ECCLESHALL.

ROUTE 966. UTTOXETER TO CHEADLE AND LEEK.

967 STAFFORD TO BURTON-ON-TRENT.

Description.—Class II. Good surface to Milford, then loose for a mile, after which fine surface to Rugeley. (Rugeley to Lichfield, 8½m., see Route 935.) After Rugeley fair surface to Alrewas, where join Route 963 to Burton.

Gradients.—At 1¾m. 1 in 13; 4m. 1 in 15; 4¾m. 1 in 18.

Milestones.—Measured from London.

Measurements.

				Stafford,* Town Hall.
9¾				Rugeley,* Market.
15¾	6			Kings Bromley.*
19¼	9¾	3¾		Alrewas,* Paul Pry Inn.
26¾	17¼	11¼	7½	Burton-on-Trent.* Bridge Street.

Principal Objects of Interest —5m., Shugborough Park. RUGELEY: Cannock Chase. Armitage: Church.

Hotels or Inns at places marked*, and at Wolseley, &c.

968 STAFFORD TO UTTOXETER.

Description. — Class III. An exceedingly steep road, continuously up and down, with dangerous hills.

Gradients.—(†*Dangerous*). At 2½m. 1 in 18; 4m. 1 in 9†; 7½m. 1 in 17; 8¾m. 1 in 10†; 9½m. 1 in 17; 10½ & 11m. 1 in 13†; 11½m. 1 in 16; 12m. 1 in 18; 12½m. 1 in 13†.

Milestones.—Measured from Town Hall, Stafford.

Measurements.

		Stafford,* Town Hall.
4½		Weston.*
13¾	9¾	Uttoxeter,* Market.

Principal Objects of Interest.—Weston: Ingestre Park, 8m., Chartley Castle ruins. UTTOXETER: Church.

969 STAFFORD TO LEEK.

Description.—Class I. & II. Splendid surface to Stone, thence good to Wetley Rocks, when the road becomes very steep, with rough surface on the hills. For Longton, turn to left at Roughclose (11¾m.).

Gradients.—(†*Dangerous*.) At 1½ & 10¾m. 1 in 25; 11½m. 1 in 17; 17½m. 1 in 16; 20m. 1 in 12†; 20¼m. 1 in 13†; 21¼m. 1 in 14; 22m. 1 in 19; 23m. 1 in 17.

Milestones.—Measured from Town Hall, Stafford; after Stone, measured from London.

Measurements.

				Stafford,* Town Hall.
7¼				Stone,* Square.
(14½)	7			Longton,* Market Hall.)
18¼	11	5¾		Wetley Rocks.*
23¼	16¼	11	5¼	Leek.*

Principal Objects of Interest.—Leek: Church.

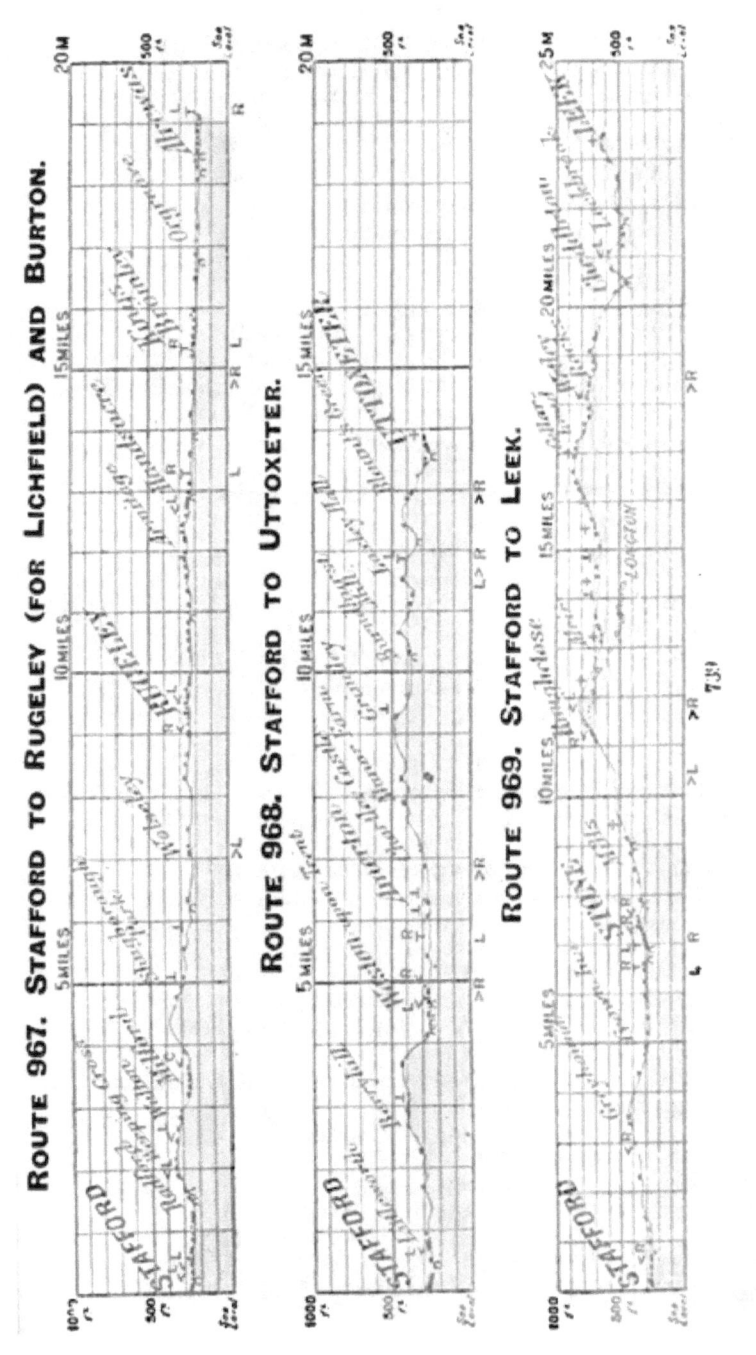

ROUTE 967. STAFFORD TO RUGELEY (FOR LICHFIELD) AND BURTON.

ROUTE 968. STAFFORD TO UTTOXETER.

ROUTE 969. STAFFORD TO LEEK.

970 STAFFORD TO CHESTER.

Description.—Class II. An excellent road to Eccleshall; thereafter slightly hilly to Woore. To Chester, R. 265.

Gradients.—At 9m. 1 in 16; 11, 11¼, & 12½m. 1 in 18; 14m. 1 in 23; 14½m. 1 in 15; 15m. 1 in 20; 15½m. 1 in 18; 16½m. 1 in 16.

Milestones.—Measured from Town Hall, Stafford, and from Eccleshall.

Measurements.

Stafford,* Town Hall.

7⅛ Eccleshall.*

14½ 7⅜ Loggerheads,* Inn. (To Market Drayton, R. 977, 4¼m.)

19¼ 12⅛ 4¾ Woore.*

48 40⅞ 33½ 28¾ Chester. R. 265.

Principal Objects of Interest. — Eccleshall Bishop's Castle, Ch. Loggerheads: Blore Heath, Battlefield, 1469.

971 NEWCASTLE TO ASHBOURNE.

Description.—Class II. The first five miles is rather unpleasant; better to go round by Trentham, joining at Meir; thereafter excellent surface, but several dangerous hills.

Gradients.—(†*Dangerous.*) At 1¾ & 13m. 1 in 14; 8¾, 9½, 9¾, 11, & 12m. 1 in 16; 13¼m. 1 in 10†; 15m. 1 in 18; 15¼m. 1 in 9†; 17½m. 1 in 16; 18 & 20m. 1 in 12†; 18¾m. 1 in 10†; 20¾m. 1 in 13†.

Measurements.

Newcastle-under-Lyme,* Town Hall.

2 Stoke-on-Trent.*

4⅜ 2⅜ Longton,* Market Hall.

11⅜ 9⅜ 7 Cheadle.*

16⅝ 14⅝ 12¼ 5¼ Alton.*

24⅜ 22⅜ 20 13 7¾ Ashbourne.*

Principal Objects of Interest.—Uninteresting through 'The Potteries.' CHEADLE: R.C. Church. Alton: Towers, Hospital. Ellaston: Calwich Abbey. Ashbourne: Church, Dovedale. Pretty road between Alton and Ashbourne.

972 NEWCASTLE TO BUXTON.

Description.—Class II. Excellent surface to Leek, but steep and dangerous hills for the first five miles, and near Leek. From Leek to Buxton, precipitous hills and poor surface. Leek to Longnor (9⅝m.), turn to right at 17⅜m.

Gradients.—(†*Dangerous*). At ¾m. 1 in 15; 1m. 1 in 10†; 2¼m. 1 in 18; 9m. 1 in 9†; 10m. 1 in 13; 10½m. 1 in 11†; thence mostly 1 in 9†. At 22¼m. 1 in 13.

Milestones.—Irregular.

Measurements

Newcastle-under-Lyme,* Town Hall.

11¾ Leek.*

24⅜ 12⅝ Buxton,* Spring Gardens.

Hotels or Inns at places marked *.

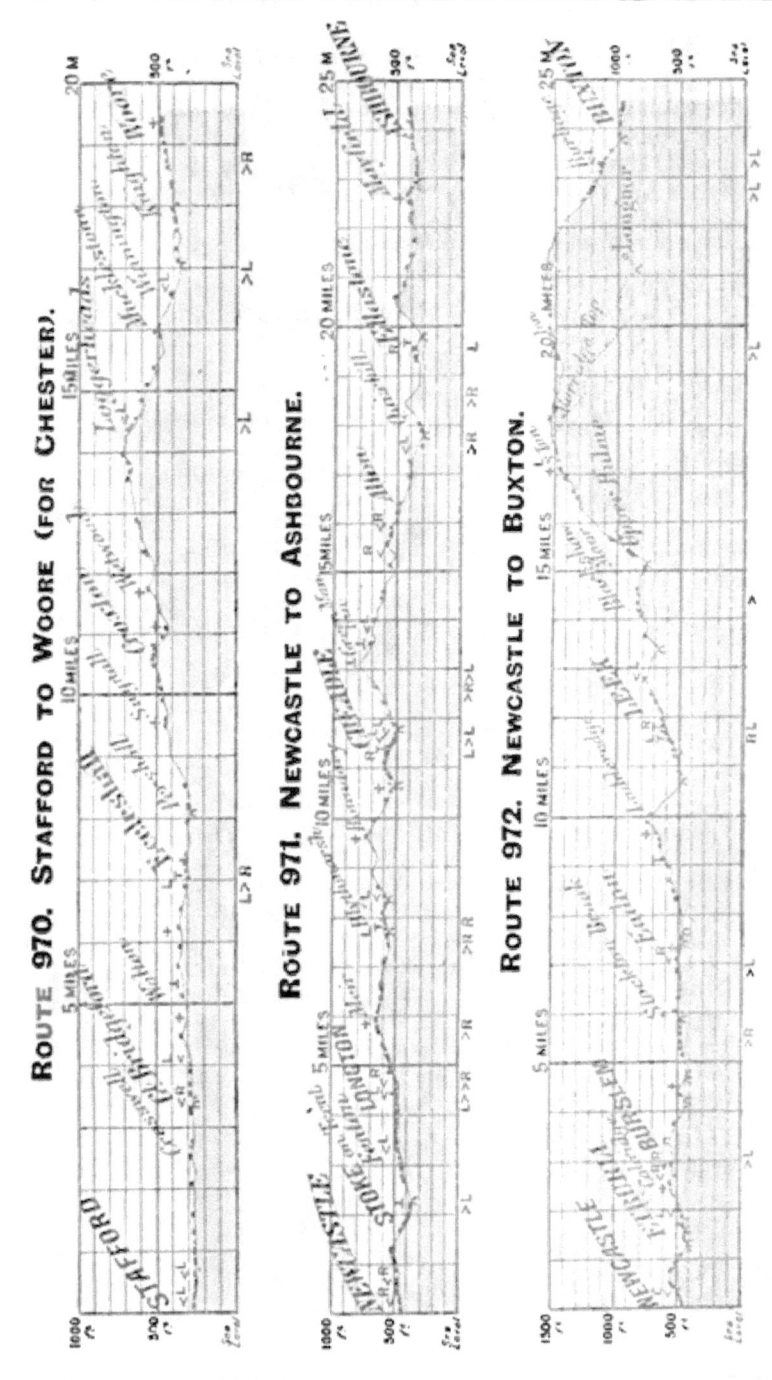

ROUTE 970. STAFFORD TO WOORE (FOR CHESTER).

ROUTE 971. NEWCASTLE TO ASHBOURNE.

ROUTE 972. NEWCASTLE TO BUXTON.

973 NEWCASTLE TO NANTWICH.

Description.—Class II. After a somewhat stiff hill to Madeley Heath, the road has very good surface all the way to Nantwich. For Crewe, keep to R. at 10¼m. The road by Audley (shown dotted) ¾m. shorter, is much steeper.

Gradients.—At 1¼m. 1 in 18; 3¼m. 1 in 20.

Milestones.—Measured from Town Hall, Newcastle.

Measurements.

Newcastle-under-Lyme.*			Newcastle-under-Lyme.*	
7¼	Betley.*		7⅞	Betley.*
15¼	7¾	Nantwich.*	13¼	5¾ Crewe,* Station.

Principal Objects of Interest.—5¾m., Heyley Castle. Betley: Court. NANTWICH: Ch. CREWE: Railway Works.

Hotels or Inns where marked*, & at Madeley Heath, &c.

974 NEWCASTLE TO WHITCHURCH.

Description.—Class II. Good surface, but a somewhat undulating road. Bar Hill is dangerous. A much better road is by Route 977 to Blackbrook (7m.), thence to Woore (3½m.), =10½m.

Gradients.—(†*Dangerous.*) At 1¼m. 1 in 18; 3¼m. 1 in 20; 6½m. 1 in 13†; 7m. 1 in 13†; 8½m. 1 in 17; 14m. 1 in 20; 14¼ & 14½m. 1 in 19; 19½m. 1 in 21.

Milestones.—Measured from Town Hall, Newcastle, and from Whitchurch.

Measurements.

Newcastle-under-Lyme,* Town Hall.				
5¾	Madeley,* Inn.			
8⅜	3¼	Woore.*		
13⅝	8¼	4¾	Audlem.*	
22	16⅜	13¼	8⅜	Whitchurch.*

Principal Objects of Interest.—Burleydam: Combermere Abbey. WHITCHURCH: Church.

Hotels or Inns at places marked*, and at Burleydam, &c.

975 NEWCASTLE TO NEWPORT.

Description.—Class II. A hilly road for seven miles, thence not quite so hilly; good surface throughout.

Gradients.—At ½m. 1 in 19; 2½m. 1 in 20; 2¾m. 1 in 16; 3½m. 1 in 14; 4½m. 1 in 18; 10¼ & 12m. 1 in 20; 15½m. 1 in 25.

Milestones.—Measured from Town Hall, Newcastle, to Eccleshall; thereafter from Newport.

Measurements.

Newcastle-under-Lyme,* Town Hall.		
11¾	Eccleshall.*	
20¾	9¼	Newport,* Town Hall.

Principal Objects of Interest.—3½m., Trentham Hall. Eccleshall: Bishop's Castle, Church. Newport: Church.

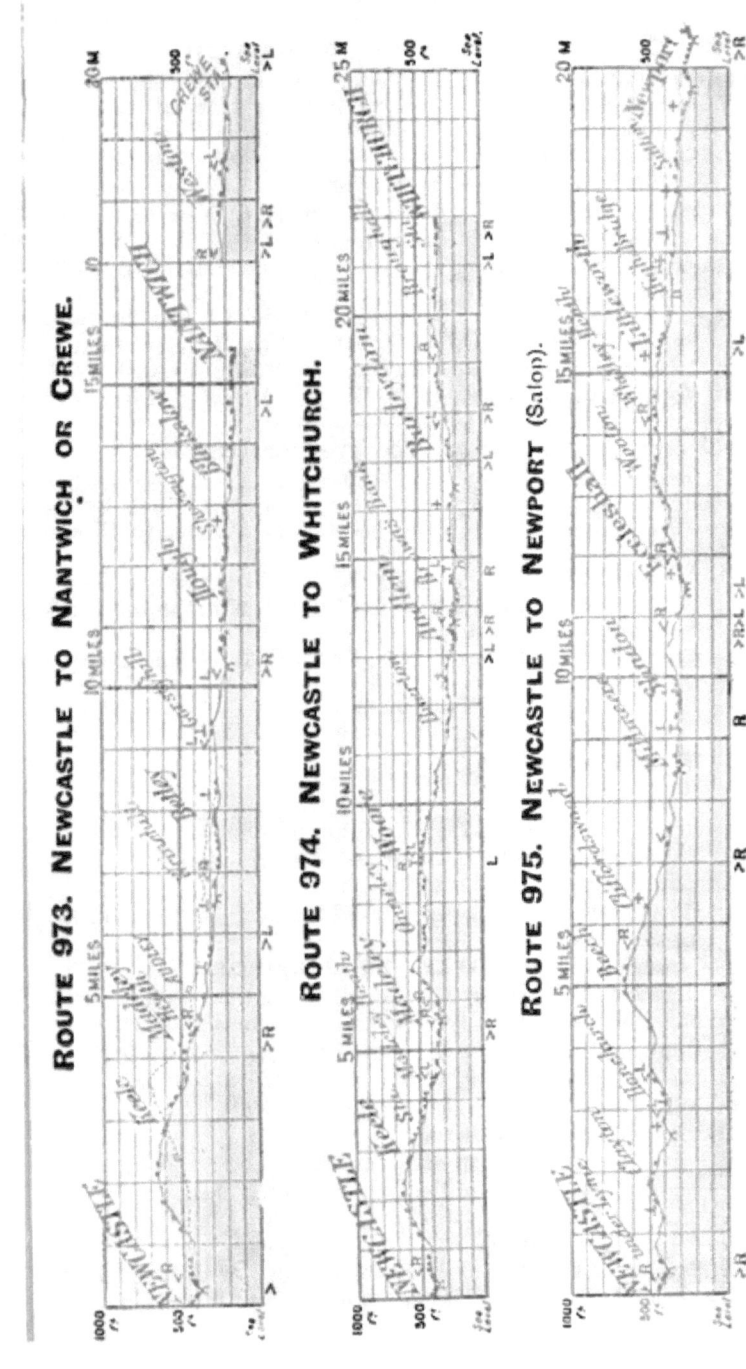

ROUTE 973. NEWCASTLE TO NANTWICH OR CREWE.

ROUTE 974. NEWCASTLE TO WHITCHURCH.

ROUTE 975. NEWCASTLE TO NEWPORT (Salop).

976 SHREWSBURY TO WHITCHURCH.

Description.—Class II. The main road is by Wem, Route 263. This road is scarcely so hilly, but the surface is slightly inferior.

Gradients.—At 7¼ & 7¾m. 1 in 22; 8½m. 1 in 17; 9m. 1 in 22; 9¾m. 1 in 21.

Milestones.—Measured from Castlegate, Shrewsbury.

Measurements.

Shrewsbury,* Market Clock.				
5¼	Hadnall.*			
9⅜	4⅛	Lee Brockhurst.*		
14⅝	9⅜	4¾	Prees.*	
19¾	14½	9⅞	5⅛	Whitchurch.*

Route 263.

Shrewsbury.*		
10¾	Wem.*	
19½	8¾	Whitchurch.*

Principal Objects of Interest.—3m., Battlefield, 1403. 11m., Hawkstone Park. WHITCHURCH: Church.

Hotels or Inns at places marked*.

977 SHREWSBURY TO NEWCASTLE.

Description.—Class I. This road is kept in splendid order, and is practically level for twenty-one miles. There are slight hills at Shawbury and Hodnet, but they are of no importance. From Market Drayton to Newcastle the road is carefully engineered, with long easy gradients, and the surface is very good. The road from Newcastle on to Burslem is very bumpy.

Gradients.—At 21¾m. 1 in 19; 24½m. 1 in 17; 25¼m. 1 in 23; 27½m. 1 in 22; 29¼m. 1 in 19; 32¾m. 1 in 24; 33½m. 1 in 25; 35¼m. 1 in 17.

Milestones.—Measured from Town Hall, Newcastle.

Measurements.

Shrewsbury,* Market Clock.									
7¼	Shawbury.*								
13½	6¼	Hodnet,* Bear Inn.							
16¼	9	2¾	Ternhill. R. 951.						
19⅛	11⅞	5⅝	2⅞	Market Drayton.*					
23⅜	16⅛	9⅞	7⅛	4¼	Loggerheads.* R. 970.				
26¼	19	12¾	10	7⅛	2⅞	Blackbrook. R. 265.			
28⅛	20⅞	14⅝	11⅞	9	4¾	1⅞	Whitmore Station.*		
33¼	26	19¾	17	14⅛	9⅞	7	5⅛	Newcastle,* Town Hall.	
36¾	29½	23¼	20½	17⅝	13⅜	10½	8⅝	3½	Burslem.*

Principal Objects of Interest.—Shawbury: Park. Hodnet: Hawkstone Park. 21¾m., Bloreheath, Battlefield, 1459. NEWCASTLE: Keele Hall, Trentham Park, Potteries, and Iron Works.

Hotels or Inns at places marked*, and at Astley, Blackbrook, &c.

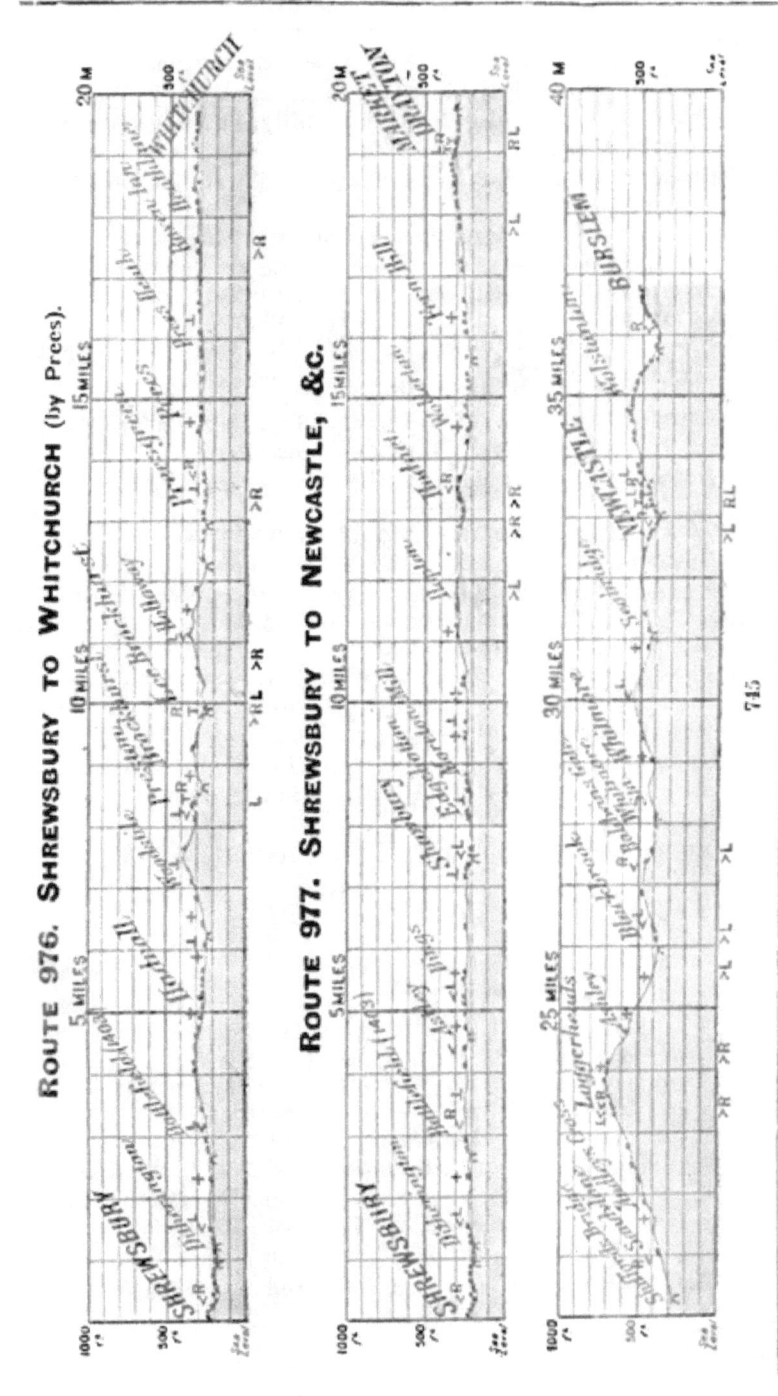

ROUTE 976. SHREWSBURY TO WHITCHURCH (by Prees).

ROUTE 977. SHREWSBURY TO NEWCASTLE, &c.

715

978 SHREWSBURY TO STAFFORD.

Description.—Class II. There are two roads between Shrewsbury and Newport; the longer, and best road, through Wellington, has splendid surface and very slight gradients for eleven miles. From Wellington to Newport the surface is also excellent, but it is not nearly so good as the first section of the road. The more direct road to Newport is shown at foot; the surface on it is very good, but several hills detract considerably from what is a very fair road. There is a dangerous descent before Newport.

From Newport to Stafford the road has very good surface, but there is a dangerous hill three miles from Stafford.

Gradients.—At ¼m. 1 in 13 (dangerous); 24m. 1 in 21; 26m. 1 in 21; 29¼m. 1 in 13, and 29½m. 1 in 15 (both dangerous).

By Ercall.—At ¼m. 1 in 13 (dangerous); 4m. 1 in 14; 10m. 1 in 23; 17½m. 1 in 24; 17¾m. 1 in 10 (dangerous).

Milestones.—Measured from Shrewsbury Town Hall to Wellington, whence from Stafford.

By Ercall.—Measured from Castlegate, Shrewsbury.

Measurements.

Shrewsbury,* Market Clock.
4 Atcham.*
11¼ 7¼ Wellington,* Market.
19½ 15½ 8¼ Newport,* Town Hall.
25⅛ 21⅛ 14¾ 5⅝ Gnosall,* Bridge.
32¼ 28¼ 21⅜ 12¾ 7⅛ Stafford,* Town Hall.

By Ercall.

Shrewsbury,* Market Clock.
8 High Ercall.*
10½ 2½ Crudgington.
18⅝ 10⅝ 8⅛ Newport,* Town Hall.
31⅜ 23⅜ 20⅞ 12¾ Stafford,* Town Hall.

Principal Objects of Interest.—1m., Lord Hill's Column. Atcham: Church, Attingham Hall. 5½m. to Uriconum (Roman city). WELLINGTON: Admaston Spa. 18m., Lilleshall Abbey. Newport: Church. 20½m., Aqualate Park. 31m., Stafford Castle. STAFFORD: Brine Baths, Shire Hall, Churches. Fine view of The Wrekin near Wellington.

By Ercall.—3m., Sundorn Castle. 4m., Haughmond Abbey, ruins.

Hotels or Inns at places marked*, and at Hadley, Haughton, &c.

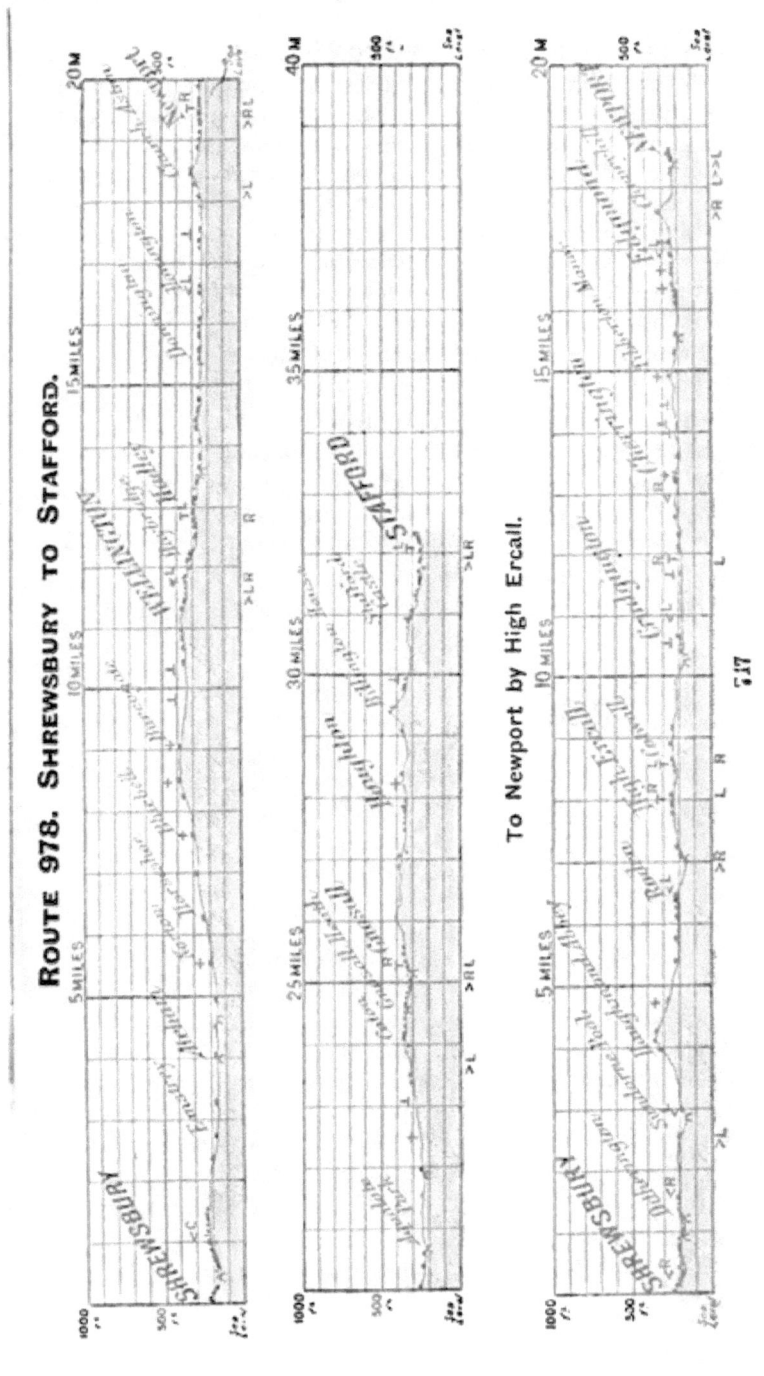

ROUTE 978. SHREWSBURY TO STAFFORD.

To Newport by High Ercall.

290

979 SHREWSBURY TO WORCESTER.

Description.—Class II. There are two roads between Shrewsbury and Bridgnorth; the direct road by Wenlock has fine surface, but there is a precipitous hill (on which innumerable accidents have happened), before Wenlock; thereafter excellent surface, but several very steep hills, to Bridgnorth. The road by Ironbridge avoids Harley Hill, and has fine surface for seven miles, then is hilly to Buildwas, after which it has good surface to Broseley, then several steep hills but good surface to Bridgnorth (Upper Town).

From Bridgnorth to Kidderminster, very good surface, but steep hills, one being dangerous. Kidderminster to Worcester, see R. 952. The branch to Bewdley at 33¼m. is very steep.

Gradients.—(† *Dangerous.*) At ¼m. 1 in 13†; 9m. 1 in 17; 10½m. 1 in 16; 11½m. 1 in 8†; 12¼m. 1 in 14; 13½m. 1 in 16; 14½m. 1 in 11†; 14¾m. 1 in 12; 15m. 1 in 14; 17¾m. 1 in 16; 20m. 1 in 12†; 20¾m. 1 in 16; 23½ & 24m. 1 in 15; 24½ & 26m. 1 in 16; 27¼m. 1 in 22; 31½m. 1 in 17; 32¼m. 1 in 12†.

By Ironbridge.—At 8m. 1 in 24; 9¾ & 10¼m. 1 in 13; 14½m. 1 in 19; 16m. 1 in 24; 16½m. 1 in 20; 17½m. 1 in 11†; 18m. 1 in 14; 19m. 1 in 22; 21m. 1 in 15; 31¼m. 1 in 22.

Milestones.—Measured from Shrewsbury Market House to Bridgnorth, thereafter from Kidderminster Town Hall. *By Ironbridge:* from Shrewsbury, & Bridgnorth Market.

Measurements.

Shrewsbury,* Market Clock.							
8¾	Cressage,* Eagle Inn.						
12⅝	3⅞	Wenlock,* Town Hall.					
20½	11¾	8⅛	Bridgnorth,* Market.				
21¼	12½	8⅝	¾	Bridgnorth,* Lower.			
27½	18¾	15⅛	7	6¼	Birdsgreen.		
(36	27¼	23⅜	15½	14¾	8½	Bewdley.*)	
34⅜	25⅝	22¼	14⅛	13⅜	7⅛	Kidderminster,* Town Hall.	
49⅞	40⅝	36¾	28⅝	27⅞	21⅝	14½	Worcester.* R. 952.

By Ironbridge.

Shrewsbury,* Market Clock.			
11¾	Buildwas,* Bridge Inn.		
13¾	2	Ironbridge,* Bridge.	
21½	9¾	7¾	Bridgnorth,* Market.

Principal Objects of Interest.—Wenlock: Town Hall, Abbey. Morville: Ch. BRIDGNORTH: Cas., Bridge. Buildwas: Abbey. Ironbridge: Bridge. KIDDERMINSTER: Ch., Baxter's Statue, Town Hall. Splendid view from Wenlock Edge. Pretty road near Ironbridge, at Bridgnorth, & near Quatford.

Hotels or Inns at places marked *, and at Cross Houses, Morville, &c.

ROUTE 979. SHREWSBURY TO WORCESTER. (Two routes to Bridgnorth.)

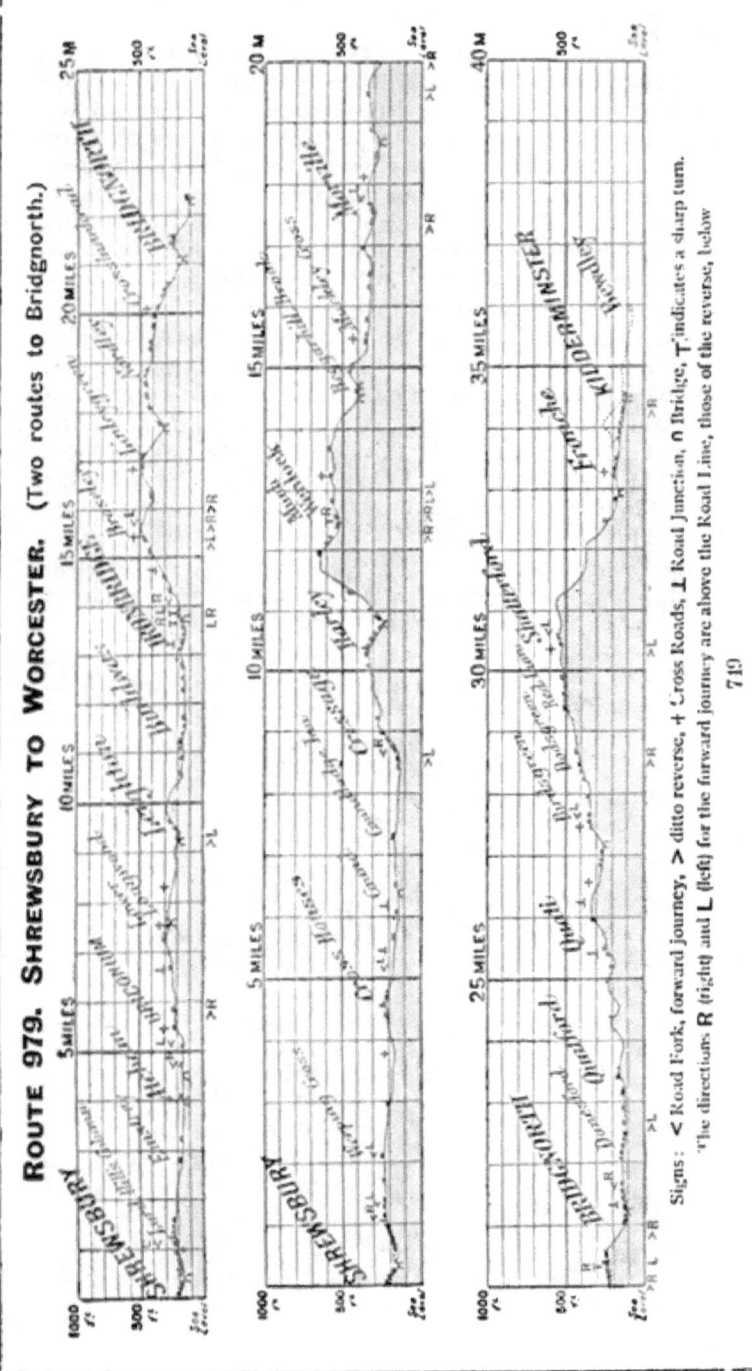

Signs: < Road Fork, forward journey, > ditto reverse, + Cross Roads, ⊥ Road Junction, ∩ Bridge, ⊤ indicates a sharp turn. The directions R (right) and L (left) for the forward journey are above the Road Line, those of the reverse, below.

719

980 SHREWSBURY TO HEREFORD.

Description.—Class I. After the dangerous descent in Shrewsbury the road has splendid surface, rising steadily to Church Stretton, with several slight hills at various points; thereafter it is a long descent of fifteen miles to Ludlow, fine surface and very slightly undulating. At Ludlow there is a steep ascent to the town, then a dangerous descent through the old gateway to the bridge, then after a slight hill it is a first-class road to Wooferton, beyond which it becomes slightly hilly to Leominster. From Leominster to Hereford the road has splendid surface, but is hilly approaching Hereford. The main road goes over Dinmore Hill, but this slightly dangerous hill is avoided by going round by Bodenham; or by Bodenham Moor and Sutton.

Gradients.—(†*Dangerous.*) At 2¾m. 1 in 24; 4¾m. 1 in 17; 6m. 1 in 17; 11¼m. 1 in 18; 23¼m. 1 in 16; 28¾m. 1 in 12†; 29m. 1 in 15; 33¾m. 1 in 22; 37m. 1 in 22; 47m. 1 in 18; 48m. 1 in 13; 49m. 1 in 17; 52½m. 1 in 16; 54¼m. 1 in 24. (Bodenham Hill 1 in 15†).

Milestones.—Measured from Shrewsbury to Church Stretton, whence from Ludlow on to Wooferton; thence from Hereford *via* Dinmore Hill.

Measurements.

Shrewsbury,* Market Clock.									
6¾	Dorrington.*								
13⅛	6⅜	Church Stretton,* Hotel.							
20⅞	14⅛	7¾	Craven Arms,* Hotel.						
28⅝	21⅞	15½	7¾	Ludlow,* Bull Ring.					
32⅝	25⅞	19½	11¾	4	Wooferton,* Inn.				
39¾	33	26⅝	18⅞	11⅛	7⅛	Leominster,* Town Hall.			
46¾	40	33⅝	25⅞	18⅞	14⅛	7	Bodenham.		
50¼	43½	37⅛	29⅜	21⅝	17⅜	10½	3½	Wellington,* Bridge Inn.	
55½	48¾	42⅜	34⅝	26⅞	22¾	15¾	8¾	5¼	Hereford,* Market.

Leominster to Hereford, by Dinmore Hill, 2¾m. less.

Principal Objects of Interest.—Church Stretton: Long Mynd, Wenlock Edge. Stokesay: Castle, Bromfield, Church. LUDLOW: Castle, Church, Richard's Castle. 37m., Berrington Park. LEOMINSTER: Town Hall, Butter Cross, Ch. 44m., Hampton Court. HEREFORD: Cathedral, Shire Hall, Castle Green, Bridge, Free Library, &c., &c.

Hotels or Inns at places marked*, and at Bayston Hill, Leebotwood, Strettons, Brimfield, &c.

ROUTE 980. SHREWSBURY TO LUDLOW AND HEREFORD.

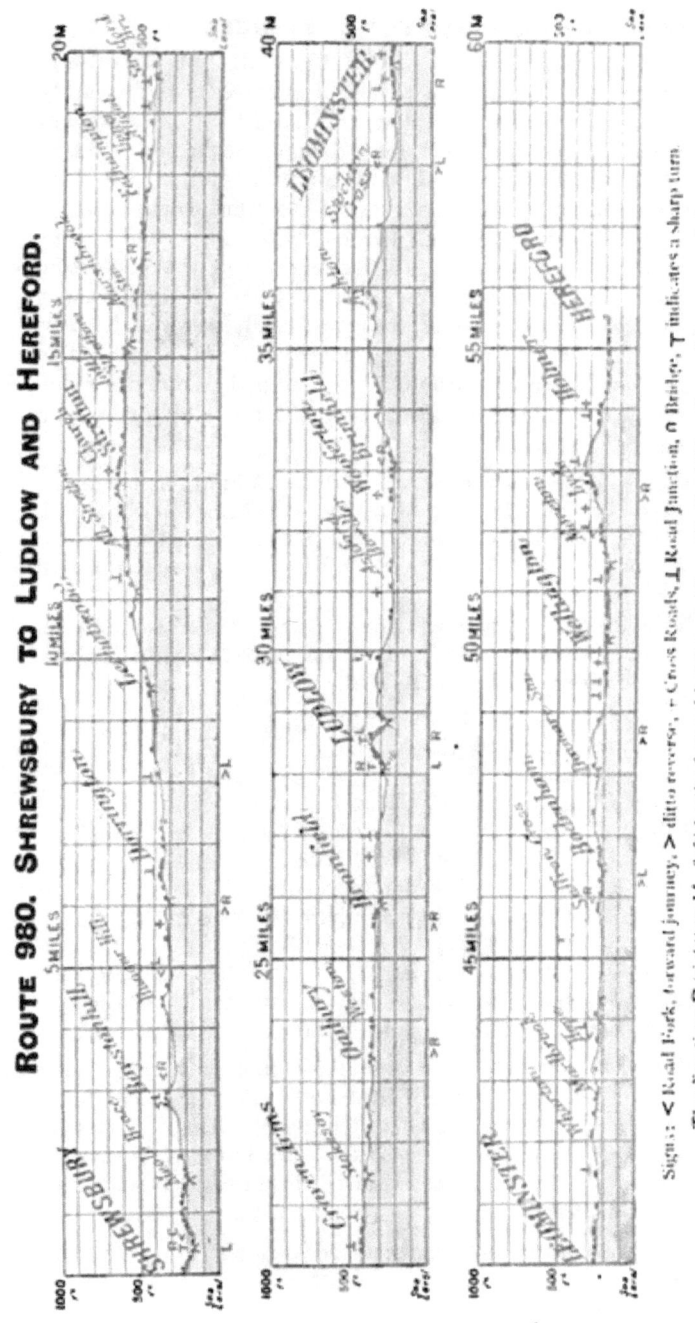

Signs : < Road Fork, forward journey, > ditto reverse, + Cross Roads, ⊥ Road Junction, ○ Bridge, ┬ indicates a sharp turn

The directions R (right) and L (left) for the forward journey are above the R al Line, those of the reverse, below.

981 SHREWSBURY TO BISHOPS CASTLE.

Description.—Class II. Good surface to Minsterley, then fairly good to Gravels, where it is poor, then good to Bishops Castle. The direct road (21m.), shown dotted, is a bad road.

Gradients.—At ¼m. 1 in 13†; ¾m. 1 in 14; 8½m. 1 in 16; 13¼m. 1 in 17; 18½m. 1 in 19; 22¼m. 1 in 15.

Milestones.—Measured from Shrewsbury & Bishops Castle

Measurements.

Shrewsbury,* Market Clock.			
9⅝	Minsterley.*		
14⅜	4¾	Gravels.*	
22⅝	13	8¼	Bishops Castle,* Clock.

Principal Objects of Interest.—Bishops Castle: Town House.

982 SHREWSBURY TO MONTGOMERY.

Description.—Class II. Fine surface. If going on to Newtown, turn to right at 21⅜m., entering Montgomery.

Gradients.—At 6m. 1 in 25; 10¾, 13¼, & 13½m. 1 in 17; 15½m. 1 in 16; 16m. 1 in 21; (21½m. 1 in 9†); 23m. 1 in 13†.

Milestones.—Measured from Shrewsbury.

Measurements.

Shrewsbury,* Market Clock.					
8⅝	Westbury.*				
18½	9⅞	Chirbury.*			
21⅜	12¾	2⅞	Montgomery.*		
24⅛	15¼	5⅜	2⅞	Garthmyl. R. 1002.	
31¼	22⅝	13	10½	7⅛	Newtown.*

Principal Objects of Interest. — Chirbury: Church. 20½m., Offa's Dyke. Montgomery: Castle.

Hotels or Inns at places marked*, and at Yockleton, Worthen, and Marton.

983 SHREWSBURY TO WELSHPOOL.

Description.—Class II. The road has splendid surface, but is undulating for the first eight miles; dangerous descent at Trewern.

Gradients.—At 7¾m. 1 in 21; 13½m. 1 in 14 (dangerous).

Milestones.—Measured from Shrewsbury.

Measurements.

Shrewsbury,* Market Clock.			
5⅝	Cross Gates,* Inn.		
12¾	7⅛	Middletown,* New Inn.	
18¾	13⅛	6½	Welshpool,* Cross.

Principal Objects of Interest. — Buttington: Church. WELSHPOOL: Powis Castle, Church.

Hotels or Inns at places marked*, & at Bicton Heath, &c.

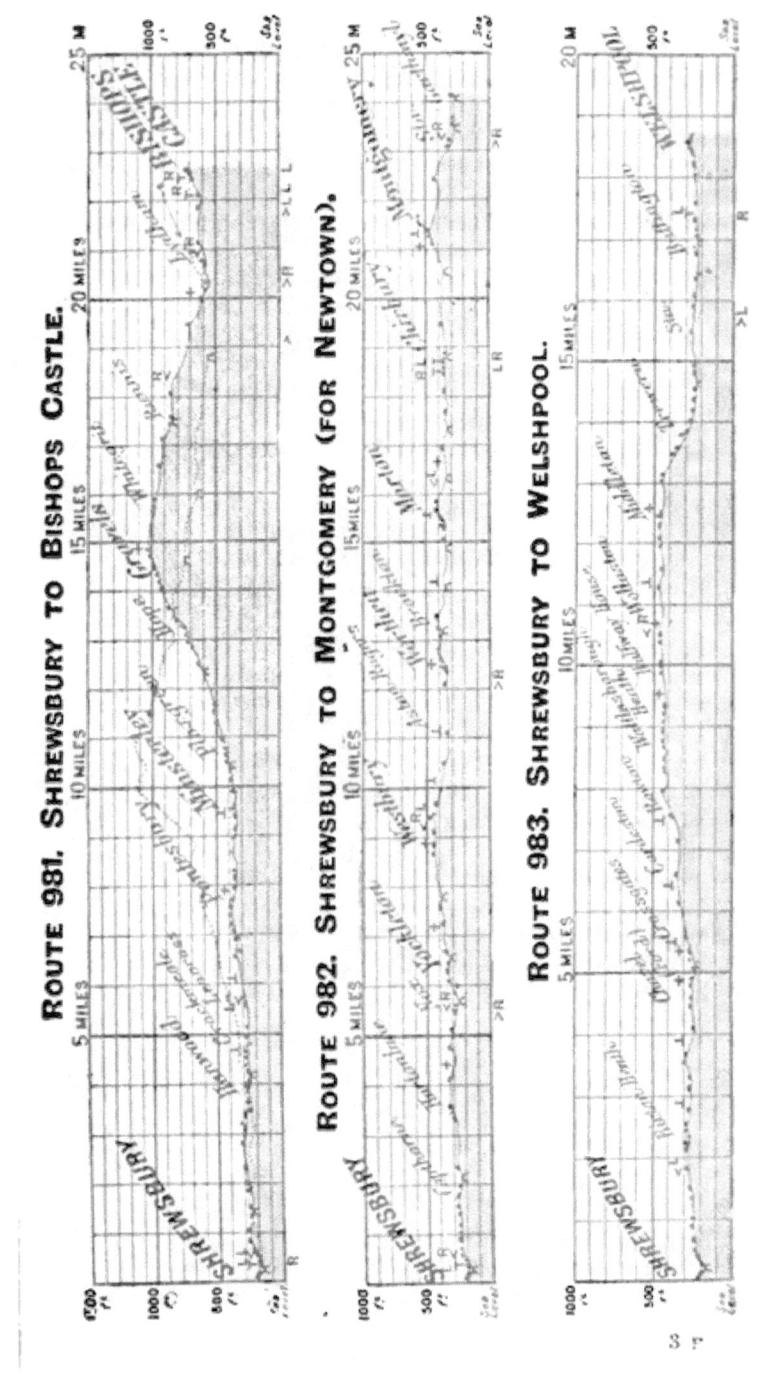

ROUTE 981. SHREWSBURY TO BISHOPS CASTLE.

ROUTE 982. SHREWSBURY TO MONTGOMERY (FOR NEWTOWN).

ROUTE 983. SHREWSBURY TO WELSHPOOL.

3 P

984 SHREWSBURY TO VYRNWY.

Description.—Class II. This is an excellent undulating road through Alberbury to Llansantffraid; practically flat near Four Crosses, then with easy undulations to Llanfyllin. Up to this point the road has good surface, but afterwards while the surface is very fair, the hills are very steep, and there is a dangerous descent, with an awkward turn, shortly before Vyrnwy. On the higher parts of the road the surface is rather loose. The road goes round the lake, and is level, with good surface (distance 11¼m.).

Gradients.—(†*Dangerous.*) At 8¾m. 1 in 22; 9¼m. 1 in 16; 17m. 1 in 25; 28½m. 1 in 12†; 29½m. 1 in 14; 30¾m. 1 in 13†; 32m. 1 in 15; 32½m. 1 in 12†.

Milestones.—Measured from Shrewsbury.

Measurements.

Shrewsbury,* Market Clock.					
8⅞	Alberbury.*				
15⅜	6⅝	Four Crosses.*			
18⅞	10⅛	3½	Llansantffraid,* Lion Hotel.		
24⅜	15⅝	9¼	5¾	Llanfyllin.*	
34⅜	25⅝	19¼	15¾	10	Vyrnwy Hotel.*

Principal Objects of Interest.—Llansantffraid: Church. Llanfyllin: Church. Views of Rodney's Pillar, near Four Crosses, otherwise uninteresting. The scenery begins after Llansantffraid. Vyrnwy: Liverpool Reservoir.

Hotels or Inns at places marked *, and at Cross Gates, Crew Green, Llandrinio, &c.

984a. SHREWSBURY TO LLANRHAIADR.

Description.—Class II. Splendid surface to Wolfs Head; thereafter a fair undulating road. The direct road to Llansantffraid is shown above.

Gradients.—At 4m. 1 in 23.

Milestones.—Measured from London.

Measurements.

Shrewsbury,* Market Clock.				
8¼	Nesscliff,* Inn.			
12⅛	3⅞	Knockin,* Hotel.		
15¾	7½	3⅝	Lynclys.*	
(20¾	12½	8⅝	5	Llansantffraid,* or)
26⅜	18⅛	14¼	10⅝	Llanrhaiadr.*

Principal Objects of Interest.—Uninteresting road to Lynclys. Llanrhaiadr: Waterfall.

Hotels or Inns at places marked *, and at Penybont.

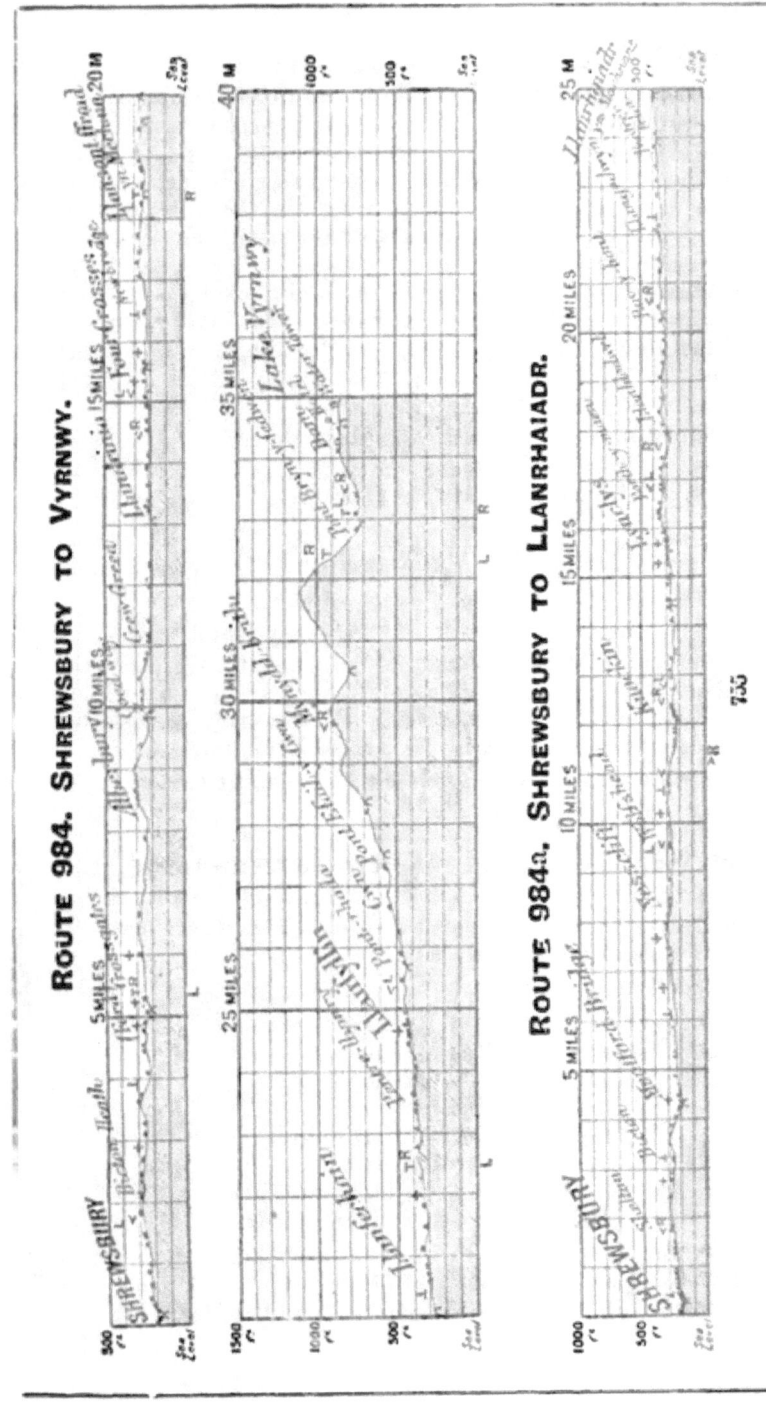

ROUTE 984. SHREWSBURY TO VYRNWY.

ROUTE 984a. SHREWSBURY TO LLANRHAIADR.

755

985 SHREWSBURY TO WREXHAM.

Description.—Class II. The road is undulating for eight miles, but after that it is practically level, except approaching Ellesmere. From Ellesmere to Wrexham exceptionally good surface, but there is a steep hill at Overton Bridge, and also a mile before Wrexham. Some prefer to follow Route 986, through Chirk, to Wrexham.

Gradients.—At 6½m. 1 in 19; 15¾m. 1 in 18; 22¼m. 1 in 19; 23m. 1 in 16; 23¼m. 1 in 17; 27½m. 1 in 18; 27¾m. 1 in 15.

Milestones.—Measured from Castle Gate, Shrewsbury, and from Ellesmere Town Hall.

Measurements.

Shrewsbury,* Market Clock.					
8¼	Harmerhill.*				
12	3¾	Cockshutt.*			
16⅝	8⅜	4⅝	Ellesmere,* Town Hall.		
21¾	13⅜	9⅝	5⅛	Overton.*	
28⅜	20⅜	16⅝	12⅝	7	Wrexham,* Town Hall.

Principal Objects of Interest.—Ellesmere: Church, Oteley Park. WREXHAM: Church. Very pretty near Ellesmere, and at Overton Bridge.

986 SHREWSBURY TO LLANGOLLEN.

Description.—Class I. The Holyhead road. Splendid surface throughout, and almost always in perfect condition; the hills are finely engineered, and the only one that is stiff is that at Chirk. There is a more direct road, avoiding Oswestry, between Queen's Head and Gobowen, 1¼m. shorter, but the surface on it is not so good. For Wrexham, turn to R. at 25m.

Gradients.—At 4m. 1 in 23; 22½m. 1 in 25; 23¼m. 1 in 18.

Milestones.—Measured from Holyhead.

Measurements.

Shrewsbury,* Market Clock.				
17⅝	9¾	Oswestry,* Fountain.		
23¼	15½	5⅝	Chirk,* Hand Hotel.	
30	21¾	12⅜	6⅝	Llangollen,* Town Clock, or
(33¾	25½	16¼	10⅜	Wrexham.*)

Principal Objects of Interest.—Pretty road near Montford Bridge. OSWESTRY: Castle Mound, Church. (Whittington: Castle). Chirk: Castle, Viaduct, Aqueduct. Fron: Collieries. LLANGOLLEN: Valle Crucis Abbey, Eliseg's Pillar, Bridge, &c. The fine scenery is beyond Llangollen.

Hotels or Inns at places marked*, and at Montford Bridge, Queen's Head, Fron, &c.

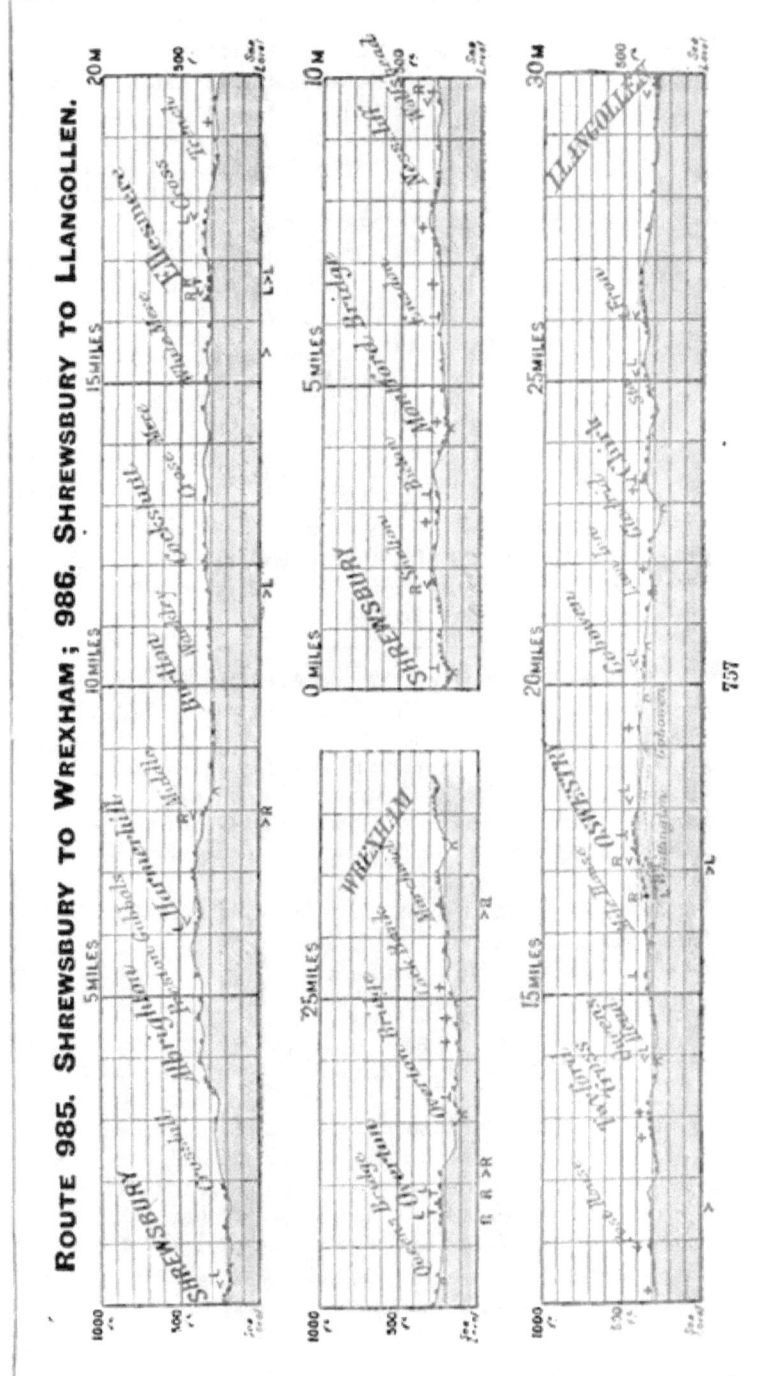

ROUTE 985. SHREWSBURY TO WREXHAM; 986. SHREWSBURY TO LLANGOLLEN.

757

987 BRIDGNORTH TO LUDLOW.

Description.—Class II. The road by Weston has good surface, and becomes very good approaching Ludlow. The direct road (shown dotted) has steep hills of 1 in 10, and poor surface.

Gradients.—At ½m. 1/12 (dangerous); 2¾m. 1/16; 3¾m. 1/19; 4¼m. 1/24; 12m. 1/15; 14¼ & 16¾m. 1/16; 7¼m. 1/14.

Milestones.—Measured from Bridgnorth, & from Ludlow.

Measurements.

Bridgnorth,* Market House.			By Direct Road.		
14½	Munslow.* R. 991.		Bridgnorth,* Market.		
(20¾	6⅝	Craven Arms,* Hotel.)	6⅝	Neenton.	
23¾	9⅝	Ludlow,* Bull Ring.	19⅝	12⅞	Ludlow.*

Principal Objects of Interest.—Brown Clee Hills. LUDLOW: Castle, Church.

Hotels or Inns at places marked *.

988 BRIDGNORTH TO CLEOBURY, &c.

Description.—Class III. An exceedingly hilly road, with poor surface. This road to Bewdley is not so good as R. 979.

Gradients.—(†*Dangerous.*) At 1 & 2¼m. 1/13†; 2½m. 1/14; 3½m. 1/17; 3¾m. 1/15†; 4¾m. 1/13†; 5¼m. 1/14; 7¼m. 1/12†; 7¾m. 1/10†; 11m. 1/12†; 11½, 12, & 13m. 1/14.

Milestones.—Measured from Bridgnorth Market.

Measurements.

Bridgnorth,* Market.			Bridgnorth,* Market.		
9¾	Kinlet,* Eagle and Serpent.		9¾	Kinlet.*	
14	4¼	Cleobury Mortimer.*	15¼	5½	Bewdley.*

Hotels or Inns at places marked*.

989 BRIDGNORTH TO NEWPORT (Salop).

Description.—Class II. After the dangerous descent to Bridgnorth (Lower), good surface to Shifnal, thence hilly.

Gradients.—At 3½m. 1 in 16; 10m. 1 in 19; 13½m. 1 in 17; 14 & 14¾m. 1 in 18; 16m. 1 in 19.

Measurements.

Bridgnorth,* Market.					
¾	Bridgnorth,* Lower.				
5¾	5	Norton.*			
11¼	10½	5½	Shifnal,* Bridge.		
13⅝	12⅞	7⅜	2⅛	Crackleybank.* R. 936.	
19⅝	18⅞	13⅜	8⅛	6¼	Newport,* Town Hall.

Principal Objects of Interest.—Shifnal: Church.

Hotels or Inns at places marked*.

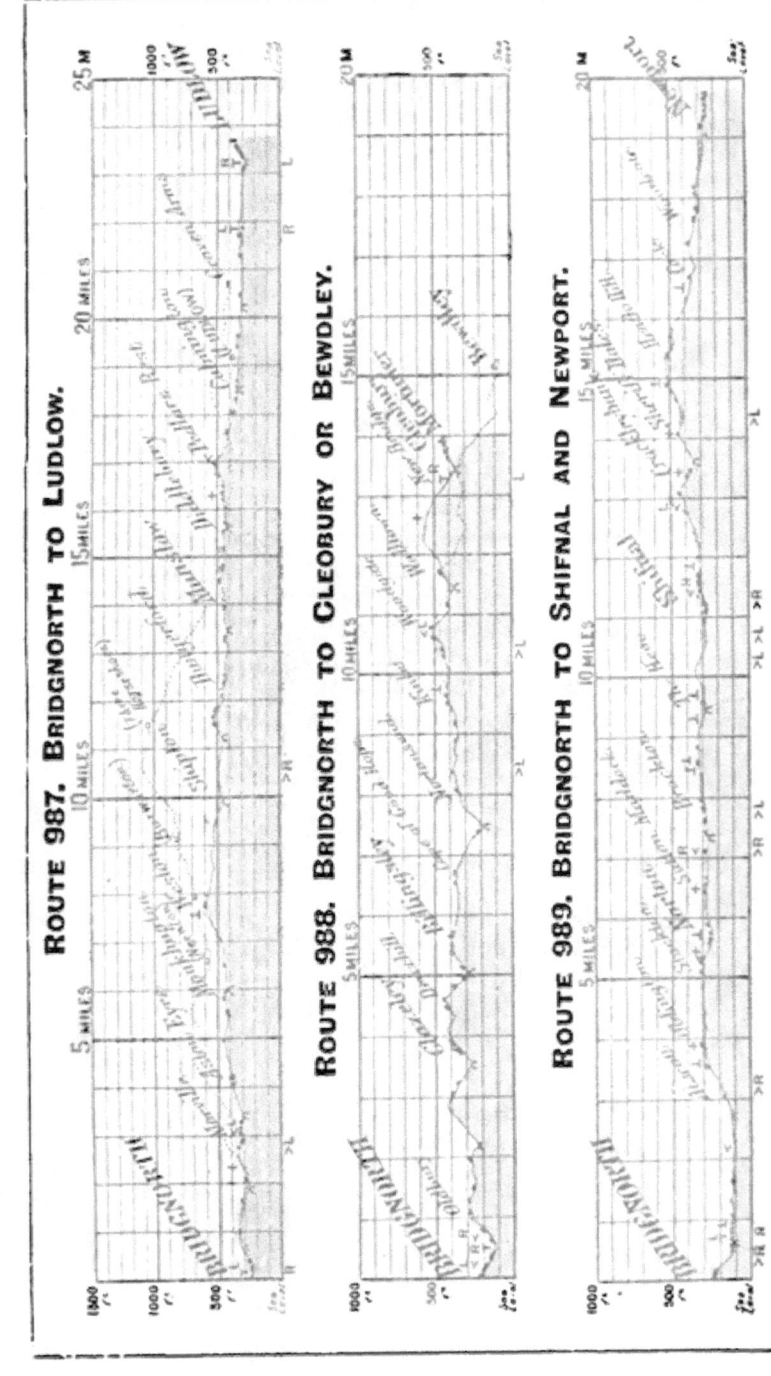

ROUTE 987. BRIDGNORTH TO LUDLOW.

ROUTE 988. BRIDGNORTH TO CLEOBURY OR BEWDLEY.

ROUTE 989. BRIDGNORTH TO SHIFNAL AND NEWPORT.

990 SHIFNAL TO IRONBRIDGE, &c.

Description.—Class II. Good surface, but steep and very dangerous hills.

Gradients.—(†*Dangerous.*) At 4¾m.1/17; 5½m.1/10†; 9½m. 1/10†; 10½m.1/12†; 12½, 17½, & 21m.1/17; 23m.1 14; 23¾m.1/13†.

Milestones.—Irregular.

Measurements.

Shifnal,* Bridge.						
4¼	Madeley.*					
6	1¾	Ironbridge.*				
8	3¾	2	Buildwas,* Bridge Inn. R. 979.			
11½	7¼	5½	3½	Wenlock,* Town Hall. R. 991.		
18¾	14½	12¾	10⅜	6⅝	Longville,* Station Inn.	
24½	20¼	18½	16½	13	6⅛	Church Stretton.*

Principal Objects of Interest. — IRONBRIDGE: Bridge. Buildwas: Abbey. Wenlock: Abbey, Town Hall. Pretty near Buildwas. Fine view near Longville.

991 WELLINGTON TO WENLOCK, &c.

Description.—Class II. A very hilly road, with steep and dangerous hills. Good surface, except in Coalbrookdale. R. 977 is joined at Shipton.

Gradients.—(†*Dangerous.*) At 1m.1/19; 2m.1/17; 3m.1/21; 4½m.1/13; 8½m.1/10†; 9¼m.1/12†; 11¼m.1/9†; 13½m.1/17; 13¾m.1/11†; 15¼m.1/12†; 18¾m.1/15.

Milestones.—Measured from the Market, Wellington.

Measurements.

Wellington,* Market.					
4⅞	Coalbrookdale.*				
(6	1⅛	Ironbridge,* Bridge.)			
7⅛	2¼	Buildwas,* Bridge Inn. R. 990.			
10⅝	5¾	3½	Wenlock,* Town Hall. R. 990.		
15½	10⅝	8⅜	4⅞	Brockton.*	
21	16⅛	13⅞	10⅜	5½	Munslow.* R. 987.

Principal Objects of Interest.—Buildwas, &c., as above.

992 WELLINGTON TO WEM.

Description.—Class II. An excellent cross-country road (difficult to follow at night, owing to numerous forks).

Gradients.—At 3½m. 1 in 19; 13m. 1 in 25; 14½m. 1 in 19.

Milestones.—Measured from Watling Street.

Measurements.

Wellington,* Market.			
6	High Ercall.* R. 978.		
9¾	3¾	Shawbury.* R. 977.	
16	10	6¼	Wem,* Church.

Principal Objects of Interest.—2m., Admaston Spa.

Hotels or Inns at places marked *.

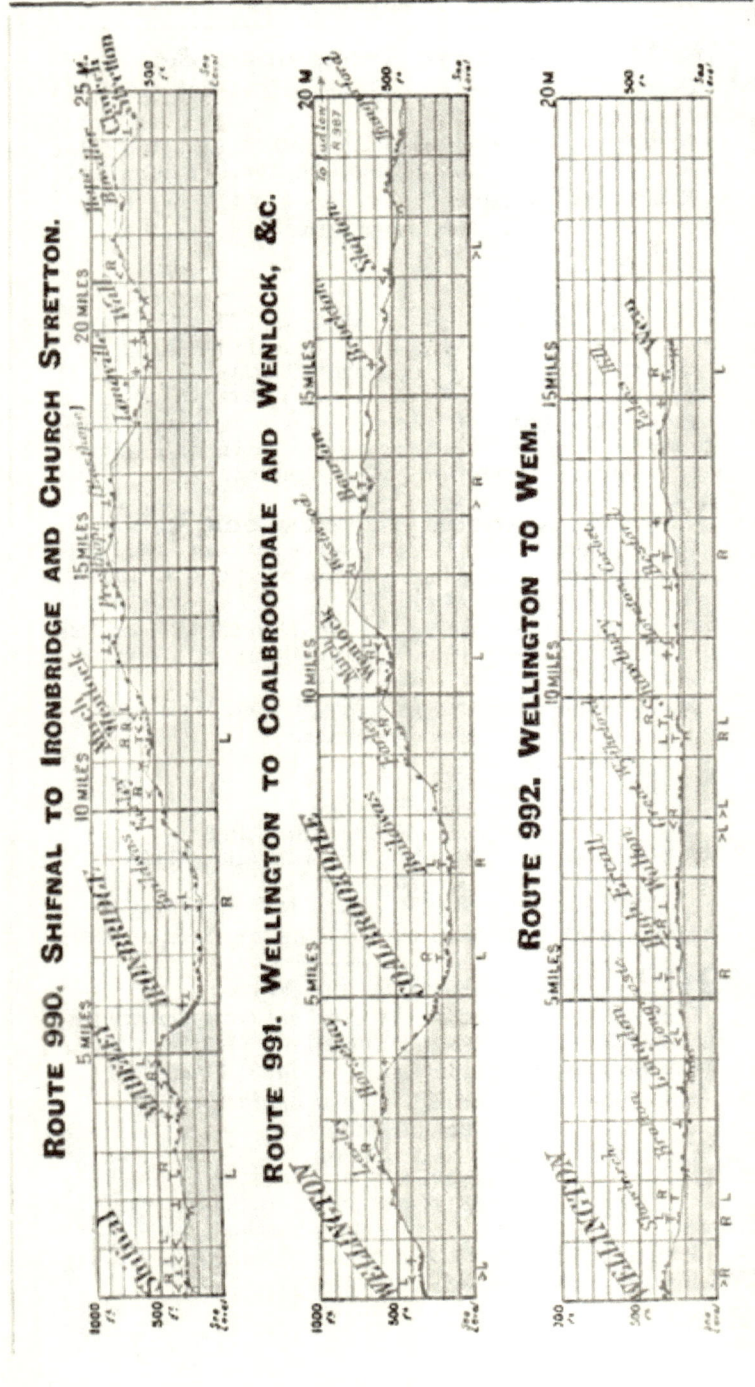

ROUTE 990. SHIFNAL TO IRONBRIDGE AND CHURCH STRETTON.

ROUTE 991. WELLINGTON TO COALBROOKDALE AND WENLOCK, &C.

ROUTE 992. WELLINGTON TO WEM.

993 NEWPORT TO NANTWICH.

Description.—Class II. An undulating road, with excellent surface; dangerous hill at Market Drayton.

Gradients.—At 6¼m. 1 in 14; 7¼m. 1 in 20; 10¾m. 1 in 16; 11¼m. 1 in 13 (dangerous); 16½ & 17¼m. 1 in 19; 22m. 1 in 22.

Milestones.—Measured from Wolverhampton,—irregular.

Measurements.

Newport,* Town Hall.
11¼ Market Drayton.*
17¾ 6½ Audlem.*
25 13¾ 7¼ Nantwich,* Church.

Principal Objects of Interest. — Nantwich: Church. Pretty approach to Market Drayton.

994 MARKET DRAYTON TO ELLESMERE.

Description.—Class II. Fine surface to Hodnet, then a somewhat loose road through Hawkstone Park (by courtesy), after which good surface to Ellesmere.

Gradients.—At 5¾m. 1 in 16; 6¼ & 7m. 1 in 13; 8½m. 1 in 16; 9m. 1 in 17; 14m. 1 in 22; 21m. 1 in 13; 21½m. 1 in 22.

Milestones.—Measured from Shrewsbury, and from Wem.

Measurements.

Market Drayton.*
5¾ Hodnet,* Bear Inn.
13 7¼ Wem,* Church.
22½ 16¾ 9½ Ellesmere,* Town Hall.

Principal Objects of Interest. — Ellesmere: Church, Mere, Oteley Park. Very pretty through Hawkstone Deer Park, and at Ellesmere.

995 WHITCHURCH TO LLANGOLLEN.

Description.—Class I. The road by Bangor has splendid surface to Ruabon; the direct road through Overton is continuously undulating, with steep hills. Poor surface about Acrefair, where there is a level crossing.

Gradients.—At 2m. 1 in 18; 5m. 1 in 19; 6m. 1 in 20; 9¾m. 1 in 16; 10½m. 1 in 13 (dangerous); 12m. 1 in 20; 14m. 1 in 22; 14½m. 1 in 19; 16¼m. 1 in 20; 18¼m. 1 in 20; 19½m. 1 in 22; 20¼ & 21m. 1 in 16; 22¾m. 1 in 19.

Milestones.—Measured from Whitchurch.

Measurements.	By Overton.
Whitchurch.*	Whitchurch.*
10¾ Bangor-on-Dee,* Star Hotel.	12¼ Overton.*
18 7¼ Ruabon,* Church.	17¼ 4¾ Ruabon.*
24½ 13¾ 6½ Llangollen.*	23¼ 11 6½ Llangollen.*

Principal Objects of Interest.—Bangor: Bridge. Ruabon: Wynnstay Park. LLANGOLLEN: as Route 986.

Hotels or Inns at places marked *.

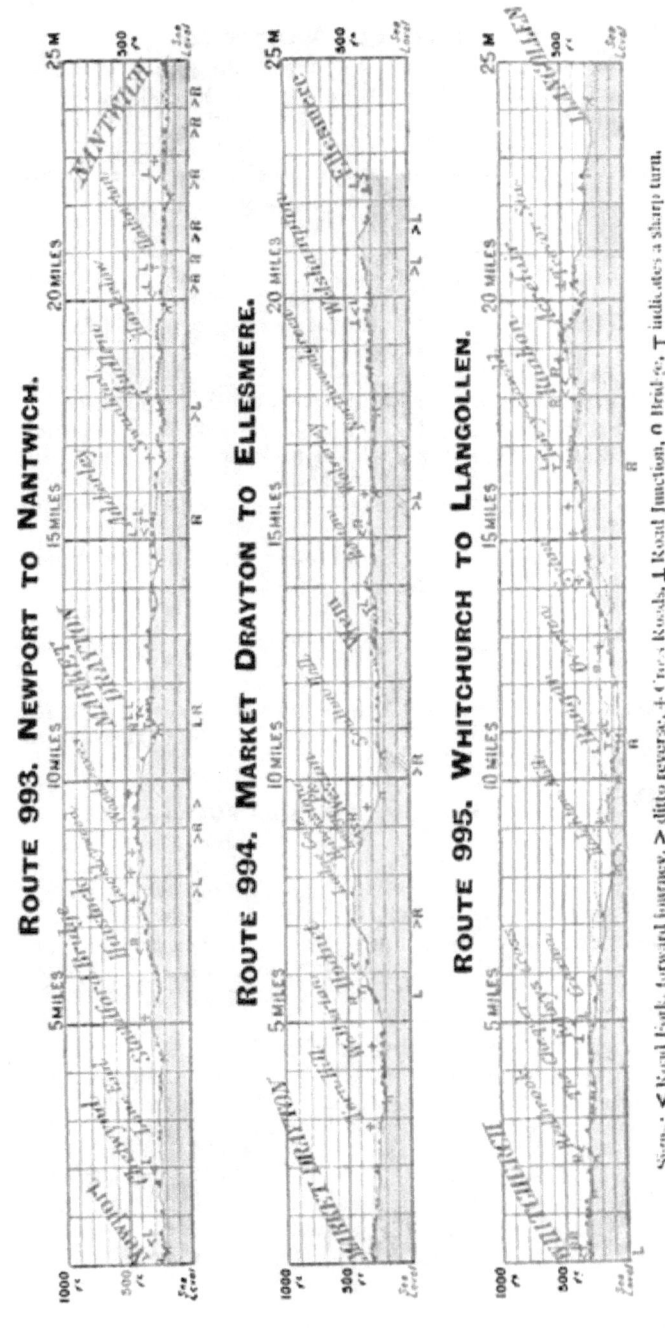

ROUTE 993. NEWPORT TO NANTWICH.

ROUTE 994. MARKET DRAYTON TO ELLESMERE.

ROUTE 995. WHITCHURCH TO LLANGOLLEN.

Signs : < Road Fork, forward journey, > ditto reverse, + Cross Roads, ⊥ Road Junction, ∩ Bridge, T indicates a sharp turn.
The directions R (right) and L (left) for the forward journey are above the Road Line, those of the reverse, below.

996 WHITCHURCH TO BRIDGNORTH.

Description.—Class II. The "record" route to Worcester. Splendid surface to Wellington, then poor for five miles to Cuckoo Oak, after which fine surface again. Level crossings at Lawley and Dawley. For Worcester (R. 979), turn to left in Lower Bridgnorth.

Gradients.—At 8½ & 9¼m. 1 in 15; 10m. 1 in 16; 23m. 1 in 19; 23½m. 1 in 17; 25½m. 1 in 16; 26¾m. 1 in 14; 32½m. 1 in 16.

Milestones.—Irregular.

Measurements.

Whitchurch.*							
10	Hodnet,* Bear Inn.						
16⅜	6⅜	Waters Upton.*					
21⅝	11⅝	5¼	Wellington,* Market. R. 991.				
25⅛	15⅛	8¾	3½	Dawley,* Town Hall.			
30⅞	20⅞	14	8¾	5¼	Norton.*		
35⅞	25⅞	19	13¾	10¼	5	Bridgnorth,* Lower.	
36⅛	26⅛	19¾	14½	11	5¾	¾	Bridgnorth,* Market; or
63¼	53¼	46⅞	41⅝	38⅛	32⅜	27⅜	Worcester.* R. 979.

Principal Objects of Interest. — Hodnet: Hawkestone Park. WELLINGTON: Admaston Spa, The Wrekin. Collieries and Iron Works from Wellington to Cuckoo Oak. BRIDGNORTH: Bridge, Castle. Pretty scenery near Bridgnorth. "The Wrekin" stands out prominently near Wellington.

Hotels or Inns at places marked *.

997 WHITCHURCH TO HOLT, &c.

Description.—Class II. A good road, with one very steep hill. From Holt to Wrexham, fine surface.

Gradients.—At 2m. 1 in 25; 4m. 1 in 15; 4¼m. 1 in 23; 5¼m. 1 in 23; 6½m. 1 in 12 (dangerous); 16¼m. 1 in 21.

Measurements.

Whitchurch.*				
5¼	Malpas.*			
12¼	7	Farndon.*		
12¾	7½	½	Holt,* Cross.	
18⅛	12⅞	5⅞	5⅜	Wrexham,* Town Hall.

Principal Objects of Interest.—Farndon: Castle. Holt: Bridge. WREXHAM: Church. Pretty scenery about Holt.

Hotels or Inns at places marked *.

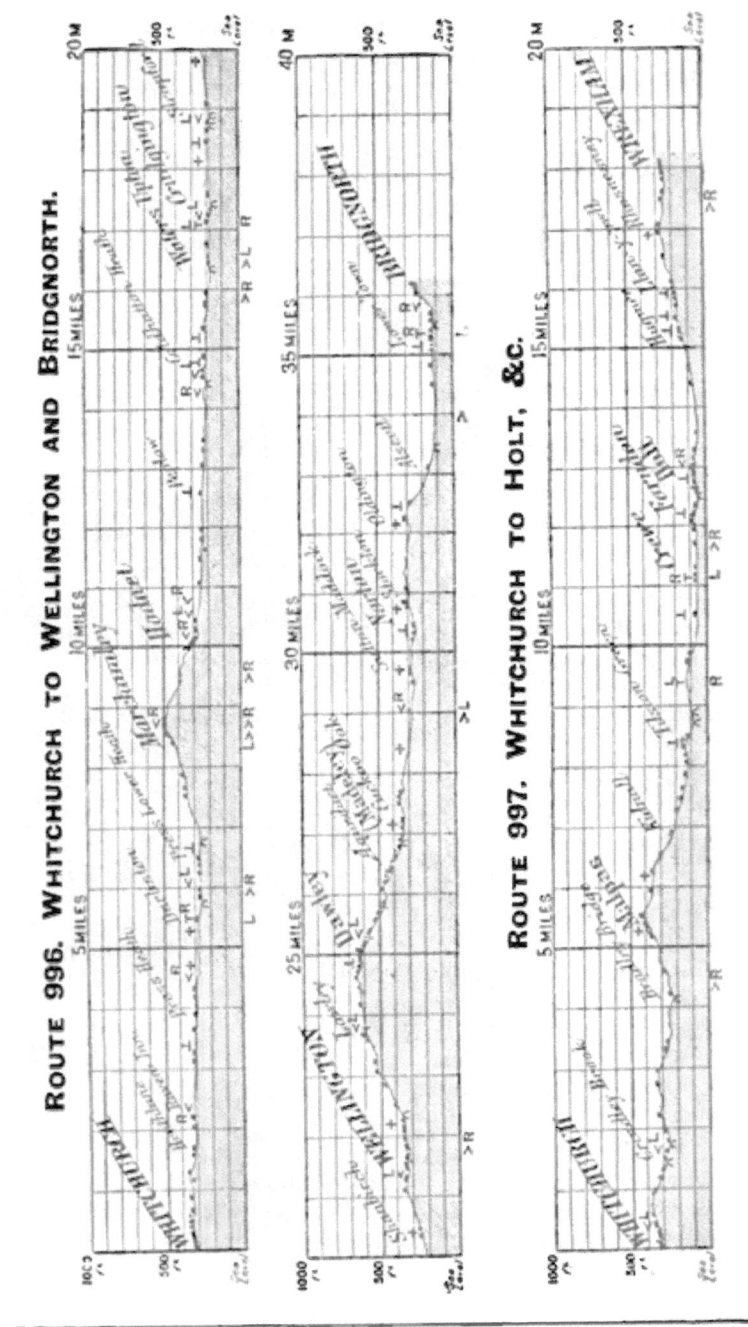

ROUTE 996. WHITCHURCH TO WELLINGTON AND BRIDGNORTH.

ROUTE 997. WHITCHURCH TO HOLT, &c.

998 OSWESTRY TO WHITCHURCH.

Description.—Class II. Good surface, but with a stiff hill to Ellesmere, thereafter an easy, undulating road. Note the two turns in Whittington.

Gradients.—At 5m. 1 in 22; 5½m. 1 in 25; 6m. 1 in 16; 9m. 1 in 22; 9½m. 1 in 13; 12m. 1 in 18.

Milestones.—Measured from Whitchurch.

Measurements.

Oswestry,* Fountain.			
2¾	Whittington.*		
8	5¼	Ellesmere,* Town Hall.	
19⅝	16⅞	11⅝	Whitchurch.*

Principal Objects of Interest.—Whittington: Castle. Ellesmere: Church, Mere, Oteley Park. WHITCHURCH: Church. Pretty road near Ellesmere.

999 OSWESTRY TO BANGOR-ON-DEE.

Description.—Class III. Fine surface at first to Gobowen, then a poor cross-country road.

Gradients.—(† *Dangerous.*) At 3¾m. 1 in 15; 4¼m. 1 in 17; 8m. 1 in 15; 8¼m. 1 in 11 †; 11¾m. 1 in 10 †.

Measurements.

Oswestry,* Fountain.			
2¾	Gobowen.*		
10¼	7	Overton.*	
13	10	2¾	Bangor-on-Dee,* Star Hotel.

Principal Objects of Interest.—Bangor: Bridge.

Hotels or Inns at places marked*, and at Street Dinas.

1000 OSWESTRY TO LLANFAIR.

Description.—Class II. Fine surface to Llynclys, then it is a good country road to Llansantffraid, after which it becomes slightly hilly, with a stiff hill over to Llanfair. This latter part has fair surface.

Gradients.—At 1m. 1 in 23; 11m. 1 in 18; 12½m. 1 in 14; 12¾m. 1 in 18; 13m. 1 in 16; 17¼m. 1 in 11; 17¾m. 1 in 16.

Measurements.

Oswestry,* Fountain.				
3⅜	Lynclys.* R. 984.			
8¼	5¼	Llansantffraid,* Lion Hotel. R. 984.		
14⅞	11¼	6⅛	Meifod.*	
20¾	17¼	12	5⅞	Llanfair,* Bridge.

Principal Objects of Interest.—Llansantffraid: Church A pretty road up the Vyrnwy Valley.

Hotels or Inns at places marked*.

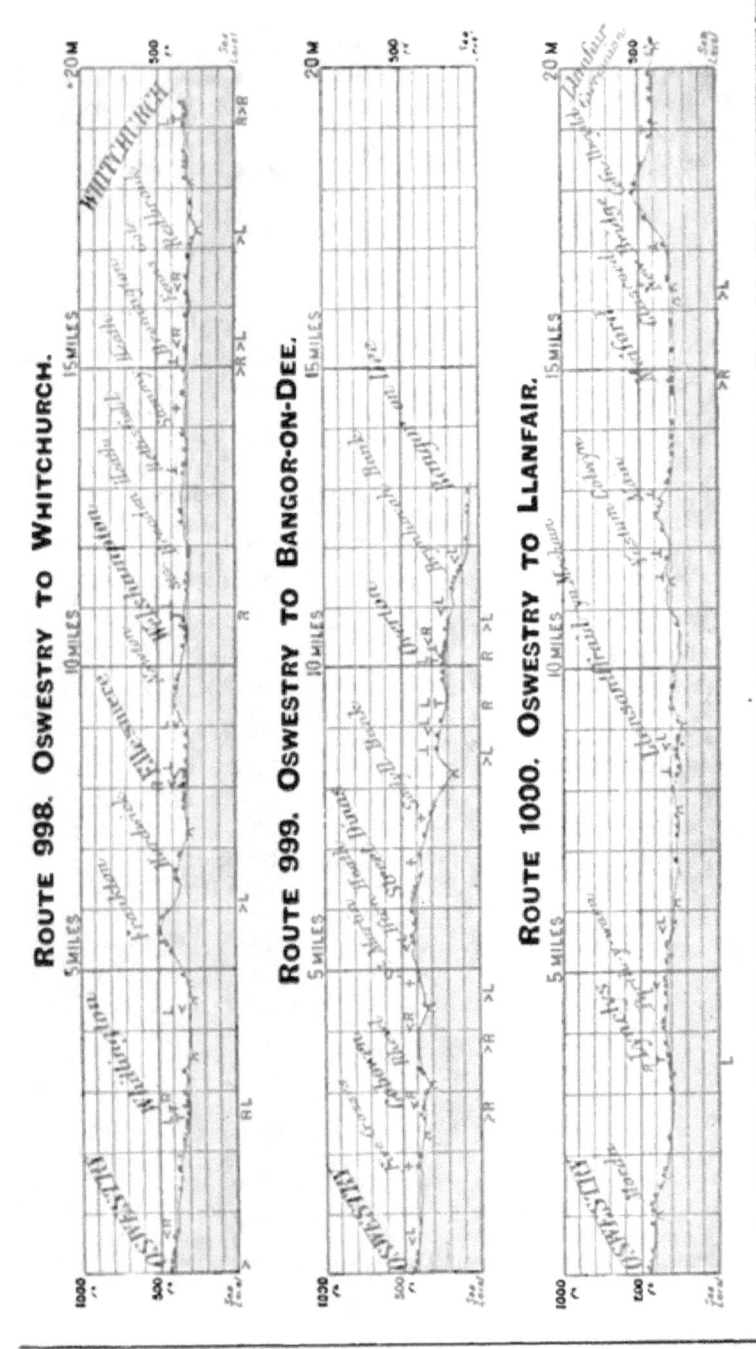

ROUTE 998. OSWESTRY TO WHITCHURCH.

ROUTE 999. OSWESTRY TO BANGOR-ON-DEE.

ROUTE 1000. OSWESTRY TO LLANFAIR.

1 CHESTER TO LLANGOLLEN. [1001]

Description.—Class I. Splendid surface to Wrexham, then fairly good, with tram rails at side, to Ruabon; bumpy past Acrefair (level crossing) to Trevor, then splendid surface to Llangollen.

Gradients.—At 7m. 1 in 25; 10m. 1 in 17; 17m. 1 in 20; 18m. 1 in 22; 18¾ and 19½m. 1 in 16; 21¼m. 1 in 19.

Milestones.—Measured from Chester Cross, to Marford, then from Wrexham.

Measurements.

Chester,* Cross.				
5½	Pulford.*			
11½	6¼	Wrexham,* Town Hall.		
16½	11¼	5	Ruabon,* Church.	
22⅝	17⅛	11⅛	6⅛	Llangollen,* Town Clock.

Principal Objects of Interest.—WREXHAM: Church. Ruabon: Wynnstay Park. Acrefair: Collieries and Iron Works. LLANGOLLEN: Bridge, Valle Crucis Abbey, Eliseg's Pillar. The fine scenery is beyond Llangollen.

Hotels or Inns at places marked*, and at Rosset, &c.

---

2 CHESTER TO NEWTOWN (Montgomery). [1002]

Description.—Class I. As above to Ruabon, whence indifferent surface to Newbridge; here the splendid surface begins, and for the next thirty-five miles, with the exception of a slight hill at Chirk, the road is either flat or has almost imperceptible undulations. For Montgomery (51¾m.), turn to left at Garthmyl. For Kerry, turn to left at Abermule.

Gradients.—From Ruabon.—At 2¼m. 1 in 19; 5½m. 1 in 18; 6m. 1 in 25; 12¼m. 1 in 23; 17m. 1 in 17.

Milestones.—Measured from Oswestry & from Welshpool.

Measurements.

Chester,* Cross.								
11½	Wrexham,* Town Hall.							
16½	5	Ruabon,* Church.						
21⅞	10⅜	5⅜	Chirk,* Hand Hotel.					
27¾	16¼	11¼	5⅞	Oswestry,* Fountain.				
33⅝	22⅛	17⅛	11¾	5⅞	Llanymynech,* Hotel.			
43	31½	26½	21⅛	15¼	9⅜	Welshpool,* Cross.		
48⅞	37⅜	32⅜	27	21⅛	15¼	5⅞	Garthmyl. R. 982.	
56½	45	40	34⅝	28¾	22⅞	13½	7⅝	Newtown.*

Principal Objects of Interest.—Wrexham and Ruabon as above. Newbridge: Viaduct. Chirk: Castle, Viaduct, Aqueduct. OSWESTRY: Castle Mound, Church, Whittington Castle. WELSHPOOL: Powis Castle, Church. NEWTOWN: Church. Views of the Shropshire and Welsh hills.

Hotels or Inns at places marked*.

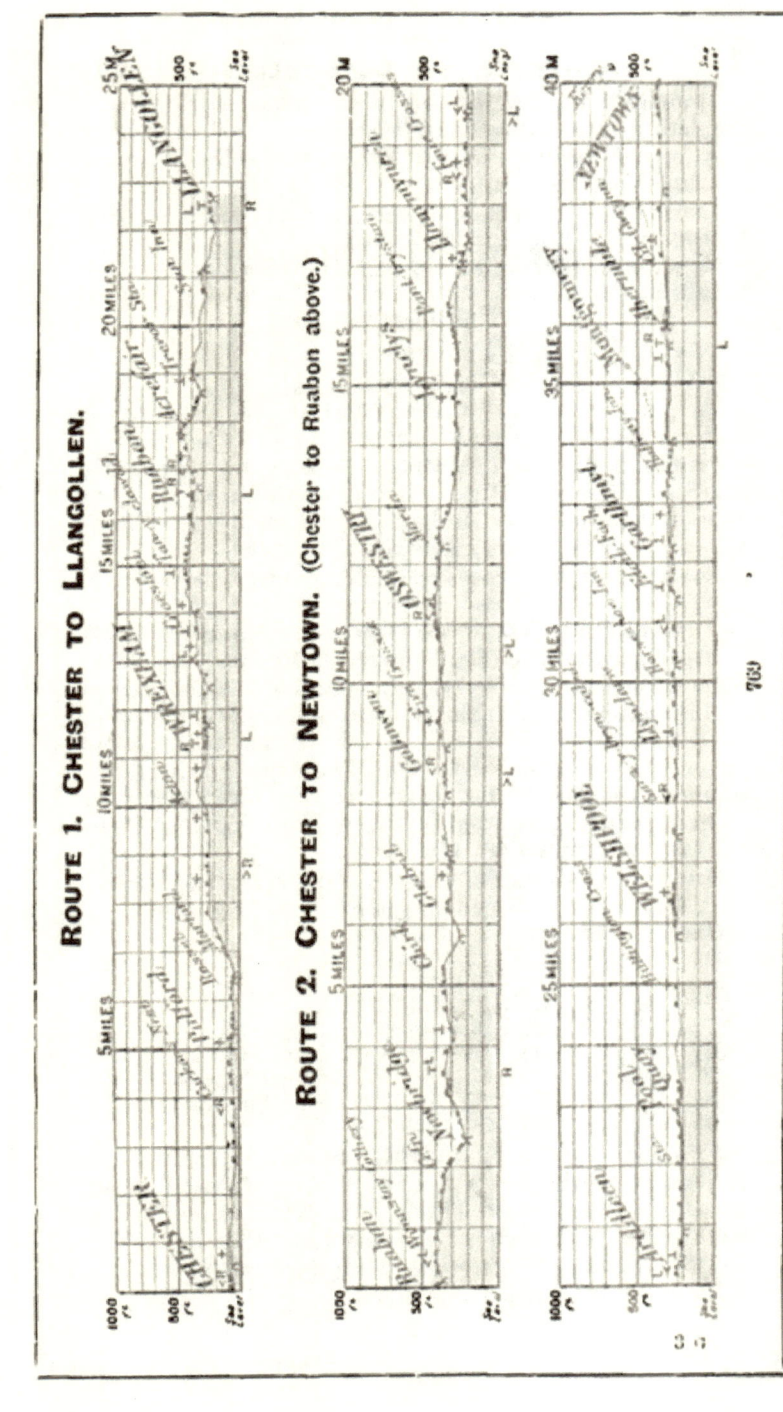

ROUTE 1. CHESTER TO LLANGOLLEN.

ROUTE 2. CHESTER TO NEWTOWN. (Chester to Ruabon above.)

3 CHESTER TO DENBIGH. [1003]

Description.—Class I. The road is somewhat bumpy, and has car lines as far as Saltney, after which it has splendid surface to Denbigh. At times the surface is a little loose in the colliery district, near Mold. For St. Asaph, turn to R. at 25¼m. This is the best route to St. Asaph.

Gradients.—At 6m. 1 in 21; 8¾m. 1 in 23; 13¾m. 1 in 22; 28m. 1 in 11.

Milestones.—Measured from the city wall, Chester, to Mold; thereafter from Town Hall, Denbigh.

Measurements.

Chester,* Cross.				
5	Broughton.*			
12	7	Mold,* Town Hall.		
21⅝	16⅝	9⅝	Caerwys Station.*	
28	23	16	6⅝	Denbigh,* Town Hall; or
29¾	24¾	17¾	8⅝	St. Asaph,* Cathedral.

Principal Objects of Interest.—½m., Grosvenor Bridge. MOLD: Church, College, Bailey Hill. DENBIGH: Castle, Church (ruin). Cefn Caves. St. Asaph: Cathedral. Uninteresting road to Mold, pretty near Caerwys.

Hotels or Inns at places marked*. and at Padeswood, Rhydymwym Station, Bodfari, Blue Hand, Trefnant, &c.

4 CHESTER TO RUTHIN. [1004]

Description.—Class II. This route to Mold is used when coming from Liverpool (R. 232); the usual road from Chester to Mold is Route 3, thence to Ruthin, as this route, 22¾m. Fairly good surface, but rather stiff hills from Queensferry to Mold. From Mold to Ruthin fair surface, but steep hills.

Gradients.—(† *Dangerous.*) From Queensferry.—At 1½ & 5½m. 1 in 18; 7¾m. 1 in 13†; 9¼m. 1 in 17; 9½m. 1 in 16; 10¼m. 1 in 13†; 12m. 1 in 18; 13m. 1 in 13†; 13½m. 1 in 14†; 14½m. 1 in 16; 15m. 1 in 12†; 16¾m. 1 in 16.

Milestones.—Measured from Cross-roads, Queensferry, and from Ruthin.

Measurements.

Liverpool.	Chester,* Cross.				
15¾	6	Queensferry,* Hotel.			
22¼	12½	6½	Mold,* Town Hall.		
26⅝	16⅞	10⅞	4⅜	Llanferris Inn.*	
32½	22¾	16¾	10¼	5⅞	Ruthin.*

Principal Objects of Interest. — MOLD: as above. Ruthin: Castle, School. Fine views between Mold and Ruthin.

Hotels or Inns where marked*, and at Loggerheads, &c.

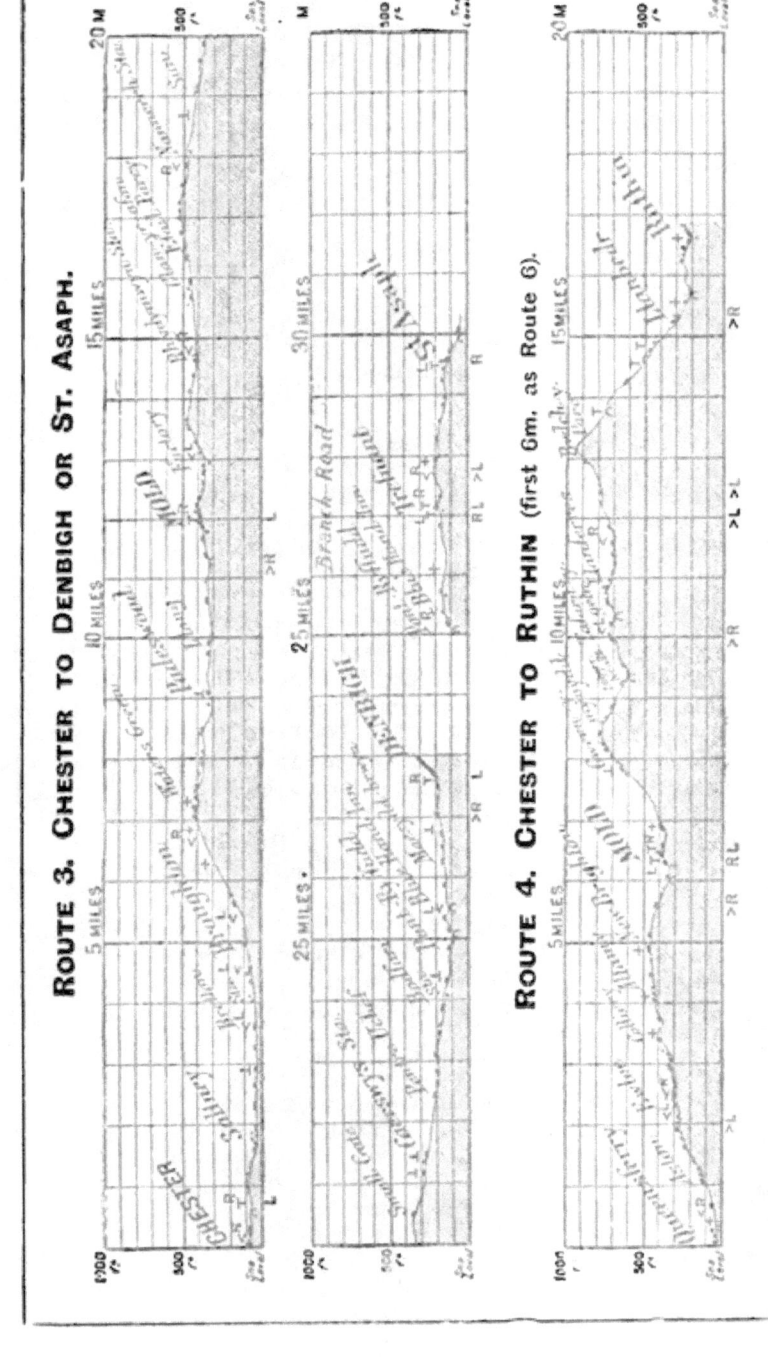

ROUTE 3. CHESTER TO DENBIGH OR ST. ASAPH.

ROUTE 4. CHESTER TO RUTHIN (first 6m. as Route 6).

5 CHESTER TO HOLYWELL. [1005]

Description.—Class II. The road is bumpy, and has car lines as far as Saltney, after which it has fine surface, but with a stiff hill, to Hawarden; thereafter fairly good surface to Holywell. Route 6 is an easier road, but the surface is scarcely so good.

Gradients.—At 5¼m. 1 in 20; 6¾m. 1 in 16; 8¾m. 1 in 20; 17m. 1 in 17; 18m. 1 in 9 (dangerous).

Milestones.—Measured from the city wall, Chester, and from Holywell.

Measurements.

Chester,* Cross.					
6⅝	Hawarden,* Fountain.				
11½	4⅞	Northop.*			
17⅝	11	6⅛	Holywell.*		
19⅛	12½	7⅝	1½	Greenfield.*	
34⅛	27½	22⅝	16½	15	Rhyl.* Route 7.

Principal Objects of Interest.—Hawarden: Castle, Fountain, Church. 14m., Halkin Castle. Holywell: Well. Greenfield: Abbey.

Hotels or Inns at places marked*, and at Saltney, Broughton, Halkin, &c.

6 CHESTER TO ST. ASAPH, &C. [1006]

Description.—Class II. The best road to St. Asaph is Route 3. This road is bumpy, and has car lines to Saltney, thence excellent surface, but with a tendency to be bumpy, to Bagillt. From Holywell to St. Asaph the road is undulating, with fairly good surface, but with a steep descent to that town; thence splendid surface to Abergele. The road from Holywell to Rhuddlan (11½m.), shown dotted, has a dangerous hill near Dyserth. For the other road to Queensferry by the bridge, see Route 7.

Gradients.—At 16½m. 1 in 17; 17¼m. 1 in 18; 17¾m. 1 in 19; 21½m. 1 in 15; 24½m. 1 in 14; 25¼m. 1 in 16; 26¾m. 1 in 17; 27¼m. 1 in 16; 27¾m. 1 in 14; 28½m. 1 in 19.

Measurements.

Chester,* Cross.				
13	Flint,* Court House.			
17½	4½	Holywell.*		
27⅝	14⅝	10⅛	St. Asaph,* Cathedral.	
34⅛	21⅛	16⅝	6½	Abergele.*

Principal Objects of Interest.—FLINT: Castle. Holywell: Well. St. Asaph: Cathedral. Bodelwyddan: Church. Abergele: Monuments, Gwrych Castle.

Hotels or Inns at places marked*, and at Sandycroft, Queensferry, Connah's Quay, Bagillt, &c.

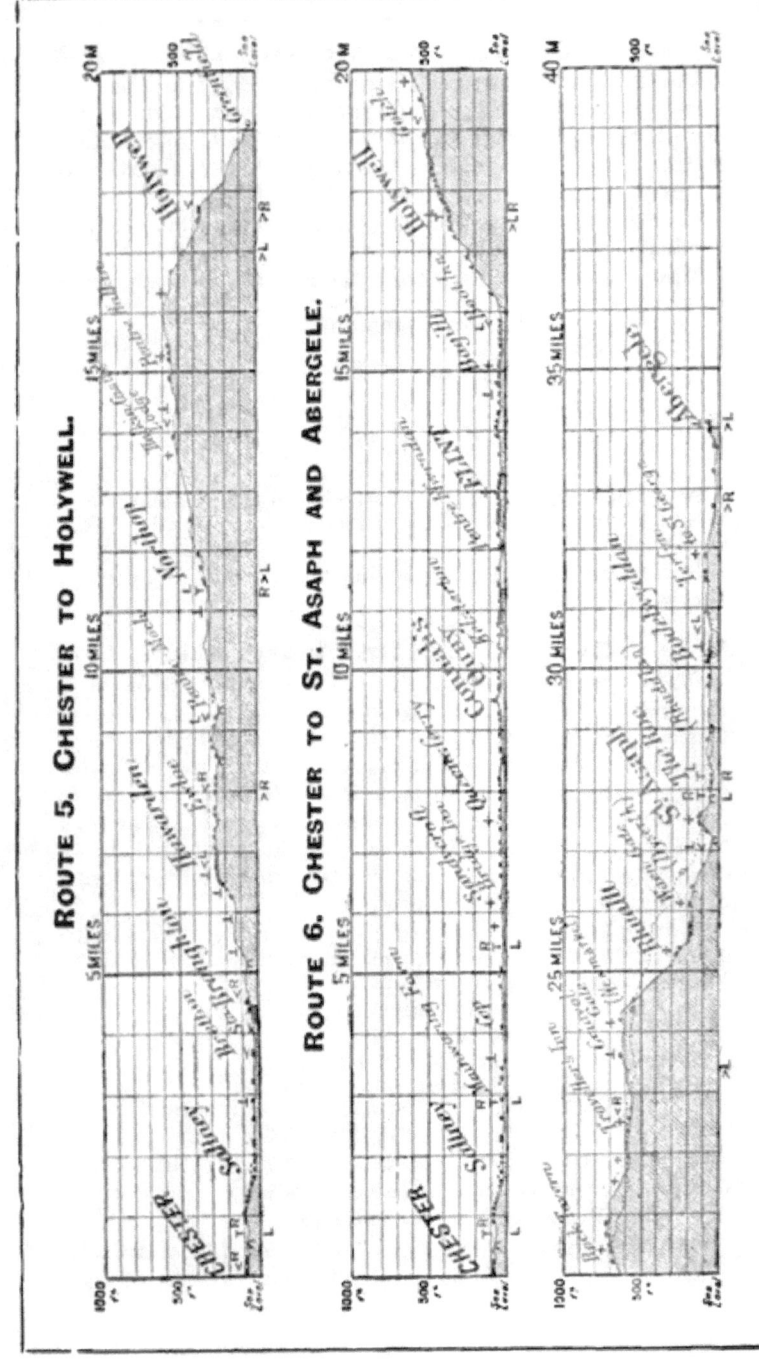

ROUTE 5. CHESTER TO HOLYWELL.

ROUTE 6. CHESTER TO ST. ASAPH AND ABERGELE.

7   CHESTER TO BANGOR.   [1007]

Description.—Class I. The Holyhead road. Fair surface to Queensferry toll bridge, (R. 6 shows another road). Excellent surface thereafter, to three miles beyond Mostyn, then poor, but improving again at Gronant, after which uniformly good surface to Bangor, but with a dangerous hill at Llanfairfechan. The branch roads to Rhyl and Llandudno are shown at foot. The road to Rhyl is flat, but not easily followed. To Llandudno has dangerous hills on both sides.

Gradients.—(† *Dangerous.*) At 24 & 26m. 1/14; 27¾m. 1/19; 38½m.1/23; 39¾m.1/19; 41m.1/17; 52½m.1/14; 53m.1/12†; 60m. 1/20. *Llandudno branch:* 42¾ & 43½m.1/16; 44½m.1/10†; 45m. 1/14; 48½m. 1/10†; 49½m. 1/14†.

Milestones.—Measured from Chester, and from Holywell.

Measurements.

Chester,* Cross.
11? Flint,* Town Hall.
16   4½ Greenfield.*
25? 14   9? Prestatyn.*
30 18½ 14   4½ Rhuddlan.*
(31 19½ 15   5½ Rhyl,* Esplanade.)
35½ 23? 19½ 9? 5½ Abergele,* Market.
41½ 29½ 25½ 15? 11? 6½ Colwyn Bay.*
(46? 35 30? 21 16½ 11? 5½ Llandudno,*Tudno Cas. Hotel.)
46? 35½ 30? 21½ 17 11? 5? 3½ Conway,* Square.
51½ 39? 39? 25? 21½ 16½ 9? 8½ 4½ Penmaenmawr.*
54½ 42? 38½ 28? 24½ 19 12½ 11   7½ 2? Llanfairfechan.*
61½ 50½ 45? 36½ 32 26? 20? 18? 15 10½ 7? Bangor,*Cathedral

Principal Objects of Interest.—FLINT: Castle. Greenfield: Abbey ruin, Holy Well. (RHYL: Town Hall, Pier.) Rhuddlan: Cas. 36m., Gwrych Cas. 38m., Limeworks. (Llandudno: Pier, St. Tudno's Ch., Happy Valley, Great Orme's Head.) Conway: Bridges, Cas. Penmaenmawr: Fine cliff scenery. Aber: Falls. BANGOR: Penrhyn Cas., Cathedral,&c.

Hotels or Inns at places marked *, & at Connah's Quay, &c.

8   WREXHAM TO FLINT.   [1008]

Description.—Class II. Fine surface to Mold, then fair.

Gradients. — At 6½m. 1 in 22 ; 14m. 1 in 18 ; 15m. 1 in 15 ; 15½m. 1 in 17 ; 17m. 1 in 18.

Measurements.

Wrexham,* Town Hall.
5⅝ Caergwrle.*
11¼ 6½ Mold,* Town Hall.
17⅝ 12¼ 6½ Flint,* Town Hall.

Principal Objects of Interest.—Caergwrle: Castle ruin. Mold: Church, College, Bailey Hill. FLINT: Castle.

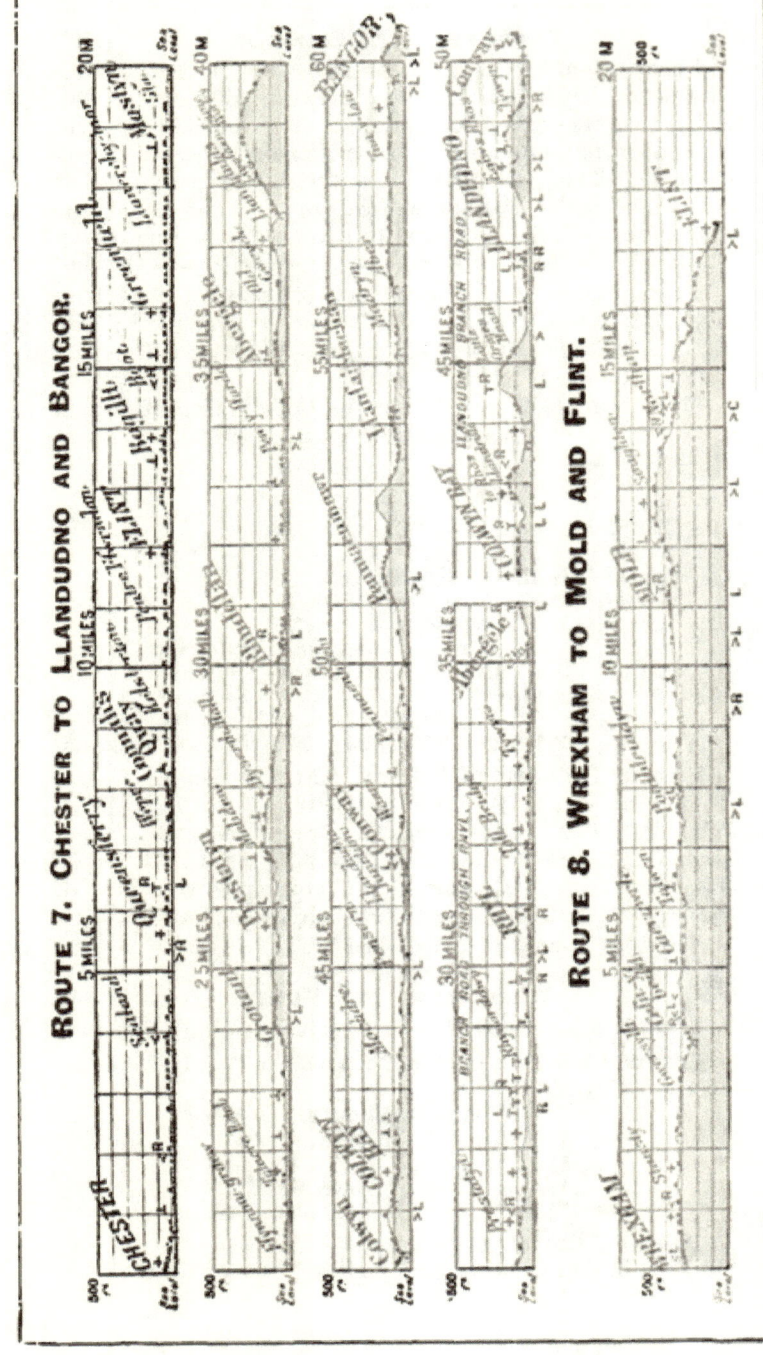

ROUTE 7. CHESTER TO LLANDUDNO AND BANGOR.

ROUTE 8. WREXHAM TO MOLD AND FLINT.

9   WREXHAM TO HAWARDEN, &c.   [1009]

Description.—Class II. Fine surface for four miles, then a good undulating road; dangerous hill at Hawarden.

Gradients.—At 7¼m. 1 in 21; 10½m. 1 in 22; 10¾m. 1 in 13.

Milestones.—Measured from Wrexham.

Measurements.

Wrexham,* Town Hall.
7¾   Hope Station.*
10½   2¾   Hawarden,* Fountain.
17½   9¾   7   Flint,* Town Hall.

Principal Objects of Interest. — Hawarden: Castle, Fountain, Church. FLINT: Castle.

Hotels or Inns where marked*, and at Queensferry, &c.

---

10   WREXHAM TO WHITCHURCH.   [1010]

Description.—Class II. Steep hills in the first mile and a half, and near Bangor. Fine surface.

Gradients.—At ½m. 1 in 18; 1m. 1 in 21; 1½m. 1 in 19; 4m. 1 in 17; 5¼ and 5½m. 1 in 13; 6m. 1 in 16; 10m. 1 in 20; 11m. 1 in 19; 13¾m. 1 in 18.

Milestones.—Measured from Whitchurch,—irregular.

Measurements.

Wrexham,* Town Hall.
5   Bangor,* Star Hotel.
11   6   Eglwys Cross.
15¾   10¾   4¾   Whitchurch.*

Principal Objects of Interest.—Bangor: Bridge. WHITCHURCH: Church.

Hotels or Inns at places marked*, and at Marchwiel.

---

11   WREXHAM TO DENBIGH.   [1011]

Description.—Class II. A steep and rather poor road for the first ten miles, thence better surface, and well engineered to Ruthin. Splendid surface from Ruthin to Denbigh. The best road is by Mold, 27¼m.

Gradients.—(†*Dangerous.*) At 2½m. 1 in 14; 3½m. 1 in 13†; 4¼m. 1 in 20; 5 & 13m. 1 in 23; 18½m. 1 in 11†; 26m. 1 in 11†.

Milestones.—Measured from Wrexham.

Measurements.

Wrexham,* Town Hall.
10½   Llandegla,* Crown Inn.
18¾   8¼   Ruthin,* Fountain.
26   15¾   7¾   Denbigh,* Town Hall.

Principal Objects of Interest. — Collieries and Iron Works for five miles. Ruthin: Castle, School. Denbigh: Castle. A rather bleak road.

Hotels or Inns at places marked*.

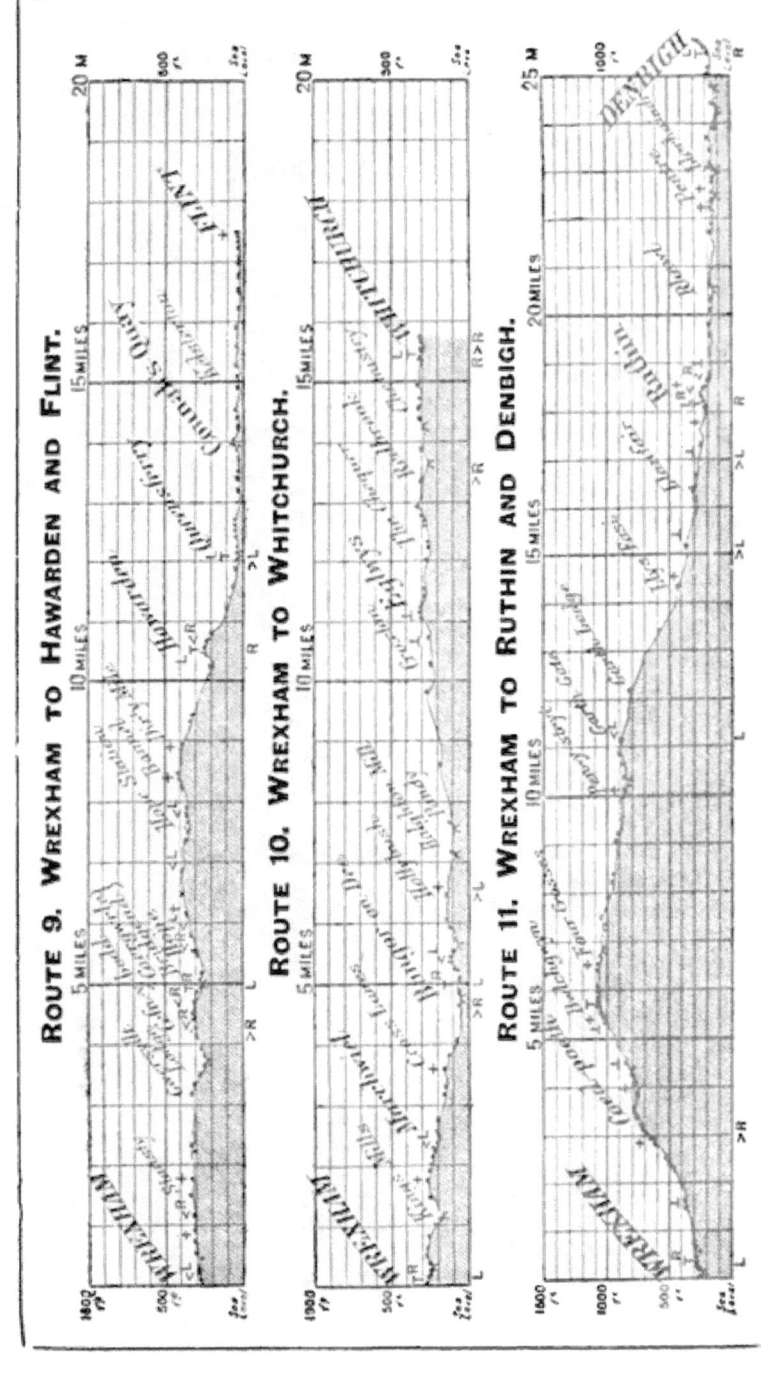

ROUTE 9. WREXHAM TO HAWARDEN AND FLINT.

ROUTE 10. WREXHAM TO WHITCHURCH.

ROUTE 11. WREXHAM TO RUTHIN AND DENBIGH.

12   LLANGOLLEN TO BANGOR, &C.   [1012]

Description.—Class I. The Holyhead road. The surface to Bettws-y-Coed is in first-class condition, but the road is slightly hilly from Llangollen to Corwen. From Bettws-y-Coed to Bangor is the stiffest part of the route, the hill out of Bettws being slightly steep, as is also the hill before and after Bethesda. The road from Bangor to Beaumaris has splendid surface to Menai Bridge (toll), but after that is narrow, with short, steep hills, continuously undulating. Bangor to Beaumaris, by Garth Ferry, 3½m. There is a Corporation steamer from Bangor to Beaumaris.

Gradients.— At 2m. 1 in 17 ; 4¾m. 1 in 18 ; 30¾m. 1 in 21 ; 33¼m. 1 in 15 ; 34 & 36m. 1 in 21 ; 43m. 1 in 18 ; 46¼m. 1 in 16 ; 48¼m. 1 in 15 ; 51m. 1 in 17 ; 56m. 1 in 19.

Milestones.—Measured from Holyhead. Cernioge on the milestones, once a noted hotel, is now a farm.

Measurements.

Llangollen,* Town Hall.

10	Corwen,* Owen Glyndwr Hotel.								
19¾	9¾	Cerrig-y-Druidon,* Saracen's Head Hotel.							
25¼	15¼	5½	Pentre Voelas,* P.O.						
(35½)	25½	15¾	10¼	Llanrwst,* Bridge.)					
32	22	12¼	6¾		Bettws-y-Coed,* Gwyder Hotel.				
37½	27½	17¾	12¼	5½		Capel Curig,* P.O.			
47	37	27¼	21¾	15	9½		Bethesda.*		
52¼	42¼	32¼	27	20¼	14¾	5½		Bangor,* Cathedral.	
54¾	44¾	35	29¼	22¾	17¼	7¾	2½		Menai Bridge.*
59½	49¼	39¾	33¾	27¼	21¾	12¼	6¾	4¾	Beaumaris.*

Principal Objects of Interest.—1¾m., Berwyn Bridge. Carrog: Glyndwr Mound. Corwen: Church. Rug: Chapel. 14m., Maesmor. 30¼m., Conway Falls. 31¼m., Waterloo Bri. Bettws-y-Coed: Dolwyddelan Castle, Llanrwst. 34¼m., Swallow Falls. 36¼m., Cyfyng Falls. Bethesda: Penrhyn Slate Quarries. BANGOR: Penrhyn Castle, Colleges, Cathedral, Recreation Ground. 54¼m., Menai Bridge, Anglesea Monument. Beaumaris : Castle, Baron Hill, Bulkeley Monument, Buffin Island.

The best scenery on this road is near Llangollen, at Maerdy, and in the wooded hills near Bettws. View of Snowdon from Capel Curig. The "Devil's Kitchen" is visible from Llyn Ogwen. The Penrhyn Slate Quarry is an immense excavation.

Hotels or Inns at places marked *, and at Glyn-Dyfrdwy, Maerdy, Glasfryn, Conway Falls, Swallow Falls, &c.

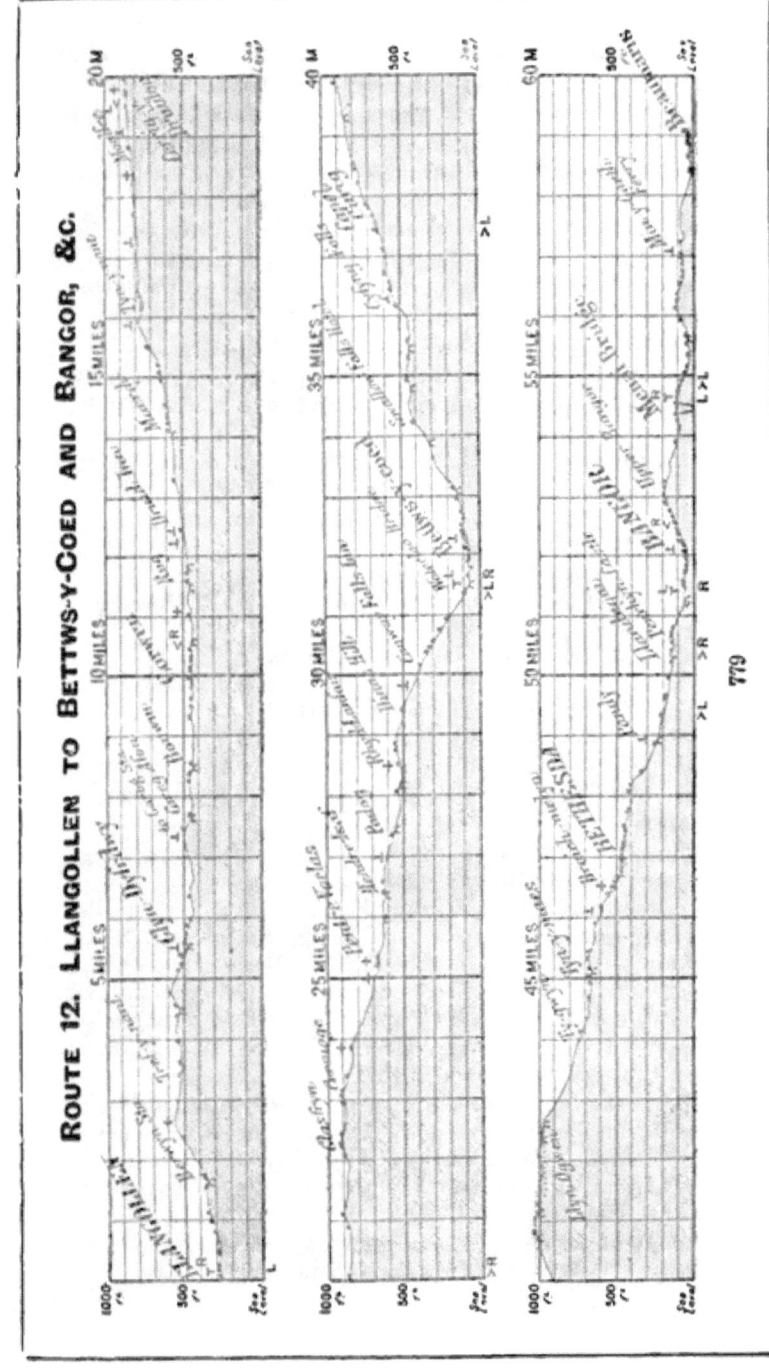

ROUTE 12. LLANGOLLEN TO BETTWS-Y-COED AND BANGOR, &C.

779

13   LLANGOLLEN TO RUTHIN.   [1013]

Description.—Class II. The best road is round by Corwen, Route 15; this road has excellent surface for the first two miles, but after that it becomes very steep, and is not particularly good until Garth Gate, when it joins the Wrexham Road; thence good surface on to Ruthin. The hills on this road are exceedingly steep, and there is a sharp turn at Britannia Inn.

Gradients.—At 1m. 1/18; 1¼m. 1/20; 1½m. 1/14; 2½m. 1/16; 2¾m. 1/12 (dangerous); 4m. 1/14; 4½m. 1/10 (dangerous); 6m. 1/15; 7m. 1/23; 7½m. 1/15; 7¾m. 1/20; 10m. 1/23.

Milestones.—Measured from Llangollen.

Measurements.

Llangollen,* Town Clock.
1¾			Valle Crucis Abbey.
6½	4¾		Pentre Bwlch.*
15¼	13¼	9	Ruthin,* Fountain.

Principal Objects of Interest.—1¾m., Valle Crucis Abbey. 2m., Eliseg's Pillar. 4m., Old Quarries. Ruthin: Castle, School, Llanbedr Church. The views of the Welsh hills obtainable from this road, are the only compensations for the arduous work.

Hotels or Inns at places marked*, and at Britannia Inn.

---

14   DENBIGH TO PENTRE VOELAS.   [1014]

Description.—Class III. This is a rough hill road of indifferent surface, and at times all patches of stones. The surface is good for the first three miles near Denbigh, and near Pentre Voelas, but the rest is much as described. The usual road is Route 15.

Gradients.—(†*Dangerous.*) At ½m. 1/13†; 1½m. 1/18; 2½m. 1/9†; 4m. 1/14; 4¾m. 1/15; 6m. 1/15; 8m. 1/9†; 10¾m. 1/13†; 12m. 1/17; 14m. 1/18; 15½m. 1/22; 16m. 1/15†.

Measurements.

Denbigh,* Town Hall.
3⅛				Groes.
8⅞	5¾			Sportsman Inn.
16¼	13	7¼		Pentre Voelas,* P.O.
23¼	20¼	14¾	6¾	Bettws-y-Coed,* Gwyder Hotel.

Principal Objects of Interest.—Fine views of the Welsh hills.

Hotels or Inns at places marked*.

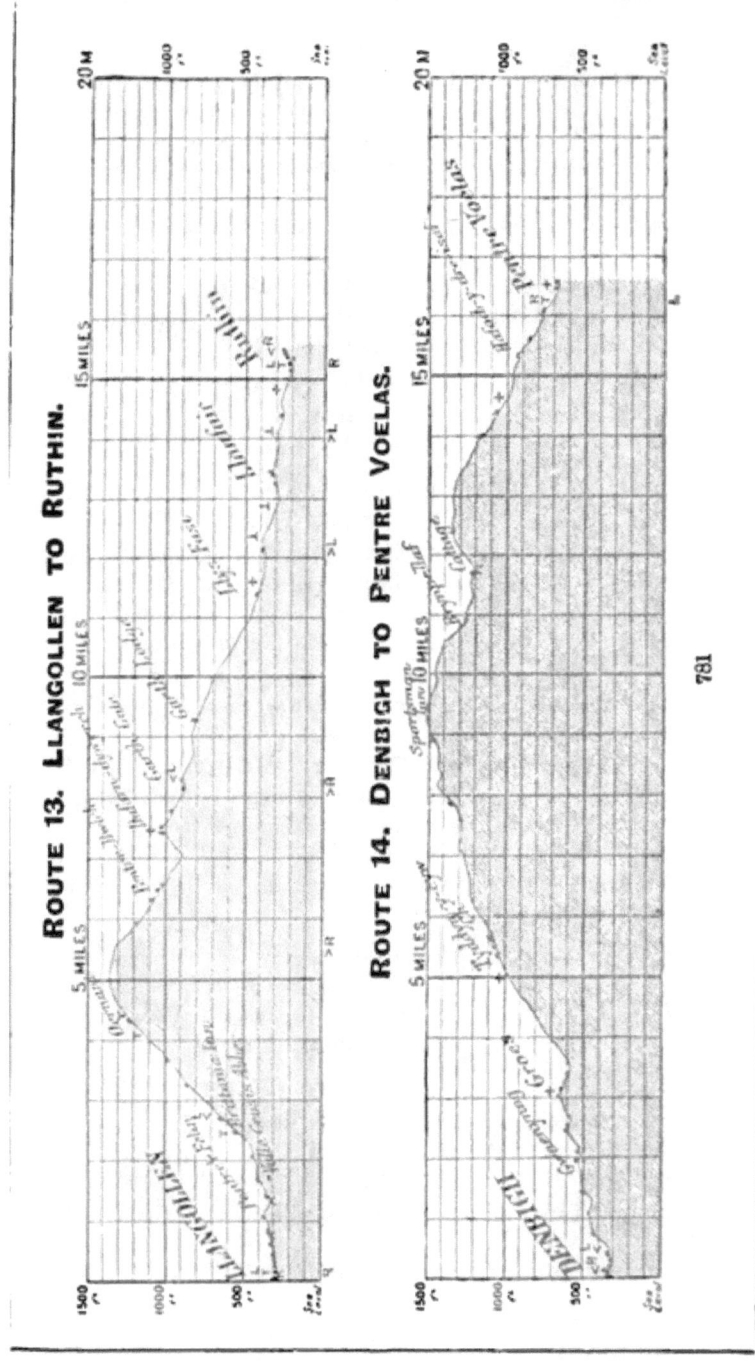

ROUTE 13. LLANGOLLEN TO RUTHIN.

ROUTE 14. DENBIGH TO PENTRE VOELAS.

15 RHYL TO CORWEN. [1015]

Description.—Class II. The road has fine surface throughout, and is kept in very good order, but there is a dangerous hill before Trefnant, and a steep hill in Ruthin. This road is followed from Denbigh or Ruthin, rather than any of the more direct roads to Llangollen, or Bettws-y-Coed. For Bala or Cerrig, turn to right at 30m.

Gradients.—(†*Dangerous.*) At 7½m. 1 in 14†; 12m. 1 in 23; 18¾m. 1 in 11†; 20½m. 1 in 18; 25½m. 1 in 19; 29½m. 1 in 13.

Milestones.—Irregular. Measured from Rhuddlan and Ruthin.

Measurements.

Rhyl,* Esplanade.							
2¾	Rhuddlan.*						
(5⅞	3⅛	St. Asaph,* Cathedral.)					
(11½	8¾	5⅝	Denbigh,* Town Hall.)				
18½	15¾	12⅝	7⅝	Ruthin,* Fountain.			
27⅞	25⅛	22	17	9⅜	Gwyddelwern.*		
31	28¼	25⅛	20⅛	12½	3⅛	Corwen,* Owen Glyndwr Hotel.	
41	38¼	35⅛	30⅛	22½	3⅛	10	Llangollen.*
39½	36¾	33⅝	28⅝	21	11⅝	Bala,* White Lion Hotel.	
37¾	35	31⅞	26⅞	19¼	9⅞	Cerrig-y-Druidon.*	

Principal Objects of Interest.—Rhuddlan: Castle. St. Asaph: Cathedral. DENBIGH: Castle, Cefn Caves. Llanrhaiadr: Church. Ruthin: Castle, School. 29½m., Rug. Corwen: Church, Vale of Llangollen.

Hotels or Inns at places marked*, and at Trefnant, &c.

16 RHYL TO BETTWS-Y-COED. [1016]

Description.—Class II. Fairly good surface to Abergele, thence a good road, but rather steep to Llanfair; after which excellent surface, but a dangerous winding descent to Llanrwst. Good surface, but short steep hills to Bettws, but a better route is shown on next page.

Gradients.—At 5½m. 1 in 21; 6¾m. 1 in 15; 9m. 1 in 21; 19¾m. 1 in 14; 20½m. 1 in 12; 23m. 1 in 12 (both dangerous).

Measurements.

Rhyl,* Esplanade.					
5¼	Abergele,* Market.				
10	4¾	Llanfair Talhaiarn,* Bridge.			
14¾	9½	4¾	Llangerniew.*		
21⅞	16⅝	11⅞	7⅛	Llanrwst,* Bridge.	
25¾	20½	15¾	11	3⅞	Bettws-y-Coed,* Gwyder Hotel.

Principal Objects of Interest.—Abergele: Gwrych Cas. Llanrwst: Bridge, Gwydir Chapel and Castle. Bettws-y-Coed: Waterloo Bridge, Conway Falls, Swallow Falls, &c.

Hotels or Inns at places marked*.

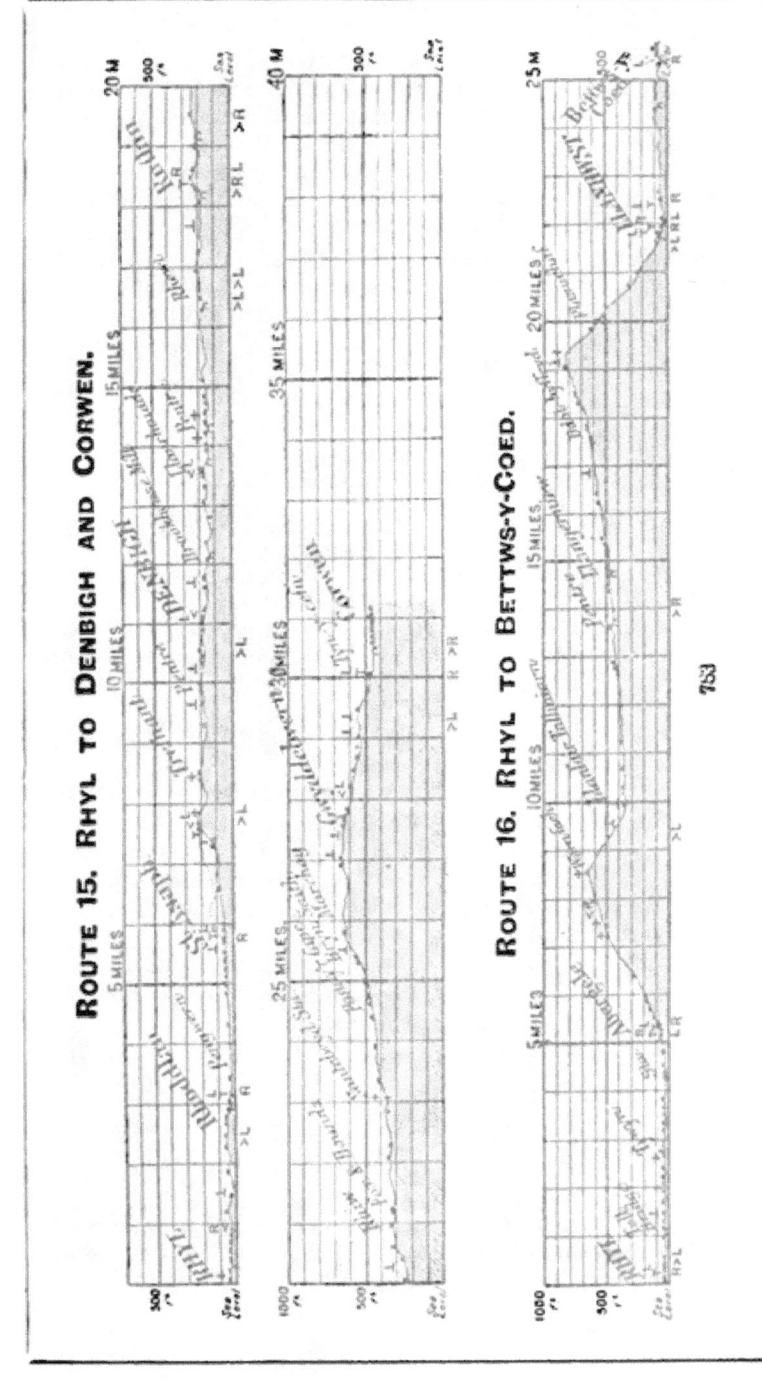

ROUTE 15. RHYL TO DENBIGH AND CORWEN.

ROUTE 16. RHYL TO BETTWS-Y-COED.

753

17 LLANDUDNO TO BETTWS-Y-COED. [1017]

Description.—Class II. Of the two routes, the one on the east side of the River Conway is the best, as, although it has two dangerous hills in the first eight miles, after that it is practically level, and has magnificent surface. The road by the west side has numerous short, steep, and dangerous hills. The first is the best road from Llanrwst to Bettws.

Gradients.—(†*Dangerous.*) At 2m. 1 in 10†; 2½ & 6½m. 1 in 14; 7¾m. 1 in 12†. *By Trefriw.*—At 4¼m. 1 in 9; 6 & 6¼m. 1 in 11†; 7¾m. 1 in 13†; 10¼m. 1 in 13†; 16¾m. 1 in 12†.

Milestones.—Measured from Llanrwst.

Conway.	*Colwyn Bay.*	**Measurements.**				
—	—	Llandudno,* Tudno Castle Hotel.				
2¾	4⅛	5⅛	Glan Coway.*			
6¾	7⅞	8¾	3⅝	Talycafn.*		
13	14½	15⅜	10¼	6⅝	Llanrwst,* Bridge.	
17⅞	19⅛	20	14⅞	11¼	4⅝	Bettws-y-Coed.*

By Trefriw.

Llandudno.*				
3¾	Conway.*			
13⅞	10⅛	Trefriw,* Bridge.		
(15	11¼	1½	Llanrwst.*)	
18⅞	15⅛	5	3⅞	Bettws-y-Coed.*

Principal Objects of Interest.—Conway: Bridge, Castle. Llanrwst: Bridge, Gwydir Cas. & Chapel. Bettws-y-Coed: Waterloo Bridge, Conway Falls, Swallow Falls. *By West Bank.*—8½m., Caer Hun. Porthllwyd: Falls. Trefriw: Spa, Dolgarrog Falls.

Hotels or Inns where marked*, & at Llandudno Junc., &c.

18 BETTWS-Y-COED TO FFESTINIOG. [1018]

Description.—Class III. A good road for seven miles, then there is a rough precipitous hill to Blaenau. Thence to Harlech good surface, but a steep descent.

Gradients.—(†*Dangerous*). At 2½m. 1/14; 6m. 1/17; 7¾m. 1/8†; 8¾m. 1/10†; 10½m. 1/8†; 13m. 1/17; 14¼m. 1/14†.

Measurements.

Bettws-y-Coed,* Gwyder Hotel.					
6	Dolwyddelan,* Hotel.				
(7¾	1¾	Roman Bridge Station.)			
11½	5½	Blaenau Ffestiniog.*			
16¾	10¾	5¼	Maentwrog,* Bridge.		
21⅞	15⅞	10⅜	5⅛	Talsarnau.* R. 35.	
25⅞	19⅞	14⅜	9⅛	4	Harlech.*

Principal Objects of Interest.—Dolwyddelan: Castle. 7¾m., 'Roman' Bridge. BLAENAU: Slate Quarries. Maentwrog: Stone. Harlech: Castle. Pretty near Maentwrog.

Hotels or Inns at places marked*.

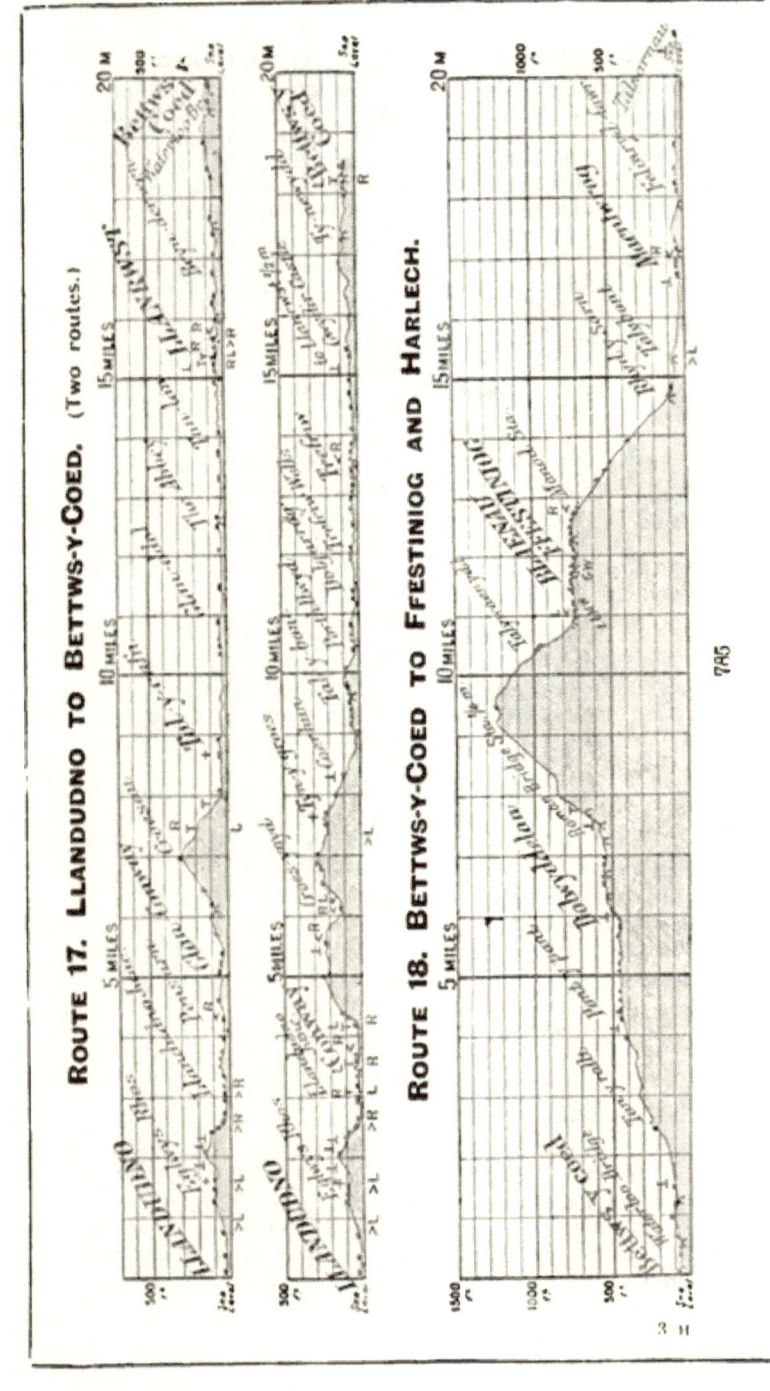

ROUTE 17. LLANDUDNO TO BETTWS-Y-COED. (Two routes.)

ROUTE 18. BETTWS-Y-COED TO FFESTINIOG AND HARLECH.

19   BANGOR TO PWLLHELI, &C.   [1019]

Description.—Class II. Splendid surface to Carnarvon, then excellent surface, but rather a hilly road, for several miles. From Clynnog to Pwllheli the surface is hardly as good,—there are several loose parts, but as a rule it is in good condition. There is a steep descent before Pwllheli. From Pwllheli to Llanbedrog the road is practically level, but after that it is very steep, and with indifferent surface.

Gradients.—(† *Dangerous.*) At $7\frac{1}{2}$m. 1 in 19 ; 9m. 1 in 18 ; $9\frac{3}{4}$m. 1 in 15 ; 11m. 1 in 20 ; $14\frac{3}{4}$m. 1 in 23 ; $19\frac{1}{4}$m. 1 in 21 ; 22m. 1 in 14 ; 25m. 1 in 19 ; $28\frac{1}{2}$m. 1 in 12 † ; $33\frac{1}{4}$m. 1 in 10 † ; 34m. 1 in 16 ; $34\frac{1}{2}$m. 1 in 17 ; 35m. 1 in 16 ; $35\frac{3}{4}$m. 1 in 12 †.

Milestones.—Continuation of those from Llangollen. After Carnarvon measured from the Town Hall there.

Measurements.

Bangor,* Cathedral.

$8\frac{3}{4}$	Carnarvon,* Castle Square.				
$18\frac{3}{4}$	$9\frac{1}{2}$	Clynnog Fawr,* Hotel.			
$26\frac{1}{4}$	$17\frac{1}{2}$	$7\frac{3}{4}$	Four Crosses.* R. 29.		
$29\frac{1}{4}$	$20\frac{1}{2}$	$10\frac{3}{4}$	3	Pwllheli,* P.O.	
$36\frac{1}{4}$	$27\frac{3}{4}$	$17\frac{3}{4}$	$9\frac{3}{4}$	$6\frac{3}{4}$	Abersoch.*

Principal Objects of Interest.—$3\frac{1}{4}$m., Vaynol Park. Port Dynorwic: Slate Harbour. CARNARVON: Castle, Esplanade. $14\frac{1}{4}$m., Glynllifon Park. Clynog: Cromlech, Church. Pwllheli: Gimlet Rock. Llanbedrog: Manor House.

Hotels or Inns at places marked *, and at Llanwnda, &c.

20   BANGOR TO HOLYHEAD.   [1020]

Description.—Class I. Fine surface throughout, but it is a most monotonous, undulating road after Menai Bridge. Poor surface near Valley.

Gradients.—At $9\frac{1}{2}$m. 1 in 22 ; 15m. 1 in 20.

Milestones.—Measured from Holyhead Arch.

Measurements.

Carnarvon.	Bangor,* Cathedral.				*Beaumaris.*
$7\frac{3}{4}$	$2\frac{1}{2}$	Menai Bridge,* Inn.			$4\frac{1}{2}$
$13\frac{1}{4}$	8	$5\frac{1}{4}$	Holland Arms Inn.*		$9\frac{5}{6}$
$25\frac{1}{2}$	$20\frac{1}{4}$	$17\frac{3}{4}$	$12\frac{1}{4}$	Valley,* Hotel.	$21\frac{3}{4}$
$29\frac{1}{4}$	24	$21\frac{1}{2}$	16	$3\frac{3}{4}$	Holyhead,* P.O.	$25\frac{3}{4}$

Principal Objects of Interest.—Menai Bridge: Bridge. Anglesea Monument, Britannia Bridge. Valley: Embankment. HOLYHEAD: Harbour, Breakwater, Holyhead Mountain, Signal Tower, South Stack Lighthouse.

Hotels or Inns at places marked * (Mona Hotel in ruins).

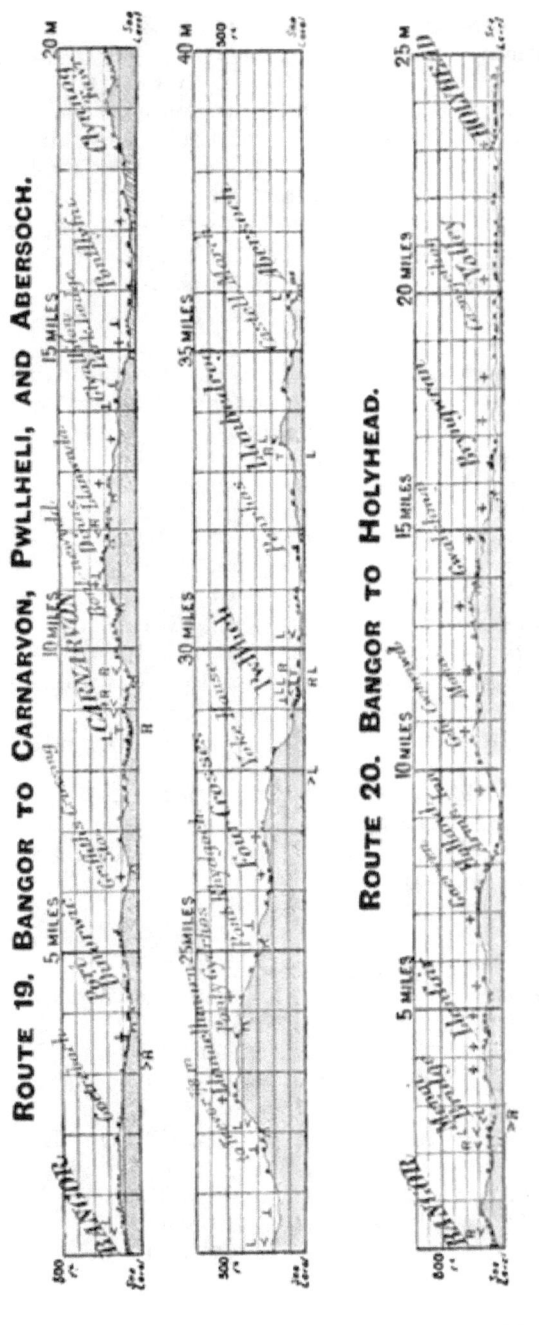

ROUTE 19. BANGOR TO CARNARVON, PWLLHELI, AND ABERSOCH.

ROUTE 20. BANGOR TO HOLYHEAD.

Signs: < Road fork, 1st and journey, > ditto, return, + 4 cross Roads, ⊥ Road Junction, ⊙ Railway, T indicates a sharp turn. The direction L - shut and L (left) for the forward journey are above the Road Line, those of the reverse, below.

787

21 BEAUMARIS TO AMLWCH. [1021]

Description.—Class III. A narrow road with fair surface, but short, steep hills.

Gradients.—At $\frac{3}{4}$m. 1 in 7 (very dangerous); others mostly 1 in 12, or 1 in 15. Care required on all.

Measurements.—Beaumaris,* Town Hall.
6 Pentraeth,* Inn.
($8\frac{1}{4}$ $2\frac{1}{4}$ Red Wharf Bay,* Hotel.)
$18\frac{1}{4}$ $12\frac{1}{4}$ 11 Amlwch.*

Amlwch to Bull Bay, $1\frac{1}{2}$m.; to Cemmaes Bay, $4\frac{1}{2}$m.

Principal Objects of Interest.—Red Wharf Bay.

22 AMLWCH TO LLANGEFNI, &c. [1022]

Description.—Class III. A narrow hilly road; fair surface.

Gradients.—Mostly 1 in 13; care required on all.

Measurements.—Amlwch.*
6 Llanerchymedd.*
$13\frac{5}{8}$ $7\frac{5}{8}$ Llangefni.*
$16\frac{5}{8}$ $10\frac{5}{8}$ 3 Holland Arms.* R. 20.

Principal Objects of Interest.—2m., Parys Mountain.

23 HOLYHEAD TO AMLWCH. [1023]

Description.—Class III. Fair surface to Valley, then a continuously undulating narrow country road.

Gradients.—Mostly 1 in 13; care required on all.

Measurements.—Holyhead,* P.O.
$3\frac{3}{4}$ Valley,* Hotel.
$14\frac{5}{8}$ $10\frac{7}{8}$ Rhosgoch,* Hotel.*
$17\frac{7}{8}$ $14\frac{1}{8}$ $3\frac{1}{4}$ Amlwch.*

Principal Objects of Interest.—Amlwch: Bull Bay, Parys Mountain Copper Works.

24 CARNARVON TO BEAUMARIS. [1024]

Description.—Class I. & II. Splendid surface to Menai Bri., thence good surface, but a continually undulating road.

Gradients.—At 5m. 1 in 19; $7\frac{1}{4}$m. 1 in 17.

Milestones.—Measured from Holyhead and Beaumaris.

Measurements.—Carnarvon,* Castle Square.
$4\frac{1}{4}$ Port Dinorwic.*
$7\frac{3}{4}$ $3\frac{1}{2}$ Menai Bridge,* Inn.
$12\frac{1}{8}$ $7\frac{7}{8}$ $4\frac{3}{8}$ Beaumaris,* Town Hall.

Principal Objects of Interest.—Menai Bridge: Bridge, Angelsea Monument, Britannia Bridge. Beaumaris: Castle.

Hotels or Inns at places marked*.

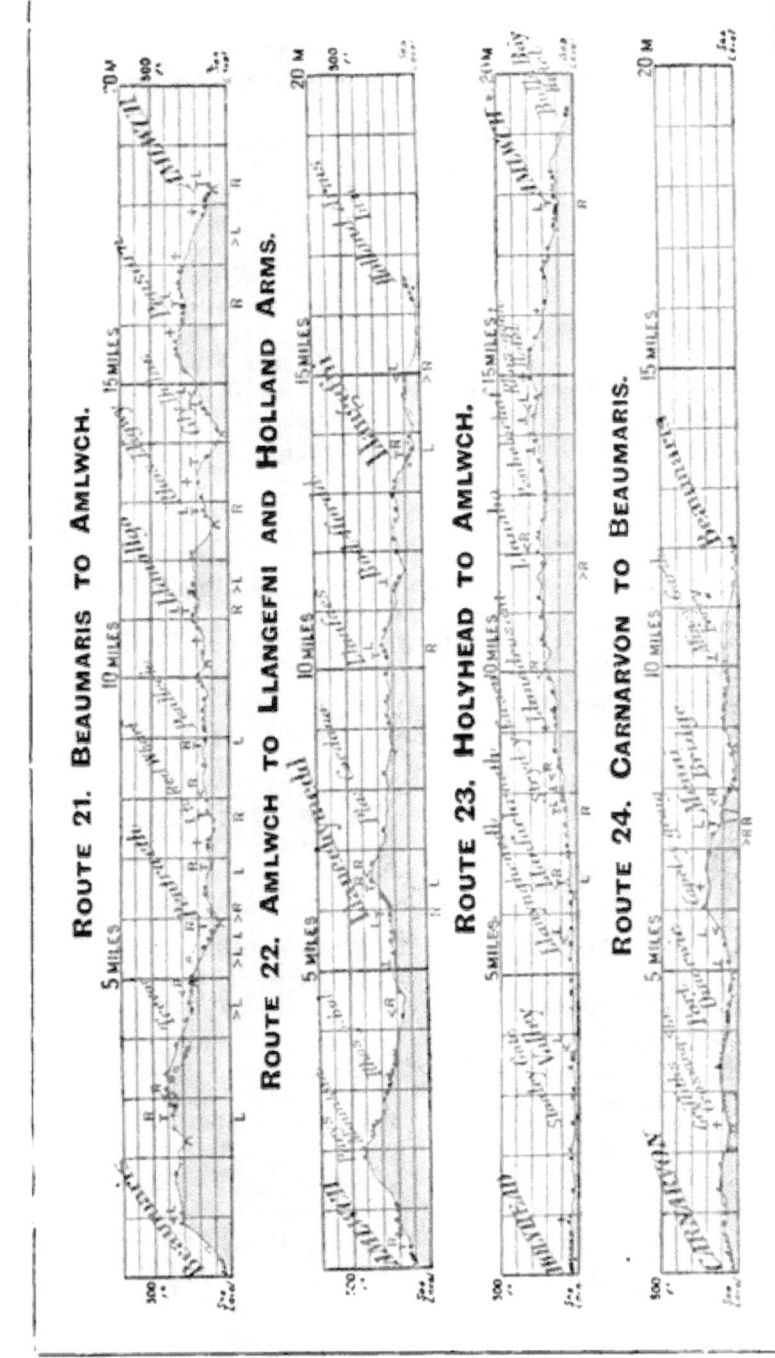

ROUTE 21. BEAUMARIS TO AMLWCH.

ROUTE 22. AMLWCH TO LLANGEFNI AND HOLLAND ARMS.

ROUTE 23. HOLYHEAD TO AMLWCH.

ROUTE 24. CARNARVON TO BEAUMARIS.

25 CARNARVON TO BETTWS-Y-COED. [1025]

Description. Class II. Fine surface, but a hilly road to Llanberis, then good, but of variable quality to Capel Curig, thence as Route 12.

Gradients.—At 6½m. 1 in 15; 11½m. 1 in 14; 12¾m. 1 in 10 (dangerous); 13½m. 1 in 17; 15m. 1 in 18; thence as Route 12.

Milestones. Measured from Llanberis Road, Carnarvon.

Measurements.

Carnarvon,* Castle Square.				
7½	Llanberis.*			
13	5½	Pen-y-gwrhyd Hotel.* R. 30.		
18¼	10¾	5¼	Capel Curig,* P.O.	
23¾	16¼	10¾	5½	Bettws-y-Coed.*

Principal Objects of Interest.—Llanberis: Dolbadarn Castle, Waterfall, Slate Quarries, Mountain Railway. 12m., The Cromlech. Bettws-y-Coed: as Route 12. Views of Snowdon and the precipices.

26 CARNARVON TO BEDDGELERT, &C. [1026]

Description.—Class II. Steep hills for four miles, then easy gradients and good surface. Fine surface between Beddgelert and Penrhyn, but there are two dangerous hills.

Gradients.—(†*Dangerous.*) At ¼, ¾, & 1½m.1/16; 2m.1/12†; 2½m.1/14; 2¾ & 3¾m.1/12†; 9 & 11½m.1/17; 12¼m.1/18; 14¾ & 15¼m.1/11†; 15½m.1/10†; 19½m.1/11†; 20m.1/10†

Measurements.

Carnarvon,* Castle Square.					
7¾	Snowdon Ranger Hotel.*				
9½	1¾	Rhyd-ddu Station.			
12¾	5	3¼	Beddgelert,* Bridge.		
20¼	12½	10¾	7½	Penrhyn Deudraeth,* Griffin Hotel.	
26¾	19	17¼	14	6½	Harlech.* R. 35.

Principal Objects of Interest.—Splendid views of Snowdon precipices. 10m., 'Pitt's Head.' Beddgelert: Gelert's Grave, Church. 14m., Aberglasyn Pass and Bridge. Penrhyn: Ffestiniog Railway, Deudraeth Castle. The prettiest part of this road is near Beddgelert.

Hotels or Inns where marked *, & at Bettws Garmon, &c.

27 CARNARVON TO PORTMADOC. [1027]

Description.—Class II. A good undulating road.

Gradients.—(†*Dangerous.*) At 1/15; 2m.1/20; 5¾m.1/18; 7¾m.1/15; 8½m.1/12†; 10½m.1/19; 15m.1/16; 17½m.1/11†.

Measurements.

Carnarvon,* Castle Square.			
6½	Penygroes.*		
18½	12	Tremadoc.*	
19¾	13¼	1¼	Portmadoc,* Town Hall.

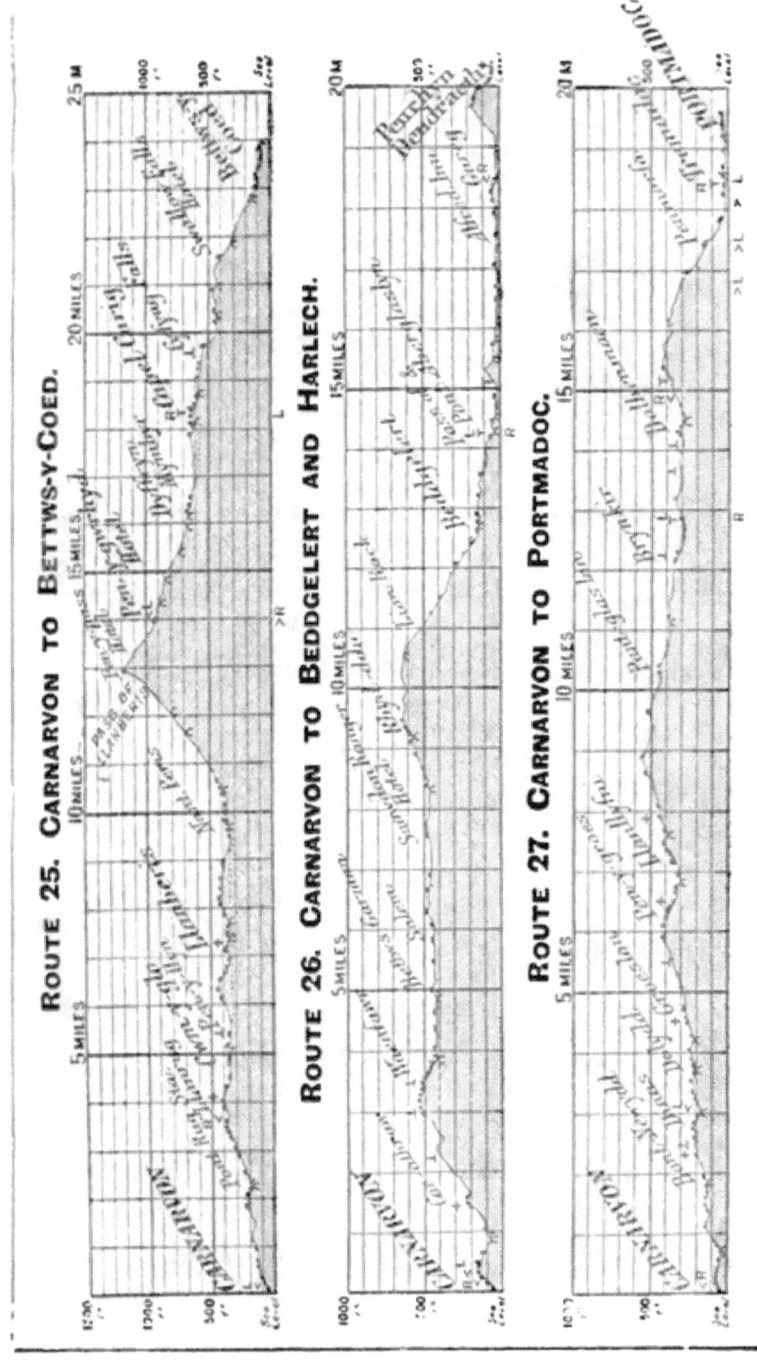

ROUTE 25. CARNARVON TO BETTWS-Y-COED.

ROUTE 26. CARNARVON TO BEDDGELERT AND HARLECH.

ROUTE 27. CARNARVON TO PORTMADOC.

28 PORTMADOC, &C., TO PWLLHELI. [1028]

Description.—Class II. Good surface, but short steep hills to Pwllheli; thereafter a fair, but somewhat hilly road to Aberdaron. Good surface from Pwllheli to Nevin.

Gradients.—Mostly 1 in 17; but 18¾m. 1 in 12; 24m. 1 in 13; 32m. 1 in 13·9 (dangerous).

Milestones.—Measured from Tremadoc, and Pwllheli.

Measurements.

Maentwrog.* Bridge.
4 Penrhyn Deudraeth,* Griffin Hotel. R. 35.
7 3 Portmadoc,* Town Hall.
(8⅛ 4⅛ 1⅛ Tremadoc.*)
11⅞ 7⅞ 4⅞ 4½ Criccieth.*
20½ 16½ 13½ 13⅛ 8⅝ Pwllheli,* P.O.
37⅝ 33⅝ 30⅝ 30½ 26 17¼ Aberdaron.*

Principal Objects of Interest.—Criccieth: Cas. Pwllheli: Gimlet Rock. Pretty near Criccieth, and Aberdaron.

Hotels or Inns at places marked *, and at Sarn.

---

29 PORTMADOC TO NEVIN. [1029]

Description.—Class III. Fairly good surface. Pwllheli to Nevin (7m.). Good surface.

Gradients.—Mostly 1 in 13.

Measurements.

Portmadoc,* Town Hall.
4⅞ Criccieth.*
11⅝ 6¾ Four Crosses.* R. 19.
19¼ 14⅜ 7⅝ Nevin.*

---

30 PORTMADOC TO BETTWS-Y-COED. [1030]

Description.—Class II. Good surface, and an easy road to four miles beyond Beddgelert; thence poor surface to Pen-y-gwrhyd, where join Route 25.

Gradients.—At 6¾m. 1 in 11; 12¾m. 1 in 14; 13½m. 1 in 20; 15¼m. 1 in 12; 16½m. 1 in 18; 19½, 21, & 23m. 1 in 21; 24m. 1 in 15.

Measurements.

Portmadoc,* Town Hall.
1¼ Tremadoc.*
7¾ 6½ Beddgelert,* Bridge.
15⅝ 14⅜ 7⅞ Pen-y-gwrhyd Hotel.* R. 25.
20⅞ 19⅝ 12⅞ 5¼ Capel Curig,* P.O.
26¼ 25 18⅝ 10¾ 5½ Bettws-y-Coed,* Gwyder Hotel.

Principal Objects of Interest.—Pass and Pont Aberglasyn. Beddgelert: Gelert's Grave, Church. Pen-y-gwrhyd: Cwmdyli Waterfalls. Bettws-y-Coed: as Route 12. Remarkably pretty near Beddgelert, views of Snowdon and Moel Siabod.

Hotels or Inns at places marked *.

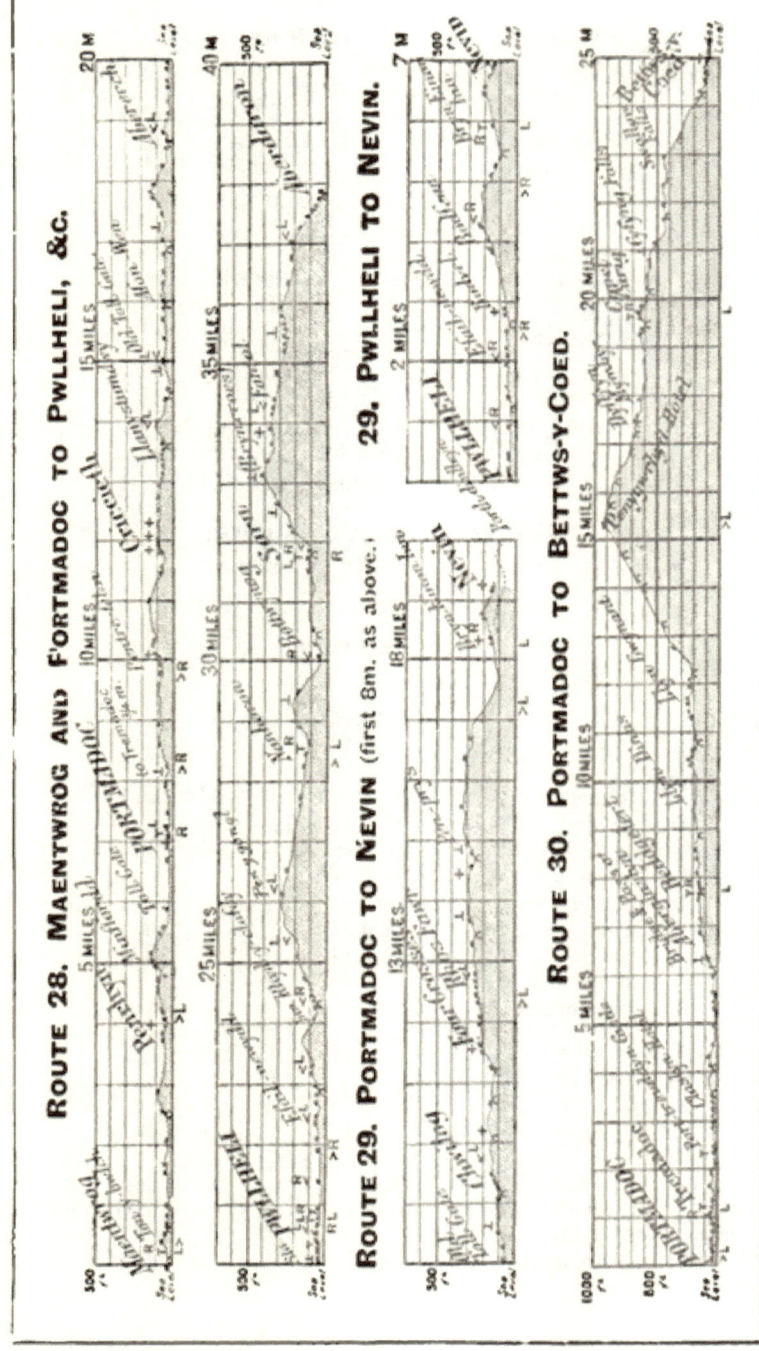

31 CORWEN TO BARMOUTH. [1031]

Description.—Class II. The shortest and best road from Corwen to Bala is by Druid. and although the surface is a little loose, the perfect engineering makes this a fast road, as the rise is very gradual. The route by Llandrillo has steeper hills, but prettier scenery. From Bala to Dolgelley the road is very good, as far as Llanuwchllyn, where turn to right at fork, along a bad road. From this point, for about six miles, the road is all loose stones and grass; but the cyclist can usually find a narrow track. After Drwsynant Station the surface at once improves, and is in good condition all the way to Dolgelley, which lies on the other side of the river from the road. From Dolgelley to Barmouth the surface is also very good, but there are a number of short steep hills, and those near Barmouth are slightly dangerous. The distance round Bala Lake is eleven miles. West side, good surface; east side, fair.

Gradients.—At 2½ & 10m. 1 in 17; 15m. 1 in 17; 15½m. 1 in 25; 21m. 1 in 24; 23m. 1 in 16; 23½m. 1 in 19; 33¼m. 1 in 18; 34m. 1 in 18; 37½m. 1 in 15; 38¾m. 1 in 13.

By Llandrillo.—At ½m. 1 in 13 (dangerous); 3½m. 1 in 15; 8¾m. 1 in 20; 9¼m. 1 in 13; 10¼m. 1 in 17; 11¼m. 1 in 18.

Milestones.—Measured from Bala, and from Dolgelley County Hall.

Measurements.

Llangollen.								
10	Corwen,* Owen Glyndwr Hotel.							
16¾	6¾	Boot Inn.*						
21½	11½	4¾	Bala,* White Lion Ho.					
(27	17	10¼	5½	Llanuwchllyn.*)				
32⅝	22⅝	15⅞	11⅛	6⅜	Drwsynant Station.			
(39⅝	29⅝	22⅞	17⅞	13⅛	6¾	Dolgelley,* Square.)		
44¼	34¼	27½	22¾	18	11⅝	5⅛	Bontddu.*	
49¼	39¼	32½	27¾	23	16⅝	10⅛	5	Barmouth,* P.O.

By Llandrillo.

Llangollen.			
10	Corwen.*		
15⅛	5⅛	Llandrillo*	
23	13	7⅞	Bala.*

Principal Objects of Interest.—Bala, College, Mound, Lake. 16m., Caergai. Llanuwchllyn: Church. DOLGELLEY: County Hall, Cader Idris, Torrent Walk, Precipice Walk, Gold Mines. Hengwrt: Cymmer Abbey. Bontddu: Waterfall. Barmouth: Bridge, Quay, Panorama Walk, Llanaber Church. A pretty road along Bala Lake. Views of Cader Idris on the descent to Dolgelley; pretty near Barmouth, with fine views of the mountains. The uninteresting parts are between Druid and Bala; and Llanuwchllyn and Drwsynant.

Hotels or Inns at places marked*, and at Druid.

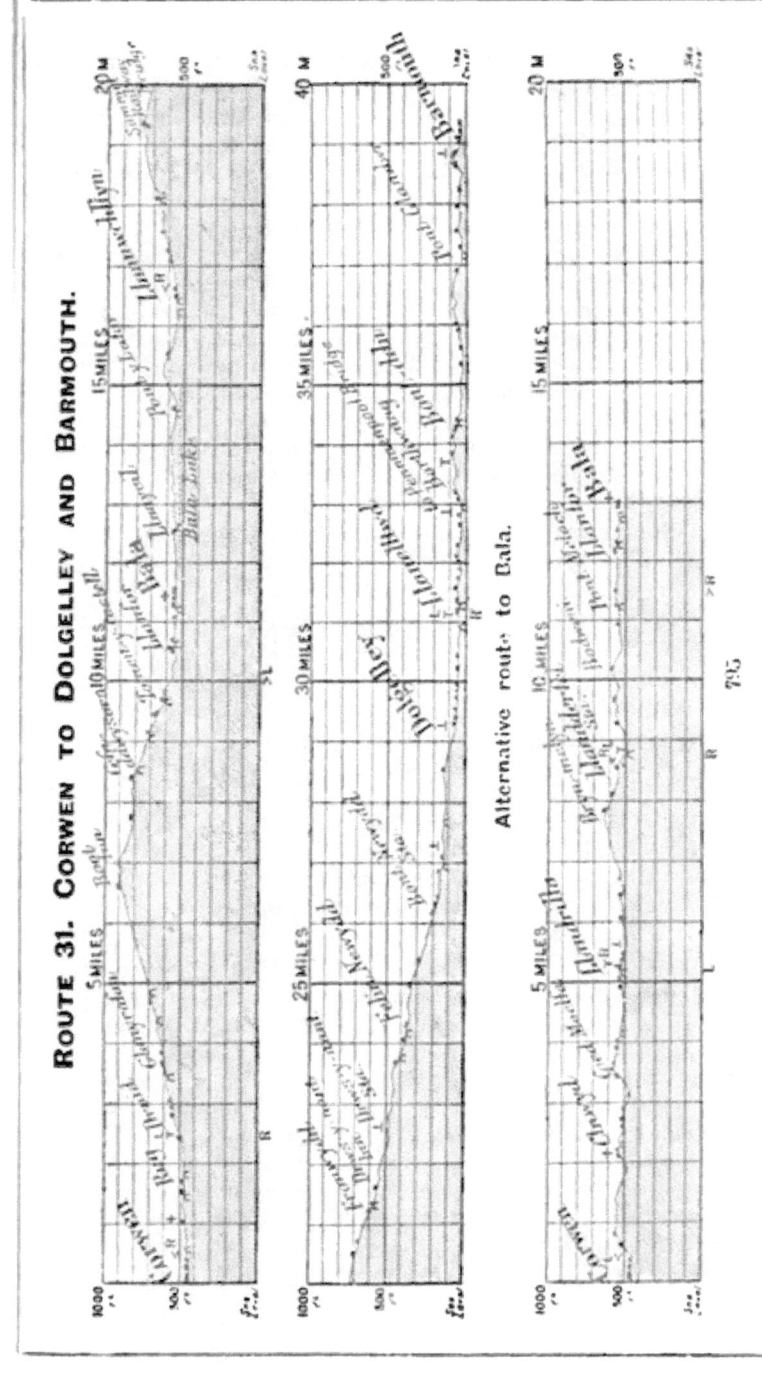

ROUTE 31. CORWEN TO DOLGELLEY AND BARMOUTH.

Alternative route to Bala.

785

32   BALA TO FFESTINIOG.   [1032]

Description.—Class III. A very bad road. For the first six miles the surface is fairly good, but after that, until Ffestiniog is reached, the hills are steep and the surface wretched. After Ffestiniog there is a very dangerous hill, thence fine surface to Maentwrog.

Gradients.—(† *Dangerous.*) At 4m. 1 in 16; 7m. 1 in 19; 9m. 1 in 17; 10 & 11m. 1 in 14; 11¾m. 1 in 12†; 14¼m. 1 in 18; 15¼m. 1 in 13†; 16¼m. 1 in 11†; 18m. 1 in 9†.

Measurements.

Bala,* White Lion Hotel.
   8¼   Rhydyfen Hotel.*
   17¾   8¾   Ffestiniog.*
   20   11¾   2¾   Maentwrog,* Bridge.
   27   18¾   9¾   7   Portmadoc,* Town Hall.   R. 28.

Principal Objects of Interest.—Fine mountain scenery. Ffestiniog: Falls. Very pretty near Maentwrog.

Hotels or Inns at places marked *.

32a.   BALA TO CERRIG-Y-DRUIDON, 10½m.

Description.—Class III. (Shown dotted on Route 32). Indifferent surface.

Gradients.—At 9½m. 1 in 15.

---

33   BALA TO LLANRHAIADR.   [1033]

Description.—Class III. A bad road; good surface for three miles, then rough and steep to Llangynog, whence excellent to Llanrhaiadr. (The road to Llanfyllin is very steep).

Gradients.—(† *Dangerous.*) At 1m. 1 in 12†; 4½m. 1 in 9†; 10½m. 1 in 13†; 12¼ & 14¾m. 1 in 10†; 15¾m. 1 in 16.

Measurements.

Bala,* White Lion Hotel.
   12¼   Llangynog,* Bridge.
   19¾   6¾   Llanrhaiadr.*   R. 98a.
   (21¾   8⅝   Llanfyllin.*)

Principal Objects of Interest.—Pretty road near Llangynog.

Hotels or Inns at places marked *.

33a.   BALA TO VYRNWY HOTEL, 14½m.

Description.—Class III. (Shown dotted on Route 33). Good surface, but more or less steep for five miles, then rough for four miles; after which it is a perfect road along Lake Vyrnwy.

Gradients.—All 1 in 8, or 1 in 9 (dangerous).

Principal Objects of Interest.—Lake Vyrnwy (Reservoir).

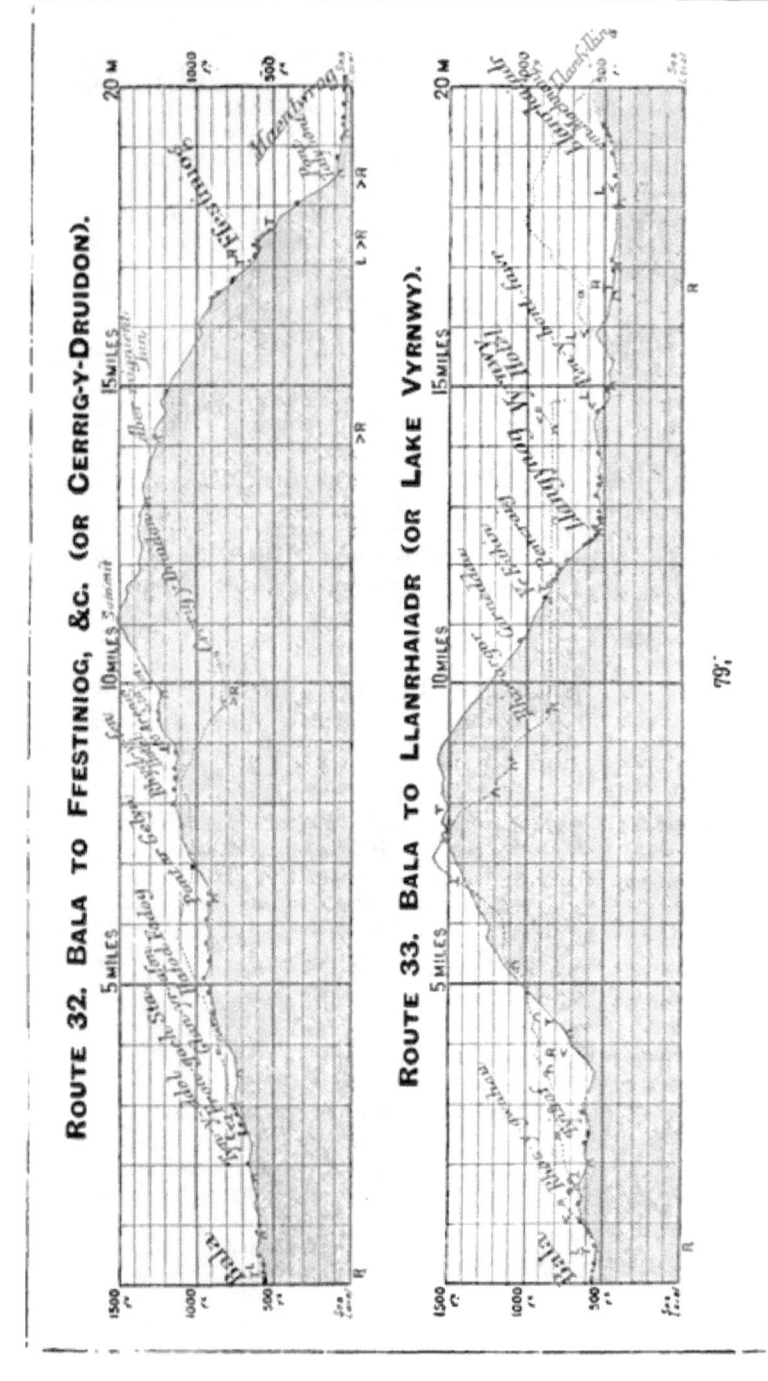

ROUTE 32. BALA TO FFESTINIOG, &C. (OR CERRIG-Y-DRUIDON).

ROUTE 33. BALA TO LLANRHAIADR (OR LAKE VYRNWY).

79.

34   BALA TO DINAS MAWDDWY.   [1034]

Description.—Class III. Good surface for five miles, then a poor road, gradually getting worse, and with a sheer descent to the Dovey Valley; thence fair surface, but numerous hills.

Gradients.—(† *Dangerous*). Mostly 1/13 to summit. 10m. 1/10†; 10¾m. 1/5†; 11m. 1/7†; thence 1/10†, or 1/12†.

Milestones.—Measured from Bala.

Measurements.

Bala,* White Lion Hotel.
(5½   Llanuwchllyn.*)
13¼   8¼   Llan-y-Mawddwy.*
18   13¼   4½   Dinas Mawddwy,* Buckley Arms Hotel.

Hotels or Inns at places marked *.

35   BARMOUTH TO PORTMADOC.   [1035]

Description.—Class II. A continuously undulating road to Harlech, with a dangerous hill at Llanfair; thereafter excellent surface all the way to Portmadoc.

Gradients.—At ¾m. 1 in 20; 6½m. 1 in 13; 6¾m. 1 in 16; 7¾m. 1 in 20; 9¼m. 1 in 10 (dangerous); 12¼m. 1 in 14.

Measurements.

Barmouth,* P.O.
11   Harlech,* Cross-roads.
15   4   Talsarnau.*   R. 18.
17½   6½   2½   Penrhyn Deudraeth,* Griffin Hotel.
20¾   9¾   5¾   3   Portmadoc,* Town Hall, or
25   14   10   7½   Beddgelert.*   R. 26.

Principal Objects of Interest.—Llanaber: Church. Llanddwywe: Church, Cors-y-gedol Cromlechs. Llanbedr: Cwm Bychan, Roman Steps. Harlech: Castle. Penrhyn: Deudraeth Castle. PORTMADOC: Embankment, Town Hall.

36   TOWYN TO CORRIS.   [1036]

Description.—Class II. The direct route to Abergynolwyn is R. 39. This road passes the prominent "Bird Rock"; fair surface, but dangerous hills.

Gradients.—(† *Dangerous*.) At 3½m. 1 in 15; 9½m. 1 in 9†; 10m. 1 in 6†; 14½m. 1 in 7†; 15½m. 1 in 16.

Measurements.

Towyn.*
3¾   Cefn Coch Hotel.*   Abergynolwyn.*
7½   3½   Bird Rock.   2½   Tal-y-llyn.*
10¼   6½   3   Abergynolwyn.*   6¾   4½   Corris.*

Principal Objects of Interest.—Bird Rock.

Hotels or Inns at places marked *.

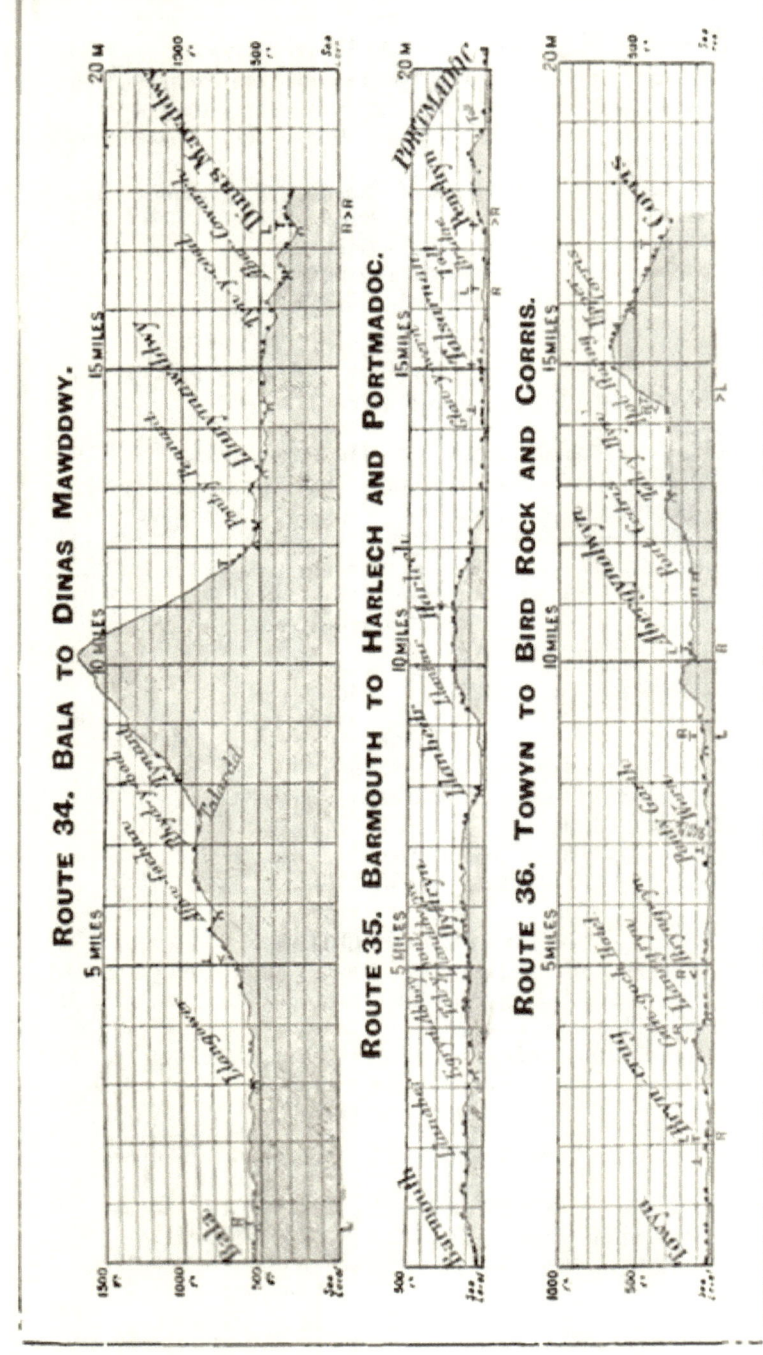

ROUTE 34. BALA TO DINAS MAWDDWY.

ROUTE 35. BARMOUTH TO HARLECH AND PORTMADOC.

ROUTE 36. TOWYN TO BIRD ROCK AND CORRIS.

37 DOLGELLEY TO FFESTINIOG. [1037]

Description.—Class II. Good surface for the first seven miles from Dolgelley; after Trawsfynydd the road is all short, steep hills, mostly dangerous.

Gradients.—(† *Dangerous.*) At 4½m. 1 in 12; 6m. 1 in 16; 8m. 1 in 13; 12½m. 1 in 16; 13¼m. 1 in 10†; 15½m. 1 in 15; 16¼m. 1 in 16; 17m. 1 in 10†; 17¼ & 18m. 1 in 8†; 19¼m. 1 in 16.

Milestones.—Measured from Dolgelley, County Hall.

Measurements.

Dolgelley,* Square.
12¾ Trawsfynydd.*
18¾ 5¼ Ffestiniog.*
21½ 8¾ 3¼ Blaenau Ffestiniog.*

Principal Objects of Interest.—1m., Hengwrt. 2m., Cymmer Abbey. 6m., Gold Mines, Mawddach Falls. Ffestiniog: Falls.

38 DOLGELLEY TO MACHYNLLETH. [1038]

Description.—Class II. The surface is excellent to Corris, after which it is in splendid condition: dangerous hills near Dolgelley, and near Minffordd.

Gradients.—(† *Dangerous.*) At 1½m. 1/15-11; 3m. 1/19; 5¼m. 1/14; 5¾m. 1/13; 6½m. 1/17; 7¼m. 1/12†; 8½m. 1/10†; 9¼m. 1/16.

Milestones.—Measured from Dolgelley and Machynlleth.

Measurements.

Dolgelley,* Square.
3¾ Cross Foxes Inn.*
7½ 4¼ Minffordd. R. 39.
11 7¾ 3½ Corris,* Braichgoch Inn.
16¾ 13 8¾ 5¾ Machynlleth,* Clock.

Principal Objects of Interest.—Views of Cader Idris, and Tal-y-llyn. Corris: Slate Quarries. Fine scenery.

Hotels or Inns at places marked *.

39 DOLGELLEY TO TOWYN. [1039]

Description.—Class III. The best road is Route 47. This road is steep to Minffordd, but has excellent surface.

Gradients.—(† *Dangerous.*) To 7½m. as Route 38. At 10¼m. 1 in 12†; 13m. 1 in 13†; 16m. 1 in 19.

Measurements.

Dolgelley,* Square.
7½ Minffordd. R. 38.
9¾ 2¾ Tal-y-llyn,* Hotel.
12½ 5 2½ Abergynolwyn.*
19¾ 12½ 9¾ 7¼ Towyn,* Town Hall.

Principal Objects of Interest.—Splendid scenery.

Hotels or Inns at places marked *.

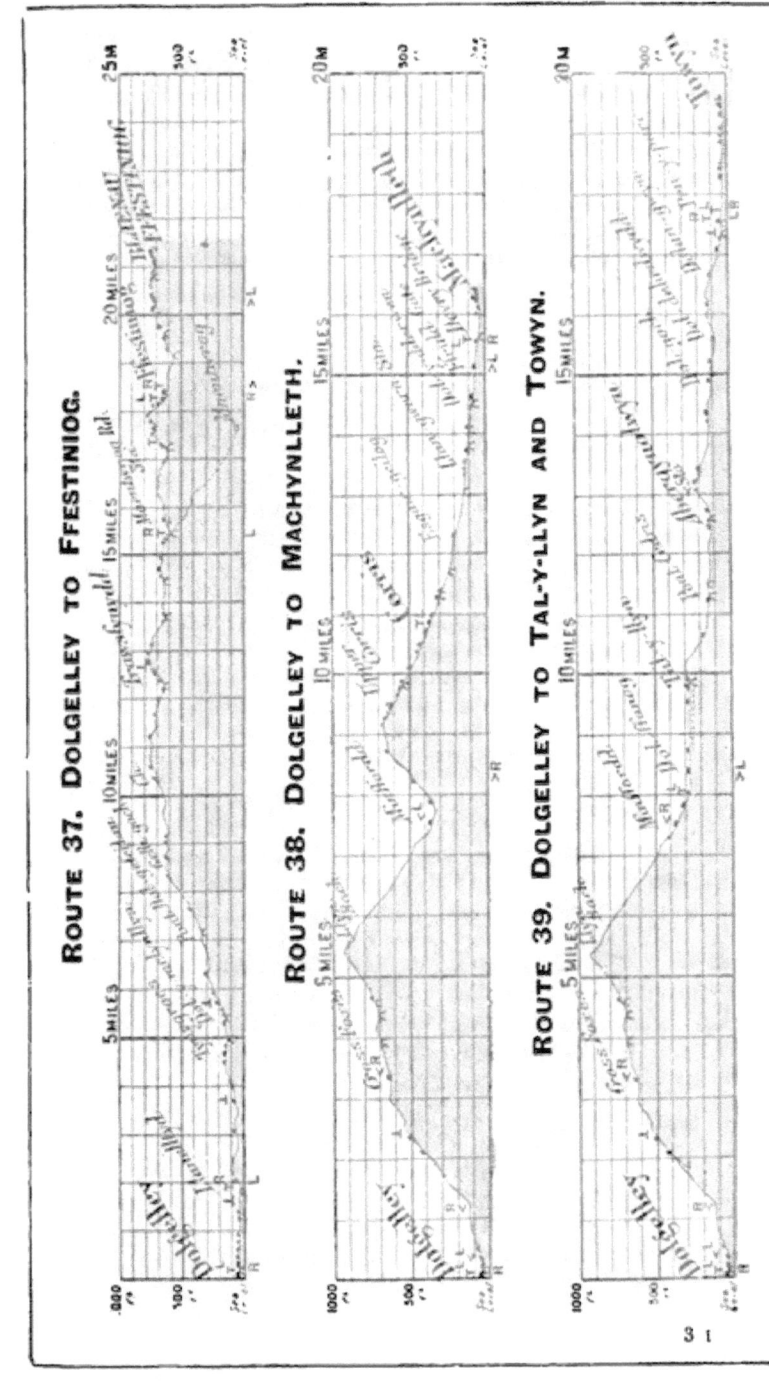

ROUTE 37. DOLGELLEY TO FFESTINIOG.

ROUTE 38. DOLGELLEY TO MACHYNLLETH.

ROUTE 39. DOLGELLEY TO TAL-Y-LLYN AND TOWYN.

40 WELSHPOOL TO DOLGELLEY. [1040]

Description.—Class II. A well engineered road, with very good surface as far as Cann Office, after which it is poorer, but it improves again near Dinas Mawddwy. Thence to Dolgelley the road is over a precipitous hill, but is in tolerably good condition, the dangerous descent to Dolgelley having excellent surface.

Gradients.—(† *Dangerous.*) At 1½m. 1 in 16; 4¼m. 1 in 17: 8¼ & 13¼m. 1 in 14; 14 & 19½m. 1 in 18; 22½m. 1 in 22; 26¾m. 1 in 17; 27¼m. 1 in 11 †; 27½m. 1 in 17; 31¼m. 1 in 7 †; 32m. 1 in 8 †; 32¾m. 1 in 8 †; 33¾m. 1 in 13 †; 35m. 1 in 19; 36½m. 1 in 11-15 †.

Milestones.—Measured from Welshpool, irregular.

Measurements.

Welshpool,* Cross.
8⅞ Llanfair,* Bridge.
15⅝ 6¾ Cann Office Hotel.*
26½ 17⅝ 10⅞ Mallwyd.* R. 48.
27½ 18⅝ 11⅞ 1 Dinas Mawddwy,* Buckley Arms Ho.
34½ 25⅝ 18⅞ 8 7 Cross Foxes.* R. 38.
37⅞ 29 22¼ 11⅜ 10⅜ 3⅜ Dolgelley,* Square.

Principal Objects of Interest.—A pretty road as far as Cann Office, then bleak and shut in, but with a fine view before Mallwyd; there is also a splendid view from the summit between Dinas Mawddwy and Dolgelley. Dinas Mawddwy: The Plas, Aran Mowddwy. Dolgelley: Torrent Walk, Precipice Walk, Cymmer Abbey, Gold Mines.

Hotels or Inns at places marked*.

41 WELSHPOOL TO BISHOPS CASTLE. [1041]

Description.—Class III. While the surface of this road is in good condition, the hills are very steep, and several of them are dangerous. For Montgomery (7½m.), turn to R. at 4m. (shown dotted), but a better road is Route 1002.

Gradients.—(† *Dangerous*). At 3m. 1 in 13 †; 4¾m. 1 in 12 †: 5¾m. 1 in 15; 9½m. 1 in 11; 10¼m. 1 in 19; 10¾m. 1 in 13 †; 13¼m. 1 in 15; 14½m. 1 in 12 †; 15¼m. 1 in 10 †.

Milestones.—Measured from Welshpool, & Bishops Cas.

Measurements.

Welshpool,* Cross.
6⅞ Chirbury.* R. 892.
9¾ 2⅞ Churchstoke.*
15¼ 8⅜ 5½ Bishops Castle,* Clock.

Principal Objects of Interest.—2¼m., River Severn. 1m., Offa's Dyke. Chirbury: Ch. Bishops Castle: Town House.

Hotels or Inns at places marked*.

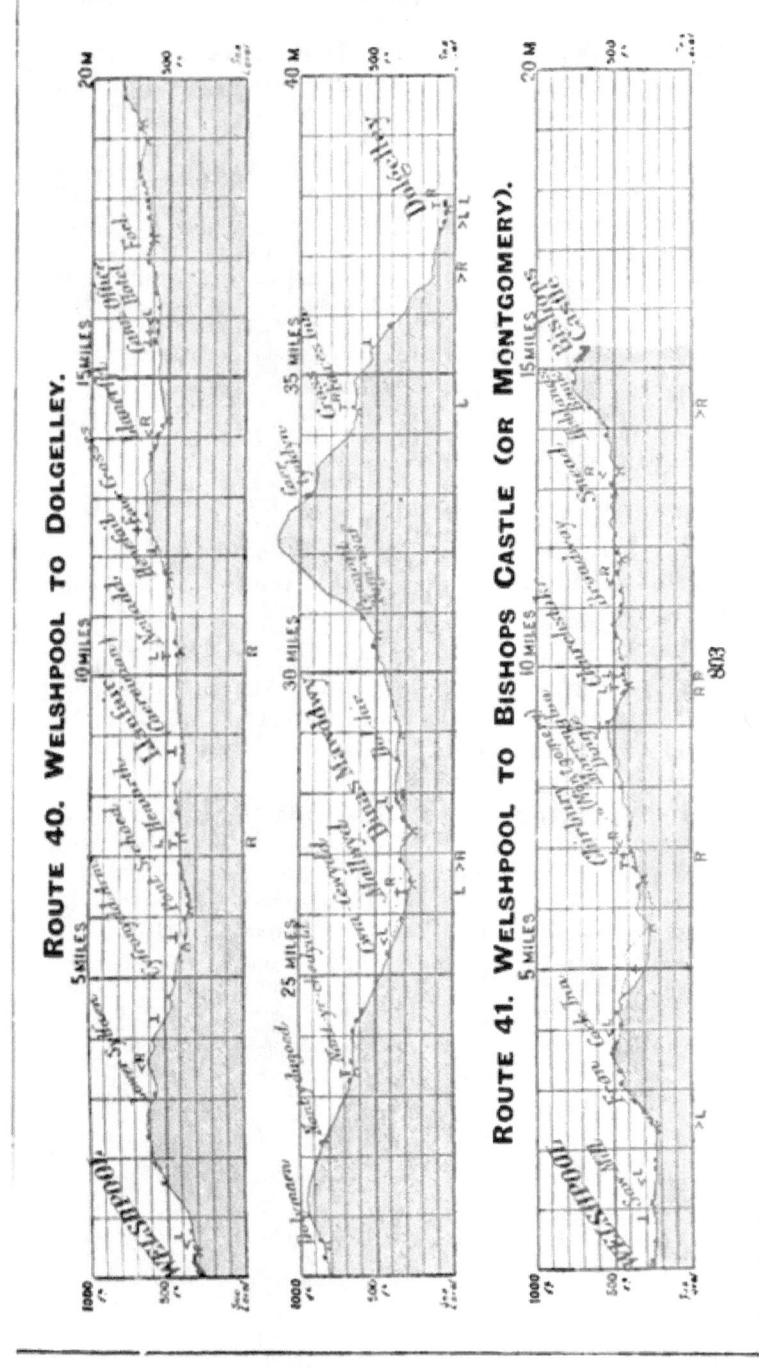

ROUTE 40. WELSHPOOL TO DOLGELLEY.

ROUTE 41. WELSHPOOL TO BISHOPS CASTLE (OR MONTGOMERY).

42 NEWTOWN TO BISHOPS CASTLE. [1042]

Description.—Class II. Steep to Kerry, thence good surface. Dangerous hill at Bishops Castle. The road from Montgomery (shown dotted) joins in at Brompton.

Gradients.—(† *Dangerous.*) At ¾m. 1 in 9†; 1½m. 1 in 9†; 2m. 1 in 14; 5½m. 1 in 22; 7¼m. 1 in 14; 12m. 1 in 13; 15½m. 1 in 12†; 16¾m. 1 in 10†.

Milestones.—Measured from Shrewsbury,—irregular.

Measurements.

Newtown.*
— Montgomery.*
10½ 2¾ Brompton.*
16¾ 9 6¼ Bishops Castle,* Clock.

Principal Objects of Interest.—Kerry: Church. Bishops Castle: Town House.

43 NEWTOWN TO KNIGHTON. [1043]

Description.—Class II. & III. Good surface on the long gradual ascent to Dolfor, thence rough for five miles, after which it is a good undulating country road.

Gradients.—(† *Dangerous.*) At ½m. 1 in 24; 5m. 1 in 9†; 6¾m. 1 in 15; 7¼m. 1 in 11†; 8½m. 1 in 12†; 10¾m. 1 in 11†; 12½m. 1 in 16; 14½m. 1 in 14; 15½m. 1 in 18.

Measurements.

Newtown.*
12¼ Felindre.*
18½ 6¼ Lloyney.*
22¾ 10⅞ 3¾ Knighton,* Norton Arms Hotel.

Principal Objects of Interest.—Pretty near Knucklas.

Hotels or Inns at places marked*, and at Beguildy, &c.

44 NEWTOWN TO LLANFAIR. [1044]

Description.—Class III. The direct road (shown dotted) consists of a series of precipitous hills, mostly 1 in 7. The better road by Berriew has splendid surface to that place, then a steep 5m., after which excellent surface to Llanfair.

Gradients.—(† *Dangerous.*) At 9m. 1 in 17; 10½m. 1 in 11†; 10½ & 12m. 1 in 10†; 13½ & 13¾m. 1 in 11†.

Measurements.

Newtown.*				Direct Road.
7¼	Garthmyl.*			Newtown.*
9¼	1¾	Berriew.*		5¾ Tregynon.
18¼	10½	9⅞	Llanfair,* Bridge.	11¼ 5¾ Llanfair.*

Principal Objects of Interest.—Berriew: Falls. 13m., Castle Caereinion.

Hotels or Inns at places marked*.

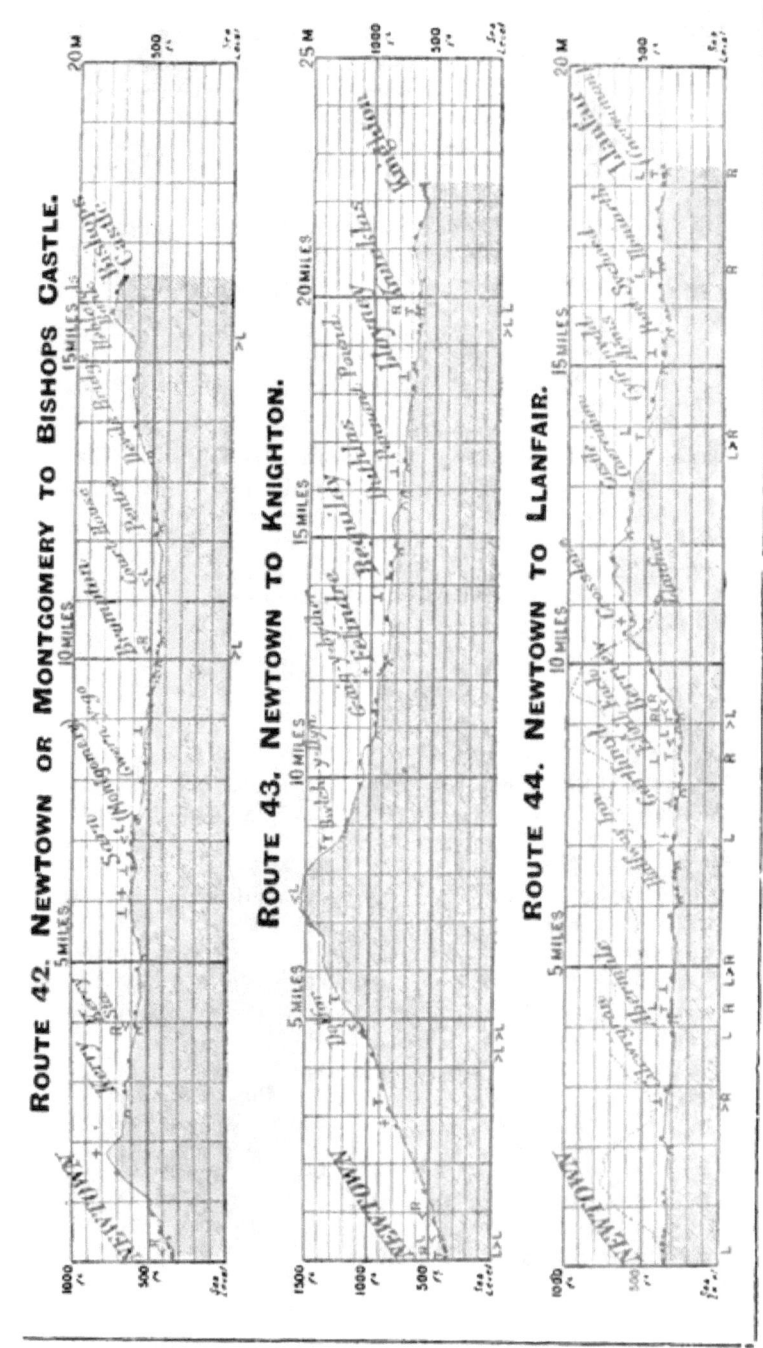

ROUTE 42. NEWTOWN OR MONTGOMERY TO BISHOPS CASTLE.

ROUTE 43. NEWTOWN TO KNIGHTON.

ROUTE 44. NEWTOWN TO LLANFAIR.

45 NEWTOWN TO ABERDOVEY. [1045]

Description.—Class I. A perfect road for the first eight miles, then good to Talerddig, where there is a dangerous descent; thence good surface, improving near Commins Coch, after which, splendid surface to Machynlleth. From Machynlleth to Aberdovey the surface is in exceedingly good condition, but there are a few slight hills. The road along the north bank of the Severn to Pontdolgoch is not so good as this route.

Gradients.—At 8 & 13¾m. 1 in 20; 14½m. 1 in 12 (dangerous); 17¼m. 1 in 18; 17½m. 1 in 23; 21m. 1 in 14; 30¼m. 1 in 17; 31¼m. 1 in 18; 35½m. 1 in 15; 36½m. 1 in 18; 37¾m. 1 in 20.

Milestones.—Measured from Newtown. After Commins Coch from Machynlleth Clock, on to Pennal, whence irregular.

Measurements.

Newtown.*							
6	Caersws.*						
11¾	5¾	Carno,* Alleppo Merchant.					
17¾	11¾	6	Llanbrynmair,* Hotel.				
23	17	11¼	5¼	Cemmaes Road.* R. 48.			
28¾	22¾	17⅛	11¼	5¾	Machynlleth,* Clock.		
33¾	26¾	21	15	9¾	3¾	Pennal,* Church.	
39½	33½	27¾	21¾	16½	10½	6¾	Aberdovey.*

Principal Objects of Interest.—Caersws: Roman station. Talerdigg: Rock Arch. Machynlleth: Clock, N.G. Railway, Lyfnant Valley. Aberdovey: College, Quay. Pretty near Llanbrynmair, also near Aberdovey.

Hotels or Inns where marked*, and at Penegoes.

46 MACHYNLLETH TO LLANIDLOES. [1046]

Description.—Class III. An impracticable road. It consists of a series of precipitous hills, utterly unrideable up, and highly dangerous down. The ordinary route is by Caersws, 31m.,—a splendid road.

Gradients.—1 in 8; 1 in 9; 1 in 7; 1 in 8; 1 in 8; 1 in 9; 1 in 8; 1 in 14; 1 in 11; 1 in 10; 1 in 11; 1 in 10; 1 in 10; 1 in 9; 1 in 7; 1 in 8; 1 in 12; 1 in 10.

Milestones.—Measured from Machynlleth.

Measurements.

Machynlleth,* Clock.		
12⅞	New Inn.*	
20¾	7⅞	Llanidloes.*

Principal Objects of Interest.—Splendid wild scenery. Van: Lead Mines. Llanidloes: Church.

Hotels or Inns at places marked *.

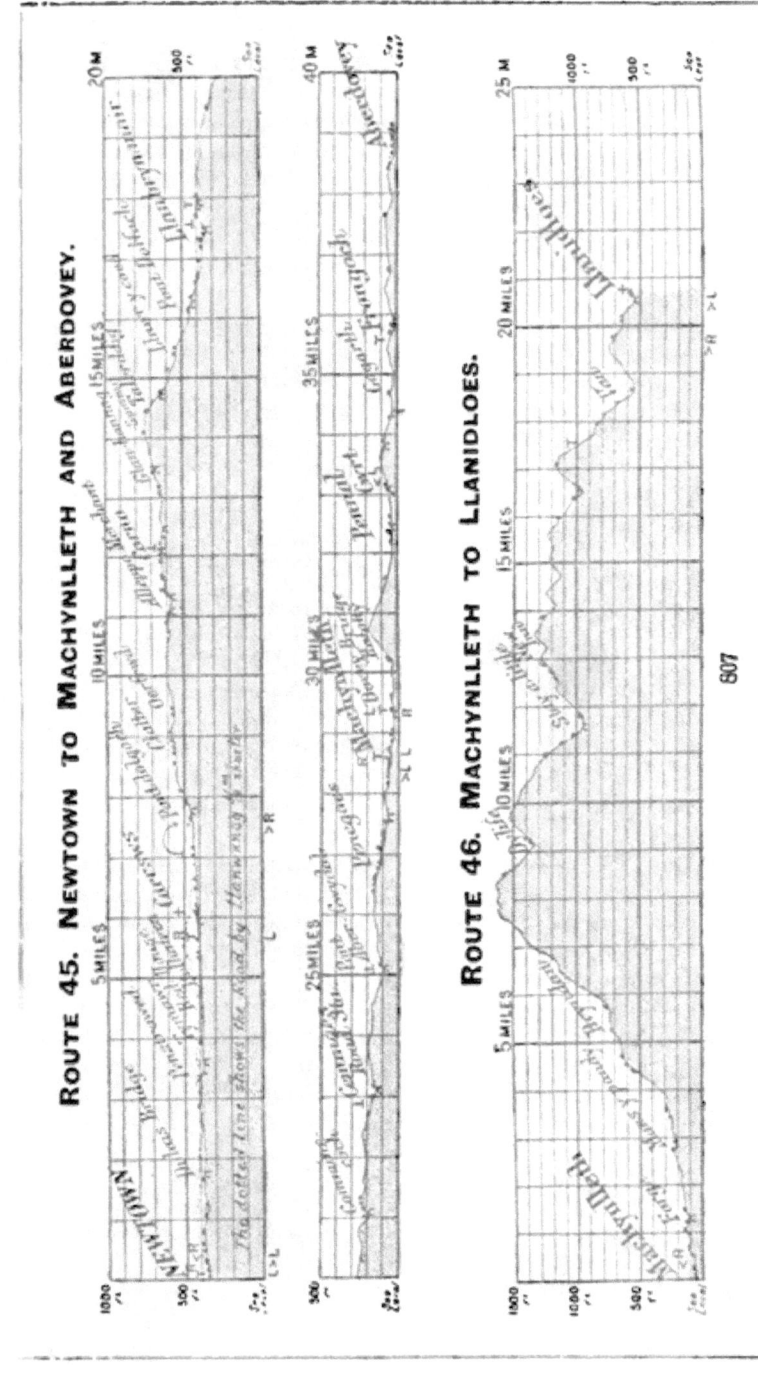

ROUTE 45. NEWTOWN TO MACHYNLLETH AND ABERDOVEY.

ROUTE 46. MACHYNLLETH TO LLANIDLOES.

607

47　ABERYSTWYTH TO BARMOUTH.　[1047]

Description.—Class II.　Dangerously steep to Bow Street (R. 48, 2½m. further, is the best road), then good, but hilly, to Borth, where ferry to Aberdovey.　From Aberdovey the road has splendid surface past Towyn to Cefncoch, when the road becomes hilly and the surface degenerates, but improves again at Llwyngwril, after which it is a very good road to Dolgelley.　Dangerous hills at Friog and Arthog.　For Barmouth, turn L. along the tram rails (no road) at 27½m. to Barmouth Junc., thence over the sand and bridge (Toll).

Gradients.—(†*Dangerous.*)　At 1m. 1 in 9†; 1¾m. 1 in 10†; 2¾m. 1 in 11†; 3½m. 1 in 16; 5¼ & 19½m. 1 in 15; 24¼m. 1 in 17; 26¾m. 1 in 14†; 29¼m. 1 in 10†; 30¼m. 1 in 17; 31½m. 1 in 14.

Milestones.—Measured from Clock Tower, Aberystwyth, and from Towyn, and Dolgelley.

Measurements.

Aberystwyth,* P.O						Barmouth to
11½	Aberdovey.*					Llywngwril, round by
15½	4¼	Towyn,* Town Hall.				Penmaenpool Bri., 16½m.
19½	7¾	3¾	Cefncoch Hotel.*			R. 36.
24	12½	8¾	4½	Llywngwril.*		
(29¼)	18¼	14¼	10½	5¼	Barmouth,* P.O.)	
35½	24	19⅜	16¼	11½	10	Dolgelley,* Square.

Principal Objects of Interest.—Aberdovey: College, Pier.　Towyn: Cadfans Pillar and Well.　Cefncoch: Bird Rock.　21m., Fine view of Carnarvonshire.　Barmouth: Bri., Panorama Walk.　Arthog: Falls, Llysbrawden.　Dolgelley: Torrent Walk, Precipice Walk, Cymmer Abbey, &c.

48　ABERYSTWYTH TO MACHYNLLETH, &C. [1048]

Description.—Class II.　The direct road to Bow Street (Route 47) is dangerously steep.　This route has short hills, and is more or less steep for the first thirteen miles, but the surface is good; thereafter magnificent surface till within a few miles of Dinas Mawddwy when the road becomes hilly.

Gradients.—At 5½m. 1/16; 7½m. 1/17; 8½m. 1/11; 9½m. 1/14; 12m. 1/13; 12½m. 1/22; 26m. 1/20; 31m. 1/17; 32½m. 1/11.

Milestones.—Measured from Aberystwyth & Machynlleth.

Measurements.

Aberystwyth,* P.O.					
9½	Talybont,' Black Lion Hotel.				
20½	10¾	Machynlleth,* Clock.			
25½	16¼	5½	Cemmaes Road,* Hotel.		R. 45.
31¼	22¼	11¾	6¼	Mallwyd,* Hotel.	R. 40.
32¼	23¼	12¾	7½	1	Dinas Mawddwy,* Buckley Arms.

Principal Objects of Interest.—Glandovey: Castle. Machynlleth: Clock Tower, Lyfnant Valley.　Pretty road.

Hotels or Inns at places marked *.

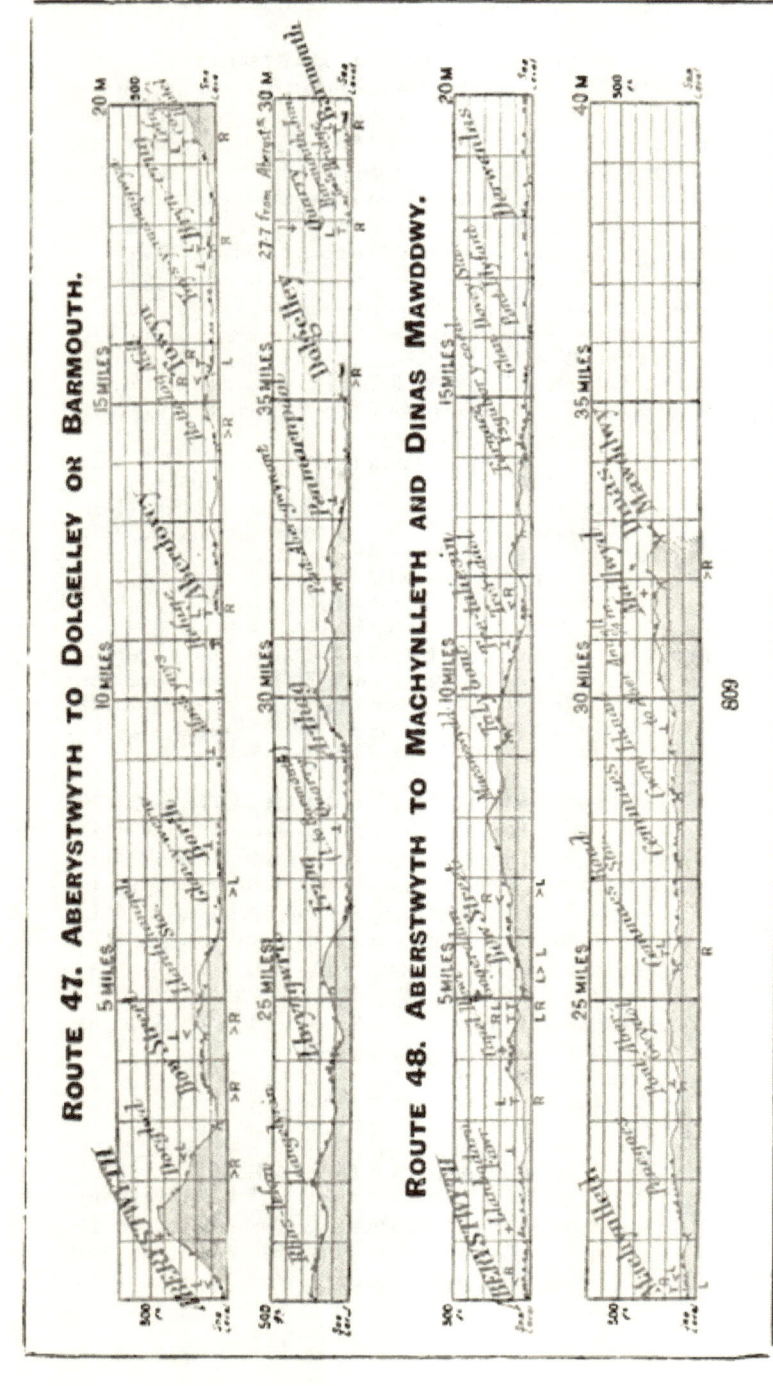

ROUTE 47. ABERYSTWYTH TO DOLGELLEY OR BARMOUTH.

ROUTE 48. ABERSTWYTH TO MACHYNLLETH AND DINAS MAWDDWY.

809

49   ABERYSTWYTH TO NEWTOWN.   [1049]

Description.—Class I. For the first twelve miles the road has splendid surface, after that it is more or less loose all the way to Llangurig, but as the ascent is very gradual, and as there is usually a good strip of surface at the sides, it is generally counted a first-class road. After Llangurig the surface is fair until Llanidloes is reached, thence it is a perfect road to Newtown.

The road by Devil's Bridge has excellent surface, but is steep. After Devil's Bridge to the junction with the main road at Dyffryn-Castell, it is rather rough, and has a ford.

Gradients.—At 6½m. mostly 1 in 22; 9m. 1 in 18; 10, 11½, 16m. 1 in 22; 19½m. 1 in 21; 26m. 1 in 16; 27¾m. 1 in 13.

By Devil's Bridge.—(†*Dangerous.*) At ¾m. 1 in 19; 1½m. 1 in 11†; 3¾m. 1 in 17; 4½m. 1 in 12†; 6½m. 1 in 18; 7½m. 1 in 12†; 10½m. 1 in 19; 11½m. 1 in 15; 12½m. 1 in 16; 14m. 1 in 13†; 14½m. 1 in 10†.

Milestones.—Measured from Aberystwyth Town Hall, from Llanidloes, and from Newtown.

Measurements.

Aberystwyth,* P.O.							
7⅝	Goginan,* Druid Inn.						
11¾	4⅛	Ponterwyd,* Gogerddan Arms Hotel.					
13¾	6½	2¼	Dyffryn-Castell Hotel.*				
24⅜	17	12⅞	10½	Llangurig.*			
29¾	22	17⅞	15½	5	Llanidloes.*		
35⅜	28	23½	21½	11	6	Llandinam.*	
(37¾	30⅜	26	23¾	13¾	8⅜	2¾	Caersws.* R. 45.)
43	35½	31¼	29½	18½	13¼	7½	Newtown.*

By Devil's Bridge.

Aberystwyth, P.O.			
7¼	Henffordd Arms.*		
12	4⅞	Devil's Bridge Hotel.*	
16¼	9	4⅛	Dyffryn-Castell Hotel*; or
15¼	8⅜	3¼	Ponterwyd,* Gogerddan Arms Ho.

(as above.)

Principal Objects of Interest.—Llangurig: Church, abandoned railway. Llanidloes: Church, Van Mines. 37½m., Moat. NEWTOWN: Church. The best scenery is to be had on the road past the Devil's Bridge. The main route is somewhat uninteresting, owing to the lack of ruggedness of the hills bordering the valley. Devil's Bridge. Punch Bowl, Parson's Bridge, &c. This part of the district is finely wooded.

Hotels or Inns at places marked*.

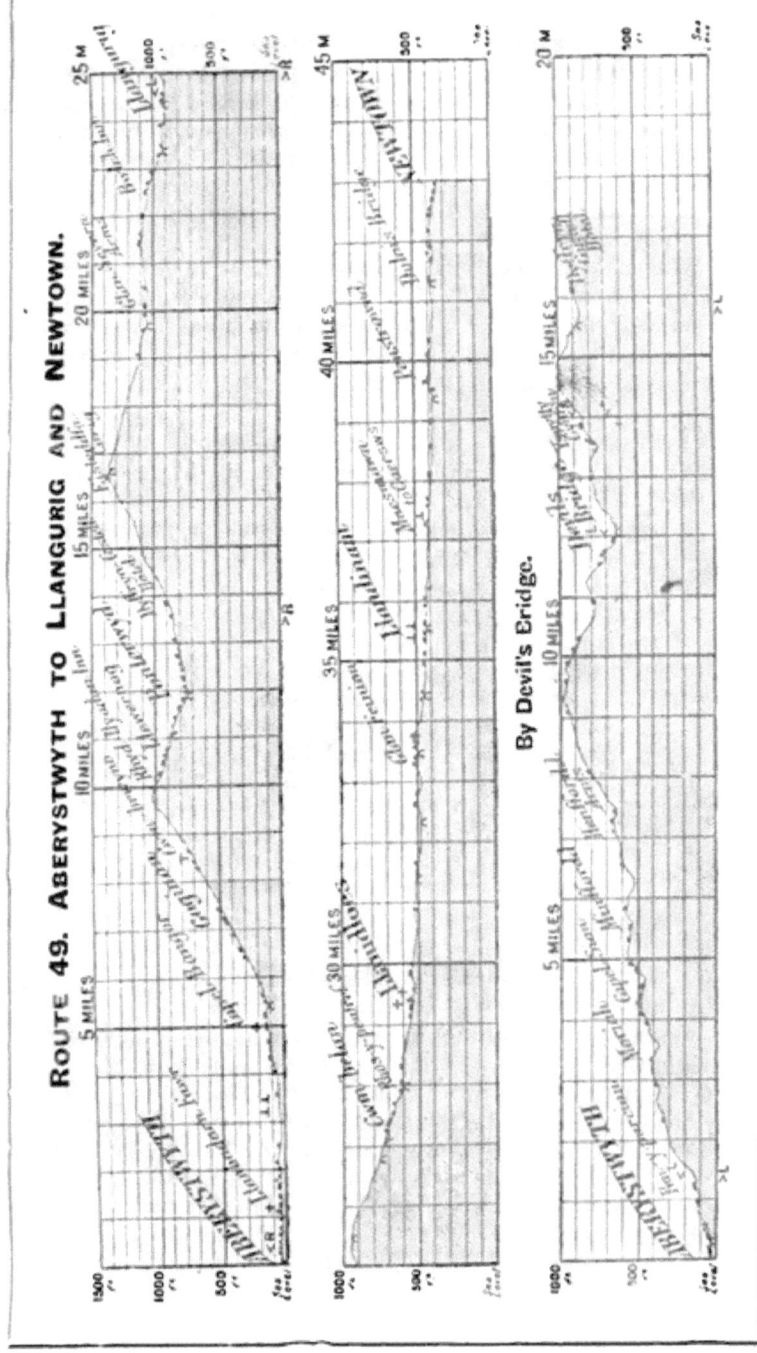

ROUTE 49. ABERYSTWYTH TO LLANGURIG AND NEWTOWN.

By Devil's Bridge.

50 Aberystwyth to Pont-rhyd-y-groes.

Description.—Class III. This route shows the direct road to Trawscoed,—a hilly steep road. Route 51 shows an easier way. From Trawscoed to Pont-rhyd-y-groes, good surface.

Gradients.—(†*Dangerous.*) At ½m. 1 in 19; 3m. 1 in 12†; 5¼m. 1 in 7†; 12m. 1 in 15; 13m. 1 in 13.

Measurements.

Aberystwyth,* P.O.			
4¾	New Cross Inn.*		
8⅝	3⅞	Trawscoed Bridge. R. 51.	
13¾	9	5⅛	Pont-rhyd-y-groes.* R. 55.

Hotels or Inns at places marked*.

51 Aberystwyth to Tregaron. [1051]

Description.—Class III. Steep hills for three miles, then a good country road, but with one very dangerous hill.

Gradients.—(†*Dangerous.*) At ½m. 1 in 19; 1¾m. 1 in 10†; 2¼m. 1 in 12†; 2¾m. 1 in 14; 3¼ & 4½m. 1 in 15; 11½m. 1 in 8†; 13¾ & 14m. 1 in 14.

Measurements.

Aberystwyth,* P.O.					
6	Llanilar,* Falcon Inn.				
9⅛	3⅛	Trawscoed Bridge. R. 50.			
14⅜	8⅜	5¼	Strata Florida Station.		
16	10	6⅞	1⅝	Pont-rhyd-fendigaid.*	
21½	15½	12⅜	7⅛	5½	Tregaron,* Bridge.

Principal Objects of Interest.—Strata Florida: Abbey. Ystrad Meurig: School. Pont-rhyd-fendigaid: Spa.

Hotels or Inns at places marked*.

52 Aberystwyth to Lampeter. [1052]

Description.—Class III. This route is shown merely to indicate its steepness. The usual road is R. 54, which has fine surface throughout. This road, after Llanrhystyd, is somewhat rough, and all the hills are dangerous.

Gradients.—(*All dangerous.*) First 9m. as R. 53. At 9½m. 1 in 8; 11m. 1 in 11; 15¼m. 1 in 8; 17m. 1 in 7; 19m. 1 in 9, &c., &c.

Milestones.—Measured from Aberystwyth, Clock.

Measurements.

Aberystwyth,* P.O.			
8⅜	Llanrhystyd.		
18	9⅝	Talsarn.*	
24¼	15⅞	6¼	Lampeter.*

Principal Objects of Interest.—Lampeter: College.

Hotels or Inns at places marked*.

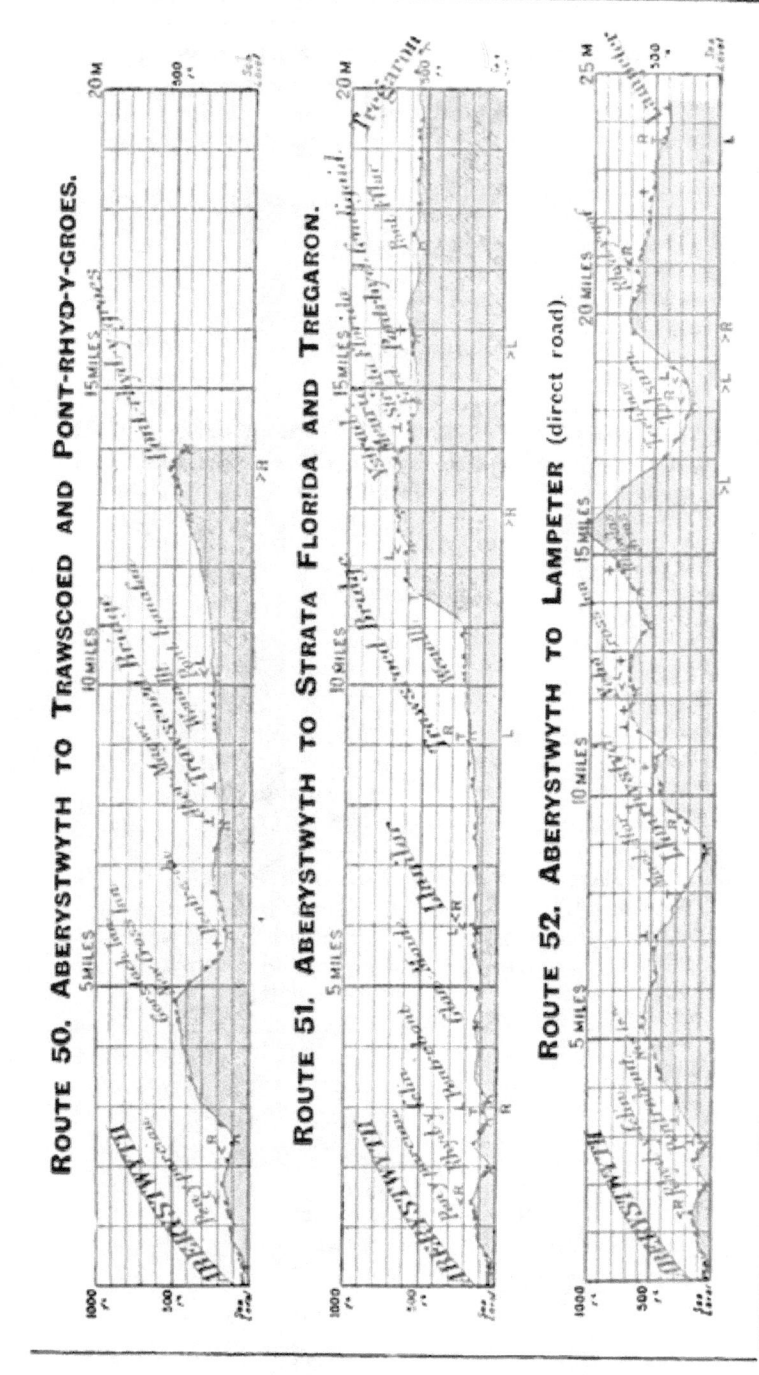

ROUTE 50. ABERYSTWYTH TO TRAWSCOED AND PONT-RHYD-Y-GROES.

ROUTE 51. ABERYSTWYTH TO STRATA FLORIDA AND TREGARON.

ROUTE 52. ABERYSTWYTH TO LAMPETER (direct road).

53 ABERYSTWYTH TO CARDIGAN. [1053]

Description.—Class II. The surface is exceedingly good, even on the steep hills, but the numerous dangerous hills,—mostly of some length,—make this a very trying road. Going north the gradients are more favourable than going south, although even then most of them are very stiff. Between Aberaeron and Cardigan the road is almost more hilly, but the surface is in fine condition.

Gradients.—(† *Dangerous.*) At ½m. 1/19; 1¾m. 1/10†; 2¼m. 1/12†; 2¾m. 1/14; 3 & 4m. 1/10†; 6, 7½, & 8½m. 1/17; 12½m. 1/10†; 13¼m. 1/16; 14¼m. 1/9†; 14½m. 1/11†; 15½, 16½, 17½, & 18¼m. 1/14; 18½m. 1/11†; 18¾m. 1/13†; 20 & 20¼m. 1/10†; 20¾m. 1/9†; 22¼m. 1/17; 22½m. 1/11† 23m. 1/14; 27¼m. 1/15; 21¾m. 1/16; 34½m. 1/12†; 35¼m. 1/14; 36½m. 1/13; 37½m. 1/14.

Milestones.—Measured from Aberystwyth Clock Tower to Aberaeron, thence from Cardigan Town Hall.

Measurements.

Aberystwyth,* P.O.					
11¼	Llannon.*				
15¾	4½	Aberaeron.*			
22⅜	11⅝	6⅝	Synod Inn.* R. 58.		
27¼	16	11½	4⅞	New Inn.*	
38¼	27	22½	15⅞	11	Cardigan,* Town Hall.

Principal Objects of Interest.—Cardigan: Cas., Church, St. Dogmael's Abbey, Kilgerran Castle. For the first nine miles there is a range of hills between the road and the sea; thereafter sea views, until a little beyond Aberaeron, when it becomes a monotonous inland road.

Hotels or Inns at places marked*, and at Llanarth, &c.

54 ABERAERON TO LAMPETER. [1054]

Description.—Class II. Splendid surface throughout, but the hills are very steep. This, with R. 53, is the main road from Aberystwyth to Lampeter.

Gradients.—*From Aberaeron.*—(† *Dangerous.*) At 1 & 1½m. 1/18; 2¼m. 1/16; 3½m. 1/12†; 4m. 1/17: 7m. 1/16; 7¼m. 1/10†: 8m. 1/12†; 8¼m. 1/10†; 9m. 1/12†; 9½m. 1/16; 12¼m. 1/11†.

Milestones.—Measured from Aberystwyth.

Aberystwyth, P.O. **Measurements.**

15¾	Aberaeron,* Feathers Hotel.		
22¼	6½	Llanfihangel Ystrad.*	
28¾	13	6½	Lampeter.*

Principal Objects of Interest.—Fine views of the hills and Valley of the Aeron. Lampeter: College.

Hotels or Inns at places marked*.

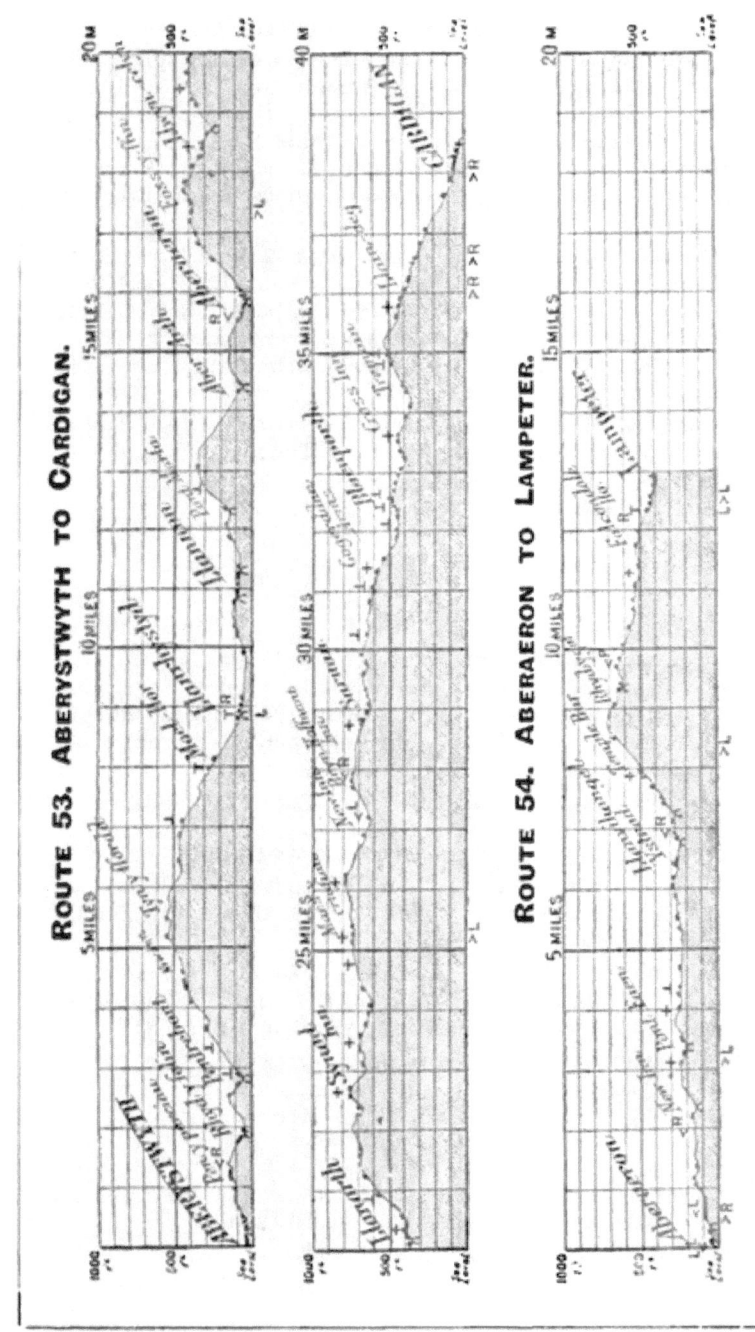

ROUTE 53. ABERYSTWYTH TO CARDIGAN.

ROUTE 54. ABERAERON TO LAMPETER.

55 Lampeter to Devil's Bridge. [1055]

Description.—Class III. Good surface to Tregaron, fair to Pont-rhyd-fendigaid, then a rough, precipitous road to Devil's Bridge. The dangerous hill near Hafod can be avoided by following the private road (shown dotted) through the park.

Gradients.—(†*Dangerous.*) At 1¼m. 1 in 15; 1½m. 1 in 16; 6¼m. 1 in 19; 9m. 1 in 16; 10¾m. 1 in 15; 17m. 1 in 10†; 18½m. 1 in 11†; 19m. 1 in 13; 19¾m. 1 in 10†; 20½ & 21¼m. 1 in 12†; 22m. 1 in 9†; 23½m. 1 in 10†; 24½m. 1 in 11†; 26m. 1 in 12†.

Measurements.

Lampeter,* Fountain.
10⅞ Tregaron,* Bridge.
16⅜ 5½ Pont-rhyd-fendigaid.*
21⅛ 10¼ 4¾ Pont-rhyd-y-groes.*
26⅞ 16 10½ 5¾ Devil's Bridge,* Hotel.

Principal Objects of Interest.—22¼m., Hafod. 25m., Arch. Devil's Bridge: Bri., Punch Bowl. Splendid scenery.

56 Lampeter to Llandovery. [1056]

Description.—Class I. This well engineered road is in fine condition. For Llangadock or Llandilo (24½m.), turn to R. at Llanwrda.

Gradients.—At 1m. 1 in 18; 2½m. 1 in 24; 4¾m. 1 in 18; 5½m. 1 in 19; 7¼ & 10m. 1 in 17.

Milestones.—Measured from Llandovery.

Measurements.

Lampeter,* Fountain.
8¼ Pumpsaint,* Inn.
16¼ 8 Llanwrda.*
20½ 12¼ 4¼ Llandovery,* Market, or
19⅝ 11⅜ 3⅜ Llangadock,* Castle Hotel.

Principal Objects of Interest.—Llandovery: Castle.

57 Lampeter to Llandilo. [1057]

Description.—Class III. Fine surface to Pumpsaint, then a narrow country road with steep hills and three fords.

Gradients.—(†*Dangerous.*) As R. 56 for 10m. 11¾m. 1/13†; 12¼m. 1/12†; 17⅝m. 1/14; 19 & 20¼m. 1/12†; 21m. 1/11†.

Measurements.

Lampeter,* Fountain
8¼ Pumpsaint,* Inn.
14¼ 6 Cross Inn.*
21⅝ 13⅜ 7⅜ Llandilo.*

Principal Objects of Interest.—Cross Inn: Talley Abbey. Llandilo: Dynevor Castle, Golden Grove.

Hotels or Inns at places marked*.

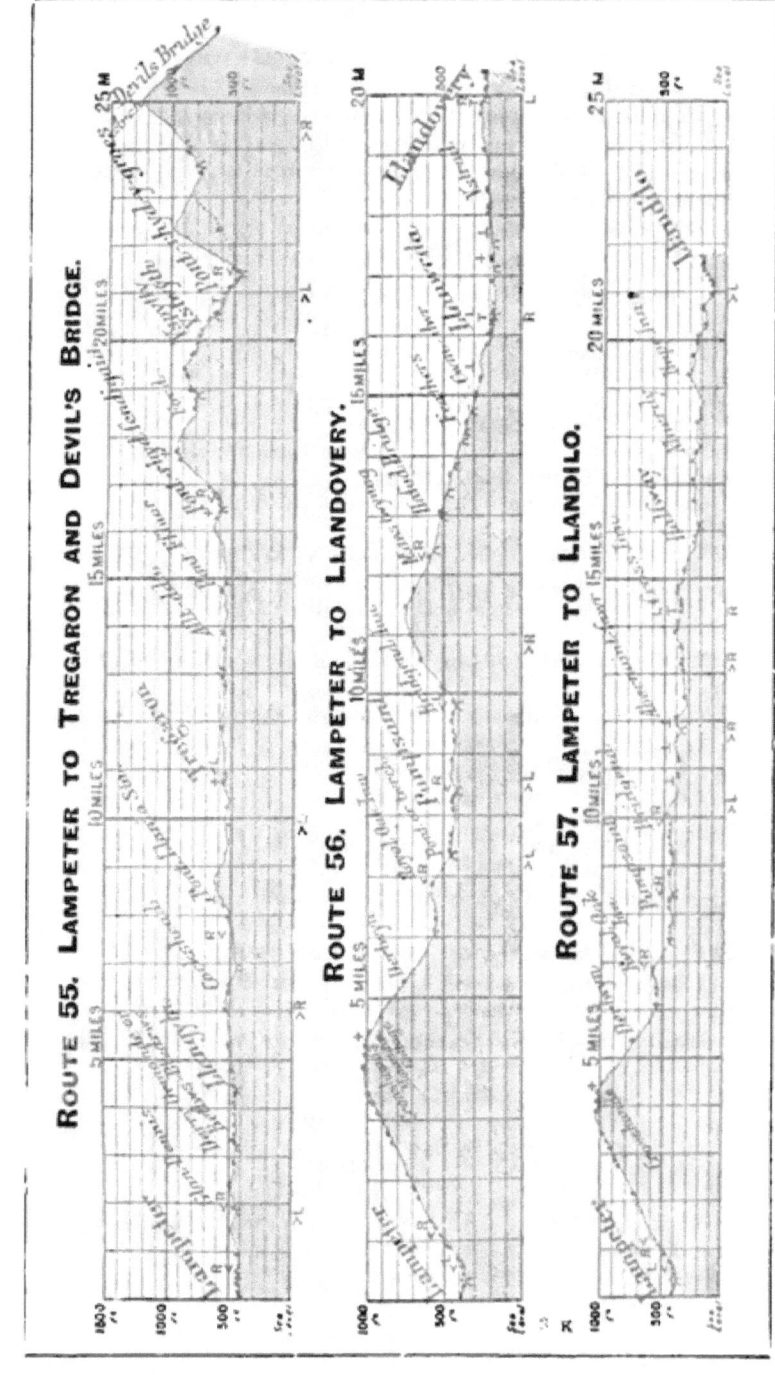

ROUTE 55. LAMPETER TO TREGARON AND DEVIL'S BRIDGE.

ROUTE 56. LAMPETER TO LLANDOVERY.

ROUTE 57. LAMPETER TO LLANDILO.

58 NEW QUAY TO CARMARTHEN. [1056]

Description.—Class III. Although the surface is kept in good order, this is a very hilly road throughout, either to Llandyssil or Allt Wallis. Route 88 is joined at Llandyssil: Route 89 at Allt Wallis.

Gradients.—(† *Dangerous.*) At ½m. 1 in 8†; 1¾m. 1 in 14; 6½m. 1 in 14; 8 & 9m. 1 in 12†; 10¼m. 1 in 13†; 15½m. 1 in 9†; 18½m. 1 in 14; 20m. 1 in 15; 20½m. 1 in 11†.

Measurements.

New Quay.*				
4¼	Synod Inn.* R. 53.			
18¼	14	Pencader.*		
21¼	17	3	Allt Wallis.*	
29⅝	25⅜	11⅜	8⅜	Carmarthen.*

New Quay.*				
4¼	Synod Inn.*			
9⅝	4⅜	Penlan Inn.*		
14⅜	10⅜	5¼	Llandyssil.*	
31¾	27½	22⅛	17½	Carmarthen.

Hotels or Inns at places marked *.

59 RHAYADER TO DEVIL'S BRIDGE, 18¼m.

Description.—Class III. The old Aberystwyth road. This route is only given for reference. It has long been almost disused, and is partly grass-grown, and all loose stones. The gradients are mostly 1 in 10 or 1 in 12, and there are three fords.

60 BISHOPS CASTLE TO KINGTON. [1060]

Description.—Class II. Fine surface for three miles, then for the next fifteen miles more or less precipitous, over four ranges of hills. All the hills are dangerous, but the surface is good. From Presteign to Kington is an excellent undulating road. The quickest, though longer road from Bishops Castle to Clun, is R. 910 (12⅞m.); to Knighton is R. 910, 62, and 909 (22⅞m.); to Presteign, R. 910 and 62 (25½m.); to Kington, R. 910, 62, and 60 (31m.). These roads avoid the big hills.

Gradients.—All 1 in 8-10 to 17m., then 18¼m. 1 in 13; 21m. 1 in 14; 22m. 1 in 13; 23¼m. 1 in 22; 24m. 1 in 18.

Milestones.—Measured from Knighton & from Presteign.

Measurements.

Bishops Castle,* Clock.				
5⅞	Clun.*			
12⅞	7	Knighton,* Norton Arms Hotel.		
19⅜	13½	6½	Presteign.* Clock.	
26¼	20⅜	13⅜	6⅞	Kington,* Clock.

Principal Objects of Interest.—Clun: Castle. 15¼m., Offa's Dyke. A pretty road at several points.

Hotels or Inns at places marked *.

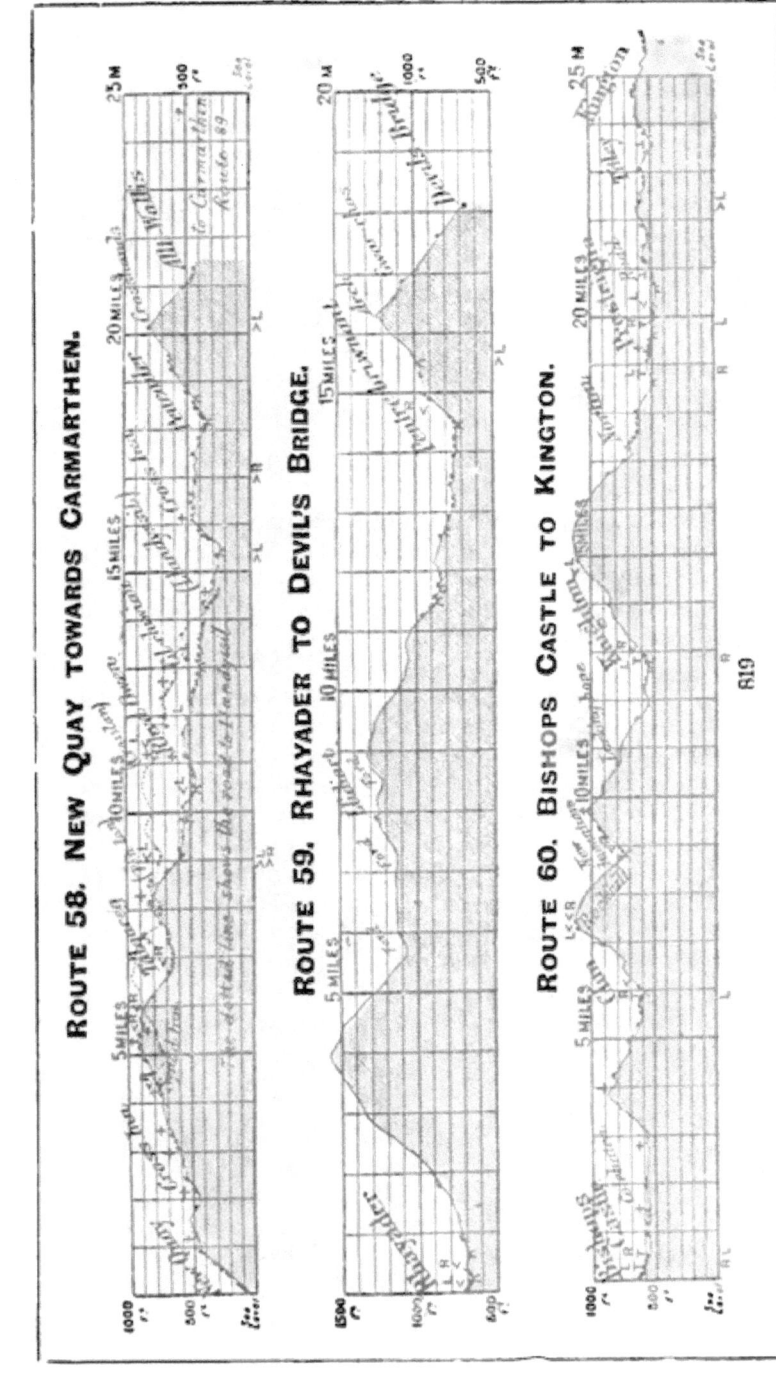

ROUTE 58. NEW QUAY TOWARDS CARMARTHEN.

ROUTE 59. RHAYADER TO DEVIL'S BRIDGE.

ROUTE 60. BISHOPS CASTLE TO KINGTON.

819

61   KNIGHTON TO LLANDRINDOD.   [1C61]

Description.—Class II. Fair surface, but inclined to be rough. Steep hills all the way.

Gradients.—(† *Dangerous*). At ¾m. 1 in 13†; ¾m. 1 in 10†; 1¼m. 1 in 9†; 3¾m. 1 in 18; 4¾m. 1 in 21; 5½m. 1 in 16; 7½, 10½, 11½, & 11¾m. 1 in 15; 14m. 1 in 14; 14½m. 1 in 16; 16½m. 1 in 18.

Milestones.—Measured from the Clock, Knighton.

Measurements.

Knighton,* Norton Arms Hotel.
    7½   Bleddfa,* Old Hundred House Inn.
    14   6½   Penybont,* Hotel. R. 64.
    19½   12   5½   Llandrindod.*

Principal Objects of Interest.—Fair scenery. Birmingham Aqueduct Works. Llandrindod: Spa, The Lake.

Hotels or Inns at places marked *, and at Crossgates.

62   PRESTEIGN TO CRAVEN ARMS.   [1062]

Description.—Class III. A narrow country road, fair surface, but with short, steep hills. This is the easiest road between Presteign and Clun (22m.), and Bishops Castle (25½m.); for which keep to left at Broome.

Gradients.—(† *Dangerous.*) At 3½m. 1 in 12†; 4¾m. 1 in 18; 6½m. 1 in 22; 11½m. 1 in 14; 11½ & 12½m. 1 in 12†; 12½m. 1 in 9†; 13½m. 1 in 16.

Measurements.

Presteign,* Clock.
    9½   Walford.* R. 909.
    10½   1½   Leintwardine,* Lion Hotel.
    17¾   8½   7½   Craven Arms,* Hotel. or
    (16   6½   5½   Aston-on-Clun.* R. 910.)

Principal Objects of Interest.—Lingen: Castle.

Hotels or Inns at places marked *, and at Lingen, &c.

63   KINGTON TO BUILTH.   [1063]

Description.—Class II. Splendid surface to Forest Inn, Then fairly good. There are four dangerous hills.

Gradients.—(† *Dangerous.*) At ½m. 1 in 12†; ¾m. 1 in 18; 2½m. 1 in 12†; 3½m. 1 in 10†; 8½m. 1 in 18; 9½m. 1 in 15; 10m. 1 in 9†; 12m. 1 in 11†; 13½m. 1 in 14; 15½m. 1 in 12†; 18m. 1 in 11†.

Milestones.—Measured from Radnor, and Builth Bridge.

Measurements.

Kington,* Clock.
    6½   Radnor,* P.O.
    20½   14   Builth,* Market House.

Principal Objects of Interest.—Radnor: Lewis Memorial. Sm., "Water Break its Neck." Builth: Wells, Wye rapids.

Hotels or Inns at places marked *, and Forest Inn, &c.

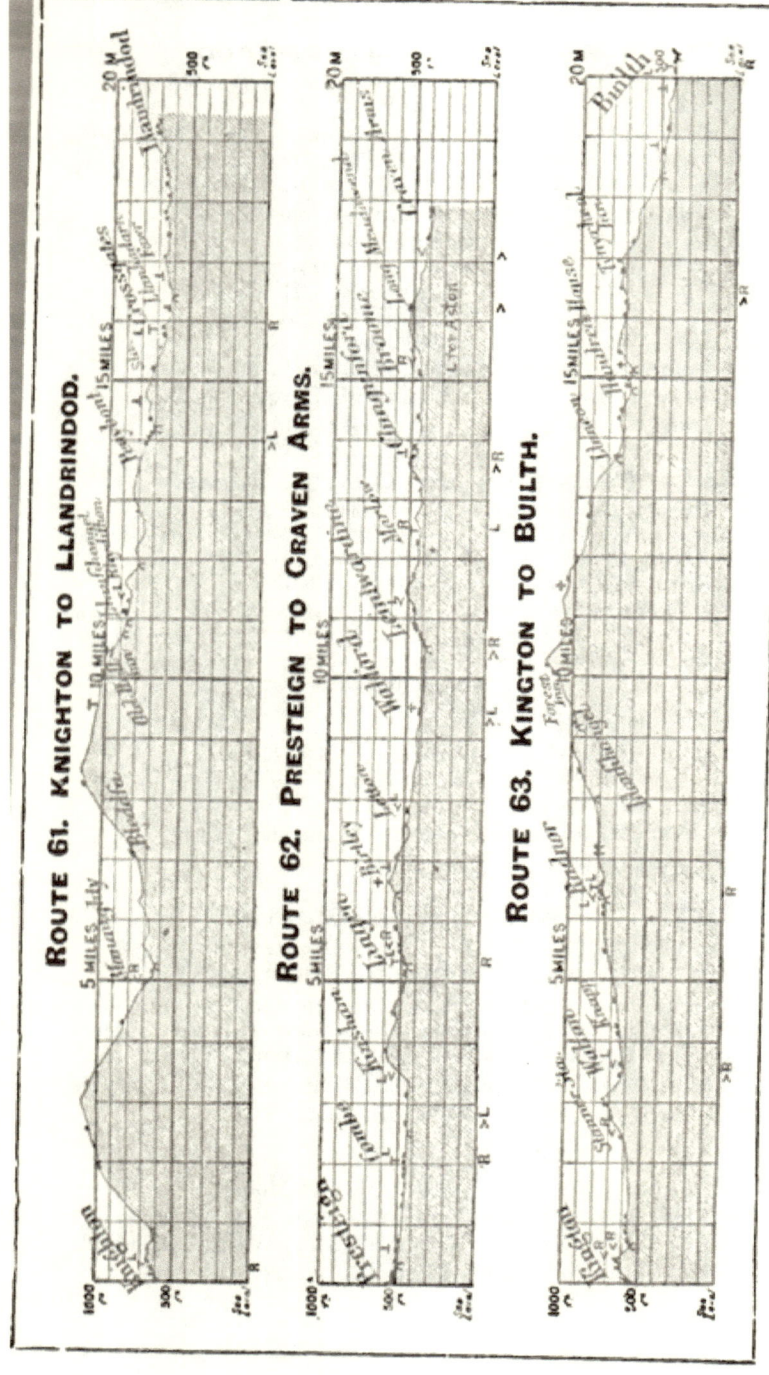

ROUTE 61. KNIGHTON TO LLANDRINDOD.

ROUTE 62. PRESTEIGN TO CRAVEN ARMS.

ROUTE 63. KINGTON TO BUILTH.

64   KINGTON TO ABERYSTWYTH.   [1064]

Description.—Class I. Splendid surface from Kington to Pen-y-bont, then very bumpy, owing to Water Works traffic. Dangerous hills between Kington and Radnor. From Rhayader to Aberystwyth: see next route, and R. 49.

Gradients.—(† *Dangerous.*) At ½m. 1 in 12†; ½m. 1 in 18; 2½m. 1 in 12†; 2½m. 1 in 10†; 8½m. 1 in 18; 9½m. 1 in 15; 10m. 1 in 21; 12m. 1 in 18; 12½m. 1 in 16; 16m. 1 in 16; 19½m. 1 in 14; 22½m. 1 in 16; 25m. 1 in 14.

Milestones.—Irregular, and from different points.

Measurements.

Kington,* Clock.
6½   Radnor,* P.O.
15½   9½   Pen-y-bont,* Hotel.
17½   11   1½   Cross Gates.*   R. 66.
(20½   14½   5½   3½   Llandrindod.*   R. 66.)
25½   19½   10   8½   11½   Rhayader.*   (*See below.*)
59½   52½   43½   41½   45   33½   Aberystwyth.*   R. 65 & 49.

Principal Objects of Interest.—Fine scenery. Radnor: Lewis Memorial. 8m., "Water Break its Neck."

Hotels or Inns at places marked*.

65   HAY TO ABERYSTWYTH.   [1065]

Description.—Class I. This road has exceptionally good surface, but is a trifle hilly near Erwood; thereafter fine surface to Builth, after which slightly hilly, but with beautiful scenery to Rhayader. Thence the road, while a trifle loose in the centre, is usually in good condition at the sides. This is the prettiest main route to Aberystwyth.

Gradients.—At 5m. 1 in 19; 10m. 1 in 14; 11 & 11½m. 1 in 19; 13½m. 1 in 15; 14½m. 1 in 13; 17½ & 18½m. 1 in 17; 21½m. 1 in 21; 23½m. 1 in 14; 24m. 1 in 20; 24½m. 1 in 17.

Milestones.—Measured from Market Hall, Builth, and from Rhayader.

Measurements.

Hay,* Market House.
7½   Llyswen,* Griffin Inn.
19   11½   Builth,* Market Hall.
24½   16½   5½   New Bridge on Wye.*
32½   24½   13½   8   Rhayader.*
41½   34½   22½   17½   9½   Llangurig.*   *Thence R. 49 to—*
66½   58½   47½   41½   33½   24½   Aberystwyth.*   R. 49.
(46½   38½   27½   22   14   Llanidloes.*   R. 49.)

Principal Objects of Interest. — Pretty scenery from Llyswen to Rhayader. 9½m., Llangoed Castle. 10m., Llanerch-coedlan Wells. Builth: Wells. Wye: Rapids. Rhayader: Birmingham Reservoirs. Llangurig: Church.

Hotels or Inns at places marked *, and at Three Cocks.

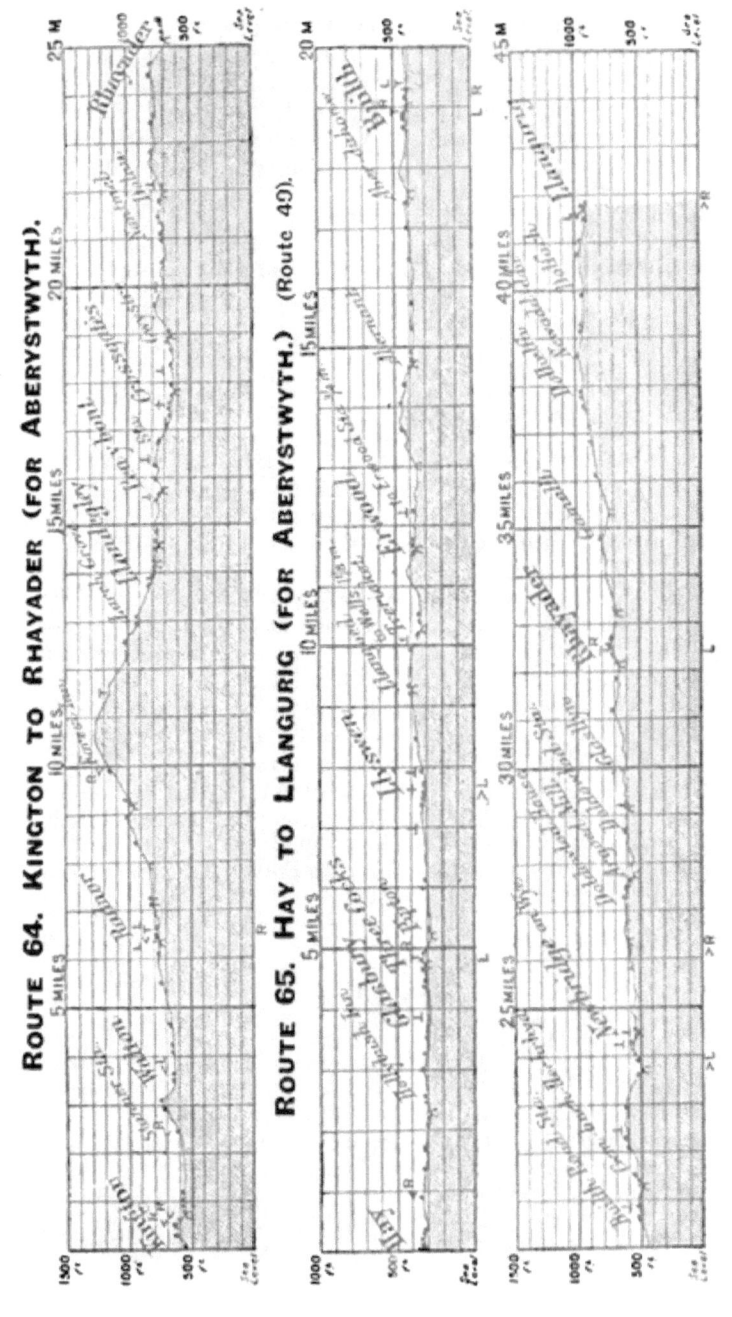

ROUTE 64. KINGTON TO RHAYADER (FOR ABERYSTWYTH).

ROUTE 65. HAY TO LLANGURIG (FOR ABERYSTWYTH.) (Route 40).

66 BUILTH TO NEWTOWN. [1066]

Description.—Class II. A somewhat hilly road, with a dangerous hill to Llandrindod, then very bumpy to Cross Gates; where the surface is rather better. After Llanddewi there is a gradual ascent, and gentle descent to Newtown. For scenery a better road is by Rhayader. For Abbey Cwm-hir (16m.), turn to left at 11¾m. Fair surface.

Gradients.—(† *Dangerous.*) At ¾m. 1 in 14†; 1½m. 1 in 18; 2m. 1 in 13†; 2½m. 1 in 20; 3m. 1 in 15; 5½, 9¼, & 9¾m. 1 in 17; 10½m. 1 in 25; 12m. 1 in 22; 12¼m. 1 in 17; 12¾m. 1 in 17; 33½m. 1 in 22.

Milestones.—Measured from Builth, Market Hall, to Camnant; thereafter from Newtown.

Measurements.

Builth,* Market Hall.						
7¼	Llandrindod,* Bridge Hotel.					
10½	3¼	Cross Gates. R. 64.				
17⅜	9⅞	6⅝	Llanbister,* School.			
21⅜	14⅛	10⅞	4¼	Llanbadarn Fynydd,* New Inn.		
29¼	22	18¾	12⅛	7⅜	Dolfor.*	
34	26¾	23½	16⅝	12⅝	4¾	Newtown.*

Principal Objects of Interest.—Llandrindod: Spa, The Lake. Pretty scenery, at first, in the Ithon Valley.

Hotels or Inns at places marked *.

---

67 BUILTH TO LLANDOVERY. [1067]

Description.—Class III. Of the two routes to Llandovery the longer, but better road, is by Llanwrtyd. This road has fair surface, but is a continuous series of short, very steep hills. Level crossing at 6m., ford at 10m. The other road is of the same character to Llangammarch, but after that it becomes very loose and rough, with dangerous hills, joining the other route at Glan-bran Arms Inn.

Gradients.—At 1m. 1 in 11; 3m. 1 in 13; 4¼m. 1 in 8; 5½m. 1 in 11; 6m. 1 in 12; 10m. 1 in 14; 17¼ & 18½m. 1 in 15; 21½m. 1 in 13.

Milestones.—Measured from Little Hall Toll, Builth, and from Llandovery Market.

Measurements.

Builth,* Market Hall.					
6¼	Garth Inn.*				
8¾	2½	Beulah.			
13⅝	6⅞	4⅜	Llanwrtyd Wells,* Hotel.		
20⅛	13⅞	11⅜	7	Glan-bran Arms Inn.*	
24½	18¼	15¾	11⅝	4⅜	Llandovery,* Market. [*over.*

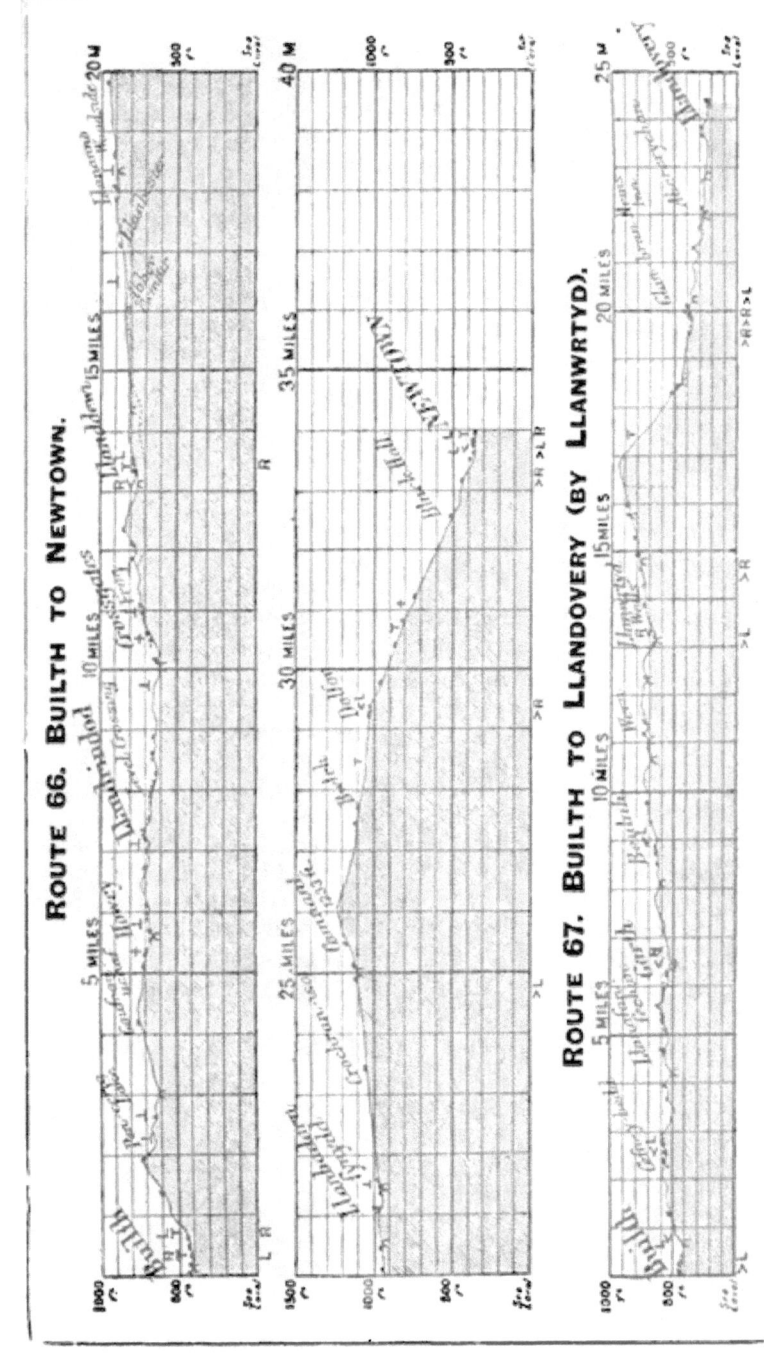

ROUTE 66. BUILTH TO NEWTOWN.

ROUTE 67. BUILTH TO LLANDOVERY (BY LLANWRTYD).

67 BUILTH TO LLANDOVERY (Contd.).

Gradients.—*By Llangammarch.*—First 6m. as previous page. 8m. 1/10; 10m. 1/17; 11m. 1/19; 11¾m. 1/13; 13½m. 1/9; 15¼m. 1/10; 16¾m. 1/10; 17½m. 1/13, &c,

Measurements.

Builth,* Market Hall.
6¾ Garth Inn.*
8 1¼ Llangammarch Wells,* Hotel.
22 15¼ 14 Llandovery,* Market.

Principal Objects of Interest.—Cefn-y-bedd: Prince Llewelyn slain, 1282. Llanwrtyd and Llangammarch, Wells.

68 BRECON TO BUILTH. [1068]

Description.—Class II. The road by Llyswen has fine surface, but has one dangerous hill with rough surface. The direct road (shown dotted) has good surface for nine miles, but then becomes precipitous and rough.

Gradients.—At 1m. 1 in 16; 4½m. 1 in 17; 9¼m, 1 in 17; 10m. 1 in 8 (dangerous); 13¼m. 1 in 14; 14¼ & 14¾m. 1 in 19; 17m. 1 in 15; 17¾m. 1 in 13; 21 & 21½m. 1 in 17. Direct road. mostly 1 in 8.

Milestones.—Measured from Brecon, and from Builth.

Measurements.

Brecon,* Guildhall.
8¼ Bronllys.
10⅞ 2⅝ Llyswen.*
22¼ 14 11⅜ Builth.*

Direct Road.

Brecon.*
9 Upper Chapel.*
16⅜ 7⅜ Builth.*

Principal Objects of Interest.—Pretty scenery near Llyswen. 12½m., Llangoed Castle. 13½m., Llanerch-coedlan Wells. Builth: Wells, Public Hall, Wye Rapids.

69 BRECON TO ABERDARE, &C. [1069]

Description.—Class II. Splendid surface for 10m., then a rough road to Penderyn, after which bumpy, with level-crossings, to Aberdare. This is a better road to Swansea than that through Ystrad-fellte to Glyn-Neath (shown dotted).

Gradients.—At 1m. 1 in 19; 4½m. 1 in 22; 6m. 1 in 25; 10m. 1 in 18; 15½m. 1 in 18.

Milestones.—Measured from Guildhall, Brecon.

Measurements.

Brecon,* Guildhall.
8¾ Storey Arms Inn.*
19½ 10¾ Hirwain.* R. 80.
23⅛ 14⅜ 3⅝ Aberdare.*

Brecon.*
15½ Ystrad-fellte.*
21¼ 5¾ Glyn-Neath.*
39¾ 24¼ 18½ Swansea.*

Principal Objects of Interest.—9½m., Reservoir. (Ystrad-fellte: Waterfalls and Caverns.)

Hotels or Inns at places marked*.

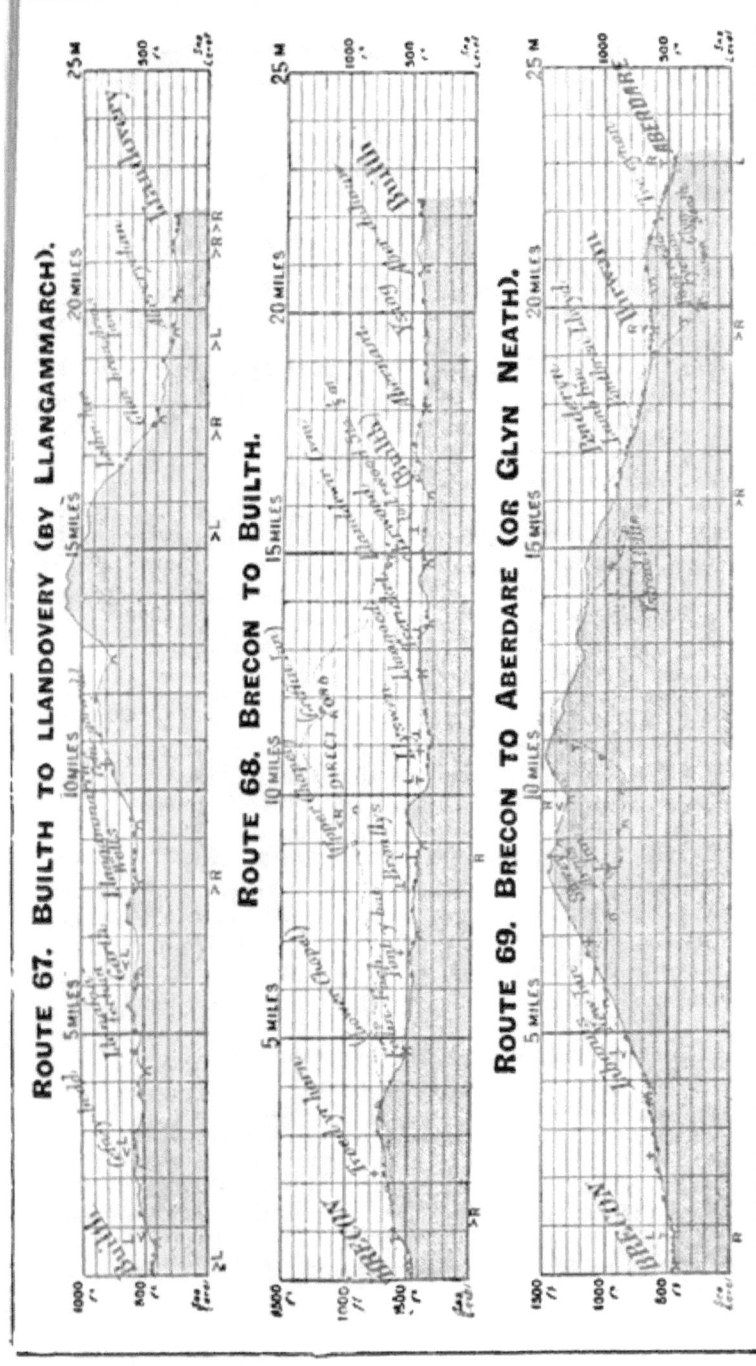

ROUTE 67. BUILTH TO LLANDOVERY (BY LLANGAMMARCH).

ROUTE 68. BRECON TO BUILTH.

ROUTE 69. BRECON TO ABERDARE (OR GLYN NEATH).

70 BRECON TO CARMARTHEN. [1070]

Description.—Class I. The Pembroke Road. Splendid surface and easy gradients the whole way from Brecon to Carmarthen. There is another road (shown dotted) between Llandovery and Llandilo, on the north bank of river Towy, by Llanwrda, equally good, but ¼m. further. The road from Llandilo to Carmarthen by the south bank of the river is good, but not equal to the main road.

Gradients. At 11m. 1 in 23; 11¾m. 1 in 19; 27½m. 1 in 21; 33m. 1 in 19; 33½m. 1 in 21; 40½m. 1 in 23; 42m. 1 in 17.

Llandilo to Carmarthen, *by Llanarthney.* (†*Dangerous.*) At ½m. 1 in 13†; 3¼ and 8½m. 1 in 19; 14½m. 1 in 12†.

Milestones.—Measured from Guildhall, Brecon, to Carmarthen.

Measurements.

Brecon,* Guildhall.
8¼ Devynock,* Usk and Railway Hotel.
11¾ 3¼ Trecastle.*
20¾ 12¼ 9 Llandovery,* Market.
26¾ 17¾ 14¾ 5¾ Llangadock,* Castle Hotel.
33 24¼ 21¼ 12¼ 6¼ Llandilo,* King Street.
41½ 33 29¾ 20¾ 15¼ 8¼ Pontarcothi.*
47¾ 39½ 36 27 21¾ 14¾ 6¼ Carmarthen,* Guildhall.

By Llanwrda.	By Llanarthney
Llandovery.*	Llandilo.*
4¼ Llanwrda.*	6¾ Llanarthney.*
12¼ 8¼ Llandilo.*	14¾ 8 Carmarthen,* Guildhall.

Principal Objects of Interest.—18½m., Obelisk. Llandovery: Castle. Llandilo: Dynevor Castle. Nelson Tower prominent near Pontdulas. Abergwili: Bishop's Palace. CARMARTHEN: Castle, Guildhall, Church, Picton Monument. A pretty road.

71 CARDIFF TO CAERPHILLY, &C. [1071]

Description.—Class II. Good surface, but there is a precipitous hill (rough) to Caerphilly. The road round by Nantgarw, R. 72 and 889, 10½m., is a little easier.

Gradients.—At 5 & 5½m. 1 in 7; 6½m. 1 in 8 (both highly dangerous); 12½m. 1 in 14; 15¾m. 1 in 15.

Milestones.—Measured from Town Hall, Cardiff, and Caerphilly.

Measurements.

Cardiff,* Castle.
7¾ Caerphilly.* R. 889.
12 4½ Ystrad Bridge.* R. 892.
16¼ 8¾ 4¼ Quakers Yard.* R. 72.

Principal Objects of Interest.—Caerphilly: Castle.

Hotels or Inns at places marked*.

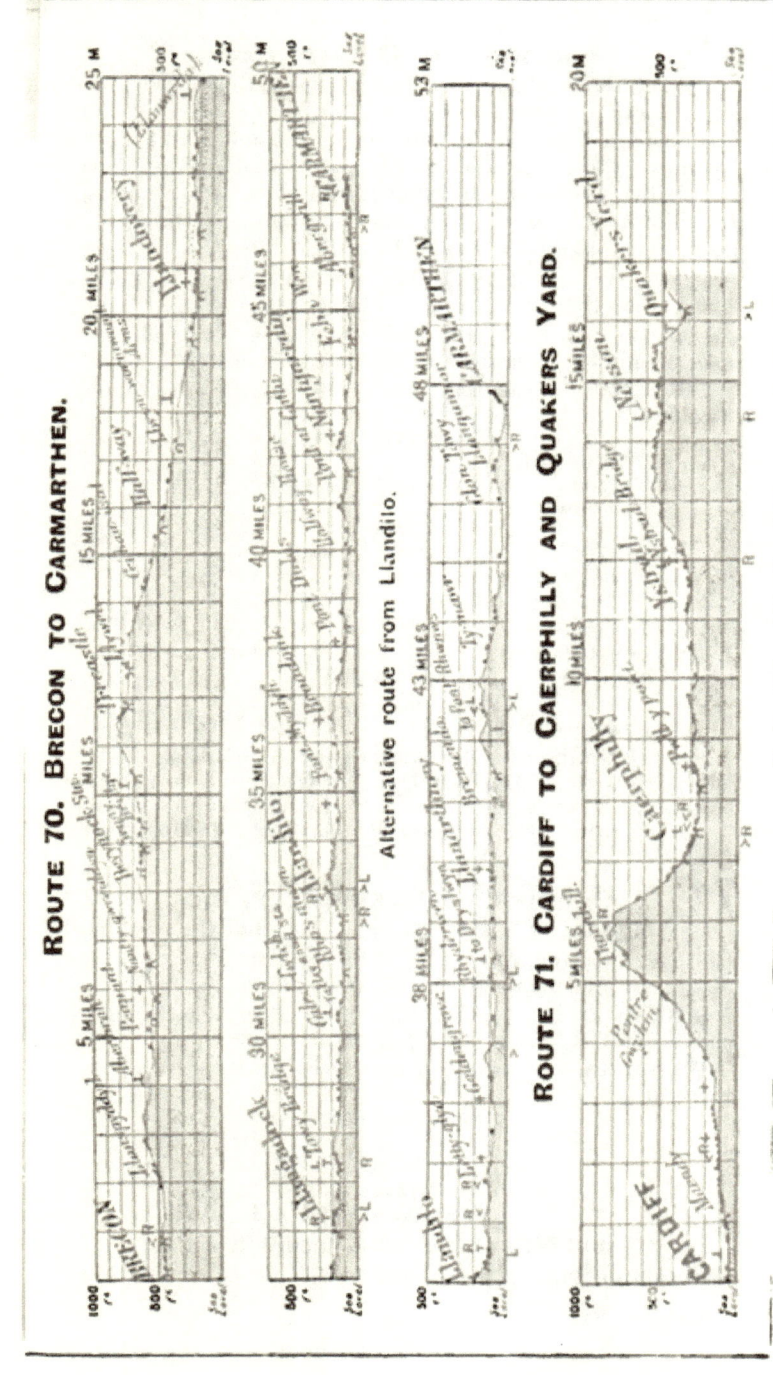

ROUTE 70. BRECON TO CARMARTHEN.

Alternative route from Llandilo.

ROUTE 71. CARDIFF TO CAERPHILLY AND QUAKERS YARD.

72   CARDIFF TO BRECON.   [1072]

Description.—Class I.   Fine surface, but sometimes bumpy to Pontypridd (which lies to west of the road); thence fairly good, through colliery district to Merthyr, with a number of level crossings near that town.   From Merthyr to Brecon the road has good surface, but there are two bad hills before the summit, after which magnificent surface to Brecon.   This road in the reverse direction is not difficult.

Gradients.—(†*Dangerous.*)   At 4m. 1 in 17; 11½m. 1 in 20; 13½m. 1 in 17; 16½m. 1 in 15; 20m. 1 in 19; 25½m. 1 in 15; 30¾m. 1 in 13†; 31¾m. 1 in 9†; 32½m. 1 in 12; 37m. 1 in 25.

Milestones.—Measured from Cardiff Town Hall to Merthyr; thereafter from Brecon Guildhall.

Measurements.

Cardiff,* Castle.

7½	Nantgarw.*	R. 889.			
(12½	4¾	Pontypridd,* Market.)			
14½	7¼	3¾	Travellers Rest Inn. R. 73.		
16¼	9	5¼	1¾	Quakers Yard.*	
23¾	16½	12¾	9¼	7½	Merthyr,* Town Hall.
33¾	26½	22¾	19¾	17¾	10½ Storey Arms Inn.*
42¾	35¾	31¾	28¼	26¾	18¾ 8¾ Brecon,* Guildhall.

Principal Objects of Interest.—5m., Castle Coch. 6m., Taff's Well.   PONTYPRIDD: Old Bridge.   16m., Old Wagon Way Bridge.   Collieries and Iron Works near Merthyr.   MERTHYR: Town Hall, Cyfarthfa Iron Works and Castle.   33m., Reservoirs.   BRECON: Guildhall, Castle, Shire Hall, Barracks.

Hotels or Inns where marked*, and innumerable others.

73   CARDIFF TO ABERDARE, &c.   [1073]

Description.—Class II.   Cardiff to Pontypridd, as R. 72; thence fair surface, but inclined to be bumpy, and with a number of level crossings.

Gradients.—*From Pontypridd.*—At ½m. 1 in 8; (dangerous); 2½m. 1 in 17; 3½m. 1 in 15.

Milestones.—Measured from Cardiff Town Hall.

Measurements.

Cardiff,* Castle.

(12¼	Pontypridd,* Market.)			
14½	3¾	Travellers Rest Inn. R. 72.		
18½	7½	4½	Mountain Ash,* Bridge.	
22¾	11¼	8½	4	Aberdare,* Commercial Street.
26¼	15¼	11¾	7½	3¾ Hirwain,* Globe Inn. R. 80.

Principal Objects of Interest.—Pontypridd: Bridge.   ABERDARE, &c.: Collieries and Iron Works.

Hotels or Inns at places marked*, and at Cap-coch.

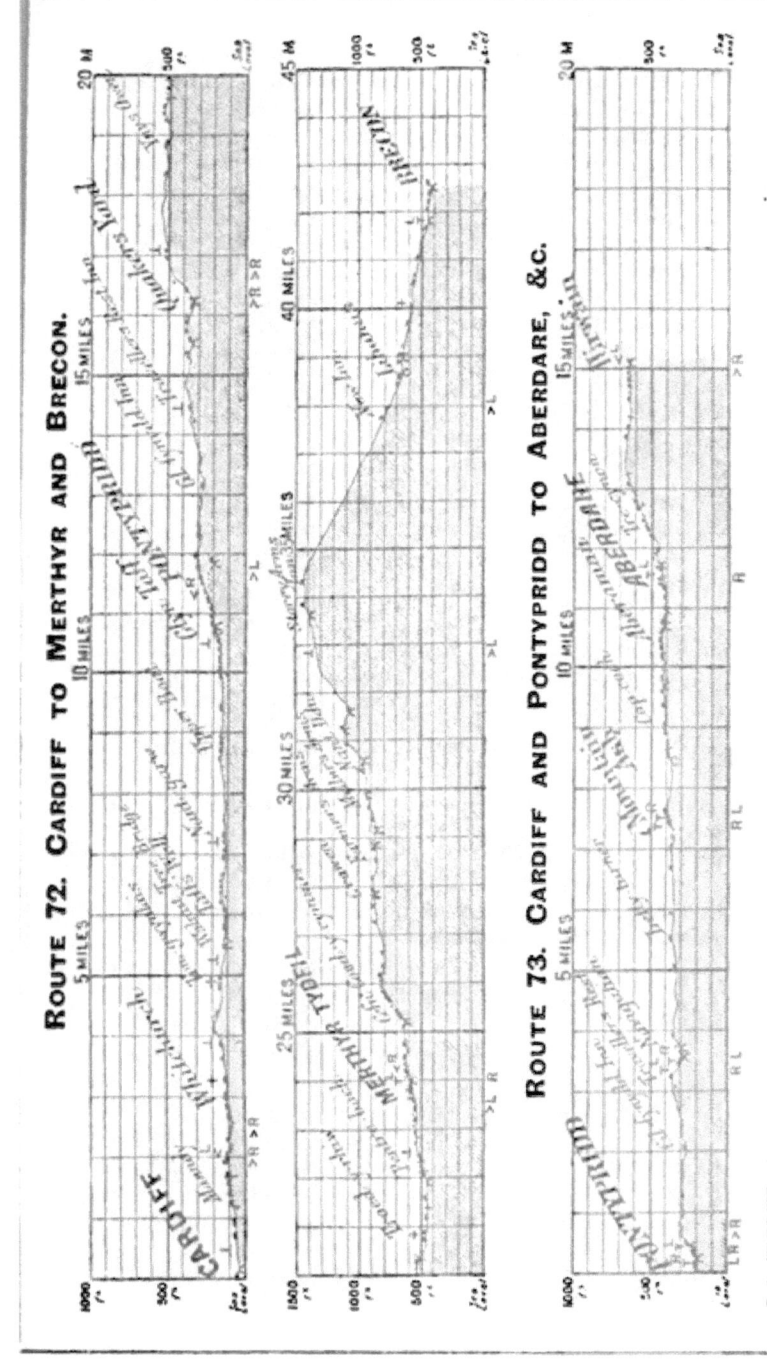

ROUTE 72. CARDIFF TO MERTHYR AND BRECON.

ROUTE 73. CARDIFF AND PONTYPRIDD TO ABERDARE, &C.

74 CARDIFF TO SWANSEA. [1074]

Description.—Class I. Good surface, but a hilly road to Bridgend, with one dangerous hill; thereafter undulating to Briton Ferry, then bumpy, and mostly with car lines.

Gradients.—(†*Dangerous.*) At 5m. 1 in 14†; 8m. 1 in 17; 11½m. 1 in 14; 13m. 1 in 12†; 14 and 16m. 1 in 16; 20m. 1 in 15; 25¾m. 1 in 15; 31½m. 1 in 19; 38¾m. 1 in 16; 40¾m. 1 in 25.

Milestones.—Continuation of those from Newport.

Measurements.

Cardiff,* Castle.
(— Llandaff.*)

12⅜	11⅛	Cowbridge,* Town Hall.							
19⅛	17⅞	6¾	Bridgend,* Town Hall.						
25⅛	23⅞	12¾	6	Pyle, Inn.*					
31¼	30	18⅞	12⅛	6⅛	Aberavan, Bridge.				
34½	33¼	22⅛	15⅜	9⅜	3¼	Briton Ferry.*			
37	35¾	24⅝	17⅞	11⅞	5¾	2½	Neath,* Angel Street.		
42⅛	40⅞	29¾	23	17	10⅞	7⅝	5⅛	Morriston.*	
45¼	44	32⅞	26⅛	20⅛	14	10¾	8¼	3⅛	Swansea.*

Principal Objects of Interest.—(Llandaff: Cathedral.) Cowbridge: South Gate, Castle. BRIDGEND: Castle. Ewenny Priory, Coyty Castle. NEATH: Abbey, Castle. SWANSEA: Castle, Royal Institution, Docks, Mumbles.

Hotels or Inns at places marked *.

75 CARDIFF TO BARRY, &C. [1075]

Description.—Class III. A fair country road, but with steep and dangerous hills of 1 in 14, and 1 in 10. For Penarth (4m.), turn to left at 2⅞m.

Measurements. Cardiff,* Castle.

9	Barry Docks.*		
16½	7½	St. Athan. R. 79.	
21½	12½	5	Cowbridge,* Town Hall.

Principal Objects of Interest.—Penarth and Barry Docks. St. Athan: Orchard Castle.

76 CARDIFF TO LLANTRISANT. [1076]

Description.—Class II. Good surface, but stiff hills.

Gradients.—At 3¼m. 1 in 19; 4m. 1 in 18; 4¾m. 1 in 14; 5½, 7, & 7¾m. 1 in 19; 8½m. 1 in 17; 10½m. 1 in 12 (dangerous).

Measurements.—Cardiff,* Castle.

2	Llandaff,* Black Lion.	
10¾	8¾	Llantrisant.*

Principal Objects of Interest.—Llandaff: Cathedral.

77 LLANTRISANT TO COWBRIDGE, 7½m. [1077]

Description.—Class II. Good surface, but a rather hilly road.

Gradients.—At ¼m. 1/12 (dangerous); 2½, 3¼, & 4m. 1/17.

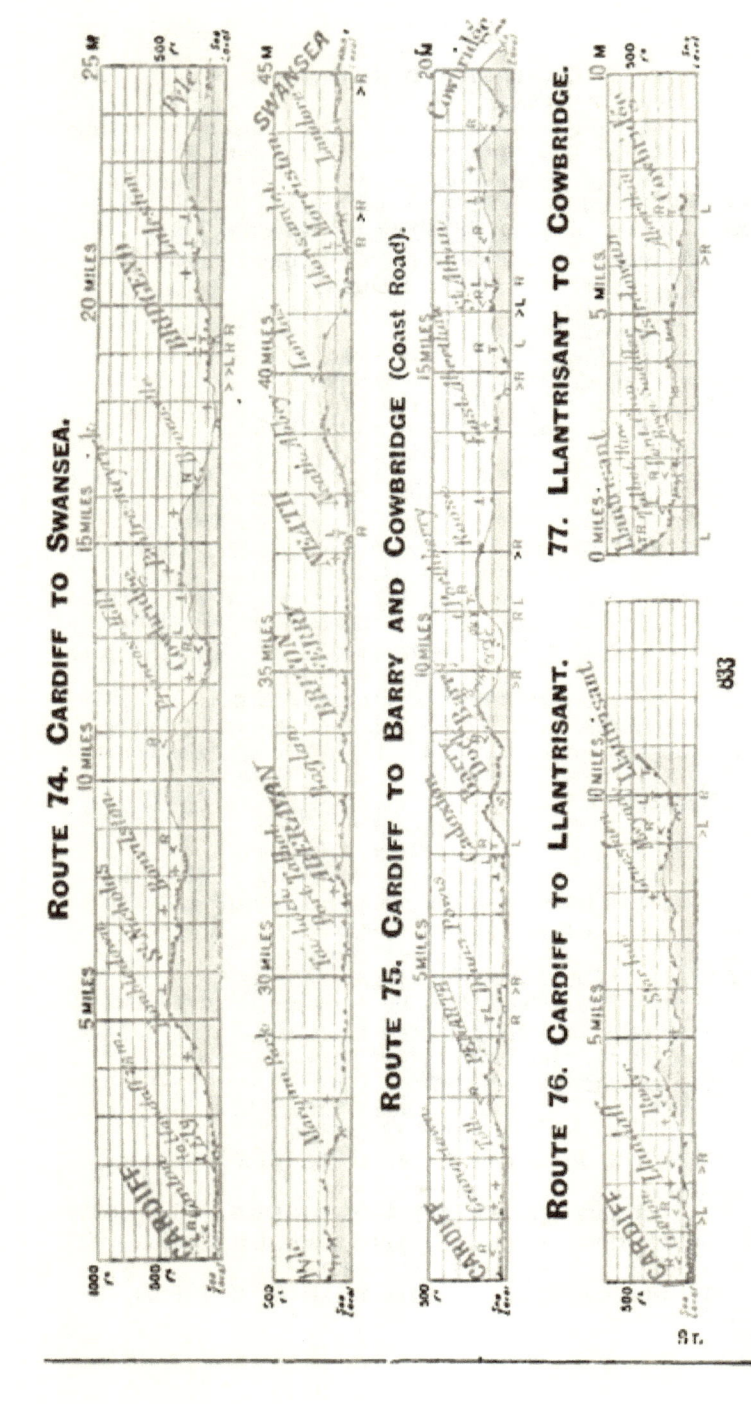

ROUTE 74. CARDIFF TO SWANSEA.

ROUTE 75. CARDIFF TO BARRY AND COWBRIDGE (Coast Road).

ROUTE 76. CARDIFF TO LLANTRISANT.

ROUTE 77. LLANTRISANT TO COWBRIDGE.

633

78 FONTYPRIDD TO BRIDGEND, &c. [1078]

Description.—Class II. A good road, but with dangerous hills. From Bridgend to Porthcawl, only fairly good surface.

Gradients.—(† *Dangerous.*) At 7½m. 1 in 12†; 11m. 1 in 10†; 11⅞m. 1 in 19; 21¼m. 1 in 15; 21¾m. 1 in 18; 22¾m.1 in 14.

Milestones.—Measured from Bridgend.

Measurements.

Pontypridd,* Market.
7¾ Llantrisant.*
18¼ 11 Bridgend,* Town Hall.
24¾ 17½ 6½ Porthcawl,* P.O.

Principal Objects of Interest.—Coychurch: Church. BRIDGEND: Castle, Coyty Castle. Porthcawl: Harbour.

79 MAESTEG TO BRIDGEND, &c. [1079]

Description.—Class III. Indifferent surface. This route merely shows the connections between various places.

Gradients.—At 2½m. 1/11 (dangerous): 16½m. 1/14, &c.

Measurements.

Maesteg.* Church.
9 Bridgend,* Town Hall.
12½ 3½ St. Brides Major. (To Southerndown, 1m.)
20¼ 11¼ 7¼ Llantwit Major,* Inn.
23¼ 14¼ 10¾ 3¼ St. Athan. R. 75.

Principal Objects of Interest.—Southerndown: Dunraven Castle. St. Donats: Castle. Llantwit: Church, Castle, Town Hall, Castle Ditches. St. Athan: Orchard Castle.

Hotels or Inns at places marked *.

80 NEATH TO MERTHYR. [1080]

Description.—Class II. Very good surface for eleven miles, then steep, but with fair surface to Hirwain, after which dangerously steep to Merthyr. The road from Merthyr to Aberdare (shown dotted) is dangerously steep,—1 in 10.

Gradients.—(† *Dangerous.*) At 2½ & 3½m. 1 in 19; 11½m. 1 in 14†; 13¾m. 1 in 19; 17½ & 19m. 1 in 11†; 19¾m. 1 in 19; 21m. 1 in 13†.

Milestones.—Irregular.

Measurements.

Swansea,* *Royal Hotel.*
8¼ Neath,* Angel Street.
18¼ 10¾ Glyn Neath.* R. 69.
23¾ 15½ 4¾ Hirwain,* Globe Inn.
30 22¼ 11½ 6½ Merthyr,* Town Hall.
(27 19¼ 8½ 3¾ 7 Aberdare,* Commercial Place.)

Principal Objects of Interest.—Glyn Neath: Falls and Caverns. Merthyr: Town Hall, Iron Works.

Hotels or Inns at places marked*, and numerous others.

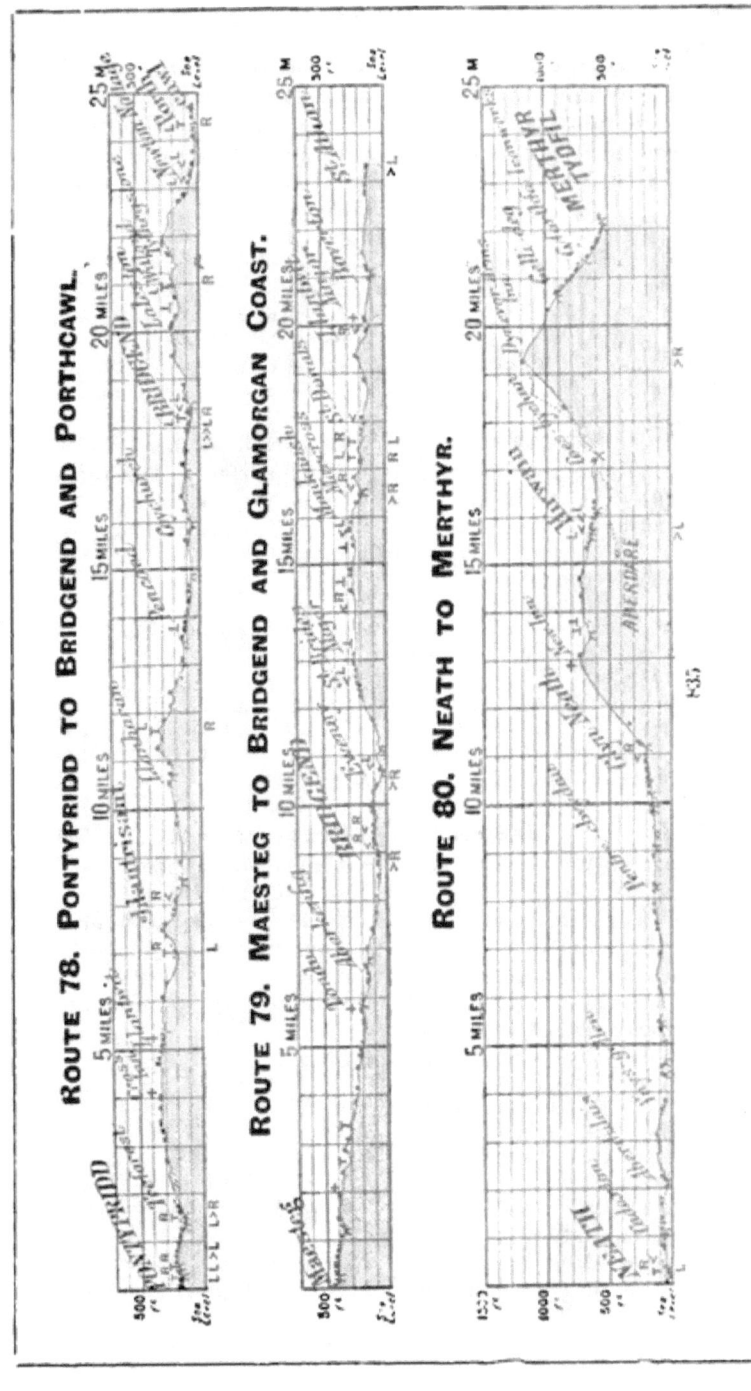

ROUTE 78. PONTYPRIDD TO BRIDGEND AND PORTHCAWL.

ROUTE 79. MAESTEG TO BRIDGEND AND GLAMORGAN COAST.

ROUTE 80. NEATH TO MERTHYR.

81 SWANSEA TO LLANDILO. [1081]

Description.—Class II. Bumpy to Morriston, then good surface, but stiff hills, and numerous level crossings.

Gradients.—At 8½m. 1 in 11 (dangerous); 10m. 1 in 16; 14m. 1 in 17; 21½m. 1 in 13.

Milestones.—Measured from Neath, and Swansea.*

Measurements.—Swansea,* Royal Hotel. (*Neath.*)

8¾			Pontardawe,* Bridge.	5½
18¾	10¼		Cross Inn.*	16
26½	18½	7¾	Llandilo.*	23¾

Principal Objects of Interest.—Collieries & Iron Works. Llandilo: Dynevor Castle.

82 SWANSEA TO BRECON. [1082]

Description.—Class III. Route 81 to Pontardawe; thence a poor road, joining Route 70 at Devynock Sta.

Gradients.—Mostly 1 in 15, or 1 in 11.

Measurements.

Swansea,* Royal Hotel.

8¾				Pontardawe.*
12¾	4½			Ystalfera.*
31½	23¼	18¾		Devynock Station.* R. 70.
40¾	31¾	27¼	8¾	Brecon,* Guildhall.

Principal Objects of Interest.—20¼m., Craig-y-nos Cas.

83 SWANSEA TO GOWER. [1083]

Description.—Class III. A good, but steep country road. The road by Reynoldston (shown dotted) is even more hilly.

Gradients.—(† *Dangerous.*) At 2m. 1 in 12†; 3¾m. 1 in 10†; 4¾m. 1 in 13†; 9m. 1 in 11†; 17½m. 1 in 11†, &c.

Milestones.—Measured from Swansea Castle.

Measurements.

Swansea,* Royal Hotel.

8¼			Gower Inn.*
18¾	10½	4½	Rhossili.

Swansea.*

12			Reynoldston,* Inn.
17¾	5¾	4½	Rhossili.

Principal Objects of Interest.—Fine coast scenery. 12m., Penrice Castle. 14m., Scurlage Castle. Rhossili: Worms Head.

84 SWANSEA TO CARMARTHEN. [1084]

Description.—See next page.

Gradients.—(† *Dangerous.*) At 1¾m. 1/17; 2¾m. 1/20; 4m. 1/16; 5¼m. 1/11†; 6¾m. 1/19; 8m. 1/15; 9¼m. 1/15; 11½ & 13½m. 1/19; 15¾m. 1/14; 19m. 1/20; 20m. 1/13; 20¾m. 1/13; 23¾m. 1/10†; 24¾m. 1/12†; 25½m. 1/17; 26½m. 1/9†.

Measurements (Direct road).

Neath. Swansea,* Royal Hotel.

8¾	9			Pontardulais.*
14½	15¼	6¼		Cross Hands.* R. 86.
26½	26¾	17¾	11½	Carmarthen,* Guildhall.

[over.

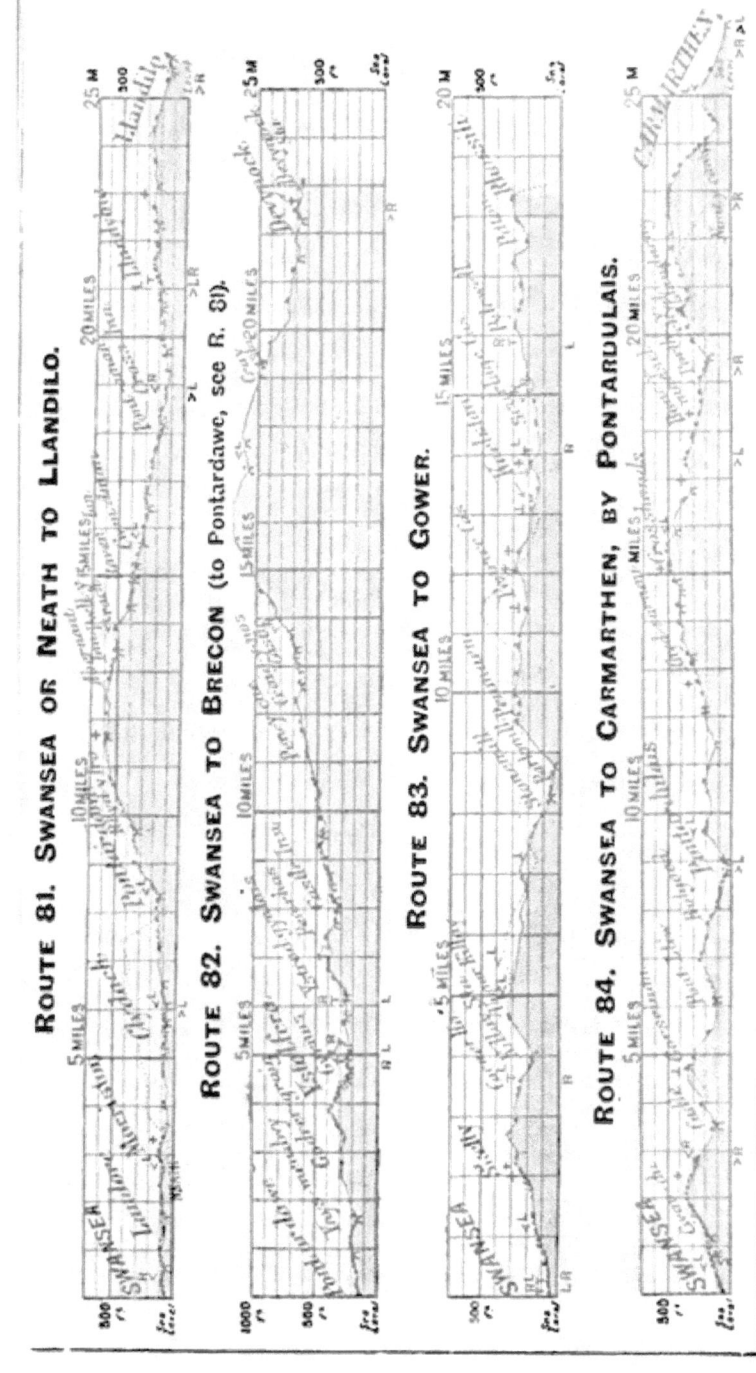

ROUTE 81. SWANSEA OR NEATH TO LLANDILO.

ROUTE 82. SWANSEA TO BRECON (to Pontardawe, see R. 81).

ROUTE 83. SWANSEA TO GOWER.

ROUTE 84. SWANSEA TO CARMARTHEN, BY PONTARDULAIS.

84 SWANSEA TO CARMARTHEN (Contd.). [1084]

Description.—Class I. The direct road by Pontardulais, while it has splendid surface, is much more hilly than the road by Llanelly; which, though continuously undulating, and with several stiff hills, has splendid surface throughout. The more direct roads between Llanelly and Carmarthen, and Llanelly and Kidwelly, are very steep.

Gradients.—(†*Dangerous.*) At 2¾m. 1 in 20; 3m. 1 in 17; 4m. 1 in 19; 5m. 1 in 16; 5¾m. 1 in 20; 6½m. 1 in 18; 7 & 21½m. 1 in 17; 23¼m. 1 in 14; 24m. 1 in 10†; 26m. 1 in 18; 27¼m. 1 in 22; 30¼m. 1 in 9†.

Milestones.—Measured from Swansea, Castle; and from Carmarthen, Bridge.

Measurements (By Llanelly).

Swansea,* Royal Hotel.
  7½   Loughor.*
 11¼   4¼   Llanelly.*
 15¼   8¾   4¼   Burry Port,* Station.
 20¼   13¾   9¼   5¼   Kidwelly.*   R. 92.
 30¼   23¾   19   14½   9½   Carmarthen,* Guildhall.

Principal Objects of Interest.—LLANELLY: Town Hall, Copper Works. Kidwelly: Church, Castle. CARMARTHEN: Guildhall, Castle, Parade, Church, Picton Monument. An uninteresting road, although often close to the sea.

Hotels or Inns at places marked *, and at Pembrey, &c.

---

85   SWANSEA TO MUMBLES, 5m.   [1085]

Description.—Class I. Fine surface, but tram rails at side.

Principal Objects of Interest.—Mumbles: Oystermouth Castle, &c.

Hotels or Inns at Mumbles, and at Langlands Bay, &c.

---

86   LLANELLY TO LLANDILO.   [1086]

Description.—Class II. The road is steep, but has good surface to Cross Hands, thence better surface, and easier hills. The road by Pontardulais is not so good.

Gradients—(†*Dangerous.*) At 1½m. 1 in 10†; 4m. 1 in 14; 5¼m. 1 in 10†; 8¾m. 1 in 11†; 9½m. 1 in 19; 12½m. 1 in 14; 16m. 1 in 22; 17½m. 1 in 13†.

Milestones.—Measured from Llandilo.

Measurements.

Llanelly.*
 9¼   Cross Hands.*   R. 84.
 17½   8¾   Llandilo.*

Principal Objects of Interest.—Good scenery at 2m., and at 15m. Llandilo: Dynevor Castle.

Hotels or Inns at places marked *.

Routes 84 & 85. Swansea to Carmarthen, & Swansea to Mumbles.

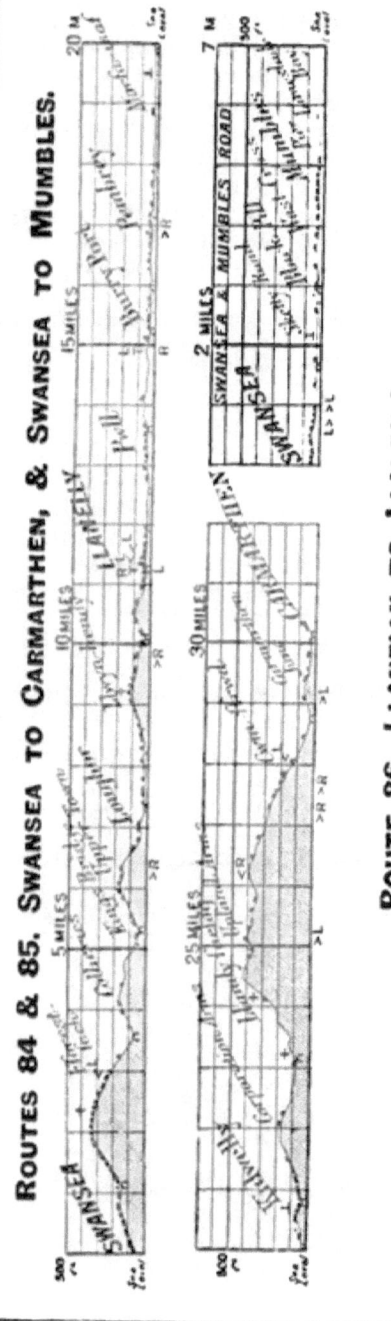

Route 86. Llanelly to Llandilo.

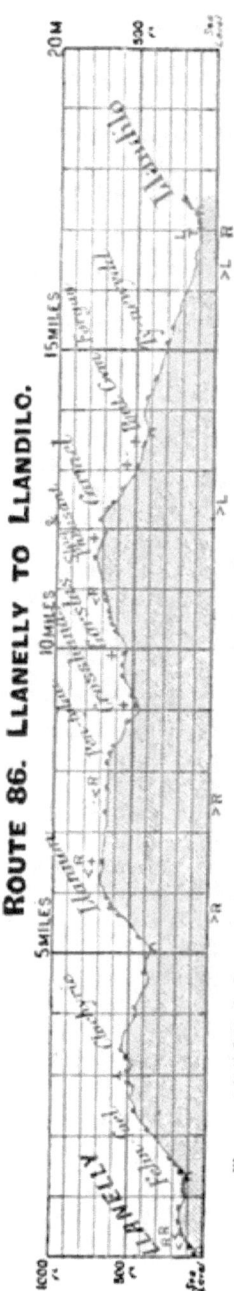

Signs: < Road Fork, forward journey, > ditto reverse, + Cross Roads, ⊥ Road Junction, ∩ Bridge, ⊤ indicates a sharp turn. The directions R (right) and L (left) for the forward journey are above the Road Line, those of the reverse, below

839

87   NEWCASTLE TO LAMPETER.   [1087]

Description.—Class II. Fine surface to Llandyssil, then very steep and dangerous to Route 89, after which splendid surface, but a hilly road. This route is only a connecting piece of road between the last 14m. of Route 88 and the last 9½m. of 89; and is shown at end of Route 88.

Gradients.—*From Farmers Arms.*—At 4½m.1 in 10 (very dangerous); 7m. 1 in 11 : 7½m. 1 in 14.

Measurements.

Cardigan,* Town Hall.
10½   Newcastle Emlyn,* Clock
(18½   8½   Llandyssil.*)
27½   17½   9½   Llan-y-byther.*
32½   22½   20½   5½   Lampeter,* Fountain.

88   CARMARTHEN TO CARDIGAN.   [1088]

Description.—Class I. Magnificent surface, but two dangerous hills; the road is one of the best in the district. For Llandyssil* 17½m. (R. 58) turn to right at 13½m.

Gradients.—(†*Dangerous.*) At 10m.1 in 14†; 12½m.1 in 19; 15½m. 1 in 11†; 22½m. 1 in 16; 27m. 1 in 11†; 28½m. 1 in 14.

Milestones.—Measured from Carmarthen, Bridge.

Measurements.

Carmarthen,* Guildhall.
7½   Conwil Elvet.*
(20   12½   Newcastle Emlyn,* Clock.
22½   15½   3½   Cenarth.*
30½   22½   10½   7½   Cardigan,* Town Hall.

Principal Objects of Interest.—A very pretty route to Conwyl, and picturesque at Cenarth. Cardigan : Cas., Ch.

Hotels or Inns at places marked*, and numerous others.

89   CARMARTHEN TO LAMPETER.   [1089]

Description. — Class II. Fine surface for 8m., then steep and dangerous hills for 5m., whence splendid surface, but an undulating road to Lampeter.

Gradients.—(†*Dangerous.*) At 4¾m.1 in 18; 7m.1 in 15; 9m.1 in 11†; 11m.1 in 10†; 12m.1 in 9†; 12¾m.1 in 11†; 13 & 13½m. 1 in 10†; 16¾m. 1 in 12†.

Milestones.—Measured from Carmarthen Bri.,—irregular.

Measurements.

Carmarthen,* Guildhall.
8½   Allt Wallis.*   R. 58.
18½   9½   Llan-y-byther.*
23½   14½   5½   Lampeter,* Fountain.

Principal Objects of Interest.—Lampeter: College.

Hotels or Inns at places marked *.

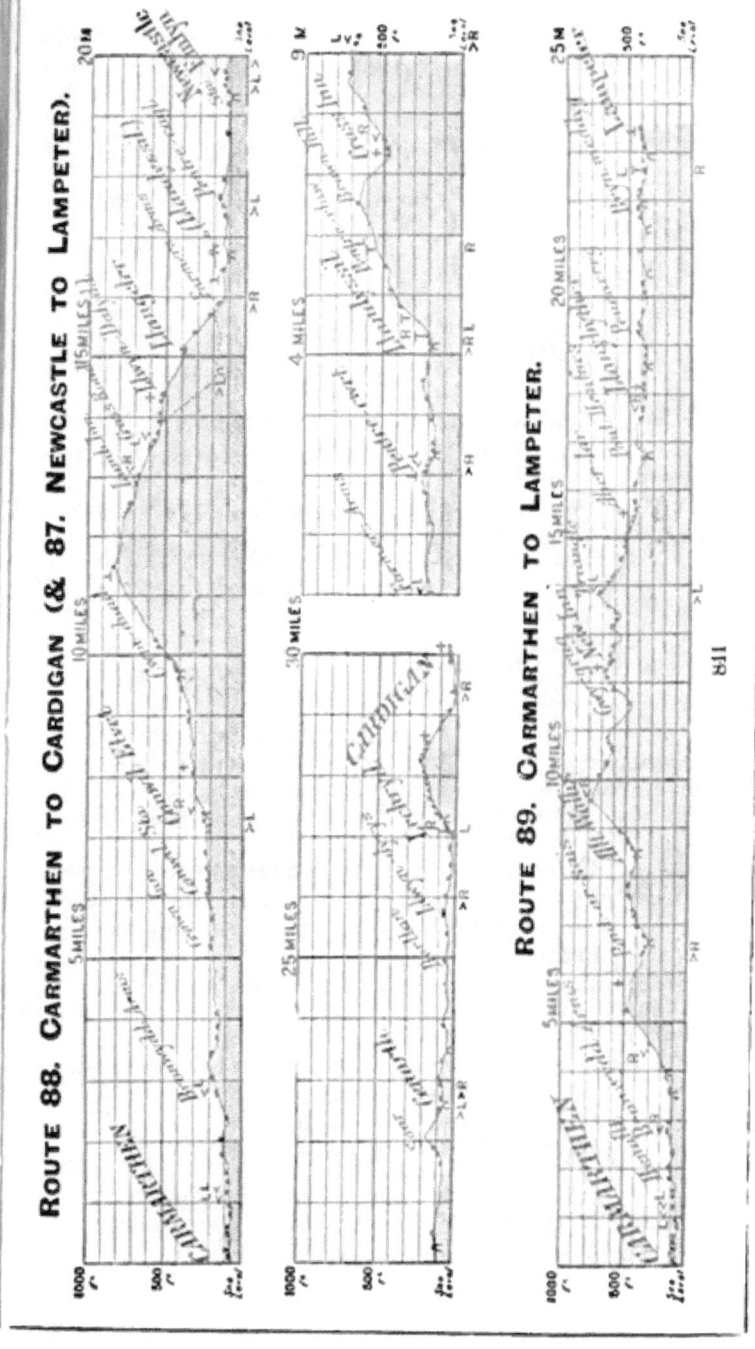

ROUTE 88. CARMARTHEN TO CARDIGAN (& 87. NEWCASTLE TO LAMPETER).

ROUTE 89. CARMARTHEN TO LAMPETER.

841

90 CARMARTHEN TO PEMBROKE. [1090]

Description.—Class I. This road is a little rough at first, but after three miles the surface improves, and continues of the best quality to Pembroke. The long ascent to Red Roses is fairly easy. For Tenby (26m.), turn to left at 21½m., R. 93. To Pembroke, turn to left at 29m.

Gradients.—At ¾m. 1 in 17; 15 & 16m. 1 in 20; 18½m. 1 in 17; 21m. 1 in 17.

Milestones.—From Brecon, and from Pembroke Dock.

Measurements.

Carmarthen,* Guildhall.

8¾	St. Clears.*			
14¾	6	Red Roses Inn.* R. 91.		
21½	12⅞	6½	Kilgetty Station.*	
32½	23¾	17¾	11⅛	Pembroke Dock.*
(31½	22¾	16½	10½	Pembroke,* Clock.)

Principal Objects of Interest.—½m., Picton Monument. 27½m., Carew Castle, and Cross. PEMBROKE DOCK: Dockyard, Milford Haven. PEMBROKE: Cas., Lamphey Palace.

Hotels or Inns at places marked*.

91 CARMARTHEN TO MILFORD. [1091]

Description.—Class II. To Red Roses, as Route 90; thence a very hilly road, but with fine surface.

Gradients.—(† *Dangerous.*) At 18½m. 1 in 12; 19¾m. 1 in 16; 20m. 1 in 13; 22½m. 1 in 9†; 23½m. 1 in 12; 24m. 1 in 13; 26m. 1 in 17; 28⅞m. 1 in 13†; 31m. 1 in 16; 32½m. 1 in 12†; 32¾m. 1 in 10†; 34¾m. 1 in 15; 37½m. 1 in 14; 38½m. 1 in 16; 39m. 1 in 17.

Milestones.—Measured from Haverfordwest, Boundary.

Measurements.

Carmarthen.* Guildhall.

14¾	Red Roses Inn.*		
21⅞	7	Narberth,* Market.	
31¼	17	10½	Haverfordwest,* Castle Hotel.
39½	24½	17¾	7½ Milford.*

Principal Objects of Interest.—Narberth: Cas. Haverfordwest: Castle, Priory, Church. Milford: Docks.

92 CARMARTHEN TO LAUGHARNE. [1092]

Description.—Class II. A fine road to Llanstephan, then dangerous hills to Laugharne (Ferry, ½m.); thereafter good surface, but dangerous hills. Kidwelly to Llanstephan, by Ferryside (Ferry, 1m.), good surface, but dangerous hills.

Gradients.—(† *Dangerous.*) At ¾m. 1 in 17; 5½m. 1 in 16; 8½ & 10¼m. 1 in 8†; 12m. 1 in 10†; 13m. 1 in 11†; 14½m. 1 in 12†.

Measurements.

Carmarthen,* Guildhall.			Kidwelly.* R. 84.	
8¼	Llanstephan.*		5 Ferryside.*	
11½	3¾	Laugharne.*	6 1 Llanstephan.*	
15¾	7½	4 St. Clears.* R. 90.	9¾ 4½ 3½ Laugharne.*	

[over.

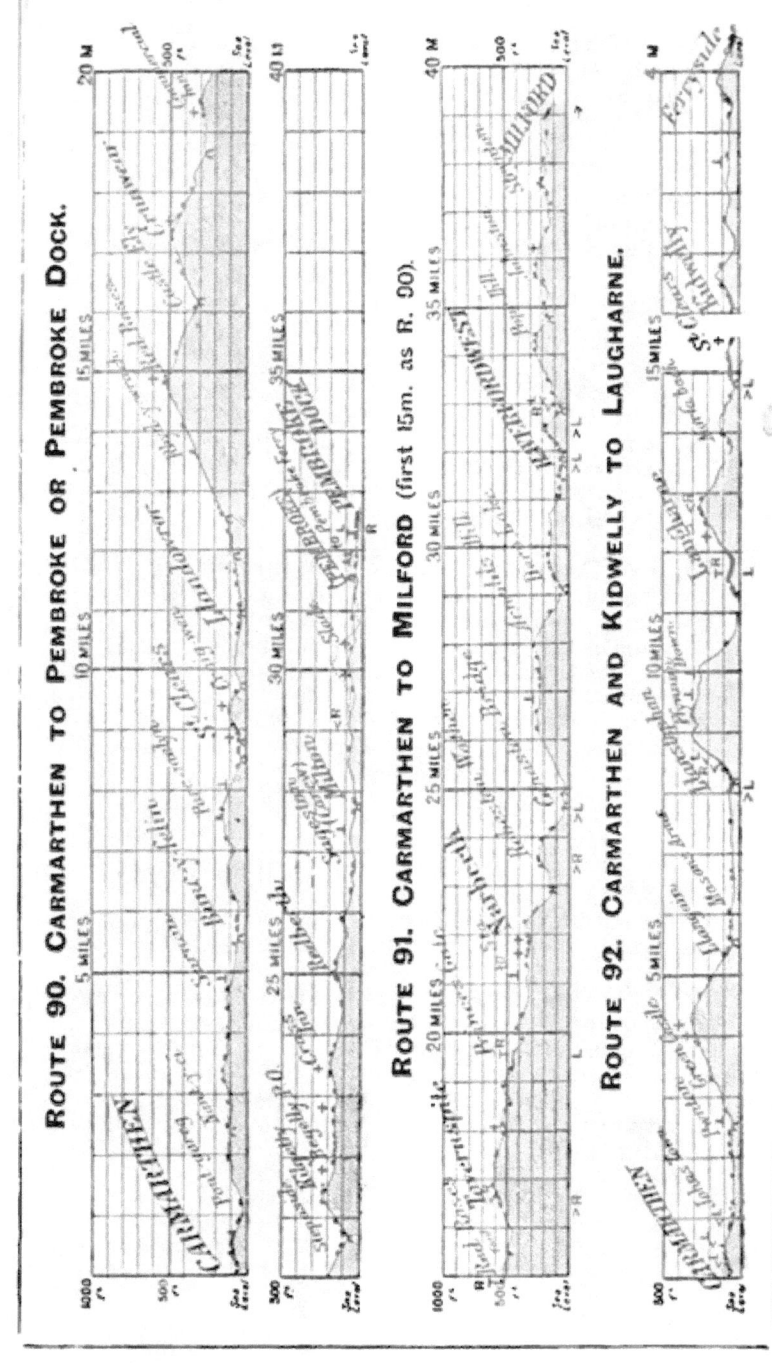

ROUTE 90. CARMARTHEN TO PEMBROKE OR PEMBROKE DOCK.

ROUTE 91. CARMARTHEN TO MILFORD (first 15m. as R. 90).

ROUTE 92. CARMARTHEN AND KIDWELLY TO LAUGHARNE.

Route 92—Continued.

Principal Objects of Interest.—Llanstephan: Castle ruins.

Hotels or Inns at places marked*.

93 TENBY TO CARDIGAN. [1093]

Description.—Class II. Good surface but very hilly; dangerous hill at Begelly, &c. The direct road to Narberth is dangerously steep; better follow the road by Princes Gate as shown on diagram—it is much easier.

Gradients.—(†*Dangerous.*) At ½m. 1 in 16; 2¼m. 1 in 15; 3¾m. 1 in 11; 5½m. 1 in 10†; 6¾m. 1 in 15; 7¾m. 1 in 12; 8¼m. 1 in 13; 10¼m. 1 in 13; 10½m. 1 in 15; 14m. 1 in 12†; 14¾m. 1 in 14; 15¼m. 1 in 16; 26¾m. 1 in 16; 27m. 1 in 12†; 28m. 1 in 19; 30¼m. 1 in 11†; 31½m. 1 in 13†; 34¼m. 1 in 11†, &c.

Milestones.—Measured from Narberth.

Measurements.

Tenby,* Church.
12½ Narberth,* Market.
26¼ 13¾ Crymmych Arms Inn.*
34⅝ 22 8⅜ Cardigan,* Town Hall.

Principal Objects of Interest.—Uninteresting road. Narberth: Church. Cardigan: Castle, Church.

Hotels or Inns at places marked*, and at Templeton, Clynderwen, Llandissilo, Bromwydd Arms, &c.

94 CARDIGAN TO FISHGUARD. [1094]

Description.—Class III. & II. A bumpy road to Newport, then fine surface. Most of the hills in this route are dangerous. There is a more direct road to Newport, by Nevern, but this route is usually preferred.

Gradients.—(†*Dangerous.*) At ½m. 1 in 11†; 4¼m. 1 in 17; 5¾m. 1 in 11†; 8¼m. 1 in 8†; 9m. 1 in 12†; 9¼m. 1 in 11†; 10m. 1 in 15; 10½m. 1 in 13†; 13m. 1 in 12†; 13¼m. 1 in 11†; 13¾m. 1 in 10†; 16¼m. 1 in 16; 17m. 1 in 14; 18¼ & 18½m. 1 in 7†.

Milestones.—Measured from Fishguard, Lower Town.

Measurements.

Cardigan,* Town Hall.
6 Eglwswrw.*
11⅜ 5⅜ Newport.*
18¾ 12¾ 6⅜ Fishguard,* Square.

Principal Objects of Interest.—Newport: Castle. Fishguard: Goodwick Sands, Careg-gwastad. Beautiful scenery at Fishguard, and at Velindre.

Hotels or Inns at places marked*.

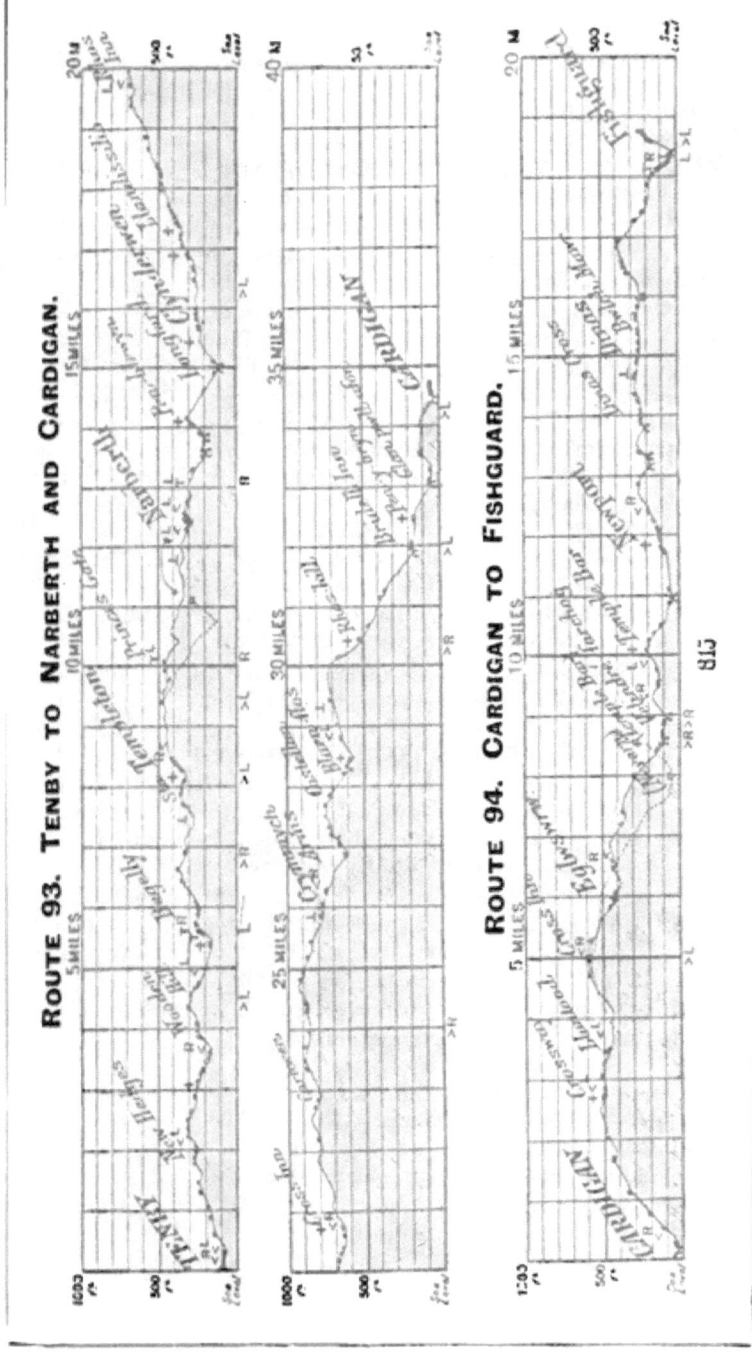

ROUTE 93. TENBY TO NARBERTH AND CARDIGAN.

ROUTE 94. CARDIGAN TO FISHGUARD.

95 HAVERFORDWEST TO FISHGUARD. [1095]

Description.—Class II. Splendid surface throughout, but there is a very dangerous turn at Wolf's Castle.

Gradients.—(† *Dangerous.*) At ¼m. 1 in 17; 3 & 3¼m. 1 in 14; 5¾m. 1 in 19; 7¼m. 1 in 11 †; 10½m. 1 in 12†; 11¼m. 1 in 9†; 11¾m. 1 in 14; 12½m. 1 in 21; 15½m. 1 in 8†.

Milestones.—Measured from Haverfordwest, Boundary.

Measurements.—Haverfordwest,* Castle Hotel.
7 Ford,* Inn.
15 8 Fishguard,* Square.

Principal Objects of Interest.—Fine scenery at 5½m. Fishguard: Goodwick Sands, Careg-gwastad.

96 HAVERFORDWEST TO ST. DAVIDS. [1096]

Description.—Class III. Very good surface, but all dangerous hills. Easier by Letterston (R. 95), 23½m.

Gradients.—(† *Dangerous.*) At ¼m. 1/12†; 1½ & 2½m. 1/13†; 4¾m. 1/11†; 8¼m. 1/8†; 9m. 1/9†; 12½m. 1/10†; 13¾m. 1/11†, &c.

Measurements.—Haverfordwest,* Castle Hotel.
12¼ Solva,* Cambrian Hotel.
15⅞ 3⅝ St. Davids,* Cross.

Principal Objects of Interest.—Reeston Castle. 6½m., Roche Castle. 10½m., Pointz Castle. St. Davids: Cathedral, College, Palace, &c. A pretty road near Solva.

97 HAVERFORDWEST TO PEMBROKE (no ferry.)

Description.—Class II. Fine surface, but dangerous hills.

Gradients.—(† *Dangerous.*) At 1m. 1 in 16; 3½m. 1 in 13; 6m. 1 in 17; 8m. 1 in 10†; 8½m. 1 in 13; 12¼m. 1 in 19; 12¾m. 1 in 11 †; 13½m. 1 in 14; 14m. 1 in 12†; 15m. 1 in 14; 18m. 1 in 10†; 19m. 1 in 14.

Milestones.—Measured from Haverfordwest, Boundary.

Measurements.—Haverfordwest,* Castle Hotel.
7¼ Canaston Bridge.
15¼ 8 Carew,* Castle Inn.
19¾ 12½ 4½ Pembroke,* Town Hall.
20¾ 13½ 5½ Pembroke,* Dock.

Principal Objects of Interest.—Carew Castle: Cross.

98 ST. DAVIDS TO FISHGUARD. [1098]

Description.—Class III. A good, but uninteresting road.

Gradients.—At 12¼m. 1 in 16.

Measurements.—St. Davids,* Cross.
5⅞ Croes Goch Inn.*
15⅝ 9¾ Fishguard,* Square.

Principal Objects of Interest.—The coast scenery is to the west of road.

Hotels or Inns at places marked*.

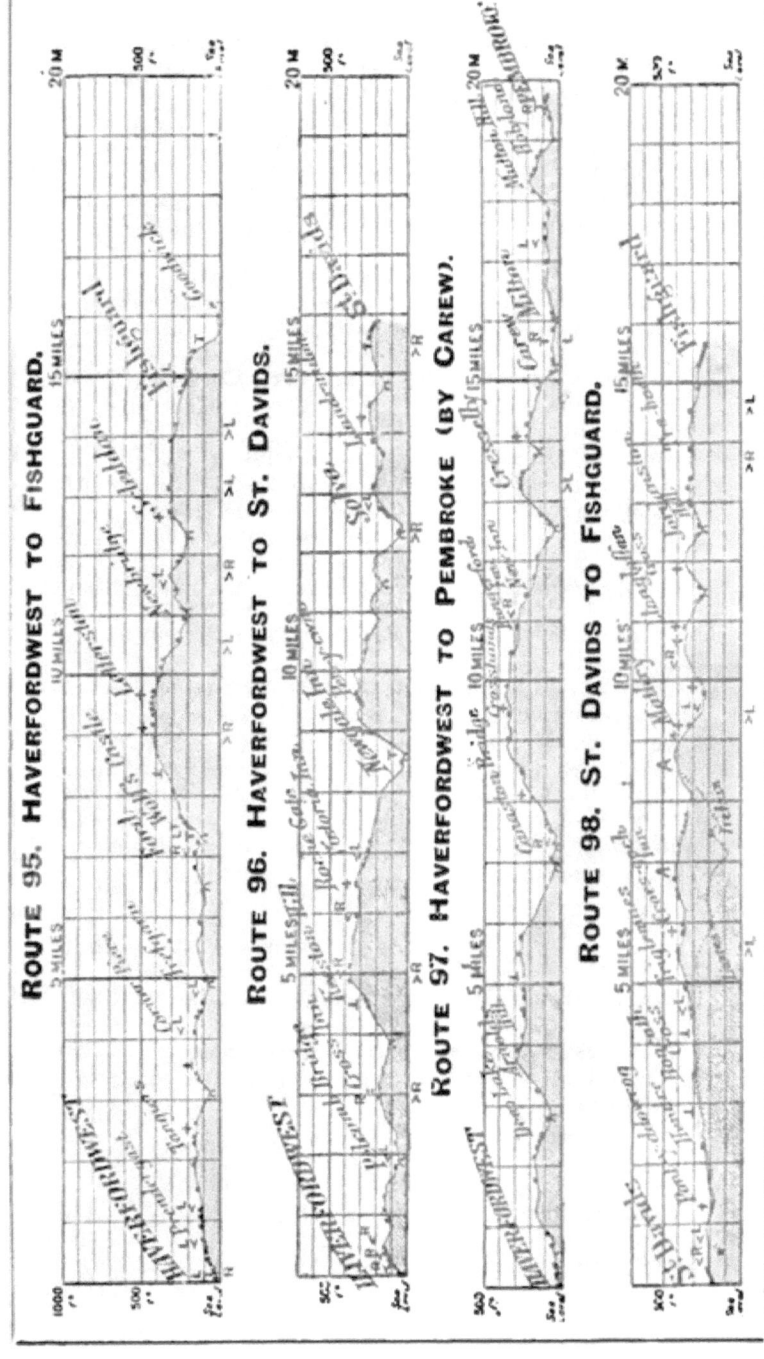

ROUTE 95. HAVERFORDWEST TO FISHGUARD.

ROUTE 96. HAVERFORDWEST TO ST. DAVIDS.

ROUTE 97. HAVERFORDWEST TO PEMBROKE (BY CAREW).

ROUTE 98. ST. DAVIDS TO FISHGUARD.

99 HAVERFORDWEST TO PEMBROKE. [1099]

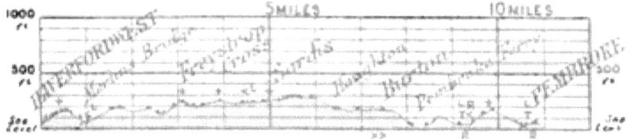

Description.—Class II. Fine surface, but steep hills to Pembroke Ferry (Ferry ½m.), thence very steep to Pembroke. For New Milford turn R. at 4½m.,—an indifferent road.

Gradients.—(† *Dangerous*.) At ½m. 1 in 12†; ¾m. 1 in 10†; 1¼ & 2m. 1 in 15; 2½m. 1 in 18; 3m. 1 in 13; 8m. 1 in 12†; 8½m. 1 in 8†; 9m. 1 in 9†; 9½m. 1 in 11†; 10m. 1 in 12†.

Milestones.—Measured from Merlins Bridge.

Measurements.

	Haverfordwest.
Haverfordwest.	5½ Rosemarket.
8½ Pembroke Ferry.	8 2¾ New Milford.
10¾ 2 Pembroke,* Town Hall.	9½ 3½ 1½ Pembroke Dock.*

100 PEMBROKE TO TENBY. [1100]

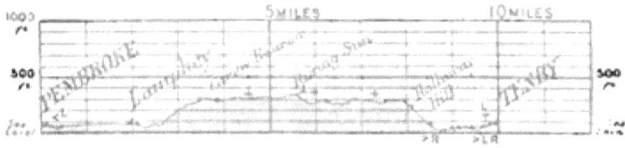

Gradients.—(† *Dangerous*.) At 3m. 1 in 12†; 5¾m. 1 in 10†; 8m. 1 in 12†.

Description.—Class II. The direct road to Tenby, by the "Ridgeway", has good surface, but dangerous hills.

The more popular route by Lydstep (shown below), although it has good surface, is narrow and rather intricate, and should not be chosen in the evening.

Gradients.—At 7½m. 1 in 19; 8½m. 1 in 14; 10m. 1 in 15.

Measurements.

Pembroke,* Town Hall.		Pembroke,* Town Hall.	
5¾ Rising Sun.		5 Jamestown.	
10 4¼ Tenby,* Church.		11½ 6½ Tenby,* Church.	

Principal Objects of Interest.—Lamphey: Bishops Palace. Lydstep: Caverns, &c. Penally: Hoyles Mouth. Tenby: Castle, St. Catherines Rock, &c.

INDEX.

1

Printed and Bound by Gall and Inglis, Edinburgh.

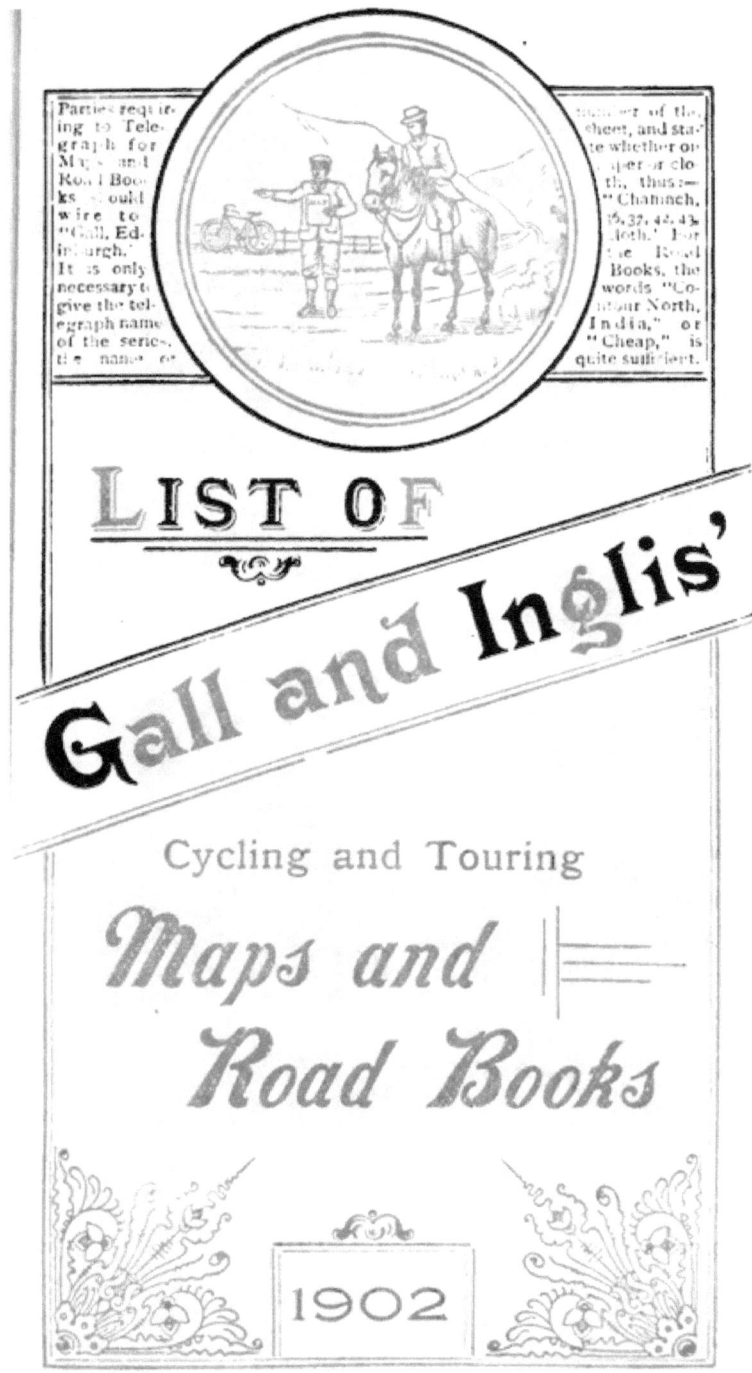

Parties requiring to Telegraph for Maps and Road Books should wire to "Gall, Edinburgh." It is only necessary to give the telegraph name of the series.

number of the sheet, and state whether paper or cloth, thus:— "Channoch, 36, 37, 42, 43, cloth." For the Road Books, the words "Contour North, India," or "Cheap," is quite sufficient.

LIST OF

Gall and Inglis'

Cycling and Touring

Maps and
Road Books

1902

GALL & INGLIS, 25 Paternoster Sq., London, E.C.; & 20 Bernard Ter., Edinburgh.
TELEGRAMS: "GALL, EDINBURGH"

THE "HALF INCH" MAP OF

ENGLAND & SCOTLAND

71 SHEETS PUBLISHED. (See Index.)

Each Sheet covers an Area of 40 × 50 Miles.

Telegraph Name for this Series,—" CHAFFINCH."

SCALE: HALF AN INCH TO A MILE.

The Fishing Gazette says : "We know these Maps to be invaluable, and that we are doing anglers good service in recommending them to their notice."

The Cyclists' Touring Club Gazette says : "Their value has long been admitted."

Tourists and Cyclists, Walking and Driving Parties, Anglers and Sportsmen can have no clearer and handier Maps for finding their way about the country ; the Main Roads are coloured, and the Cross Roads, Lanes, and Footpaths distinctly marked.

These Maps are printed on thin, but tough paper, and are therefore light and strong ; while the cloth edition can be folded to lie open at any particular part—a great advantage to Cyclists.

— PRICES —

Printed on Strong Paper, Roads Coloured, each sheet, 1/-

Cycling Edition.—Mounted on Cloth, and folded
    neat pocket size,   each sheet, 1/6

For hanging on Wall   on cloth, rollers, and var-
    nished,   each sheet, 2/8

SPECIAL LARGE SHEETS are also issued, to suit places near the joining of several sheets.—BRIGHTON, CAMBRIDGE, DARLINGTON, GLAMORGAN, LEEDS, OXFORD, READING, and SOUTHAMPTON. 1/- & 2/-

HALF SHEETS for the convenience of Tourists, with the following places in the centre, are issued at 6d. each ; mounted on Cloth, 1/- :—

ENGLAND.—BOURNEMOUTH, CANTERBURY, DOVER, EASTBOURNE, HASTINGS, ISLE O' WIGHT, PEMBROKE, PLYMOUTH, PORTSMOUTH, RAMSGATE, SCARBOROUGH, WINDSOR, &c.

SCOTLAND.—ALLOA, ARRAN, BLAIRGOWRIE, CLYDE, FALKIRK, MELROSE, PITLOCHRY, STIRLING, & TROSSACHS.

The above Maps are to be had in nearly every town and watering-place, often with a local publisher's name. In that case, the words " Gall & Inglis, Edinburgh" appear at the right-hand bottom corner.

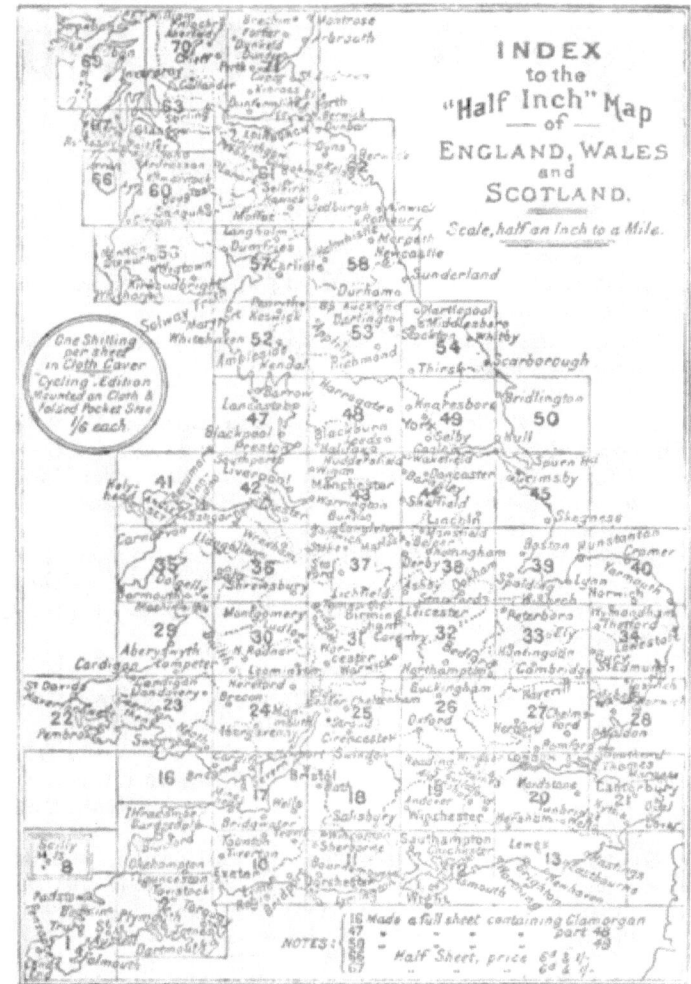

INDEX
to the
"Half Inch" Map
— of —
ENGLAND, WALES
and
SCOTLAND.
Scale, half an inch to a Mile.

One Shilling
per sheet
in Cloth Cover
Cycling Edition
Mounted on Cloth &
Folded Pocket Size
1/6 each

SIXTY MILES

NORTH, SOUTH, EAST, & WEST OF LONDON.

These four Maps have have been specially prepared to suit the
requirements of Cyclists residing in the suburbs of London. They
show London to Bedford, Cambridge, &c., London to Brighton,
Hastings, &c., London to Clacton, Margate, &c., and London to
Oxford, Newbury, &c. respectively. Scale: Half an Inch to a Mile.

PRICE 1S. EACH.; ON CLOTH, 2S. EACH.

THE "SAFETY" CYCLING MAPS.

Telegraph Name for this Series,—"SAFETY."

These Maps Show by distinct colourings the different classes of Roads, Difficult and Dangerous Hills, the Unrideable Roads, as well as the approximate speed over which each road can be travelled, and are invaluable to the tourist in planning a tour, and in selecting the best roads point to point, or across the country.

Price 1s.; mounted on Cloth, 1s. 6d.

ENGLAND. —In one sheet. Scale, 15 miles to an inch.

SCOTLAND. —In one sheet. Scale, 10 miles to an inch

"Compiled with great care."—*Scotsman.*

"The best Map of Scotland we have ever had the pleasure to examine."—*C. T. C. Gazette.*

England on a Larger Scale.

IN FOUR SHEETS.

Scale : 10 Miles to an inch.

Showing the best Cycling Roads, Dangerous Hills, &c.

Mounted on Cloth, 1/- each.

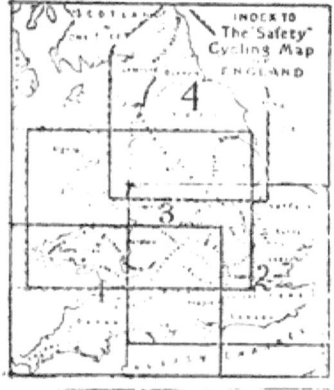

1. Southern Division.
2. South-East Division.
3. Central Division.
4. Northern Division.

Each sheet shows an area of 160 × 220 miles.

THE
"Strip" Maps,

By H. R. G. INGLIS.

*Telegraph Name for these Maps,
"STRIP."*

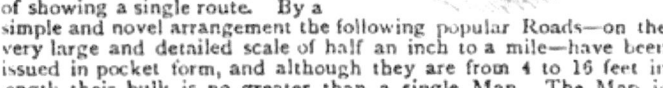

On a long Tour everyone has felt the nuisance of carrying a large number of Maps for the purpose of showing a single route. By a simple and novel arrangement the following popular Roads—on the very large and detailed scale of half an inch to a mile—have been issued in pocket form, and although they are from 4 to 16 feet in ength their bulk is no greater than a single Map. The Map is

JUST LIKE A BOOK,

And never requires to be unfolded.

[OVER

LAND'S END TO JOHN O' GROATS, 5/-

Land's End to Birmingham, 1 6. Edinburgh to Inverness, 1/-
Worcester to Edinburgh, 1.6.   Inverness to John o' Groats, 1/-

3. { 'Brighton Road,' London to Brighton, } 1/-
   { 'Portsmouth Road,'   „   Portsmouth, }
4. 'Southampton Road,' London to Bournemouth, 1/-
5. 'Exeter Road,' London to Exeter, 1/-
6. 'Bath Road,' London to Bristol, 1/-
8. 'Holyhead Road,' London to Dublin, 1/-
10. 'Great North Road,' in two parts.
        London to York, Leeds, or Harrogate, 1/-
        York to Edinburgh, 1/-
15. 'Land's End Road,' Bristol to Land's End, 1/-
16. { 'Worcester Road,' Bristol to Birmingham, } 1/-
    { Worcester to Lancashire, }
20. 'Great North Road,' Edinburgh to York, 1/-
21. 'Carlisle Road,' Edinburgh to Lancashire, 1/-
23. 'Highland Road,' Edinburgh to Inverness, 1/-
28. 'John o' Groat's Road,' Inverness to Caithness, 1/-

The Combination of several of these sheets gives :—
London to Land's End, London to John o' Groats.

Edinburgh | Dunbar | Berwick | Alnwick | Newcastle | Durham | Darlington | Thirsk | York | Selby | Doncaster | Newark | Grantham | Stamford | St. Neots | Hitchin | Hatfield | London

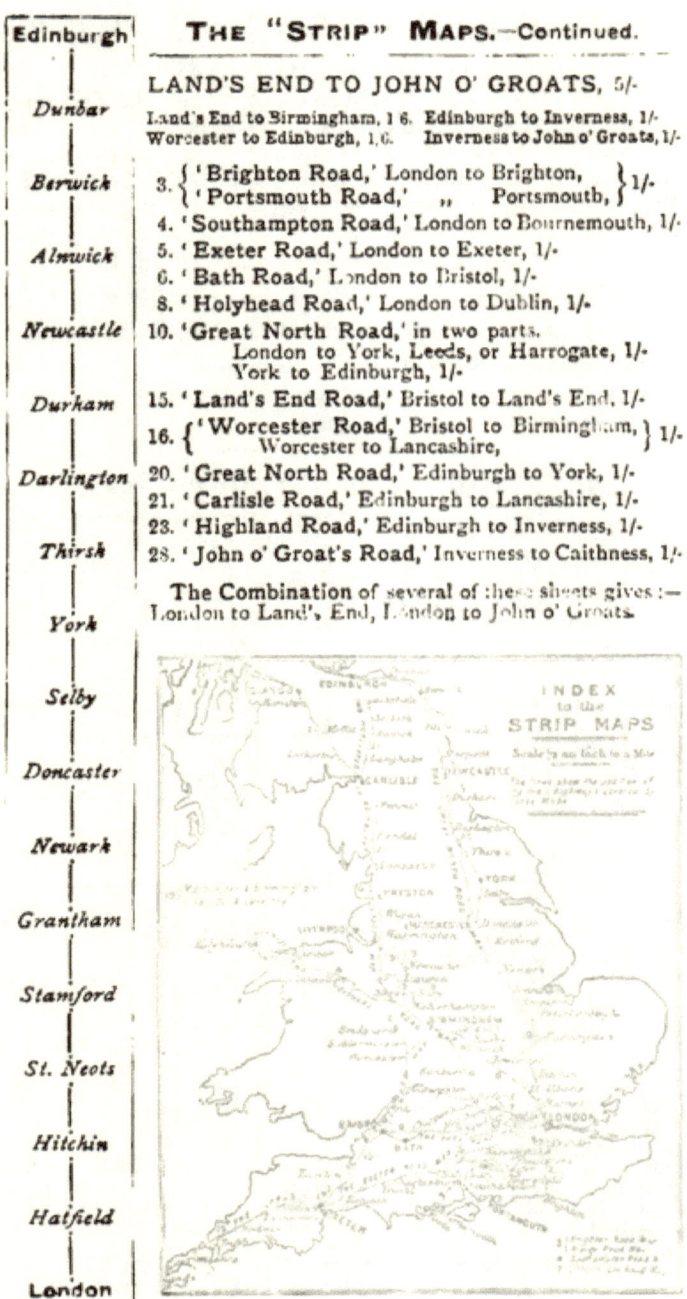

CYCLING
Guides and Guide Books.

The Scottish Borders and Galloway, by JAMES
LENNOX, Chief Consul, Cyclists' Touring Club.

1/- net, or Cloth, with numerous Illustrations, 1/6 net.

This handy volume is both a Cyclist's Guide and a Guide Book.
The roads are very fully described, and there are footnotes containing interesting information relating to all that can be seen *en route*.

Short Spins Round London (South of the Thames).
by ARTHUR C. ARMSTRONG and HARRY R. G. INGLIS.

With 50 Maps and Plans, 1/- net.

Deals minutely with nearly every road and cross road within a
radius of 20 miles of London. Fully illustrated with Maps and
"Contour" Plans. A delightful companion for choosing "Short
Spins."

Short Spins Round Edinburgh, by H. R. G. INGLIS.

Price 6d. with 50 Maps and Plans.

A local Supplement to "The 'Contour' Road Book of Scotland,"
dealing with all the roads close to Edinburgh, and copiously illustrated with Maps and Plans.

Pollock's Guide to the Lothians.

Price 6d. with Maps and Illustrations.

This admirable work is a concise description—arranged alpha-
betically—of the places in the neighbourhood of Edinburgh, as
well as in the Counties of Stirling, Linlithgow, Edinburgh, and
Haddington, also Callander and the Fife coast towns.

Pollock's Guide to the Clyde.

Price 6d. with Maps and Illustrations.

Contains full information about the towns and watering-places
on the river Clyde, as well as in the County of Lanarkshire.

The Forth Bridge.

A popular Penny Guide giving full information about this great
structure, with maps and numerous illustrations.

THE "ROYAL" ROAD BOOKS
1/- each. With "Contour" Plans.

These books, abridged from the "Contour" Road Books, contain
the main routes through the country, and for Tourists along the
principal roads are all that are required. Each book is fully illustrated with "Contour" Plans.

England.—Complete in one volume, containing nearly 300 "Contour" Plans.

Scotland.—Complete in one volume, with numerous illustrations.

Ireland.—One volume.

OTHER WORKS IN PREPARATION.

CRUCHLEY'S
COUNTY MAPS
OF ENGLAND.

44 Maps, each about 20 by 23 Inches.

Telegraph Name for this Series,—"COUNTY."

The Publishers' Circular, referring to "Surrey," says :
" An excellent Map, as we have found on many occasions
when walking in that county."

The average scale of these Maps being considerably less
than that of the Half Inch Map, this forms a much cheaper
Map of England, but as each sheet, as a rule, covers a
much larger area, the amount of detail is considerably less.

Price 6d. each, printed on strong paper, Coloured.

*Price 1s. each, mounted on cloth, Coloured, and folded
in neat Cloth Cover.*

Bedford	.. ..	1	Shropshire ..	30	Westmuld.&LakeDist. 37
Berkshire ..	..	2	Somerset ..	31	Wiltshire 38
Buckingham	..	3	Stafford ..	32	Worcestershire .. 39
Cambridge	..	4	Suffolk ..	33	Yorkshire.. 40
Cheshire ..	..	5	Surrey ..	34	North Wales .. ..
Cornwall ..	..	6	Sussex ..	35	Mid Wales .. ..
Cumberland	..	7	Warwick.. ..	36	South Wales .. ..
Derbyshire	..	8			
Devonshire	..	9			
Dorsetshire	..	10			
Durham ..	..	11			
Essex	..	12			
Gloucester..	..	13			
Hampshire	..	14			
Hereford	..	15			
Hertford	..	16			
Huntingdon	..	17			
Kent ..	..	18			
Lancashire	..	19			
Leicester	..	20			
Lincoln ..	..	21			
Middlesex	..	22			
Monmouth	..	23			
Norfolk ..	..	24			
Northampton		25			
Northumb'rland		26			
Nottingham	..	27			
Oxfordshire	..	28			
Pembroke..	.. ..				
Rutland ..	..	29			

GALL & INGLIS'
MAPS OF LONDON.

Extended Edition.

REDUCED ORDNANCE MAP of LONDON.

Showing the 'Bus, Car, and Steamer Routes, divided into Half-Mile Squares; with Handbook containing Index to 5000 Streets, &c., Guide to the principal places of interest, and 3 useful Maps. Additional strips on the North, South, and East have been added, making the area of the Map nearly 40 by 50 Inches. The Map is very minute, and shows not only the streets, but the narrow lanes and alleys of the "city," and is of infinite value on account of its great detail. The Handbook contains a small Map of the City, which can be readily referred to in the street, without opening up the large Map.

PRICE 1S.; MOUNTED ON CLOTH, 2S. 6D.

The largest and most detailed Map sold at this price.

HANDY MAP & GUIDE TO LONDON,
20 by 30 INCHES.

This Handy Map is beatifully Coloured, and with a new Illustrated Guide and Index to the Streets, forms a neat Pocket Companion to the City.

MOUNTED ON CLOTH, PRICE 1S.

THE SIXPENNY PLAN OF LONDON,
20 by 30 INCHES.

Folded in Cover, Showing the Streets, Railways, Steamer Routes, &c.

THE ENVIRONS OF LONDON,
SCALE: HALF AN INCH TO A MILE.

Shows the country 25 miles on each side of St. Paul's, and is a splendid Cycling Map.

MAIN ROADS COLOURED, 1S.; ON CLOTH, 2S.

THE SUBURBS OF LONDON.

Shows the country from Croydon to Enfield, and Hampton to Romford, on a large scale—1 inch to mile. To do justice to the roads, this scale is absolutely necessary in this area. A capital Map for Rambling, and for short runs.

PRICE 6D. ON CLOTH, 1S.

www.ingramcontent.com/pod-product-compliance
Lightning Source LLC
Chambersburg PA
CBHW021343110726
47900CB00005B/1587